Si igitur sit aliquod agens, quod non in genere contineatur, effectus eius adhuc magis accedent remote ad similitudinem formae agentis: non tamen ita quod participent similitudinem formae agentis secundum eandem rationem speciei aut generis, sed secundum aliqualem analogiam, sicut ipsum esse est commune omnibus. Et hoc modo illa quae sunt a Deo, assimilantur ei inquantum sunt entia, ut primo et universali principio totius esse.

— Thomas Aquinas, *Summa theologiae* I, q. 4, a. 3

Fear of scholasticism is the mark of a false prophet.

— Karl Barth, *Church Dogmatics* I/1, §7.2

The Analogy of Being

Invention of the Antichrist
or the Wisdom of God?

Edited by

Thomas Joseph White, O.P.

WILLIAM B. EERDMANS PUBLISHING COMPANY
GRAND RAPIDS, MICHIGAN / CAMBRIDGE, U.K.

Published 2011 by
Wm. B. Eerdmans Publishing Co.
2140 Oak Industrial Drive N.E., Grand Rapids, Michigan 49505 /
P.O. Box 163, Cambridge CB3 9PU U.K.

Printed in the United States of America

17 16 15 14 13 12 11   7 6 5 4 3 2 1

Library of Congress Cataloging-in-Publication Data

The Analogy of being: invention of the Antichrist or the wisdom of God? /
    edited by Thomas Joseph White.
        p.   cm.
    Proceedings of a conference held in Apr. 2008 in Washington, D.C.
    Includes bibliographical references (p.   ) and index.
    ISBN 978-0-8028-6533-5 (pbk.: alk. paper)
        1. Przywara, Erich, 1889-1972. Analogia entis — Congresses.
        2. God (Christianity) — Knowableness — Congresses. 3. Analogy (Religion) —
        Congresses. 4. Barth, Karl, 1886-1968 — Congresses. 5. Catholic Church —
        Doctrines — Congresses.   I. White, Thomas Joseph, 1971-

    BT103.P793A53   2011
    231′.042 — dc22

                                                      2010037718

www.eerdmans.com

Dedicated to the memory of

Fr. Erich Przywara, S.J.

and

Karl Barth

two earthen vessels, two witnesses to Christ

Contents

Contents

Foreword

When Erich Przywara died in 1972, he left behind sixty books and hundreds of articles, as well as a solid reputation in the European intellectual world and a lasting influence in the work of theologians like Karl Rahner and Hans Urs von Balthasar. In the English-speaking world, however, Przywara's work has remained relatively and undeservedly unknown. The *New Catholic Encyclopedia* (published in 1964 and in a second edition in 2002), for example, contains no entry on Przywara.

Ironically, what continues to assure him a durable readership among English-speaking scholars — as this remarkable collection of essays demonstrates — is Karl Barth's blistering attack on the theory of analogy that he rightly or wrongly associated with Przywara's 1932 book *Analogia Entis*. "I regard the *analogia entis* as the invention of Antichrist," Barth famously wrote, "and I believe that because of it it is impossible ever to become a Catholic."[1]

The consensus seems to be that Barth misunderstood Przywara. Przywara certainly thought so, and most careful readers of his work agree. Von Balthasar wrote a whole book to show that, far from being at odds, Barth and Przywara were, in their different ways, endeavoring to make the same point. Although Barth is said to have considered von Balthasar's book to be the best book ever written about his work, it does not seem to have changed his mind about Przywara, for he never in print revised his judgment of the *analogia entis*.

---

1. Karl Barth, *Church Dogmatics*, trans. G. W. Bromiley and T. F. Torrance (London: T. &T. Clark; New York: Continuum, 2004), I/1, p. xiii.

There is reason to think that, whether or not he acknowledged that he had misread Przywara, Barth had found in the notion of the *analogia entis* a foil with which to reiterate the Reformation negation of Catholic natural theology — a task made all the more urgent by what he took to be liberal theology's retrieval of all that was wrong with traditional natural theology. Expressed in terms, whether of a metaphysics of the created order (à la classical theology), or of an ontology of the structures of consciousness (à la liberal theology), the assertion or postulation of a human access to God prior to and independently of God's free revelation in Christ and the Holy Spirit were, for Barth, absolutely to be excluded in Christian dogmatics. One could say that, after Schleiermacher, natural theology, whatever its provenance, had irreversibly lost its innocence in Barth's eyes. Rightly or wrongly, Barth construed the *analogia entis* — or, perhaps more accurately, perceived that it could be construed — as positing just the sort of preexistent relation between God and creatures that he believed to be ruled out by authentic Christian faith.

Readers of the fascinating essays collected in this volume will learn much about the *analogia entis* controversy, which has assured Erich Przywara's fame among anglophone readers of Karl Barth. But they will learn a great deal besides. Among other things, they will gain a deepened appreciation of Przywara's not inconsiderable legacy. But here it is not simply a matter of learning more about these particular thinkers but, more important, of entering into a more profound understanding of the philosophical and theological issues that lend such a lively interest to the controversy between them and their interpreters. One could mention, among the more prominent topics, the following: the possibility and nature of metaphysics in postmodern thought, the place of religious desire in the economy of salvation, the role of metaphysical thinking in theology, the logic of analogous discourse in theology, the nature and grace of human knowledge of God, and the trinitarian structure of divine revelation and action.

It is rare that so unified a set of papers should be the outcome of a theological symposium with twelve different speakers. In this case — perhaps precisely because of the care with which the topic was defined — the result is a stimulating and focused conversation into which thoughtful readers will find themselves irresistibly drawn.

Archbishop J. Augustine Di Noia, O.P.
Vatican City

Acknowledgments

The majority of the essays in this volume derive from presentations originally given at a theological conference in April 2008 in Washington, D.C., one bearing the same title as this volume. The event was generously sponsored by the two institutions that hosted it: the Pontifical Faculty of the Immaculate Conception of the Dominican House of Studies, and the John Paul II Cultural Center. The editor, who organized the conference, would therefore like to thank all those who encouraged and supported this event: especially Fr. Steven Boguslawski, O.P., the president and acting director (respectively) of the aforementioned institutions, and Fr. Gabriel O'Donnell, O.P., the dean of the Pontifical Faculty. I would also like to thank especially Mr. William B. Eerdmans, whose generous sponsorship of the conference helped to make the event possible. The Dominican community in Washington was very generously involved in helping in this event, and I would also like to thank Ms. Honya Weeks, who assisted in the preparations for the conference and devoted a great deal of work to this task.

In the editing of this text, Reinhard Hütter has kindly offered me very helpful advice on regular occasions. In particular, I should also especially like to thank Ms. Monica Bond, whose work for some months as an assistant editor on this book greatly helped to improve its textual cogency and clarity.

This project would not have been envisaged to begin with had it not been for the recent work of David Bentley Hart and John Betz, both of whom have done much to promote an increased awareness in the English-speaking world of the richness of the thought of Erich Przywara, S.J. Their ongoing translation of his work *Analogia Entis* into English and conversations with them concerning the subject matter were in many ways the impetus for the beginnings of the project. Finally, I would like to thank the contributors to this volume for their splendid theological essays. Their perspectives on the mystery of Christ lead us to reflect anew and more deeply on the gift of faith and its relationship to human reason, as do their constructive engagement of each other's diverse traditions of doctrinal reflection. May their substantive and often quite complementary interpretations of the role of the analogy of being in Christian theology serve as a model of ecumenical encounter at a profound level.

THOMAS JOSEPH WHITE, O.P.
The Solemnity of Christmas, 2008

The *Analogia Entis* Controversy and Its Contemporary Significance

Thomas Joseph White, O.P.

It seems strange that the disputes between Erich Przywara and Karl Barth between the years 1929 and 1932 concerning *analogia entis,* "analogy of being," should have given rise to the single most important ecumenical controversy of the twentieth century.[1] After all, the term itself was rarely employed in medieval scholasticism or in the writings of the Reformation, and it can hardly refer to a locus classicus of traditional Roman-Reformed discord or doctrinal dispute. Moreover, the theory itself, as exposited by Przywara — though foreshadowed in Baroque scholasticism — was highly original and extremely complex, such that its nature could be grasped by few.[2] Yet both

---

1. On the nature of the original controversy, see the varying interpretations of Eberhard Jüngel, "Die Möglichkeit theologischer Anthropologie auf dem Grunde der Analogie," in *Barth-Studien* (Gütersloh: Benziger, 1982), pp. 210-32; Eberhard Mechels, *Analogie bei Erich Przywara und Karl Barth. Das Verhältnis von Offenbarungstheologie und Metaphysik* (Neukirchen: Neukirchener Verlag, 1974); Bernhard Gertz, *Glaubenswelt als Analogie. Die theologische Analogie-Lehre Erich Przywaras und ihr Ort in der Auseinandersetzung um die analogia fidei* (Düsseldorf: Patmos Verlag, 1969), as well as the now-classic reflections of Hans Urs von Balthasar, *Karl Barth. Darstellung und Deutung seiner Theologie* (Cologne: Verlag Jakob Hegner, 1951; ET *The Theology of Karl Barth,* trans. Edward Oakes [San Francisco: Ignatius Press, 1992]).

2. See Julio Terán-Dutari, "Die Geschichte des Terminus 'Analogia entis' und das Werk Erich Przywara," *Philosophisches Jahrbuch der Görres-Gesellschaft* 77 (1970): 163-79.

I would like to thank John Betz for his great help concerning the choice and translations of key texts of Erich Przywara in this essay.

Przywara and Barth insisted upon the fundamental importance of the concept for understanding the nature of Christian thought as such in ways that
were uncharacteristic with regard to their respective preceding theological
traditions, allotting the idea a structural theological significance (either positive or negative).[3] This seems, on the surface of things, idiosyncratic. Why,
then, has this controversy been so important?

The now-historic dispute between the two great thinkers is significant
because it concerns the attempt by each to redefine the significance of Christianity in confrontation with an acutely modern, post-Enlightenment crisis
of meaning. Succinctly stated, the Enlightenment was characterized by the
rise of the empirical sciences and a corresponding culture of technology;
philosophical concentration on the meaning and autonomy of the experi-
encing subject over and against the classical Western metaphysical tradition;
and a political and cultural relativization of the importance of appeals to
Christian revealed truth.[4] Meanwhile, modernity — from Hume and Kant
to Nietzsche — challenged the Enlightenment conditions for philosophy by
introducing a more radical form of questioning into the cultural landscape
of the academy and the broader society of an increasingly secular Europe:
Are we intellectually capable of any form of knowledge of God? Can man attain to any knowledge of transcendent moral ideals? Are there any overarching, perennial metaphysical truths, such as unchanging characteristics pertaining to human nature?[5] What it seemed possible to know in the
Enlightenment concerning God, morality, or human nature became increasingly uncertain or dubious in modernity.

This questioning of foundations, already prefigured in such nineteenth-
century figures as Dostoyevsky and Nietzsche, underwent a broad expansion
and cultural intensification in western Europe because of the mass slaughters
of World War I and the political and fiscal crises in its wake, giving rise to
widespread moral and existential disorientation, especially in Germany be-

---

3. Von Balthasar, *The Theology of Karl Barth*, p. 35: "In designating this principle [of
the analogy of being] as the touchstone for everything Catholic, Barth is in essence adopting
the usage first adumbrated by Erich Przywara. . . . But Barth is also explicitly accepting
Przywara's own estimation of analogy of being as an expressly *formal* principle, something
Przywara was the first to do."

4. Cf. the description of Jonathan I. Israel, *Radical Enlightenment: Philosophy and the
Making of Modernity, 1650-1750* (Oxford: Oxford University Press, 2001), pp. 3-22.

5. See the insightful, if not uncontroversial, survey of this historical period in Charles
Taylor, *Sources of the Self: The Making of the Modern Identity* (Cambridge, Mass.: Harvard
University Press, 1989), esp. pp. 305-455, 495-521.

tween the two World Wars.[6] Przywara and Barth were the inhabitants of a profoundly unsettled world, one quite different from that of late nineteenth-century Christian thinkers such as Matthias Joseph Scheeben or John Henry Newman. In a sense, then, Przywara and Barth, two of the first great "postsecular" Christian thinkers, each sought to identify a profound and adequate understanding of Christianity, not only over and against the claims of its theological alternative (i.e., Catholic vs. Protestant) or in response to the secularizing, rationalist criticisms of the Enlightenment, but also over and against, and in critical confrontation with, the seeming absence of meaning in modern Europe, a modernity that had lost confidence in both its Christian heritage and in the Enlightenment vision of man.

Otherwise stated, in these two theologies something more fundamental was being discussed than particular Christian doctrines or the status of rational belief in the existence of God. Rather, what was at stake was the identification of the conditions of possibility for Christian belief and discipleship in a deeply secularized age. This required in turn a clarification of the sources of the irremediable otherness of Christianity with respect to secular modernity. What is the deepest source of the underlying tension between the two? How might the strangeness of Christianity emerge afresh from within the questions or problems of modernity, but also over and against its mistaken preconceptions? And, therefore, how might the message of Christianity "ever ancient, ever new" represent itself transparently as both the judgment upon and salvation of a postreligious humanity? Embodied in Przywara's notion of the *analogia entis* and Barth's early dialectical theology was each thinker's response to these difficult questions.

The writings of Przywara and Barth were to influence a generation of theologians in both the Catholic and the Protestant spheres in immense ways, and these influences still underlie any number of contemporary theological disputes. How, then, might we characterize the issues that came to light in the exchanges between Przywara and Barth? As a way of sketching out the basic topology of these issues, and as an introduction to this collection of essays on the *analogia entis* controversy and its significance, three chief loci of dispute can be mentioned. Each was to unfold in the wake of Przywara and Barth as a topic central to theology in the twentieth century:

---

6. On this historical background, see Bruce L. McCormack, *Karl Barth's Critically Realistic Dialectical Theology: Its Genesis and Development, 1909-1936* (Oxford: Clarendon, 1995), pp. 31-125, 208-90; Thomas O'Meara, *Erich Przywara, S.J.* (Notre Dame, Ind.: University of Notre Dame Press, 2002).

(1) the relationship between Christianity and the metaphysics of being; (2) the relationship between Christological grace and our understanding of the meaning and purpose of human nature, and (3) the relationship between Christian faith and modern human reason. In each of these domains, we can find both differences and likenesses between Przywara and Barth that prefigure and foreshadow the unfolding poles of later Catholic and Protestant theology in the twentieth century. A consideration of these three loci serves as an appropriate introduction to the essays in this volume, then, as their positions also alert us to substantive challenges and interests that inhabit contemporary theology.

I. Christianity and the Metaphysics of Being: How Should We Diagnose the Modern, Postreligious Malaise?

The notion of an "analogy" of being has its origins in pre-Christian Greek antiquity.[7] The term *analogia* had originally been used to express proportions between mathematical numbers but was employed creatively by Aristotle in the context of metaphysical discussions in order to express ontological similitudes between diverse beings or states of being.[8] In addition, the Stagirite would claim that the word "being" itself, like the words "oneness" and "goodness," did not have a univocal signification but had differing (what he called "equivocal") senses, such that "being is said in many ways."[9] The term can connote "substances," "qualities," "quantities," "relations," and so on. Aristotle's development of the categories was an initial attempt to outline a kind of analogical way of signifying being, over against the uniformity of Plato's Ideas.[10]

In late antiquity and the Middle Ages, however, this concept of an analogical way of signifying "being" was to be rethought with a view toward explicitly reflecting upon the metaphysical and logical grounds for our discourse concerning God.[11] The classic example is the analogical theory of

7. See the study by Hampus Lyttkens, *The Analogy between God and the World: An Investigation of Its Background and Interpretation of Its Use by Thomas of Aquino*, trans. Axel Poignant (Uppsala: Almqvist & Wiksells, 1952), pp. 15-18.

8. See *Metaphysics* 12.5.1071a4-17; 9.6.1048a25–1048b9.

9. Ibid. 4.2.1003a32–1003b25.

10. See, for example, the analogous treatment of "the good" as a criticism of Platonic Ideas in *Nic. Ethics* 1.6, esp. 1096a23-29.

11. See the recent study of this historical development by Jean-François Courtine, *Inventio analogiae. Métaphysique et ontothéologie* (Paris: J. Vrin, 2005), esp. pp. 109-290.

Thomas Aquinas, who understood discourse concerning God to be analogical, as opposed to univocal or equivocal.[12] In univocal discourse we claim to predicate things of God in the same sense in which we say them of creatures, while an equivocation theory rejects the idea that there is anything that carries over from our language about creatures into God. For St. Thomas the terms "being," "goodness," and "unity" are predicated of God neither in the same way that they are predicated of creatures nor in such a way as to be wholly unintelligible.[13] Rather, with reflective adjustment, such terms can be made to rightly designate in a particular fashion what God is, even while respecting the transcendence of God's divine essence, which remains always utterly incomprehensible to human thought.[14] The Fourth Lateran Council (which took place in 1215, a generation before Aquinas's career began) would express this in its own way: "For between the Creator and the creature there can be noted no similarity so great that a greater dissimilarity cannot be seen between them."[15]

Barth and Przywara were to disagree profoundly about the importance of the use of this metaphysical tradition within Christian doctrine, and on its relationship to Christology. In its metaphysical component, the early project of Erich Przywara was profoundly original. While deeply influenced by Augustine and Aquinas, the German Jesuit was also indebted to the thought of Scotus and Suárez, whose reflections he saw as complementing in many instances the seminal metaphysics of the Angelic Doctor. He also sought to respond comprehensively from within Catholicism to the unfolding of German theological thought since Kant, not omitting German idealism (Hegel, Schelling), as well as subsequent German atheism (Nietzsche and the early Heidegger).[16]

At base, the metaphysical thought of St. Augustine in the *Confessions* is axiomatic for Przywara, who perceives in Augustine's discoveries of the simultaneous transcendence and immanence of God the key to understanding the dynamic mystery of the analogy of being, of the created order as entirely from God, and yet utterly distinct from God, as like God and yet

---

12. *ST* I, q. 13, a. 5.

13. *De pot.*, q. 7, aa. 5 and 7.

14. *ST* I, q. 13, aa. 2 and 3.

15. Denzinger, *Enchiridion Symbolorum*, 806: "Quia inter creatorem et creaturam non potest [tanta] similitudo notari, quin inter eos maior sit dissimilitudo notanda."

16. Cf. the discussion of Przywara's influences by John Betz, "Beyond the Sublime: The Aesthetics of the Analogy of Being," *Modern Theology* 21 (July 2005): 367-411 and 22 (January 2006): 1-50.

radically dissimilar to God, as given to be itself and yet as wholly ordered toward God.[17] For Przywara, this dynamic movement of all things from God and back to him is given voice in an acutely metaphysical way by Aquinas, whose articulation of the likeness between creation and God avoids both the agnosticism of equivocation theory and the seeming rationalism of univocity theory.[18] In losing sight of this profound truth of classic metaphysics (which was embodied in the *maior dissimilitudo* formula of Lateran IV),[19] post-Christian modern thought tends inevitably in one of two directions: toward either univocal or equivocal reflection concerning God. Univocal thinking (which problematically understands God in terms of the world) tends either toward the pantheological deification of the world (which Przywara sees exemplified in a thinker like Hegel) or toward an absolutization of God, which sees the world as a merely ephemeral expression of the divine life of God (which Przywara terms "theopanism" and which he sees exemplified in thinkers such as Luther or Barth).[20] Equivocal thinking (which is evidenced in thinkers such as Kant and the early Heidegger) makes God in his alterity literally unthinkable and tends inevitably toward a way of philosophizing that is antitheological. It results in an evacuation from the world of all meaning that could be sacred, or derived from God.[21]

Between the absolutization of intraworldly becoming as itself a development of the divine, and a banishment of God from the world, the *analogia*

---

17. See Przywara, "Gott in uns und Gott über uns?" in *Ringen der Gegenwart. Gesammelte Aufsätze, 1922-1927* (Augsburg: Benno Filser, 1929), pp. 543-78; cf. idem, *Analogia Entis. Metaphysik*, vol. 1 (Munich: Kösel & Pustet, 1932), pp. 117-24; cf. rev. ed., *Analogia Entis. Metaphysik; Ur-struktur und All-Rhythmus* (Einsiedeln: Johannes Verlag, 1962), pp. 163-71. Pagination to the original 1932 edition hereafter included in parentheses.

18. See *Analogia Entis*, pp. 171-202 (124-49).

19. *Analogia Entis*, p. 138 (97).

20. For early indications of Przywara's concept of "theopanism," see Erich Przywara, *Gottgeheimnis der Welt. Drei Vorträge über die geistige Krisis der Gegenwart* (Munich: Theatiner-Verlag, 1923); reprinted in *Schriften*, 3 vols. (Einsiedeln: Johannes Verlag, 1962), 2:207ff.; *Gott. Fünf Vorträge über das religionsphilosophische Problem* (Munich: Oratoriums-Verlag, 1926), pp. 66ff.; reprinted in *Schriften*, 2:285ff. For Przywara's mature understanding of the *analogia entis* vis-à-vis the respective extremes of pantheism and theopanism, see *Analogia Entis*, pp. 67-71, 123-24 (38-42, 85-86).

21. See, for example, the reflections on Hegel and Heidegger by Erich Przywara in *Analogia Entis*, esp. pp. 92-109; "Essenz- und Existenz-Philosophie. Tragische Identität oder Distanz der Geduld," *Scholastik* 14 (1939); reprinted in *Schriften*, 3:213-46. See also, for more on Przywara's estimation of Heidegger, "Drei Richtungen der Phänomenologie," *Stimmen der Zeit* 115 (1928): 252-64, and "Wende zum Menschen," *Stimmen der Zeit* 119 (1930): 1-10.

entis permits the reaffirmation of the nonabsolute, but true, meaning of the creation, and of the simultaneous polarization of all things back toward the ever greater and incomprehensible mystery of God. Theocentrism and a profound Christian humanism are thus completely compatible and, in theological thought, must mutually reinforce one another. In one respect, this dynamic and analogical rapport between creatures and God finds its most fundamental expression for Przywara in creation. For, as the Creator, God is at once "in" the world, which in turn resembles him, and "above" the world, as the ever greater source and end of all things.[22] Yet in another respect analogy is present in an even more ultimate way in the dynamics of grace and Christological sanctification. Christ himself is the dynamic ground in which the human and divine are both united and differentiated.[23] For in Christ, God is both present in creation and yet ever greater than the humanity in which he is revealed. Simultaneously, then, the Son incarnate reveals the analogical mystery of the life of God (the Son, who is like the Father) *and*, as the union of God and man, is the ultimate realization of the analogical likeness-in-difference of man and God. The consideration of the *analogia entis*, for Przywara, then, is not something limited to a *philosophical* metaphysics; on the contrary, it opens up at its highest level into the Christian understanding of revealed mysteries. It designates the relation between God and man that is embodied in the incarnation. It also obtains in the life of grace at the highest level of supernatural unity — of participation in the divine nature — between Christ and his church, understood as the *corpus Christi mysticum*.[24] As Przywara puts it,

> The spiritual realm constitutes, to be sure, the most exalted aspect of creation, but between this realm and God there remains an inviolable and insuperable difference. The decisive form of unity with Christ in the *corpus Christi mysticum* — the form according to which alone any unity between God and creature can be conceived — is that of the Fourth Lateran Council (1215). This form of unity is solely and exclusively one in which an "ever greater dissimilarity (and hence distance and differ-

22. *Analogia Entis*, pp. 121ff. (83ff.).
23. See, for example, the 1940 essay "Die Reichweite der Analogie als katholischer Grundform," reprinted in the later edition of *Analogia Entis* in *Schriften*, 3:247-301. See also "Weg zu Gott," in *Ringen der Gegenwart*, vol. 1 (Augsburg: Benno Filser, 1929), pp. 389-539, reprinted in *Schriften*, 2:3-120; and "Katholizismus," in *Ringen der Gegenwart*, vol. 2 (Augsburg: Benno Filser, 1929), pp. 543-725.
24. *Analogia Entis*, pp. 38ff., 58ff.

ence)" is to be observed within every "similarity (and hence every proximity and unity), however great." According to the council, this law is
valid not simply for every "natural relation" between God and creature
(which is supernaturally crowned in "complete unity"), but obtains, as
the council explains, precisely with regard to the most exalted, supernatural unity and indeed for any unity whatsoever.[25]

In the famous expression of Przywara, then, the analogy of being is to be
considered "the formal principle of Catholic thought"[26] precisely because
the difference of being between the creature and God (and the metaphysical
openness of the creature toward God that it implies) is preserved even in
man's relation-by-grace to the higher reaches of reality: in the mystery of
Christ and his church, and in man's graced relationship to the inner life of
the Trinity itself.

Przywara's own explorations of a theory of analogy would become
controversial even in Catholic theological circles (not least his affirmation
just mentioned, that the analogy of being is the fundamental form of Catholic thought). For Barth, however, they were an important stimulus (among
others) in his quest to confront the crisis of modernity in a distinctly Protestant theological way. In essence, we find in Barth's early work an interest in
bringing into focus (1) the conditions for authentic knowledge of God in a
postreligious world, (2) the manner in which one might identify a similitude
or likeness between God and his creatures, and (3) a genealogy of diagnosis
for the modern malaise of unbelief. In addition, he is interested in doing this
while (4) attempting to evaluate the long-standing importance of the metaphysics of being and the analogical knowledge of God found in the Catholic
tradition. Such parallels are far from insignificant, and yet, as is well known,
Barth's solutions to these enigmas contain avid marks of contrast from (and
rejection of) Przywara's project on virtually every point. What was to
emerge instead was a distinct, revelatory epistemology that Barth claimed
was faithful to the deepest theological prerogatives of the Reformation, and
which was of great creative import.

First of all, while Przywara would seek to understand the *philosophical*
and *metaphysical* origins of the malaise of modernity and thereby to propose

25. Przywara, "Corpus Christi Mysticum — eine Bilanz" (1940), in *Katholische Krise*
(Düsseldorf: Patmos Verlag, 1967), p. 148.
26. The phrase is used in particular in "Die Reichweite der Analogie" but can be
found, in variants (e.g., as "das katholische *Urprinzip*"), in earlier works and essays, such as
"Neue Theologie," from 1926, in *Ringen der Gegenwart*, p. 725.

certain countermeasures, Barth would attempt to locate the basis for knowledge of God *uniquely* in the revelation of God given on the cross and in the
resurrection.[27] But this meant also explaining godlessness in modernity *not*
by recourse to a philosophical or metaphysical explanation, even in a secondary sense (e.g., through a philosophical genealogy of atheism as a complement to the theological understanding of the effects of sin on human reason). Rather, Barth's diagnoses sought to be more radical: They depicted the
state of modern atheism as only a more or less vivid unveiling of what has already, always been the case in fallen human nature. "The image of God [in
fallen man] is not just . . . destroyed apart from a few relics; it is totally anni-
hilated. . . . Man has completely lost the capacity for God."[28] We are in truth
beings without authentic knowledge of God, incapable of rejoining God in
any way by our own powers.

Second, Barth did seek, even from the early commentaries on Romans
(as Bruce McCormack shows in his essay in this volume), a way of finding
symmetry (or analogy) between God and the world established in Christ
(which, in the early *Church Dogmatics,* he termed an *analogia fidei*),[29] and this
quest was to develop through the span of Barth's theological career. Nevertheless, the similitude is established uniquely by the unilateral activity or initiative
of God in Christ, without parallel or analogy to be found in human agency
outside of Christ.[30] Such a viewpoint was already thematic in *Church Dogmatics* I/1 and was to become a centerpiece of Barthian theological reflection.

Third, then, for Barth metaphysical reflection on the analogy between
creation and God in the Catholic tradition plays a role similar to that of religious experience and Christian ethics in the liberal Protestantism from
Schleiermacher to Harnack: it marks a human way of approaching God
from comparison with creatures that fails to recognize (1) the radicality of
the gulf that separates us from God and (2) the primal requirement of a divine initiative (in revelation) that stands at the font of any true human response to God.[31] Whereas Przywara sought to prescribe remedies to Kant's
agnosticism and Feuerbach's atheism by a revisionist philosophical interpretation of the origins of *their* plight, Barth sought in their iconoclastic refusal

---

27. *Church Dogmatics* I/1, pp. 239-40. (All citations of the *CD* are taken from the English translations by G. W. Bromiley and T. F. Torrance [London: T. & T. Clark, 2004].)
28. Ibid., p. 238.
29. See, for example, ibid., pp. 12, 243-44, 437, 457.
30. Ibid., pp. 239-40, 243-47.
31. See the comparisons of Roman Catholicism and "modernist Protestantism" in
ibid., pp. 36-44.

of all authentic divine symbols an indication of the irremediably fallen character of human existence.[32] Theirs was an implicit (if indirect) confirmation of the *sola fide* of the Lutheran tradition. It is metaphysical speculation as such — in the fallen human being — that plays a role of distracting us from the truth of revelation. Consequently the Catholic *analogia entis* is seen as a constant attempt to domesticate the transcendence of God and distort the revelation. In the famous words of Barth himself: "I regard the *analogia entis* as the invention of Antichrist, and I believe that because of it it is impossible ever to become a Roman Catholic, all other reasons for not doing so being to my mind short-sighted and trivial."[33] Over and against this background, the light of Christ shines out as man's only true possibility for knowledge of God, and his grace is the unique condition for the development of an authentic human freedom, which is itself possible only as a result of God's grace and in response to the ethical commandments of God given in faith.[34]

At stake in this dispute is the basic question of whether or in what way a *ressourcement* of classical metaphysics is required *within modern theology,* as a dimension of one's response to secular modernity. Is the final differentiation of Christian faith and modern unbelief determined in part by the metaphysical substructure of comprehension of the world to which each in turn subscribes? If so, does the Christian affirmation that the world is created and is an outward mirror of the inward glory of God require a contemporary retrieval of medieval, pre-Kantian metaphysical thinking? Does the importance of this metaphysical heritage in fact extend even into the comprehension of the most ultimate mysteries of faith, and if so, how? Conversely, can the modern critiques of every speculative intellectual aspiration toward divine transcendence (exemplified by Kant's *Critique of Pure Reason*) find their place within a post-Kantian, Reformed theology of human fallenness and redemption in Christ? In the wake of postmodernity's antifoundationalism (its acknowledgment of the absence of acceptance of common grounds for the

32. Ibid., pp. 41, 130-31, 192. See the remarks on Kant and Feuerbach in Barth's work *Die protestantische Theologie im 19. Jahrhundert. Ihre Vorgeschichte und ihre Geschichte* (Zürich: Evangelischer Verlag, 1947), composed mainly of coursework from his teaching in 1932-33. ET *Protestant Theology in the Nineteenth Century: Its Background and History,* trans. Brian Cozens and John Bowden (London: SCM Press, 1973), pp. 266-312, 534-40.

33. *CD* I/1, p. xiii.

34. See ibid., pp. 200-201, 207. John Webster has shown how this theme of freedom under grace in response to revelation was developed in successive volumes of the *Church Dogmatics.* See in particular his *Barth's Moral Theology: Human Action in Barth's Thought* (Edinburgh: T. & T. Clark, 1998), esp. pp. 99-124.

evaluation of human meaning), does Christology offer the unique possibility for the understanding of our existence as creatures? Is the resolution to first foundations possible only by means of Christology? These inquiries bring us to the second major theme announced by the Przywara-Barth debate: that concerning the relationship between Christological grace and our understanding of the meaning and purpose of human nature.

II. Christological Grace and Human Nature: How Can One Discern What Is Authentically Human?

Speaking somewhat schematically, one can juxtapose Przywara and Barth by speaking of the thought of the former as an ascending anthropology that is resolved only Christologically, and of the thought of the latter as a descending Christology that is employed architectonically to determine the content of anthropology. Przywara the Christian metaphysician presents a theological ontology and anthropology of the created order that opens up toward Christ (in whom the former find their only perfect realization). Barth develops a Christology that understands the agency of God in Christ breaking into the created order such that the revelation of God alone makes clear what creation is, and, in a final way, what the election, nature, and vocation of the human creature is. In one case, the efforts of human reason find their most comprehensive achievement only in Christ, once they are perfected by divine grace. In the other case, the presence of Christ is the unique condition of possibility for a rational understanding of the created order as created and is therefore the basis for a uniquely theological explanation of the meaning of human existence. Both thinkers are profoundly Christological, and both are taken with ontological questions of creation and the theology of ultimate human purposes. Yet the balance and relation of these two poles (Christology/anthropology) is diverse in the thought of each. In a sense, their diverse "solutions" are suggestive of two distinct trends in modern theology. Here let us briefly consider each in turn.

The religious disorientation of early twentieth-century western Europe was coupled with a deep sense of spiritual and cultural restlessness, and this not unsurprisingly led to a revival of interest among Catholic theologians in Augustinian anthropology. For in Augustine's thought one finds a vivid and insightful description, not only of the profound human need for God, but also of how the human capacity for godlessness is itself a sign of the irresolution of a human existence lived without grace. At the outset of the *Confessions,* Augustine announces his famous theme that "our hearts are restless until they rest in Thee," signaling the true final end for which God has destined human beings by grace (the vision of God).[35] And yet Augustine also recognized in his own journey of unbelief (borrowing a phrase from Platonic philosophy) a "region of dissimilarity" in which human beings might linger or fall, a place or state of tormenting remoteness from God.[36] "Your rays beamed intensely upon me, beating back my feeble gaze, and I trembled with love and dread. I knew myself to be far away from you in a region of unlikeness. . . . And I recognized that you have chastened man for his sin and caused my soul to dwindle away." A paradox unfolds: On the one hand, the human person is made in the image of God and seemingly called to the highest dignity of union with the divine. On the other hand, having lost sight of this dignity, man might come to no longer reflect God's likeness, becoming dissimilar not only from God but also thereby alienated from his or her true self, from what is most authentically human. The restless desire for God results from the tension between these two poles of godliness and seeming godforsakenness. And this tension is indicative in one sense of man's nothingness, as he leans toward the abyss, even while in another respect it suggests the hidden dignity and ever present possibility for salvation of a creature called to the life of grace.

Przywara perceived in such Augustinian themes the resources for a profound analysis of and response to the torturing enigmas of the modern self. God is immanent to the broken and bewildered spirit of man by virtue of the mystery of creation, as the radical transcendence of God is necessarily accompanied by his omnipresence and immanence.[37] God never abandons his creature and in fact is closer to each of us than we are to ourselves, calling us to himself.[38] Human contingency, which is in one sense an indication of our ontological possibility for nothingness and for the absence of meaning, is in another sense the sign par excellence of our vertiginous relativity to God. Therefore where the self seems the most irrefragably separated from God (most godless), there the wholly other dissimilarity of God in his tran-

---

35. Augustine, *Confessions* 1.1.1.

36. Cf. *Confessions* 7.10.16, trans. Maria Boulding, *The Confessions* (Hyde Park, N.Y.: New City Press, 1997).

37. See "Gott in uns und Gott über uns," in *Ringen der Gegenwart,* pp. 543-78. Cf. *Confessions* 3.6.11. See Przywara's early reflections on this in his *Religionsphilosophie katholischer Theologie* (Munich: R. Oldenbourg, 1927) (e.g., p. 83), which were in turn to reappear as a fundamental theme of *Analogia Entis.*

38. See *Analogia Entis,* p. 122 (84), p. 167 (121).

scendence may also appear anew: not necessarily as a recognized presence, but at least as an inescapable need, reflected (however paradoxically) in the human person's deep sense of the absence of meaning. Even in a culture infected by nihilism, then, it is impossible to efface in human persons the ontological possibility of redemption. For Przywara, however, the anthropological enigma of man — and the unfolding of his inner life — is never ultimately resolved except Christologically.[39] The aspiration to the transcendence of God naturally inhabits the human spirit, pointing it toward that which alone can satisfy its craving for the uncreated. But in the fallen state of man, this craving can be recognized for what it is, and lived out in the agonies of this world effectively in view of God, only in the light that Christ has cast upon human nature and with the grace that Christ affords.[40] The "philosophical" plight of the human person is resolved Christologically.

Simultaneously, this latter mystery (of Christ incarnate and crucified) recapitulates and exemplifies the union-in-differentiation of God and the human that the *analogia entis* originally suggests. In Christ the "original relation" of the creature to God is both restored and perfected. Just as the human creature is made for union with the transcendent God by grace and can cease to recognize its true self if it forgets this vocation, so also the union of God with humanity in Christ exposes the falsehood of the human forgetfulness of God (and all of the merely secular philosophies that are derivative therefrom) and through the experience of suffering turns created human nature "from within" back toward God, in a way that simultaneously glorifies in love both God and the human creation.[41] Otherwise stated, God's transcendent mystery is given anew to a wounded humanity in the mysteriously immanent presence of Christ crucified. In him, God's unknown otherness comes to be known *in* human brokenness as love. The dissimilarity between humanity and God deepened by sin finds a mysterious saving image of itself in the agony of the Son born in love. The Son's being united to what is furthest from God — human suffering and alienation — is the means to unite man to God.[42] And yet here the mystery of analogy is only deepened,

---

39. As John Betz, Kenneth Oakes, and Richard Schenk make clear in their essays in this volume, this Christological understanding of analogy was to intensify in Przywara's later work in the 1940s; see also von Balthasar, *The Theology of Karl Barth*, pp. 326-34.

40. See Przywara, "Die Reichweite der Analogie," pp. 352ff. Compare *Confessions* 7.17.23–18.24.

41. This theme is developed in depth in Przywara's later work *Deus Semper Maior* (Freiburg: Heider, 1938).

42. *Analogia Entis*, pp. 161ff.

not destroyed: for if Christ's human life is in one sense a bridge across the gulf of dissimilarity between God and creatures, in another sense the incarnation and passion deepen an awareness of the transcendence and incomprehensibility of God: the presence of God in Christ is a new form of incomprehensible mystery.[43] The "ever greater" character of God is revealed anew, even in the reconciling love of Christ.

Similar, if not identical, metaphysical and spiritual projects were being developed in the early twentieth century alongside Przywara's, most eminently by the French philosopher Maurice Blondel and by the Belgian Jesuit Joseph Maréchal.[44] In each of these thinkers we see the emergence of a modern anthropology guided by profoundly Augustinian themes, in which the aspirations of the self toward the transcendent are inevitable, even when they are not consciously acknowledged (or are willfully suppressed). Of course all three of these thinkers were to influence decisively the thought of Karl Rahner, whose original anthropological and Christological reflections are not wholly dissimilar from those of Przywara (as Richard Schenk suggests in his essay in this volume). In Rahner's ambitious modern theological anthropology (much more indebted to Kant than is Przywara's), the natural aspiration of the human person to transcendence is the locus for the perpetual unveiling of the meaning of Christian mystery. Only because we are always, already open to a self-communication on God's part is the revelation of Christ capable of being meaningful to us.[45] But precisely because only such a revelation on God's part can complete or fulfill us as human is the mystery of Christ essential to unlocking the puzzle of human existence.[46] Consequently, whereas metaphysical reflections can ascend toward God through analogical reflection, for Rahner these same re-

---

43. Ibid.

44. See, in particular, Maurice Blondel, *L'action* (1893 ed.) (Paris: Presses universitaires de France, 1995); Joseph Maréchal, *Le point de départ de la métaphysique*, vol. 5 (Paris: Librarie Félix Alcan, 1926).

45. See Karl Rahner, *Hörer des Wortes*, ed. J. B. Metz (Munich: Kösel, 1963; ET *Hearers of the Word*, trans. Michael Richards [New York: Herder & Herder, 1969]), esp. chaps. 4–5 and 13, pp. 45-68, 150-63.

46. See the conclusion of *Hearers of the Word*, pp. 175-76: "Philosophy, rightly understood, is always a *praeparatio evangelii* and is intrinsically Christian — not in the sense of a retrospective baptism, but because it forms a man who is able to hear God's message to the extent that he can do this for himself." Christ alone achieves our philosophical search for meaning, thereby allowing us to make sense of our personal history. See also Karl Rahner, "History of the World and Salvation-History," in *Theological Investigations*, vol. 5, trans. K. H. Kruger (London: Darton, Longman & Todd, 1966), pp. 97-114.

flections find their ultimate support and meaning existentially because of an already, always given "ground" of Christological grace, the supernatural-existential gift of divine presence and indwelling offered in Christ, through the Holy Spirit.[47] While the parallels noted here between Przywara and Rahner are obviously intended to be merely suggestive, it is clear that there are likenesses, and that the respective responses of these two great thinkers to the problem of antireligious alienation in modernity are indicative of an important strand of modern Catholic theology. For each, anthropology is understood most ultimately in light of a metaphysics of creation, and the meaning of the metaphysical dynamism of the human creature is resolved only in its ultimate pinnacle, who is the God-man, Christ. The philosophical mystery of the human person, then, is like a mountain whose summit approaches God but which trails off into the mists of faith. It is only in Christ, and by the light of faith, that the apex can be navigated and that the whole may be surveyed from a complete perspective, as seen from its Christological heights.

One can contrast this strand of theology with the descending Christological perspectives of Karl Barth, which were in turn to influence not a few Catholics. Barth's early work bears the influence of his pondering of the existential testimony of St. Augustine and expresses skepticism at a key juncture.[48] Speaking of the ascent toward God in the reflections of Augustine and Monica at Ostia (*Confessions* 9.10), he discusses the seductive attraction of a human way of reflection unto God, of the identification of a natural way of tending toward the divine that would be awakened, stimulated, and crowned by the workings of Christian grace. Over and against such a conception he declares that:

> What Augustine describes in *Conf.* IX, 10 is, according to his own account, the consequence of an *ascendere* and *transcendere* of all the limitations and restrictions of man's existence and situation. . . . [It] is certain that this *ascendere* and *transcendere* means abandoning, or at any rate wanting to abandon, the place where God encounters man in His revelation and where He gives Himself to be heard and seen by man. . . . If we really soar up to these heights . . . it simply means that we wilfully hurry past God, who descends in His revelation into this world of ours. Instead of finding Him where He Himself has sought us — namely, in

---

47. See Karl Rahner, *Foundations of Christian Faith: An Introduction to the Idea of Christianity,* trans. W. V. Dych (New York: Crossroad, 1978), pp. 24-43, 138-75, 178-81, 206-12.
48. *CD* II/1, pp. 10-12.

Thomas Joseph White, O.P.

His objectivity — we seek Him where He is not to be found, since He on His side seeks us in His Word.[49]

In his commentary on Romans, Barth had insisted, famously, that the revelatory action of God comes to the creature like a tangent line to a circle, signifying the human nonpossession of knowledge of God and the dialectically other, almost incomprehensible, character of grace, as regards all prior, natural dispositions or inner-human tendencies.[50] In the early *Church Dogmatics* (where Barth also reacts most vehemently to Przywara's theories), this is recomposed in terms of a revelatory actualism, by which the inbreaking revelation of God's action in Christ provides the unique basis for the knowledge of God but finds within man no corollary of an epistemological predisposition to revelation.[51] Famously, Barth rejects in just this respect Emil Brunner's notion of a fitting "point of contact" (*Anknüpfungspunkt*) in man by virtue of his created human nature, to which divine revelation is addressed.[52]

Long after the Przywara debate, Barth would go on to revive and rethink his Christological criteria for all knowledge in a thorough and very original way. After interpreting the knowledge of divine attributes in distinctly Christological terms in *Church Dogmatics* II/1 (so that none of the classical "attributes" of God might be considered except from and within reference to Christ), he would creatively reinterpret the doctrine of election in universalistic terms by rethinking it Christologically (in *Church Dogmatics* II/2).[53] In *CD* III/1 he would then interpret the doctrine of creation itself

49. Ibid., p. 11.

50. "In the Resurrection the new world of the Holy Spirit touches the old world of the flesh, but touches it as a tangent touches a circle, that is, without touching it" (Karl Barth, *The Epistle to the Romans,* 6th ed., trans. Edwyn C. Hoskyns [Oxford: Oxford University Press, 1968], p. 30).

51. See, for example, *CD* I/1, p. 41: Catholic theology errs because "grace here becomes nature, the action of God immediately disappears and is taken up into the action of the recipient of grace, that which is beyond all human possibilities changes at once into that which is enclosed with the reality of the Church." Behind this lies the problem that "Roman Catholic faith . . . affirms an *analogia entis,* the presence of a divine likeness of the creature even in the fallen world."

52. Ibid., pp. 27-36.

53. On this facet of Barth's thought, see Bruce McCormack, "Grace and Being: The Role of God's Gracious Election in Karl Barth's Theological Ontology," in *The Cambridge Companion to Karl Barth,* ed. John Webster, pp. 92-110 (Cambridge: Cambridge University Press, 2000).

in light of Christology and the election. Herein, the world is comprehended by and in the light of Christ, such that an understanding of the created order *as created* and *as utterly relative to God* is given only in and through the biblical revelation of the Son made man.[54] As Bruce McCormack argues eloquently in this volume, this process was completed, in some real sense, in the Christological ontology of Barth's later period (in *Church Dogmatics* IV/1-3). Whereas for Przywara, the human being is perfectly understood only *in Christ* as a creature ontologically turned toward God, for Barth, from beginning to end, Christ is the foundational condition for authentic understanding of what it is to be human, and how and under what conditions the human being may be said to relate to God or to resemble God analogically. In Christ alone is the human being truly confronted with true knowledge of God and of his or her election to life with God. But also, only in Christ is the human person even capable of understanding his or her true nature as *creature* and *as person*.[55] Throughout the development of Barth's thinking, the conversation with the Catholic doctrine of the *analogia entis* was never abandoned, but it received numerous reconsiderations and clarifications, which in turn did not leave Barth's thought unaffected.[56] Yet these reflections also always received a Christological form.

The notion of a Christological context for all philosophizing concerning the human person was an idea that was to resonate with a branch of Catholic thought in the twentieth century, most notably with Hans Urs von Balthasar. In the interim between himself and Barth there stands the important figure of Gottlieb Söhngen, the lay scholar of medieval Augustinianism and the mentor of the young Joseph Ratzinger. Söhngen was to perceive in

54. See, for example, *CD* III/1, pp. 11-12: "[I]t is again as this Eternal Father, and not in any other way, that He reveals Himself as the Creator, i.e., in Jesus Christ His Son by the Holy Ghost, in exact correspondence to the way in which He has inwardly resolved and decided to be the Creator. As He cannot be the Creator except as the Father, He is not known at all unless He is known in this revelation of Himself."

55. See, for example, ibid. III/2, pp. 222ff. (sect. 45, pt. 2: Jesus Christ as "The Basic Form of Humanity"); pp. 225-26: "For all the disparity [between ourselves and Christ] there is here presupposed a common factor, a parity, not merely between Jesus and other men, but, because between Jesus and other men, between God and man generally. When we ask: What is humanity, human creatureliness? we must first ask: What is its basic form? In other words, to what extent does human essence correspond to the determination of man to be the covenant-partner of God [by election]? Our criterion in answering this question is the humanity of the man Jesus."

56. On the *analogia entis*, see in particular *CD* II/1, pp. 81-85, 232, 529ff., and III/3, pp. 89-154.

Barth's own language of an "analogia fidei," in distinction from the *analogia entis,* the possibility of a dialogue, and he pursued this line of inquiry in a series of articles that were to become of significant ecumenical importance:[57] first, because Barth would write that he could accept this view of the *analogia entis,* were it to be understood as acceptable in the Catholic Church;[58] second, because this vision was in turn to influence in diverse ways a younger generation of Catholic theologians (among whom were von Balthasar and Ratzinger). Söhngen — by an implicit appeal to the patristic and medieval Augustinian tradition — aspired to present a Catholic understanding of reality as a total theological unity, in which ontological and philosophical discourse (the *analogia entis*) was always contextualized by Christology and a higher and more ultimate understanding of the Christian mystery (the *analogia fidei*).[59] Restated in more contemporary terms, the vocation of the Catholic intellectual in the modern world is to articulate a total worldview that is simultaneously theological and philosophical in the face of a human culture in which philosophical and scientific discourses and forms of understanding are multiple, partial, disunified, and sometimes incompatible. Christ is the condition for a final discernment and total integration of all lesser truths within the one saving truth that gives perspective to the whole, and that perspective is theological. Far from conflicting with the disciplines of science and philosophy, then, theology offers an irreplaceable gift of coherence, as the deeper and more total meaning invested in all things is brought forth to our knowledge in Christ and is unveiled in faith.

Evidently, one finds diverse echoes of this Christological form of reflection in the works of Hans Urs von Balthasar, whose great theological trilogy of the *Theo-Logic, Theological Aesthetics,* and *Theo-Drama* is an attempt to reread ontological reflection on the transcendentals (being as truth, beauty, and goodness, respectively) in light of Christ. Here the dual influences of Barth's Christocentrism and the classical metaphysics of being (not least of all as understood by Aquinas) are placed in critical correlation and are integrated into a unified whole in a highly original way. Joseph Ratzinger (now Pope Benedict XVI), meanwhile, has emphasized in a variety of writings the primacy of the divine Logos as the keystone to a Christian rationality in modernity.[60] The crisis of meaning in modernity is intimately related

57. Gottleib Söhngen, "Analogia fidei," *Catholica* 3 (1934): 113-36 and 176-208; and "Wunderzeichen und Glaube," *Catholica* 4 (1935): 145-64.

58. See *CD* II/1, pp. 81-84.

59. See the analysis of von Balthasar, *The Theology of Karl Barth,* pp. 311-19.

60. See, for example, Joseph Ratzinger (Benedict XVI), *Introduction to Christianity,*

to the loss of an overarching religious perspective, one in which the pursuit of knowledge is understood to have a final, and transcendent, purpose. Yet with Christ, the "rationality" that underlies creation is disclosed as a rationality of personal love and divine wisdom, thereby sanctioning in the most preeminent way the human desire for meaning and the pursuit of ultimate truth.[61] In the light of the cross, one can also have "faith in reason," in a search for a unifying perspective that is not in vain.[62] These reflections bring us to the last of our considerations: The question of the relationship between Christian faith and modern human reason as it was framed by the debate between Przywara and Barth.

III. Faith, Reason, and Natural Theological Knowledge of God

Of course both preceding sections of this Introduction point to an underlying issue concerning the traditional Catholic interpretation of natural knowledge of God and its relationship to faith. Patristic thinkers such as Gregory of Nazianzus, Augustine, or John of Damascus taught unambiguously that human reason has the natural capacity to obtain to some real knowledge of the existence of God and of some of his attributes as Creator, however imperfectly.[63] Aquinas, meanwhile, had developed quite an ambitious reflection on the human mind's inherent possibility for the metaphysical naming of God, by way of analogical comparison with creatures.[64] Furthermore, in his articulation of the *praeambula fidei,* the Angelic Doctor had argued that certain truths accessible in principle to natural reason (such as the truth of the existence of God or the incorruptibility of the human soul) were taught by divine revelation.[65] This is *not* because they are inaccessible

---

trans. J. R. Foster (San Francisco: Ignatius, 2000), pp. 74-79, 137-61; and *"In the Beginning . . .": A Catholic Understanding of the Story of Creation and the Fall,* trans. Boniface Ramsey (Grand Rapids: Eerdmans, 1998); Pope Benedict XVI, encyclical *Deus caritas est* (2005), sects. 10 and 13.

61. See, for example, Ratzinger, *Introduction to Christianity,* p. 143.

62. Ratzinger, *"In the Beginning . . . ,"* pp. 15-18, 79-100.

63. See, for example, Gregory of Nazianzus, *Orat.* 28; Augustine, *De lib. arbitrio* 2.7-33; *Serm.* 141; *Confessions* 7.10.16; 10.6.4; John Damascene, *De fide. orth.* 1.1 and 1.3.

64. *SCG* 1.32-34; *De pot.,* q. 7, aa. 5-7; *ST* I, q. 13. See the helpful study by Rudi te Velde, *Aquinas on God* (Aldershot: Ashgate, 2006).

65. *In Boeth. De Trin.,* q. 2, a. 3. See the study of this subject by Ralph McInerny, *Praeambula fidei: Thomism and the God of the Philosophers* (Washington, D.C.: Catholic University of America Press, 2006).

to philosophical thought but, rather, because they are truths that pertain immediately to human salvation and can be known by ordinary human reason only with great difficulty, such that they have been understood naturally only by a few, after a long time, and often admixed with error.[66] To attain to the heights of reason in a stable fashion, we have need of revelation. Nevertheless, Aquinas also inverted this claim to make clear that, while philosophy and metaphysical arguments for the existence of God develop best within the context of a Christian theological culture, they also do have a role to play *within* theological reflection, first as a means of understanding the mystery of faith more deeply, but also as a manner of demonstrating that Christianity — if it transcends the scope of natural human reason — is in no way *irrational*.[67] Theology itself has need of a reasonable philosophy to show the profound harmony and compatibility of divine revelation with ordinary human realism.

> The gifts of grace are added to nature in such a way that they do not destroy it, but rather perfect it. So too the light of faith, which is imparted to us as a gift, does not do away with the light of natural reason given to us by God. . . . Accordingly we can use philosophy in sacred doctrine in three ways. First, in order to demonstrate the preambles of faith, which we must necessarily know in [the act of] faith. Such are the truths about God that are proved by natural reason, for example, that God exists, that he is one, and other truths of this sort about God or creatures proved in philosophy and presupposed by faith. Second, by throwing light on the contents of faith by analogies, as Augustine uses many analogies drawn from philosophical doctrines in order to elucidate the Trinity. Third, in order to refute assertions contrary to the faith, either by showing them to be false or lacking in necessity.[68]

In the nineteenth century, and in the background of the Przywara-Barth debate, there lies the event of the First Vatican Council, in which the declaration *Dei Filius* declared (over and against the rationalist skepticism associated with Hume and Kant) that "God, the source and end of all things, can be known with certainty from the consideration of created things, by the natural power of human reason (Rom. 1:20)." And with somewhat solemn fi-

66. *SCG* 1.4-5; *ST* I, q. 1, a. 1.
67. *In Boeth. De Trin.*, q. 2, a. 3.
68. *Expos. de Trin.*, q. 2, a. 3 (trans. Ralph McInerny, *Aquinas: Selected Writings* [London: Penguin, 1998]).

nality the council added, "If anyone says that the one, true God, our Creator and Lord, cannot be known with certainty from the things that have been made, by the natural light of human reason, let him be anathema."[69] Subsequent to the council, the pontifical program of Leo XIII (1878-1903) insisted on the revival of Thomistic studies as a means to engage the secularization of modern academic culture, and this program was given an expanded ecclesial-legislative status at the beginning of the twentieth century under the influential pontificate of Pius X (1903-14).[70] This history, and the Thomistic revival to which it gave rise, is no doubt an influence of great underlying importance in the later discussions between Przywara and Barth in the 1920s.

On the one hand, Przywara saw himself as a defender of Vatican I precisely in his interpretation of the *analogia entis;* this council's insistence on the rationality of belief in God is associated by the Jesuit thinker directly with the analogical knowledge of God drawn from creatures, and also with the teaching of Lateran IV.[71] Even as we approach God philosophically or rationally, an "ever greater dissimilarity" between God and creatures emerges, so that while reason points us toward God, it also leaves us before an incomprehensible mystery that can be accepted and ultimately embraced fruitfully only in the Christological light of faith. Yet in offering this form of interpretation, Przywara was also suggesting the possibility of a more theological and Augustinian interpretation of Vatican I, one that would become more explicit in his later, midcentury writings.[72] According to this view, the wounded self can emerge from its godlessness *in view of* the true knowledge of God (both natural and supernatural) only if the heart is healed so as to

69. *Dei Filius,* chap. 2, and anathema 1 (trans. Norman Tanner, *Decrees of the Ecumenical Councils* [London: Sheed & Ward; Washington, D.C.: Georgetown University Press, 1990]).

70. On the nineteenth- and twentieth-century revival of modern Thomism, see Russell Hittinger, "*Pascendi Dominici Gregis* at 100: Two Modernisms, Two Thomisms; Reflections on the Centenary of Pius X's Letter against the Modernists," *Nova et Vetera,* Engl. ed., 5, no. 4 (2007): 843-80.

71. See *Analogia Entis,* pp. 73ff. (43ff.), 92-93 (82-83), 208-9 (153-54). See also "Die Reichweite der Analogie," in *Schriften,* 3:274-75, 293-94.

72. As von Balthasar points out in *The Theology of Karl Barth,* pp. 256-57, 328-29. P. 256 (citing Przywara's essay "Philosophie," *Philosophisches Jahrbuch,* 1949, pp. 1-9): "Insofar as [philosophy] has for its final form the form of the Cross, it preserves its natural form. Concretely existing philosophy in the one, single concrete order of original sin and redemption occurs to *the* extent, as authentic philosophy, that the Pauline dynamic 'we are called dead men and yet we live' (2 Cor. 6:9) is its working principle. The either/or of existing philosophy stands between 'originally sinful philosophy' and 'redeemed philosophy.'"

seek God willingly as its true end. Correspondingly, in a world that has forgotten Christ, is there a true knowledge of God (by natural reflection) that remains? Perhaps in a post-Christian civilization even the natural knowledge of God of which the human person is capable becomes obscured and effaced.[73] And correspondingly, perhaps it is only in an ecclesial cultural world in which Christ is known explicitly by grace and sought with all the resources of the human mind and heart that an authentic speculative metaphysical reflection about God and creatures can be safeguarded and rightly developed.

Such perspectives were to figure in important ways into subsequent reflection on Vatican I in the twentieth century, particularly in the thought of Hans Urs von Balthasar and subsequently in that of Walter Kasper.[74] These men have sought to hold together a dual affirmation of *both* the natural possibility of genuine metaphysical knowledge of God *and* the understanding that such knowledge may never have been achieved successfully outside of the Christian world of theology. The ecumenical potential for a rapprochement between this Augustinian perspective and the classical Protestant tradition should be evident, even if this perspective cannot be identified with that of the Barthian as such.

On the other hand, Barth was willing not only to renew Luther's critique of metaphysical speculation concerning God (termed diagnostically "theologia gloriae") but also to radicalize this critique, linking it to the criticisms of all possible natural theology as forms of merely human projection that are alien to the gospel.[75] Even as Barth sought to recenter all claims to

---

73. See von Balthasar on Przywara, *The Theology of Karl Barth,* pp. 256-57.

74. See von Balthasar's own reflections on the subject in *The Theology of Karl Barth,* pp. 302-25; Walter Kasper, *The God of Jesus Christ,* trans. Matthew O'Connell (New York: Crossroad, 1989), pp. 65-115, esp. p. 69.

75. This viewpoint is particularly manifest in Luther's Heidelberg Disputation: "That person is not rightly called a theologian who looks upon the invisible things of God as though they were clearly perceptible through things that have actually happened. . . . He deserves to be called a theologian who understands the visible and manifest things of God seen through suffering and the Cross. A theology of glory calls evil good and good evil. A theology of the Cross calls the thing what it actually is. That wisdom which sees the invisible things of God in works as perceived by man is completely puffed up, blinded, and hardened" (*Luther's Works,* ed. J. Pelikan [vols. 1-30] and H. Lehmann [vols. 31-55] [Philadelphia: Fortress Press, 1955-], 25:167). This aspect of Luther's thought became a subject of renewed interest in the early twentieth century. See the representative and influential study by Walther von Loewenich, *Luther's Theology of the Cross,* trans. Herbert Bouman (Belfast: Christian Journals, 1976). See Barth's *Church Dogmatics* I/1, pp. 14, 167, where he cites von Loewenich,

knowledge of God upon Christ and the revelatory action of God alone, he also claimed that all natural theology (whether Catholic or Protestant) stood as an obstacle to the right interpretation of Scripture.[76] Nor was he unaware that this stance conflicted directly with Vatican I, a truth he not only acknowledged but emphasized.[77] Of course, not all of Barth's Protestant contemporaries would agree with him in this respect, as evidenced by his famous controversy with Emil Brunner.[78] And even among Barth's students in a later generation there have been important disagreements in this regard. For example, while both Eberhard Jüngel and Wolfhart Pannenberg have been critical of analogy theory as they understand it (differently) to be articulated by Thomas Aquinas, Pannenberg, in contrast to Jüngel, has increasingly insisted in his later work upon the veracity of some form of human natural knowledge of God.[79]

While both Protestant and Catholic theologians have explored possibilities for some form of ecumenical convergence on the question of "natural theology" in the twentieth century, the magisterium of the Catholic Church has not remained neutral in the discussion. Without excluding the Augustinian tradition's insistence upon the damaging effects of sin on the human intellect, the pontificates of Pius XII (1939-58), Paul VI (1963-78), and John Paul II (1978-2005), as well as the Second Vatican Council, all insisted in the face of secularism on the natural human capacity to arrive at some form of knowledge of God, however imperfect.[80] In particular, the pa-

---

and 178-79, on Luther's distinction between a *theologia gloriae* and a *theologia crucis* as applied to the possibility of natural theology.

76. See in particular *CD* II/1, pp. 63-178.

77. Ibid., pp. 79-84.

78. See Emil Brunner, *Natur und gnade. Zum gespräch mit Karl Barth* (Zürich: Zwingli-Verlag, 1935), and Karl Barth, "Nein! Antwort an Emil Brunner," *Theological Existenz Haute* 14 (1934): 4-63.

79. See Wolhart Pannenberg, *Systematic Theology*, vol. 1, trans. Geoffrey W. Bromiley (Grand Rapids: Eerdmans, 1991), pp. 63-118 on the distinction between "natural theology" and "natural knowledge of God," contrasted with Eberhard Jüngel, *God as the Mystery of the World: On the Foundation of the Theology of the Crucified One in the Dispute between Theism and Atheism*, trans. Darrell L. Guder (Grand Rapids: Eerdmans, 1983), pp. 261-98. For these authors' contrasting interpretations of Aquinas, see the essay by Reinhard Hütter in this volume.

80. See in particular Pius XII, *Humani generis* (1950), *Acta apostolicae sedis* 42 (1950): 561, Denzinger, *Enchiridion Symbolorum*, 3875, which is cited anew in the 1994 Catechism of the Catholic Church, sects. 37-38: "Though human reason is, strictly speaking, truly capable by its own natural power and light of attaining to a true and certain knowledge of the one personal God, who watches over and controls the world by his providence, and of the natu-

pal encyclical of John Paul II *Fides et ratio* (1998) strongly insisted upon the "metaphysical range" of the human intellect that is capable even of analogical knowledge of God, commending in particular toward this end a renewal of study of the thought of Thomas Aquinas.[81]

Such pronouncements should be contextualized by reference to the twentieth-century revival of Thomistic studies, inspired by the renewal of scholastic studies launched by Leo XIII.[82] In response to the rise of modern atheistic philosophical trends, thinkers such as Étienne Gilson, Jacques Maritain, Cornelius Fabro, Bernard Montagnes, Ralph McInerny, Gustav Siewerth, and Ferdinand Ulrich have all directly addressed a range of issues that touch in some way directly upon the Przywara-Barth debate: from natural knowledge of God, to analogical predication, to the question of the *praeambula fidei* and of their relationship to supernatural faith. Siewerth and Ulrich in particular have also reflected directly upon the role of the analogy of being *in* Christology, the latter in dialogue with the thought of Hans Urs von Balthasar.[83] In all of these thinkers, we find a robust insistence on the natural human capacity for metaphysical and analogical knowledge of God, derived from a philosophical consideration of creatures. This Thomistic tradition of reflection represents an influential strand of thought in the Catholic Church, as it seeks to present viable rational arguments for the existence of God as a means of interpreting the position of Vatican I. As

ral law written in our hearts by the Creator; yet there are many obstacles which prevent reason from the effective and fruitful use of this inborn faculty. For the truths that concern the relations between God and man wholly transcend the visible order of things, and, if they are translated into human action and influence it, they call for self-surrender and abnegation. The human mind, in its turn, is hampered in the attaining of such truths, not only by the impact of the senses and the imagination, but also by disordered appetites which are the consequences of original sin. So it happens that men in such matters easily persuade themselves that what they would not like to be true is false or at least doubtful." Both texts refer in turn to *ST* I, q. 1, a. 1, and *Dei Filius*. See also *Dei Verbum*, sect. 6, and the commentary on this passage in the encyclical *Fides et ratio* (1998) of John Paul II, sects. 8ff.

81. Cf. *Fides et ratio*, sects. 43-44, 83-84; n. 84: "Faith clearly presupposes that human language is capable of expressing divine and transcendent reality in a universal way — analogically, it is true, but no less meaningfully for that. Were this not so, the word of God, which is always a divine word in human language, would not be capable of saying anything about God."

82. See the observations on this phenomenon by Alasdair MacIntyre, *Three Rival Versions of Moral Enquiry* (Notre Dame, Ind.: University of Notre Dame Press, 1990), pp. 58-81.

83. See, in particular, Gustav Siewerth, *Der Thomismus als Identitätssystem* (Frankfurt: Verlag Schulte-Bulmke, 1939), and Ferdinand Ulrich, *Homo abyssus. Das Wagnis der Seinsfrage* (Einsiedeln: Johannes Verlag, 1998).

such, it helps us to identify a major point of outstanding difference between Barth and classic Catholic theology. Consequently, a treatment of the "analogy of being" in contemporary Roman Catholic theology merits the reception of substantive input from the modern Thomistic tradition, precisely so as to deepen and prolong the ecumenical character of the Przywara-Barth debate.

Finally, underlying the question of faith and reason as related to the analogy of being is the issue of the Christian response to the conflict in contemporary culture between the extreme secularization of the academy (with its prescribed forms of postreligious rational discourse as those that are uniquely normative) and emergent forms of religiosity (particularly in Islamic forms, but by no means exclusively so) that find secular culture intolerable or incomprehensible. As Benedict XVI, the former student of Gottlieb Söhngen, argued pointedly in his Regensburg address of 2006, the renewal of the intellectual health of the modern academy requires the development of an intellectual *via media* between the extremes of secularism and the religious rejection of the engagement with modernity.[84] A merely empiricist reason that refuses to confront the metaphysical dimensions of reality and the question of the existence of God sterilizes the intellect and imprisons the human spirit within an artificially constraining horizon of immanence. Such a truncated form of rationality cannot understand the genuinely religious aspirations of the human heart and mind and, consequently, is itself easily misunderstood in turn by genuinely religious adherents.[85] However, one must equally avoid the promotion of a religious sense of transcendence that refuses to engage sufficiently the rational complexity of modern science and history, the immanent sphere of human democratic culture and society.[86] Both of these forms of thought are plagued by an excessively univocal form of reflection: either all is understood in terms of the limited forms of this finite world that empirical reason seeks endlessly to master (so that the transcendence of God is ignored or uncomprehended). Or, everything is un-

---

84. Benedict XVI, "Faith, Reason, and the University: Memories and Reflections," University of Regensburg speech, September 12, 2006.

85. Ibid.: "In the Western world it is widely held that only positivistic reason and the forms of philosophy based on it are universally valid. Yet the world's profoundly religious cultures see this exclusion of the divine from the universality of reason as an attack on their most profound convictions. A reason which is deaf to the divine and which relegates religion into the realm of subcultures is incapable of entering into the dialogue of cultures."

86. Ibid.: "The decisive statement in this argument against violent conversion is this: not to act in accordance with reason is contrary to God's nature."

derstood as ultimately relative to the intelligibility of God and God's will, such that the inner "difference" of the world, of human freedom, and of the scientific and historical complexity of modern thought is not acknowledged sufficiently or permitted to emerge fully within a true dialogue of ongoing theological reflection.[87]

Between these two extremes lies the way of analogy — namely, the view that the world is itself invested with meaning, ethical purpose, and intelligibility, of which it cannot be (rationally) divested, even in the name of God and religion. However, the world invested with such meaning, purpose, and intelligibility is itself suggestive of a higher, and more mysterious, Logos, or reason, that underlies the creation and has given it being out of love. The world thus speaks by analogy of a higher wisdom — the wisdom of God — that is not wholly extrinsic to natural human rationality and that is not wholly unintelligible. "The faith of the Church has always insisted that between God and us, between his eternal Creator Spirit and our created reason there exists a real analogy, in which — as the Fourth Lateran Council in 1215 stated — unlikeness remains infinitely greater than likeness, yet not to the point of abolishing analogy and its language. God does not become more divine when we push him away from us in a sheer, impenetrable voluntarism; rather, the truly divine God is the God who has revealed himself as *logos* and, as *logos,* has acted and continues to act lovingly on our behalf."[88] A purely equivocal account of our knowledge of God leads to an extrinsicism of faith to reason, and therefore gives rise either to an irrational faith or to a truncated reason that is alienated from belief. The heart of the human person remains in either case an unresolved puzzle. Only by understanding all things in the light of the uncreated Logos who is love — the Logos who became flesh — is the rationality of the creation and of the human person fully manifest, such that this same rationality is opened up from within to its plenary fulfillment in God.

---

87. Ibid.: "This gives rise to positions which . . . might even lead to the image of a capricious God, who is not even bound to truth and goodness. God's transcendence and otherness are so exalted that our reason, our sense of the true and good, are no longer an authentic mirror of God, whose deepest possibilities remain eternally unattainable and hidden behind his actual decisions."

88. Ibid.

IV. Conclusion: The Analogy of Being: Invention of the Antichrist or the Wisdom of God?

All of the essays in this volume address in various ways each of the themes that were sketched out above, and all of them discuss in greater detail one or more of the thinkers previously mentioned. As such, they attempt to address the seemingly stark contrast of the initial phase of the Przywara-Barth debate: Is the analogy of being the "invention of the Antichrist," or is it the signature in creation of the wisdom of God? Furthermore, how did this highly nuanced discussion between the great Jesuit and the Swiss Reformed theologian play itself out in successive generations, and how should our interpretation of it be colored by the Thomistic revival of the twentieth century, as well as by the concerns of contemporary theology? Because the essays contained herein focus on the significance of this debate with a view toward its actual theological significance, they are arranged primarily by their thematic content insofar as it pertains to chronology.

The first section of the book contains studies by John Betz and Bruce McCormack on the original dispute between Przywara and Barth. Both of these contemporary theologians have striven in exemplary fashion to reevaluate the thought of these theological mentors, demonstrating in clear and newly revealing ways the substance and relevance of this initial debate. For his part, John Betz offers a clear and enlightening view of the early work of Przywara on the *analogia entis,* showing how this thought is at once deeply rooted in the Augustinian and Thomistic traditions and simultaneously very original. He discusses some of the important ways in which Przywara's thought developed in successive decades after the Barth debate and argues convincingly that this great theological achievement has been problematically ignored, even as it offers to contemporary theology extremely profound resources.

Bruce McCormack presents an insightful contextual study of the early Barthian rejection of the analogy of being and then details masterfully the ways in which Barth's thought on analogy developed. He does this in lucid and critical confrontation with von Balthasar's theories on Barth's development, and then details how the Christology of *Church Dogmatics* IV/1-3 has given rise in recent German Barth scholarship to a new form of reflection on the relationship between election and the triune identity of God. McCormack offers a forceful and eloquent, if not uncontroversial, account of why and how this reading of Barth's later thought helps us to make sense of Barth's deepest intuitions on the relation between election, Christology, and analogy, intuitions that McCormack believes should contribute to constructive contemporary theological work.

The second section of the book considers the ecumenical fruits of the Przywara-Barth debate as they unfolded during the generation after the initial debate, and looks at how these conversations affect the landscape of contemporary Catholic theology in particular. Kenneth Oakes, following a theological insight from the work of Joseph Ratzinger, offers a careful ecumenical reevaluation of Przywara as a theologian of the cross. Beginning from a consideration of Przywara's interpretation of the distinctly doctrinal importance of analogy as understood by Lateran IV, Oakes demonstrates that the German theologian's understanding of the *analogia entis* is endemic to his *theological* understanding of Christ, and of the divine-human communion that is realized within the divine economy. He then goes on to show how Przywara's later reflections on the *commercium,* or grace-filled "exchange" between Christ and ourselves in the mystery of the crucifixion, both presupposes and deepens an appreciation of the analogy between God and creatures.

Richard Schenk compares and contrasts the work of Erich Przywara with that of Gottlieb Söhngen and shows how the differing reactions to Barth of each contributed to the development of modern Catholic theology in differing directions. Schenk insightfully identifies foreshadowings of Rahner's work in the writing of Przywara and of von Balthasar's work in the theories of Söhngen. He does this while offering an insightful Thomistic rejoinder to the theological concerns of each of these strands of modern Catholic theology. Peter Casarella details ways in which Hans Urs von Balthasar, in his famous study of Karl Barth, sought not only to understand the Reformed theologian in a sympathetic Catholic light but also to set the bases for a new form of Catholic theological reflection, in contradistinction to (but also in simultaneous dependence upon) both Przywara and Barth. Von Balthasar's reconsideration of the analogy of being in a Christological light and his simultaneous reconsideration of Christology as it relates to classic metaphysics gives his thought a distinct richness and profundity, as he is self-consciously the inheritor of both Barth and Przywara and attempts to resituate the concerns of each within a yet greater whole.

The third section of the book invites representatives from the contemporary Thomistic world to weigh in on the theological significance of the Barth-Przywara debate, with reference to twentieth-century Thomistic scholarship. In response to the criticisms of both Pannenberg and Jüngel to the thought of Aquinas, Reinhard Hütter offers an architectonic account of

St. Thomas's analogy theory of divine names, appealing in particular to the influential modern research of the French Dominican Bernard Montagnes.[89] This understanding of Aquinas examines ontological similitudes among creatures and the way these creatures are in turn related to the causality of God as Creator. Analogical discourse concerning God is seen to have its foundation in an ontology of participated being. Aquinas's theory of analogy avoids, Hütter claims, the excesses of both equivocal and univocal discourse that Jüngel and Pannenberg problematically attribute to it.

The essay in the volume by Thomas Joseph White examines Aquinas's thought on the distinctly theological analogy of the Son of God as the "Word" incarnate, and it attempts to ask St. Thomas a Barthian-Przywarian question: in what sense is the *analogia fidei,* or the analogical knowledge of Christ as the Word of God given in faith, itself dependent implicitly upon an *analogia entis,* or the analogical knowledge of God by metaphysical reflection? Does Christology require a natural theology? To these contemporary questions, the essay attempts to offer responses that are inspired by the reflection of St. Thomas, answering in the affirmative.

Bruce Marshall, meanwhile, adopts as his guide to analogy in Aquinas the theories of Ralph McInerny (centered primarily on the use of logical predication rather than ontology),[90] using this approach to emphasize simultaneously (1) the utter transcendence of God with respect to our natural human knowledge and (2) the utter immanence and presence of God in Christ as a human like ourselves. This interpretation of St. Thomas's texts stresses the near-inaccessibility of God for natural human thought, while underscoring the unique proximity and intelligibility of God as he is made known to us in Christ. As such, it suggests important points of convergence between Aquinas and the Protestant tradition.

Martin Bieler offers a rich and intriguing presentation of the metaphysical thought of the German Thomist Ferdinand Ulrich, who was a close friend of von Balthasar and an influence upon the latter. Ulrich addresses in a direct and profound way a number of the key themes of the Przywara-Barth debate, placing these ideas in dialogue with contemporary European philosophy as well. Most notably, Ulrich's thought understands the analogy of being to be expressive of God's gift of creation, as a gift of love. Yet this gift

---

89. See Bernard Montagnes, *La doctrine de l'analogie de l'être d'après Saint Thomas d'Aquin* (Louvain: Publications Universitaires, 1963).

90. See in particular Ralph McInerny, *Aquinas and Analogy* (Washington, D.C.: Catholic University of America Press, 1996).

of existence to all beings is itself suggestive of a more ultimate mystery (known only to the theologian) of the gift of God the Son to the world by the goodness of God the Father.

The fourth and final section of the book considers the *analogia entis* debate immediately in the context of contemporary theology. Michael Hanby considers ways in which the implicit *philosophical* presuppositions of modern science hamper our attempt to understand integrally the beauty and integrity of the physical world as the creation of God. A metaphysical and theological retrieval of the analogical naming of God from creatures leads to a deepened consideration of creation as reflective of the beauty of God. It does so while facilitating the recovery of a more complete epistemology, one that can better appreciate the integrity of the natural sciences, while envisaging their methodological practices within the context of a broader theology of creation.

John Webster offers a beautiful consideration of the theology of the letter to the Ephesians and explains how a Reformed theology can take into account the dignity and freedom of the created order of human persons, while simultaneously understanding this order as itself summoned in Christ toward fulfillment in the filial adoption that is proper to the children of God. This filiation has its source, measure, and term in the mystery of God revealed in Christ, so that a vivid doctrine of Christological election allows a simultaneous understanding of the freedom and goodness of God, and of the freedom and goodness of a redeemed humanity. The two coexist in a mutual likeness without rivalry, but also in a subordinated and beautiful order.

Finally, David Bentley Hart, perhaps the most well-known contemporary interpreter and defender of Erich Przywara,[91] argues that an orthodox understanding of the divinity of the Logos that emerged in the wake of the Council of Nicaea required of Christianity in turn the self-conscious development of an analogical metaphysics of creation, one that could articulate vividly the nonreciprocal relativity of creation with respect to God. This metaphysical tradition is of perennial importance precisely so as to preserve a distinctly Christian sense of the transcendent distinction between God and creatures, and the simultaneous reference of the latter to the former, a distinction made most manifest in the mystery of the incarnation. Only such an ontology can permit us to avoid a metaphysics of identity that reductively enfolds the created order into the absolute, or that seeks problematically to

---

91. See David Bentley Hart, *The Beauty of the Infinite: The Aesthetics of Christian Truth* (Grand Rapids: Eerdmans, 2003), pp. 155-249, esp. pp. 241ff.

elevate God by banishing all trace of him from the world. Christology invites a purification, then, of our mistaken views of creation and a corresponding liberation from a reductively intraworldly ontology, inviting us instead to see all creatures as contingently meaningful expressions of God's infinite goodness, and as beings dynamically recapitulated in the Logos incarnate.

Each of the essays in this volume bears eloquent witness to the ongoing significance of the Przywara-Barth debate and to the perduring vitality of their respective theological projects. In particular, the ecumenical fruitfulness of this initial and historic modern attempt at Roman-Reformed dialogue led to greater mutual understanding, constructive criticism, and self-clarification. These qualities are echoed in the ecumenical character of the essays in this volume. For herein one finds a dense and complex assortment of mutual influences: of modern Protestant, Orthodox, and Roman Catholic theological traditions speaking to one another, in critical dialogue and controversy. The debate concerning the analogy of being in modern theology is not resolved, and though it has led to the identification of some important points of convergence, it has also helped to underscore places of outstanding difference. These differences are of course not always a hindrance to greater theological reflection, but when they are a source of ecclesial division, they are also an invitation to identify accurately the true sources of discord and to locate the deeper grounds of unity. Unity among Christians is the will of Christ, "so that they may be one, as [Christ and the Father] are one" (John 17:22). As Erich Przywara rightly noted, it was within the context of an ecclesiological and trinitarian (and therefore distinctly theological) dispute concerning the meaning of this very passage from Scripture that the doctrinal formula of the *analogia entis* took shape at the Fourth Lateran Council, precisely so as to recognize the unity of the church as both a gift of grace (and therefore as a true participation in the life of the triune God) and yet simultaneously as a merely created participation in this same life, not identical with the transcendent mystery of the deity as such. Debate about the analogy of being in modern theology is of importance, not only that we might become more aware of the intellectual structure of the Christian tradition as it relates to a post-Christian modernity, but also so that in a world that is increasingly secular, and that increasingly risks finding Christianity incomprehensible, Christians can seek to bear witness with a united, scriptural, and apostolic voice to the mystery of the triune Creator, who has redeemed the world in Christ, and whose creation resounds with his glory.

PART I

RECONSIDERING THE THEOLOGICAL CONTOURS OF THE ORIGINAL DEBATE

CHAPTER 1

After Barth: A New Introduction to Erich Przywara's *Analogia Entis*

John R. Betz

> As a consequence of Erich Przywara's work — which cannot be
> admired enough — the term *analogia entis* developed into a con-
> troversial theological formula that has doubtless been invoked
> more often than it has been even remotely understood.
>
> — Eberhard Jüngel[1]

It is, of course, not unheard of in the history of Christianity for theological
doctrines to turn upon a single phrase — such as *homoousios* (concerning
the divinity of Christ as the incarnate Son), *filioque* (concerning the eternal
procession of the Holy Spirit from the Son), and the Reformation's shibbo-
leth *sola fide* (concerning salvation), to name some of the most obvious examples. In the first decades of the twentieth century, however, at least in Germany, no single phrase was the subject of more theological controversy than
the seemingly innocuous metaphysical term *analogia entis*.[2] Compared with

---

1. Eberhard Jüngel, *Gott als Geheimnis der Welt*, 6th ed. (Tübingen: Mohr Siebeck,
1992), p. 357. At the outset I would like to express my thanks to Eberhard Jüngel for the pleasure of occasional conversations about Przywara, and also to Hans-Anton Drewes for a seminar on this topic in Tübingen in the summer semester of 1997.

2. For some of the more notable contributions to the debate, see Hermann Diem,
"Analogia fidei gegen analogia entis. Ein Beitrag zur Kontroverstheologie," *Evangelische
Theologie* 3 (1936): 157-80; Gottlieb Söhngen, "Analogia fidei I: Gottähnlichkeit allein aus
Glauben?" and "Analogia fidei II: Die Einheit in der Glaubenswissenschaft," *Catholica* 3

the significance of these other catchphrases, the *analogia entis* might not seem especially important. Indeed, an outsider to this controversy might legitimately think it a suitable matter of discussion for specialists and academic theologians who have the time to be exercised by abstruse metaphysical questions, but hardly relevant to the church — and the beliefs of Christians — at large.

And yet, as the participants in the debate recognized, what was at issue with the *analogia entis* was not just any theological doctrine, but in some sense the most basic of all doctrines: the doctrine of the relation between God and creation. To Erich Przywara, S.J., its most important and brilliant proponent, it was a succinct way of stating the Catholic understanding of creation over against what he perceived to be the dialectical extremes of "pantheism" (ancient and modern) and Lutheran-Reformed "theopanism" (as he saw exemplified in the theology of the early Barth).[3] To Karl Barth, however, its most vociferous critic, the *analogia entis* represented everything that was wrong with natural theology and, by extension, the Catholic Church. In fact, in the preface to his *Church Dogmatics,* he went so far as to denounce the *analogia entis* as "*the* invention of Antichrist," and to say that, by comparison, all other reasons for not becoming Catholic were "short-sighted" and "frivolous."[4]

The tenor of these remarks is familiar; Barth expresses himself with similar vehemence in such works as his *Römerbrief* (1922) and his *Nein! Antwort an Emil Brunner* (1934). On the face of it, therefore, one could rea-

---

(1934): 113-36 and 176-208; idem, "Analogia entis oder analogia fidei?" in *Die Einheit in der Theologie* (Munich: K. Zink, 1952); Hans Urs von Balthasar, "Analogie und Dialektik. Zur Klärung der theologischen Prinzipienlehre Karl Barths," *Divus Thomas* 22 (1944): 171-216; *Karl Barth. Darstellung und Deutung seiner Theologie*, 4th ed. (Einsiedeln: Johannes Verlag, 1976); Emil Brunner, *Dogmatik: Die Christliche Lehre von der Schöpfung und Erlösung* (Zürich: Theologischer Verlag, 1950), pp. 54-56.

3. The specific meaning of these terms in Przywara's vocabulary will be explained in what follows.

4. Karl Barth, *Kirchliche Dogmatik* (Munich: C. Kaiser; Zurich: TVZ, 1932-67) (hereafter *KD*), I/I, p. viii. (All translations of the *KD* are by the author.) While Barth clearly has Przywara's doctrine of the *analogia entis* in mind, as Bruce McCormack has pointed out, it is important to observe that in the context of his preface Barth was not so much addressing Przywara as his Protestant confreres, intending by this statement to repudiate absurd charges of crypto-Catholicism (on the part of Georg Wobbermin) and to take Brunner and other Protestant theologians to task for too readily mixing in the Catholic business of natural theology. See in the present volume, Bruce McCormack, "Karl Barth's Version of an 'Analogy of Being': A Dialectical No and Yes to Roman Catholicism."

sonably take such remarks as simply another example of his characteristically bombastic, hyperbolic style — as exaggerated rhetoric and nothing more. And yet, as was the case with these other works, it is clear that Barth was quite serious. Indeed, from the programmatic nature of his preface, there is no denying that he viewed the *analogia entis* (metonymically identified with the Catholic Church) as antithetical to the entire project of his *Church Dogmatics*, in which he proposes to steer his own *via media* between the supposed Scylla of Roman Catholicism and the Charybdis of liberal Protestantism. For any number of reasons, therefore, his charges against the *analogia entis* continue to warrant careful consideration — on the part of Catholic theologians, who would want to defend or clarify the teachings of the church; on the part of Reformed theologians, who may wish to reassess their own position; and on the part of anyone interested in the possibility of ecumenical dialogue, which Barth's peremptory verdict perhaps prematurely foreclosed.

Of course, it may turn out upon more careful examination of Przywara's doctrine that Barth was mistaken about the *analogia entis;* it may be, in von Balthasar's judgment, that "nothing whatever can be found of that ogre Barth has made of the analogy of being."[5] Before any final judgments can be made, however, it would seem obligatory to know what Przywara himself understood by the *analogia entis,* since it was Przywara whom Barth had in mind in rejecting it — and, with it, the Catholic Church. Is the *analogia entis* a refurbished version of natural theology, which gives the creature a metaphysical "hold" on God and thereby compromises the novelty and due theological priority of faith and revelation, as Barth seems to have feared? Or is it, beyond the sphere of natural theology, a formal principle that pertains even to the content of faith and revelation, as Przywara tirelessly insisted? To put it as sharply as possible, is the *analogia entis* "*the* invention of Antichrist," or is it in fact a doctrine based in and commended by Scripture, which declares in a passage echoed in Paul's letter to the Romans: "From the greatness and beauty of created things comes a corresponding perception of their Creator" (Wis. 13:5; cf. Rom. 1:20)?

Unfortunately, any effort to answer these questions today is greatly hindered by the fact that what the *analogia entis* actually means (or at least what it meant to Erich Przywara) has to a great extent been forgotten —

---

5. Hans Urs von Balthasar, *The Theology of Karl Barth,* trans. E. Oakes (San Francisco: Ignatius Press, 1992), p. 50.

along with any memory of Przywara himself, around whom, like the quiet center of a storm, this great theological controversy turned. Admittedly, the term *analogia entis* is not original to Przywara; it can be traced back to Cajetan and can be found thereafter as a *terminus technicus* among the religious orders.[6] But it was Przywara who reintroduced the term and gave it a more comprehensive meaning, transforming it, in the words of Karl Rahner, "from a scholastic technicality into the fundamental structure of Catholic theology."[7] And, importantly, it was in this form that the *analogia entis* became the subject of ecumenical debate.[8] In the following, therefore, as a matter of necessity, given his current obscurity, I will first give a brief account of Przywara's place in modern theology. Second, going back to the roots of the *analogia entis* in the philosophical and theological tradition, I will discuss its provenance both as a term and as a metaphysical concept. Third, I will set forth the meaning of the *analogia entis* as Przywara himself understood it: in his early work and lectures from 1922 to 1925, and then in his *Religionsphilosophie katholischer Theologie* (1926) and *Analogia Entis* (1932). Finally, with the real *analogia entis* in view, and not some chimera or caricature, I will assess the legitimacy of Barth's criticisms of it, asking whether Przywara was, after all, right to consider it a "fundamental form" of Catholic theology.

I. Erich Przywara (1889-1972)

In view of Przywara's prominence as a Catholic theologian among the intellectual elite of Europe during the first half of the twentieth century, it is somewhat baffling that he is so little known and studied today.[9] To give some

6. See Julio Terán-Dutari, "Die Geschichte des Terminus 'Analogia entis' und das Werk Erich Przywaras," *Philosophisches Jahrbuch der Görres-Gesellschaft* 77 (1970): 163-79.
7. Karl Rahner, "Laudatio auf Erich Przywara," in *Gnade als Freiheit. Kleine theologische Beiträge* (Freiburg: Herder, 1971), p. 270.
8. See von Balthasar, *The Theology of Karl Barth*, p. 35: "In designating this principle [of the analogy of being] as the touchstone for everything Catholic, Barth is in essence adopting the usage first adumbrated by Erich Przywara. . . . But Barth is also explicitly accepting Przywara's own estimation of the analogy of being as an expressly *formal* principle, something Przywara was the first to do."
9. See, however, the important recent work of Thomas O'Meara, *Erich Przywara, S.J.: His Theology and His World* (Notre Dame, Ind.: University of Notre Dame Press, 2002), which provides the best introduction to Przywara and the larger context of his theology to date. See also the studies in English by James Collins, Niels Nielsen, and James Zeitz (noted

indication of his importance, he was a leading editor of the Jesuit journal *Stimmen der Zeit* from 1922 until it was shut down by the Nazis in 1941; he was a regular public lecturer (e.g., at the famous Davos seminar in 1928); and he was the prolific author of over forty monographs and as many as 800 articles and reviews. Aside from the *Analogia Entis* (1932), arguably the most important work of Catholic metaphysics in the twentieth century, these works include studies of Kierkegaard (1929), Kant (1930), and Hölderlin (1949); popular anthologies of Augustine and Newman (Przywara was also the editor of the first German edition of Newman's translated works); a massive three-volume commentary on Ignatius's *Spiritual Exercises,* entitled *Deus Semper Maior* (1938); an equally massive 900-page compilation *Humanitas* (1952), which covers a shocking range of thinkers and literary figures of the Western tradition from Heraclitus to Thomas Wolfe; several works of biblical exegesis, including *Christentum gemäß Johannes* (1954) and *Alter und Neuer Bund* (1956); a fascinating if somewhat arcane metaphysical anthropology, simply titled *Mensch* (1959); ecclesiological works such as *Kirche in Gegensätzen* (1962) and *Katholische Krise* (1967), not to mention several collections of hymns, prayers, liturgical reflections, and works of religious poetry.

Simply put, there is no German Catholic theologian of the first half of the twentieth century who can match the range of Przywara's erudition or the remarkable acuity of his intellect. And so it stands to reason that Barth felt compelled, in one way or another, to be in conversation with him — inviting him to his seminar in Münster in 1929 and in Bonn in 1931.[10] As Barth describes Przywara in a letter from this time:

> He also knows everything, everything which we think we know, except that, always right at the proper moment, he does not make use of it. The

---

in O'Meara's bibliography), and for a summary of Przywara's thought (and its possible implications for a theological aesthetics) vis-à-vis Barth and other critics of the *analogia entis,* John R. Betz, "Beyond the Sublime: The Aesthetics of the Analogy of Being" (pt. 2), *Modern Theology* 22 (January 2006): 21-30.

10. I am indebted to Christophe Chalamet and Keith Johnson for helpful conversations about Barth's relationship with Przywara at this time. See Johnson, *Karl Barth and the Analogia Entis,* forthcoming with T. & T. Clark. For the most extensive treatments of Barth and Przywara, see Bernhard Gertz, *Glaubenswelt als Analogie. Die theologische Analogie-Lehre Erich Przywaras und ihr Ort in der Auseinandersetzung um die analogia fidei* (Düsseldorf: Patmos Verlag, 1969), and Eberhard Mechels, *Analogie bei Erich Przywara und Karl Barth, Das Verhältnis von Offenbarungstheologie und Metaphysik* (Neukirchen: Neukirchener Verlag, 1974).

Catholic Church is becoming for me more and more *the* amazing phenomenon. In comparison, our Protestant opponents look very much like dwarfs, don't you think? . . . This Jesuit was really something I had never seen before. He also told me that I too am for him *the* opponent *par excellence.* He is a little man with a large head, but that doesn't mean he is not the giant Goliath incarnate.[11]

As C. Chalamet has commented, it would be "an understatement to say that Barth was impressed by Przywara," who remained for Barth as well *the* opponent *par excellence,* against whom even Barth's late doctrine of an *analogia fidei (relationis)* is defined.[12]

If Przywara was this highly regarded by the most famous Protestant theologian of the twentieth century, he was no less admired by Karl Rahner and Hans Urs von Balthasar, his most famous students, who speak glowingly of Przywara as a teacher and clearly reflect in their own theologies particular aspects of his work and thought.[13] Consider, for example, von Balthasar's remarkable statement in 1945 that Przywara was "the greatest spirit I was ever permitted to meet";[14] or the words of Rahner in 1965: "One must not forget Father Erich Przywara. For the Catholics of Germany in the twenties, thirties, and forties he was considered one of the greatest minds. He had a great influence on all of us when we were young."[15]

It would seem that Rahner and von Balthasar first came into contact with Przywara during their philosophical studies at the Jesuit *Berchmanskolleg* (at the time in Pullach), just outside of Munich. In von Balthasar's case the fruit of his study with Przywara between 1930 and 1932 is reflected in his

11. I am indebted to Christophe Chalamet for this quote (here in his translation) and for the following references. See Barth, Letter to Pastor Horn, February 13, 1929; Karl Barth-Archiv (Basel); see also Barth's letters to Eduard Thurneysen in *Karl Barth–Eduard Thurneysen Briefwechsel,* vol. 2, *1921-1930* (Zurich: TVZ, 1974), p. 638 and pp. 651-54.

12. See Christophe Chalamet, "*Est Deus in nobis?* The Early Years of Karl Barth and Erich Przywara's Debate," published in German in Martin Leiner-Michael Trowitzsch, eds., *Karl Barths Theologie als europaeisches Ereignis* (Göttingen: Vandenhoeck & Ruprecht, 2008).

13. Most basically, at a purely formal level, one sees in Rahner a similar philosophical rigor, subtlety, and penetrating ability to analyze theological questions; in von Balthasar, on the other hand, one sees a reflection both of Przywara's enormous literary range as a man of letters and his prophetic pathos as a critic of modern culture.

14. Quoted in O'Meara, *Erich Przywara,* p. 134; see von Balthasar, "Es stellt sich vor," *Das neue Buch* 7 (1945): 43-44.

15. O'Meara, *Erich Przywara,* p. 139; see Paul Imhof, ed., *Karl Rahner in Dialogue: Conversations and Interviews 1965-1985* (New York: Crossroad, 1986), p. 14.

philosophical dissertation from 1933, "Erich Przywaras Philosophie der Analogie," and his thorough assimilation of Przywara's *Analogia Entis,* which he reviewed the same year in the *Schweizerische Rundschau.*[16] By all accounts, von Balthasar's early study with Przywara, including his later collaboration with him as an editor of *Stimmen der Zeit* between 1936 and 1938, was formative. Indeed, as Werner Löser points out, Przywara's doctrine of analogy not only was fundamental to von Balthasar's own theology but remained throughout, allowing for certain modifications, at the center of von Balthasar's theology: "Von Balthasar never wavered from the conviction that the doctrine of the 'analogia entis' was of decisive significance for every right-thinking philosophy and theology. It determines, whether implicitly or explicitly, all the expressions of his thought."[17] We should not be surprised, then, that von Balthasar speaks warmly of Przywara as the "old master," or that Przywara, in turn, speaks of von Balthasar as his friend and "old student."[18] Their friendship is reflected, furthermore, in the fact that von Balthasar defended Przywara in his book on Barth, that he apparently cared for Przywara during periods of illness, and that he edited and published the three-volume edition of his *Schriften,* which appeared in 1962.[19] Though the extent of Rahner's early contact with Przywara is less clear, one can gauge something of his esteem and their later friendship from the fact that Rahner apparently made regular trips to Murnau to visit him until Przywara's death in 1972.

Another important Catholic figure he influenced was the recently canonized philosopher Edith Stein. Przywara was not only friend and spiritual director but also an important philosophical interlocutor. It was Przywara, for instance, in the capacity of a friend and spiritual director, who first suggested that Stein take up more intensive study of Aquinas by way of a translation of Aquinas's *De veritate* — a suggestion that decisively

---

16. Von Balthasar, "Die Metaphysik Erich Przywaras," *Schweizerische Rundschau* 33 (1933): 489-99.

17. Werner Löser, S.J., "Weg und Werk Hans Urs von Balthasars," in Philosophisch-Theologische Hochschule Sankt Georgen, www.sankt-georgen.de/leseraum/loeser12.pdf; see also Löser, *Kleine Hinführung zu Hans Urs von Balthasar* (Freiburg: Herder, 2005): "Die Überzeugung, daß die Lehre von der 'Analogia entis' für jede rechte Philosophie und auch Theologie von maßgebender Bedeutung ist, ist bei von Balthasar fortan stets lebendig geblieben. Sie bestimmt verborgen oder ausdrücklich alle Äußerungen seines Denkens."

18. See von Balthasar's introduction to Leo Zimny, ed., *Erich Przywara. Sein Schrifttum, 1912-1962* (Einsiedeln: Johannes Verlag, 1963), p. 18; Przywara, *In und Gegen. Stellungnahmen zur Zeit* (Nürnberg: Glock & Lutz, 1955), p. 279.

19. Erich Przywara, *Schriften,* 3 vols. (Einsiedeln: Johannes Verlag, 1962).

shaped the development of her philosophy, as is evident from her subsequent comparison of Husserl and Thomas, which appeared in Husserl's *Festschrift* in 1929. So, too, Przywara's *Analogia Entis,* which we know Stein to have read and to have commented upon, clearly pointed the way from phenomenology to metaphysics, given that (as a metaphysics) it begins precisely with phenomenological questions. And in general, it seems that throughout their friendship Przywara consistently encouraged Stein to develop her own philosophy. Not surprisingly, therefore, she notes in the preface to *Finite and Eternal Being* that the exchange of ideas that took place between them between 1925 and 1931 decisively influenced this work and continued to be a "powerful stimulus" when she subsequently resumed her philosophical research.[20]

In any case, it is clear that Rahner, von Balthasar, and Stein all learned from Przywara and considered him a model Christian intellectual. For their part, Rahner and von Balthasar even indicate that Przywara's thought possesses an abiding significance — indeed an abiding novelty — that remains to be appreciated and is important for the future of the church. As von Balthasar puts it, "Whoever goes through [Przywara's] school, wherever one's own path may eventually lead, will bear the marks of this encounter in one's thought and life."[21] Moreover, he says that "every return to the old master will leave one oddly shaken, perhaps because one comes to realize how much younger this old master has remained than all who have come after him."[22] Elsewhere, von Balthasar spells out more precisely the ways in which Przywara's thought both anticipated the Second Vatican Council and remains a necessary "corrective" to some of its (perhaps) unintended effects:

> [Przywara] had long anticipated the opening of the Church to the world [*das All*] that came with the council, but he possessed in addition the corrective that has not been applied in the way that the council's [teachings] have been inflected and broadly put into practice: namely, the elemental, downright Old Testament sense for the divinity of God, who is a consuming fire, a death-bringing sword, and a transporting love. In-

---

20. Edith Stein, *Finite and Eternal Being,* trans. Kurt F. Reichardt; vol. 9 of *The Collected Works of Edith Stein* (Washington: ICS Publications, 2002), p. xxix. This work, which was originally a development of Stein's *Habilitationsschrift,* was more or less completed in 1937, but for ominous circumstantial reasons was not published until after her death in 1950. See pp. xiv-xv.

21. Przywara, *Sein Schrifttum,* p. 18.

22. Ibid.

deed, he alone possessed the language in which the word "God" could be heard without that touch of squeamishness that has led to the tepid, half-hearted talk of the average theology of today. He lives like the mythical salamander in the fire: there, at the point where finite, creaturely being arises out of the infinite, where that indissoluble mystery holds sway that he baptized with the name *analogia entis*.[23]

Rahner also recognized the novelty of his "old teacher" and his importance to the contemporary church. In his *laudatio* from 1967, for example, he admits that in the noisy marketplace of ideas Przywara's voice is hardly heard anymore. And yet he asks, "Does this mean that the Catholic generation of today has learned what it had to learn from him and, now that it is able to forget the old teacher, can continue nonchalantly to march along the path of the future of the Church without him?"[24] "Without being a prophet," Rahner adds, "I feel compelled to say that we, the generation after him, as well as future generations still have critical things to learn from him."[25] Indeed, he says, "The whole Przywara, especially the late Przywara, is yet to come. He stands at a place in the road that many in the church have yet to get past."[26] Rahner then concludes his *laudatio* with the words of von Balthasar: "It is almost unthinkable that Przywara could have founded a school, but Przywara himself never reckoned with one. He remains an incomparable teacher — every thinker should have to think through what he shows us — and yet he must content himself with letting those who have caught something of his fire go their own way."[27]

And, true enough, Stein, Rahner, and von Balthasar all went their own way; they are not simply imitations of the "old master." Nevertheless, it is notable that they continued to regard Przywara's thought as a stimulus and touchstone for their own philosophical and theological investigations; moreover, in the view of Rahner and von Balthasar, as something unsurpassed — something that could have provided "critical therapy" for Christian thought in our time. As von Balthasar poignantly put it, "Erich Przywara's immense theological undertaking — whose profundity and

23. Von Balthasar, "Erich Przywara," in *Tendenzen der Theologie im 20. Jahrhundert,* ed. Hans Jürgen Schulz (Stuttgart and Berlin: Kreuz Verlag, 1966), pp. 354-55.

24. Karl Rahner, *Gnade als Freiheit. Kleine theologische Beiträge* (Freiburg: Herder, 1968), p. 271.

25. Ibid.

26. Ibid., p. 272.

27. Ibid., p. 273; von Balthasar, "Erich Przywara," p. 359.

breadth is without comparison in our time — could have provided critical therapy for Christian thought in our day. Yet our age has taken the easier path of not engaging him" — indeed, of "ignoring him."[28]

II. The Philosophical Roots of the *Analogia Entis* and Its Development into a Theological Term

Given such remarkable testimony on the part of Rahner and von Balthasar, it would seem all the more important to know what exactly Przywara taught and, above all, what he understood by the *analogia entis*. To get to this point, however, one must first appreciate the extent to which Przywara stands in and consciously reflects upon a tradition of thought that goes all the way back to the origins of Greek philosophy.[29] For as Eberhard Jüngel, another Przywara admirer,[30] has argued, the *concept* of analogy (if not the term itself) can already be found in Heraclitus and Parmenides, namely, as a *Denkform* governing the metaphysical relation between the One (or, in

28. Ibid., p. 271 (quoted by Rahner); Przywara, *Sein Schrifttum*, p. 18. While this circumstance may be lamentable, there are understandable reasons why Przywara has been neglected. Chief among them is that, though he was also a poet and capable of beautiful expressions, Przywara's philosophical works are at times so dense and idiosyncratic that reading him, even for the most patient of readers, can be excruciatingly difficult. As von Balthasar observed in his review of the *Analogia Entis:* "An exposition of this thought-world, which is compressed into 150 pages, would require perhaps 1000 normal pages of philosophical epic" (von Balthasar, "Die Metaphysik Erich Przywaras," p. 489).

29. See in this regard Hampus Lyttkens, *The Analogy between God and the World: An Investigation of Its Background and Interpretation of Its Use by Thomas of Aquino*, trans. A. Poignant (Uppsala: Almqvist & Wiksells, 1952), pp. 15-110. In this respect I would suggest that whatever differences Protestants and Catholics may have concerning the *analogia entis* ultimately trace back to more general differences concerning the relationship between philosophy and Christian theology. Whereas for Catholics (and some Protestants, such as Wolfhart Pannenberg) one may speak of an invigorating but qualified assimilation of philosophy by Christian theology — in the way that the Church Fathers commonly speak of a "despoiling of the Egyptians" (Exod. 12:36) — for many Protestants, following Luther, one can speak only of a dubious and problematic relationship between them (continuing, as it were, the mutual suspicion of the poets and the philosophers in Greek antiquity). Thus, as a rule, in modern Protestant theology dialectic tends to have priority over analogy, whether in the matter of the relationship between God and world or in the way that Christian theology relates to pre-Christian philosophy, mythology, and religion. In any case, it is clear that if Barth has a problem with the *analogia entis*, his hostility toward it is fed by his suspicion of the philosophical tradition in general, from which the concept of analogy originally derives.

30. See, for example, Jüngel, *Gott als Geheimnis der Welt*, p. 357.

Heraclitus's case, the Logos), which "is" and abides, and the many, which by comparison "are not."[31]

But even if Jüngel is right and the philosophies of Heraclitus and Parmenides are implicitly governed by analogy, the explicit development of analogy as a philosophical concept arose in view of the differences traditionally ascribed to them.[32] To put it simply, for Parmenides there is only being; change is an illusion (εἰ γὰρ ἔγεντ', οὐκ ἔστ'), for Heraclitus there is no being, no permanence, but only becoming (πάντα ῥεῖ καὶ οὐδὲν μένει).[33] As historically received, the philosophies of Parmenides and Heraclitus thus came to represent dialectical extremes — "all is being" and "all is becoming" — with no *analogia entis* in sight: on the one hand, a monistic philosophy of absolute identity (to the point that change is an illusion), on the other hand, a philosophy of absolute change and difference (to the point that permanence is an illusion and all that is real is the revolution of opposites). Granted, Heraclitus holds that there is a Logos, which is manifested in the world of change as the abiding ground and measure of its change, and to this extent he too has a doctrine of being, even, mutatis mutandis, a kind of analogy of being — given an implicitly analogical relation between the abiding of the Logos and the constancy of change. Likewise, following Jüngel, one could argue that Parmenides' philosophy is also governed by an implicit analogy, in this case between thought and being, as well as between the realm of truth and the realm of opinion. That being said, however, the *explicit* philosophical use of analogy clearly arises out of the attempt to solve the metaphysical conundrum inherited from them.[34] And it arises, specifically, in the works of Plato and Aristotle.

---

31. Thus, for example, according to his reading of the B 3 fragment, Jüngel finds analogy implied in Parmenides' understanding of the relation between thought and being: "Parmenides setzt in B 3 Denken und Sein in einen Selbigkeitsbezug. Es geht ihm dabei um mehr als um die Auskunft 'A = A'. Es geht ihm auch nicht um die Ineinssetzung von einander Widersprechendem. Parmenides lehrt vielmehr einen Selbigkeitsbezug von einander Entsprechendem. Das Denken entspricht dem Sein. Denn das Sein spricht sich dem Denken zu." See "Zum Ursprung der Analogie bei Parmenides und Heraklit," in *Entsprechungen: Gott — Wahrheit — Mensch*, 3rd ed. (Tübingen: Mohr Siebeck, 2002), p. 67.

32. See *Analogia Entis*, in *Schriften*, 3:143-44.

33. [For if it came into being it is not]. See Plato, *Cratylus* 402a: "Heraclitus somewhere says that all things are in process and nothing stays still, and likening existing things to the stream of a river he says that you would not step twice into the same river." Quoted in *The Presocratic Philosophers*, 2nd edition, ed. G. S. Kirk, J. E. Raven and M. Schofield (Cambridge: Cambridge University Press, 1983).

34. See, for example, Plato, *Theaetetus* 180e; Aristotle, *Metaphysics* 1.5.986b–987b; 4.5.1010a, and elsewhere.

On the one hand, Plato and Aristotle affirmed that our experience of finite being is not an illusion and that finite things do, in fact, change; in short, they affirmed the commonsense view that there is a world that is in process, in becoming *(in fieri),* and that things really do come into being and pass away. On the other hand, they recognized that this world of change, though real, is not real in any ultimate sense but points to some kind of being or substance that exists truly, immutably, and eternally. Simply put, they navigated between the extreme positions represented by Heraclitus and Parmenides. Thus, at the conclusion of book 5 of the *Republic,* Plato speaks of the world of change as something "intermediate": as something between being and nonbeing, and likewise as something between the forms and the formless. All of which is developed in books 6 and 7 into an essentially analogical understanding of finite things as so many images of the archetypal forms.[35]

It is in Aristotle, however, that we first see analogy employed in a more technical sense in connection with ontological questions.[36] At the beginning of book 4 of the *Metaphysics,* for example, he prepares the way for an analogical understanding of being when he famously says that "being can be said in many ways" (τὸ δὲ ὂν λέγεται μὲν πολλαχῶς) and then proceeds to elaborate precisely in this connection what has come to be known as a *pros hen* (πρὸς ἕν) analogy.[37] To give Aristotle's own example, "Some things are said to be because they are substances, others because they are affections of substance, others because they are a process towards substance, or destructions or privations or qualities of substance, or productive or generative of substance, or of substance itself. It is for this reason that we say even of non-being that it *is* non-being."[38] To be sure, being is predicated in the truest sense only of substance, the primary analogate, which is why being *qua* substance is the proper object of the science of metaphysics. The point here, though, is that

35. So too, therefore, in the *Republic* (511e), Plato arranges his "line" precisely according to an analogy (ἀνὰ λόγον) between the order of knowledge and the order of being, whereby the relation between opinion and knowledge is said to mirror the relation between image and archetype. In short, as Lyttkens puts it, for Plato, "Being bears the same relation to becoming as truth does to belief." See *op. cit.,* p. 24.

36. See Lyttkens, *The Analogy between God and World,* p. 52.

37. *Metaphysics* 4.1.1003a32; cf. 5.1.1028a10. This type of analogy is so called for the reason that diverse things sharing a common denomination (e.g., several things sharing the denomination "being") are analogically related "to one" primary analogate from which their different meanings derive.

38. Ibid., 4.2.1003b6-11, trans. W. D. Ross, in *The Complete Works of Aristotle,* ed. Jonathan Barnes (Princeton: Princeton University Press, 1984).

analogy functions to indicate some kind of loosely similar relation among otherwise disparate things. Thus, after naming some of the more direct ways that things can be related (namely, unity in number, species, and genus), Aristotle names analogy as a fourth kind of unity, according to which things are only indirectly related, as one thing to another (ὡς ἄλλο πρὸς ἄλλο).[39] And to this extent, as a way of talking about a relation between otherwise unequal or even opposing things, analogy can be said to be a kind of "mean" (τὸ γὰρ ἀνάλογον μέσον).[40]

Still, though, what Aristotle had to say about analogy is rather obscure. Fortunately, therefore, Aquinas's commentary on the above passage from the *Metaphysics* (1016b-1017a) is illuminating and helps to clarify the two basic kinds of analogy that have come down to us from Aristotle and his medieval commentators. Aquinas says that analogy can be understood here in two ways: either as two things being related to a third (the classic example being that of health, which is predicated differently but not equivocally of man, urine, and medicine, where man is the primary analogate), or in the sense that two things are proportionally similar to two other things (as in the relation of the tranquility of the sea to the serenity of the air).[41] The first kind of analogy is what we have already identified as a *pros hen* analogy, since two things are ordered "to one" primary thing (in this case, man), whereas urine and medicine are "healthy" only in an analogical sense, as, respectively, a sign and cause of health. Since Cajetan, this kind of analogy has also come to be known as an analogy of attribution *(analogia attributionis),* which can be distinguished further according to whether the attribution is intrinsic or extrinsic.[42] The second kind of analogy, which Cajetan favors, is known as an

---

39. *Metaphysics* 5.6.1016b. See *Analogia Entis*, pp. 149-50.

40. See *Nicomachean Ethics* 5.3.1131b.

41. Aquinas, *In Duodecim Libros Metaphysicorum Aristotelis Expositio* V, lec. 8; *Commentary on Aristotle's Metaphysics,* trans. John P. Rowan (Notre Dame, Ind.: Dumb Ox Books, 1961), p. 317.

42. For example, "health" is attributed extrinsically to "urine" and "medicine," since these things are not in themselves, strictly speaking, "healthy." If, however, one is talking about such concepts as *ens* or *bonum,* and if it is God who causes these perfections in creatures, and if, as for Aquinas and the medievals in general, effects in some way resemble their causes, according to the principle *omne agens agit sibi simile,* then it is clear that, while these concepts refer primarily to God, they also refer to something, however deficient, intrinsic to creatures themselves. See, for example, *De veritate,* q. 21, a. 4: ". . . omne agens invenitur sibi simile agere; unde si prima bonitas sit effectiva omnium bonorum, oportet quod similitudinem suam imprimat in rebus effectis; et sic unumquodque dicetur bonum sicut forma inhaerente per similitudinem summi boni sibi inditam, et ulterius per bonitatem

analogy of proportionality *(analogia proportionalitatis),* since it is based
upon a comparison of two different proportions and recalls the origins of
analogy in Greek arithmetic. While it cannot be decided here which of these
analogies is more proper, the second analogy *(analogia proportionalitatis)*
clearly comports with metaphor and, as such, could be said to indicate a
greater dissimilarity between the things compared. And this, in fact, is how
Przywara understands this type of analogy. In any case, what is common to
both forms of analogy is that both point to a kind of middle ground between
univocity and equivocity, witnessing, once again, to Aristotle's definition of
analogy as a "mean."[43]

But what, one might ask, does any of this have to do with the modern
theological debate about the *analogia entis?* Without going into the details of
Aquinas's own doctrine of analogy[44] or the subsequent tradition of interpretation (e.g., in Cajetan and Suárez), the answer is: everything. For what is at
stake is how the foregoing *philosophical* use of analogy applies to and in
some sense predetermines on the basis of reason the *theological* relation between God and creation. For, clearly, the same analogical logic that for Aris-

---

primam, sicut per exemplar et effectivum omnis bonitatis creatae." See Lyttkens, *op. cit.,* pp.
207-8, 246ff.

43. *Nicomachean Ethics* V, 3, 1131b.

44. Among the most important treatments of Aquinas on analogy, see Lyttkens, *op.
cit.;* George Klubertanz, *St. Thomas Aquinas on Analogy* (Chicago: Loyola University Press,
1960); Bernard Montagnes, *The Doctrine of the Analogy of Being according to Thomas Aquinas,* trans. E. M. Macierowski (Milwaukee, Wis.: Marquette University Press, 2004). It is
sometimes objected, however, that Thomas never used the term *analogia entis* and that for
Thomas analogy was merely a way of understanding the appropriate theological use of certain words. As Herbert McCabe puts it in his translation of *Summa theologiae,* vol. 3:
Knowing and Naming God (London: Eyre and Spottiswoode, 1964), p. 106: "Analogy is not a
way of getting to know about God, nor is it a theory of the structure of the universe, it is a
comment on our use of certain words." See, however, in addition to the works cited above, as
well as Przywara's own treatment of Aquinas in *Analogia Entis,* pp. 171-202, W. Norris Clarke,
Explorations in Metaphysics (Notre Dame, Ind.: University of Notre Dame Press, 1994), p. 45:
"It is a strange fact, well enough known to Thomistic scholars familiar with the whole of St.
Thomas's thought, that the great underlying themes, the central structural principles orga-
nizing his philosophical worldview, are not ordinarily highlighted explicitly in their own
right, as a modern philosopher would tend to do. [. . .] The central governing principles are
used constantly, and indeed quite explicitly, to solve these problems, but St. Thomas does not
ordinarily thematize them directly in a full-fledged exposition of them in their own right as
universal principles." Among these central, governing principles, one might add, is the
analogia entis, which is plainly implied (whether or not he uses the term) in Thomas's affirmation of an *analogia proportionalitatis* between the being of God and the being of creatures
(see *De veritate,* q. 2, a. 11).

totle applies to diverse modes of being (substance, quality, etc.) also extends to the different kinds of substances themselves, in such a way that analogy could be said to govern the hierarchy of different substances, each according to its particular manner of being. Thus, following Aristotle, being is said primarily of eternal, unmovable, divine substance, secondarily of eternally moving substances (e.g., Aristotle's spheres), and in a still more removed sense of substances, like ourselves, which are moving but finite and perishable. Accordingly, as a matter of metaphysics or philosophical theology, philosophy could be said to establish in advance some kind of relation between God and the world, specifically, some kind of *analogy* between the "being" of God and the "being" of creatures. The all-important question, then, that was passed down from Greek philosophy to Christian theology, answered in some way by every great theologian of the church from Augustine to Aquinas, and revisited in the modern debate concerning the *analogia entis,* was what to make of the relationship between philosophy and theology — indeed, what also to make of the relationship between reason and faith, nature and grace.[45] Consequently, the debate concerning the *analogia entis,* far from being a minor academic or ecumenical dispute — as Barth rightly grasped — was really a debate about everything.

But if, as discussed, the concept of the *analogia entis* can be found already in Plato and Aristotle and thence passes into the tradition of Christian reflection on the relation between God and creation, the term itself does not appear until the sixteenth century. It appears first, so far as we know, in Cajetan, at which point, as Julio Terán-Dutari has shown, it became something of a *terminus technicus* in the schools of the orders — in part among the Dominicans, in John of St. Thomas, for example, but especially among the Jesuits, beginning most obviously with Suárez's *Metaphysical Disputations* (e.g., disputations 28 and 32). Thereafter the term can be found among seventeenth-century Jesuits such as Mendoza and Arriaga, and nineteenth-century Jesuits such as Schiffini, de Mandato, and Remer.[46] Indeed, the term can be traced all the way up to the Jesuit manuals in use around the turn of the twentieth century. In no sense, therefore, is the term original to

---

45. Not surprisingly, therefore, at the heart of Przywara's *Analogia Entis* one finds precisely a discussion of these relationships, specifically, a discussion of the noetic principle *fides (theologia) non destruit, sed supponit et perficit rationem (philosophiam),* and its ontic correlate *gratia non destruit, sed supponit et perficit naturam* — both of which, taken together, express the basic "methodological principle" for the metaphysical worldview of Thomas and, following Przywara, the Catholic Church. See *Analogia Entis,* pp. 83-84.

46. See n. 6 above.

Przywara, even if he mints it anew and gives it a fuller meaning than it hitherto possessed. It is — and Barth is right to have recognized this — very much a part of the Catholic tradition.

III. The *Analogia Entis* and the Natural Knowledge of God in Przywara's Early Work

Having briefly traced the history of the *analogia entis* as a concept and a term, we are now in a better position to understand Przywara's own doctrine — both its continuity with and innovation upon the philosophical and theological tradition. In an early essay from 1922, for example, "Gottes-erfahrung und Gottesbeweis," Przywara more or less identifies the *analogia entis* with "the metaphysical insight that everything 'mutable' or *in fieri* (and hence everything 'finite') can exist and act only by virtue of the fact that the ultimate ground of its existence and action is a being [*ein Seiendes*] that exists absolutely (and, as such, is 'infinite')."[47] As a result, he goes on to say, "There remains fundamentally only this choice: either one identifies the mutable and finite with what is immutable and infinite" (which is what happens in the case of pantheism and, perhaps unwittingly, in what Przywara calls "theopanism," which I will discuss in the next section), "or one recognizes the actual state of affairs that the *philosophia perennis* describes by the *analogia entis*."[48] In short, the *analogia entis* is based upon the metaphysical insight "that mutable and finite things are grounded in their ultimate essence in something immutable and infinite, which is essentially distinct from them."[49] To this extent, the *analogia entis* is simply an abbreviated way of formulating a traditional philosophical insight.

At the same time, however, if the *analogia entis* figures as a philosophical principle, it clearly comports with what is traditionally understood by natural theology — with the kind of natural knowledge of God that one finds in book 12 of Aristotle's *Metaphysics,* is clearly taught by Paul (Rom. 1:20), is thereafter commonly espoused by the Church Fathers, is set forth in the traditional demonstrations of God's existence (most famously in Aquinas's "five ways"), and is reaffirmed by the First Vatican Council. (And so Barth is by no means wrong to see a connection between the *analogia entis*

47. *Religionsphilosophische Schriften,* vol. 2, p. 7.
48. Ibid.
49. Ibid.

and natural theology, even if, as we shall see, the one cannot be reduced to the other). As the council declares, "The same Holy mother Church holds and teaches that God, the source and end of all things, can be known with certainty from the consideration of created things, by the natural power of human reason," citing in this connection the well-known words of the apostle that "ever since the creation of the world, his invisible nature has been clearly perceived in the things that have been made (Rom. 1:20)."[50] Accordingly, in keeping with this tradition, Przywara says that "all the perfection of the creature is but an image — an analogy [!] — of the infinite perfection of the Creator," and that the "Creator declares himself in creatures on the basis of being this essential ground of being."[51] Once again, therefore, far from constituting some novel doctrine, the *analogia entis* is simply a succinct way of stating what the Catholic Church has always believed. In this regard one is reminded of Augustine in book 9 of the *Confessions,* where he imagines the totality of creatures crying out with one voice, "We did not make ourselves; we were made by him who abides for eternity."[52] In fact, Przywara cites Augustine precisely in this context, saying that the content of God's self-declaration in creation is none other than the concept of God that one finds in Augustine — the concept of a God who is "in all things and yet, at the same time, beyond all things, a God who is tangibly present [*faßlich*] in creatures, who are his image, and yet incomprehensible in his inmost being [*Wesen*]."[53]

Here, then, we have the foundation of Przywara's understanding of the *analogia entis* as a basic metaphysical principle and a basic truth of our natural knowledge of God. As he puts it in the same early essay from 1922, "The *analogia entis* is the origin, ground of truth, content, and extent of our natural knowledge of God."[54] Accordingly, the *analogia entis* serves to describe a wide variety of concrete religious experience. As Przywara puts it, "The

50. *Dei Filius, Dogmatic constitution on the Catholic faith,* chapter 2. Thus, affirming the *duplex ordo* of Vatican I, Przywara says that the knowledge of God's existence is, strictly speaking, a matter of reason, since it is "positively reasonable" — as opposed to matters of faith in mysteries, which can merely be shown to be "not contrary to reason" (*Schriften,* 2:8).

51. Ibid.

52. *Confessions* 9.10.25. Admittedly, Augustine reports having this experience during his famous vision at Ostia — and so it would seem that he was in a state of supernatural illumination at the time he had this perception — but for Przywara, following the apostle, no special illumination should be required to recognize that creatures are not the Creator.

53. *Schriften,* 2:7.

54. Ibid., p. 10.

more specific ways in which God is known can be very different: at one moment one might ascend from the perfections of finite things to the infinite source of all perfection; at another moment one might catch a glimpse of the majesty of the immutable shining through the flitting back and forth of mutable things; at another moment one's experience of other persons may give one a lively sense of the personality of God as the fulfillment of everything we intimate in personal greatness; or, at yet another moment, we may happen to perceive in the restless activity of creation the 'active repose and reposing activity' of the Creator."[55] In other words, in such experiences we intimate something of the distinction — the analogy — between the being of God and the being of creation.

But if the *analogia entis* is essentially a code word for our natural knowledge of God, this knowledge, as merely natural knowledge, is severely limited. Indeed, this is why natural theology, without the light of revelation, is always on the verge of idolatrously collapsing the distinction between Creator and creature that the *analogia entis* holds open.[56] In other words, positively stated, it is only in the light of revelation that the full scope of the *analogia entis,* both the radical immanence *and* transcendence of God, appears.[57] Thus, even in his early works we see that, for Przywara, the fundamental structure of the *analogia entis,* the "Ur-Struktur," as he later described it

---

55. Ibid.

56. See, in addition to what follows, Przywara's fascinating footnote on Romans 1:21ff. *(Analogia Entis,* p. 118), where, following Aquinas, he makes a fundamental distinction between formal and material knowledge of the divine. In light of this passage it is clear that, for Przywara, one can have a formal knowledge of the divine as something shared in by Catholics and pagans, in the minimal sense of recognizing a divine ground of the world that is distinct from the world (cf. *ST* I, q. 13, a. 10, ad 5; q. 13, a. 9, ad 2), and yet fail to "recognize" God as God. Indeed, the problem with natural theology, for Przywara no less than for Barth, is that the distinction between God and world is all too easily blurred. Thus, for Przywara, vis-à-vis the one triune God of Christianity, even Aristotle's "God" is ultimately an *idol,* being merely the immanent unity of the cosmos: the unity of the ontic cosmic cycle (κυκλοφορία) with the noetic cycle of thought in and to itself (νόησις νοήσεως). Had Barth read this passage prior to making his remarks in the preface (and it seems that he did not), it would have demanded a qualification, one would think, if not a retraction of his position concerning the *analogia entis.*

57. For this reason one could legitimately debate to what extent the *analogia entis* is a principle of natural theology or whether it remains, strictly speaking, a doctrine of the faith, i.e., whether one must then speak, following Söhngen, of an *analogia entis* within an *analogia fidei.* Przywara, however, clearly sees the natural knowledge of the *analogia entis* as something perfected in light of faith, according to the Thomistic maxim adduced above, *fides non destruit, sed supponit et perficit rationem* (see n. 45).

(which is only dimly and imperfectly perceived at the level of natural theology), is that of an "in-and-beyond" (*in-über*), a phrase that could be rendered more literally as an "in-over" or "in-and-above."[58] For the God who is immanent to creation, in the sense of declaring himself "in it" as the ground and cause of its being, is at the same time transcendent of creation, or "beyond it." In the words of Augustine and Thomas, whom Przywara frequently cites as progenitors of the *in-über* structure of the *analogia entis,* God is at once *interior omni re* and *exterior omni re,* both "*in* all things as the cause of their being" and "*above* all things by the excellence of his nature."[59]

In no sense, therefore, can the *analogia entis* be said to establish an immediate ontological or epistemological connection between God and creatures, as Barth seems to have feared. On the contrary, for Przywara, the *analogia entis* prohibits any such immediacy, whether ontological or noetic, precisely by virtue of this fundamental, dynamic, even explosive rhythm of the "in-and-beyond," which militates against every form of pantheism, every secular doctrine of pure immanence, and every form of titanic human presumption. Thus von Balthasar, noting the irony of Barth's criticisms of the *analogia entis,* points out that "both [Barth and Przywara] took a stand against Kantianism and Hegelianism, against Schleiermacher's (or the modern) method of immanence, against every scheme by which the human being, whether devout or not, might attempt to lay hold of the living God."[60] Granted, the *analogia entis* admits some kind of *relation* between God and creation, as we shall see in greater detail in what follows; otherwise it would not be an analogy. But in no way can this relation be construed as comprehensible, which would equally constitute a misunderstanding of the nature of analogy. Rather, the final word of the analogy, as Przywara tirelessly emphasizes, is God's incomprehensible *transcendence.* Thus, even if the *analogia entis* affirms a natural knowledge of God on the basis of God's self-declaration in creation, one must be clear that, for Przywara, this knowledge is *only* analogical. For to know God at all is to know that he transcends un-

---

58. For more on this idiosyncratic phrase and its significance to Przywara's thought, see Thomas Schumacher, *In-Über. Analogie als Grundbestimmung von Theo-Logie* (Munich: Institut zur Förderung der Glaubenslehre, 2003).

59. See Augustine, *De Gen. ad litt.,* viii, 26; 48: "interior omni re, quia in ipso sunt omnia, et exterior omni re, quia ipse est super omnia"; cf. *ST* I, q. 8, a. 1, c. et ad 1 (my emphasis): "Deus sit in omnibus rebus, et intime. Ad primum ergo dicendum quod Deus est supra omnia per excellentiam suae naturae, et tamen est in omnibus rebus, ut causans omnium esse, ut supra dictum est."

60. Przywara, *Sein Schrifttum,* p. 6.

derstanding. As Przywara frequently puts it, quoting Augustine, "Si comprehendis, non est Deus."[61] In other words, as soon as one thinks one has comprehended God, it is not God whom one comprehends, but merely an idol of one's imagining. Przywara understood this as well as Calvin, but he learned it from Ignatius's conception of the Divine Majesty as the God who is *semper maior,* or "ever greater." And this is why he understands the *analogia entis,* contra Hegel, precisely as a *reductio in mysterium.*[62]

In no sense, therefore, does the *analogia entis* form some kind of natural bridge between God and creatures, according to a common, truncated understanding of analogy only in terms of similarity and not also in terms of dissimilarity: as though the *analogia entis* granted one traversable access to the divine (which occurs only in Christ, who is the Way). This would be a complete misunderstanding of Przywara's doctrine, and would seem to be the kind of misunderstanding involved in Barth's repudiation of it. On the contrary, having the form of an ultimate "in-and-*beyond*," the *analogia entis* is essentially a form of negative theology in the tradition of the Areopagite. For here too, as for Pseudo-Dionysius, every positive, luminous similarity, "however great," is ultimately conducted into the apophatic night of an "ever greater" dissimilarity.[63] Indeed, for Przywara, the dynamic rhythm of the *analogia entis* (between positive and negative theologies) is never stilled — not even at the heights of mystical union. And for this reason alone, inasmuch as it spans both natural and supernatural knowledge (and experience) of God, qualifying as a rule every *unio caritatis in gratia,* the *analogia entis* cannot be reduced to a form of natural theology.

IV. "Dynamic Polarity": The Augustinian Rhythm of the *Analogia Entis*

All of this is further explicated in a 1923 essay entitled "God in us and God above us," where Przywara says that the God of the *analogia entis* is none other than the God of Augustine — a God who is *interior intimo meo* but at the same time *superior summo meo,* "more inward than my inmost [part]" and "higher than my highest."[64] "*Deus interior* and *Deus exterior,*" Przywara

61. *Serm.* 107.3.5 ("if you understand it, it is not God").
62. See *Analogia Entis,* pp. 88-89.
63. Ibid., p. 137.
64. *Confessions* 3.6.11.

writes — "'God in all and above all,' God more inward than we are to ourselves, and yet surmounting and transcending [all things] as infinite and incomprehensible."[65] And for this reason, he concludes, precisely "because
God reveals himself as at once a God of blessed, mystical intimacy and a God
of the coolest distance, the fundamental disposition of the believing soul
should be one of 'fearing love and loving fear' — a fear that springs from
love inasmuch as love fears to lose the beloved; and a love that through fear
maintains a holy sobriety and a tender reverence."[66] Thus, for Przywara, not
only does the *analogia entis* sum up the Catholic concept of God (as a God
who is both immanent and transcendent), it is also the measure of authentic
religious experience.

At this point, given the centrality of the *analogia entis* to Przywara's
theology, and given above all that it would seem to determine in advance,
prior to any special revelation, both the God-world relation and the nature
of authentic faith, one must be careful to avoid misunderstandings. For, as
with Barth, it is easy to receive the impression that the *analogia entis*, as a
systematic principle, has somehow displaced the priority of revelation in determining our theological conceptions. The reason why such fears are un-
founded, Przywara repeatedly points out, is that the *analogia entis* is precisely not an a priori principle from which anything could be derived.[67] In
fact, it is not even a principle in the strict sense of the word. Rather, he says, it
is an abbreviated way of expressing a posteriori the fundamental structure of
something *factual,* something expressed in Scripture and confirmed by religious experience: that God is encountered "in" the world (in the soul) as
"transcending" the world (the soul).[68] In short, God is at once "near" and
"far away" — near in the words of the psalmist, "Where can I go from your
Spirit? Or where can I flee from your presence?" (Ps. 139:7); near in the sense
of the apostle's dictum that "in him we live and move and have our being"
(Acts 17:28); near in the sense of the yet more inward and mysterious presence of the Holy Spirit "*in*" the disciples (John 14:17), or of "Christ *in* you,
the hope of glory" (Col. 1:27).[69] At the same time, however, Scripture and the

65. *Ringen der Gegenwart. Gesammelte Aufsätze 1922-1927* (Augsburg: Benno Filser
Verlag, 1929), vol. 2, p. 543.
66. Ibid.
67. See *In und Gegen*, p. 279.
68. See Przywara, *Religionsbegründung. Max Scheler — J. H. Newman* (Freiburg:
Herder, 1923), p. 142.
69. To be sure, for Przywara, there is an analogical interval between God's presence to
creation as the Creator and God's saving presence to the soul through faith — just as there is

"dark nights" of the saints also attest that God is inscrutably "far off" (see Eccl. 7:24), that he "dwells in unapproachable light" (1 Tim. 6:16), that his ways are not our ways and his thoughts are not our thoughts (Isa. 55:9). In the words of the First Vatican Council, God is "Re et essentia mundo distinctus . . . et super omnia, quae praeter ipsum sunt et concipi possunt, ineffabiliter excelsus."[70] Thus, summing up the rhythm of the *analogia entis,* Przywara says that the experience of God's intimacy ("Inne-Sein") goes hand in hand with an experience of his infinite transcendence ("Über-Sein").[71]

Importantly, however, the rhythm of the *analogia entis* is not that of a stable back-and-forth between the poles of divine immanence and divine transcendence, which could lead one to posit an ultimate equilibrium between them. On the contrary, as we have seen, the rhythm of the *analogia entis* is an explicitly dynamic one. As Przywara puts it, recalling the theme of divine infinity in Gregory of Nyssa and Augustine, "Even if we were to have the most sublime experience of mystical union, would we then have any right to come to a stopping point and dream of having finally attained a state of 'immediacy' or a state of 'maximal knowledge' or a state of 'ultimate proximity'"? He answers with a single paradoxical phrase from Augustine: *Invenitur quaerendus!* ("That which is found is yet to be sought!"). In other words, with respect to God, "Even the greatest finding is but the beginning of a new searching."[72]

But if "God in us" and "God above us" together constitute the fundamental rhythm of the *analogia entis,* and if this rhythm, dynamically conceived, is basic to the Catholic concept of God, it is also clear where, as Przywara sees it, things can go wrong. This can happen in one of two ways, each of which denies the "and" in "God in us and God above us." On the one hand, if one makes "God in us" absolute, denying divine transcendence, one ends up with pantheism, in which case there is no God because everything is

---

an analogical interval between nature and grace, reason and faith. This has never been in question. The point here is simply that, as an expression of the first moment of the rhythm of the *analogia entis,* "the Lord is near," as Paul says (Phil. 4:5) — whether he be experienced merely as the Creator in his works or, at the same time, salvifically and more intimately, as the Bridegroom and lover of the soul.

70. *Dei Filius, Dogmatic constitution on the Catholic faith,* c. 1. Trans.: "who in reality and by his nature is distinct from the world . . . and ineffably exalted above all things that are outside of him and anything that could be conceived."

71. *Schriften,* 2:281.

72. Ibid., p. 231.

univocally God. On the other hand, if one makes God equivocally "other," denying divine immanence (to a real creation), one ends up either with a Gnostic world that is essentially independent of God (paving the way for modern secularism) or, in a second type of Gnosticism, one so devalues the integrity of creation as a natural realm of secondary causes as to absorb the creature (whether inadvertently or not) into the divine life. In this case we have what Przywara, in view of the Lutheran doctrine of God's *Allein-wirksamkeit,* calls "theopanism": "For if God is only something 'above or beyond me,' the human being ends up being either independent of God, and thus himself God, or he becomes a pure emanation of this transcendence."[73] In either case, Przywara says, "both lead to the dissolution of the concept of God" — whether through the "mystical delirium of a unity without difference," or through the fearful reverence of the unknown God who is "always other." Indeed, both "are equally perversions of the genuine mystery of God — both the objectivism that militates against any notion of 'God in me,' as well as the subjectivism that shrinks back from any notion of 'God beyond me.'"[74] What is needed therefore is what in his 1923 work *Gottgeheimnis der*

---

73. *Ringen der Gegenwart,* vol. 2, p. 544.

74. Ibid. Though Przywara has not named any names here, from remarks made elsewhere it is clear that he is thinking, on the one hand, of Kant, Schleiermacher, and the general trend of modern liberal Protestantism (as essentially forms of pantheism), and, on the other hand, of the God of Luther, Calvin, Hegel, and Barth (as essentially forms of theopanism). When Barth positions himself over against Przywara in the *Church Dogmatics,* it is therefore only after his own dialectical theology has been positioned by Przywara as an unwitting form of theopanism, namely, inasmuch as (ontologically) it is predicated upon a rejection of the *analogia entis,* and (epistemologically) the creature is denied any knowledge of God that is not God's own self-interpretation. See, for example, *Schriften,* 2:285-86. See also Przywara's portrait of Barth in *Humanitas: Der Mensch gestern und morgen* (Nürnberg: Glock & Lutz, 1952), pp. 172ff. Whether or not Przywara's charge of theopanism is fair, and whether or not it would have to be qualified in view of the later volumes of the *Church Dogmatics* (esp. vol. 3 on creation), cannot be decided here. See, though, in this regard von Balthasar, "Analogie und Natur. Zur Klärung der theologischen Prinzipienlehre Karl Barths," *Divus Thomas* 23 (1945): 3-56, in which von Balthasar shows that Barth does, in fact, have a formal concept of nature and thus is at least implicitly committed to what Przywara means by the *analogia entis.* See, for example, p. 18: "Wer aber Gott und Geschöpf sagt, der sagt (wie wir im ersten Aufsatz sahen) *Analogia Entis.*" See also the recent fine article by Kenneth Oakes, "The Question of Nature and Grace in Karl Barth: Humanity as Creature and as Covenant-Partner," *Modern Theology* 23 (October 2007): 595-616, in which Oakes shows (and rightly reminded me) that the *late* Barth ("the new Barth"! in Brunner's phrase), having abjured the doctrine of God's *Alleinwirksamkeit* and come to see the human being as a genuine covenant-partner, may be exculpated from charges of theopanism. If Bruce

Welt Przywara calls a philosophy of "dynamic polarity" — a philosophy that would do justice to the poles of divine immanence and divine transcendence.

V. The "Suspended Middle" of Creaturely Being: The Full Form of the *Analogia Entis*

Przywara's mature doctrine of the *analogia entis* is set forth in two principal works: first in his *Religionsphilosphie katholischer Theologie* (1926) and then, more thoroughly, in his *Analogia Entis* (1932).[75] The difference between these and earlier works is that here Przywara takes a further, bolder step, attempting to lay a systematic foundation for the *analogia entis* in the structures of consciousness and, indeed, in the principles of thought itself. And to this extent, and to the extent that Przywara attends to the question of the intentionality of consciousness, Przywara could be said to adopt more of a phenomenological approach.[76] Thus, for instance, *Religionsphilosophie katholischer Theologie* begins with a rigorous examination of the possible orientations of consciousness as such, from which the possible types of specifically religious consciousness (and corresponding philosophies of religion) emerge.[77] Likewise, in *Analogia Entis* Przywara begins to unfold the

---

McCormack is right, however, and Barth's doctrine of election is ultimately a doctrine of God's eternal *self-determination,* as though in Christ (and therefore through human history) God were somehow determining his own being and nature, then Przywara's original intuition stands and Barth's theology, having rejected any *analogia entis,* is, in fact, ultimately a form of trinitarian Gnosticism, since history is then a function of God's own "history" and inner life.

75. *Religionsphilosphie katholischer Theologie* (reprinted in *Schriften,* vol. 2) was originally translated as *Polarity: A German Catholic's Interpretation of Religion* by A. C. Bouquet (London: Oxford University Press, 1935). The *Analogia Entis,* which until now has never been translated into English (having appeared in French and Italian), will be forthcoming (trans. John Betz and David Bentley Hart) with Eerdmans Publishers.

76. In this regard it is important to recall that Przywara was well acquainted with Husserl, and was also a close friend of Edith Stein. In fact, Stein not only read *Analogia Entis* prior to publication, but also recommended certain changes, for example, that Przywara should have begun with his historical treatment of analogy instead of leaving it where it currently stands in the penultimate section of the work.

77. For example, if consciousness is fundamentally oriented to itself as the unity of its own experience, this will tend to be expressed in a religious philosophy of *immanence;* if consciousness is fundamentally oriented toward an external unity beyond it, this will tend to be expressed in a religious philosophy of *transcendence;* if, finally, consciousness can dis-

concept of "metaphysics as such" precisely by attending to the evident tensions between a transcendental philosophy of consciousness (which attends to essences) and a philosophy of being (which attends to the question of being and our historical-existential being-in-the-world), thereby implicitly touching upon the conflict that had recently emerged from within the school of phenomenology (and from Przywara's perspective, inevitably so) between Husserl and his one-time assistant, Heidegger. In general, both of these works are highly attuned to the tensions that animate *all* philosophical reflection. What makes these works especially interesting, however, certainly for anyone interested in the relationship between philosophy and theology, is how for Przywara the *analogia entis* emerges from within philosophy as the liberating (ultimately theological) solution to philosophy's own inherent contradictions.

Needless to say, it is impossible here to go through all the steps required to see how the *analogia entis* in fact emerges from the problems intrinsic to philosophy. Following only the general lines of Przywara's argument in *Analogia Entis* (§§1-4), however, one might summarize these steps as follows. First, in §1 Przywara begins with the epistemological problem of the relation between being and consciousness — a problem that is reflected at the level of methodology in one of two basic options (which again reflect the difference within phenomenology between Heidegger and Husserl): either a "meta-ontics," which begins with the question of being, or a "meta-noetics," which begins with consciousness or, more specifically, the act of consciousness. He then shows that neither of these methodological starting points is pure, absolute in itself, but that each points to the other and is, in fact, implied in the other. Thus any rigorous philosophy will have to take into account this dynamic tension and ultimate correlation between a meta-ontics and a meta-noetics.

Przywara's next step is to argue that this dynamic epistemological tension is ultimately rooted in a dynamic ontological tension between essence and existence, which is ontologically prior to any methodological considerations. In other words, for Przywara, the epistemological instability that

---

cover no unity, internal or external, nor any rest, but conceives of unity as an infinite task, never to be finished, this will tend to be expressed in a *transcendental* philosophy of religion. The first type, represented by Schleiermacher, tends in the direction of an aesthetic religion of pure "condition" (*reinen "Zustandes"*); the second type, represented by deism, tends in the direction of an intellectual religion of "objects" (*der "Gegenstände"*); the third type, whose purest instantiation Przywara sees in Cohen's Neo-Kantianism, tends in the direction of an ethical, voluntaristic religion of the "imperative" (*"des Sollens"*).

manifests itself in the ineluctable back and forth between a meta-ontics and a meta-noetics is ultimately a reflection, at the level of method, of the inherent instability of creaturely being as such. For just as epistemology is without any firm footing, so too is the being of the creature itself. For, unlike God, whose essence is to exist, the essence of the creature is precisely not identical to its existence. Rather, essence and existence are related in the creature in such a way that the essence of the creature is never fully given — that is, never identical or collapsible to its existence — but is always on the horizon of its existence as something to be attained. This is more or less what Przywara means by his otherwise cryptic formula "essence in-and-beyond existence," understood as the basic formula of a creaturely metaphysics as such.[78] To be sure, the essence of the creature informs the *fact* of the creature's existence, making it *what* it is; therein lies the "in" of "essence *in*-and-beyond existence." Radically speaking, however, the creature is never fully there, since its essence is at the same time always that *to which* it is underway.[79] Indeed, to draw out the metaphysical implications of Scripture, the creature cannot even be said to be *what* it is, for "*what* we will be has not yet been revealed" (1 John 3:2).

But as Przywara goes on to argue in §2, what is meant by meta-noetics and meta-ontics stands in need of further clarification. For just as νοῦς (from which "noetic" is derived) ultimately designates in Aristotle the "crowning" of a hierarchy that includes scientific, ethical, and artistic modes of consciousness — modes that are aimed, respectively, at the true, the good, and the beautiful — so too ὄν (from which "ontic" is derived), far from indicating a pure, factual presence, turns out to be similarly bound up with the transcendentals.[80] Consequently, according to Przywara, we find that the

---

78. See *Analogia Entis*, §§1-4, pp. 23-97 *passim*.

79. Thus Przywara speaks of "a tension (that can never be mastered in thought) between a being that is 'such' [*so*] and 'there' [*da*], yet whose 'such' in fact always remains 'to be attained,' so that in its purity it is never really 'there.'" See Przywara, "Die Problematik der Neuscholastik," in *Kant-Studien* 33 (1928): 81. In this respect the *analogia entis* bears comparison to the existentialism of Heidegger. The difference here is that this dynamic of *Dasein*, to use Heidegger's expression, is analogous to Being — to *Sein* — itself. It is an image of the God, whose essence is to exist. And for this reason the ecstatic projection of *Dasein* — or of Przywara's "essence in-and-beyond existence" — does not ultimately run up against death or Nothing (as for Heidegger), but against the One of whom it is an image, and in whose active repose its restless mutability finds its supernatural rest.

80. See *Analogia Entis*, pp. 29-30. For instance, the nature of creaturely being is so constituted in terms of *potentia* and *actus* (δύναμις and ἐνέργεια) as to be directed to a truth, an essence, beyond it (as is even the case, mutatis mutandis, with the "*je seine*

tension between a meta-ontics and a meta-noetics is inevitably inflected in the form of a tension between a "transcendental metaphysics," as predominates in antiquity (with its predominantly meta-ontic starting point), and a "metaphysical transcendentalism," as predominates in modernity (with its predominantly meta-noetic starting point). What we discover from this inevitable correlation, however, is no foundation but only a further confirmation of the creaturely tensions that no philosophy has yet resolved (or even can resolve).

According to Przywara, these tensions manifest themselves further (§3) in the tension between an a priori metaphysics (with its emphasis upon the purity of a transcendental subject and its alleged capacity for timeless, superhistorical truth) and an a posteriori metaphysics, which takes history, the senses, tradition, and embodiment seriously as that through which any superhistorical truth is discerned. In short, for Przywara, we see here the difference — and the tension — between Kant and Thomas Aquinas.[81] If the one direction tends (in its extreme rationalistic form) to deprive history of any truth, the other tends (in extreme forms of historicism) to dissolve truth into history. Rightly understood, however, truth, which is "beyond history," is known only "in history," and thus, according to Przywara, we arrive at the formula "truth in-and-beyond history."[82] But truth, Przywara goes on to say, belongs to the region of essence; and history, to the region of existence. Thus, in the formula "truth in-and-beyond history," and in the historical aporetic it involves, we again encounter the more basic formula "essence in-and-beyond existence." That is to say, we once again discover that the creature is ultimately and irreducibly a nonidentity of the ideative and the real, the essential and the existential, and that truth and history must therefore be understood in correlative terms.

At this point, having laid bare the tensions intrinsic to philosophy — from the tension between a meta-ontics and a meta-noetics (§1), to the tension between a transcendental metaphysics and a metaphysical transcendentalism (§2), to the tension between an a priori and an a posteriori metaphysics (§3) — Przywara shows that the concept of God is already implied in any

---

Möglichkeit" of Heidegger's *Dasein*). Thus here again we see an instantiation of the formula "essence in-and-*beyond* existence." So too, if one emphasizes the practical aspect of this dynamic, as pertains to the life of virtue, the same formula once again appears, though now under the form of an "ontic good." And, finally, the beautiful appears as the realization or ideal unity of essence and existence in the work of art.

81. See *Analogia Entis*, p. 48.
82. Ibid., p. 57.

formal consideration of metaphysics as such; and thus we come to the question of the relation between philosophy and theology (§4). The concept of God (of theology) is implied, most obviously, in the metaphysical question of the relation between that which is "grounded, directed, and determined" and its "ground-end-definition [*Grund-Ziel-Sinn*]."[83] In short, it is implied in any consideration of the relation between the absolute and the relative; as Aquinas puts it, "res divinae . . . prout sunt principia omnium entium."[84] The all-important question, however, is whether God is reducible to the absolute of a *philosophical* metaphysics (whether in the form of an a priori or an a posteriori metaphysics).[85] If this should be the case, then philosophy would already be theology. Indeed, it would mean that the absolute posited by the creature would be the absolute of God himself. But a *theological* metaphysics, Przywara points out, is concerned not with God as conceived philosophically but with God as he has freely revealed himself, transcending all philosophical conceptions. Thus we come to a fundamental choice: "either the absolutizations of the immanent poles of the creaturely (as we saw in the cases of absolute a priori and absolute a posteriori metaphysics) or the absolute beyond-and-in them."[86] The problem with the absolutizations, however, is that they fail to do justice to the creaturely quality of finite being as a dynamic unity (in the form of "in-and-beyond") of essence and existence. In the first case, that of an absolute a priori metaphysics, "the creaturely solidifies (into an eternity of essence: in the systematic rigidity of a pure apriorism); in the second case it dissolves (into the *apeiron* of existence: in the '*in infinitum*' of purely a posteriori experience)."[87] In short, in neither

---

83. Ibid., p. 63.

84. Ibid., p. 68; see *In Boeth. De Trin.*, q. 5, a. 4, corp. (things divine . . . insofar as they are the principles of all beings).

85. Whereas an a priori metaphysics proceeds deductively from the ideative to the real (in which case the world appears to pure eidetic vision as a more or less direct expression of divine ideas), an a posteriori metaphysics proceeds inductively from the empirical, from the breadth of the many, to a concept of their unity, to a concept of the universe, understood as the perfection of the whole. Whereas the former tends in its extreme form to theopanism, the latter tends in its extreme form to pantheism. See *Analogia Entis*, p. 70: "In a purely a priori metaphysics, philosophy amounts to a theology of the 'God of the ideas' within the absoluteness of eidetic vision and mathematical deduction — in a purely a posteriori metaphysics, on the other hand, it amounts to a theology of a 'God of the all' within the absoluteness of the purely empirical and of a perfection that, rounding itself out, returns to itself."

86. Ibid., p. 65.

87. Ibid.

case do we truly have a creature. Thus, through the failures of the respective absolutes of a philosophical metaphysics, and through a concern to achieve a metaphysics that is adequate to creaturely being, we come to the prospect of a genuinely *theological* metaphysics — a metaphysics that does justice to the creature *qua* creature, as well as to divine freedom and transcendence. In sum, to spell out the matter according to Przywara's peculiar terminology, we come to see that the tension intrinsic to creaturely being ("essence in-and-beyond existence") points to and is "vertically intersected" by the still more basic formula "God *beyond*-in creation."

Now we are finally in a position to see why, for Przywara, creaturely being is inherently *analogical,* and why philosophy itself leads to a conception of the *analogia entis.* In order to understand Przywara's somewhat idiosyncratic use of the term "analogy," however, it is important first to observe the particular way in which he appropriates Aristotle's definition of analogy as a "mean," or something "intermediate" (τὸ γὰρ ἀνάλογον μέσον).[88] When Aristotle gives this definition in the *Nicomachean Ethics,* it is in the context of a discussion of justice. Here, however, it is applied to the nature of creaturely being and, specifically, to the characteristic tensions (between extremes) that we have just described. Accordingly, in view of the way that creaturely being is constituted by a dynamic tension between essence and existence (according to the formula "essence in-and-beyond existence"), Przywara speaks of creaturely being as a kind of "middle." More specifically, given the way that creaturely being, that is, its actuality (ἐνέργεια) at any moment, is suspended between its potentiality (δύναμις) and end (τέλος) — an end that is curiously "in" but at the same time "beyond" the creature (ἐν-τελέχεια) — he speaks of creaturely being as a kind of "*suspended* middle [*schwebende Mitte*]."[89] Indeed, for Przywara, the creature only "is" in this *rhythmic* "back and forth": back to the infinite of potentiality, which is limited in every act, and forth to the end "in-and-beyond" every actuality. Therein lies the first aspect — what Przywara calls the "immanent analogy" — of the *analogia entis.*

But given that, according to the terms of this "immanent analogy," creaturely being has no firm footing in itself, given that its essence is precisely not identical to its essence, given that it is therefore not self-possessed (see 1 Cor. 6:19-20) but ecstatically constituted — given, moreover, that it essentially "is and is not" (in Augustine's phrase, *est non est*),

88. See *Nicomachean Ethics* V, 3, 1131b. See *Analogia Entis,* pp. 149-50.
89. See *Analogia Entis,* pp. 115-16.

"being" only in constant movement — the very being of the creature also points beyond itself to that which "IS."[90] And thus, given the traditional identification of God with being (Exod. 3:14), we are driven to the question of a further analogy — a "theological analogy" — between God and creation (in the form of "God in-and-beyond creation"). At this point we come to see that the first analogy, which points beyond itself toward a transcendent participation (as a "teilnehmendes Über-hinaus-bezogensein"), presupposes and is vertically intersected by the grace of a second, profounder analogy, understood in donative terms as a "*'self-imparting-relation-from-above'* of the divine Is (Truth, etc.)."[91] In other words, whereas the first analogy emphasizes a participatory "sharing," even "taking" *(teil-nehmend),* of creaturely being in the divine (and thus accords with a strictly Platonic understanding of analogy), the second analogy emphasizes that being "is" only *as* the "im-parting" of a gift, moreover, that the creature only "is" insofar as it is between nothing and the "Creator *ex nihilo.*" Accordingly, for Przywara, the full form of the *analogia entis* must be understood in terms of the intersection of these *two* analogies — the latter of which fills out the former with its properly theological height and depth — and thus, by implication, in terms of an intersection of philosophy and theology.

VI. The *Analogia Entis* at the Intersection of Philosophy and Theology

The nature of the relationship between philosophy and theology, however, stands in need of further clarification. On the one hand, as we have already seen, some form of *theologia naturalis* is immanent to the concept of metaphysics as such — both in terms of the question of the creature's origin *(principium)* and end *(finis),* and in terms of the suggestion of a divine identity of essence and existence, a divine "IS," to which the real distinction of essence and existence in creaturely being (as "essence in-and-beyond existence") obscurely points.[92] Thus Przywara affirms the teaching of Vatican I

90. See Augustine, *In Ps.* 121.12; *Confessions,* 12.6; see *Analogia Entis,* pp. 118-19.
91. *Analogia Entis,* p. 119. In Przywara's own idiosyncratic phrasing, "Die Analogie als teilnehmendes Über-hinaus-bezogen-sein hat also zu ihrer tieferen Voraussetzung eine *Analogie als teilgebendes Sich-von-oben-hinein-beziehen* der göttlichen Identität des Ist (Wahrheit usw.)."
92. Ibid., p. 65.

that God, at least as a "positive limit-concept," can be known by the natural light of reason.[93] And to this extent, one may say, theology is always already "in" philosophy.[94] On the other hand, as we have also seen, contra Hegel, theology is not reducible to philosophy. For theology's proper concern is with the supernatural mystery of "things divine as they are in themselves" *(res divinae prout sunt in se).*[95] This is not to say that theology is able to make the supernatural mysteries of faith comprehensible, that it succeeds where philosophy fails. On the contrary, for Przywara, following Augustine, theology is precisely a *reductio in mysterium,* "an entry into the mystery of God in order more deeply 'to grasp his incomprehensibility as such.'"[96] As Augustine puts it, "He is hidden in order that you might seek him; and in order that you might not cease in your search once you have found him, he is infinite. Thus is it said . . . 'Seek his face evermore'" (Ps. 105:4).[97] Quite the opposite, therefore, of reducing to a concept, to a *Begriff,* theology is, properly speaking, a reduction to the *Deus tamquam ignotus* of Aquinas and to the "superluminous darkness" (ὑπέρφωτος γνόφος) of the Areopagite.[98] And so, while theology is always already positively "in" philosophy, it is always also "beyond" its grasp; hence Przywara's succinct formula "theology in-and-beyond philosophy."[99]

But if theology is beyond philosophy, it is also that at which philosophy aims. Indeed, for Przywara, theology is not only formally in philosophy but also the proper *telos* of philosophy; more precisely, in view of the familiar *"in-über"* structure, theology is the *en-telechy* (ἐντελέχεια) of philosophy.[100] For to the extent that philosophy is as incomplete and unstable as the being of the creature it describes, it ineluctably points beyond itself and its own inherent tensions to a region of mystery — precisely in the way that the *pro-fane* points to the sacredness of the temple *(fanum).* But to this extent, like the sacred and the profane, they also truly belong together. Thus, for Przywara, essentially following Thomas, the relation of philosophy to theol-

93. Ibid., p. 74; Denzinger, *Enchiridion Symbolorum,* 1799.

94. *Analogia Entis,* pp. 72ff.

95. Ibid., p. 87; Aquinas, *In Boeth. De Trin.,* q. 5, a. 4, c.

96. *Analogia Entis,* p. 87; *De Trin.* 15.2.2.

97. *In Jo. Tract.* 63.1: "Ut inveniendus quaeratur, occultus est; ut inventus quaeratur, immensus est. Unde alibi dicitur, 'Quaerite faciem ejus semper'" (Ps. 105:4).

98. *Analogia Entis,* p. 88; Aquinas, *In Boeth. De Trin.,* q. 1, a. 2, c. et ad 1; Pseudo-Areopagite, *Mystical Theology* 1.1.

99. *Analogia Entis,* pp. 95-96.

100. As Przywara puts it, "It is through the theological, as its 'inner telos' (ἐντελέχεια), that the 'ascending movement' (δύναμις) of metaphysics reaches its 'final actualization' (ἐνέργεια)" (*Analogia Entis,* p. 80).

ogy is ultimately configured in the same way as the relation of reason to faith: *fides (theologia) non destruit, sed supponit et perificit rationem (philosophiam)*.[101] Following Przywara (and Thomas), one may thus speak of an analogical ordering of philosophy to theology — as of natural desire to its fulfillment. One must be clear, however, that this does not mean that philosophy is able of itself to make out the mysteries with which theology is properly concerned — no more than Adam could envision Eve before she was given to him. For as of yet, from a purely philosophical perspective, nothing whatsoever can be made out about who God is or what he has revealed, or even that there is such thing as revelation. All that can be made out metaphysically with any degree of certainty apart from revelation is that creaturely being is not its own ground, that it is not being itself, that it "is" only in the form of becoming, and that theology, that is, the science of a God of revelation, is a reasonable possibility or, to put it in still more minimalist terms, a "nonimpossibility."[102]

VII. The Logical Foundation of the *Analogia Entis* in the Principle of Noncontradiction

Thus far we have seen how analogy emerges from within philosophy as the operative principle of metaphysics as such; we have also seen how philosophy points to theology, and how a theological analogy fills out the "in-and-beyond" of the so-called immanent analogy with its properly theological height and depth. Now, in §§5-6, Przywara returns to the subject of analogy and shows how analogy is reflected even in the foundations of logic, specifically, in the principle of noncontradiction. As Aristotle formulates this foundational principle, "Just as the same attribute cannot simultaneously be affirmed and denied of the same subject, neither can one simultaneously take something to be and not to be" (τὸ γὰρ αὐτὸ ἅμα ὑπάρχειν τε καὶ μὴ ὑπάρξειν ἀδύνατον τῷ αὐτῷ καὶ κατὰ τὸ αὐτό . . . ἀδύνατον γὰρ ὁντινοῦν ταὐτὸν ὑπολαμβάνειν εἶναι καὶ μὴ εἶναι).[103] The reason why this principle is fundamental to Przywara's argument for the *analogia entis* — indeed, why he goes so far as to call it the foundation for the *analogia entis* — is that in

101. Ibid., p. 83.

102. Ibid.

103. Ibid., p. 105; *Metaphysics* 4.3.1005b19-24 ("for the same attribute cannot, in the same way, both belong and not belong to a thing . . . for it is not possible to believe something both to be and not to be"). Cf. *Metaphysics* 10.5.1061b–1062a.

this principle (as the most basic principle of thought) we see precisely the kind of interpenetration of ontic and noetic forms that Przywara claimed was the case in §1 with regard to an inevitable co-implication and interpenetration of a meta-ontics and a meta-noetics. Thus we have a solid basis in logic for the entire argument developed thus far. Indeed, vis-à-vis the various philosophies of identity (pure logic) and contradiction (pure dialectic), which either hubristically seek a more basic logic of identity ($A = A$) or, under the pretence of humility, deny even the minimalist position that the principle of noncontradiction affords, it turns out that the principle of noncontradiction is preserved in analogy alone, since both analogy (as the fundamental form of being) and the principle of noncontradiction (as the fundamental form of thought) fall precisely *between* the extremes of contradiction and identity.[104]

VIII. The Theological Foundation of the *Analogia Entis* as an Explication of Lateran IV

But if the *analogia entis* is grounded in the principle of noncontradiction — if, that is, it may be substantiated philosophically — it is, once again, only from a theological perspective that it fully appears. For, as we have seen, the full form of the *analogia entis* consists precisely in an intersection of two analogies — the immanent (in the form of "essence in-and-beyond existence") and the theological (in the form of "God in-and-beyond creation"). Indeed, here too the Thomistic maxim *fides (gratia) non destruit, sed supponit et perficit rationem (naturam)* holds true, inasmuch as the former analogy, which is presupposed, points to and is fulfilled in the latter. The problem with the first analogy, taken by itself, is that the creature ends up cramped in itself — in its own possibility (Heidegger's "je seine Möglichkeit"). Seen in light of the theological analogy, however, the potentiality of creaturely being appears more radically, between nothing and the "Creator out of nothing," as a *potentia oboedientialis*. That is to say, the potentiality of the creature now appears as a potentiality for a supernatural end *(finis ad quem homo a Deo praeparatur)*.[105] But it is not, contra Pelagius, a potentiality in the creature's power.[106] Nor is it an end to which

---

104. *Analogia Entis*, p. 105.
105. Ibid., p. 132; *De ver.*, q. 27, a. 1, c.; cf. *Analogia Entis*, p. 141.
106. *Analogia Entis*, p. 133; *De ver.*, q. 8, a. 3, c.; *Summa contra Gentiles* 3.52-53.

the natural desire of the creature could lay any claim. On the contrary, it is expressly a "free gift from above."[107] At the same time, however, the creature is not displaced or reduced to inactivity with regard to its own end (as would be the case with a full-blown theopanism). Rather, the wonder of creaturely being (as seen from the perspective of the theological analogy) is that the maximum of God's proximity to creation (God "in" creation) is at the same time "the greatest liberation of the creature for active, free self-movement" *(quanto aliqua natura Deo vicinior, tanto minus ab eo inclinatur et nata est seipsam inclinare).*[108] Indeed, the more the human being is "in" God by virtue of the gift of God (see John 4:10), that is, by virtue of the gift of the Holy Spirit, who is received "from on high" (Luke 24:49), the more humanity comes into *its own* as the active *image* of God it was always intended to be — to the point of sharing, not only in God's own causal agency as the "origin of all good" *(quod sint causa bonitatis aliorum),*[109] but also in God's own providential office *(non solum quod sint provisae, sed etiam quod provideant).*[110]

Thus, from a consideration of potentiality — having come to see more clearly how profoundly God is "in" creation, communicating to creatures his own perfections — we naturally come back to the question of the theological analogy between God (as the cause of creaturely perfections) and creation (now understood as a realm of analogous, secondary causes). In short, we now see more clearly how creation, in human beings, is truly made in the image of God (Gen. 1:26-27) and therefore is rightly understood to constitute an analogy, a similitude, to God. But as we have seen throughout and as it is crucial to observe here, for Przywara the stress of the theological analogy falls not on the side of proximity, similarity, and immanence but rather on the side of distance, dissimilarity, and transcendence. Thus Przywara can claim that the *analogia entis* is simply an explication of the Fourth Lateran Council's edict against Joachim of Fiore: "Inter creatorem et creaturam non potest tanta similitudo notari, quin inter eos non maior sit dissimilitudo notanda [No similarity can be observed between Creator and creature, however great, that would not require one to observe a greater dissimilarity be-

107. *Analogia Entis,* p. 134.
108. Ibid.; *De ver.,* q. 22, a. 4, c. ("the nearer any nature is to God, the less inclined it is to be moved by another and the more capable it is of moving itself").
109. *Analogia Entis,* p. 134; *De ver.,* q. 5, a. 8 c. ("that they might be the cause of goodness in others").
110. *Analogia Entis,* p. 134; *De ver.,* q. 6, a. 5 c. ("that they be not only provided for, but provident").

tween them]."[111] And it is precisely in order to emphasize this point that, at the conclusion of §6, Przywara elaborates the theological analogy in terms of the two traditional models of analogy that were discussed above: an *analogia attributionis,* otherwise known as a *pros hen* (πρὸς ἕν) analogy, and an *analogia proportionalitatis,* understood not, as in the *analogia attributionis,* as an ordering to one *(ad aliquid unum),* but rather as *"a relation of mutual alterity,"* as one proportion to *another* (ὡς ἄλλο πρὸς ἄλλο).[112] Whereas the former emphasizes a degree of similarity between God and creation (inasmuch as the creature can point to God as the ground and cause of its perfections), the latter emphasizes an ultimate dissimilarity. For in the latter case one can speak only of a suspended analogy between two radically different proportions, that is, two radically different ways of being: on the one hand, in the creature a relation of essence and existence, which has the form of a "unity-in-tension" [*Spannungseinheit*]; on the other hand, in the case of God, an essential identity [*Wesenseinheit*] of essence and existence.[113] Accordingly, the most one can say is that there is some kind of relation, some kind of analogy between being and becoming, which are related *not directly* but as one proportion to another.

Properly understood, therefore, the *analogia entis* (in the form of the theological analogy) comprises two moments: a *tanta similitudo* expressed in the *analogia attributionis* and a *maior dissimilitudo* expressed in the *analogia proportionalitatis.* Accordingly, "analogy lies between univocity *(univocatio)* and complete equivocity *(aequivocatio)."*[114] But two things are crucial to observe here, upon which a proper understanding of Przywara's doctrine depends. First, for Przywara, following Thomas (*De ver.,* q. 2, a. 11), the stress falls on the second analogy, the *analogia proportionalitatis.* For one must always observe the "alterity *(diversas proportiones)* within whatever *one* term is predicated *of* both God and creature *(ad aliquid unum:* e.g., being, good, etc.)."[115] Second, in giving due priority to the *analogia proportionalitatis,* it is not as though the similarity implied by the *analogia attributionis* is "simply

111. See *Schriften,* 2:402; *Analogia Entis,* p. 138. See Denzinger, *The Sources of Catholic Dogma,* trans. Roy J. Deferrari (St. Louis: Herder, 1957), p. 171 (432). N.B.: Some manuscripts seem to include the "tanta" in *tanta similitudo,* while others do not. In any case, Przywara generally reads it as *tanta similitudo;* he also tends to read the Ignatian "ever greater" *(semper maior)* into the Lateran *maior dissimilitudo.*

112. *Analogia Entis,* p. 136; Aristotle, *Metaphysics* 5.6.1016b.

113. *Schriften,* 2:403; cf. p. 39; cf. *ST* I, q. 80, a. 1.

114. *ST* I, q. 13, a. 5, corp.

115. *Analogia Entis,* pp. 136-37.

John R. Betz

'balanced out' by the dissimilarity of the mode [*modus*] whereby this same *one* is in both God and creature (like and unlike, *simile 'et' dissimile*)."[116] For then, "it would not be the divine Is (Truth, etc.) that is ultimately decisive, but instead this suspended equilibrium between God and creature."[117] "No," Przywara says, "the positive commonality of the *ad aliquid unum* is led beyond itself into the genuinely Areopagitic 'dazzling darkness' of the *diversas proportiones* — into, that is, an 'ever greater dissimilarity': *creaturae . . . quamvis aliquam Dei similitudinem gerant in seipsis, tamen maxima dissimilitudo subest*."[118] Indeed, the simple point of the *analogia entis* (as far as its ultimate stress is concerned) is that any analogy between God and creatures is ultimately *only* an analogy — one that at a certain point fails, breaks off, pointing beyond every similitude, "however great," to an "ever greater" God, who is expressly "beyond all analogy." As Przywara put it, already in 1927, "God is the one who is 'ever greater,' transcending all analogy. . . . What is meant by *analogia entis* is precisely this: that in the very same act in which the human being comes to intimate God in the likeness of the creature, he also comes to intimate him as the one who is beyond all likeness."[119]

IX. After Barth: Some Final Clarifications

At this point, with the actual doctrine of the *analogia entis* in view, it may be hoped that we are in a better position to assess the merits of Barth's criticism of it.[120] That being said, given that Barth's remarks about the *analogia entis*, while strident, are few and far between — indeed, given that he nowhere presents a substantive refutation of the doctrine — identifying his actual criticisms is in itself a difficult task. In the rest of the essay, therefore, I will attempt first to identify a particular reason for Barth's objection to the *analogia entis*, and then to respond to the particular objection on the basis of Przywara's actual doctrine.

116. Ibid., p. 137; *De ver.*, q. 2, a. 11, ad 1.

117. *Analogia Entis*, p. 137.

118. Ibid.; *De ver.*, q. 1, a. 10, ad 1 in contr. ("although creatures bear within themselves a certain likeness to God, there is nevertheless present the greatest unlikeness"). For this reason, Przywara says that the "resonance" of the first analogy gives way to the "silence" of the second (see *Analogia Entis*, p. 210).

119. *Schriften*, 2:404.

120. For a more extensive defense of Przywara vis-à-vis Barth's criticisms of the *analogia entis*, see the section on Barth in my article "Beyond the Sublime: The Aesthetics of the Analogy of Being" (pt. 2), pp. 3-12.

70

As for the basis of Barth's understanding of Przywara's doctrine, we know that he and Przywara met (at Barth's invitation) at Barth's seminar in Münster in February 1929, in which context Przywara delivered a lecture entitled "Das katholische Kirchenprinzip"; we also know that they met again at Barth's seminar, this time in Bonn, in December 1931.[121] And there is every reason to believe that they were on friendly terms — and even remained so. In fact, as Keith Johnson has shown, in May 1932 Przywara wrote to Barth to ask if he would review his *Analogia Entis*. Barth, however, declined — apparently claiming that he did not have time to do it justice. It is therefore quite possible that Barth never read the *Analogia Entis,* having formed his judgment of the *analogia entis* on the basis of Przywara's previous work, in particular his *Religionsphilosophie katholischer Theologie,* and a couple of evenings of conversation. Nevertheless, Barth was apparently confident enough in his understanding of Przywara's doctrine to issue his famous anathema only a few months later. So the question remains: Why did Barth make the alienating pronouncement that he did?

However one answers this question, one can be sure that Barth's reasons for rejecting the *analogia entis* were bound up with his rejection of natural theology — especially to the extent that he was still operating within the mind-set of his early dialectical theology and had not made any explicit turn toward analogy, in the form of an *analogia fidei (relationis),* that would mark the later volumes of the *Church Dogmatics.*[122] For if for Barth the problem with natural theology lay in the presumption that we can know something about God apart from faith (and apart from God's self-revelation), the *analogia entis* seems to have represented in his view a corresponding presumption: namely, that we are always already ontologically related to God on the basis of our being, our mere nature, apart from God's free self-relating to us by grace. In other words, both natural theology and the *analogia entis* seem to have represented in Barth's view Promethean attempts to lay hold of God

---

121. For Przywara's lecture and Barth's response, see *Zwischen den Zeiten* 7 (1929): 277-302. For more on the historical background of their encounter, see Chalamet, "Est Deus in nobis?" See also two books that have just appeared: Keith Johnson, *Karl Barth and the Analogia Entis* (London: T. & T. Clark, 2010), and Amy Marga, *Karl Barth's Dialogue with Catholicism in Göttingen and Münster: Its Significance for His Doctrine of God* (Tübingen: Mohr-Siebeck, 2010).

122. See Eberhard Jüngel, "Die Möglichkeit theologischer Anthropologie auf dem Grunde der Analogie. Eine Untersuchung zum Analogieverständnis Karl Barths," in *Barth-Studien* (Gütersloh: Benziger, 1982), pp. 210-32; see also in the same volume, "Von der Dialektik zur Analogie. Die Schule Kierkegaards und der Einspruch Petersons," pp. 127-79.

— the one from the subjective-noetic side, the other from the objective-ontic side, the one usurping the role of faith, the other the role of grace. And sure enough, in his short work from 1929 *The Holy Spirit and the Christian Life,* Barth indicates precisely this: that his problem with the *analogia entis* is that it establishes a continuity between God and creation already at the level of nature; whereas, in his view, any relationship the creature may have to God is not something to which we always already have a claim but solely the result of an "incomprehensible, unmerited divine *giving*."[123]

Given the date of this last-named work, we can be fairly sure that this is Barth's main criticism of the *analogia entis,* and that this is what he had in mind in so adamantly rejecting it a few years later. In response to this criticism, however, one would minimally have to point out the following: (1) that for Przywara, as for any Christian, creation *itself* is the result of an "incomprehensible, unmerited divine *giving*"; (2) that any attempt to turn creation into a "given," a "datum," would be to misunderstand what it means to be a creature; (3) that, for Przywara, the analogy of creation is precisely *only* an analogy, and to this extent an *unstable* likeness, admitting no direct knowledge of the divine whatsoever; (4) that similitude, therefore, according to Przywara's understanding of the *analogia entis,* in no way entails "continuity" or some kind of metaphysical "bridge-building" in the way that Barth seems to have feared; and (5) that for Catholic theology in general God's more intimate self-relating to us by grace is not something competing with God's self-revelation in nature (to say otherwise would be to embrace a form of Manichaeism), but an unanticipated deepening and clarification of this initial self-revelation.

In any case, it should be clear that this first and oft-repeated criticism of the *analogia entis* has remarkably little to do with Przywara's actual doctrine — in either its early or its mature form. To know that this is so, one need only recall how vigorously, from early on, Przywara combats every form of pantheism (ancient or modern), that is, every conflation of the divine with the creature. This is why von Balthasar could unequivocally say, as already noted, that "both [Barth and Przywara] took a stand against Kantianism and Hegelianism, against Schleiermacher's (or the modern) method of immanence, against every scheme by which the human being, whether devout or

---

123. I am indebted here to Christophe Chalamet for alerting me to this passage and for his clarification of Barth's position. See Barth, *Vorträge und kleinere Arbeiten, 1925-1930,* ed H. Schmidt (Zürich: TVZ, 1994), pp. 480-81, published in English in 1938 as *The Holy Ghost and the Christian Life,* trans. R. B. Hoyle, and reprinted in 1993 in a revised edition by Westminster/John Knox Press. For the full translation of this passage, see Chalamet, "Est Deus in nobis?"

not, might attempt to lay hold of the living God."[124] In no sense, therefore, can the doctrine of the *analogia entis,* the doctrine of a mysterious similitude of creation, be construed as giving the creature some kind of "hold" on God. As Przywara plainly says in *Religionsphilosophie katholischer Theologie,* "*analogia entis* means neither a calculation of God nor a limiting of God within the limits of the creature, but a reverent looking to God as the one whose self-condescension is already [what constitutes] this creation as creation."[125] To be sure, for Przywara (as for Thomas and the medievals in general), creation remains a *similitude,* some kind of likeness, but once again, as he explains, in no way does this put God within the creature's grasp:

> The [most] basic and decisive feature of the Catholic grounding of religion . . . can be described as follows: it conceives of the relation between God and creature as "upwardly open." This entails two things. On the one hand, this means that God is neither the absolute positing of any particular aspect of creation — neither the spiritual [*des Geisthaften*] nor the cosmic [*des Allhaften*], neither will nor thought, neither the personal nor the ideal — nor is he the ideal "unity" of the antitheses of these "sides" of creation. He is absolutely transcendent, as Thomas Aquinas puts it, *tamquam ignotus,* beyond all conceivable contents. Seen from this perspective, the creature is that which is never "completed"; it is the inconclusive "openness" of its tensions. On the other hand, this totality of the creaturely — in its antitheses and in the ever renewed attempts to bring together the tensions of its antitheses — is a "revelation" of God "from above"; that is, it is not an analogy [*Gleichnis*] into which God could in any way be "compelled" [*"vernotwendigt"*], as though by means of this analogy he could be arrived at [*errechnet*] in his living essence and activity . . . but an analogy that points beyond itself to a God who is beyond all analogy [*übergleichnishaft*], who happened to choose this particular "analogy" according to an inscrutable decree and could choose thousands of others. God is thus, on the one hand, the mysterious "meaning" to which the totality of creation points. . . . At the same time, however, he is neither the "inner" sense [*Sinn*] of creaturely reality . . . nor is "this" creaturely reality in any way a "necessary" revelation of his nature and activity or a limitation of new ways of his self-revelation.[126]

124. Przywara, *Sein Schrifttum,* p. 6.
125. Ibid., p. 442.
126. *Schriften,* 2:400ff. Przywara refers here to the first chapter of the *Constitutio*

John R. Betz

In view of these statements, which are wholly characteristic of
Przywara's thought at this time and whose basic point (that of the *maior
dissimilitudo* between God and creatures) is given, if anything, only greater
emphasis in his *Analogia Entis* (which Przywara introduces in 1932 as an explicitly negative theology in the tradition of the Areopagite), one is at a loss
to know what here could conceivably be construed as "*the* invention of
Antichrist." For in no sense can it lie in a supposed attempt to get a metaphysical "hold" on God or in a supposed failure to do justice to God's radical
transcendence. Nor, for that matter, as is commonly thought, can the
analogia entis be identified with a form of natural theology (even if it is inti-
mated at the intersection of philosophy and theology), precisely because the
analogia entis pertains as a fundamental form, as Przywara frequently points
out, even to the most exalted supernatural knowledge and experience of
God in a *unio caritatis in gratia.*[127]

Having encountered so much misunderstanding of his doctrine, in
1940 Przywara responded to his critics, Barth included, in an essay entitled
"The Scope of Analogy as a Fundamental Catholic Form" ("Die Reichweite
der Analogie als katholischer Grundform").[128] Von Balthasar, too, entered
the fray, defending the "old master" in lengthy articles in *Divus Thomas* (and
later in his book on Barth).[129] Still, though, Barth persisted in his opinion,

---

dogmatica de fide catholica of the [First] Vatican Council (Denzinger 1782): "Re et essentia a
mundo distinctus . . . et super omnia, quae praeter ipsum sunt et concipi possunt,
ineffabiliter excelsus . . . ad manifestandam perfectionem suam per bona, quae creaturis
impertitur, lieberrimo consilio . . . de nihilo condidit creaturam." ("In his being and essence
distinct from the world . . . and ineffably exalted beyond everything that is outside him and
anything that can be conceived . . . [God] created the world out of nothing in the perfect
freedom of his counsel for the sake of manifesting his perfection through the good things
bestowed upon creatures.")

127. *Analogia Entis,* p. 138. In other words, no supernatural knowledge or experience
of God would obviate the need to recognize God as "ever greater." Therein lies the simple
point of the *analogia entis,* which the saints seem most to comprehend, inasmuch as it is
they who most understand both how intimate God is to his creatures and also how exceed-
ingly transcendent he is and remains.

128. See *Schriften,* 3:247-301. At the heart of this work is Przywara's reminder to Barth
and other critics that the *analogia entis* is, at the end of the day, simply a philosophical-
theological explication of the Fourth Lateran Council's dogmatic statement against Joachim
of Fiore (as was discussed above).

129. See nn. 5 and 71; see also *The Theology of Karl Barth,* p. 257, where von Balthasar
says that one must "flatly deny Barth's charge . . . that it tries to 'overpower' God (since the
analogy of being is precisely the 'principle' that was formulated to exclude and immobilize
any such attempt to usurp God, and that from the very roots)."

denying as late as 1948 that there is "any correspondence and similitude of being, any *analogia entis;* for the being of God and that of man are and remain incomparable."[130] Clearly, this is a caricature of the *analogia entis* and cannot be said to be an adequate representation of Przywara's doctrine. For as we have seen, the *analogia entis* is not a metaphysical superstructure connecting the being of God to the being of creatures; nor does it compromise divine transcendence; nor is it reducible to a form of natural theology. On the contrary, as "fundamental form" of "dynamic transcendence," it applies beyond natural theology even to the greatest, most supernatural revelations, ever again reinstating God's dynamic transcendence.

In a final clarification of his position from 1952, Przywara thus relates feeling grossly misunderstood, saying that Barth's representation of his doctrine amounted to a "grotesque distortion" of his views.[131] "If [my *Analogia Entis*] is the invention of Antichrist . . . (and if his use of this phrase is something other than a joke to be received in the spirit of camaraderie [*eine kameradschaftliche Sottise*], as I have long taken it to be), then my dear old friend Karl Barth should reenroll himself in the school of the old Greek monks and relearn from them the meaning of the phrase 'discernment of spirits.'"[132] In the same context he gives a summary of his doctrine that is worth quoting in full, adding that the doctrine is ultimately so "simple" — the idea that God is "ever greater" — that it too, in fulfillment of the gospel (Matt. 11:25), is "hidden from the wise and the intelligent, but revealed to babes":

> *Analogia entis* is an abbreviated way of stating what the Fourth Lateran Council — and thus a Christianity that was still unified — defined in 1215: that even in the most extreme regions of the supernatural (as was here at issue in the trinitarian mysticism [of Joachim of Fiore]), "one cannot note any similarity between Creator and creature — however great — that would not require one always to note an ever greater dissimilarity." Thus *analogia entis* in no way signifies a "natural theology"; on the contrary, it obtains precisely in the domain of the supernatural and the genuinely Christian. Nor does it signify a "theological-

---

130. *KD* III/2, p. 262. Instead Barth now argues, according to the terms of his new doctrine of an *analogia relationis,* that there is no analogy between God and human beings except a relational analogy (an *analogia proportionalitatis!*) between the self-relationality of God in the immanent Trinity and God's relating to us in Christ.

131. *In und Gegen,* p. 277.

132. Ibid., p. 278.

philosophical doctrine, according to which the created world is ordered to God"; still less does it signify a comprehensible ontological nexus between Creator, creation, and creature. On the contrary, *analogia entis* signifies that what is decisive in "every similarity, however great," is the "ever greater dissimilarity." It signifies, so to speak, God's "dynamic transcendence," that is, that God is ever above and beyond [*je-über-hinaus*] "everything external to him and everything that can be conceived," as was stressed in the "negative theology" of the Greek fathers and transmitted like a "sacred relic" from Augustine to Thomas to the [First] Vatican Council. My dear friends — from Karl Barth to Söhngen to Haecker to Balthasar — have apparently never grasped that "analogia," according to Aristotle, is a "proportion between two *X*[s]" (see my *Analogia Entis!*).[133]

Leaving aside the question of how Przywara may have felt misunderstood even by von Balthasar,[134] Przywara's point is again that the final analogy between God and creatures is not an *analogia attributionis* but an *analogia proportionalitatis,* precisely in the sense of a mutual alterity (ἄλλο πρὸς ἄλλο). Whereas the first analogy grounds the similarity, the relationship, between God and creatures, inasmuch as creaturely perfections point to God as their cause, the second analogy highlights the "ever greater dissimilarity" between God and creatures, beyond every similarity, "however great." Thus Przywara says in the *Analogia Entis,* "In everything that is said of God and creatures in common (being, true-good-beautiful, etc.), it is not the case that God and creatures are thereby related to something common. Instead, here everything reduces to the irreducible priority of God."[135] Indeed, "the creature [points] in every respect beyond itself to God as the one who is prior, without any 'possibility of appeal' to a third (e.g., being) . . . *(cum Deo nihil sit prius, sed ipse sit prior creatura).*"[136] As a result, unable to point to any *tertium comparationis* (not even to being, as is commonly thought) as something in which God and creatures both share, creation is

133. Ibid., pp. 277ff.
134. Przywara suggests here that von Balthasar's elucidation of his position was ultimately not simple enough in the manner just described. As for any substantive differences between Przywara and von Balthasar, there seems to be only one, which is hinted at in von Balthasar's *Theodramatik:* that the rhythm of the *analogia entis* is ultimately so dynamic as to compromise the givenness of the *form* — the *Gestalt* — of Christ. See *Theodramatik* II/1 (Einsiedeln: Johannes Verlag, 1976), p. 325.
135. *Analogia Entis,* pp. 137-38; *De pot.,* q. 7, a. 7, corp.
136. *Analogia Entis,* pp. 137-38.

left radically suspended.[137] In short, before God it has nothing left to stand on. And for this reason, given that the *analogia entis* ultimately leaves the creature suspended before a God who is confined to no genus *(Deus non est in genere!)*, Przywara says that the final form of the *analogia entis,* or rather its final moment, is a "suspended analogy" between the creature (out of nothing) and the "Creator out of nothing."[138]

So again, how could any of this be considered "*the* invention of Antichrist"? Is it possibly that, according to Barth's apocryphal late teaching, "the *analogia entis* misconstrues the difference between God and human beings in that it overlooks God's *proximity*"?[139] But this too — aside from being a volte-face — makes little sense, given that Przywara affirms not only God's immanence to creation (the first moment of "God in us and God above us") but also the Thomistic doctrine of infused grace *(gratia infusa et inhaerens).* Or is the problem with the *analogia entis* the mere suggestion that there is some kind of relation, some kind of similitude, however distant and remote, between Creator and creature, which can be discerned by the natural light of reason: minimally, that the creature is not its own cause, that it is an effect of the Creator and, as such, bears some remote likeness to its cause (according, say, to the medieval principle *omne agens agit sibi simile*)? Indeed, it would seem that here we are closer to Barth's real concern.[140] As he puts it in *The Holy Spirit and the Christian Life,* referring to the very passage from Przywara's *Religionsphilosophie katholischer Theologie* that was quoted above: "The human as creature is not in a place from which he can establish

137. To be sure, this is one of the most common, if misguided, criticisms of the *analogia entis:* that it supposedly subordinates God to some "being," that is, to some third term, which is shared in, however differently, by God and creatures. See, for example, Henri Bouillard, S.J., *The Knowledge of God,* trans. Samuel D. Femiano (New York: Herder & Herder, 1968), pp. 101ff., who follows Barth in identifying Przywara with Quenstedt, claiming that (allegedly for both of them) "there exists between the creature and the Creator a relationship which resides in a *being* which is common to both of them, a relationship which can be known independently of revelation in Jesus Christ." In this case, it would seem particularly unfortunate that Przywara was not even understood by a member of his own order, when those misunderstanding him were legion, but was instead subjected to the same misplaced criticism.

138. *Analogia Entis,* p. 141.

139. See Jüngel, *Gott als Geheimnis der Welt,* p. 385.

140. See in this regard Archie J. Spencer, "Causality and the *analogia entis:* Karl Barth's Rejection of Analogy of Being Reconsidered," *Nova et Vetera,* Engl. ed., 6, no. 2 (2008): 329-76, and the response of Thomas Joseph White, O.P., "How Barth Got Aquinas Wrong: A Reply to Archie J. Spencer on Causality and Christocentrism," *Nova et Vetera,* Engl. ed., 7, no. 1 (2009): 241-70.

and survey his relation to God (e.g., in a scheme of a unity of similarity and dissimilarity) and, on that basis, understand himself as 'open upwards,' and therefore he is not able to attribute his knowing to a revealedness [*Offenbarsein*] of God proper to him as such."[141]

The point of Barth's criticism, then, to judge from this last statement, is that the *analogia entis* is an Archimedean point from which one can securely infer one's relation to God and give a neat and tidy accounting, a ledger, of similarities and differences between God and creatures — whereby the similarities are credited to our own account, as safely in our possession, and the differences constitute the remainder that is not. But — and this seems to be the main point — we need not fear the differences because we have enough similarities in our account to feel comfortable about ourselves and our relationship to God, which is also a given. Accordingly, just as natural theology gives us epistemological security, the *analogia entis* provides "ontological security."[142] Of course, if this is the *analogia entis,* then Barth has legitimate reasons for rejecting it — reasons having largely to do with the cultural and political circumstances of the time. But it is not; it is a caricature that misses entirely the spirit and pathos of Przywara's actual doctrine, which is precisely to humble human pride and every proud system of thought by *depriving* being of any firm footing, any Archimedean point. Indeed, the irony in all of this, as von Balthasar noted, is that Przywara's doctrine of the *analogia entis* (far from being a mere scholastic technicality) was his own calculated response to the ills brought on by the immanentism of modern philosophy and culture — a wedge driven into the prevailing immanentism as a reminder

---

141. *The Holy Spirit and the Christian Life,* p. 5 (Chalamet's translation).

142. For Barth, then, it would seem that, once again, the real issue with the *analogia entis* was that he saw it as an extension of natural theology, moreover, as making natural theology possible by positing an ontological relationship with God that is proper to the creature as such. Were Barth not so concerned about the developments of modern culture after the First World War, the *analogia entis* would have seemed innocuous enough; it might even have struck him as nothing other than a highly sophisticated exposition of what the church through the ages has always taught in light of Genesis 1:26-27, Wisdom 13:5, and Romans 1:19-20. Given his understandable cultural and political concerns, however, any weight that the *analogia entis* might give to natural theology — which he saw as ultimately abetting the conflation of the divine with modern humanism — was too much to bear. To him the only road open for theology was not one that showed how we are always already "in touch" with God on the basis of our being but one that showed how we are contradicted by the revelation of the Word of God, which reveals the depths of our sin, blindness, and *incapacity* for anything properly divine. Therein, it seems, lies the heart of the matter and the reason why Barth was reluctant to make any qualifications of his criticism.

that created being is inherently analogical and therefore in no way reducible to the secular terms of modern humanism. In any case, for Przywara, it is nothing to stand on that could be cause for human pride or Promethean self-assertion; on the contrary, it is a cause for humility, showing that to be a creature is to be suspended between nothing and the Creator out of nothing.

But if Barth's criticism that the *analogia entis* provides some kind of Archimedean point has no basis with regard to Przywara's doctrine, the passage quoted above contains another aspect of his criticism that merits further consideration: namely, his denial that created being at the level of nature (presumably since it is fallen) is in any sense "upwardly open" to transcendence (since it is closed by sin).[143] Part of Barth's point here is that such a perspective upon created being (that of the *analogia entis* as a scheme of similarity within ultimate dissimilarity) is unavailable from a purely natural standpoint (and this is a debatable point). But his criticism runs deeper than this and is connected to his denial that there is any natural openness of the creature to God, any point of contact — any *Anknüpfungspunkt* (to use Brunner's term) — whatsoever. Indeed, Barth's concern is that from the perspective of the *analogia entis,* creation is always already dynamically open to God, in spite of sin, and to this extent always already "prepared" for God. And in this regard he refers explicitly to the following passage from Przywara's *Religionsphilosophie katholischer Theologie* (which happens to be the only passage from Przywara that Barth cites in the whole of the *Church Dogmatics*):[144]

> In the Catholic *analogia entis* we find the possibilities for a genuine *Menschwerdungskosmos,* which brings together body and soul, community and individual, inasmuch as in their totality (taking into consideration, of course, the upward relation from dead matter to pure spirit) they are "open" to God. From the standpoint of a Catholic *analogia entis,* the creature in its totality presents a perspective within analogy that goes beyond all analogy, a perspective regarding the God who *transcends all analogy;* and in this respect the creature is a receptive preparation for him: in its ultimate essence it already cries out, as it were, "Be-

---

143. Of course, rightly understood, Przywara's point in the passage to which Barth alludes is simply that God cannot be reduced to any aspect of created being, not even the totality of created being, but infinitely transcends it as the *Deus tamquam ignotus.* In other words, to say that created being is "upwardly open" is simply to observe this analogical interval between created being and the God who is beyond all analogy.

144. See *KD* I/2, §15, pp. 158-59.

hold the handmaid of the Lord: may it be done unto me according to thy Word!"[145]

In view of Barth's unequivocally negative reaction to this text in the context of an extended intratextual polemic against Catholic theology in general, we can now be reasonably sure that his chief problem with the *analogia entis,* aside, that is, from his tendency to conflate it with natural theology, was the Mariology he saw in it, that is, the notion that creation is fundamentally Mariological, always already looking to God and always already intended for God — indeed, always already in touch with God on the basis of its mere being, inasmuch as creation itself is already a *self*-revelation of God. We can also be sure that, from Barth's Reformed perspective, the doctrine of the *analogia entis,* inasmuch as it takes Mary, conceived without sin, as a model, fails to appreciate sufficiently the predicament of sin, which precisely "closes" any openness to transcendence that the creature, on the basis of its mere being, could be said to possess (which is why, for the explosive Barth, the door of any openness, which may have existed prior to the fall, must now be "blasted open" by the dynamite of grace). Finally, it seems that, from Barth's perspective, the *analogia entis* amounted to an illegitimate philosophical anticipation of the incarnation. And admittedly, in the same context, Przywara says that the incarnation is the "crowning of the movement of God's self-condescension" in creation; that "religion, in the ultimate sense of the *analogia entis,* means the active consciousness of the divine ori-

---

145. *Schriften,* 2:441-42 (emphasis mine). Importantly, this passage occurs in the context of Przywara's discussion of two basic ways of construing the God-world relation that he says are alien to a Catholic perspective and, specifically, to a Catholic understanding of the incarnation. The first way is one in which God is reducible to some aspect of the world — even the highest, absolute unity of the world. Here we have what is essentially the God of Aristotle and, mutatis mutandis, Hegel. (See n. 56 above.) In this case, Przywara says, the incarnation is made impossible precisely because God and world are already "melted together" and God possesses no freedom vis-à-vis the world. The second way of construing the God-world relation safeguards God's transcendence but is characterized by an essentially Docetic-Gnostic view of the incarnation as touching only upon the "invisible interior" of the soul, in which case the incarnation is rendered essentially invisible. Whereas in the first case God is so much "in" the world as ultimately to be a part (or the whole) of the world, in the second case, God, though free with respect to world, does not enter into it profoundly enough (and here Przywara seems to have the tendency of Reformed theology, including Barth, in mind). Against both forms of religion, each of which in some way fails to do justice to the "in-and-beyond" of "God in-and-beyond creation," Przywara argues that a proper understanding of the incarnation is preserved only in the Catholic understanding of the *analogia entis.*

gin of the creature, the consciousness that in its ultimate essence it is a self-revelation and self-condescension of God"; and that this makes the creature, "already in this 'natural' form of religion, an objective preparation for the actual incarnation."[146]

But leaving aside the question of sin and how this might be said to qualify any *analogia entis*,[147] to say that the creature is ontologically a preparation for the incarnation (how could it be otherwise?) is not to say that a natural knowledge of God can *anticipate* the incarnation. On the contrary, for Przywara, following Aquinas and the explicit teaching of the Catholic Church, the fundamental mystery of the incarnation and the mystical body of Christ — and the mystery of a universe always intended for this, that is, a *Menschwerdungskosmos* — is in no way visible from the vantage of the creature apart from *faith* in what has been *revealed*. As he puts it, "The final mystery of Catholic religion is not visible from the perspective of the creature by way of calculation from below to above, but from God alone, in reverent looking to him who is beyond all creation."[148] To be sure, for Przywara, there remains some analogy, some kind of connection, between the orders of creation and of redemption — which must obtain if God is the author of both — but they are not confused. For "the incarnation of God is, on the one hand, nothing that could in any way be calculated; but, on the other hand, neither is it something contradictory."[149] Rather, they are related in the same way as the orders of nature and grace. As Przywara puts it, in God these or-

146. Ibid., p. 442.

147. While it is true that original sin is not a prominent feature of the *analogia entis,* it is hardly the case that Przywara denies it, or that the openness of which he speaks is not, in his view, severely compromised by sin; see *Analogia Entis,* pp. 168-69. That being said, it is undoubtedly the case that whereas Barth was, from at least 1922 onward, far more pessimistic about any created openness to God or the inherent goodness of creation, it was only gradually that Przywara came to sense the depths of human sin. See, for example, his far darker *Alter und Neuer Bund,* which was penned during the Second World War.

148. *Analogia Entis,* p. 443. To illustrate this point, one might again take the example of Adam and Eve. While the union of Adam and Eve presupposes both Adam's existence and his essence, it is not as though Eve could be envisioned before she was *given* to him. So too, while the whole of creation is ontologically a preparation for the incarnation, for union with God in Christ, this is not to say that the hypostatic union, much less the ultimate mystery of the mystical body of Christ, the *totus Christus,* could in any way be conceived or realistically anticipated — apart from the grace of prophecy — before Christ himself was given. Something similar could be said of the much-disputed doctrine of a natural desire for the supernatural, for the fulfillment of human longing in the divine, and why a natural desire is not some kind of claim on God.

149. Ibid., p. 442.

John R. Betz

ders, "in their objective essence," are one and inseparable, given that the supernatural "gift of participation" in God through Christ is simply "the *unanticipated* and *unmerited* completion of that analogous 'gift of participation' which is the essence of nature"; accordingly, "the 'participation in the divine nature' [should be seen] as the blessed crowning of 'in him we live and move and have our being.'"[150]

Such, then, is Przywara's basic contribution to theological considerations of nature and grace: that he always thinks in terms of analogy (in the sense of the "greater dissimilarity within any similarity") and not in terms of identity or contradiction; and that he does not view grace as concurring with nature so much as completing and perfecting it.[151] Accordingly, one need not deny a natural desire for God, a vague openness, a kind of longing on the part of the creature, in order to preserve the novelty of revelation. In short, one need not denigrate the glory of God's creation (in Mary) in order to safeguard the glory of God (in Christ). Nor, from Przywara's Catholic perspective, must one deny human cooperation in redemption (as is paradigmatic in Mary) in order to safeguard divine sovereignty. On the contrary, for Przywara, God is glorified precisely in liberating the creature for active, cooperative "service."[152] But here Barth differs — as is clear from the rest of his polemical excursus. And for this reason, and to the extent that at this point he still maintains the doctrine of God's *Alleinwirksamkeit* — to the extent, that is, that he embraces a form of "theopanism" — one may conclude that Barth's objection to the *analogia entis* is ultimately not so much an objection to any particular aspect of Przywara's carefully formulated doctrine as it is a fundamental objection to Thomas Aquinas and the Thomistic principle at its core: *gratia (fides) non destruit, sed supponit et perficit naturam (rationem).*[153] Thus, in rejecting the *analogia entis*, he is indeed rejecting the Catholic Church, having rightly concluded that the *analogia entis* is a consistent expression of its basic theology.

But perhaps we have still not stated Barth's objection to the *analogia entis* in its strongest possible form. As von Balthasar formulates it, "He accuses [the Catholic Church] of possessing a systematic principle that is not

150. *Schriften*, 2:34; Przywara, "Natur und Übernatur," in *Ringen der Gegenwart: Gesammelte Aufsätze, 1922-1927*, vol. 1 (Augsburg: Benno Filser Verlag, 1929), p. 429 (my emphasis).
151. "Natur und Übernatur," p. 429. For more on Przywara's view of the relationship between the natural and the supernatural, see pp. 445ff. and pp. 27-45.
152. *Analogia Entis*, pp. 134-35.
153. Ibid., pp. 83-84.

in itself Christ the Lord but an abstract theory — namely, the *analogia entis* — from which one can determine the relation between God and creatures in advance, according to a prior philosophical understanding (i.e., of natural theology), so that the revelation of God in Jesus Christ appears ultimately as the fulfillment of an already existing reality and knowledge."[154] In other words, "the place that Christ assumes in fulfillment of [such a system] is already designated in advance: in an ontology that is prior to the order of revelation and cannot be shattered by it."[155] Accordingly, in Barth's view, the *analogia entis* becomes the measure, the yardstick, of any possible revelation; what is worse, it would seem to displace Christ as *the* analogy — *the* relation — between God and creatures.[156] This, it seems, is the ultimate challenge. For indeed what does the *analogia entis,* as a doctrine of creation, have to do with Christ? If it turns out to have nothing to do with him, then perhaps we should be concerned, and perhaps Barth had reason to call it the "invention of Antichrist."

At face value, Barth has a point. For if we boil down the *analogia entis* to its core, we find the ultimate structure (and rhythm) of the "in-over" or "in-and-beyond" — a structure (and rhythm) that is present both in the for-

---

154. *Karl Barth. Darstellung und Deutung seiner Theologie,* pp. 46-47 (my translation); *The Theology of Karl Barth: Exposition and Interpretation,* trans. Edward Oakes (San Francisco: Ignatius Press, 1992), p. 37.

155. Ibid. Cf. *KD* II/1, §31, pp. 656-57.

156. And Barth has a point here; for as Scripture variously attests, creation is founded upon and *ultimately* unintelligible apart from Christ, the Alpha and Omega (John 1:3; Col. 1:15ff.; Rev. 1:8). In other words, as any Christian must affirm, in Christ and his hypostatic union lies the *real* relation, within whom the rest of creation is always already comprised, and in whom it is always already loved (John 3:16). It may be, therefore, that the entire point of Barth's rejection of the *analogia entis* is dramatically to emphasize that no metaphysics, no ontology, however pious, can be conceived apart from Christ, just as Barth refuses to entertain any anthropology apart from the God-man. But if this is so, then Barth's problem with the *analogia entis* is ultimately a problem not with Przywara so much as with the *duplex ordo* of Vatican I. Consequently, the question comes down to this: Is there (as for Barth) no natural knowledge of God but *only* theologically inspired knowledge of God (in which case secularism would seem justified in unbelief), or is there (as for Przywara and the Catholic Church) a limited natural knowledge of God on the basis of Romans 1 (which leaves secularism without excuse), which remains to be filled out and perfected by faith? For in the end, it is not the question of whether creation must *ultimately* be understood from a Christological standpoint (see, for example, Przywara's *Logos* or *Christentum gemäß Johannes*), but whether the *analogia entis,* as a creaturely metaphysics, is already adumbrated within philosophy, to the light of natural reason, as the answer to philosophy's own inherent contradictions.

mula for a creaturely metaphysics ("essence in-and-beyond existence") and in the formula for an explicitly theological understanding of creation ("God in-and-beyond creation"). So the question remains, when Christ is revealed does he — or does he not — already fit into this preestablished metaphysics? The first response must be that the *analogia entis* is not a preconceived armchair metaphysics (as we have seen) but an explicitly *descriptive* metaphysics, namely, a metaphysics descriptive of the actual tensions characteristic of creaturely being and thought as such, whose fundamental point is that creaturely being and thought are not self-identical but fundamentally "open," "suspended," existing in a state of "tension," and that, to this extent, the whole of creation, which no philosophy can master, points beyond itself. It is therefore completely the opposite of a "closed" system into which Christ is made to fit. At the same time, though, it is indeed a metaphysical description of the state of affairs that Christ fulfills, inasmuch as Christ is the satisfaction of human longing and the only one who can resolve the tensions of our nature. And in this respect, if this is the supposed problem with the *analogia entis,* namely, that it is committed to an understanding of creaturely being in terms of type and fulfillment, then once again Barth's problem with the *analogia entis* is simply a problem with the Catholic Church, which rejects any conception of the incarnation in dialectical terms as a negation of creation.

But if Christ is, in fact, the fulfillment of the metaphysics of the *analogia entis* — with its fundamental structure of the "in-and-beyond" — in what respect might this be true? While it would far exceed the scope of this essay to show in detail how Przywara's metaphysics ties in to his Christology,[157] which is developed in his subsequent exegetical works, one can at least say the following. God's self-revelation in Christ does not contradict God's self-revelation in creation (as "God in-and-beyond creation") but answers to the creature's deepest needs (as expressed in the formula "essence in-and-beyond existence"). For it is in Christ that the creature finally finds its essence — in him who is the "firstborn of all creation" (Col. 1:15), the reason and archetype of its existence. So too it is in Christ that the restless heart of the creature finds its rest (Matt. 11:28-29). Moreover, it is in Christ that the "in-and-beyond" of the theological analogy (of "God in-and-beyond creation") is deepened and heightened in hitherto unimaginable ways:

157. See, however, in the present volume, Kenneth Oakes, "The Cross and the *analogia entis* in Erich Przywara."

But each of us was given grace according to the measure of Christ's gift. Therefore it is said, "When he ascended on high he made captivity itself a captive; he gave gifts to his people." (When it says, "He ascended," what does it mean but that he also descended into the lower parts of the earth? He who descended is the same one who ascended far above all the heavens, so that he might fill all things.) (Eph. 4:7-10)

That it to say, it is in Christ that we see the measure and scope of all creation. For it is in Christ, who redeems humanity by his death, condescending, so to speak, even to the primal void of creation, that we see just how interior God, in fact, is: *interior omni re.* Indeed, so great and deep is the mystery of divine love in Christ that nothing escapes God's presence (see Ps. 139), not even the soul that is otherwise far from him. As the resurrected Lord puts it to every soul, as it were, from the inside of the soul: "Listen! I am standing at the door, knocking; if you hear my voice and open the door, I will come in to you and eat with you, and you with me" (Rev. 3:20). At the same time, it is in Christ that we truly see God's transcendence of creation, that God is *exterior omni re,* as the one who "ascended far above all the heavens," in order to draw all of humanity to himself (see John 12:32). As the apostle puts it, speaking of Christ's ineffable majesty, "Therefore God also highly exalted him and gave him the name that is above every name, so that at the name of Jesus every knee should bend, in heaven and on earth and under the earth, and every tongue should confess that Jesus Christ is Lord, to the glory of God the Father" (Phil. 2:9-10). In sum, it is in Christ, who is "the way" (John 14:6) — in the words of Heraclitus, "the way up and the way down" (ὁδὸς ἄνω κάτω μία καὶ ωὐτή) — that we see the ultimate revelation and fulfillment of the truth: that God is at once *in*-and-*beyond* creation. And to this extent Christ himself is and remains the ultimate measure — the ultimate *analogy* — of being; which is to say that it is in Christ, as experienced by the saints in the depth of his love *(interior intimo meo)* and the height of his glory *(superior summo meo),* that the full, breathtaking scope of the *analogia entis* appears. Thus, the *analogia entis,* far from being unrelated to Christ, turns out to be all about him.[158]

158. Not surprisingly, therefore, as Kenneth Oakes's essay in this volume shows, Przywara's thought becomes increasingly concerned with Christ. For it is in Christ that the analogy of being (as a *relation* ultimately of mutual *otherness* in terms of the ἄλλο πρὸς ἄλλο of the *analogia proportionalitatis*) is inconceivably fulfilled in a marvelous exchange *(commercium admirabile)* between ἄλλο and ἄλλο. Indeed, for Przywara, following Augustine (and Luther!), *this* is the proper meaning of redemption: "reconciliation" in Christ be-

Admittedly, all of this needs to be developed; it is not clear from the first pages of the *Analogia Entis,* which remains, much like the first two parts of Aquinas's *Summa,* a prolegomenon to Christ and the mysteries of salvation. But surely prolegomena are not to be rejected because they are prolegomena — no more than it would be theologically sensible to cut John the Baptist out of the gospel, or, for that matter, like Marcion, to reject the Old Testament altogether. Yet this, if one may use this analogy, seems to be what Barth demands: that Christians not even try to show how Christ is always already *in* philosophy (i.e., in pagan wisdom), though hidden, just as he is always already *in* the Old Testament, though hidden. Instead, it would seem far more reasonable to conclude that both ways of doing theology are legitimate: both a philosophical theology, as one sees in Przywara, which shows how theology presupposes philosophy and fulfills it, and a properly dogmatic theology, as one sees in Barth. Admittedly, to the Corinthians Paul preaches nothing but Christ crucified (1 Cor. 1:23), which comes with "a demonstration of the Spirit and of power" (1 Cor. 2:4). But the same apostle was also an apologist to the Greeks, and what was his argument if not some kind of appeal to an *analogia entis?* "For 'In him we live and move and have our being'; as even some of your own poets have said, 'For we too are his offspring'" (Acts 17:28). Thus, it may be hoped, Scripture itself answers the entire question, resolving any imagined conflict between an *analogia entis* and an *analogia fidei.*

Now, finally, regarding the question of whether or not the *analogia entis* remains a "fundamental form" of Catholic theology, one cannot fail to point out that there have been several Catholic theologians who have dis-

---

tween God and creatures in the form of exchange (καταλλαγή): an exchange of human sin for divine friendship and glory. See 2 Corinthians 5:18-19. Hence it is in Christ that the *analogia entis* is fulfilled in a still more foundational analogy of love — or rather one should say that this ultimate analogy, as *commercium,* always lay at the basis of the *analogia entis,* inasmuch as it was in Christ, the lamb who was "slain from the foundation of the world" (Rev. 13:8), and in view of the reconciliation that he would accomplish, that all things were made (John 1:3; Col. 1:15-16). Thus Christ is truly the Alpha and the Omega (Rev. 1:8). In any case, it is "unfortunate," as von Balthasar observes, "that Barth failed to see that Przywara's thought as a whole, including the entire structure of the *analogia entis,* is fundamentally Christological" (Przywara, *Sein Schrifttum,* p. 5). In this regard, see esp. Przywara's *Summula* (Nürnberg: Glock & Lutz, 1946). See also von Balthasar, *Karl Barth. Darstellung und Deutung seiner Theologie,* pp. 337ff. The same must also be said of the Catholic understanding of the relationship between nature and grace, namely, that Christ is at the center of it: for apart from him, as the only mediator (1 Tim. 2:5), there simply *is no analogy* between the orders of nature and grace, creation and redemption.

puted this, most notably, Gottlieb Söhngen.[159] Unlike Barth, Söhngen did not dispute the *analogia entis* as such; he recognized that it was necessary to articulating a Christian doctrine of creation in light of Genesis 1:26-27. In his view, therefore, it was senseless to speak of an *analogia fidei* contra an *analogia entis.* Contra Przywara, however, Söhngen allowed the *analogia entis* only *within* an overarching *analogia fidei*.[160] From Przywara's perspective, however, Söhngen seems to have missed his point. For the guiding question of his *Analogia Entis* is precisely whether the *analogia entis* can be discerned on the horizon of philosophy. For that matter, as Przywara saw it and frequently pointed out, the *analogia entis* holds even for any *analogia fidei* inasmuch as no revelation, however definitive, and no rule of faith, however authoritative, would obviate the need to observe the principle of the *analogia entis* — namely, the principle of the "greater dissimilarity" between God and creatures within every similarity, however great. And in this sense, for Przywara, the *analogia entis* retains its legitimacy as a fundamental form of Catholic theology.

159. See n. 2 above.

160. What is meant by "analogy of faith," however, is itself a matter of dispute. Strictly speaking, the phrase refers to Romans 12:6, where Paul says that the "analogy of faith" must hold for the prophets; in other words, what prophets say must be "proportionate" to the rule of faith. This is the primary sense in which Przywara understands the term, though, following Augustine, he also speaks of the *analogia fidei* in terms of the analogy between Old and New Testaments. In Barth, however, it tends to mean either that there is no analogy between God and creatures apart from the analogy that God himself causes in the creature by faith — whereby alone we are made like God — or it refers to the self-correspondence of God in Christ. See *KD* I/1, pp. 251ff. For the definitive discussion of what is at issue here, see Gertz, *Glaubenswelt als Analogie;* for Przywara's discussion of the relation between *analogia entis* and *analogia fidei,* see *Schriften,* 3:247-301.

CHAPTER 2

Karl Barth's Version of an "Analogy of Being": A Dialectical No and Yes to Roman Catholicism

Bruce L. McCormack

I. Introduction

The analogy of being: invention of the Antichrist or the wisdom of God? The question posed by the subtitle of this volume of essays is surely rhetorical. For taken strictly, it seems to invite a decision between a form of radical Protestantism represented by Karl Barth during the early stages of his dogmatic reflections and the form of the analogy of being represented by the early Erich Przywara (up through his 1932 book *Analogia Entis*).[1] I suspect that the framers of our theme knew full well the problems that surround such a decision. There is, first of all, the fact that Catholics are not united among themselves with regard to Przywara's version of the *analogia entis* — and never have been. As long ago as 1951, in his influential book on Karl Barth's theology, Hans Urs von Balthasar wrote, "Przywara is *not* the 'Crown witness' of Catholic doctrine, let alone a modern Church Father, even of the Catholic doctrine of '*analogia entis*,' if by that we mean that the undoubtedly ingenious formula introduced by Przywara has now become *the* key to Catholic doctrine incumbent on all to use. We must not forget that Przywara formulated his doctrine during Barth's early thought, that is, against Barth's dialectical theology."[2] And these words were written at a time when von

---

1. Erich Przywara, *Analogia Entis. Metaphysik* (Munich: Kösel & Pustet, 1932).
2. Hans Urs von Balthasar, *The Theology of Karl Barth: Exposition and Interpretation*, trans. Edward Oakes (San Francisco: Ignatius Press, 1992), p. 39.

Balthasar still shared much in common with Przywara! As the years passed, von Balthasar's own version of the *analogia entis* became increasingly Christological in its orientation, and his distance from the early Przywara grew.[3] And if that is the case with von Balthasar, what of other Catholic theologians? My sense is that divisions of opinion within Catholicism with respect to the precise *nature* of the *analogia entis* as well as its *status* in Catholic theology continue to exist on into our own day. If so, then, a choice for the early Przywara is not one that many Catholics would be willing to make. It is even a question whether the later Przywara himself would want them to do so.[4] All of that is on the one side.

But, second, the either-or that is apparently posed by our theme misleads because it fails to acknowledge the extent to which Barth himself changed his mind. The change of mind that I have in view is *not*, however, as is customarily thought, a change with respect to Barth's attitude toward the version of the analogy of being represented by Przywara. Barth did not, as is sometimes alleged, change his mind on that score.[5] When he ceased speaking of the *analogia entis*, it was not because he had come to the conclusion that he had misunderstood Przywara. He ceased speaking of it because Gottlieb Söhngen[6] and Hans Urs von Balthasar had given him reason to believe that there were other versions of the analogy of being to be found among Catholics that were more amenable to Barth's talk of the *analogia fidei*.[7] If Catholics

3. Hans Urs von Balthasar, *Theo-Drama: Theological Dramatic Theory*, vol. 3: *The Dramatis Personae: The Person in Christ*, trans. Graham Harrison (San Francisco: Ignatius Press, 1992), p. 222.

4. Przywara was not left untouched by the 1934 debate between Barth and Gottlieb Söhngen. In his later years, Przywara sought to narrow the distance between his early version of the *analogia entis* and Barth's *analogia fidei* by folding the latter into the former, a move which was the very opposite of that made by Söhngen and von Balthasar, both of whom tried to locate the *analogia entis* in the *analogia fidei*. On this point, see Keith Johnson, "Analogia Entis: A Reconsideration of the Debate between Karl Barth and Roman Catholicism, 1914-1964" (PhD diss., Princeton Theological Seminary, 2008), p. 200, n. 58.

5. As this is the burden of Keith Johnson's fine dissertation, I will not undertake the questions surrounding Barth's critique of Przywara here — or the question of whether Barth had rightly understood Przywara. See Johnson, "Analogia Entis."

6. See Söhngen, "Analogia fidei I. Gottähnlichkeit allein aus Glauben?" and "Analogia fidei II. Die Einheit in der Glaubenswissenschaft," *Catholica* 3 (1934): 113-36 and 176-208. Because of considerations of space, I will not be treating Söhngen here.

7. Of the forty-three references to the *analogia entis* in the German edition of the *Church Dogmatics*, thirty-eight of them appear in the first three part-volumes; only five appear after *Kirchliche Dogmatik* II/1 — and none of them are to be found in the doctrine of reconciliation.

wished to embrace the commitments resident in his *analogia fidei,* he would
no longer speak ill of them. So no, that is not the change I have in mind. The
change of mind of which I speak has to do with developments internal to the
Church Dogmatics.

When Barth revised his doctrine of election in *Church Dogmatics* II/2,
he put in place the ontological basis of a Christology that was finally elabo-
rated only in *Church Dogmatics* IV/1 through IV/3. I will explain the nature
of this revision (and the divine ontology to which it gave rise) in the course
of my reflections on Barth in the third section of this essay. Suffice it here to
say that the relation of Barth's doctrine of election to his later Christology
may be rightly described as follows: Christology is the epistemological basis
of election, and election is the ontological basis of Christology. But to put it
that way is also to say that Barth's doctrine of revelation (as it was first elabo-
rated in Göttingen and maintained unchanged through *Church Dogmatics*
II/1) was recentered (through a shift from a focus on the event in which faith
takes its rise in the believer to a focus on Christology). Formally, the basic
structure of Barth's doctrine of revelation remained unchanged. But materially, it experienced a considerable expansion and deepening. As von
Balthasar puts it, "As Barth continued to publish succeeding volumes of the
Church Dogmatics, he gradually and without fanfare, but no less inexorably,
replaced the central notion of 'the Word of God' with that of 'Jesus Christ,
God and man.' What emerges as this great Summa unfolds is the insight that
'God's Word' is not the most comprehensive term for the essence and con-
tent of revelation."[8]

Now this particular description of the development that took place in
Barth's thought within the bounds of the *Church Dogmatics* is indeed a
happy one, though, as we shall see, even von Balthasar did not fully grasp the
significance of this change — *and could not.* It is easily forgotten that when
von Balthasar wrote his book on Barth, he had access only to the first seven
part-volumes, up through *Church Dogmatics* III/3. I would submit that it is
impossible to understand the ontological implications of Barth's doctrine of
election in the absence of his later Christology (found in *Church Dogmatics*
IV/1-3). It is impossible to lay hold of the version of an "analogy of being"
that was made possible by the twin doctrines of election and Christology —
unless one has access to the later Christology. The Christology of *Church
Dogmatics* I/2 won't do the trick, for it is superseded in important ways by
the subsequent revision of election. Moreover, Barth's talk of an *analogia*

8. Von Balthasar, *The Theology of Karl Barth,* p. 114.

relationis in *Church Dogmatics* III/1 — which von Balthasar made to be the basis for finding the Catholic *analogia entis* in Barth's *analogia fidei* — will be rightly understood only when seen on the basis of the theological ontology necessitated by Barth's later Christology. I will argue in this essay that von Balthasar's claim (following the earlier work of Gottlieb Söhngen) that Barth's *analogia fidei* contains a version of an "analogy of being" is formally correct but materially incorrect. The version of the "analogy of being" that truly is contained in Barth's *analogia fidei* can be recognized only where the relation of God to the human Jesus is kept in view, and that means: on the basis of his later Christology. Hence, Barth's version of the "analogy of being" is *not* the one von Balthasar tried to carve out of the *analogia relationis* of *Church Dogmatics* III/1.

Third and finally, our theme brings immediately before us a phrase that has caused great consternation in many quarters but has rarely been understood in its literary and historical contexts. "I regard the *analogia entis* as the invention of Antichrist, and I believe that because of it it is impossible ever to become a Roman Catholic."[9] Barth is, to be sure, intending a rejection of the early Przywara's version of the *analogia entis* with this statement. I would not deny that for a second. But it is important not to miss the clause that immediately follows this one: "all other reasons for not doing so being to my mind short-sighted and trivial."[10] This clause entails a sharp criticism of liberal "neo-Protestantism." *It is liberal Protestantism, not Roman Catholicism, that is the real target of this statement.* Certainly, the passion (even anger) that this statement brings to expression has its source in Barth's frustrations with liberal Protestantism.[11] Therefore, nothing of any value for ecumenical dialogue will be gained by spending too much time worrying over Barth's language in the preface to *Church Dogmatics* I/1. The basis for a fruitful ecumenical engagement lies in the later Barth, not here.

So much by way of introduction. I have set forth a number of theses; the time has come to defend them. In what follows, I direct my attention in the second section to the development of Karl Barth's doctrine of the *analogia fidei*. To do so will help to clear the ground of a number of misreadings of Barth's *Romans* commentary, which have contributed massively to misunderstandings on the Catholic side that still plague attempts to

9. Barth, *Church Dogmatics,* trans. G. W. Bromiley and T. F. Torrance (London: T. & T. Clark; New York: Continuum, 2004) (henceforth *CD*), I/1, p. xiii.

10. Ibid.

11. See below, pp. 106-7.

understand the significance of debates over the *analogia entis*. I then turn in the third major section to an evaluation of von Balthasar's critique of Barth's *analogia fidei*. My justification for choosing von Balthasar rather than Przywara lies in the fact that it is really von Balthasar's book on Barth that has left its stamp on current Catholic attempts to engage Barth — even those that try to bring Barth into conversation with Przywara. The "Barth" to which recourse is had is invariably von Balthasar's. In the fourth and final section, I will turn to the later Barth's version of an "analogy of being."

It should be noted that I will not be speaking here of a version of the *analogia entis* in Barth. That terminology has a technical significance that is tied too closely to the Catholic tradition to be used for Barth. I will speak more generally of an "analogy of being" — thereby seeking to get at the ontological implications of Barth's later, materially enriched theological epistemology.

II. Determining the Context for a Critical Evaluation of von Balthasar's Reading of Barth: The Origins of Barth's "Analogia Fidei" and His Later Debate with Przywara

From his turn to "theological objectivism" sometime between 1915 and 1916 and on through *Church Dogmatics* II/1, Barth's attention was directed above all to the problem of the knowledge of God. It was theological epistemology, in other words, that was his dominant concern. In relation to this problem especially, it is crucial for anyone interested in the later debates over the *analogia entis* to know something of the historiography of research related to Barth's so-called dialectical theology.

Prior to Ingrid Spieckermann's 1985 book on Barth's doctrine of the knowledge of God, it had been widely assumed that Barth's second *Romans* of 1922 had left him in a situation of more or less complete skepticism.[12] Knowledge of God on the soil of the second *Romans* was thought to be an impossibility. The conclusion that was typically drawn from this was that no real relation between God and the human is possible. Spieckermann's break-through was her discovery in *Romans* of an "analogy of the cross," which she rightly characterized as an *Urgestalt* of the *analogia fidei*.[13] For if the point of

12. See, for example, Paul Althaus, "Theologie und Geschichte. Zur Auseinandersetzung mit der dialektischen Theologie," *Zeitschrift für systematische Theologie* 1 (1923/24): 746.

13. Ingrid Spieckermann, *Gotteserkenntnis. Ein Beitrag zur Grundfrage der neuen Theologie Karl Barths* (Munich: C. Kaiser, 1985), pp. 129, 143.

the *analogia fidei* in *Church Dogmatics* I/1 was to insist that "in faith there takes place a conformity of man to God . . . i.e. an adapting of man to the Word of God . . . a similarity for all the dissimilarity implied by the distinction between God and man,"[14] then it cannot be denied that such a conformity was already affirmed in *Romans* — albeit in a different form. For the Barth of the second *Romans,* revelation takes place in that the meaning of the cross is understood by the recipient of revelation in the light of the resurrection. Or, with greater elaboration: the unintuitable God, who raised Jesus from the dead, gives himself to be known in the intuitability of the historical event of the crucifixion, which is received and understood by the human in the power of the Spirit.[15] To be sure, Barth here stretches human knowledge of God in this book to the breaking point. But he does not think such knowledge impossible. His point is rather that the knowledge of God is always and at every point a divine possibility, rather than a human possibility — not that it is impossible altogether.

In sum: the "analogy of the cross" is a highly actualistic form of analogy that results in a conformity of human knowledge of God to God's knowledge of himself. That it does not require a doctrine of the incarnation in order to be explained certainly distinguishes it materially from Barth's subsequent elaboration of the *analogia fidei* (starting in the Prolegomena to his Göttingen lectures on dogmatics in the summer semester of 1924). But formally, structurally, these two forms of analogy are identical.

I should add: this is no longer a disputed question among Barth specialists, so far as I am aware. If disagreement remains, it has been largely silent. Certainly, no refutation has been undertaken. So for the time being, I think we may count this problem as resolved. But that then has important ramifications for the attempt by Przywara and (later) by von Balthasar to find evidence of "theopanism" in the second *Romans,* as we shall now see.

Erich Przywara first came to Barth's attention in the fall of 1923. On September 30 Thurneysen wrote to Barth, "Acquire for yourself a copy of number 11 of *Stimmen der Zeit,* August 23, Herder Freiburg. There you will find a remarkable and extensive essay about us from the side of the Catholic partner. It is interesting because he makes the Catholic standpoint very clearly visible. Along the way, essential and penetrating remarks on Augus-

---

14. Barth, *CD* I/1, p. 238.

15. On this point see Bruce McCormack, *Karl Barth's Critically Realistic Dialectical Theology: Its Genesis and Development, 1909-1936* (Oxford: Clarendon Press, 1995), pp. 245-62.

tine occur. It is an expert who speaks there. We come off very well, even though our real concern has not been seen."[16] The essay in question is Erich Przywara's justly famous "God in us or God above us?"[17] That the dialectical theologians "came off well" in this essay is certainly true. Przywara judged the dialectical theology centered on Karl Barth to be a "rebirth of genuine Protestantism." And he added, "If Luther belongs to any group in present-day Protestantism, then he belongs to them and is their father."[18] Of course, it must be observed that Przywara did not intend this as a compliment! But given the battle then underway between the dialectical theologians and their liberal Protestant critics, this judgment especially was most welcome in the camp of the dialectical theologians.

The situation Przywara was seeking to address in this early essay was one created by Catholic responses to the crisis in German intellectual life, which was the consequence of the Armistice, the abdication of the emperor, and the advent of a Weimar government that had proven incapable of coping with the effects of the Versailles Treaty. In relation to the final point, what I have in mind was the inability of the Weimar government to keep up with the reparation payments required by the treaty to the victorious Entente Powers; the occupation of the *Ruhrgebiet* by French troops in January 1923; French takeover of the management of German industries in that region to ensure that the payment schedule be met, and the inflation of the Mark, to which that precipitous action led, culminating in massive unemployment and food riots in the major German cities in August that year. This situation provides the immediate background of Przywara's analysis of the crisis of Western thought in "God in us or God above us" — as it does of Barth's writings in this period as well — and we make a mistake if we discount its effects on what any theologian of the time had to say at this time on the subject of "crisis."

Seen in this light, it is understandable that Przywara's most pressing concern was not with the dialectical theologians. In many ways, they were, for him, a sideshow. His most pressing concern, as the fourth section of this essay reveals, is with the response of German Catholic theologians (esp. Hermann Hefele) to the *intellectual* crisis that the factors just described had produced. Przywara was convinced that Catholic theology

16. Eduard Thurneysen to Karl Barth, September 30, 1923, in *Karl Barth–Eduard Thurneysen Briefwechsel*, vol. 2, *1921-1930*, ed. E. Thurneysen (Zürich: TVZ, 1974), p. 190.

17. Erich Przywara, "Gott in uns oder Gott über uns? (Immanenz und Transzendenz im heutigen Geistesleben)," *Stimmen der Zeit* 105 (1923): 343-62.

18. Ibid., p. 350.

alone had the resources to provide an adequate response to this crisis — and it was crucial that they should draw upon these resources. Protestant theology, in contrast, in both of its leading forms (the anthropocentric theology of the liberals and the theocentric theology of the dialectical theologians) was far too deeply implicated in creating the conditions that had given rise to the intellectual crisis in the first place for the Protestants to respond adequately.

Przywara's thesis, in a nutshell, is this. The roots of the intellectual crisis in the West was to be found in the sixteenth century — most especially in Luther's concept of God. According to Przywara, Luther had understood God as an all-determining reality, as the only real and only effective reality, which leaves no room for a genuine freedom in the human.[19] "Transcendence and immanence are no longer bound together in a 'tension of opposites,'" as they had been in Augustine, "but have been made identical. In that the hidden, incomprehensible God, the *Deus absconditus* as Luther liked to say, is not merely 'all in all' but rather 'everything alone.' He is the essence of the creature, and all activities of the creature, insofar as they are understood to be 'essential,' are his work alone."[20]

The net effect of this allegedly one-sided emphasis upon divine transcendence was to set aside a proper understanding of the Creator-creature relation — one in which transcendence and immanence are maintained in a healthy balance. The result was that Protestant philosophers in the modern period went in one of two directions. Either they followed Luther in making all that takes place in nature and history to be the consequence of divine activity without remainder (thereby collapsing the world into God). Or, in reaction against such an outcome, they collapsed divine activity into creaturely activity. The first path is the one taken by Spinoza and Hegel. The second is the one advocated by Kant and Nietzsche.[21] But both are a function of an *exclusive* transcendence, and they are united in affirming the *identity* of God and the world. Przywara does not yet employ the contrast of "theopanism" and naturalistic pantheism in this essay, but the basis has here been clearly laid for that distinction.

What is important for our purposes here is that Barth and his friends

---

19. Ibid., p. 347. It is important to note that Przywara does not base this judgment on his own reading of Luther. He is relying here on essays by Franz Xavier Kliefl (Catholic theologian at the University of Wurzburg) and Ernst Troeltsch (Protestant theologian at the University of Heidelberg) that had appeared simultaneously in October 1917.

20. Ibid., p. 348.

21. Ibid., pp. 347-48.

are clearly seen to belong to the theopanistic pole of this modern Protestant divide. I already noted that Przywara's judgment that Luther "belongs to them" was not intended as a compliment — and my reason for saying this should now be clear. The Barth of the second *Romans* commentary is guilty of a one-sided emphasis on divine transcendence. His God is the "wholly other" God of Luther.[22] The only possible relation that such a God can have to the human is that of negation, the "Absolute No," as Friedrich Gogarten put it.[23] Barth's theology is clearly a reaction against the experiential theologies of liberal Protestants. What Barth does not realize, Przywara says, is that it is precisely one-sidedness like his that made an overemphasis on the other side both possible and necessary. At the end of the day, the root of Barth's theology is precisely the same as the root of Rudolf Otto's theology, Barth's protestations to the contrary notwithstanding.

Przywara's answer to the intellectual crisis created by an exclusive emphasis upon divine transcendence is the "God in us and God above us" of Augustine. Augustine was able to maintain transcendence and immanence in a proper balance because he understood that God can be closer to us than we are to ourselves, even while remaining "the infinite and incomprehensible."[24] And the key to this "in us and above us" lies in the concept of analogy. God and the human are two, Przywara says, not one. But they stand over against each other not in a relation of antithesis (as in Barth) but in a relation of analogy. Przywara's name for this analogy is the "analogia entis"[25] — a term he defines here largely in terms of the "similarity within a [greater?] dissimilarity" formula of the Fourth Lateran Council.

What are we to make of all this? Well, I suppose the first thing to be said is that most readers of this essay today would have difficulties with Przywara's attempt to reduce so many problems in modern philosophy to a single source. I tend myself to take a more pragmatic view. "Grand metanarratives" are very helpful in times of societal upheaval in bringing much-needed order into the chaos. And there are a number of important insights that appear along the way. I do think Przywara has the Rudolf Otto–Friedrich Heiler school dead to rights. In the second place, I can well imagine that any reader today who knows anything about Luther research since 1923 will have enormous difficulties with the portrayal of Luther's theology

22. Ibid., p. 350.
23. Ibid.
24. Ibid., p. 344.
25. Ibid.

that appears here. But that is not something I am going to concern myself with here either. My interest lies in what we learn about Przywara's conception of Barth's theology. Von Balthasar would later concede to Przywara the validity of the latter's reading of the second *Romans* — and on that basis, von Balthasar would go on to drive a wedge between its theology and the theology of the *Church Dogmatics*. But that then means that Przywara's interpretation of *Romans* has had (through von Balthasar) a lasting impact on the Catholic reception of Barth. So some comment is needed.

Przywara understands the "opposition" or "antithesis" of God and the human described by Barth as metaphysical in nature. In doing so, he has failed to see that the antithesis is fundamentally a *soteriological* one. To be sure, Barth had at his disposal a rich battery of images that in any other context would clearly be metaphysical — the time-eternity dialectic topping the list. It is also true that it would be possible to carve a metaphysic out of Barth's talk of an original "immediacy" that characterized the God-human relation — if one wished to do so. And the fact that this category could be so understood (against his intentions) led Barth to abandon it very quickly after the second edition of *Romans* had been published. Or again: images like that of the tangent and the circle do strongly suggest either an inability or unwillingness on the part of God to act in this world.[26] But appearances can deceive. Already in *Romans,* Barth understands the resurrection of Jesus to have been "bodily."[27] On that basis, one must at least grant that he held that the divine causality is operative in the realm of nature and history. And even the dialectic of time and eternity stood in the service of a doctrine of revelation whose outcome was the conformity of the creature's knowledge of God to God's knowledge of himself and, with that, the reconciliation of the creature with God.[28] And finally, though Barth was not yet in a position to sort out the ontological implications of his theological epistemology (and would not be until he revised his doctrine of election in *Church Dogmatics* II/2), he had laid the basis for the very

26. Karl Barth, *Der Römerbrief, 1922* (Zürich: TVZ, 1940), p. 6.
27. Ibid., p. 183.
28. Cf. Michael Beintker, *Die Dialektik in der "dialektischen Theologie" Karl Barths* (Munich: C. Kaiser, 1987), p. 33: "The 'infinite qualitative distinction' between God and the human does not arise out of a metaphysically conceived time-eternity dualism as is sometimes maintained but rather out of the radical placing-in-question of sin by divine grace." See also my *Karl Barth's Critically Realistic Dialectical Theology,* pp. 262-66. The truth is that Barth's second *Romans* is the most powerful antimetaphysical manifesto ever to appear in the history of theology. See ibid., pp. 245-62.

quick emergence of an *analogia fidei* in the strict sense in his first lectures on dogmatics just two years later.

But that then also means that Przywara's critique fell on already pre-pared soil. So it would be a mistake to think that this critique — or perhaps the conversations between Barth and Przywara in 1929 in Münster — some-how moved Barth to develop his *analogia fidei*. For that development was al-ready underway in *Romans*. What Barth in all likelihood gained from his reading of Przywara was an incentive to develop a doctrine of the incarna-tion adequate to the needs of his then-emerging doctrine of analogy. But even there, Przywara was not the only influence. Barth's studies of Zwingli and the Reformed confessions (in the winter semester of 1922/23 and the summer semester of 1923, respectively) had already alerted him to that need.[29]

The *analogia fidei* in the strict sense is first found in the Prolegomena to the Göttingen Dogmatics. At its root, Barth's *analogia fidei* rests upon the understanding that creaturely media that have, in themselves, no capacity to be adequate bearers of revelation are made to be so by the use God makes of them in revelation. The context is a reflection on the relation of human lan-guage to God's speech in revelation. Human language, Barth says, is lan-guage created by humans for speaking of the things and persons of their ex-perience. As such, it has no capacity in itself to be the vehicle of God's speech. But in that God takes it up and makes use of it in revealing himself, it is "qualified" to be God's Word. Commenting on Heinrich Bullinger's state-ment in the Second Helvetic Confession — "The preaching of the Word of God is the Word of God"[30] — Barth raises the following rhetorical question:

> Should one not at least gather from this confident assertion the *question* of whether there might not be words that (although they are human words, mere words like all others) are, at the same time, more than that; namely, for the sake of the knowledge out of which they arise, are com-

29. In my book on Barth's development, I made the claim that Przywara's talk of the incarnation in this essay may have contributed to Barth's elaboration of that theme in his Göttingen Dogmatics. See McCormack, *Karl Barth's Critically Realistic Dialectical Theology*, p. 321. But I had not read Barth's lectures on Zwingli or his lectures on the Reformed confes-sions at that time because they were only available in his (for me) indecipherable handwrit-ing. Subsequent to the completion of my book, both sets of lectures were transcribed and published in the critical edition of Barth's works.

30. See the Second Helvetic Confession, chapter 1, in *Reformed Confessions of the Six-teenth Century*, ed. A. C. Cochrane (Philadelphia: Westminster Press, 1966), p. 225.

munication of truth from one person to another? Becoming human is, therefore, not yet humanization, and Protestantism meant originally to believe in the becoming-human of the Logos precisely in spoken human words.[31]

And so Barth speaks of the human words of Scripture and of a preaching based on Scripture as "qualified words" — words made to correspond in the event of revelation to the divine reality to which they point. This was the original home of Barth's *analogia fidei* in the strict sense — the problem of the relation of language to divine reality and, with that, the problem of the conformity of human knowledge of God to God's knowledge of himself. To the question "but doesn't divine use of human language *demand* the existence of a 'capacity' for such use in language itself?" I would say this: Language performs this function, for Barth, in the event in which God makes use of it in his self-revelation. What Barth has in view here is a highly concrete relationship that *exists* only in that God actively speaks to a community or an individual. Apart from the relation established in *this* divine activity, there can be no meaningful talk of a "capacity" in language. For if we were to speak of a "capacity" apart from this relation, we would no longer be talking of a "capacity" for precisely *this* relation. We would be talking instead about a "capacity" proper to the creaturely as such and, therefore, about a generally valid relation rooted not in God's self-revelation in Jesus Christ but in creation.

In the years that intervened between the Prolegomena lectures on dogmatics in Göttingen in the summer of 1924 and the publication of the first part-volume of the *Church Dogmatics* in 1932, Barth continued to read Przywara with appreciation. Upon Barth's move to the predominantly Catholic city of Münster in 1925, he also participated in a Catholic-led discussion group that included the future founding editor of *Catholica*, Robert Grosche.[32] During these years, he actively sought to narrow the distance between his own conception of analogy and that which he found in Przywara. He made close study of the latter's 1926 work *Religionsphilosophie katholischer Theologie* — a book that contained Przywara's most mature ex-

---

31. Karl Barth, *Unterricht in der christlichen Religion*, vol. 1, *Prolegomena, 1924*, ed. Hannelotte Reiffen (Zürich, TVZ, 1985), p. 40; ET *The Göttingen Dogmatics*, vol. 1, *Instruction in the Christian Religion*, trans. Geoffrey W. Bromiley (Grand Rapids: Eerdmans, 1990), pp. 32-33.

32. See McCormack, *Karl Barth's Critically Realistic Dialectical Theology*, pp. 376-77; W. H. Neuser, "Karl Barth in Münster, 1924-1930," *Theologische Studien* 130 (1985): 37-40.

position yet of the *analogia entis* and its implications.[33] The effect of this study was to move Barth to seek to find a way to take on board the concept of the *analogia entis* in his own work, without effecting a departure from the commitments we have already seen. The fruits of these efforts are to be found, first, in the still unpublished portions of Barth's lectures on dogmatics in Münster — in which Barth employs the *analogia entis* in his own constructive work — and second, in two essays published in the late 1920s. The essays in question bear the titles "Fate and Idea in Theology" and "The Holy Spirit and the Christian Life."[34]

These materials are best interpreted together, as a unit — since the light they shed individually on Barth's relationship to Catholic theology in this period can be fully appreciated only when placed alongside other efforts with similar aims. But that does create an interesting problem for the Catholic reception of Barth. Von Balthasar had no access to Dogmatics I of the Münster cycle (in which Barth experimented with treating the doctrine of God under the heading of creation); they remain unpublished to this day.[35] He worked closely with "Fate and Idea," but for reasons not known to me, he passed over "The Holy Spirit and the Christian Life." The omission is significant. "Fate and Idea" sets forth only Barth's critique of Przywara's version of the *analogia entis*. An attempt to make positive use of the concept within his own theological frame of reference, however, appears in print only in "The Holy Spirit and the Christian Life."

The occasion for both of these essays was the historic visit of Erich Przywara to Barth's seminar on Thomas's *Summa theologiae* on February 5-

---

33. Erich Przywara, *Religionsphilosophie katholischer Theologie* (Munich: R. Olderbourg, 1926). Barth was invited to do a companion volume in this series on the philosophy of religion, which arises most naturally in connection with evangelical theology, but declined. The invitation was then extended to Emil Brunner, whose volume appeared two years later. See Brunner, *Religionsphilosophie evangelischer Theologie* (Munich: R. Oldenbourg, 1928). On Barth's invitation, see Karl Barth to Eduard Thurneysen, June 8, 1924, in *Barth-Thurneysen Briefwechsel*, 2:259. See also Thurneysen's response, to the effect that the "spirit of Erasmus" was somehow at work in this proposal (Thurneysen to Barth, June 11, 1924, in ibid., p. 260).

34. Karl Barth, "Schicksal und Idee in der Theologie," in *Theologische Fragen und Antworten,* 2d ed. (Zürich: TVZ, 1986), pp. 54-92; idem, *The Holy Spirit and the Christian Life: The Theological Basis of Ethics,* trans. R. Birch Hoyle (Louisville, Ky.: Westminster/John Knox Press, 1993).

35. Permission to work with these materials has been given by the Karl Barth Nachlaßkommission to Dr. Amy Marga (Luther Seminary). Marga's dissertation is currently being revised and expanded for publication. See Marga, "Partners in the Gospel: Karl Barth and Roman Catholicism, 1922-1932" (PhD diss., Princeton Theological Seminary, 2006).

6, 1929, where he patiently answered questions prepared by Barth's students. It is worth pondering Barth's effusive comments on this visit in his letters to Thurneysen:

> Erich Przywara, SJ, gave a two-hour-long lecture on the church that, considered from the point of view of its skilled craftsmanship, was simply a dainty morsel, a masterpiece. He then shone in my seminar, once again for two hours, answering our carefully prepared questions. And finally, he "overwhelmed" me here for two evenings' worth, just as, according to his doctrine, the dear God overwhelms people with grace (at least within the Catholic Church) so that the formula "God in-above humankind from God's side" is, at one and the same time, the motto of his existence, as well as the dissolution of all Protestant and modernist, transcendentalist and immanentist stupidities and constraints in the peace of the *analogia entis*.[36]

Barth returned to his theme later in the same letter, this time with even greater enthusiasm:

> *Ja, Eduard, was war das wohl?* And what is the meaning of this Catholicism that, in spite of our [400th anniversary] celebrations of the Reformation, so alertly puts in an appearance? Was that an angel of the Antichrist or a chosen instrument of the Lord? The Grand Inquisitor or really a disciple of the "apostle of the peoples"? Or both at the same time or neither . . . ? Obviously, this possibility too exists: there are people like us who . . . no longer burn [people] as was done 400 years ago, but simply *laugh* down from a sovereign height; like us in that *they too* do so with a calling upon God (with all Kutterish emphasis!). In the name of the church, with the Bible under one arm, knowing as we do (and perhaps even better) of death and the devil, time and eternity, with the real human being of today in view. Is it the most cunning world that laughs there, or is there something in it of the laughter of the One who dwells in heaven? Is it perhaps fitting that in this year in which we celebrate the 200th anniversary of Lessing's birth, we turn our attention for a change to the parable of the three rings?[37]

36. Karl Barth to Eduard Thurneysen, February 9, 1929, in *Barth-Thurneysen Briefwechsel*, 2:652. The lecture to which Barth refers here was subsequently published by him in the pages of *Zwischen den Zeiten*. See Erich Przywara, "Das katholische Kirchenprinzip," *Zwischen den Zeiten* 7 (1929): 277-302.

37. Barth to Thurneysen, February 9, 1929, in *Barth-Thurneysen Briefwechsel*, 2:654-55.

The questions raised here are indeed serious ones — and not to be answered too quickly on either side! But we must not miss the sheer *delight* that Barth takes in being able to ask them. He is very aware that even to ask such questions was unthinkable in the preceding four centuries — and still unthinkable for vast numbers of his then contemporary Protestants and Catholics. Truly, the visit of Erich Przywara to Barth's seminar and indeed his *home* in Münster is an episode that deserves prominent mention in any history of ecumenical engagement in the twentieth century.

In the light of this promising opening, we must consider what Barth then says of the *analogia entis* in "The Holy Spirit and the Christian Life." This essay first saw life as a lecture given at a gathering of Reformed pastors in Elberfeld on October 9, 1929. Barth had devoted a free semester that summer to the reading of Augustine and Luther, doubtless in an effort to better understand the underpinnings of Przywara's paradigm for construing the history of theology in the West. The fruit of that reading is to be found here.

The point at which Barth wants to take issue with Przywara is clearly that of the alleged "continuity" that joins Creator and creature as a consequence of creation. Since Barth accepts Przywara's claim that it is Augustine who is the guarantor of his own views on the subject of the God-human relation, Barth begins with the bishop of Hippo. Augustine rightly saw, Barth says, that the Holy Spirit "is not identical with what we recognize as our own created life of the spirit or the soul."[38] But Augustine did try to find a relation of continuity between the Holy Spirit and created spirit. And Barth's question is: Can this do justice to the Creator/creature distinction? "According to his teaching, God is not the 'soul' *(animam):* he is above the 'spirit' (of man), and more than it, and still, according to Augustine, he is primarily *in* the soul, its proper origin, but now forgotten, and very probably is only to be recalled to memory when grace gives its aid."[39] Such an understanding of "God in us" then lays the foundation for the Platonic notion of *anamnesis* — and provides the justification for equating that for which the human heart seeks (namely, the Eternal, the Good, or — we might say — the Infinite) with God. Barth's question was whether this construal could do justice to the Creator/creature distinction. He argued that a well-ordered doctrine of creation will hold in balance continuity and discontinuity in the God-human relation established in creation. "The discontinuity between God the Creator and man, when one considers the relation of Creator and creature, must

---

38. Barth, "The Holy Spirit and the Christian Life," p. 3.
39. Ibid., pp. 3-4.

mean that between being Lord and being lorded over there exists an irreversibility such as excludes the idea of God as an object of whom, in Platonic fashion, we have a reminiscence, as 'Ancient Beauty.'"[40] And he continues, "If [the] creature is to be strictly understood as a reality willed and placed by God in distinction from God's own reality, that is to say, as the wonder of a reality that, by the power of God's love, has a place and persistence alongside God's reality, then the continuity between God and it (the true *analogia entis,* by virtue of which he, the uncreated Spirit, can be revealed to the created spirit) — this continuity cannot belong to the creature itself but only to the Creator *in his relation* to the creature. It cannot be taken to mean that the creature has an original endowment in his makeup, but only as a second marvel of God's love, as the inconceivable, undeserved, divine *bestowal* on his creature."[41] Thus creation, as an act of God in which the creature does not and cannot share, is an expression of divine lordship. It is a unilateral act. No orthodox Christian theologian would say that the creature cooperates in its creation. What happens? God speaks — and worlds come into being. But that then also means that the act of creating establishes only a discontinuity, a *distinction* in the God-human relation. It does not yet establish continuity in that relation. For continuity to exist, something else must take place. The something else is that God graciously enters into a concrete and personal relation to the human. To be sure, the fall then disrupts this relation. But God does not cease to engage the human lost in sin. In revelation, God (repeatedly) reestablishes that gracious relation.

But now notice: in order for this gracious relation to do justice to the element of discontinuity proper to creation (and the lordship of God, which we have seen that element to entail), the element of continuity cannot simply be a *given.* "Man as *creature* is not in a position from which he can establish and survey (e.g., in a scheme of the unity of like and unlike) his relation to God and thereby interpret himself as 'open upward,' as Erich Przywara says, and consequently describe his own knowledge as if it meant that God's revealedness were within the compass of his own understanding by itself."[42] The element of continuity in the God-world relation is not something the human can find in himself or herself. Even in the unfallen state, that is not true. It is all the more true subsequent to the fall. The element of continuity — if it is to honor the element of discontinuity — can-

---

40. Ibid., pp. 4-5.
41. Ibid., p. 5.
42. Ibid.

not be found in anything proper to the human *as such*. If it were, the relation between God and the human would indeed be reversible. It could not help but be reversible, a fact that shows itself in the efforts made by philosophers to mount up to knowledge of God from their knowledge of the created world as such. But then, in that case, the element of discontinuity would have been denied — and the proper balance between discontinuity and continuity set aside:

> Revelation is to be understood as the occurrence of the Creator Spirit's coming to us in the future, of him-who-exists-for-us, and so it is not a *datum* but a *dandum* (Lat. "to be given"), not as fulfillment but as promise. Grace is our having been created, but it is also [our being] "created for God." But grace is ever and in all relations God's *deed* and *act,* taking place in this and that moment of time in which God wills to be gracious to us, and is gracious, and makes this grace manifest. It is never at all a quality of ours, inborn in us, such as would enable us to know of it in advance.[43]

Two comments on this fascinating series of observations are in order. First, Barth has shifted the *basis* for a concept of analogy from creation as such to revelation (understood in Catholic terms as "special," reconciling and redeeming, revelation). In doing so, he has also offered a challenge to Przywara's claim that his version of the *analogia entis* alone is capable of holding transcendence and immanence in balance. To this Barth says that only his version is capable of accomplishing what Przywara wants. Second, Barth is quite willing at this time to speak of the analogy established in the event of revelation as a form of the *analogia entis.* The term is not so problematic that it cannot be put to a good use.

It is important to see that Barth was seeking to engage Przywara on the soil of the latter's understanding of the *analogia entis* and that this attempt was carried out in a quite friendly manner. We do not yet see the rhetorical pyrotechnics of the preface to *Church Dogmatics* I/1. Obviously, something must have changed if Barth would reach the point of describing the *analogia entis* just three years later as the "invention of the Antichrist." So what changed?

Well, for starters, the stock market crash took place just fifteen days after Barth's Elberfeld lecture. Its effects were especially devastating on a German economy that was already in deep recession. The Weimar government,

43. Ibid., pp. 5-6.

led by SPD Hermann Müller, resigned on March 27, 1930, and was replaced by a government prepared to invoke the emergency-powers provision of the Weimar Constitution — that would allow for the dissolution of Parliament by decree of the president. And that is, in fact, what took place in July 1930. New elections were called for on September 14. The worst came to pass: the Nazis, until then a minuscule party operating on the fringes of German politics, became the second largest faction in the new Parliament. By early 1931 Barth was on "high alert" where the political consequences of theological commitments were concerned — and he began to worry about the consequences of natural theology, which he felt opened the door to the unwarranted legitimation of human experiences and feelings in the name of God.[44] He had been aware for some time that his erstwhile fellow-travelers in the dialectical theology movement — above all, Friedrich Gogarten and Emil Brunner — were now engaged in various forms of natural theology that were joined, in the case of each, with a right-wing political outlook. Had the political situation not changed so dramatically, Barth might have remained content to allow them to develop in their own directions and say little. But the times did not allow for that.

In the midst of these developments, Georg Wobbermin (Barth's former colleague in Göttingen and a proponent of laying a foundation for theology in the psychology of religion) lobbed a sizable bomb into Barth's backyard. In a series of articles published in May 1932, Wobbermin set forth the thesis that Professor Erik Peterson and Swiss pastor Oskar Bauhofer, both of whom had recently converted to Catholicism, had begun their movement toward Rome with an attachment to the "dialectical theology" of Barth. The implication was clear: Barth's theology turns Protestants into Catholics. In response, Barth wrote a fiery "Open Letter" to Wobbermin that was published in the pages of *Theologische Blätter* in June.[45] It was an "untruth," he said, that either of these men had ever had a commitment to the "dialectical theology" — as Wobbermin well knew. Peterson was fully formed theologically before "dialectical theology" appeared on the scene. And Wobbermin had to know of Peterson's manifesto against the theology of Karl Barth under the title "What Is Theology?" in 1925.[46] Where Bauhofer was concerned, Barth had refused a request by Bauhofer's publisher to rec-

---

44. See McCormack, *Karl Barth's Critically Realistic Dialectical Theology*, p. 414.

45. Karl Barth, "Offener Brief an Professor D. Dr. G. Wobbermin," *Theologische Blätter* 11 (1932): 186-87.

46. Erik Peterson, "Was ist Theologie?" in *Theologische Traktate* (Munich: Kösel, 1951), pp. 9-44.

ommend his 1930 book *Das Metareligiöse*[47] — an invitation that had then been accepted by "my friend Emil Brunner, who has a fatal interest in apologetics."[48] But, Barth insisted, the fact that Brunner was able to take up a positive stance toward this book had nothing whatsoever to do with him or his theology. Wobbermin had said it was the dialectical theology of Karl Barth that made Catholics out of Protestants, not the dialectical theology of Emil Brunner! And, in any case, Bauhofer was coming from the theology of Ernst Troeltsch, not Brunner. Barth concluded by calling upon Wobbermin to cease and desist in his efforts to discredit Barth's theology by innuendo and assertion and to try to prove his case through careful comparison of the writings of Barth, Peterson, and Bauhofer. Until that happened, he could count on it that Barth had "*no* respect" for anything he had to say on the subject.[49]

Barth was still hot about Wobbermin's charge in August, as his preface to *Church Dogmatics* I/1 demonstrates. He is clearly rankled by the charge of "crypto-Catholicism," particularly insofar as it comes from those liberal Protestants who stand on the ground of a "natural knowledge of God" rather than the understanding of the Word of God that gave rise to Protestantism in the first place. And it is the atmosphere that this charge has created that finally explains the invocation of the spirit of the Antichrist:

> I can see no third alternative between that exploitation of the *analogia entis* which is legitimate only on the basis of Roman Catholicism, between the greatness and misery of a so-called natural knowledge of God in the sense of the *Vaticanum,* and a Protestant theology which draws from its own source, which stands on its own feet, and which is finally liberated from this secular misery. Hence I have had no option but to say No at this point. I regard the *analogia entis* as the invention of Antichrist, and I believe that because of it it is impossible ever to become a Roman Catholic, all other reasons for not doing so being to my mind short-sighted and trivial.[50]

47. Oskar Bauhofer, *Das Metareligiöse. Eine kritische Religionsphilosophie* (Leipzig: J. C. Hinrichs, 1930).

48. Barth, "Offener Brief an Professor D. Dr. G. Wobbermin," p. 186.

49. Ibid., p. 187. Thurneysen's comment on Wobbermin's performance in this affair is telling. "Was ist das doch für ein unaufrichtiger Mensch!" Eduard Thurneysen to Karl Barth, June 14, 1932, in *Barth-Thurneysen Briefwechsel,* 2:236.

50. Karl Barth, *CD* I/1, p. xiii.

The protest that is expressed in these pointed words is directed *not* to Roman Catholicism per se but to a liberal Protestantism that shared with Roman Catholicism a commitment to a natural knowledge of God — a natural knowledge that the so-called German Christians were already using to defend the proposition that there existed a "deep religious significance in the intoxication of Nordic blood and their political *Führer*."[51] Even as Barth penned these words, Germany was hurtling toward cataclysm, a descent into a barbarism unheard of in the history of the world. What, then, is truly "barbarous"[52] is not what Barth says here. After all, it was Przywara himself who had taught him that the *analogia entis* is truly basic to all Catholic teaching. And Barth was convinced that something similar was basic to liberal Protestantism in all of its varieties. What would have been "barbarous" on his part, believing what he did, would have been to remain silent about any of this. Von Balthasar's comment on the furor created by these words is instructive and salutary. "These startling remarks have aroused a great deal of unjustifiable surprise or ridicule. Such reactions would be understandable if it were only a question of some particular material doctrine of Catholicism and not an attempt to formulate the decisive formal consideration that is the basis of everything Catholic."[53]

Now whether Barth had understood Przywara correctly is a question by itself. Given that this essay has as its focus von Balthasar's critique of Barth and the development of a version of the *analogia entis* by the later Barth, I cannot resolve that issue here.[54] But in one important respect, the answer we give to this problem doesn't matter. Having become convinced that the root of Catholic theology and the root of liberal theology were much the same — and given the tendency of Wobbermin and others to simply pass by that contention in silence in order then to accuse him of "crypto-Catholicism" — that had to be addressed, and addressed forcibly. Could I wish that he had found other words to express the connection he thought himself to see and to give voice to his indignation? Certainly. But that is easy to say in hindsight.

Far too much ink has already been spilled over this passage. The time

51. Ibid., p. xiv.

52. I am here referring, of course, to David Bentley Hart's judgment on what he calls "Barth's notorious, fairly barbarous rejection of the *analogia entis* as the invention of antichrist" as an "example of inane (and cruel) invective." See Hart, *The Beauty of the Infinite: The Aesthetics of Christian Truth* (Grand Rapids: Eerdmans, 2003), p. 241.

53. Von Balthasar, *The Theology of Karl Barth*, p. 49.

54. But see the dissertation by Keith Johnson, "Analogia Entis."

has come, in the name of Christian unity, to put it aside and move on to more profitable points of departure for a discussion. I turn then to von Balthasar's critique of Barth's theology, in the hope of uncovering those points of departure.

III. *Analogia Entis* in *Analogia Fidei?*

Hans Urs von Balthasar's book on Karl Barth remains to this day a classic — not only in Barth studies but in ecumenical theology. It is a simply brilliant book, one that rests on a real depth of understanding.[55] Such mistakes as are made in it are intelligent ones that rest on the fact that Barth had yet to write his mature Christology when von Balthasar wrote his book. So I, for one, do not fault him for his mistakes but think of him always with gratitude for his willingness to treat Barth charitably, and with gratitude, especially, for his magnificent theology of Holy Saturday, to which I owe so much in my own constructive work.[56]

Von Balthasar's critique of Barth is bound up with and dependent upon the story he tells of Barth's development. So it is with that story that we must begin.

A. *Von Balthasar's Depiction of Barth's Theological Development*

Von Balthasar shared Przywara's judgment of the second *Romans:* it was an exercise in an existentialized version of identity philosophy. Its basic decisions are to be found in the idea of an original relation of "immediacy" of the human to God and an equally primordial disruption of that relation, resulting in an unbridgeable chasm between the two. The "fall" is thus treated as metaphysical in nature. "Fallenness" is proper to the creature as such. "To be a creature is coterminous with being guilty."[57] The concept of "nature" is,

55. To give just one example, von Balthasar's recognition that both Kierkegaardian and Hegelian forms of dialectic are at work in *Romans* and that the two function cooperatively is most insightful. See von Balthasar, *The Theology of Karl Barth,* pp. 82-83.

56. See Bruce McCormack, "'With Loud Cries and Tears': The Humanity of the Son in the Epistle to the Hebrews," in *The Epistle to the Hebrews and Christian Theology,* ed. Richard Bauckham, Daniel R. Driver, Trevor A. Hart, and Nathan MacDonald, pp. 37-68 (Grand Rapids: Eerdmans, 2009).

57. Von Balthasar, *The Theology of Karl Barth,* p. 70.

on this showing, caught in a contradiction. "Nature" is good insofar as it co-incides with grace in the immediacy of the origin. But "nature just as neces-sarily coincides with the condition of sin as such."[58] The "theopanism" of Barth's early theology follows quite naturally from this state of affairs:

> The best way of characterizing this ideology is by describing it as a dy-namic and actualist *theopanism,* which we define as a monism of be-ginning and end (protology and eschatology): God stands at the be-ginning and at the end, surrounding a world-reality understood in dualistic and dialectical terms, ultimately overcoming it in the mathe-matical point of the miracle of transformation. . . . This monism of the Word of God . . . threatens time and again to swallow up the reality of the world. Though the world (which does after all stand in relation to the Word of God) is certainly something and not nothing, it looks so forlorn and hopeless under this harsh glare that one might just as well wish it did not exist.[59]

It goes without saying that the human cannot come into its own in a revela-tion event that is construed against this background.

As suggested earlier, everything in this interpretation finds a strong root in Barth's rich battery of images touching upon the God-world rela-tion in *Romans.* The problem with it lies in what is left out of the account. What is missed, above all, is the fact that the revelation of God really does reach its goal in the human precisely in *this* world, so that the human is al-ready here and now what it will be eschatologically; not a creature absorbed into an all-consuming divine being but a truly free creature able to stand before God.

To his credit, von Balthasar admits "Barth's later journey is a paradoxi-cal rehabilitation of *The Epistle to the Romans,* insofar as it now becomes clear what this strange book *was trying to say all along.* In retrospect, we now learn that this book was not trying to be a philosophy decked out as a theology but a theology dressed out as a philosophy, yet easily detached from the latter."[60] That much is certainly right. And the only adjustment I would make is that the philosophy in question is not so much a form of idealism as it is a form of romanticism. It is closer to Schleiermacher than either Barth or von Balthasar realized. Von Balthasar came closest to the truth when he described *Romans*

---

58. Ibid.
59. Ibid., p. 94.
60. Ibid., p. 85.

as an exercise in "theological expressionism."[61] That is exactly right, and because it is, the images Barth employed cannot be taken quite so literally without risk of completely missing the point.

We come then to what von Balthasar regarded as the second and decisive stage of Barth's development: the "turn" to analogy:

> Just as Augustine underwent two conversions, the one from gross error to the true God and to Christianity and the other (much later) from the religious Neoplatonism of his early writings to an authentic theology, so too in Barth we may find two decisive turning points. The first, his turn from liberalism to radical Christianity, occurred during the First World War and found expression in *The Epistle to the Romans*. The second was his final emancipation from the shackles of philosophy, enabling him finally to arrive at a genuine, self-authenticating theology. This second conversion was a gradual process, indeed a struggle, that lasted nearly ten years, ending at about 1930: "Actually, the real work that documents my farewell to . . . the remnants of a philosophical or anthropological . . . grounding and exposition of Christian doctrine . . . is not my much-read little book against Emil Brunner but my 1931 book on Anselm of Canterbury's proof for the existence of God."[62]

The second "conversion" described in this passage is said to have taken ten years but to have been completed sometime around 1930.

Now I have already provided sufficient reason to think that the *analogia fidei* first emerged in 1924. So von Balthasar is right to sense that it was beginning to appear in the years prior to 1930. His language of a second "conversion" misleads, of course, but that is a negligible mistake, easily corrected. More interesting is what comes next:

61. Ibid., p. 83.

62. Ibid., p. 93. It should be noted that von Balthasar is here citing from Barth's 1939 contribution to the *Christian Century* series "How My Mind Has Changed," which was first translated and published in German under the title "Parergon" in 1948 (as a Beiheft to the journal *Evangelische Theologie*). It should also be noted that I have lightly revised the translation of the citation offered in Edward Oakes's translation of von Balthasar's *The Theology of Karl Barth*. Barth does not speak of a "conversion"; that is von Balthasar's term. Barth speaks of a "farewell to" the remnants of a philosophical grounding, not a "conversion" from such a grounding. Indeed, this sentence appears in the context of Barth's description of his work in the period stretching from 1928 to 1938 in terms of a "deepening" and an "application" of the knowledge he had acquired in the years prior to 1928. Still, Barth does bear responsibility for pointing von Balthasar (and others) to the book on Anselm as the "document" of this "farewell."

Barth did not suddenly replace dialectics with analogy. We cannot isolate any one particular text as *the* sign of this shift, for it happened gradually. Not even mentioned in the first volume of the *Church Dogmatics*
[i.e., *CD* I/1], the second volume (1938 [i.e., *CD* I/2]) merely notes it
without having the opportunity to test it. But with the third volume
(*The Doctrine of God,* 1940 [i.e., *CD* II/1]) . . . it starts to take on definitive form, so that the doctrine of analogy unfolds more and more clearly
with each succeeding volume. Indeed so victorious does it become that
by the time of the later volumes on creation, anthropology, and providence (1945, 1948, and 1950), it has become the central theme of his theology. So one will search in vain for a fully developed version of this doctrine in the early stages of the *Church Dogmatics.*[63]

So the "conversion" is complete for von Balthasar by 1930, and yet one
looks in vain for a "fully developed" version of analogy in early volumes of
the *Church Dogmatics.* Von Balthasar then further muddies the waters by
saying (a page later) that the "classical definition of analogy" does indeed appear in *Church Dogmatics* I/1.[64] So what is going on here?

The reason for the apparent inconsistencies in these various formulations is that von Balthasar is struggling with the relation of the *analogia
fidei* and Christology in the early volumes of the *Church Dogmatics.* Consider the
following passage:

> Of course, the first volume (1932 [*CD* I/1]) does energetically overcome
> the existential and anthropological starting point of the *Prolegomena*
> [*Die Christliche Dogmatik im Entwurf*] to offer a purely theological doc-
> trine of the Word of God, that is, one firmly rooted in the Word of God
> itself. But the Christology remains in the background. Nonetheless,

63. Von Balthasar, *The Theology of Karl Barth,* p. 93. It should be noted that I have
lightly altered Oakes's translation. Oakes makes the "third volume" to be "Doctrine of the
Word of God" rather than, as von Balthasar has it, the "Doctrine of God." I should add that
von Balthasar made the task of following him much more difficult than it needed to be, because he chose to ignore the fact that Barth divides his volumes into part-volumes and calls
CD I/2 the "second volume," *CD* II/1 the "third volume," and so on.

64. Von Balthasar, *The Theology of Karl Barth,* p. 108. Von Balthasar thinks the "classical definition" emerges in *CD* I/1 at the point at which Barth says, "By the power of faith and
its profession, the Word of God becomes a human thought and a human word, certainly in
infinite dissimilarity and inadequacy, but not in total human strangeness with its model.
The human copy [*Abbild*] is a *real* copy of its divine counterpart." For this formulation, see
Barth, *KD* I/1, p. 201.

within this doctrine on the Word of God there does emerge in this first
volume the concept of the analogy of faith, *though cut off from even a
trace of its connection with Christology.*[65]

Now I would say that this comment rests upon a sound instinct. Barth does
have a Christology, of course, one he has been tinkering with since writing
the Göttingen Dogmatics. But it is highly formal in character, drawn up to
meet the needs and requirements of his doctrine of revelation.[66] And that
observation leads us to a very important, preliminary conclusion.

*It is in Barth's doctrine of revelation that the basic decisions were made
that control all his theologizing from 1924 through around 1940.* The basic
structure of that doctrine is provided by a dialectic of veiling and unveiling.
According to Barth, God reveals himself in that he establishes a relation of
indirect (noncontinuous) identity with a creaturely medium — first and
foremost through the *assumptio carnis.* Now notice: indirect identity is a
strictly epistemological concept. It doesn't yet say anything about ontology.
All it says is that God the Son veils or hides himself by joining himself
hypostatically to human flesh. So the true Subject of this human life is divine
in nature, but that is not a state of affairs that is outwardly perceptible to a
human observer. The true Subject is veiled by the flesh. If, then, God is to
disclose himself to a human being, God must "lift the veil," so to speak. He
does so in that, by the power of the Holy Spirit, he gives us spiritual "eyes
and ears" to see what lies hidden beneath the surface of the flesh.[67]

In its way, this is a *trinitarian* concept of revelation. God the Father reveals himself in the person of the Son by the power of the Holy Spirit. But,
again, it is trinitarian only in a highly formal sense. It is not yet trinitarian in
a material sense because a Christologically based divine ontology does not
yet control Barth's thinking about the Trinity. Many critics have pointed out

---

65. Barth, *KD* I/1, p. 201.

66. That is just as true of the material elaboration of Christology in ¶28 of the
Göttingen Dogmatics as it is of ¶6 on the incarnation. To be sure, Barth does touch upon the
problems of the relation of the "natures" to the "person of the union" and of the "natures" to
each other in ¶28 — and that is Christology in the strict sense of the ancients. But the decisions he makes even in ¶28 are clearly in service of his theological epistemology. See Barth,
Unterricht in der christlichen Religion, 1:160-206; idem, *Unterricht in der christlichen Religion,*
vol. 3, *Die Lehre von der Versöhnung; Die Lehre von der Erlösung, 1925/1926* (Zürich: TVZ,
2003), pp. 26-74.

67. The situation is actually more complicated than I have described, since it also involves an act of God in bearing witness to himself in and through the words of Holy Scripture. But this much will do to make my point.

just how formal the doctrine of the Trinity found in *CD* I/1 is — with its derivation of the Trinity from the grammatical logic of the proposition "God reveals himself as Lord." What many overlook is the fact that the reason for this is that Barth does not yet have a fully worked out theological ontology.

From 1924 on through *Church Dogmatics* I/1, Barth understands the doctrine of the Trinity to be an answer to a question posed by his doctrine of revelation. The question is how to safeguard the hiddenness of God in a self-revelation that is complete, whole, and entire. And the answer is: through a particular understanding of the proper role of the doctrine of the Trinity in dogmatics. "I understand the Trinity as the problem of *the indissoluble subjectivity of God in his revelation*."[68] My point is this: Barth's doctrine of the Trinity would remain formal until he was in a position to so identify the being of the triune God with his being in his self-revelation that Christology could control his thinking even about the Trinity. And that would not happen until he carried out his massive revision of the Reformed doctrine of election in *Church Dogmatics* II/2. And if that is true of the doctrine of the Trinity, it makes sense that it would be true of the treatment of Christ's person found in *Church Dogmatics* I/2 as well — since he is still working within the bounds of his Prolegomena in what he writes about Christology in I/2.[69]

We may return, then, to von Balthasar, who, I have said, understood quite well that the doctrine of analogy in *CD* I/1 had yet to be brought into a connection to Christology. That much is right — and it helps us to resolve the apparent inconsistency in von Balthasar's developmental paradigm. What he wanted to say is that, although the "classical definition" of the *analogia fidei* appeared in I/1, its "fully developed" form could emerge only after it had been brought into a connection with Christology, when, in fact, Christology was made to provide the material basis for the doctrine of analogy — something that von Balthasar thought to have happened in I/2 (with Barth's robust affirmation of Chalcedon). It was that development that then enabled the emergence of the fully developed form of analogy in II/1. Now that is a coherent picture and one that, as I have said, rests on a sound instinct. But the picture,

---

68. Karl Barth to Eduard Thurneysen, May 28, 1924, in *Barth-Thurneysen Briefwechsel*, 2:254. Cf. Barth, *Unterricht in der christlichen Religion*, 1:120; idem, *CD* I/1, p. 382.

69. One of the exercises I undertook in writing my dissertation back in the 1980s was to do a synchronic study of all the individual sections of the three versions of Barth's Prolegomena (Göttingen, Münster, and Bonn/Basel) in order to determine exactly what had changed. I filled ten quadrille-lined books with notes from this study. My conclusion was that such changes as had occurred had all been of the nature of "deepening" and "clarifying"; no fundamental changes occurred in this period.

nonetheless, is wrong. Von Balthasar's mistake was to think that a "Christological foundation"[70] for the doctrine of analogy emerged in I/2.

The problem is that the Christology of I/2, like the doctrine of the Trinity in I/1, is controlled by Barth's doctrine of revelation. It is a Christology that takes up the ancient teaching on the *an-* and *enhypostasis* of the human nature of Christ solely for the purpose of further explicating the dialectic of veiling and unveiling in Barth's doctrine of revelation. But it is not yet the kind of Christology that would be capable of giving rise to the version of the *analogia entis* that is commensurate with the theological ontology Barth would begin to develop in *CD* II/2.[71] And so, having not seen the later Christology, von Balthasar is forced to try to carve a version of the *analogia entis* out of an *analogia fidei* that is still not controlled materially by Christology. On the contrary: the doctrine of analogy is still more basic to Barth's thinking than Christology is — precisely because he is still concerned first and foremost with theological epistemology. The result is that von Balthasar seeks to find the basis for an *analogia entis* in the highly formalized Chalcedonianism of *CD* I/2 in order then to criticize the doctrine of analogy in its "fully developed" form for not recognizing the presuppositions contained in *that* particular Christology. In doing so, he misses the fact that Barth does not yet have a theological ontology.

B. Von Balthasar's Critique

It is best to begin with von Balthasar's understanding of the *analogia fidei* in Barth's theology. Seen in terms of the classic definition offered in *CD* I/1, von Balthasar understands the *analogia fidei* to have two central features:

> First, it is not an analogy that can be understood from the standpoint of an observer who surveys all before him and then synthesizes what he surveys. It is not Being as such that the creature has in common with God, despite their fundamental dissimilarity. Rather it is an *action* (inaccessible to all theory); it is a human decision that is similar to God's action, despite their fundamental dissimilarity. . . . Second, analogy of

---

70. Von Balthasar, *The Theology of Karl Barth*, p. 114.

71. I explored the material differences between the Christologies of *CD* I/2 and *CD* IV/1-2 in considerable detail in a lecture given at the Karl-Barth-Tagung on the Leuenberg in 2002. See Bruce McCormack, "Barths grundsätzlicher Chalcedonismus?" *Zeitschrift für dialektische Theologie* 18 (2002): 138-73.

faith also means, in contrast to the analogy of being, a similarity that is established by God in relation to the creature, in a direction that is irreversible, in an establishment from above, in the being-grasped of the creature by God.[72]

Now that, I would submit, is an apt enough description of the *analogia fidei* in *CD* I/1 — which is all that it intends to be at this point.

But, as already stated, this description remains unconnected to Christology in *CD* I/1. Even more important: it *still* does not find its material basis in Christology in *CD* I/2! *The analogia fidei remains — through CD II/1! — a description of the epistemological consequences of a doctrine of revelation that finds its focus in the event of faith.* In faith, human knowledge of God is conformed to God's knowledge of himself. Barth knew that such a claim had ontological implications, but he was not yet in a position to explore them. And so, when von Balthasar came to the Christological material in *CD* I/2, he simply *supplied* what was missing. But he did so on the basis of the Chalcedonian formula as such, not on the basis of the developmental trajectory that would soon lead Barth to construct his theological ontology in the light of election.

Analogy, von Balthasar says, means:

> a compatibility between God and creature. . . . [In I/2] Barth establishes this insight on its ultimate foundation: the miracle of the Incarnation. And what better foundation could there be than this most improbable of miracles! Because Christ is the measure of all things, no contradiction between God and the world can break in upon the depths of this compatibility.[73]

There is a "compatibility" between God and the human, in other words, that sin has not overcome, a "compatibility" that continues to exist even in human fallenness. Thus, according to von Balthasar, the incarnation does not establish for the first time a "compatibility" that did not exist prior to it. On the contrary, the incarnation requires the existence of this basic "compatibility" if God and the human are to be united in the one divine-human person. As he puts it, "we can glimpse" in God's self-revelation in Jesus Christ "a *presupposition* lying at its foundations that makes revelation possible in the first place."[74] What is presupposed is the "compatibility" of the divine and the human as es-

---

72. Von Balthasar, *The Theology of Karl Barth*, p. 108 (revised).
73. Ibid., p. 114.
74. Ibid., p. 112.

tablished in creation. "The order of the Incarnation presupposes the order of creation."[75] Thus, the two natures of Christ cannot *exclude* each other. They cannot be so related that they "correspond to Yes and No, thesis and antithesis, statement and contradiction. Otherwise his humanity would not be authentic, and sinful humanity would not be redeemed through his Incarnation."[76] What is needed, von Balthasar adds, is a unity that preserves the diversity of natures. And precisely this is what Chalcedon gives us. And so, he concludes, "Volume 2 [i.e., *CD* I/2] begins with a ringing affirmation that the teachings of the Council of Chalcedon still hold true and are binding, which implies the same for the concept of nature, *physis*."[77]

What von Balthasar thinks that he discovered in Barth is an *analogia entis* that is presupposed by the *analogia fidei* — once Barth had (as he thought) founded it upon the Chalcedonian Christology. But again: von Balthasar has really discovered this in the Chalcedon Definition, not in Barth. Even in *Church Dogmatics* I/2, Barth's adherence to Chalcedon is not *that* strict (and would become much less so with the passage of time). Barth's "confessionalism" was always and at every point a confessionalism of the spirit, not the letter.[78] Such "confessionalism" did not require adoption of the categories employed in the Chalcedonian Formula but only the attempt to understand the subject matter under discussion and to present that subject matter in his own words, under the guidance of the formula. To put a finer point on it: even in *CD* I/2, Barth did not take the validity of the abstract definitions of divine and human "natures" contained in the Chalcedonian Formula for granted, though as yet he had nothing to replace them with. So it is true to say that Chalcedon presupposes a concept of nature. But it is not true to say that Barth does. But I continue for the moment with von Balthasar.

Having found what he thinks to be the basis for an *analogia entis* in Barth's *analogia fidei,* von Balthasar can then ask of Barth's most elaborate explanation of his *analogia fidei* along the lines of an *analogia attributionis extrinsicae* (in *CD* II/1): "Why extrinsic? Because the relationship that grace establishes between God's Word and the creature is not intrinsic or inherent (*proprie*)."[79] And then he adds:

75. Ibid., p. 163.
76. Ibid., p. 88.
77. Ibid., p. 115.
78. Barth, *Church Dogmatics* I/2, p. 838; cf. idem, *Unterricht in der christlichen Religion*, 1:357; idem, *Die christliche Dogmatik im Entwurf,* ed. Gerhard Sauter (Zürich: TVZ, 1982), p. 564.
79. Von Balthasar, *The Theology of Karl Barth*, p. 110.

The trouble is that this insistence leads to contortion and contradiction. For if it is in fact true that the 'authentic' truth of the creature resides in God, then it is indeed *God's* truth, created and established by God. In other words, it is the very expression of the creature's essence that it be God's creature.[80]

But precisely here we encounter a problem that would finally be resolved only by Barth's doctrine of election. In what does "creatureliness" consist? What is "essential" to the concept of the human *after* Barth's doctrine of election is in place is *not* some abstract definition of "creatureliness"; what is truly essential is the fact that human beings have been chosen from eternity to be God's covenant partners. That election is the internal ground of creation means (among other things) that the "creatureliness" of the human derives from this state of affairs and is rightly *defined* by it. If it is only in the activity characterized by faith and obedience that the human is what he or she is "essentially," then one cannot look away from this actualistically realized relation to define the human. And in one important sense, that is already true, even prior to the revision of election. When Barth says in his Gifford Lectures that "God's revelation presupposes that there exists a world distinct from himself and that there is someone to whom he can disclose himself,"[81] he means it only in the sense that the world must necessarily be there and the human recipient of revelation must necessarily be there if revelation is to occur. But to say this is not at all to say, as von Balthasar puts it, that this is "a presupposition . . . that makes revelation *possible* in the first place."[82] That would be like saying that if a woman who cannot swim throws herself into the lake, she has "contributed" to the rescue that follows by the mere fact that she is "there" in the lake![83] But the ground of the "there-ness" of the creature is to be found in the covenant of grace, not in an act of creation that has no reference to the covenant.

80. Ibid.

81. Karl Barth, *Gotteserkenntnis und Gottesdienst nach reformatorische Lehre* (Zürich-Zollikon: Verlag der Evangelischen Buchhandlung Zollikon), p. 69.

82. Von Balthasar, *The Theology of Karl Barth,* p. 112 (emphasis mine).

83. See on this point, Karl Barth, "No! Answer to Emil Brunner," in *Natural Theology: Comprising "Nature and Grace" by Professor Dr. Emil Brunner and the Reply "No!" by Dr. Karl Barth,* trans. P. Fraenkel (Eugene, Ore.: Wipf & Stock, 2002), p. 79: "If a man had just been saved from drowning by a competent swimmer, would it not be very unsuitable if he proclaimed the fact that he was a man and not a lump of lead as his 'capacity for being saved'? Unless he could claim to have helped the man who saved him by a few strokes or the like!"

IV. Barth's Version of an "Analogy of Being"

A. *Setting the Stage*

The root of Karl Barth's theological ontology is to be found in his doctrine of election in *Church Dogmatics* II/2. The ground for the moves he makes in that part-volume are prepared for, to some extent, by elements found in the second half of *Church Dogmatics* II/1 — which makes that volume to be something of a transitional document. The elements I have in mind appear in the anticipations of the doctrine of election that come to expression in the opening paragraph of Barth's treatment of the reality of God.

Here already Barth says that, in our efforts to answer to the question "what or who 'is' God?"

> we cannot for a moment turn our thoughts anywhere else than to God's act in His revelation. We cannot for a moment start anywhere else than from there. . . . What God is as God, . . . the *essentia* or "essence" of God, is something which we shall encounter either at the place where God deals with us as Lord and Saviour, or not at all.[84]

And the reason he gives for this state of affairs is that God's being in act is a being in the act of his self-revelation. "We are in fact interpreting the being of God when we describe it as God's reality, as 'God's being in act,' namely, in the act of His revelation."[85] What God is in the act of interpreting himself to us in his self-revelation, he truly is:

> We are dealing with the being of God: but with regard to the being of God, the word "event" or "act" is *final*, and cannot be surpassed or compromised. To its very deepest depths God's Godhead consists in the fact that it is an event — not any event, not events in general, but the event of His action, in which we have a share in God's revelation.[86]

Furthermore, the act in which God has his being is utterly unique in kind. "In speaking of the essence of God we are concerned with an act which utterly surpasses the whole of the actuality that we have come to know as act, and compared with which all that we have come to know as act is no act at

---

84. Barth, *CD* II/1, p. 261.
85. Ibid., p. 262.
86. Ibid., p. 263.

all, because as act it can be transcended. This is not the case with the act of God that happens in revelation."[87] What makes this act unique? Barth's answer is: the divine freedom with respect to his own being:

> The specific freedom of the event, act and life of God *in His revelation and in eternity* is, of course, the freedom of the spirit. It is not, therefore, accident or necessity. . . . It is the freedom of a knowing and willing I.[88]

In speaking of a *free* divine act in eternity that grounds God's being in act in time, Barth is gesturing toward God's gracious election and the covenant of grace that is its content. Most important, Barth says with respect to both God's being in act in eternity and his being in the act of revelation in time that they are neither "necessary" nor "accidental." Not necessary: we have in view a free act of God. Not accidental: this act is the act that defines what God is essentially.

For all of these reasons, Barth says that the ancient definition of God as *actus purus* is finally inadequate. What is needed in order to cut this definition off from all general definitions (rooted in a prior understanding of what "being in act" might mean elsewhere) is concreteness. "*Actus purus* is not sufficient as a description of God. To it there must be added at least *et singularis*."[89] And again, the singularity in which God has his true being is to be found in the act of his self-revelation in time, so that we are right to conclude that "God is *in Himself* free event, free act and free life."[90]

Barth sums up the foregoing reflection with the following rather striking statement:

> [God's being] is His own conscious, willed and executed decision. . . . No other being exists absolutely in its act. No other being is absolutely its own, conscious, willed and executed decision.[91]

Absolutely his conscious, willed, and executed decision? How could this be — if the decision in question were not utterly basic not only to what God is in time, but also to what he is in eternity, in himself? But that must then mean that the decision in question is not something new to God when, in time, he

---

87. Ibid.
88. Ibid., p. 267 (emphasis mine).
89. Ibid., p. 264.
90. Ibid. (emphasis mine).
91. Ibid., p. 271.

addresses himself to the human recipient of revelation; when in time, he has his being in the act of revelation. It must mean that the decision in question is something that takes place in himself, in eternity. It must mean that it is illegitimate to posit anything in God as ontologically prior to the decision in which God gives himself the being that he then actualizes in time.[92]

It should be noted that throughout this discussion of God's being in act in *Church Dogmatics* II/1, Barth is speaking of the divine person in relation to a self-revelation that is conceived of in terms of an address of a divine I to a human thou:

> The particularity of the divine event, act and life is the particularity of the being of a person. We speak of an action, of a deed, when we speak of the being of God as a happening. Indeed the peak of all happening in

92. George Hunsinger has suggested that the "decision" referred to by Barth is a decision made by the triune God in eternity to be what he "necessarily" is as triune. "As Father, Son and Holy Ghost, God is necessarily who and what he is to all eternity. God eternally affirms and confirms himself, in an executed decision, as the Holy Trinity" ("Election and the Trinity: Twenty-five Theses on the Theology of Karl Barth," *Modern Theology* 24 [2008]: 185). There are at least four problems with this conclusion. First, an affirmation and confirmation by God of a being that is truly "necessary" to him could not be a free act in any ordinary sense of the word. It would have to be a necessary act — unless God were thought to be free to depart from his true being. Second, such a view overlooks the emphasis placed throughout this section on the freedom of God with respect to his own essential being. God, Barth says, is an event, a happening, both in time and in eternity. And with respect to this event that God is, Barth says (as already quoted above; see n. 88), ". . . the specific freedom of the event, act and life of God in His revelation and in eternity is, of course, the freedom of the spirit. It is not, therefore, accident or necessity." Third, to eliminate (as Hunsinger does) the element of freedom from the decision that is basic to God's essential being is to render incomprehensible Barth's protest against the insufficiency of the formula *actus purus* as a description of God. For the act described traditionally by the formula *actus purus* was, like Hunsinger's act, a necessary one. Barth's, on the other hand, is free — which is why he describes God as *actus purus et singularis*. Fourth, Hunsinger undertakes this forced exegesis in an effort to provide further support for the claim that "the Trinity is ontologically prior to and logically presupposed by the pre-temporal act of election" (p. 181). He seems not to have noticed that this claim contradicts his earlier proposition, in accordance with which "act and being are each ontologically basic. Act for Barth is no more prior to or constitutive of God's being than the reverse. . . . They are equally and primordially basic" (p. 180). Now I would regard that last claim as true — true not only for Barth but for myself as well. But Hunsinger contradicts the latter claim when he goes on to posit in God a necessary being above and prior to the being that God freely gives himself in election. What is that if not to give "being" "ontological priority" over act? I will have more to say about Hunsinger's critique of my reading of Barth — and his own reading! — in "Election and the Trinity: Theses in Response to George Hunsinger," *Scottish Journal of Theology* 63 (2010): 203-24.

revelation, according to Holy Scripture, consists in the fact that God speaks as an I, and is heard by the thou who is addressed. The whole content of the happening consists in the fact that the Word of God became flesh and that His Spirit is poured out upon all flesh.[93]

Barth is still focused in this section on the event of the Word. He has not yet learned to say "Jesus Christ" instead of "the Word." The Christocentricity for which he is justly famous has yet to emerge in its fully refined form. But all of that would change rather quickly once he undertook reflection upon the doctrine of election.

B. Barth's Doctrine of Election as the Root of a Wholly Revised "Analogy of Being"

1. Introduction: The Content of Barth's Doctrine of Election

The analogy of being developed by Karl Barth takes the form of an analogy between *a divine act* in which God gives himself his true being, and *a human act* in which the human receives his or her true being. It thus consists in a relation of correspondence between the divine being-in-act and a corresponding human being-in-act. The divine act in question is God's free election; the human act is an equally free electing of election (i.e., faith and obedience). The analogy thus has freedom at its heart — a freedom for self-sacrificial service to others.

The doctrine of election that provides the ontological ground of this analogy may be described with deceptive simplicity as follows. In a "primal decision"[94] that constitutes the beginning of all of God's works *ad extra*, God chose to be God in a covenant of grace with a human race still to be created. He chose suffering, death, and perdition for himself, and grace, mercy, and peace for the human race. What makes this description to be deceptively simple is the fact that Barth makes Jesus Christ to be the *subject* of election, rather than a Logos or Son, whose identity is complete in itself apart from and prior to the determination to assume human flesh in time. That Jesus Christ might be the *object* of eternal election would seem to be a straightforward proposition and one that does not require much in the way of explana-

93. Barth, *CD* II/1, p. 267.
94. Ibid. II/2, pp. 9, 50, 51, 72, 91, 92, 103, 167, 168.

tion. For to speak in this way is simply to say that the consequence of this eternal act of self-determination is the incarnation. But how can *Jesus Christ* be the subject of his own election? How can that which is apparently the consequence of the eternal act also be presupposed in it? It would seem, on the face of it, to be illogical.

If Barth is right to speak in this (admittedly) *somewhat* improper way, the justification for it will be found in two considerations. First, the basic structure of his doctrine of the Trinity — one divine subject in three modes of being — must hold true even after the revision of election. That is, God must be as fully God (the one divine subject) in his second mode of being as in his first. Second, and more important, there can be no being of the eternal Son or Logos in which he is not already the Son or Logos determined for enfleshment. To put it this way is to suggest that the eternal act of self-determination is *constitutive* of God's essential being, so that what is acquired through enfleshment is as proper to his eternal being as anything else that might be ascribed to him. And that is precisely the step Barth would eventually take (in *Church Dogmatics* IV/1).

But even now the picture needs to be made more precise. Jesus Christ is the electing God and the elect human. That is the most basic content of Barth's doctrine of election. But if God is to *be* "God for us," then God is also the object of election. Jesus Christ is the *elected* God. And if the human Jesus in whom this eternal decision is fully realized in time is to be free in corresponding to the determination given to him in his eternal election, then he must elect his election. Thus, as Hans Theodore Goebel has rightly pointed out, Barth's doctrine gives rise to two sets of two propositions that help to make sense of his emerging concept of analogy. On the one side: (1) Jesus Christ is the electing God, and (2) Jesus Christ is the elected human. And on the other side: (3) Jesus Christ is the electing human, and (4) Jesus Christ is the elected God.[95] What binds these two sets of propositions into a unity is the fact that Jesus Christ (in his deity and his humanity) is both subject and object of the eternal decision. He is subject — with regard to both his deity and his humanity. And he is object — again, with regard to both his deity and his humanity. He is both on both sides of the equation because both sides are given in the eternal decision.

The concept of analogy emerges clearly from the foregoing consider-

95. Hans Theodore Goebel, *Vom freien Wählen Gottes und des Menschen. Interpretationsübungen zur "Analogie" nach Karl Barths Lehre von der Erwählung und Bedenken ihrer Folgen für die Kirchliche Dogmatik* (Frankfurt: Peter Lang, 1990), pp. 26-27.

ations. The humility and obedience of the God-human in time, in which true humanity is realized, finds its ontological ground in an eternal humility and obedience of the self-same Son, Jesus Christ. When, in faith, other men and women correspond to the humility and obedience of Jesus Christ, they are corresponding to his own correspondence in time to his eternal *being*. In other words, it is precisely by making this relation of correspondence to be realized actualistically and giving it a grounding in an eternal act of decision that Barth makes his concept of analogy (as correspondence) to be an analogy of *being*.

Now the picture of Barth's understanding of God's eternal being that has here been sketched in outline has been called into question in recent English-language Barth research — even though it has a considerable pedigree in the German literature.[96] Because that literature is largely unknown, it will help in making the case that needs to be made here if we engage next in a historiographical excursus. It is important for English-language students of Barth to understand that the interpretation offered here stands squarely within the bounds of a received interpretive tradition, even as it deepens and extends the critical correction of Barth inaugurated within that tradition.

2. The Historiography of a Disputed Question: The Electing God Is Jesus Christ

The real pioneer in understanding Barth's theological ontology was Eberhard Jüngel in his 1965 book *God's Being Is in Becoming*.[97] Here, in a summary statement, is what he says about the pivotal role of divine election in that ontology:

96. See Hunsinger, "Election and the Trinity," p. 179: "How the Holy Trinity and election are related has become a hot topic in Barth studies. On the one hand are the 'traditionalists' (for lack of a better term), who contend that throughout the *Church Dogmatics* Karl Barth never changed his mind that the triune life of God was prior to the divine decision of election. On the other hand there is a growing tribe of 'revisionists' who maintain that for the later Barth the situation was much the reverse in that God's pre-temporal decision of election actually gave rise to the Trinity." I hope to show in this section that what Hunsinger here characterizes as "revisionism" is anything but.

97. Eberhard Jüngel, *God's Being Is in Becoming*, trans. John Webster (Grand Rapids: Eerdmans, 2001). See also idem, ". . . keine Menschenlosigkeit Gottes . . . ," *Evangelische Theologie* 31 (1971): 376-90; reprinted in *Barth-Studien* (Gütersloh: Benziger, 1982), pp. 332-47. What follows here in this subsection of my essay is rightly regarded as a lengthy excursus on the historiography of Barth interpretation. But such a detour is absolutely necessary if Barth's version of the *analogia entis* is to be understood with clarity.

God's being-in-act was understood [in earlier portions of Jüngel's book] to mean that God is his decision. Decision sets in relation, for it is as such a setting-oneself-in-relation. Part of the peculiarity of Barth's *Dogmatics* is that God's setting-himself-in-relation points in both an inward and an outward direction at the same time. This is grounded in Barth's understanding of revelation as the self-interpretation of God in which God is his own "double." And so it is not surprising that this double structure of the one being of God also finds a place in the doctrine of election. . . . We understood the one being of God in its double structure as a being in correspondence. And in the statement "God corresponds to himself" we saw the grounding of God's being as the one who loves in freedom. In just this way, the statement defines the historicality of the being of God which reiterates itself in the historicality of revelation. This point is expressed by Barth's talk of God's primal decision, which is coupled — not by chance — with the concept of primal history. God's primal decision is understood by Barth as God's *election of grace.*[98]

The "correspondence" of which Jüngel speaks is a correspondence of God's being in the temporal act of revelation to his being in the eternal act of election. That is the "double structure" of God's being that Jüngel finds in Barth — a repetition of God's eternal being in his act of self-interpretation (i.e., revelation) in time. Most important, however, it is the act of election that grounds and secures this "correspondence" and "double structure," since election is a decision that "points in both an inward and an outward direction at the same time." It is an *opus Dei ad extra internum* [an external work of God directed inward] at the same time that it is an *opus Dei ad extra externum* [an external work of God directed outward]. There is no other kind of "correspondence" — and, in the nature of the case, there cannot be, since the decision we are speaking of is one in which God gives himself his own being. If we wished to speak, for example, of a correspondence between an *indeterminate* being of the triune God in eternity (as complete in itself above and prior to the decision of election) and a *determinate* being of the triune God (as given in the decision of election), then we would make ourselves guilty of "becoming mythological or slipping into metaphysics."[99] No,

98. Jüngel, *God's Being Is in Becoming*, p. 83.

99. Ibid., p. 33. George Hunsinger claims that he is following Jüngel in making the "double structure" and "double historicity" of God to consist in the very traditional relation of the immanent and economic Trinities. "The Holy Trinity, for Barth, therefore enjoys a

what makes the doctrine of the Trinity to have antimetaphysical force, for Jüngel, is the fact that it describes the God who has freely set himself in relation to the human race in Jesus Christ. So, in his view, the triunity of God has, at most, a *logical* priority over election (as the "inward" element that appears *in* the "primal decision"); triunity does not have *ontological* priority over election in the sense of a being behind or above election, since God simply is what he is in election.

Jüngel's understanding of the grounding of Barth's theological ontology in God's primal decision — with its implications for both who and what the true God is and who and what the true human is — finds significant confirmation in *Church Dogmatics* II/2. "It is as God's election that we must understand the Word and decree and beginning of God over against the reality that is distinct from Himself. When we say this, we say that in His decision all God's works, both 'inward' and 'outward,' rest upon His freedom."[100] What Barth means in making this claim was made abundantly clear at an earlier point in *CD* II/2, at the point at which Barth interacted with the old Reformed orthodox conception of predestination. The old Reformed theologians understood Jesus Christ to be the object of election — but only with respect to his human nature:

> With these theologians, so far as I can see, the doctrine of election was never regarded or treated as an integral part of the doctrine of God. There is a link here with the particular conception of the fathers and scholastics frequently touched on in the first part of our doctrine of God — a conception now appropriated afresh by the older Protestant orthodoxy. According to this conception God is everything in the way of aseity, simplicity, immutability, infinity, etc., but He is not the living God, that is to say, He is not the God who lives in concrete decision. God

---

double historicity. It is a matter of one and the same Holy Trinity in two simultaneous modes of existence. . . . The first mode — eternal, immanent, primordial, self-existent and necessary — is the *koinonia* of the Father with the Son as the *logos asarkos* in the Holy Spirit. This mode, which remains forever hidden from us, represents the Holy Trinity in its primary objectivity. The second mode — historical, economic, derivative, dependent and contingent — is the *koinonia* of the Father with the Son as the *logos ensarkos* in the Holy Spirit. We have noetic access to the Holy Trinity only through this mode, which represents its secondary relationship." Leaving aside, for the moment, the question of whether an indeterminate being of the triune God could be said to have a "history," Hunsinger's claim to "follow Eberhard Jüngel" in employing the latter's distinctions to serve the purposes of his own reading of Barth is clearly false.

100. Barth, *CD* II/2, p. 99.

lives in this sense only figuratively. It is not something that belongs to His proper and essential life, but only to His relationship with the world. Basically, then, it may only be "ascribed" to Him, while it is believed that His true being and likewise His true Godhead are to be sought in the impassibility that is above and behind His living activity within the universe. It was illogical, but most fortunate, that theologians still dared to speak not only of the *opera Dei ad extra externa* but also, with reference to the divine decrees, of the *opera Dei ad extra interna.* They could speak, then, of the concrete forms and directions and aims of the divine will and the divine being. They could define the concept of the decree as *interna voluntatis divinae actio,* in spite of the fact that God, as *ens simplex et infinitum,* was not properly or by definition capable of such *opera ad extra interna,* of such *interna actio. . . .* But what these theologians did not dare to do was this. From the fact that God is the living God, that He is the living God inwardly as well as outwardly, a quality expressed and attested in concrete decision, they did not dare to deduce the further fact that clearly God does not exist otherwise, and that He does not will to be understood otherwise, than in the concreteness of life, in the determination of His will, that is as such a determination of His being. Strangely enough, they did not feel driven to make such a deduction even by their doctrine of the Trinity. They spoke of the three persons, of their interrelationship, of their common work *ad extra,* without ever realising the implications of the fact that this triune being does not exist and cannot be known as a being that rests or moves purely within itself. God is not *in abstracto* Father, Son and Holy Ghost, the triune God. He is so with a definite purpose and reference.[101]

The object of election, then, is not merely Jesus Christ with respect to his humanity, but the God-human in his divine-human unity. That is why the doctrine of election belongs to the doctrine of God — because the act of self-determination that occurs in election defines what God is *essentially:*

In no depth of the Godhead shall we encounter any other but Him [i.e., Jesus Christ]. There is no such thing as Godhead in itself. Godhead is always the Godhead of the Father, the Son and the Holy Spirit. But the Father is the Father of Jesus Christ and the Holy Spirit is the Spirit of the Father and the Spirit of Jesus Christ.[102]

101. Ibid., pp. 78-79.
102. Ibid., p. 115.

Or as Barth would put it later, "At no level or time can we have to do with God without having also to do with this man."[103]

What has happened here is that Barth's earlier claim in *Church Dogmatics* II/1 — "God's Godhead consists in the fact that it is an event — not any event, not events in general, but the event of His action, in which we have a share in God's revelation"[104] — has now been rendered far more precise. The transition from a concentration on the event of the Word addressed to the believer to a concentration on Jesus Christ has taken place. At no depth of the Godhead will we find any other.

Now admittedly, Barth's reflections on this theme are anything but uniform and self-consistent.[105] For that reason, a second view of the matter soon emerged to compete with Jüngel's. In 1975 Wilfried Härle published a large book on Barth's theological ontology that departs from Jüngel's account in two important respects. First, Härle does not like the word "becoming." This is not a word Barth uses, he notes. Instead, he prefers to speak simply of God's being as "act."[106] But which act? This leads us directly to the second point of divergence (which also explains the first). Härle wants to find the ontological root of the being in act of God in time not so much in God's being in the act of election but rather in an "inner-trinitarian being"[107] of God that stands (as yet) in no relation to election, that is, in a state of indeterminacy (since determination is given to the being of God only in election).

Härle's analysis of Barth's ontology takes as its starting point the fact that Barth conceives of revelation as *self*-revelation, as a revelation of God that is complete, whole, and entire. God's whole being is present in revela-

---

103. Ibid., IV/2, p. 33.

104. Ibid., II/1, p. 263 (see p. 118 above).

105. See, for example, Barth, *CD* II/2, p. 102: "He [Jesus Christ] was not at the beginning of God, for God has indeed no beginning. But He was at the beginning of all things, at the beginning of God's dealings with the reality which is distinct from Himself." The problem that such statements create for Barth is that they seem — contrary to his own intentions — to open up a metaphysical gap between God's being and the act of election, which, as he would eventually say (in IV/1), is a determination of the divine "essence." See below, pp. 140-41. But a determination of a divine essence that previously had existed in a different "state" would involve change and, by definition, an *essential* change, change on the level of being (ontology) — and Barth wanted always to uphold immutability. The only way he can escape this difficulty is by identifying the act in which God constitutes himself as God with the act in which he chooses to be God "for us."

106. Wilfried Härle, *Sein und Gnade. Die Ontologie in Karl Barths "Kirchliche Dogmatik"* (Berlin: de Gruyter, 1975), pp. 50-52.

107. Ibid., p. 48.

tion; nothing is left behind. "As 'self-unveiling,' revelation is for Barth 'a repetition of God' — or, otherwise expressed: God is 'His own double.'"[108]

Now, as Härle rightly observes, the impression could easily be given from this starting point in epistemology that "the being of God has been collapsed into His being-revealed."[109] And indeed, Barth can say that "the essence and the activity of God are not two things, but one."[110] But he also distinguishes the two:

> Although the activity of God is the essence of God, it is necessary and important to *distinguish* His essence as such from His activity as a reminder that this activity of God is a free divine decision, as a reminder also that we are only able to know God because and insofar as He gives Himself to be known by us. God's activity is certainly the activity of the whole essence of God. God gives Himself completely in His revelation to the human. But He does not do so in such a way that He makes Himself the prisoner of the human. He remains *free,* in that He works, in that He gives Himself.[111]

But a distinction is not yet a difference; it is not yet another being of God "before and after and above His activities."[112] And yet, Barth seems to Härle to want to say that there is indeed a being of God "above" his activities in a different and stronger sense. The stronger sense comes into view at the point at which Härle thematizes the question that he finds embedded in the affirmation of a being of God above his works. The question is: Who is the *subject* who reveals himself? "The question of the *being* of God is therefore for Barth the question of the subject of revelation that, from the very first, makes the activity that takes place in revelation to be the activity of *God.*"[113]

108. Ibid., pp. 21-22 (here quoting Barth, *CD* I/1, p. 299, 316; I have revised the second of these quotes).

109. Härle, *Sein und Gnade*, p. 22.

110. Barth, *CD* I/1, p. 371 (lightly revised); cited by Härle, *Sein und Gnade*, p. 22.

111. Barth, *CD* I/1, p. 371 (very lightly revised); cited (less fully) by Härle, *Sein und Gnade*, p. 22.

112. Barth, *CD* II/1, p. 260; cited by Härle, *Sein und Gnade*, p. 24. It should be noted that the larger context of this quote gives it a slightly different meaning than appears in its use by Härle. "When we ask questions about God's being, we cannot in fact leave the sphere of His action and working as it is revealed to us in His Word. God is who He is in His works. He is the same even in Himself, even before and after and above His works, and without them." The stress here falls on *sameness,* not another mode of being and existence.

113. Härle, *Sein und Gnade*, p. 25.

But as Härle rightly observes, it is not at all clear whether, on the basis of Barth's epistemology, an answer to this question is even possible. Barth, it would seem, is caught in a "circle"[114] that has been created by his epistemology. "On the one hand, the question of the being of God can only be answered by reference to 'God's act in His revelation'; on the other hand, revelation will only be known and understood as 'real revelation' where it is known and understood as '*God's* work and activity.'"[115] To inquire after the subject of an act is to make the former a subject of interest in its own right. It introduces precisely the kind of distinction between the divine essence and the divine activity, between "God's being in His activity and God's being above His activity,"[116] that has to lead to the further question of whether the circle has in fact been transcended. Barth would seem to have landed himself with the following dilemma: Either he stays within the circle — which would appear to render an answer to the question of the subject of revelation impossible (it being the case that the only thing that can be discussed on the basis of Barth's epistemology is God in his self-revelation, not God in himself). Or he transcends the circle by positing the existence of another source of knowledge of the subject apart from his self-revelation.

Härle's answer is: Barth does indeed transcend the circle created by his epistemology by means of his highly formal derivation of the doctrine of the Trinity in *CD* I/1 — and herein lies his second and most momentous departure from Jüngel's account of Barth's theological ontology. Barth makes use of a formalized *concept* of revelation in *CD* I/1 in order to derive the doctrine of an immanent Trinity analytically from that concept. But such a formalized concept of revelation constitutes a departure from material attention to the *history* of God's self-revelation — and, to just that extent, a breaking open of Barth's tightly drawn epistemological circle has occurred. "Our result comes close to Jüngel's but at the decisive point departs from it. Jüngel remains within the circle of the knowledge of God and the knowledge of revelation. With Barth, however, this circle appears to be broken *de facto* by means of a retreat to a *concept* of revelation."[117]

With the breaking open of Barth's epistemological circle identified by Härle, there also takes place, in his view, a "reversal" in the order of knowing.[118] Where Barth's doctrine of revelation requires that everything said of

114. Ibid.
115. Ibid. (here citing Barth, *CD* II/1, pp. 261, 259 respectively).
116. Härle, *Sein und Gnade*, p. 26.
117. Ibid., p. 29, n. 92.
118. Ibid., p. 26.

God find its ground in that revelation, the *concept* of revelation employed in his derivation of the doctrine of the Trinity allows (requires?) the doctrine of God to now assume a certain primacy even over the doctrine of revelation (as the first and foundational moment of the latter):

> Barth formulates the "fundamental problem placed before us by Scripture with respect to revelation" as follows: "the revelation attested in Holy Scripture does not want to be understood as just any revelation, next to which there are or could be others. It wants to be understood absolutely in its particularity. That means however: it wants to be understood absolutely from its subject, from a standpoint in *God* [von *Gott*]." On this basis, Barth then decides "to begin the doctrine of revelation with the doctrine of the triune God." Herein, the primacy of the doctrine of the Trinity is unambiguously formulated.[119]

Now the fact that Barth immediately makes revelation to be the "root of the doctrine of the Trinity" might seem to run counter to the claim just made. Surely Barth is still giving the primacy to revelation? And yet the situation is anything but clear. For according to Barth, "In order to understand the concept of revelation, we have first of all to ask who God is."[120] Barth's answer to this question is: "God reveals Himself as the Lord."[121] In giving this answer, Barth also makes it clear that he is making a direct identification of lordship with the essence or deity of God. "Revelation is the revelation of *lordship* and therewith it is the revelation of *God*. For the Godhead of God, what man does not know and God must reveal to him, and according to the witness of Scripture does reveal to him, is lordship."[122] God is here equated with lordship, and revelation is made to be the announcement of that lordship.[123] That Barth seeks to justify this equation by reference to certain biblical texts is quite true. But his selection of just those texts that allow for this equation to the exclusion of others — let us say, those that equate the being of God with love or perhaps with grace — suggests strongly that he is *presupposing* an answer to the question of who God is and then using it as a filter for selecting biblical passages. In any event, a concept of God is here being made basic to the concept of revelation, and it is on the basis of this

---

119. Ibid., p. 27 (here citing Barth, *CD* I/1, pp. 295, 296).
120. Barth, *CD* I/1, p. 300 (lightly revised).
121. Ibid., p. 306.
122. Ibid., p. 307 (emphasis mine).
123. Härle, *Sein und Gnade*, p. 28.

understanding of God that Barth is then able to derive his doctrine of the Trinity from his concept of revelation.[124]

In my view, Härle is right over against Jüngel in holding that Barth breaks through the circle created by his own theological epistemology — *at least where Barth's derivation of the doctrine of the Trinity in Church Dogmatics I/1 is concerned.* By staying within that circle, Jüngel has (unconsciously?) improved upon Barth through an interpretation of the latter's doctrine of the Trinity in the light of the later Christology of *CD* IV/1-2. He has corrected Barth — by Barth. It is only because he has done this that Jüngel can believe that Barth's doctrine of the Trinity is "christologically grounded."[125] In truth, it is not. It is grounded in a highly formal concept of revelation.

Still, Jüngel's reception of Barth is the more profound of the two from a constructive point of view. For it is precisely by making Barth to be more self-consistent that Jüngel is able to avoid opening up a metaphysical gap between the being of the triune God in and for itself and the being of the triune God for us. That is the importance of his claim that election looks inward and outward at the same time. Thus, Jüngel's correction was much needed.

What neither Jüngel nor Härle seems to have considered, however, is the possibility that it was only Barth's revision of election in *Church Dogmatics* II/2 that enabled him to become more consistently faithful to his commitment to never ascribe anything to God that cannot be justified on the basis of a self-revelation of God — a self-revelation that from that point on would be conceived of strictly on the basis of the biblically narrated history of Jesus of Nazareth.[126] Härle, at least, catches sight of the fact that development has taken place within the bounds of the *Church Dogmatics* when

---

124. I think that Härle is on to something here. Already in the first subsection of ¶8, "The Place of the Doctrine of the Trinity in Dogmatics," and before he even gets to "The Root of the Doctrine of the Trinity," Barth is clearly working with the equation of God's being with lordship and freedom (which he regards as virtual synonyms), even as he seeks to describe the formal *structure* of revelation. But his understanding of the structure of revelation has remained unchanged since his second commentary on Romans — which suggests, at a minimum, that Barth's concept of revelation is designed from the outset to protect and promote the otherness — the "ontic and noetic autonomy" — of God. See *CD* I/1, p. 307. Be that as it may, what Barth is not doing here is giving his doctrine of the Trinity a strict basis in Christology — as he would later do with other doctrines (starting with *CD* II/2). He is working, in spite of himself, with "abstract" (non-Christological) conceptions.

125. Jüngel, *God's Being Is in Becoming*, p. 30.

126. Barth, *CD* II/2, p. 188: "Who and what Jesus Christ is, is something that can only be narrated, not examined and described in a system."

he says, "One can say that, beginning with *Church Dogmatics* II/1, the concept 'grace' takes over increasingly the significance and function that the concept 'lordship' had for the doctrine of God in *Church Dogmatics* I/1."[127] That insight ought to have born greater fruit in his thinking, however. For it is not possible to equate divine "being" with "grace"[128] without raising serious questions as to whether an abstract, highly formal doctrine of the Trinity can provide an adequate grounding for Barth's theological ontology. After all, the relatedness of the Father to the Son cannot be understood as "gracious" — and therefore, the triune being of God cannot be equated with "grace" — apart from the determination given to that relation to be a God for us fallen and miserable creatures in Jesus Christ. God cannot *be* grace otherwise than in election. And as we shall soon see, it could not give rise to the *analogia relationis* in the form in which it emerges in *Church Dogmatics* III/1. For that analogy is not understood by Barth to be grounded in the inner-trinitarian relations in the abstract but the inner-trinitarian relations as determined by the electing grace of God.

In sum, Härle would make the ontological root of Barth's ontology to lie in his doctrine of the Trinity (a being of God "above" his works). Jüngel closes the epistemological circle decisively with the consequence that God's "primal decision" is made to be the root of Barth's ontology. At most, the tri-unity of God — and, especially, the genetic relations between the "persons" of the Trinity — constitute for him an "immanent-trinitarian *capacity* for revelation."[129] But since even the talk of a "capacity" might seem to gesture toward a being above the *opera Dei ad extra internum* — which would clearly violate Jüngel's intentions — it probably ought to be avoided. If God's eternal decision is rightly regarded as one that looks inward and outward at the same time, then surely a *simultaneity* must be posited between God's being as triune and God's being for us in Jesus Christ? Jüngel had solved most of the problems, but not all of them.

A new stage in the history of German-language research into Barth's ontology was inaugurated in 1989, when Hans Theodore Goebel raised the question of the relation between "God being-in-himself-beforehand in his three modes of being, and his being for us in his being-in-himself-beforehand in his three modes of being." How, Goebel wanted to know, "does the transition from the one to the other come about in God himself?

---

127. Härle, *Sein und Gnade*, p. 36, n. 126.
128. Ibid., p. 37.
129. Jüngel, *God's Being Is in Becoming*, p. 38 (emphasis mine).

And is the doctrine of the Trinity *as such* the answer to this question?"[130] Goebel's answer is negative. Starting from an abstract doctrine of the Trinity, with its strong emphasis upon the *unity* of God, it is not possible to get to God's being for us, for the latter gives priority to the *differentiation* of the "persons" revealed in the history of the death and resurrection of Jesus Christ. So if there is to be a "correspondence" between the being of God in time and the being of God in eternity, then the root of that correspondence cannot be found in the "genetic relations" *as such* but only in the "genetic relations" as determined in election. Seen in this light, any attempt to talk about the genetic relations in abstraction from that determination is an exercise in speculation. *For the first time, the question of the logical relationship between Trinity and election had been placed squarely on the table.*

But this, then, led Goebel quite naturally to a second question. Is it not the case that the place given by Barth to the doctrine of the Trinity in his Prolegomena already bears within itself a certain abstraction from the epistemological commitments reflected in the subsequent doctrine of election? Ought not the question of God's capability of revealing himself have been stood "in a subordinated relationship to the question of the *will* of the subject of revelation," and ought not the answer to this question have been "determinative" for the explication of the Trinity?[131] Goebel's answer to this question is affirmative. Barth's doctrine of the Trinity undergoes a "further development" as a consequence of Barth's insistence in the doctrine of election that *Jesus Christ* is the electing God, that we shall not encounter at any depth of the Godhead any other but the One bearing this name. The doctrine of the Trinity is now developed (above all in *CD* IV/1 on the basis of the *historical* relation of the Son to the Father — the economic Trinity), so that the humility and obedience characteristic of that relation is now understood to be as proper to the eternal relation of the Son to the Father (immanent Trinity).[132]

Third, "Is the primary significance of revelation the revelation of Lordship, when revelation is viewed *concretely* as the history of the crucified and resurrected Jesus Christ? Or is it not primarily the revelation of the will (the covenant!) of God for (with) man *in* that God demonstrates his sover-

---

130. Hans Theodore Goebel, "Trinitätslehre und Erwählungslehre bei Karl Barth," in *Wahrheit und Versöhnung: Theologische and philosophische Beiträge zur Gotteslehre*, ed. D. Korsch and H. Ruddies, pp. 147-66 (Gütersloh: Gütersloher Verlagshaus Gerd Mohn, 1989), pp. 153-54.

131. Ibid., p. 154.

132. Ibid., p. 161.

eign freedom?" Not the "naked sovereignty"[133] of an absolute subject, then, but the sovereignty of the God who humbled himself in the person of His Son is the proper basis for understanding the being of God.

Fourth — and most important from the standpoint of the version of analogy that begins to emerge in *Church Dogmatics* III/1 — Goebel finds the root of all of Barth's thinking about an "analogy" between the being of God and the being of the human to lie in the divine election. "The analogy between God and the human that finds its basic form in the eternal history of the election of Jesus Christ . . . includes within itself as its first presupposition the self-determination of the electing God."[134]

It remained for Thies Gundlach to draw the obvious conclusion. The doctrine of election came "too late" in the order of presentation in the *Church Dogmatics* for it to exercise the control of Barth's doctrines of the Trinity and the divine attributes that it ought to have had.[135] Barth's doctrine of election constitutes not simply a "further development" of his doctrines of the Trinity and the attributes of God (as Goebel had put it) but their "critical correction."[136] Indeed, the ordering of Trinity before election gives a relative justification to the thesis of Trutz Rendtorff and others, who speak of a "radical autonomy of God" in Barth's theology.[137] That misunderstanding can be cleared up however, only where the freedom of God is understood not as a freedom of indifference but as a freedom for the human race, the freedom that manifests itself in gracious self-giving for the sake of the human other.

Taking a step back, it has been shown that the trend of German-language scholarship has been, for some time, in the direction of insisting that a critical correction was introduced into Barth's conception of the divine being as a consequence of his revision of election. That Barth himself did not achieve complete clarity with regard to just how revolutionary his

133. Barth, *CD* II/2, p. 49.

134. Goebel, "Trinitätslehre und Erwählungslehre bei Karl Barth," p. 164. It should be noted that Goebel's dissertation (which appeared the following year) was devoted to the explication of election as the ground of analogy. See Goebel, *Vom freien Wählen Gottes und des Menschen.*

135. Thies Gundlach, *Selbstbegrenzung Gottes und die Autonomie des Menschen* (Frankfurt: Peter Lang, 1992), p. 161.

136. Ibid., p. 167.

137. Ibid., p. 164. The reference here is to Trutz Rendtorff, "Radikale Autonomie Gottes. Zum Verständnis der Theologie Karl Barths und ihre Folgen," in *Theorie des Christentums. Historisch-theologische Studien zu seiner neuzeitlichen Verfassung* (Gütersloh: Gütersloher Verlagshaus Gerd Mohn, 1972), pp. 161-81.

doctrine of election could be is not to be denied. He simply wrote better than he knew.

3. *The Analogia Relationis*

The concept of an *analogia relationis* is employed but briefly by Barth in the context of a discussion of the *imago Dei*. The "image of God," according to Barth, is not a "dignity" that is "inherent in man."[138] It is not something that could be "lost" in the fall; nor can it be "inherited" through natural repro-duction.[139] It consists rather in a relation of *correspondence* that has been willed by God from all eternity. It is that eternal act of will that constitutes God's "intention and action" in creating human beings. And it is that eternal act of will that ensures that the image of God is the future of human beings, even in their fallenness. Human beings, subsequent to Adam, are created not *in* the image but *for* it, as their eschatological goal.[140] Thus, the image of God finds its secure ground in a promise given in the covenant of grace — a promise that was realized fully and completely in the man Jesus, is realized only provisionally and actualistically in believers, and will be realized in the latter when they are brought into complete conformity to Christ in the eschaton.

Examined more closely, the relation of "correspondence" that is made by Barth to be central to the image of God consists in an *analogia relationis* — an analogy between two, and then three — relationships in which the be-ing of God and the being of the human are actualized. The most basic of these relationships, which provides the ground of the analogy, is the "I-Thou relation" between the eternal Father and the eternal Son. Now there are statements that, if taken in isolation, could seem to imply that it is the rela-tion of the eternal Father to the eternal Son *as such* — that is to say, ab-stracted from and presupposed by the eternal covenant of grace — that pro-vides this ground. Barth can say, for example, "Is it not palpable that we have

138. Barth, *CD* III/1, p. 198.
139. Ibid., pp. 199-200.
140. Ibid., p. 197: "Man is not created to be the image of God but . . . he is created in correspondence with the image of God. His divine likeness is never his possession, but con-sists wholly in the intention and deed of his Creator, whose will concerning him is this cor-respondence." To say, as Barth does, that the human was created "in correspondence with the image" is to make the "prototype" of the image to be the man Jesus — who, from eter-nity, stood first in the intention of God — above and prior not only to the act of creation but even the intention to create. More on this in a moment.

to do with a clear and simple correspondence, an *analogia relationis,* between this mark of the divine being, namely, that it includes an I and a Thou, and the being of man, male and female?"[141] But the sentence that immediately follows places us on notice that we should not jump to such a conclusion. For the I-Thou relation of Father and Son has a concrete and definite character and direction. "The relationship between the summoning I in God's being and the summoned divine Thou is reflected both in the relationship of God to the man whom He has created, and also in the relationship between the I and the Thou, between male and female, in human existence itself." We must not, out of fear of the offense caused by Barth's treatment of the male-female relation, rush too quickly past what he says here. Because if we do, we miss the point of the comparison. The analogy between Father and Son on the one side and the man and the woman on the other consists not in an abstract concept of *love,* but in a concrete love that consists in a summoning and a being summoned, a call and a being called, a before and an after, an above and a below.[142]

The decisive point is that it is in the relation of the *summoning I* to the *summoned Thou* that Barth finds the ground of the *analogia relationis,* not in an abstract relation of the Father to the Son. If it were the latter, then an equally abstract relation of the Son to the Father would have to be mentioned immediately alongside the relation of the Son to the Father, and both relationships would (in all likelihood) be governed by an abstract concept of "equality," as happened traditionally. But that is precisely what Barth does not do. He makes the relation of the Father (as the summoning I) to the Son (as the summoned Thou) to be the ground of his analogy — which means too that he is making the covenant of grace to be the ground of the being of the triune God in the analogy.[143]

---

141. Ibid., p. 196.

142. The stone of offense is not really Barth, at this point, but Paul. For it is Paul's description of the man as the glory of God and the woman as the glory of the man in 1 Cor. 11:7 that Barth uses as a lens for teasing out the significance of the man-woman relation as central to the image of God. See ibid., p. 205. Cf. Wilfried Härle, who makes the ground of the analogy to consist in an unqualified way in the love of God (*Sein und Gnade,* p. 211).

143. Of decisive importance is the fact that the Father and the Son appear here only as determined in a particular direction — as summoning and summoned. It is true that Barth can appear to speak of a triunity of God in and for itself from time to time. But if close attention is paid to the fuller context in which such statements appear, the concept of the covenant will usually be found lurking. In *CD* III/2, where Barth takes up the concept of an *analogia relationis* a second time, he can say, "Even in His inner divine being there is relationship. To be sure, God is One in Himself. But He is not alone. There is in Him a co-

Two other considerations serve to confirm this conclusion. First, Barth clearly wishes to distance his *analogia relationis* from the Catholic *analogia entis*. The Catholic *analogia entis* refers, as he understands it, to a *given* relation, to a relatedness that is characteristic of human being *as created*. Had Barth now wished to establish an analogy between a wholly abstract relatedness internal to a divine being that is unrelated to anything outside itself and an equally abstract capacity for relatedness that is thought to be characteristic of the human *as such,* then he would indeed be guilty of offering up an "etiolated" version of the Catholic *analogia entis,* as David Bentley Hart has suggested.[144] For such a version of the analogy of being would rest decisively upon an inherent feature of divine being — which would beg for the corollary understanding that relationality is something intrinsic to human nature as such, so that its attenuation would constitute an attenuation of humanness in the one in whom it is found. Certainly, there are any number of relational ontologies on the market today. But they differ from Barth's in referring to a "relationality-in-general" — not to the wholly *concrete* relationality that is divinely *willed* in the covenant of grace. And that leads to a second point.

---

existence, co-inherence and reciprocity. God in Himself is not just simple, but in the simplicity of His essence He is threefold — the Father, Son and Holy Ghost." But the context in which this statement appears has to do with Barth's claim that God's freedom is not the freedom of caprice — that the co-humanity of Jesus is grounded in a freedom of God in which there is nothing "arbitrary or accidental." And the explanation for this is that God in His freedom is "for man." "If 'God for man' is the eternal covenant revealed and made effective in time in the humanity of Jesus, in this decision of the Creator for the creature there arises a relationship which is not alien to the Creator, to God as God, but we might almost say appropriate and natural to Him. God repeats in this relationship *ad extra* a relationship proper to Himself in His inner divine essence. Entering into this relationship, He makes a copy of Himself." There then follows the statements with which we began. "Even in His inner divine being there is relationship." But then notice the continuation. "He posits Himself, is posited by Himself, and confirms Himself in both respects, as His own origin and also as His own goal. He is in Himself the One who loves eternally, the One who is eternally loved, and eternal love; and in this triunity He is the origin and source of every I and thou, of the I which is eternally from and to the Thou and therefore supremely I. And it is this relationship in the inner divine being which is repeated and reflected in God's eternal covenant with man as revealed and operative in time in the humanity of Jesus." The triunity that is here said to provide the ground of every I-thou relationship is a *posited* triunity with an origin and a goal. It is that which is "repeated and reflected" in the covenant of grace so that the two are identical in content. The best construction to place upon these still somewhat ambiguous reflections (esp. when read in light of the considerations to be advanced in the final subsection of this essay) is, I think, Jüngel's. The eternal covenant is a decision that looks inward and outward at the same time, ensuring that God "in himself" and "God for us" are identical in content.

144. David Bentley Hart, *The Beauty of the Infinite,* p. 241.

Barth follows Dietrich Bonhoeffer in making "freedom for" the other to be basic to the *analogia relationis*. "As God is free for man, so man is free for man; but only inasmuch as God is for him, so that the *analogia relationis* as the meaning of the divine likeness cannot be equated with an *analogia entis*."[145] It should be noted that if "freedom for" can exist in the human only to the extent that the human is "for" an other in the way that God is "for" the human, then the act that grounds this freedom is itself an act that points in a definite direction, so that the freedom in question is a *determined* freedom. It is not the freedom of indifference, which would be characteristic of an abstract concept of deity in and for itself.

As applied to God, this "freedom for" is the basic posture out of which the I summons and the Thou is summoned and which has reality only in the act of summoning. It is a freedom characteristic of both the Father (in summoning) and the Son (in freely obeying this summons). Thus, it is something that falls rightly under the heading of the trinitarian axiom *opera trinitatis ad extra sunt indivisa*. The Father is free in the act of "summoning"; the Son is free in allowing himself to be "summoned." But freedom on both sides of the relation is that "freedom for" the human other that is constituted in, through, and by the covenant of grace.

One final comment: Barth locates the "prototype" of the image of God in *CD* III/1 and III/2 in the "man Jesus" (following 2 Cor. 4:4 and Col. 1:15 especially).[146] He *is* the image, and we are an image of the image that he is. We actively and willingly correspond in a discontinuous, broken fashion to his unbroken life of active and willing correspondence. For Barth, the true being of the human is made real and concrete in the faith and obedience of the man Jesus. "Paul regarded the man Jesus as the real image of God, and therefore as the real man created by God."[147] He *is* the image in that he perfectly corresponds to the humility and obedience of the eternal Son. This is a subject Barth only finally would take up in *Church Dogmatics* IV/1. When he did, another layer of "correspondence" would have been added to the picture just drawn — without which his treatment of "image-bearing" would remain incomplete.

Once the picture is complete, it will also become clear why von Balthasar was wrong to say that Barth's *analogia relationis* presupposed the sociality of the human:

145. Barth, *CD* III/1, p. 195.
146. Ibid., p. 201.
147. Ibid., p. 203.

Interhuman relationships . . . are a true presupposition for the fact that Jesus can become our brother. It is *because* man is a social being who lives in intersubjective relationships that he is capable in the first place of entering into a covenant with God, as God intended (*CD* III/2, 266-67). And *this* natural order is for its part only possible on the basis of God's own interpersonal nature, his triune nature, of that the human being is a true image.[148]

The reasons why this piece of analysis is wrong at each step should by now be clear. First, it is not because "man is a social being who lives in intersubjective relationships" that he is capable of entering into a covenant. Rather, it is because Jesus Christ lives already in eternity in the covenant and, therefore, in conformity to the covenantal will of His Father that man is then made to be a social being. Second, the basis for this correspondence is found not in an abstract intersubjectivity of God but in the concrete intersubjectivity of God that is constituted in the covenant of grace. Ultimately, von Balthasar is able to make the order of the incarnation presuppose the order of nature only because he is working with an abstract understanding of the nature of God as triune. The consequence is that the relation of correspondence that he erects is not Barth's. But again: it is worth remembering that von Balthasar had not seen Barth's later Christology when he wrote these lines. He was operating with at least one hand tied behind his back.

4. The Humility of the Eternal Son

Barth's treatment of the doctrine of the incarnation in *Church Dogmatics* IV/1 is unfolded in three movements: (1) an initial description of the mystery needing to be explained, (2) the "outer moment" of the divine self-humiliation in time, and (3) the "inner moment" of the obedience of the Son to the Father in eternity. It is the last of these three movements that is of interest to us here.[149]

148. Von Balthasar, *The Theology of Karl Barth*, p. 163.
149. The distinction between "inner" and "outer" moments in the divine self-humiliation appears in *CD* IV/1, p. 192. The treatment of the outer moment occupies Barth on pp. 177-92; the inner moment, on pp. 192-210. I have provided a much more complete exposition of the whole of this section (which bears the heading "The Way of the Son of God into the Far Country") in Bruce McCormack, "Divine Impassibility or Simply Divine Constancy? Implications of Karl Barth's Later Christology for Debates over Impassibility," in *Di-*

According to Barth, the "mystery of the inner being of God"[150] is that "it is just as natural" for God "to be lowly as it is to be high, to be near as it is to be far, to be little as it is to be great, to be abroad and to be at home. . . . The humility in which He dwells and acts in Jesus Christ is not alien to Him, but proper to Him. His humility is a *novum mysterium* for us in whose favor He executes it when He makes use of His freedom for it. . . . But for Him this humility is no *novum mysterium*. . . . He is amongst us in humility, our God, God for us, as that which He is in Himself, in the most inward depth of His Godhead."[151] When we consider the fact that in *Church Dogmatics* I/1, Barth did consider the "step" into humility and obedience to be something new in God, it quickly becomes clear just how far he has traveled in his thinking since then.[152] Even more significantly, humility and lowliness are to be found "in the most inward depth of His Godhead." Godhead is not rightly conceived as an undifferentiated "substance." Godhead consists in a relational existence that is characterized by an above and a below.

But most significantly of all, it is not only humility that is to be found in the most inward depth of the Godhead:

> If the humility of Christ is not simply an attitude of the man Jesus of Nazareth, if it is the attitude of this man because . . . there is a humility grounded in the being of God, then something else is grounded in the being of God Himself. For, according to the New Testament, it is the case that the humility of this man is an act of obedience. . . . If, then, God is in Christ, if what the man Jesus does is God's own work, this aspect of the self-emptying and self-humbling of Jesus Christ as an act of obedience cannot be alien to God. But in this case we have to see here the other and inner side of the mystery of the divine nature of Christ and therefore the nature of the one true God — that He Himself is also able and free to render obedience.[153]

Humility is something that might well be construed as a disposition, a posture or attitude, a "psychological" state of affairs. But obedience is surely something that one cannot have in the absence of a definite command and

vine Impassibility and the Mystery of Human Suffering, ed. James F. Keating and Thomas Joseph White, O.P., pp. 150-86 (Grand Rapids: Eerdmans, 2009).

150. Barth, *CD* IV/1, p. 177.
151. Ibid., pp. 192-93.
152. Ibid. I/1, p. 316.
153. Ibid. IV/1, p. 193.

with a definite goal in view. And Barth clearly makes the humility of the man Jesus to be a function of his obedience — which makes the act of obedience to be the more ontologically basic of the two. Moreover, he understands the obedience of the man Jesus to express and reflect an obedience that is as "proper" to the divine "nature" as is majesty and exaltedness. "We have not only not to deny but actually to affirm and understand as *essential* to the being of God the offensive fact that there is in God Himself an above and a below, a *prius* and a *posterius*, a superiority and a subordination. . . . It belongs to the inner life of God that there should take place within it obedience."[154]

I said earlier that Barth's later Christology would require critical corrections to be made in his earlier doctrine of the Trinity. Now it is clear why this is so. For now he is thinking about the Trinity strictly "from below" — from the obedience of the man Jesus to an "obedience" that is "proper" to the Son as Son in eternity, an obedience (and, therefore, a humility) that belongs to the Son as to his "personal properties." For to say that "it belongs to the inner life of God that there should take place within it obedience" is also to say that "His divine unity consists in the fact that in Himself He is both One who is obeyed and Another who obeys."[155] Where the *analogia relationis* was rooted by Barth in a "freedom for" the other that was *common* to the Trinity as a whole, Barth's later Christology has now taken the step of making the correspondence that has long lain at the heart of his concept of analogy to find its root in a particular exemplification of that freedom — in a "personal property" that is characteristic of the Son alone. That means, of course, that it is no longer possible to reduce the personal properties of the Son to his being generated by the Father, to genetic relations as such (as has often taken place in the Christian tradition). Obedience and humility too are the personal properties of the Son.

What does this do to the concept of divine unity? Well, it certainly does not give rise to the "myth" of "two gods of unequal divinity."[156] The unity of

154. Ibid., pp. 200-201 (emphasis mine).
155. Ibid., p. 201. It should be noted that Barth's emphasis on the fact that the oneness of the divine subject, who is "both One who is obeyed and Another who obeys," completely undermines every hint of authoritarian imposition in the use made here of the divine freedom and authority. For in order to have an authoritarian conception of freedom at work, one really does need distinct "individuals" in the Godhead — the One acting in relation to and upon the Other. But Barth's understanding of the Trinity as one subject in three modes of being does not allow for this. For him, the "commanding" and "obeying" of the one God is an act of self-relating. And the "obedience" of the Son is offered freely and joyfully. On this point, see Jüngel, "Keine Menschenlosigkeit Gottes," p. 339.
156. Barth, *CD* IV/1, p. 201.

God is not to be conceived along the lines of a "being in and for oneself, with being enclosed and imprisoned in one's own being, with singleness and solitariness. . . . What distinguishes His peculiar unity with Himself from all other unities or from what we think we know of such unities is the fact that — in a particularity that is exemplary and instructive for an understanding of these others — it is a unity that is open and free and active in itself — a unity in more than one mode of being, a unity of the One with Another, of a first with a second, an above with a below, an origin *and its consequences*."[157]

The oneness of three "persons" of the Trinity, Barth is saying, is a oneness that has an origin and that has consequences; that has, in other words, a *history*. A "history" is a movement from here to there — with a definite goal and purpose in view. If there is no such movement, there can be no history. But Barth most definitely says that there is movement — from an above to a below, from superiority to subordination — and that this movement, so far from setting aside the unity of the first two modes of being, constitutes it (in the confirming power of the Holy Spirit):

> Does subordination in God necessarily involve an inferiority, and therefore a deprivation, a lack? Why not rather a particular being in the glory of the one equal Godhead, in whose inner order there is also, in fact, this dimension, the direction downwards, that has its own dignity? . . . In equal Godhead the one God is, in fact, the One and also Another, . . . One who rules and commands in majesty and One who obeys in humility. The one God is both the one and the other. And . . . He is the one and the other without any cleft or differentiation but in perfect unity and equality *because* in the same perfect unity and equality He is also a Third, the One who affirms the one and equal Godhead through and by and in the two modes of being, the One who makes possible and maintains His fellowship with Himself as the one and the other. In virtue of this third mode of being He is in the other two without division or contradiction, the whole God in each.[158]

It is clear that Barth makes the Holy Spirit's work *ad intra* to be of decisive importance for understanding the unity of God in his three modes of being. More could be said on this theme, but that is another essay. Suffice it to say that the unity in question is a living and open unity that includes a direction downward toward the human race.

157. Ibid., p. 202 (emphasis mine).
158. Ibid., pp. 202-3.

It should be clear by now that Barth has, in effect, identified the eternal processions (the genetic relations) with the eternal missions and vice versa, so that we are no longer dealing with two eternal activities but one:

> In humility as the Son who complies, He is the same as is the Father in majesty as the Father who disposes. He is the same in consequence (and obedience) as the Son as is the Father in origin. He is the same as the Son, i.e., the self-posited God (the eternally begotten of the Father as the dogma has it) as is the Father as the self-positing God (the Father who eternally begets). Moreover in His humility and compliance as the Son He has a supreme part in the majesty and disposing of the Father. The Father as the origin is never apart from Him as the consequence, the obedient One. The self-positing God is never apart from Him as the One who is posited as God by God. . . . The Father is not the Father and the Son is not the Son without a mutual affirmation and love in the Holy Spirit.[159]

In this passage, a direct equation is made between the traditional dogmatic language of eternal begetting and the like and the activity in the covenant of grace that makes the Father to be the one who "commands" and the Son to be the one who "obeys." The two activities are in fact one. And that is why there can be a correspondence between the willed obedience of the man Jesus in time and the willed obedience that is the very being of the Son, Jesus Christ, in eternity. And because the act of obedience on both sides of this relation constitutes the being of God (in his second mode of being) and the being of the human, the analogy between them can be described only as an "analogy of being."

Moreover, when our own occasional acts of obedience conform to the obedience of the man Jesus, we too are given a part (actualistically) in the eternal history that is the being of the triune God. "His speaking and activity and work *ad extra* consist in the fact that He gives to the world created by Him, to man, a part in the history in which He is God, that there is primarily in the work of creation a reflection, in the antithesis of Creator and creature an image and likeness, and in the twofoldness of the existence of man a reflection of this likeness of the inner life of God Himself."[160] In that we are brought by God's grace into a wholly actualistic conformity to the being of the man Jesus, we too are made to conform to the being of the eternal Son.

159. Ibid., p. 209.
160. Ibid., p. 203.

And to just that extent, we too are given a share in the "analogy of being" that has been perfectly actualized in the man Jesus.

V. Conclusion

The subtitle of this article is my conclusion. Karl Barth's version of an "analogy of being" constitutes a dialectical "no" and "yes" to Roman Catholicism. The "no" — which is an emphatic "no" — is said to the version articulated by Przywara and subsequently modified and corrected by von Balthasar. Barth's version of an "analogy of being" is *not* theirs. But it is hard to avoid the impression that the care given by Barth in elaborating his very different version of the analogy of being reflects a concerted effort to erect on Protestant soil a theological ontology as self-consistent and complete as that found in Roman Catholicism. A final word of affirmation is given, then, to the belief that such penetrating and comprehensive efforts at theological construction are necessary and important. In putting it this way, I am suggesting that Barth's version of an "analogy of being" is an ecumenical achievement of the highest order.

PART II

ECUMENICAL PROPOSALS

CHAPTER 3

The Cross and the *Analogia Entis* in Erich Przywara

Kenneth Oakes

Christus also allein und einzig als "Christus der Gekreuzigte"

— Erich Przywara[1]

I. Introduction

Erich Przywara is typically known neither for his exegetical endeavors nor for being a theologian of the cross. In some ways his fate within the history of twentieth-century theology is not too different from that of a young Karl Barth, who was initially read by many as an overexcited religious metaphysician, and not as a Reformed churchman committed to the exposition of Scripture. The reasons for this general misimpression surrounding Przywara are several: the intense and oftentimes misinformed debates surrounding his own rather unique account of the *analogia entis,* the lack of English translations of his major works (except those that are among his more technical and philosophical), and the fact that the majority of secondary literature surrounding his work is in German, Italian, and Spanish.[2]

---

1. Erich Przywara, *Alter und Neuer Bund. Theologie der Stunde* (Vienna: Herold Verlag, 1956), p. 528.

2. A commendable exception to this rule is, however, John R. Betz, "Beyond the Sublime: The Aesthetics of the Analogy of Being" (pt. 2), *Modern Theology* 22 (January 2006): 1-50. For a recent and clear description of Przywara's understanding of analogy,

Nevertheless, that exegesis and commentary were always among Przywara's central concerns can readily be inferred from his commentaries on the parables and the "I am" sayings of Christ,[3] on the Johannine writings,[4] on the liturgy of the church year,[5] his selections with commentary of the writings of Augustine and Newman,[6] and most especially his three-volume exegesis of the *Ignatian Exercises*,[7] a work that Martha Zechmeister identifies as his turn from a more philosophical and fundamental theology to a theology of Scripture and history.[8] That the (very) Catholic Przywara could explain that Martin Luther's "'*sola scriptura*' was not initially a dogmatic statement but a spirited emergency call that did not accidentally ring forth from him as an Augustinian (for Augustinian theology is scriptural theology)"[9] highlights his attentiveness to the exposition of Scripture. Equally, that Przywara's theology is wholly a *theologia crucis* is clear from

---

which is almost a line-by-line commentary of the *Analogia Entis,* see Thomas Schumacher, *In-Über. Analogie als Grundbestimmung von Theo-Logie. Reflexionen im Ausgang von Erich Przywara* (Munich: Institut zur Förderung der Glaubenslehre, 2003). The absolute standard for work on Przywara, however, was and remains Bernhard Gertz, *Glaubenswelt als Analogie. Die theologische Analogie-Lehre Erich Przywaras und ihr Ort in der Auseinandersetzung um die analogia fidei* (Düsseldorf: Patmos Verlag, 1969). See also his introduction to the life and work of Przywara, "Erich Przywara (1889-1972)," in *Filosofía cristiana en el pensamiento católico de los siglos XIX y XX. Vuelta a la herencia escolástica,* ed. Emerich Coreth and trans. Eloy Rodríguez Navarro, pp. 523-39 (Madrid: Ediciones Encuentro, 1993).

3. Erich Przywara, "Himmelreich: Die Gleichnisse des Herrn" (1922/1923), in *Schriften,* vol. 1, *Frühe Religiöse Schriften* (Einsiedeln: Johannes Verlag, 1962), pp. 27-272.

4. Erich Przywara, *Christentum gemäss Johannes* (Nürnberg: Glock & Lutz, 1955). James V. Zeitz notes that this work was supposed to be "the first of a series called Christentum gemäss Offenbarung" and that Przywara's *Christentum gemäss Matthias* still exists in manuscript form (*Spirituality and analogia entis according to Erich Przywara, S.J.* [Washington, D.C.: University Press of America, 1982], pp. 262 and 286, n. 6).

5. Erich Przywara, "Kirchenjahr," in *Schriften,* 1:273-321. Przywara also penned a series of poems on the liturgical year, entitled *Nuptiae Agni. Liturgie des Kirchenjahres* (Nürnberg: Glock & Lutz, 1948).

6. Erich Przywara, ed., *An Augustine Synthesis* (London: Sheed & Ward, 1999); Erich Przywara, ed., *A Newman Synthesis* (London: Sheed & Ward, 1930), republished as *The Heart of Newman* (San Francisco: Ignatius Press, 1997).

7. Erich Przywara, *Deus Semper Maior. Theologie der Exerzitien,* 3 vols. (Freiburg: Herder, 1938), reprinted with a new appendix in 2 vols. (Vienna: Herold Verlag, 1964).

8. Martha Zechmeister, *Gottes-Nacht. Erich Przywaras Weg negativer Theologie* (Berlin: LIT Verlag, 1997), p. 71.

9. Erich Przywara, *In und Gegen. Stellungnahmen zur Zeit* (Nürnberg: Glock & Lutz, 1955), p. 397.

works such as *Crucis mysterium*,[10] *Alter und Neuer Bund*, and *Logos, Abendland, Reich, Commercium*,[11] a point that recent scholarship on Przywara has rightfully emphasized.[12] Even Joseph Cardinal Ratzinger makes note of such a feature of Przywara's work when he points his reader toward "the profound theology of the *sacrum commercium* in the late work of E. Przywara. There he first gave to his *analogia entis* doctrine its full theological form (theology of the cross), which has been unfortunately hardly noticed."[13]

Within this essay I will explore how Przywara deploys his account of the *analogia entis* within the context of his theology of the cross in several of his later works. There are a couple of reasons for pursuing this question. First, I wish to highlight Przywara's attention to scriptural exegesis in order to present him as something more than a religious metaphysician. Second, Przywara's *analogia entis*, like all pithy "rules" within theology — that "grace perfects nature," that "the economic Trinity is the immanent Trinity," that "God is simple," and so forth — is meaningful and potentially valuable only after we see how and where it is positioned within his theology taken more broadly. Analyzing why and how Przywara uses the *analogia entis* within his doctrine of the cross offers a particularly helpful case for detecting any doctrinal contortions that might arise from it. To these ends, I will analyze the cross and the *analogia entis* in two of Przywara's later works: *Alter und Neuer Bund* (1956) and *Logos, Abendland, Reich, Commercium* (1964). First of all, however, I will present some background material on the *analogia entis*

10. Erich Przywara, *Crucis mysterium. Das Christliche Heute* (Paderborn: Schöningh, 1939).

11. Erich Przywara, *Logos, Abendland, Reich, Commercium* (Düsseldorf: Patmos-Verlag, 1964).

12. See Ralf Stolina, "Die kreuzestheologische Konzeption negativer Theologie bei Erich Przywara," in *Niemand hat Gott je gesehen* (Berlin: de Gruyter, 2000), pp. 49-66; Rafael Francisco Luciani Rivero, "Analogía como Agape. Logos, Commercium, Theologia Crucis (Przywara)," in *El misterio de la diferencia. Un estudio tipológico de la analogía como estructura originaria de la realidad en Tomás de Aquino, Erich Przywara y Hans Urs Von Balthasar y su uso en teología trinitaria* (Rome: Editrice Pontificia Universitá Gregoriana, 2002), pp. 415-55; Peter Lüning, *Der Mensch im Angesicht des Gekreuzigten. Untersuchung zum Kreuzesverständnis von Erich Przywara, Karl Rahner, Jon Sobrino und Hans Urs von Balthasar* (Münster: Aschendorff, 2007); and Eva-Maria Faber, "Skandal und Torheit. Katholische Kreuzestheologie bei Erich Przywara," *Geist und Leben* 69 (1996): 338-53.

13. Joseph Cardinal Ratzinger (Benedict XVI), *Daughter Zion: Meditations on the Church's Marian Belief*, trans. John M. McDermott (San Francisco: Ignatius Press, 1983), p. 29. Ratzinger finishes this footnote by stating, "see esp. *Alter und Neuer Bund*."

through Przywara's article "Die Reichweite der Analogie als katholischer Grundform" (1940).[14]

II. The Background to Przywara's Theology of the Cross

In Przywara's theology and philosophy, the *analogia entis* is not some one thing, describes not a stable, timeless hierarchy of essences with God precariously perched atop, and is not some competitive alternative to revelation or to the person and work of Jesus Christ. Instead, Przywara's *analogia entis* is a placeholder for a bundle of decisions that are simultaneously exegetical, doctrinal, metaphysical, and ecclesial, and that, according to Przywara, express some of the fundamental tenets and concerns of Roman Catholicism throughout its diverse history. This latter point can be seen most clearly in *Religionsphilosophie katholischer Theologie,* in that Przywara peruses some of the most contentious debates within Roman Catholicism (under the admittedly pedestrian contrasts of an *Augustinustypus* and a *Thomastypus*) and attempts to unify them all by recourse to the *analogia entis.*[15] Przywara can therefore call analogy and the *analogia entis* the "Grundform" or "Struktur-Prinzip" of Catholic theology and philosophy, not because it is some unchanging philosophical metaphysic upon which doctrines sit and contort, but because he sees it expressed positively within the history and debates of Roman Catholic theologies, negatively and indirectly through the very best of pagan philosophy, and yet ultimately in the rhythm of the triune God's self-revelation and work in creation and reconciliation. Yet by far the best primary source for the deceptively multivalent nature of Przywara's own, at times idiosyncratic, understanding of the *analogia entis* is his article "Die Reichweite der Analogie als katholischer Grundform," which in turn is a

14. Erich Przywara, "Die Reichweite der Analogie als katholischer Grundform," in *Schriften,* vol. 3, *Analogia Entis. Metaphysik; Ur-Struktur und All-Rhythmus* (Einsiedeln: Johannes Verlag, 1962), pp. 247-301.

15. See Erich Przywara, *Schriften,* vol. 2, *Religionsphilosophische Schriften* (Einsiedeln: Johannes Verlag, 1962), pp. 460-511. This method once led Karl Barth to remark to his students in historical theology that "the unchallenged master of the above-mentioned art of directing all water to one's own mill in a refined combination of eirenism and polemic is not a Protestant at all, but the Catholic theologian Erich Przywara, whose historical analyses as given in his *Religionsphilosophie katholische* [sic] *Theologie* (1926) and his articles in *Stimmen der Zeit* (now collected in two volumes, *Ringen der Gegenwart,* 1929) cannot go unmentioned here" (Karl Barth, *Protestant Theology in the Nineteenth Century: Its Background and History,* trans. Brian Cozens and John Bowden [Grand Rapids: Eerdmans, 2002], p. 7).

summary of the Fourth Lateran Council (1215). As Przywara regularly notes in his work on analogy,[16] it is from this council that he derives his understanding of analogy as noting an "ever greater dissimilarity" between Creator and creation, even in "yet so great a similarity" (which he labels "the classic formula for analogy").[17]

Przywara begins this article with an account of the decision of the council to exonerate Peter Lombard's theology of the Trinity from the alleged accusations of Joachim of Fiore. These are truly "alleged accusations," for there are no extant copies of the work by Joachim that the council (perhaps?) references as *De Unitate seu essentia Trinitatis*.[18] According to the council documents, Joachim argued that the unity of the Father, Son, and Holy Spirit "is not true and proper [*veram et propriam*], but is something collective and similar [*quasi collectivam et similitudinariam*], as many men are called one people, and many faithful, one Church."[19] For his exegetical support, Joachim apparently offers these verses for consideration: "'of the multitude believing there was one heart and mind' [Acts 4:32]; and 'He who clings to God is one spirit with him' [1 Cor. 6:17]; likewise, 'He who . . . plants and he who waters are one' [1 Cor. 3:8]; and, 'we are all one body in Christ' [Rom. 12:5]; again in the Book of Kings [Ruth]: 'My people and your people are one' [Ruth 1:16]."[20] Yet the verse that impressed the council, which they call "the following most powerful expression" of Joachim's position, is Jesus' petition to the Father during the High Priestly prayer: "I will, Father, that they are one in us as we are one, so that they may be perfected in unity [John 17:22-23]."[21]

The council responds to Joachim's charges by clarifying the relationship between the divine essence and the divine persons, and by glossing some of the passages supposedly brought forward by Joachim in support of his understanding of the "unity" of the divine persons. As for John 17:22, the council explains, "But when Truth prays to the Father for his faithful saying: 'I will that they be one in us, as we also are one' [John 17:22]: this word 'one'

16. Erich Przywara, "Religionsphilosophie katholischer Theologie," in *Schriften*, 2:373-511 and 402-5.

17. Przywara, "Reichweite der Analogie," p. 251.

18. See Bernard McGinn, *The Calabrian Abbot: Joachim of Fiore in the History of Western Thought* (New York: Macmillan, 1985), pp. 164-69.

19. Heinrich Denzinger, ed., *The Sources of Catholic Dogma*, trans. Roy J. Deferrari, from the 30th ed. of *Enchridion Symbolorum* (London: B. Herder, 1957), pp. 170, 421.

20. Ibid.

21. Ibid.

indeed is accepted for the faithful in such a way that a union of charity in grace is understood, for the divine Persons in such a way that a unity of identity in nature is considered."[22] As for Jesus' prayer that the faithful "be perfected in unity," the council answers by alluding to Matthew 5:48: "as elsewhere Truth says: 'Be . . . perfect, as also your heavenly Father is perfect,' as if He said more clearly, 'Be perfect' in the perfection of grace 'as your heavenly Father is perfect' in the perfection of nature, that is, each in his own manner."[23] The rationale that the council gives for these distinctions is this: "because between the Creator and the creature so great a likeness cannot be noted without the necessity of noting a greater dissimilarity between them."[24]

Przywara reads the most basic intention of the council to be the reassertion of the difference between Creator and creation, even in their highest points of unity. Przywara had already argued this point in his 1926 *Religionsphilosophie katholischer Theologie* and his 1932 *Analogia Entis,* but here it is more fully developed, and he offers three basic points as to how the council made this reassertion.[25] First of all, the council specifies the particular unity of the Father, Son and Spirit and by doing so neatly and firmly divorces "unity with (the triune) God" from "the unity of God."[26] Second, the council depicts the unity of the faithful with God as a "union of charity in grace," thereby identifying the nature of the union, one of "charity" or love, and its source, "grace." For his third point, Przywara explains the basic rationale of the council's decisions: "Precisely in this way does the irreducible dif-

22. Ibid., pp. 171, 432.

23. Ibid. (translation modified): ". . . quemadmodum alibi Veritas ait: 'Estote perfecti, sicut et Pater vester caelestis perfectus est' (Mt 5, 48), ac si diceret manifestius: 'Estote perfecti' perfectione gratiae, 'sicut Pater vester caelestis perfectus est' perfectione naturae, utraque videlicet suo modo.' The English translation reads, "as if he said more clearly 'Be perfect' in the perfection of grace 'as your heavenly Father is perfect' in the perfection of grace," thus ruining the council's very point of differentiation. H. Denzinger, ed., *Enchiridion Symbolorum, definitionum et declarationum de rebus fidei et morum,* 37th ed. (Freiburg: Herder, 1991), pp. 806, 432.

24. Denzinger, *Sources,* pp. 171, 432.

25. Przywara, "Religionsphilosophie katholischer Theology," pp. 402-5. "The formula is used as a general justification for the fact that even the highest supernatural participation in God, meaning in the inner-divine triune life *(unio caritatis in gratia),* does not sublimate the distance to what God is in himself, beyond everything, transcending even the graced creature *(identitatis unitas in natura)*" (Przywara, *Analogia Entis* [Munich: Kösel & Pustet, 1932], p. 97). This argument also appears in Przywara's essay "Metaphysik, Religion, Analogie," in *Schriften,* 3:313-34; see esp. pp. 325-29.

26. Przywara, "Reichweite der Analogie," p. 252.

ference between God and creation emerge within the highest concepts, like 'unity' *(unum)* and 'perfection' *(perfectio)*";[27] and again, "The mystery of unity with and in the triune God (as the highest and deepest mystery of the supernatural and salvation) becomes the place of the most formal emergence of the distance between God the Creator and creation."[28] The council's formula of "yet so great a similarity" within "an ever greater dissimilarity" is thus a rule of thumb that serves as a reminder for the difference between Creator and creation, and Przywara's championing of it as a basic "rule" for theology (or as how "analogy" should be understood) has not been without its critics.[29]

If the council affirmed the necessity to distinguish the unity and perfection of God from the unity and perfection of God's creatures according to the rule "each in his own manner," thereby affirming "so great a likeness" within "a greater dissimilarity," they did so by reference to the antecedent perfection and unity of the Father, Son, and Holy Spirit in the triune life itself. Hence the difference between the Creator and creation, at least in this account, does not stem from an account of God as first cause with creation, as an effect therefore bearing dim reminiscences of this cause. Instead, Przywara explains that "thus the point of departure for the council's decision is the highest and deepest and most intimate mystery of revelation: the mystery of divinization of 'participation in the divine nature,' as children of the Father, conformed to the Son, spirit from the Holy Spirit; the mystery of salvation of the 'unity' of the church as unity with the Father who sends with the Son who is sent and thus in the unity in the Holy Spirit as the unity of the Father and Son."[30] Yet "this point of departure," the very mystery of our salvation, leads us onward "into the 'ever greater' mystery of the 'ever greater

27. Ibid., p. 253.

28. Ibid.

29. See Eberhard Jüngel, *Gott als Geheimnis der Welt. Zur Begründung der Theologie des Gekreuzigten im Streit zwischen Theismus und Atheismus,* 7th ed. (Tübingen: Mohr Siebeck, 2001), pp. 388-89, and Hans Urs von Balthasar, *Theo-Drama: Theological Dramatic Theory,* vol. 3, *The Dramatis Personae: The Persons in Christ,* trans. Graham Harrison (San Francisco: Ignatius Press, 1988), pp. 220-21, n. 51. A response to Jüngel's criticisms can be found in Martha Zechmeister, "Karsamtag. Zu einer Theologie des Gott-vermisses," in *Vom Wagnis der Nichtidentität,* ed. Johann Reikerstofer, pp. 50-78 (Berlin: LIT Verlag, 1998), esp. pp. 68-69. Equally, Steffen Lösel's defense of von Balthasar's theology of revelation against Jüngel's criticisms could also be applied, mutatis mutandis, to Przywara. See Lösel's "Love Divine, All Loves Excelling: Balthasar's Negative Theology of Revelation," *Journal of Religion* 82, no. 4 (2002): 586-616.

30. Przywara, "Reichweite der Analogie," p. 254.

dissimilarity' between the 'Creator,' as the 'incomprehensible and ineffable most excellent reality' (which is the 'Father, Son, and Spirit' in the intimacy among themselves) and 'creation,' which in itself is 'many persons one people and many believers one Church.'"[31] Here the Jesuit Przywara is a true disciple of Augustine and Ignatius of Loyola, for he reads the council's "greater" in the Ignatian sense of *Deus semper maior.*[32] By this supplement, Przywara causes a *via eminentiae* to flower within what could become a statement of increasing indifference or colorless distance between Creator and creation. Przywara had already made this point in his *Analogia Entis* when he states, concerning the basis of this "so great a likeness cannot be noted," that "the inner ground of this 'cannot' is not, however, an objective principle that controls the relationship between God and creation, for then it would stand above both and would itself be the truly divine. Rather, the inner ground is God as *Deus semper maior.*"[33] Critics like Jüngel or, at times, von Balthasar, who read Przywara as finally an agnostic regarding revelation by his placing of God at some infinitely remote distance, overlook the specific nature of this *semper maior* and the necessary accent on the "yet so great a similarity," and they hence read him as a purveyor of an eerie and menacing mysticism not unlike that of Conrad.

Przywara reexamines these points in the second main section of this article, in which he writes of analogy as the *Struktur-Prinzip* for theology.[34] He again notes that this principle or structure "proceeds from the word of revelation, in which the mystery of supernatural 'participation in the divine nature' and the supernatural incarnation and salvation expresses itself in its core and its highest point, the trinitarian unity: 'that they may be one in us as we are one' (John 17:22)."[35] There is also the following move, as seen above: "It goes beyond in the emphasis that in this twofold supernatural mystery the natural relationship between Creator and creation not only is not sublimated but remains the proportion [*Maß*] and the standard [*Richte*]."[36] By "natural relationship," Przywara only and simply means that the triune Creator always re-

---

31. Ibid., pp. 253-54.

32. Przywara, *Analogia Entis,* p. 97.

33. Ibid. Joseph Palakeel is thus mistaken when he attributes a more "positive" reading of this formula of analogy to von Balthasar rather than Przywara. See his *The Use of Analogy in Theological Discourse: An Investigation in Ecumenical Perspective* (Rome: Editrice Pontificia Università Gregoriana, 1995), pp. 318-22.

34. Przywara, "Reichweite der Analogie," p. 262.

35. Ibid., pp. 262-63.

36. Ibid., p. 263.

mains Creator, and his creatures always remain his creatures, even in the gracious, supernatural participation of the children of God in Christ.[37] Przywara can therefore argue that the council's formula, as it holds across a range of doctrinal *loci* and summarizes the mysteries of the faith, contains the "three components of the one, factual order of salvation: natural createdness, supernatural participation in the divine nature, and supernatural salvation."[38] These "three components" are the three *Sache* of theology according to Przywara, and the *analogia entis* holds true in each of them, for the irreducible difference between the triune, uncreated God and his creation will continually surface at various necessary points within their exposition.

At this point, some of the mystique surrounding the *analogia entis* can be dispelled by rephrasing the matter doctrinally, and by showing how the *analogia entis* works across the two *Sache* of "natural createdness" and "supernatural participation in the divine nature." It should now be clear that this formula picked up by Przywara comes from exegetical decisions made by a church council (as a matter of "kirchliche Diskretion"),[39] decisions that have their primary location in the doctrine of the one God, who is Father, Son, and Holy Spirit, who is "unity" and "perfection" "by nature." Przywara's *analogia entis* is thus mindful of the particularity of this God who is Father, Son, and Holy Spirit from all eternity.[40] We can see this inasmuch as our relationship, as adopted children and as wayward heirs, to the Father, through the Son, in the Holy Spirit presupposes the unique and eternal relation of the only-begotten Son to the Father in the Spirit, and thus for every so great a similarity between our relation to the Father and that of the Son, there

37. "Thus it is clear how the *analogia entis* forms the basic structure of the Catholic solution. For in it lies the decisive way between two extremes already described. Thus God can never actually cease being God, and the creature being the creature, and so there truly remains, in every yet so deep a condescension of God into the creature, and every yet so great an elevation of the creature towards God, always and necessarily the boundaries of the final likeness-difference tension between God and creature, as it is based in the *analogia entis*" (Przywara, "Religionsphilosophie katholischer Theologie," p. 452).

38. Przywara, "Reichweite der Analogie," p. 263.

39. Ibid., p. 274.

40. Przywara takes the distinction in unity of the economic and the immanent Trinity as simply nonnegotiable. On this point see esp. "Trinität" in *In und Gegen,* pp. 307-10. David Bentley Hart's talk of the "analogical interval" between the economic and immanent Trinity could aptly summarize Przywara's thought on this matter, for Przywara himself places an analogical relationship between the economic and immanent Trinity. See Hart, *The Beauty of the Infinite: The Aesthetics of Christian Truth* (Grand Rapids: Eerdmans, 2004), pp. 165-66, and Przywara, *Alter und Neuer Bund,* pp. 541-43.

arises the ever greater dissimilarity of the Son's relation to the Father.[41] Hence our inclusion into the life and mission of the Son simultaneously signals our very distinction from the Son, who eternally shares in the very being of the Father with the Holy Spirit and whose unrepeatable, singular mission to the world as this man nevertheless enables and determines the form of our own. One of the many jobs of the *analogia entis* is, then, to perpetually remind all of our theological discourse of the infinite, perfect, and majestic life of Father, Son, and Holy Spirit and to interrupt and amplify our talk of and service to this one accordingly.

Another way of phrasing these matters is to say that Przywara's doctrine of analogy succinctly expresses the claim that all of God's perfections, including God's very own being, *ousia, esse,* life, essence, and existence, are *a se,* from and in himself. As for creation, the *analogia entis* is a reiteration of the doctrine of *creatio ex nihilo,* indeed of *creatio continua,* which, among many other things, expresses the continual dependence of every facet of creation, including its very life and being, upon the gracious and free act and being of God.[42] This particular difference between Creator and creature has the capacity to run wild fairly quickly, for identifying this distinction is only the beginning of its further specification according to the demands of the gospel. For help in this regard, Przywara typically appeals to Aquinas's *distinctio realis* between essence and existence within creation and his *distinctio rationis* between essence and existence in God, albeit reinterpreted in dynamic categories. Near the end of this section on the Fourth Lateran Council, Przywara notes how Aquinas's understandings of the Trinity, analogy, and being agree with the documents from the council. He explains, "Thomas, however, roots this 'cannot' and 'must' in being as such. God is 'being through his essence' *(ens per essentiam),* creation, however, only 'through participation' *(per participationem).*"[43] Here too we can see the council's distinction of "by grace" and "by nature" reiterating itself within

---

41. This argument is remarkably similar to that of Barth in his *Church Dogmatics* III/2, trans. Harold Knight et al. (Edinburgh: T. & T. Clark, 1960), pp. 55-76 and 132-42. For more on Barth's use of similarity-greater dissimilarity judgments in linking his Christology and anthropology, see my "The Question of Nature and Grace in Karl Barth: Humanity as Creature and as Covenant-Partner," *Modern Theology* 23 (2007): 595-616.

42. See Betz, "Beyond the Sublime," part 2, p. 30. The combination of these two claims, in terms of a dynamic interpretation of Aquinas's real distinction, can be found in Przywara, *Analogia Entis,* p. 147. See also Przywara, "Religionsphilosophie katholischer Theologie," pp. 403-12.

43. Przywara, "Reichweite der Analogie," p. 260.

ontology, for creation's being as created and as re-created in Jesus Christ occurs only as grace, only insofar as it perpetually comes from another, while
the triune God's infinite being and life always just is, "by nature," and thus
always comes only from himself.

For this very reason Przywara is able to weave a threefold negative,
positive, and active *potentia oboedientialis* into the fabric of his analogy of being.[44] By "obediential potency," Przywara means nothing like the capacity
for obedience by willful exertion. Instead, Przywara's point is that the creature, no matter how destroyed, destitute, and deformed by sin, always stands
before the Creator in complete receptivity; sin can never definitely occlude
the creature from the Creator's gracious hand. Yet this entirely negative potentiality includes a "positive potentiality," meaning that the creature is always and ever directed to its Creator by its Creator. Finally, by "active potentiality" Przywara intends that the creature can indeed be freed by its Creator
for a life of service offered in the creature's own genuine spontaneity. Yet
even here Przywara and his *analogia entis* are always attentive to the "distance of the servants to the Lord,"[45] and to the perpetual difference of our
spirit from the Holy Spirit of the Son, who cries out from us "Abba, Father"
(Gal. 4:6). These statements truly concern the creature, but notice that all of
these arguments are first and foremost a testimony to the Creator, and only
faintly and secondarily, but still truly, a claim concerning the creature.

It is when Przywara further specifies the content of the third component of the analogy formula, "supernatural salvation," that we can begin to
see how he might develop a theology of the cross in light of the irreducible
difference between Creator and creation. Przywara's brief introduction to
salvation history begins with humanity's original and gracious participation
in the divine nature subsequently lost by our first parents. Our reconciliation with God is the freely given reparticipation, reconstitution, and
reconformation into the life of the divine persons, yet in such a way that this
participation is in excess to the original, since it now presupposes the Son's
taking up, judging, and sanctifying human nature. Przywara states, "The full

---

44. See Przywara, *Analogia Entis*, pp. 86-94. Apropos here is John Milbank's reading
of Przywara when he notes, "Following Erich Przywara and Hans Urs von Balthasar, I
should prefer a more dialectical account in which 'essence' no longer figures as the definitely
identifiable principle of finite limitation but marks an active, open — and not predeter-
mined — possibility sometimes transcending given actuality. This makes the dynamic nonidentity of being and essence itself the mark of finitude" (*The Word Made Strange: Theology,
Language, Culture* [Oxford: Blackwell, 1997], p. 15).

45. See Przywara, *Analogia Entis*, pp. 86-93.

concreteness of the 'participation in the divine nature' first has its basis in that it is regiven in the 'participation of God in human nature' in the 'fullness of time,' because the incarnation of God as the historically ultimate thing is the determining goal in God's plan: 'he had elected us (in Christ) before the foundation of the world (Eph. 1:4)'";[46] Jesus Christ is indeed "the second Adam, and yet more first than the first one."[47] Hence our reparticipation in God is specifically in the person of the Son, who is sent by the Father in the power of the Holy Spirit to be obedient and crucified on our behalf. The Son's mission and sending by the Father is into a whole slew of "oppositions" (John's Prologue and the *kenosis* passage from Philippians are key for Przywara here) and "thus the corresponding theology is materially such a 'descent between oppositions': God's spiritual nature (and our participation therein) in his flesh, God's riches (and our participation therein) in his poverty, God's holiness (and our participation therein) in his 'carrying the sins of the world,' God's glory (and our participation therein) in his scandal of shame."[48] Here we can already see the burgeoning of Przywara's later emphases upon the stark contradictions and oppositions inherent in the Son's mission to the world. Additionally, given that our participation is in this particular Son, Przywara even interprets our divinization as ruled by Christ on the cross: "the complete law of 'divinization' therefore runs like this: as Christ is essentially the descending God, then even our own ascent in the 'participation in God' only occurs in the participation in this descent. The glory of God (as the means of divinization) is in the scandal of the cross (as the means of salvation)."[49]

It remains to be seen, however, what effects this understanding of analogy and the *analogia entis* have upon the actual content of different areas of Christian doctrine. To this end, I will next explore how Przywara relates this understanding of the being of the Creator and the being of creature to his theology of the work of Christ upon the cross in *Alter und Neuer Bund*, and in *Logos, Abendland, Reich, Commercium*.[50]

---

46. Przywara, "Reichweite der Analogie," p. 266. This verse is a rather central one in Przywara's theology, and is the reason why he can speak of the "Kosmos Christi." See *Alter und Neuer Bund*, p. 541, and *Logos, Abendland, Reich, Commercium*, p. 40.

47. Przywara, *Logos, Abendland, Reich, Commercium*, p. 147.

48. Przywara, "Reichweite der Analogie," p. 268.

49. Ibid., p. 267.

50. An unfortunate omission within the following section is Przywara's *Christentum gemäss Johannes*. In the afterword to *Logos, Abendland, Reich, Commercium*, Przywara notes that "the theology of the *commercium*, as it had been worked out in its present form around

III. The Curse of the Law, the Curse of the Cross

Alter und Neuer Bund is a sweeping apocalyptic and exegetical work in which Przywara undertakes Christological, Mariological, and ecclesiological readings of a variety of Old Testament passages. The chapters that form this work were initially talks given during the Second World War in Berlin, Vienna, and Munich,[51] and the devastation of Europe at that time is palpable on each page. The style of direct exposition of various pericopes resembles that first seen in his *Himmelreich,* and later reencountered within *Logos, Abendland, Reich, Commercium.* While *Himmelreich* was more devotional and pastoral in tone, these two later works freely interweave exegesis and metaphysical speculation. *Alter und Neuer Bund* also reflects Przywara's growing preference for the bucolic, nuptial, fleshly, and "commercial" metaphors within Scripture, and his wariness toward overly conceptual terminologies drawn from various philosophies.[52] While there is much to discuss within this fascinating and at times bizarre work, I will focus on the afterword, for it is here that Przywara most extensively discusses the relationships between the old and the new covenant, and the *analogia fidei* and the *analogia entis.*

The overall movement of this piece is a spiraling outward from the history of the old and new covenant to the doctrine of the immanent Trinity. Przywara begins by characterizing the relationships of the old and new covenant under the familiar Pauline categories of promise, type, and fulfillment (Rom. 5:14; 1 Cor. 10:6, 10), and that of witness (Heb. 12:1). He then discusses the "Energetik," or that which propels the transitions from the old covenant to the new covenant, through an exegesis of Galatians 3–5 (a particularly rocky area of current Pauline studies).[53] Again we encounter well-known

---

1960, constitutes the true kernel of the series of sermons 'Alter und Neuer Bund,' as well as the kernel of the intended three part 'Theologie der Evangelien'" (*Logos, Abendland, Reich, Commercium,* p. 171). He could have added his *Crucis mysterium* to that sequence as well. There is no single work devoted to the content and development of Przywara's theology in these exegetical works, but for helpful analyses see Luciani Rivero, "Analogía como Agape," pp. 425-55, and Zeitz, "Elements of a Biblical Theology," in *Spirituality and analogia entis,* pp. 261-95.

51. Przywara, *Alter und Neuer Bund,* p. 13.

52. Here Przywara worries about the effects of any philosophical terminology, whether Platonic, Aristotelian, or Hegelian, upon the content of revelation. See Przywara, *Alter und Neuer Bund,* pp. 531-32.

53. Aside from the meaning and value of "the works of the law," one of the biggest disagreements in contemporary literature on Galatians surrounds the identity of those under the curse of the law: Israel as such? the Galatians? "the troublemakers"? Jew and Gentile alike? See Jeffrey R. Wisdom, *Blessing for the Nations and the Curse of the Law: Paul's Citation*

themes such as pedagogy and bondage under the law of the old covenant, and the freedom in the Spirit of those within the new covenant. Przywara next readdresses the unity of the Old and New Testaments as a unity of revelation from one God and develops the forms of theology, liturgy, morality, ascesis, and mysticism that correspond to this revelation. He finally discusses the *Rhythmus* between the *analogia fidei* and the *analogia entis* in terms of the economic and immanent Trinity and by doing so returns us to the basic movement of the Fourth Lateran Council.

At this point one should note that Przywara's account of the *analogia fidei* differs from that offered by Barth, von Balthasar, and Söhngen. Indeed, in the opening of *Alter und Neuer Bund,* Przywara somewhat grumpily distinguishes his own understanding of the *analogia fidei* from that of Barth and others: "This genuine 'analogia fidei' is not to be confused with the now fashionable pseudo-*analogia fidei,* as Barth and, following him, Haecker, Söhngen, together with their disciples, erroneously call an 'analogical knowing in faith' an '*analogia fidei.*'"[54] Przywara intends by the term *analogia fidei* the far more traditional sense of the practice or art of reading Scripture in light of Scripture, a practice first given its postapostolic expression in the works of Origen and encouraged by the First Vatican Council.[55] The *analogia fidei,* for Przywara, does not name a subject conformed to God by faith, nor is it a methodology designed to secure theology's claims to be following revelation. Rather, it is the coherence or context of the world of Scripture, a world that is no different from our own. Such an interpretation

---

of Genesis and Deuteronomy in Gal 3.8-10 (Tübingen: Mohr Siebeck, 2001); Hans-Joachim Eckstein, *Verheißung und Gesetz. Eine exegetische Untersuchung zu Galater 2,15-47* (Tübingen: Mohr Siebeck, 1996); and James D. G. Dunn, *Jesus, Paul, and the Law* (London: SPCK, 1990), pp. 215-41.

54. Przywara, *Alter und Neuer Bund,* p. 11. Interestingly, it was Przywara who wrote the article on *analogia fidei* for the *Lexikon für Theologie und Kirche,* 2d ed., vol. 1 (Freiburg: Herder, 1957), pp. 473-76.

55. "For it was him [Origen] who first undertook the program that the Vatican Council calls the primary one: the analogous coherence of the old and new covenant" (Przywara, *In und Gegen,* p. 287). Besides the obvious reference to the analogy of faith found in the Church Fathers and also the Reformers, Przywara seems to be following the nineteenth-century precedents of Pius IX and Leo XIII in viewing the *analogia fidei* as the interconnection of the two Testaments of Scripture and between the divine mysteries themselves. See "Dogmatic Constitution concerning the Catholic Faith," in Denzinger, *Sources,* pp. 442-51, 1781-1820, esp. p. 447, 1796. This view of the First Vatican Council was commended in the encyclical letter *Aeterni Patris* by Leo XIII, particularly para. 6. I owe these last points to Thomas Joseph White.

of the *analogia fidei* recently found support in a work by Benedict XVI, who directs his readers to Przywara's *Alter und Neuer Bund* for further reading on the *analogia fidei* between the two Testaments.[56]

Most decisive for Przywara's exposition of the relationship and history of the old and new covenant within the art of the *analogia fidei* is Galatians 3:13-14: "Christ redeemed us from the curse of the law by becoming a curse for us — for it is written, 'Cursed is everyone who hangs on a tree' — in order that in Christ Jesus the blessing of Abraham might come to the Gentiles, so that we might receive the promise of the Spirit through faith."[57] Przywara seizes upon the interplay between these two curses and notes that "the curse of the law and the curse of the cross form the energetic correspondence between the Old and New Testament."[58] The scope of this curse/law couplet is universal, as the whole of Israel lingers under the training and curse of the law (Przywara's reading of Gal. 4:1-3) and as the Gentiles violate the *Shema' Yisroel*, "Hear, O Israel, the LORD your God is one," by being enslaved to "that which is by nature not God" (Gal. 4:8), which nevertheless stands as their own analogous pedagogy.[59] The "energetic" of the interchange between law and promise, curse and blessing, old and new, pedagogy and "the fullness of time," the energetic that concerns and affects both Jew and Gentile, has only one name and one place: "the cross is the exclusive and sole place and execution of the 'energetic' from the old to the new covenant. Within it alone are the deadly oppositions between promise and law overcome, the curse of the law carried and borne away in and by and through Jesus Christ";[60] and again, "for the 'blessings' belong to the 'promise,' and yet the curse to the law, so that only in the curse of the cross do the blessings of the promise break through the curse of the law, and only in this way, in the 'buy out' of the cross."[61] The old and the new covenant, as Przywara dramatically puts it, are "nailed together" by "the nails of the cross."[62] Przywara labels this

---

56. Benedict XVI (Joseph Cardinal Ratzinger), *God's Word: Scripture, Tradition, Office*, trans. Henry Taylor (San Francisco: Ignatius Press, 2008), p. 60.

57. This translation is from the New Revised Standard Version.

58. Przywara, *Alter und Neuer Bund*, p. 528.

59. Przywara thus reads Gal. 4:8 in tandem with the two verses in Galatians involving "ta stoicheia tou kosmou" (Gal. 4:3; see also v. 9), and he understands the pagan philosophers concerned with the cyclical "order of the world" to be both cursed and undergoing their own *Bildung* (*Alter und Neuer Bund*, pp. 526-27).

60. Przywara, *Alter und Neuer Bund*, pp. 527-28.

61. Ibid., p. 527.

62. Ibid., p. 531.

history the "full commercium of *katallagē*" and claims it as the basic theologoumenon of Paul, Irenaeus, and Augustine.

Inasmuch as Przywara understands the *analogia fidei* to be the practice of reading the Old and the New Testament together, we can state that it is Jesus Christ crucified who is at the very center of the analogy of faith. Przywara can, with this definition in place, argue that "the mystery of God unveils itself (what *re-ve-latio* signifies) in the 'analogia fidei' between the old and new covenant to the extent and insofar as this analogia fidei is the radical 'analogy in the scandal of the cross.'"[63] Przywara identifies in the *analogia fidei* the same perpetual rhythm of his own understanding of analogy, for the togetherness of the old and new covenant and of the Old and New Testament does not present a "pure unity" or "likeness" that is at our own immediate cognitive disposal. There is an ever greater dissimilarity in the *analogia fidei* that breaks through our attempts to move beyond mere "images and parables"[64] of God's work in the world. Yet this claim is not primarily about our own reasoning but instead stems from the ever greater dissimilarity of the very "mystery of the 'unfathomable' God as he 'crosses through' [*durchkreuzt*] 'God the almighty' and 'God the wise,' in the cross of 'God the powerless' and 'God the foolish,' in order to make the scandal of the cross the scandal of God."[65] Here we can again see Przywara's growing preference for emphasizing the *sub contrario* (which here functions as the ever greater dissimilarity within the *analogia fidei*) and the inherently scandalous nature of the gospel's proclamation.[66] Przywara concludes his remarks on

63. Ibid.

64. Ibid., p. 530. This notion is one of great importance to Przywara and represents, not some general epistemological reservation, but the form of Christ's preaching to his followers. See "Bild, Gleichnis, Symbol, Mythos, Mysterium, Logos," in *Schriften*, 3:335-92; and Przywara, "Predigt in Bild und Gleichnis," in *In und Gegen*, pp. 411-18. "As a final conclusion, even Christian preaching has to have the form of preaching according to 'Christ the crucified.' For to the cross in content there corresponds the cross in the form. This 'cross' in the form of the preaching of Christ, and thus in the form of Christian preaching in general, lies in the progression from likeness, to parable, to *paroimia,* to *'esoptron'* and *'ainigma'* (mirror and mystery)" (Przywara, "Predigt in Bild und Gleichnis," p. 411).

65. Przywara, *Alter und Neuer Bund,* p. 531.

66. Przywara always maintained that the preaching of the Christ crucified is a scandal, even while holding to the Vaticanum's *duplex ordo cognitionis,* which also underwent some revisions under Przywara's own hand. Notice the relationship between the theological and the philosophical in *Analogia Entis,* p. 51, and his remarks in "Bild, Gleichnis, Symbol, Mythos, Mysterium, Logos," pp. 350-51, but esp. "Philosophie als Problem," in *Schriften,* 3:303-12.

the *analogia fidei* by stating, "The *scandal of the cross and of God is **the** essence of the analogia fidei between the old and the new covenant*."[67]

After this preparatory work Przywara finally invokes the *analogia entis* and brings it to bear upon this material. This sequence from Scripture to the *analogia fidei* and then to the *analogia entis* is no accident, as Przywara argues that this path is the only true one for any theology of revelation: "From the material interconnection between the old and the new covenant, to the formal *analogia fidei* between the two, to the radical *analogia entis* (the ever greater dissimilarity) — that alone is the way of a theology of revelation."[68] In the process, Przywara denies that he is thereby moving from scriptural exegesis to abstract speculation, for there can be no strict opposition between "theological exegesis" and "speculative theology."[69] He states, "Seeing in the mirror that is this *analogia fidei,* through the old covenant into the new and seeing their interconnection throughout in the authentic *analogia entis* between God and creation, means seeing through every 'yet so great' of a participation in being between God and creation into the 'yet ever greater' of the unfathomable mystery of God in himself."[70]

This "unfathomable mystery of God in himself," to which the *analogia entis* points and on whose behalf it both interrupts and intensifies the *analogia fidei,* is nothing other than the life of the triune God. The *analogia entis,* then, is not the final word concerning God and creation, for it too is contained within a yet greater rhythm: that of the triune life in itself. Przywara remarks, "This rhythm of a formal *analogia entis* in the material *analogia fidei* has its final depths in the rhythm . . . [of] what the formula of the Council of Florence, in the decree for the Jacobites (1441), defines as the *'relationis oppositio',* as the 'opposition of relation.'"[71] Przywara simply assumes that the sending out of the Son by the Father in the Holy Spirit within the economy is a revelation of the antecedent, eternally triune God. Yet he also denies the validity of any "pure theology of the Trinity" that would break off the Old Testament and use the New Testament only as a "steppingstone" into a trinitarian metaphysics; such an approach for Przywara is a denial of revelation itself.[72] Furthermore, as there is no other Logos than the one encountered and present in this history, Przywara can invoke Luther in

---

67. Przywara, *Alter und Neuer Bund,* p. 531 (emphases in original).
68. Ibid., p. 533.
69. Ibid.
70. Ibid.
71. Ibid., p. 539.
72. Ibid., p. 542.

arguing, "For if the divinity and humanity in Christ form an inseparable unity in one person, then no one can wish for some 'God unclothed in his naked divinity.'"[73] Przywara has, with this subordination of the *analogia entis* to the Trinity, repeated and rehearsed the movement of the Fourth Lateran Council, for it too explained the difference between the unity and perfection of creatures and the unity and perfection of God with reference to the relationships between the Father, Son, and Holy Spirit. Przywara states that "the formal-rhythm of the *analogia entis* here reaches its final form as the Fourth Lateran Council most properly expressed it: that in the yet-so-great of the similarity of the 'Trinity in us' (of the 'that they may be one like us and in us' from John 17) there arises the supra-transcendence of the ever greater of the dissimilarity of the 'Trinity in itself' (to the ever yet-so-great of every unity in the Trinity)."[74] This convoluted and infelicitous distinction of the "Trinity in itself" and the "Trinity in us" is supposed to invoke the various distinctions and relations of the unity of the multitude of believers, the unity of believers with God, and the unity of the Father, Son, and Holy Spirit already seen in his reading of the Fourth Lateran Council. One could argue, then, that Przywara even has his own *analogia relationis* alongside his own account of the *analogia fidei*.

Thus the *analogia entis* does not negate or erase the *analogia fidei*, which for Przywara is centered upon the cross, but instead intensifies and amplifies whatever we wish to say about this story of Jesus Christ and his own unique work. Luciani Rivero, playing with Przywara's important "in-über" formulations,[75] can thus speak of the "*analogia fidei* in-over the *analogia entis*," explaining that "if the *in* signifies the formal subsistence of the analogy of faith in the oscillating rhythm of the analogy of being, the *over* signifies its concretization and materialization in the divine revelation in the person of the incarnate Logos."[76] Stated differently, the *analogia fidei* resides "in" the rhythm of the *analogia entis*, for even here Creator remains

---

73. Przywara, *In und Gegen*, p. 275. The context of these remarks is Przywara's criticisms against Bultmann's *Entmythologisierung*. Przywara here alludes to Luther's well-known comments regarding a naked and a clothed God and naked and clothed divine speech, but he gives no reference to any specific work by Luther.

74. Przywara, *Alter und Neuer Bund*, p. 540.

75. See Przywara, "Gott in uns oder Gott über uns? Immanenz und Transcendenz im heutigen Geistesleben," *Stimmen der Zeit* 53 (1923): 343-62; "Gott in uns und Gott über uns," in *Ringen der Gegenwart. Gesammelte Aufsätze, 1922-1927*, vol. 2 (Augsburg: Benno Filser, 1929), pp. 543-77; "Gott in uns und über uns," in *Schriften*, 2:271-81.

76. Luciani Rivero, "Analogía como Agape," p. 448.

Creator and creature remains creature, and yet the *analogia fidei* remains "over" and in no way reducible to whatever we may wish to say regarding Creator and creature through the *analogia entis*. In this way, Betz rightfully and helpfully explains that the *analogia entis* can never disrupt or reduce the significance either of our "being in Adam" or of our "being in Christ," and the work of Christ in the Spirit under the will of Father to move humans from the former to the latter.[77]

These primary contrasts of law and promise, slavery and freedom are greatly expanded within the later *Logos, Abendland, Reich, Commercium*. Instead of speaking of the *analogia fidei*, however, Przywara's focus is the *commercium*, a concept culled from the *O admirabile commercium* sung at the Vigil of Epiphany.[78] Przywara's *commercium* is shorthand for the manifold scandalous "exchanges" present in the New Testament, and he expressly names Matthew 20:28, 2 Corinthians 5:17-21, Romans 6:6-22, and Philippians 2:5-9 as his basic inspirations.[79] Przywara contends that these contrasts and exchanges of Paul, Irenaeus, Augustine, and Luther (now among the heroes of the faith) "lead to a *theological structure of the commercium*,"[80] which, "as the true 'theology of revelation,' stands against the philosophical theology that reduces revelation to the basic concepts of Platonism and Aristotelianism."[81] Przywara stylistically depicts what he means by the *commercium* in a number of places:

77. "For the *analogia fidei* is no more compromised by the *analogia entis* than the order of grace is compromised by the fact that God is 'in-and-beyond' creation whether one is 'in Adam' or 'in Christ,' since, for Przywara, the nature of this 'in-and-beyond' is itself analogical (in the sense of an ultimate dissimilarity); and thus God's immanence to creation as the Creator (cf. Acts 17:28) is in no way to be confused with the *saving* immanence of his very own Spirit to the *believer* (1 Cor. 6:19)" (Betz, "Beyond the Sublime," pt. 2, p. 8). Here Betz is responding to criticisms from Dietrich Bonhoeffer's *Act and Being*, ed. Hans-Richard Reuter and Wayne Whitson Floyd Jr., trans. H. Martin Rumscheidt (Minneapolis: Fortress Press, 1996), pp. 73-80.

78. See Laurence Paul Hemming, *Worship as a Revelation: The Past, Present, and Future of Catholic Liturgy* (London: Burns & Oates, 2008), pp. 164-74. Hemming translates this first antiphon as "O admirable exchange: the creator of the human race, assuming a living body, deigns to have been born of the Virgin, and comes forth as a man without human seed, his divinity has been extended to us."

79. For a tight, attentive description of Przywara's *commercium*, see Joachim Negel, *Ambivalentes Opfer. Studien zur Symbolik, Dialektik und Aporetik eines theologischen Fundamentalbegriffs* (Paderborn: Ferdinand Schöningh, 2005), pp. 138-48.

80. Przywara, *Logos, Abendland, Reich, Commercium*, p. 128.

81. Ibid. For a description of Przywara's "breakthrough to the authentic Luther," see Zechmeister, *Gottes-Nacht*, pp. 206-13, and Bernhard Gertz, *Glaubenswelt als Analogie*, pp. 372-84.

The Son and Logos of the Father in the Spirit
    became the Son of Mary from Adam and Eve
    — in the form of a human word *(legein)* of a human gospel *(logia)*

so that:

the offspring of Adam and Eve in the "will of the flesh" and "will of humanity," who in themselves are capable only of a "human word,"
    might receive the "freedom of the glory of the children of God"
        "born from God"
        and thus "participate in the divine nature," "in the form" of the
        Son and eternal Word.

John 1:13; Gal. 3:23; 4:7; Rom. 8:15-16;
2 Pet. 1:4; Rom. 8:29; Heb. 2:11-12[82]

These exchanges are broader than those within *Alter und Neuer Bund,* and yet the center of the *commercium* is no different from the center of the *analogia fidei:* Christ on the cross. We can see this when Przywara emphasizes some of the themes already seen in *Alter und Neuer Bund:*

The thrice-holy, blessed, free, good God, as all-righteous, all-wise, all-loving in the fullness of his majesty
    became "the sins" of the world, "the curse" of the world, "the bondage" of the world, the hell of the world — in the scandal of its unrighteousness and foolishness and cruelty — into the "nothingness of emptiness" *(kenōsis)*

so that:

This world of sin, of curse, of bondage, of hell in the nothingness of its emptiness
    might participate and share *(koinōnia)* in the divine holiness, blessedness, freedom, goodness, righteousness, wisdom, love — in the fullness of majesty.

2 Cor. 5:21; Gal. 3:10-11; Phil. 2:7-8;
1 Cor. 1:18-25; 2 Pet. 1:4[83]

---

82. Przywara, *Logos, Abendland, Reich, Commercium,* p. 135.
83. Ibid., pp. 136-37.

This whole series of exchanges is what Przywara intends by "the *commercium*," and he argues that it stands as the center of every scriptural theology of revelation. The *commercium* "is essentially the final thing to which all must be returned (in that *reductio in mysterium* of an *ordo mysteriorum*, as the Vaticanum held [Denzinger 1796]), and which can be reduced to nothing other than itself, as is self-evident for a 'final mystery.'"[84] As "the final thing," "the *commercium* is absolutely *the* metaphysic, ethics, practice, and aesthetics, because *commercium* is the name of creation and history, and by this is the name for every relationship between Creator and creation, for the one Christ, who essentially is the *commercium*, is 'from the foundation of the world' 'the head and summation of everything in heaven and on earth' (Eph. 1:1-10)."[85] The *commercium* is, then, the name for the relationship between and the history of Creator and creation, and as such it only has one true and proper name: Jesus Christ. There are, of course, problems and tensions within Przywara's "exchange Christology,"[86] but even so, it is not fair when von Balthasar remarks, pointing to Przywara's analogy formula, that "it is no accident that Przywara never produced a Christology."[87]

The *commercium* is *das Letzte,* but like the *analogia fidei,* it too has a relationship to analogy, one that can be rather suggestive and difficult to follow in this work. Przywara's main thesis in this regard is that "this *commercium* is, however, the actual concrete reality of that *analogia* that the Fourth Lateran Council defined as the most basic law [*Ur-Gesetz*] for any order between God and creation, and that, as the *analogia entis,* is therefore the nature of being: 'being as analogy.'"[88] What follows from this statement is

---

84. Ibid., p. 128. This aspect of the *reductio in mysterium* in Przywara's account of analogy caused Wolfhart Pannenberg to admit, "Therefore one must say that Przywara's formula of a 'reduction to mystery' [*reductio in mysterium*], by attending to the ever greater dissimilarity of God bursts the intention of analogy (which aims at uncovering the common logos) since, conversely, this tendency toward coordinating the unknown into the known which is at work in the concept of analogy, is diametrically opposed to a reduction to mystery" (*Basic Questions in Theology,* vol. 1, trans. George H. Kehm [London: SCM Press, 1970], pp. 225-26).

85. Przywara, *Logos, Abendland, Reich, Commercium,* p. 128.

86. What first comes to mind is the temptation to inflate the *munus sacerdotale,* or the sacrificial, representative, and substitutionary work of Jesus Christ, at the expense of Christ's *munus propheticum* and *munus regium.* At least in the works under consideration here, Przywara does seem to have succumbed to this easy enticement. There is, however, a corresponding *munus nuptiale* (if I may be forgiven the innovation) in Przywara's doctrine of Christ.

87. Von Balthasar, *Theo-Drama,* 3:221.

88. Przywara, *Logos, Abendland, Reich, Commercium,* p. 129.

largely a series of denials and negations. The first and primary claim of this kind is that "*commercium* and analogy are not deducible from one another, for analogy is no 'principle from which something could be deduced.'" That analogy is no autonomous, independent "principle from which" truths are derived about God and the world was already made plain in both his *Religionsphilosophie katholischer Theologie* and his *Analogia Entis*.[89] Instead, "*analogy* has a negative, prohibitive relation to the *commercium*. It is *the 'proportion' [Maß] for the commercium*, which practically means the proportion for all theologies, philosophies, and mysticisms of the *commercium*,"[90] a point that merely reasserts the inevitable and irreducible difference between Creator and creation within the *commercium*.

Przywara's second point is that "on the other hand, however, the *commercium* is the *actual concreteness of analogy*."[91] Here is where we see Przywara fully integrating his account of analogy and of *Heilsgeschichte*. The "yet sharper law of the 'ever greater dissimilarity'" comes forth, not primarily as "the *maior dissimilitudo* of a negative or apophatic *theologia eminentiae*," but as "'the ever greater dissimilarity' to the degree in which God 'in his goodness and omnipotent power' (Denzinger 1783) may communicate his very self and may allow creation to participate in him, even to the extreme degree precisely of a 'God as creation' and 'Creation as God' — as it even factually occurs in the *commercium*."[92] Przywara is connecting the moment of the ever greater dissimilarity between Creator and creation to the incarnation of the Logos into the very world that opposes it, and to the being cursed of the blameless Logos for the sake of removing the curse from Jews and Gentiles. In this way the *analogia entis*, the ever greater dissimilarity between Creator and creation, is uniquely revealed in the person of Christ crucified on the cross, for this is the ever greater dissimilarity of God to creation: that God was made man, the Creator made creation, without thereby ceasing to be God and without creation ceasing to be creation, that the infinite source and fountain of life and perfection was made a life, and was cursed and crucified by the very creation he made, taking upon himself and bearing away the sins of those that sinned against him. *O admirabile commercium!*

Przywara's argument that the *commercium* itself has an "analogie-haft

---

89. Przywara, "Religionsphilosophie katholischer Theologie," pp. 452-59; Przywara, *Analogia Entis*, p. 150.

90. Przywara, *Logos, Abendland, Reich, Commercium*, p. 130.

91. Ibid.

92. Ibid., p. 133.

Struktur"[93] should at least be mildly intelligible now, for within the *commercium* we see the same rhythms of likeness and ever greater unlikeness between Creator and creation that his formula of analogy struggles to express. Rudolf Berlinger offers this comment regarding Przywara's later work, that "in the place of analogy we see the doctrine of the (incarnational) *commercium;* in the place of the *similitudo,* the *absconditum* [of the God 'seen' in human form]; and in the place of the *dissimilitudo,* the *sub contrario* [of the cross]."[94] This statement is partially correct regarding Przywara's emphases, but it is not the case that analogy is replaced with the *commercium tout court;* for it is the *commercium* that is "mirrored out" in analogy itself, analogy "mirroring" the very structure of the *commercium,* with the act of God in Christ being the "ever greater dissimilarity" between the triune God and his creation.[95] In Christ crucified the rhythm of the *commercium* and the *analogia entis* coincide.

If asked what stands in the very center of all of these various points, counterpoints, and suggestive and at times bizarre rhythms, it is Christ crucified. The body of Jesus Christ crucified on the cross is the very center of the *analogia fidei* and of the *commercium,* and thus it stands at the very center of the *analogia entis* as well, which itself is invoked for the sake of the infinite perfection, majesty, and unending and indestructible life of the Father, Son, and Holy Spirit, from whom all perfection, unity, and life come.

IV. Conclusion

As I have hopefully shown in this paper, Przywara's *analogia entis* is no simple, stable philosophical metaphysic from which one may climb an ascending scale of ever more impressive essences. Instead, the *analogia entis* is shorthand for a variety of moves, arguments, and concerns that cut through a whole swathe of doctrines. More significantly, however, we have seen how Przywara's *analogia entis* cannot crowd out, replace, or mitigate the work wrought by Christ on the cross. As demonstrated in the section on *Alter und Neuer Bund* and *Logos, Abendland, Reich, Commercium,* Przywara's analogy is empty and lifeless without the *analogia fidei* or the *commercium.* It thus

93. Ibid., p. 132.

94. Rudolf Berlinger, "Absconditum sub contrario. Philosophische Bemerkungen zur Methode Erich Przywaras," *Philosophisches Jahrbuch* 62 (1953): 92, as in Negel, *Ambivalentes Opfer,* p. 140.

95. Przywara, *Logos, Abendland, Reich, Commercium,* pp. 132-33.

has no content of its own that might compete with, replace, or diminish revelation, Scripture, or the person and work of Jesus Christ.

Equally, we have seen that the *analogia entis,* as the "form" or "proportion" of either the *analogia fidei* or the *commercium,* works to preserve the irreducible distinction between Creator and creature, Savior and saved, Sanctifier and sanctified, and to interrupt and to intensify every positive theological claim on behalf of theology's object. For the Przywara of *Logos, Abendland, Reich, Commercium,* the *commercium* is the very basis and content of any theology of revelation, and he himself contrasts a theology centered upon being with a theology whose center is the *commercium:* "a 'philosophical theology' that arranges the particular elements of revelation in the basic concepts of Aristotle or Plato or possibly of an Eastern philosophy stands opposed to the most proper 'theology of revelation' whose center is not 'being' but the *'commercium.'"*[96] Przywara's later work itself reflects that the subject and object of theology is not primarily being but the *analogia fidei* and the *commercium,* and thus the center of theology is always and irreducibly the work wrought by the God-man Jesus Christ upon the cross for the sake of creation. It is still Przywara's contention, however, that to speak of the Creator and creation well, we will need to be mindful of analogy, and of the *analogia entis.*[97] Once again the *analogia entis,* according to Przywara, ever and only reflects and radiates the glory of Jesus Christ, the incarnate God.

Battista Mondin notes that Przywara cuts "a rather solitary but decidedly important and robust figure,"[98] and thus much clarification is needed before Przywara's contribution to the life and teaching of the church can be assessed. Hopefully this essay has contributed to such a clarification by at least showing how many previous attempts to mediate between Przywara's *analogia entis* and Barth's *analogia fidei,* although no doubt charged with respectable ecumenical intentions, are somewhat redundant. A host of these

96. Ibid., p. 133. Przywara also states that *analogia entis* "is not, as Wagner believes, supported through a 'principle' of causality (as in Aristotelianism) or by 'participation in being' (as in Platonism)" (*In und Gegen,* p. 280). Here Przywara is responding to Hans Wagner, *Existenz, Analogie, Dialektik. Religio pura seu transcendentalis* (Munich: Ernst Reinhard, 1953).

97. So important are all three of these loci — the *commercium,* the *analogia fidei,* and the *analogia entis* — that in 1955 Przywara refers to them as "the author's fundamental ideas" (*In und Gegen,* p. 8).

98. Battista Mondin, *Storia della teologia* (Bologna: Edizioni Studio Dominicano, 1997), p. 498.

studies have been undertaken in order to supplement Przywara's supposedly too "philosophical" *analogia entis* with revelation, or to give Barth's dialectical theology of the Word some kind of ontological background among all the seemingly punctiliar acts of God and humanity. Peter S. Oh, following von Balthasar, has recently called Barth's *analogia fidei* and Przywara's *analogia entis* "complementary ways of viewing revelation,"[99] but even this gesture is superfluous, for Przywara's *analogia entis* needs no supplement of revelation, and Barth's theology needs no supplement of ontological claims and concerns.[100] Future discussions, therefore, between these two theologians would be most fruitful and edifying if held in other, more substantial doctrinal locations, such as their Christologies, their doctrines of God, but most of all in their exegesis of Scripture, as they themselves would no doubt agree.[101]

99. Peter S. Oh, *Karl Barth's Trinitarian Theology: A Study in Karl Barth's Analogical Use of the Trinitarian Relations* (London: T. & T. Clark, 2006), pp. 13-20.

100. See Karl Barth, *Church Dogmatics* II/1, trans. T. H. L. Parker et al. (Edinburgh: T. & T. Clark, 1957), pp. 257-321; and *Church Dogmatics* III/2, pp. 203-22.

101. I would like to extend my warmest thanks to John R. Betz and Thomas Joseph White, O.P., for their insightful and gracious comments, questions, and suggestions on an earlier draft of this essay.

CHAPTER 4

Analogy as the *discrimen naturae et gratiae:* Thomism and Ecumenical Learning

Richard Schenk, O.P.

I. Introduction

In a remark that was arguably too self-critical, Erich Przywara made the following observation in the year 1955:

> In 1923 I introduced the expression "analogia entis" in my philosophy of religion in dialogue with Scheler and in 1925 in dialogue with Karl Barth, making it the central point of my metaphysical and controversial theological writings and of my philosophy of religion. . . . It did not, however, become the point of departure of fruitful discussion but the point of departure for a great conflict.[1]

Przywara's notion of *analogia entis* certainly provided "the point of departure for a great conflict," but even in its beginnings and the first three decades of its development, the controversial discussion of the problematic surrounding this notion had proven fruitful. The chief question being vetted

---

1. Erich Przywara, *In und Gegen. Stellungnahmen zur Zeit* (Nürnberg: Glock & Lutz, 1955), p. 177, cited here in the translation of Thomas F. O'Meara, *Erich Przywara, S.J.* (Notre Dame, Ind.: Notre Dame University Press, 2002), p. 207, n. 41. Karl Hammer, "Analogia relationis gegen analogia entis," in *Parrhesia. Karl Barth zum achtigsten Geburtstag*, ed. E. Busch, pp. 288-304 (Zürich: EVZ, 1966), p. 289, refers to an even harsher side of Przywara's verdict here: that the work had become the "Ausgangspunkt einer grotesken Verzerrung . . . zuerst bei Karl Barth, dann im folgenden bei Gottlieb Söhngen und Theodor Haecker und nun anscheinend auch bei Balthasar."

in this volume is whether further discussion can bear fruit again. What are we seeking when we return to the question posed by Karl Barth's challenge to Erich Przywara, the question of *analogia entis* vis-à-vis *analogia fidei?*

Looking back at the discussion prior to the Second Vatican Council, it would be hard to deny that both sides had aimed from the beginning at "ecumenical learning." For the purposes of this paper, let me presuppose here that genuine ecumenical discussion is guided by a twofold goal, reflected in what Michael Root and others have termed "the affirmation and the admonition" of other Christian communities.[2] Its dual goal means that ecumenical discussion will blend strategies of convergence with those of a more clearly differentiating form of relationality. I am assuming here further that the entire body of the Christian faithful has been and can continue to be enriched by many of its confessional communities, and that confessional identity *can* be enriched by both convergent and differentiating relational forms of ecumenical discussion. Statements of convergence or difference can each bring blessing or curse, learning or obliviousness, friendship or disinterest. In raising questions of self-identity, they are likely to reveal as well, not without some conflict, differences within one's own confessional family.

As shown even by three sets of remarks in the first volume of *Church Dogmatics* of 1932 (*KD* I/1), Karl Barth's engagement of Przywara's use of *analogia entis* aimed at as sympathetic (or convergent) a reading of the scholastic tradition of Catholicism as the ultimate rejection of this "Catholic principle" would allow (relational).[3] This applies even to Barth's qualification of *analogia entis* as the "invention of the Antichrist," which admits a moment of attraction and temptation.[4] Already in Barth's 1929 letter to

2. Cf. Gabriel J. Fackre and Michael Root, *Affirmations and Admonitions: Lutheran Decisions and Dialogue with Reformed, Episcopal, and Roman Catholic Churches* (Grand Rapids: Eerdmans, 1998); cf. also Richard Schenk, "Eine Ökumene des Einspruchs. Systematische Überlegungen zum heutigen ökumenischen Prozess aus einer römisch-katholischen Sicht," in *Die Reunionsgespräche im Niedersachsen des 17. Jahrhunderts. Rojas y Spinola, Molan, Leibniz,* ed. Hans Otte and Richard Schenk, pp. 225-50 (Göttingen: Vandenhoeck & Ruprecht, 1999).

3. *KD* I/1, pp. viiiff., 138ff., 178-80. The latter two passages, referring to a critical review by Przywara published in 1929 in *Stimmen der Zeit* (pp. 231ff.), reject the charge of "canonizing the spirit against nature" and reducing God largely to a verbal event, but Barth can use the critique, exaggerated as it appears to him, to seek a view of Reformational theology distinct from the one urged by Friedrich Gogarten.

4. Largely with reference to the analogy debates, Grover Foley summed up well this genuinely ecumenical ambivalence: "Karl Barth dagegen sieht in Lehre und Leben des

Richard Schenk, O.P.

Eduard Thurneysen in which he reports on Przywara's lecture[5] and the following personal conversation in Münster, to which Barth had invited his Jesuit colleague, Barth showed that his reference to the Antichrist was meant to be more reflective than bold (despite the characteristic "parrhesia" of the phrase). Barth asks himself and Thurneysen whether this suggestion of the all-too-final "peace of the analogia entis" was made by "an angel of the Antichrist or a chosen armament of the Lord? By the Grand Inquisitor or by a true disciple of the Apostle to the nations?"[6] Barth is so far from an undivided rejection of Przywara's vision and its sources that he compares the situation into which he feels himself placed by encountering this form of Catholicism with the situation portrayed by Lessing's parable of the three rings.

II. Catholic Learners

Ecumenical learning on the Catholic side of the analogy debates revolved around the question of the degree to which Catholic theology could embrace what since his Heidelberg Disputation of 1518 Luther had contrasted to its scholastic heritage: a *theologia crucis*.

A. Erich Przywara

John Betz has presented Erich Przywara's views on analogy in this same volume in greater detail and precision than can be treated here. The literature on the debate begun by Przywara's writings has been extensive.[7] Here I intend to recall only one of the features of Przywara's reflections that most shaped the debate to follow: the use of a slightly reconstructed axiom on grace and nature to elucidate the desired meaning of the *analogia entis*.

One of the surprises for the reader of both Przywara's work and its dis-

---

Katholizismus sowohl eine große Verheißung wie eine ganz ernst zu nehmende Bedrohung" ("Das Verhältnis Karl Barths zum römischen Katholizismus," in *Parrhesia. Karl Barth zum achtzigsten Geburtstag am 10. Mai 1966* [Zürich: EVZ, 1966], p. 599).

5. *Zwischen den Zeiten* 7 (1929).

6. Cited here according to Bruce L. McCormack, *Theologische Dialektik und kritischer Realismus. Entstehung und Entwicklung von Karl Barths Theologie, 1909-1936* (Zürich: TVZ, 2006), pp. 324ff., from *Karl Barth–Eduard Thurneysen Briefwechsel*, vol. 2, *1921-1930*, ed. Eduard Thurneysen (Zürich: TVZ, 1974), pp. 652ff.

7. Cf. the bibliographic resources noted by O'Meara, *Erich Przywara, S.J.*, p. 245.

cussion by Protestants and Catholics alike is the degree to which analogy is treated in the context of its association with variations on the axiom that grace does not destroy nature but perfects it.[8] Przywara shows as little concern for the historical origins of the axiom as for those of the notion of *analogia entis.*[9] As would be expected from this "master of the rhythms" of polar tensions, Przywara did not intend the axiom to reflect the thought of any one thinker, much less one text. In his 1923 work *The God-Mystery of the World,* Przywara wrote of

> the unfathomable miracle of that unique foundational relationship between God and creation, the miracle of the "analogia entis," the polarity of similarity and dissimilarity between God, who according to the Apostle "is all in all" and "works all in all," . . . and the creature in its own being and workings: that is precisely the unfathomable miracle of this "analogia entis" that is stressed in the same way by Augustine, Thomas, and Scotus, that the "analogia entis" encompasses both the order of being and the order of knowing. . . . That doctrine of the "analogia entis," on which Thomas and Scotus differ, at least in their manner of expression, is not the theological doctrine of the "analogia entis" that is meant by us here.[10]

Przywara would soon develop and vary a formula for this broad sense of analogy by blending three passages from Thomas Aquinas: *De ver.,* q. 14, a. 10, ad 9; *ST* I, q. 1, a. 8, ad 2; and *ST* I, q. 2, a. 2, ad 1.[11] The discussion of

8. Cf. Richard Schenk, *Die Gnade vollendeter Endlichkeit. Zur transzendental-theologischen Auslegung der thomanischen Anthropologie* (Freiburg: Herder, 1989), pp. 370-442; and Stephan Nieborak, *"Homo analogia." Zur philosophisch-theologischen Bedeutung der "analogia entis" im Rahmen der existentiellen Frage bei Erich Przywara, S.J. (1889-1972)* (Frankfurt: Peter Lang, 1994), esp. pp. 394-403, although with a caveat as to the author's suspicions about the historical origins of the axiom, p. 386, n. 1.

9. For the late scholastic provenance of the latter, cf. Bernhard Gertz, *Glaubenswelt als Analogie. Die theologische Analogie-Lehre Erich Przywaras und ihr Ort in der Auseinandersetzung um die analogia fidei* (Düsseldorf: Patmos Verlag, 1969), pp. 235ff.; and Julio Terán Dutari, "Die Geschichte des Terminus 'Analogia entis' und das Werk Erich Przywaras," *Philosophisches Jahrbuch der Görres-Gesellschaft* 77 (1970): 163-79.

10. Erich Przywara, *Gott Geheimnis der Welt. Drei Vorträge über die geistige Krise der Gegenwart* (Munich: Theatiner-Verlag, 1923), pp. 135 and 188, n. 70. Unless otherwise stated, the English translations of German works are my own.

11. Thomas Aquinas, *De ver.,* q. 14, a. 10, ad 9: "Ad nonum dicendum, quod *fides non destruit rationem, sed excedit eam et perficit,* ut dictum est."

ST I, q. 1, a. 8, ad 2: "Ad secundum dicendum quod argumentari ex auctoritate est

"analogy," both by Przywara and by his pre–Vatican II supporters and critics, would devote at least as much attention to this axiom and its "ontological" and epistemological consequences as to the diverse medieval positions on the finer points of analogy vis-à-vis univocity. All versions of Przywara's formula are taken from an axiom on the relation of nature and grace, which most directly addresses the "order of being" but which could be altered, as Thomas and Przywara agree, to reflect the "order of knowing." In the classic statement of his position, in *Analogia Entis* (1932), Przywara sees the axiom as focusing the meaning of analogy:

> The corresponding practical method is therefore best contained in both the sentences that have been formulated from this basic understanding. For the meta-noetic side of the metaphysical problem, the sentence applies: *fides (theologia) non destruit, sed supponit et perficit rationem (philosophiam)* [Faith (theology) does not destroy but presupposes and perfects reason (philosophy)]. To the meta-ontic side belongs the second sentence: *gratia non destruit, sed supponit et perficit naturam* [Grace does not destroy but presupposes and perfects nature]. Precisely in their interconnectedness, as Thomas likes to put it (*ST* I, q. 1, a. 8, ad 2; q. 2, a. 2, ad 1), these sentences then constitute the methodological statement for the metaphysical sense of the world that expresses itself in the unity of both these sides of the metaphysical problem.[12]

---

maxime proprium huius doctrinae, eo quod principia huius doctrinae per revelationem habentur, et sic oportet quod credatur auctoritati eorum quibus revelatio facta est. Nec hoc derogat dignitati huius doctrinae, nam licet locus ab auctoritate, quae fundatur super ratione humana, sit infirmissimus; locus tamen ab auctoritate, quae fundatur super revelatione divina, est efficacissimus. Utitur tamen sacra doctrina etiam ratione humana, non quidem ad probandum fidem, quia per hoc tolleretur meritum fidei; sed ad manifestandum aliqua alia quae traduntur in hac doctrina. Cum enim *gratia non tollat naturam, sed perficiat,* oportet quod naturalis ratio subserviat fidei; sicut et naturalis inclinatio voluntatis obsequitur caritati. Unde et apostolus dicit, II ad Cor. X, *in captivitatem redigentes omnem intellectum in obsequium Christi."*

ST I, q. 2, a. 2, ad 1: "Ad primum ergo dicendum quod Deum esse, et alia huiusmodi quae per rationem naturalem nota possunt esse de Deo, ut dicitur Rom. I, non sunt articuli fidei, sed praeambula ad articulos, sic enim fides praesupponit cognitionem naturalem, sicut gratia naturam, et ut perfectio perfectibile. Nihil tamen prohibet illud quod secundum se demonstrabile est et scibile, ab aliquo accipi ut credibile, qui demonstrationem non capit."

12. Erich Przywara, *Schriften,* vol. 3: *Analogia Entis. Metaphysik; Ur-struktur und All-Rhythmus* (Einsiedeln: Johannes Verlag, 1962), pp. 82ff.; cf. p. 75ff.

Pay

Rather than historically analyzing the axiom or systematically discussing the nouns it contains, Przywara varies and interprets the verbs *(non destruit, supponit, perficere, excedere)* in often suggestive ways. But especially in his unique sense of the close unity between the two forms of thought (theology is the "form-primacy" for philosophy), Przywara begins to part company with the thought — though not yet the *termini* — of Thomas Aquinas. Philosophy and theology are equally in danger of losing the cogency proper to each. It is to this exaggerated proximity of philosophy and theology that Richard Schaeffler ascribes the lack of an extensive philosophical reception of Przywara's thought; its interpretation of the axiom had left philosophy too little autonomy.[13] Hans Urs von Balthasar was certainly right in associating Przywara with Maurice Blondel and Joseph Maréchal in their common concern for asserting a dynamism from below.[14] Unlike Blondel or Thomas, however, Przywara describes the upward dynamic from below as oblivious to its own essential finitude until it is taught this from above. Far from thematizing the self-critical experience of philosophers from Pythagoras and Aristotle to Kant and Nietzsche, Przywara's philosophy finds its fulfillment and its end in theology, from where alone it learns of its limitations and the need for its replacement by the "One Metaphysics."

> Theology is for the One Metaphysics *entelecheia,* its ultimate life-giving form, inasmuch as it also appears to be the *sterēsis* of philosophical thought, i.e., its being broken open and emptied: life in death. Indeed, as Thomas says *(De ver.,* q. 14, a. 10, ad 9), the theological stands to the philosophical in the relationship of the "excedere," breaking it open, by being

13. Richard Schaeffler, *Die Wechselbeziehungen zwischen Philosophie und katholischer Theologie* (Darmstadt: Wissenschaftliche Buchgesellschaft, 1980), pp. 42-59.

14. Hans Urs von Balthasar, "Erich Przywara," in Leo Zimny, *Erich Przywara. Sein Schriftum, 1912-1962* (Einsiedeln: Johannes Verlag, 1963), pp. 13ff. Cf. Erich Przywara, *Gottgeheimnis der Welt* (Munich: Theatiner-Verlag, 1923; reprinted in *Schriften,* vol. 2: *Religionsphilosophische Schriften* [Einsiedeln: Johannes Verlag, 1962]), p. 136: "Every complete look at the world includes its God-mystery as well, even if quite unconsciously. There is no need for a new 'deduction' from the world to God, the 'deducing' of the 'analogia entis,' in order to also know God consciously. Knowledge of the world and knowledge of God intersect each other in a mysterious way. Thus every philosophy carries with it, even if only in its own hidden foundation, its sense of God. The God-mystery is the mystery of its mysteries." For the development of analogy in Przywara's early works, cf. also Rudolf Stertenbrink, *Ein Weg zum Denken. Die "analogia entis" bei Erich Przywara* (Salzburg: Pustet, 1971). For Balthasar's reservations in 1962 about republishing Przywara's work, cf. Manfred Lochbrunner, *Hans Urs von Balthasar und seine Philosophenfreunde. Fünf Doppelporträts* (Würzburg: Echter, 2005), pp. 168ff.

beyond it and leaving it behind emptied. For the same reason, theology perfects philosophy, thoroughly brings it to an end and completion.[15]

The tension and rhythm of the polarities in-and-above, which Przywara drew upon to explicate so forcefully the *Spiritual Exercises* of St. Ignatius and the ideal of the Society of Jesus to see God as "in and above" every conflict,[16] are associated here with a more universal existential, though one discovered fully only in the duality of philosophy and theology. Only in this duality do the mottos "Ad maiorem gloriam Dei" and "Deus semper maior" complement one another, and it is here that the similarity-in-ever-greater-dissimilarity of Lateran IV's understanding of analogy first finds its full systematic expression.

Though perhaps not the most likely witness to the possibilities of a *theologia crucis,* Karl Rahner understood well the original intention of his teacher, of whom he writes:

> Through him "analogia entis" advanced from being a little esoteric scholastic distinction to being the basic structure of what is "Catholic." Arguably more than all the other Catholic thinkers of his time, Przywara was the one who brought the Reformation's radical pathos of the *theologia crucis* into Catholic thought — without ceasing to be Catholic.[17]

Przywara's peculiar interpretation of the axiom mitigated against his programmatic intention to elaborate the meaning of *analogia entis* as a locus of a Catholic *theologia crucis.* This became clear already in Przywara's own

15. Przywara, *Analogia Entis,* p. 83.

16. Cf. Erich Przywara, *Deus semper maior. Theologie der Exerzitien* (Vienna: Herold, 1964). Among the many discussions of the more ascetic, less mystical interpretation of the *Exercises* by Przywara (God less in than above our history), cf. James V. Zeitz, *Spirituality and analogia entis according to Erich Przywara, S.J.: Metaphysics and Religious Experience, the Ignatian Exercises, the Balance in Rhythm in "Similarity" and "Greater Dissimilarity" according to Lateran IV* (Washington, D.C.: University Press of America, 1982). As legitimate as it is in principle to reflect upon the mutual linkage between spirituality and systematics, especially for a thinker like Przywara, there is the danger that institutional zeal can begin to blur critical reflection (pace Klaus-Peter Fischer and Peter Eicher); cf. Peter Lüning, *Der Mensch im Angesicht des Gekreuzigten. Untersuchungen zum Kreuzesverständnis von Erich Przywara, Karl Rahner, Jon Sobrino und Hans Urs von Balthasar* (Münster: Aschendorff, 2007). The author sees all four of his writers, including Karl Rahner, as distinct but genuine variations on a primarily kenotic Christology in the Ignatian tradition.

17. Karl Rahner, "Laudatio auf Ernst Przywara," in *Gnade als Freiheit. Kleine theologische Beiträge* (Freiburg: Herder, 1968), p. 270.

further development. In 1942, in the midst of World War II, the darkness of which Przywara felt intensely, and thus ten years after his monumental monograph, Przywara qualifies the *analogia entis* for the sake of a more robust *theologia crucis*. In his essay "The Principle 'Gratia non destruit, sed supponit et perficit naturam': A History of Ideas Interpretation," published in *Scholastik,* he deepens suggestively the sense of the *non destruit,*[18] but clearly excludes Thomas Aquinas from those who leave open a staurological interpretation of the axiom. Thomas would follow a too heavily Hellenistic and harmonistic, allegedly too little an Augustinian, crucifixional sense of the axiom.[19] Not yet the axiom itself, but certainly the Thomistic interpretation of it and the sense of *analogia entis* it had explicated were dismissed. Przywara understood this as ecumenical convergence: "In this sense the Reformation was right to oppose the Reformational *theologia crucis* to a *theologia gloriae,* to stress the *status crucis* against an inadmissible, unjustified anticipation of the *status gloriae.*"[20] Not without caricatures, but in essence accurately, Bernard Gertz summed up Przywara's new direction:

> The structure of the essay of 1942 makes clear why just a few years previously Przywara, in his commentary on the *Exercises,* had employed the unusual triad "nature — supernature — salvation." It is the grand attempt to insert the newly discovered biblical theology into the neo-scholastic scheme nature — supernature. In point of fact, however, the former breaks open the latter. The schema will cease to play a role in Przywara's later writings. In this sense the essay of 1942 marks a decisive turn for Przywara. Perhaps one can say that he senses the deepest mystery of Thomas; but at the same time, he takes his leave of him. Now, if not earlier, it is for the West not the hour to be looking up to transfiguration, but it is the hour of the experience of the cross. Thomas passes leadership off to Elias. The shibboleth now is not Ordo, but Fire. "God's overflowing love, through which he shines with storming cruelty, takes on the appearance of that cruelty named humanity." All that remains of Thomas is the prayer of Carmel in the night: *Adoro te devote, latens Deitas.*[21]

18. Erich Pryzwara, "Der Grundsatz. Eine ideengeschichtliche Interpretation," in *Scholastik* 17 (1942): 178-86, esp. 181ff.

19. For earlier suggestions of this turn, cf. Julio Terán-Dutari, *Christentum und Metaphysik. Das Verhältnis beider nach der Analogielehre Erich Przywaras* (Munich: Berchmanskolleg, 1973), pp. 114, 623-41.

20. Pryzwara, "Der Grundsatz," p. 184.

21. Gertz, *Glaubenswelt als Analogie,* pp. 195ff., citing Erich Pryzwara, *Was ist Gott? Summula* (Nürnberg: Glock & Lutz, 1947; 2d ed., 1953), p. 103; cf. the notion of *analogia*

B. Gottlieb Söhngen

Two of the most prominent Catholic theologians to take a "point of departure for fruitful discussion" from the initial exchange between Przywara and Barth were Gottlieb Söhngen and Hans Urs von Balthasar. Though in some ways distinct from Przywara and one another, they followed at some length much the same basic path that Przywara had followed (and was still discovering). They embraced the discussion of analogy with the intention of ecumenical learning, in the dual sense of convergent and relational methods. They focused on the connection of analogy to *axiomata* on grace and nature: for Söhngen, the *discrimen legis et evangelii;* for Balthasar, the axiom that Przywara had placed at the center of the discussion. That axiom would remain largely uninvestigated as to its historical genesis and earlier uses; instead, its systematic possibilities were developed largely in a historical vacuum. Both sought methods to relativize the *analogia entis* in the supposed best interest of a *theologia crucis,* favoring a shift to the predominance of the *analogia fidei.* For the purposes of this paper, I will deal only with the contributions of Gottlieb Söhngen.[22]

In 1940 Karl Barth reviewed in *Kirchliche Dogmatik* II/1 the discussion of his thoughts on the dangers of a doctrine of analogy that would justify speaking of God apart from revelation. He sets a kind of counterpoint to his earlier remarks:

> It cannot yet be considered settled whether the Roman Catholic answer to our thesis of the knowability of God exclusively by his revelation truly and finally can be led back to our line of thought or rather alternatively

---

doloris in Michael Schreiter, "Zur geschichtstheologischen Ausdeutung der ignatianischen Exerzitien bei Erich Przywara und Karl Rahner," in *Zur grösseren Ehre Gottes. Ignatius von Loyola neu entdeckt für die Theologie der Gegenwart,* ed. Thomas Gertler et al., pp. 368-88 (Freiburg: Herder, 2006). This shift in Przywara's own sense of the incompatibility of the *analogia entis* and a *theologia crucis* is passed over too quickly by Eberhard Mechels, *Analogie bei Erich Przywara und Karl Barth. Das Verhältnis von Offenbarungstheologie und Metaphysik* (Neukirchen: Neukirchener Verlag, 1974).

22. The discussion of Hans Urs von Balthasar, who calls into question for the first time the opposition of *theologia crucis* and *theologia gloriae,* would look most closely at the development within his continued discussion of the axiom on grace between the two essays from the mid-1940s in *Divus Thomas* and the publication of his 1951 study on Barth, "Analogie und Dialektik. Zur Klärung der theologischen Prinzipienlehre Karl Barths," *Divus Thomas* (Fribourg) 22 (1944): 171-216; "Analogie und Natur. Zur Klärung der theologischen Prinzipienlehre Karl Barths," *Divus Thomas* (Fribourg) 23 (1945): 3-56.

to this interpretation of *analogia entis*. It must be mentioned that Gottlieb Söhngen has presented in two essays on *analogia fidei* . . . a teaching in this matter that marks a significant shift from the previous position, according to which now the knowledge of being and the *analogia entis* are subordinated to, rather than placed above, the knowledge of God's deeds and thus the *analogia fidei* in theology. . . . If *that* were the Roman Catholic teaching of *analogia entis*, then I would have to retract my earlier sentence that I hold the *analogia entis* as the "invention of the Antichrist." . . . But I am not aware that *this* teaching on the *analogia entis* is defended by anyone else in Catholic quarters or that it ever was proposed there in quite this understanding.[23]

For his part, Gottlieb Söhngen also came to identify a shift in Barth's thinking:[24]

But later, in the second edition [of *KD*], it sounds quite different: The analogy of faith has its "external basis" in an analogy of being that, strictly speaking in a Protestant understanding, should be taken as an *analogia relationis (attributionis extrinsecae?)* or rather better an *analogia operationis*, as an analogy in the order of intentional action, of the divine action in creation and salvific history.[25]

That such a sense of analogy would not yet establish the analogate formally in the creature[26] troubled Söhngen all the less, as the essays of 1934 had

23. *KD* II/1 (1940), pp. 89ff. (my translation), quoted also in the introduction to Hans Küng, "Karl Barths Lehre vom Wort Gottes als Frage an die katholische Theologie," in *Einsicht und Glaube. Festschrift G. Söhngen zum 70. Geburtstag*, ed. Joseph Ratzinger and Heinrich Fries, pp. 75-97 (Freiburg: Herder, 1962). Barth is referring to two essays in the "Quartalschrift für Kontroverstheologie": G. Söhngen, "Analogia fidei I: Gottähnlichkeit allein aus dem Glauben?" and "Analogia fidei II: Die Einheit in der Glaubenswissenschaft," *Catholica* 3 (1934): 113-36 and 176-208.

24. On Söhngen's work, cf. Josef Graf, *Gottlieb Söhngens (1892-1971) Suche nach der "Einheit in der Theologie." Ein Beitrag zum Durchbruch des heilsgeschichtlichen Denkens* (Frankfurt: Peter Lang, 1991); and Werner Böckenförde, "Das Schrifttum Gottlieb Söhngens, vollständig zusammengestellt," in Ratzinger and Fries, *Einsicht und Glaube*, pp. 479-86.

25. Gottlieb Söhngen, "Analogie," in *Handbuch theologischer Grundbegriffe*, vol. 1, ed. Heinrich Fries, pp. 49-61 (Munich: Kösel, 1962), p. 60.

26. Cf. the reflections on analogy by Wolfhart Pannenberg prior to his 1955 Habilitation, *Analogie und Offenbarung. Eine kritische Untersuchung der Geschichte des Analogiebegriffs in der Lehre von der Gotteserkenntnis* (Göttingen: Vandenhoeck & Ruprecht, 2007), esp. "Zur Bedeutung des Analogiegedankens bei Karl Barth. Eine Auseinandersetzung mit

already laid out an argument that Söhngen's later work would continue to develop for reading *analogia entis* as a product of the *analogia fidei*.[27] While the connection of Söhngen's stress on the primacy of faith in salvific history to the discussion initiated by Przywara of the axiom on grace and nature remained largely implicit in Söhngen's work,[28] he sought to further a Catholic reception of the Reformational *discrimen legis et evangelii*. His 1957 monograph *Law and Gospel: Their Analogous Unity,* which considered the theological, philosophical, and political implications of its topic, sought to steer clear of the debates that since the 1930s would continue to mark internal Protestant discussions.[29] Söhngen's attempts here to retrieve Luther's proposals for a *theologia crucis* or Geronimo Seripando's contributions to the Tridentine debates on justification underline his sympathy for the Lutheran origins of the *discrimen*. But in the end, he embraces the programmatic and affirming order "gospel and law" and the robust recovery of the *tertius usus legis* that Barth had famously proposed in his essay of the same title in 1935.[30]

Urs von Balthasar," *Theologische Literaturzeitung* 78 (1953): 17-24; and review of Hans Wagner, *Existenz, Analogie, Dialektik,* vol. 1, *Theologische Literaturzeitung* 79 (1954): 318ff.; cf. also the references of Erich Naab, *Zur Begründung der analogia entis bei Erich Przywara. Eine Erörterung* (Regensburg: Pustet, 1987), pp. 76ff.

27. Cf. Gottlieb Söhngen, "Analogia entis oder analogia fidei?" *Wissenschaft und Weisheit* 9 (1942): 91-100, reprinted in Söhngen, *Die Einheit in der Theologie* (Munich: K. Zink, 1952), pp. 235-47, and "Analogia entis in analogia fidei," in *Antwort. Karl Barth zum siebzigsten Geburtstag am 10. Mai 1956,* ed. E. Wolf, pp. 266-71 (Zurich: Evangelischer Verlag, 1956); idem, *Analogie und Metapher. Kleine Philosophie und Theologie der Sprache* (Freiburg: Alber, 1962), including the "Barthian" interpretation of being as a "sign" of God, p. 102. On Balthasar's view of the ecumenical convergence regarding the attempt by Barth to include the analogy of being within the analogy of faith, cf. Werner Löser, "Von Balthasars Karl-Barth-Buch — eine theologische Würdigung," in *Karl Barth — Hans Urs von Balthasar. Eine theologische Zwiesprache,* ed. Wolfgang W. Müller, pp. 71-96 (Zurich: TVZ, 2006), esp. pp. 79ff.

28. Cf. the essay by his student Joseph Ratzinger, "Gratia praesupponit naturam. Erwägungen über Sinn und Grenze eines scholastischen Axioms," in Ratzinger and Fries, *Einsicht und Glaube,* pp. 135-49. In this essay, closely following Söhngen's sense of a nature either fallen or healed (but not somehow both), Ratzinger sought to overcome the facile optimism of a shallow concept of nature as innocence. He would later complement these goals with others less familiar to his mentor.

29. For the inner-Protestant state of the question in the 1950s, cf. Gottlieb Söhngen, *Gesetz und Evangelium. Ihre analoge Einheit. Theologisch, philosophisch, staatsbürgerlich* (Freiburg: Alber, 1957), pp. 3-6.

30. Karl Barth, "Evangelium und Gesetz," first in *Theologische Existenz heute* 32 (1935), reprinted several times, including in *Gesetz und Evangelium. Beiträge zur gegenwärtigen theologischen Diskussion,* ed. Ernst Kinder and Klaus Haendler, pp. 1-29 (Darmstadt:

While Söhngen followed Barth as well in his reading of Anselm as a representative of a rationality built upon faith,[31] it was his introduction of the memory of Bonaventure that arguably made the greatest impression upon the Catholic imagination of a potential convergence of Catholic and Reformed thought.[32] Söhngen anticipated Przywara's suspicions that Thomas Aquinas's sense of analogy precludes a genuine appreciation of the *theologia crucis*. His call to openly shift from a Thomistic to a Bonaventurian paradigm in Catholic theology as a way to deepen the convergence not just with Reformed but with patristic theology was one that found widespread Catholic support in the years that would follow.

At first sight, the degree of sympathy for the Thomist reading on the Protestant side of the discussion might be surprising. Referring to Catholic attempts to inscribe *analogia entis* into the more fundamental *analogia fidei*, Hermann Diem, who had done much to reconcile Lutheran and Reformed positions, wrote:

> And yet for us, all this means that Bonaventure's "and" is no less fatal than that of a less "broken" *analogia entis*. One might well recall here that it was precisely the Franciscan line of Augustinianism — and not its Thomistic line — that afterward flowed into the Pelagianism of a nominalist-Jesuit doctrine of grace. Was that just by accident, or did it not have as its reason that there was a more open *theologia gloriae* promoted here than in Thomism and so had to come to a steeper fall?[33]

Wissenschaftlichen Buchgesellschaft, 1986); Gottlieb Söhngen, *Gesetz und Evangelium*, pp. 102ff.; as well as Söhngen's 1960 lecture "Gesetz und Evangelium," with its reaffirmation of the "analogia relationis" of salvific history as the basis of our access to God, in *Gesetz und Evangelium*, pp. 324-55. Cf. also Söhngen, "Natürliche Theologie und Heilsgeschichte. Antwort an Emil Brunner," *Catholica* 4 (1935): 97-114.

31. Cf. Söhngen, *Die Einheit in der Theologie*, pp. 24-35.

32. Cf. Gottlieb Söhngen, "Bonaventura als Klassiker der Analogia fidei," *Wissenschaft und Weisheit* 2 (1935): 97-111.

33. Hermann Diem, "Analogia fidei gegen analogia entis. Ein Beitrag zur Kontroverstheologie," in *Evangelische Theologie* 3 (1936): 171. Similarly favorable readings of the Thomistic sense of the axiom were developed by Ulrich Kühn, *Natur und Gnade. Untersuchungen zur deutschen katholischen Theologie der Gegenwart* (Berlin: Lutherisches Verlagshaus, 1961); idem, *Via caritatis. Theologie des Gesetzes bei Thomas von Aquin* (Göttingen: Vandenhoeck & Ruprecht, 1965); and Gerhard Ebeling, "Der hermeneutische Ort der Gotteslehre bei Petrus Lombardus und Thomas Aquinas," *Zeitschrift für Theologie und Kirche* 61 (1964): 283-326.

III. The Historical Roots of the Axiom on Grace and Nature: Renegotiating the Average Preunderstanding of the Axiom behind Analogy

The importance of Przywara's early challenges to, and Söhngen's intended rapprochement with, the thought of Karl Barth takes on all the more significance for the shape of postconciliar Roman Catholic theology if one recalls the lines that lead from Przywara's early work on the *analogia entis* and from Söhngen's primacy of the analogy of faith to the later system of Karl Rahner and the program of Hans Urs von Balthasar, respectively. As suggestive as Diem's implication is of a more "broken" (because more Thomistic) reading of analogy, there is a need to look first for a more historical account of the origins of the axiom on grace and nature.

The Neoplatonic provenance of the axiom has been largely overlooked. As studies by J. B. Beumer,[34] Bernard Stoeckle,[35] and (with reservations) Michael J. Marmann[36] have shown, we first meet the fully explicit theological axiom in the thirteenth century in the context of Bonaventure's criticism of it as a principle of Dionysian thought. While Söhngen did not concern himself with the axiom itself, this fact adds importance to his suggestion that we look to Bonaventure for a Catholic alternative to theologies stemming from a prior commitment to the *analogia entis*. The commentary by Bonaventure written around 1250 on the second book of Peter Lombard's *Sentences* takes up the question as to whether humans, like angels, are ranked from their start into different orders of hierarchical preference. A main source for speaking of angelic orders had been, along with Gregory the Great, Dionysius's work *On the Celestial Hierarchies*. Bonaventure envisions the argument that, if humans are graced in different degrees, which he grants, then this might seem to imply that they are not equal by nature either but, rather, are by a diversity of natural talents already of such distinct hierarchical orders as to predetermine the differences in graced existence: notions he strongly rejects. The anticipated objection would run as follows: This angelic kind of hierarchical order also

---

34. J. B. Beumer, "Gratia supponit naturam. Zur Geschichte eines theologischen Prinzips," *Gregorianum* 20 (1930): 381-406 and 535-52, esp. 390ff.

35. Bernhard Stoeckle, *Gratia supponit naturam. Geschichte und Analyse eines theologischen Axioms* (Rome: Orbis Catholicus, 1962).

36. Michael J. Marmann, "Praeambula ad gratiam. Ideengeschichtliche Untersuchung über die Entstehung des Axioms *gratia praesupponit naturam*" (PhD diss., University of Regensburg, 1974); cf. also Johann Auer, *Das Evangelium der Gnade,* 2d ed. (Regensburg: Pustet, 1980), pp. 189ff.

belongs to human beings by grace. But since *grace presupposes nature,* so, too, must a hierarchical order of grace presuppose a hierarchical order of nature; for, if there were not a hierarchical order of nature, there would be no such order of grace. The Minorite Bonaventure first tells us what his existential stake in the question is:

> In human beings, however, even when we can determine certain advantages in matters of nature as well as in those of grace, nevertheless the two often fail to correspond to one another. Where nature is better, grace is often less; and who today is rightly called the lesser *(minor)* might well be the greater tomorrow.[37]

Bonaventure then supplies us with a direct answer to the objection:

> That argument is not convincing which claims that, if there be no hierarchical order in nature, there could be no hierarchical order in grace. For it is not at all necessary that grace match *(adaequare)* nature, nor is it necessary that the order of grace presuppose *(praesupponere)* any order in nature, although *grace presupposes nature* in the sense that an accident presupposes a subject. And because our grace corresponds to the grace of the angels, even though our nature is not of the same species as their nature, thus, if by this (the correspondence in grace) there be in us, too, a distinction of (graced) orders, then this (alone) is to be understood as corresponding to the angelic orders.[38]

Bonaventure seems less likely to be polemicizing here against Alexander of Hales's assertion of a merely temporal precedence of nature to grace[39] than to be recalling the widespread critique of the Dominicans rallying around their Parisian *confrater,* Stephanus de Varnesia (Etienne de Vernizy/ de Venizy), who in 1241 and perhaps again in 1244,[40] together with other proponents or defenders ("et assertores et defensores" of ten theses),[41] was cen-

---

37. *In II Sent.,* d. 9, q. 1, a. 9, c. (ed. Quaracchi 1885, II 257 A).

38. Ibid., obj. 2 and ad 2 (256ff.).

39. Cf. Stoeckle, *Gratia supponit naturam,* p. 105ff.

40. On the questions of the date(s) raised by Victorin Doucet and others, cf. Jacques-Guy Bougerol, "A propos des condamnations parisiennes de 1241 et 1244," *Archivum franciscanum historicum* 80 (1987): 462-66.

41. For the possibility that these might have included Hugh of St. Cher, cf. Henri Dondaine, "Hugues de S. Cher et la condamnation de 1241," *Revue des sciences philosophiques et théologiques* 33 (1949): 170-74.

sured first by the theology faculty and the chancellor of the university (Odo of Chateauroux), then more directly and sternly by the bishop of Paris (William of Auvergne).[42] The censure may well be viewed together with a wider reaction around 1241 against the new Aristotelian influence felt at the university, since several of the theses suggest a tendency to reduce salvific-historical theology to philosophical-sapiential theology: a trend that was destined to be criticized again in the second wave of anti-Aristotelian reaction, now inspired and not just followed by Bonaventure, beginning in the late 1260s.

Quite contrary to custom and the genre of a Sentence commentary, Bonaventure cites all ten censured theses.[43] The ninth thesis suggests an origin more immediately Dionysian than Aristotelian and reminiscent of the position that Bonaventure is now criticizing less than ten years after the censure: ". . . that those, whose natural gifts are better, will by necessity also have more of grace and glory."[44] The critics of the 1240s spell out their contradictory belief, leaving open the possibility of a more individualized, more salvifically historical, and yet also more arbitrary- (or mythological-) looking form of divine providence than fits well into a sapiential theology: "We reprove this error, because we firmly believe that God will give grace and glory to each one according to what He has elected and preordained."[45] In his own commentary, Bonaventure weaves into his problematization of the

---

42. Cf. William J. Courtenay, "Dominicans and Suspect Opinion in the Thirteenth Century: The Cases of Stephen of Venizy, Peter of Tarentaise, and the Articles of 1270 and 1271," *Vivarium* 32, no. 2 (1994): 186-95; and Juergen Mietke, "Papst, Ortsbischof und Universität in den Pariser Theologenprozessen des 13. Jahrhunderts," in *Die Auseinandersetzungen an der Pariser Universität im XIII. Jahrhundert,* ed. Albert Zimmermann, pp. 52-94 (Berlin: de Gruyter, 1976), esp. pp. 63-66.

43. Among the condemned theses were positions of a negative but also rationalist theology, such as that the divine essence necessarily cannot be given in beatific vision to any created mind (thesis 1), that there are eternal truths apart from those anchored personally in the Godhead (thesis 7), that the single essential dimension of the Godhead should be given greater weight than the trinitarian persons (reflected in theses 2 and 3), that the beginning of creation should not be considered temporally (thesis 8), and that the first angelic and human sins were inevitable (thesis 10).

44. "*Nonus,* quod qui habet meliora naturalia, de necessitate plus habebit de gratia et gloria" (*Collection L'univers de la philosophie* I, no. 128, pp. 170-72, here 171); cf. Bonaventura: "Cum enim non oporteat gratiam adaequari naturae, non oportet ordinem gratiae praesupponere ordinem in natura" (*Collection L'univers de la philosophie* II 237B).

45. "Hunc errorem reprobamus, firmiter enim credimus, quod Deus secundum quod preelegit et preordinavit, dabit unicuique gratiam et gloriam" (*Collection L'univers de la philosophie* II 237B).

Dionysian notion of hierarchy the axiom *gratia praesupponit naturam.* Here, as in the slightly later formulations that will continue with the words "et non destruit eam," the reference seems to echo Dionysius's *De divinis nominibus* even more than his work *On the Celestial Hierarchies.*

The Dominican general chapter of 1243 had asked the members of the order to respect the decision of 1241. Stephen himself seems to have complied, since he was allowed to incept and serve as a master in Paris, and since he is mentioned by name in few of the surviving manuscripts.[46] But the issue apparently resurfaced in 1256, just as Thomas was in Paris finishing his commentary on the *Sentences.* The general chapter of the Dominicans meeting that year at Paris and the provincial chapter of the provence felt the need to reiterate the appeal for the brethren to comply with the earlier decision.[47] Around 1279 one of Bonaventure's prize students, William de la Mare, introduces the issue in the *correctories* dispute, claiming that Thomas Aquinas flagrantly maintains what was condemned as the ninth thesis in 1241.[48]

Dionysius's claim falls near the end of his long, internal treatise "Unde malum" in book 4, where he concludes his defense of divine providence's "coexistence" (so to speak) with — and toleration of — voluntary human failings. He rejects explicitly the "empty-headed" opinion that providence, should it exist, would have to eliminate all evils, including those caused by human liberty, thus forcing rational creatures to always make the right choices. Dionysius counters that *it does not belong to providence to destroy nature, but rather to preserve the nature of each;* in this sense, to "save" it. John Sarracenus's translation of Dionysius's free-will defense differs little at this point from Eriugena's or Hilduin's: "Etenim corrumpere naturam non providentiae. Unde, sicut providentia uniuscujusque naturae est salvativa." With but very minor revisions, Robert Grosseteste's translation will also follow the lead of his predecessors here, as indeed in most places.[49]

In the context of his argument, Dionysius applies his principle that providence is *salvativa naturae (physeōs sōstikē)* — of that nature which is "self-moved" *(to autokinēton),* an expression used by Proclus as a technical term for free human choice, referring both to the autonomous source of its own activity (*self*-moved) and to the source of its own inconstancy and its all-too-variable virtuosity (self-*moved*). What is "self-moved" takes its place

46. Cf. Courtenay, "Dominicans and Suspect Opinion in the Thirteenth Century."

47. Ibid., p. 188.

48. Cf. the remarks by William in P. Glorieux's edition of Richard Knapwell's *Le Correctorium corruptorii "Quare"* (Kain: Saulchoir, 1927), art. 21, pp. 91-95.

49. Cf. *Dionysiaca* I, ed. Philipp Chavallier (Paris: Desclée de Brouwer, 1937), p. 312.

in the hierarchy of beings between unmoved movers, with all their constancy and reliability, on the one hand, and, on the other, what is so inconstant as to be moved by others and only by others. Providence rightly provides even for what is between these two groups, preserving the *per se mobilia* as *per se mobilia*, that is, conserving their tendency toward inconstancy and occasional moral failure. To force them to constant virtue would be to destroy them as *per se mobilia.*

Only in 1895 did Josef Stiglmayr and Hugo Koch demonstrate the general dependence of the Pseudo-Areopagite upon Proclus[50] by comparing the Dionysian treatise "Unde malum" (in book 4 of *De divinis nominibus*) with Proclus's opusculum *De malorum subsistentia.* Unfortunately, Koch concludes his analysis with 4.32, ending just before the beginning of the question as to how there could be evil at all, if providence exists. Stiglmayr proceeds only one line further, breaking off before reaching the sentence that will later prove to be so suggestive: *that providence does not destroy nature but saves it.* The texts of Proclus paraphrased here by Dionysius seem to include passages from another opusculum, the sixth aporia of Proclus's *De decem dubitationibus circa providentiam.* The free-will defense of providence and the vocabulary reconstructed by Helmut Boese for the sixth aporia suggest its close reading by Dionysius: Providence *(pronoia)* saves *(sōtzousan)* nature (here *to genomenon,* not *tēn physin*), preserves especially the free choice of human beings as self-movement *(autokinēsis),* including its natural tendency to be inconstant in virtue.[51] "We are not saying that providence, which first brought freedom of choice into the whole of things, now rules in order to do away with this freedom, but rather to save and preserve it."[52] It is this statement by Proclus in its implicit citation by Dionysius that will be transformed into a key axiom about grace.

Even after the shift in perspective, moving from providence preserving a stable world order to grace's transforming history, Thomas's use of the axiom remained attentive to the implications of finitude that had been implied by the Proclan and Dionysian prehistory of the axiom. The nature that is not destroyed by grace, far from being the self-glorifying nature that the critics of analogy feared, was the nature that would experience its own failings. In

---

50. Cf. Josef Stiglmayr, "Der Neuplatoniker Proclus als Vorlage des sogenannten Dionysius Areopagita in der Lehre vom Übel," *Historisches Jahrbuch* 16 (1895): 253-73 and 721-80; and Hugo Koch, "Proklus als Quelle des Pseudo-Dionysius Areopagita in der Lehre vom Bösen," *Philologus* 54 (1895): 438-54.

51. Cf. esp. no. 39, 60-63.

52. Ibid.

numerous cases, Thomas will sum up "nature" by the principle that what can fail in principle will fail at some point in fact. Some examples of Thomas's use of the Dionysian axiom or phrases drawn from it that grace preserves rather than destroys nature:

1. *In I Sent.*, d. 39, q. 2, a. 2, that providence must be not just of the necessary, but of chance and the fallible, whose failing providence does not impede.

2. *In I Sent.*, d. 46, q. 1, a. 4, whether God want evils to occur, Thomas affirms only that he wants the world to contain the contingent and fallible, even if failings make no direct contribution to the good.[53]

3. *In II Sent.*, d. 23, q. 1, a. 1, whether God could bestow complete impeccability, that God preserves the defectibility in freedom of choice.

4. *In II Sent.*, d. 34, q. 1, a. 1, on whether anything is in fact evil, Thomas distinguishes that which God unconditionally wants from what he merely tolerates, though even that is sometimes just to preserve fallible goods in their fallible goodness.

5. *In IV Sent.*, d. 49, q. 2, a. 3, that we will not comprehend God *in patria*, like *ST* II-II, q. 19, a. 11, ad 3, that we will have *timor filialis in patria*, including a sense of God as other and the source of a gratuitous gift, preserving finitude even in the final fullness of grace.

6. *De ver.*, q. 5, a. 3, that God's providence extends to what is corruptible, not preventing its eventual corruption.

7. *De ver.*, q. 5, a. 4, with direct reference to Dionysius, that, while goods such as the martyr's patience or the sinner's contrition are not produced by the evils of cruelty or sin, it nevertheless belongs to grace not to prevent these evils but to turn them to good.

8. *SCG* 3.71-72, that evil or even contingency should not be excluded a priori from things, lest God destroy the goods of fallible and contingent natures.

9. *In De div. nom.*, on 4.33 and 8.7, obviously with direct reference to Dionysius, and similarly in *ST* I, q. 22, a. 4, that it is good that God preserve fallible freedom of choice, even though sin makes no direct contribution to the good.

10. *ST* I, q. 62, a. 7, that angels are made blessed by a grace that still pre-

---

53. Cf. in the preceding article Thomas's similar arguments, though without reference to the axiom, *In I Sent.*, d. 46, q. 1, a. 3: whether evil, since it does not directly enhance the good, is part of the world's perfection.

serves their natural knowledge and will, destroying only those imperfections that prevent the good of grace.

11. *ST* II-II, q. 165, a. 1, that God allows temptation by the devil, though the devil makes no direct contribution to our beatitude.

12. *Comp. theo.* 1.142, that it does not detract from God's grace to allow evils, since it belongs to his goodness to include the fallible and not to prevent in principle their failings.

These examples should suffice for the present to place in question the "preunderstanding" of the Thomistic axiom as an assertion of self-sufficiency. While the experience of fallibility need not come first with grace itself, grace does not destroy but deepens that experience. Grace then leads to a good that is inaccessible to nature those evils that our nature endures or even causes. Grace deepens the natural awareness that we are anything but self-sufficient.

IV. Thomism and Ecumenical Learning

Even in the best of cases, analogy in the Thomistic understanding involves just such an experience of our human finitude in the abiding dialectic (in Bruce McCormack's terms, a complementary, not a supplemental, dialectic)[54] between the signification of perfections such as, say, *ens, unum, bonum, verum,* whose full meaning must be given in God, and the woefully inadequate *modus significandi,* by which we necessarily grasp them at a level that is anything but divine.[55] In this sense, analogy remains dialectical, even under grace. The grace of revelation does not replace the dialectic of analogy with new univocity. Reminding us of the mysteriousness of God, analogy also reminds us of the mysteriousness of the world, whose final meaning could become evident only in him — evidence that is not yet a given.

Thomas seems to have feared less a natural theology aware of these limitations than a revealed theology — or a philosophy derived from it — that would claim to know too much. The contrast with Bonaventure suggested by Söhngen is indeed of help here. The best-documented dispute by

54. McCormack, *Theologische Dialektik und kritischer Realismus,* p. 154.
55. Cf., e.g., Thomas Aquinas, *ST* I, q. 13, a. 4, c.; and Gregory P. Rocca, *Speaking the Incomprehensible God: Thomas Aquinas on the Interplay of Positive and Negative Theology* (Washington, D.C.: Catholic University of America Press, 2004).

Thomas with Bonaventure, his school, and the ecclesial censures of their day is perhaps the question of whether at least the believer can come to know philosophically that the visible universe had a beginning.[56] Thomas insisted that the revelation of creation does not empower us to reach a philosophical answer to this question, which as philosophical must remain open. Thomas was thus not the most robust example of "strong reason" in his own day,[57] nor without a correspondence to what in the future would come to be known as the antinomies of reason.[58] For Thomas those antinomies included the beginning of the world and, though not the God of the world, the God of grace.

Despite all the fruitful discussion of analogy that Roman Catholic theology has been privileged to share, it has in the end arguably lost much of its facility to distinguish grace and nature. The twin futures anticipated by the early Przywara and by Söhngen would, for reasons in many ways deeply opposed to one another, agree on relativizing the *discrimen gratiae et naturae,* which is at once also the *discrimen fidei et experientiae.* Hermann Diem's hunch was not far from the mark. The Thomistic sense of "broken" analogy and the axiom on grace associated with it suggest a theology of the cross that is capable of believing in the midst of what has been called the "experience of inexperience."[59] In Thomas's understanding, faith itself remains restless. Faith, though the fruit of grace, can never put behind itself the question "Wie kriege ich einen gnädigen Gott?"

56. Cf. Richard C. Dales, *Medieval Discussions of the Eternity of the World* (Leiden: Brill, 1990); J. M. B. Wissink, ed., *The Eternity of the World in the Thought of Thomas Aquinas and His Contemporaries* (Leiden: Brill, 1990); Richard C. Dales und Omar Argerami, eds., *Medieval Latin Texts on the Eternity of the World* (Leiden: Brill, 1991); and Rolf Schönberger's introduction "Der Disput über die Ewigkeit der Welt," in *Über die Ewigkeit der Welt. Bonaventura, Thomas von Aquin, Boethius von Dacien,* ed. Peter Nickl (Frankfurt: Klostermann, 2000).

57. Cf. Richard Schenk, "Option für den Thomismus in der Enzyklika?" in *Die Vernunft des Glaubens und der Glaube der Vernunft. Die Enzyklika Fides et Ratio in der Debatte zwischen Philosophie und Theologie,* ed. P. Koslowski and A. M. Hauk, pp. 59-81 (Munich: W. Fink, 2007).

58. Cf. Anton Antweiler, *Die Anfangslosigkeit der Welt nach Thomas von Aquin und Kant* (Trier: Paulinus, 1961).

59. Joseph Ratzinger, "Glaube und Erfahrung," in *Theologische Prinzipienlehre. Bausteine zur Fundamentaltheologie* (Munich: Wewel, 1982), pp. 359-71, esp. 367; and Leo Scheffczyk, "Die Frage nach der 'Erfahrung' als theologischem Verifikationsprinzip," in *Dienst der Vermittlung,* ed. Wilhelm Ernst, pp. 353-73 (Leipzig: Benno, 1977).

CHAPTER 5

Hans Urs von Balthasar, Erich Przywara's *Analogia Entis,* and the Problem of a Catholic *Denkform*

Peter Casarella

I. Introduction

The aim of this essay is quite modest. I will survey a few selected texts and contexts in which Hans Urs von Balthasar engages the work of Erich Przywara. I am interested in showing how Balthasar interprets Przywara and how that interpretation sheds light on Balthasar's own development as a thinker.

I have decided to highlight the question of a Catholic *Denkform* in order to make two points. First, Balthasar came to the study of theology from *Germanistik,* but he never abandoned the methods or thought patterns of his own area of academic expertise. Much of this paper will focus on the book Balthasar wrote on Karl Barth, which many consider his most lasting achievement as an academic theologian. But even in this work we can see Balthasar testing the limits of the genre by alluding to questions of theological style.

My second reason for introducing some elements of a formal analysis into the discussion concerns the purpose of the book on Barth and the general approach adopted by Balthasar as an author of theological works. Balthasar was well aware of a debate that was raging about the *analogia entis* and recounts the positions of Karl Barth, Przywara, Gottlieb Söhngen, and others. By introducing questions of style, Balthasar, I will argue, is also trying to shift the terms of the debate. His book on Barth was intended as an experiment in ecumenical theology, and the general approach in this book and in the many other writings he produced in this period of his life is not one that is intended to prolong or exacerbate the polemics of the academy. Balthasar's method is one of Catholic integration. I am not saying that Balthasar as a rule avoided polemics or even that the book on Barth is free of polemics. Balthasar as a rule submerges his polemical instincts into the text. They are certainly there, but you have to read between the lines in order to see them. My goal in this essay is simply to highlight an important irenic strand in the author's own self-description that may even shed some light upon our common deliberations about Przywara's *analogia entis.*

II. On Theological Styles

The book *Karl Barth. Darstellung und Deutung seiner Theologie* (1951; 2d ed., 1961) is not just about Karl Barth.[1] One-third of its pages are dedicated to the comparison of "the Catholic form of thought" to that of Barth. Balthasar's use of the terms "thinking" *(Denken)* and "form of thought" *(Denkform)* rather than "theology" could be construed as nothing more than the pretense of a literary scholar who had crossed the border into dogmatic theology without wanting to leave behind all traces of his original home in literary studies. However, considerations of theological styles dominate the book, especially the part that considers the need to develop a Catholic response to the Barthian style of thinking. In fact, Balthasar opens his part 3 with the observation: "There is not only a history of styles of beauty; there is also one for the true."[2] This comment is quite typical of Balthasar's early writings on philosophy and literature, a vast corpus that has now been surveyed in synoptic fashion by Aidan Nichols.[3] Balthasar thus approaches the question of the comparison of Barth and Catholic theology through the lens of a *Stilgeschichte des Wahren.* He does not thereby reduce theological accomplishments to hollow rhetorical performances or postmodern gestures. Balthasar is focused on theological styles, which basically means that he is taking into consideration both the form and the content of what is being proposed.

The comparative section of the book highlights the disparity between

1. All internal citations are from Hans Urs von Balthasar, *Karl Barth. Darstellung und Deutung seiner Theologie* (Einsiedeln: Johannes Verlag, 1976).

2. Ibid., p. 263.

3. Aidan Nichols, *Scattering the Seed: A Guide through Balthasar's Early Writings on Philosophy and the Arts* (Washington, D.C.: Catholic University of America Press, 2006).

Peter Casarella

the Barthian style and a Catholic style.[4] Balthasar does not juxtapose his interpretation of Barth as an individual theologian with that of the entire Catholic style of thought. Moreover, he notes, Barth's interpretation of the Catholic tradition is in many ways at odds with the angle on Catholicism developed by other Protestant theologians such as Emil Brunner or Rudolf Bultmann. Balthasar assumes that what Barth takes to be the specific difference between Protestantism and Catholicism is Barth's private theological opinion.

This broadening of perspective on the diversity of Protestant authors also has its repercussions with respect to the Catholic position. Balthasar does not assume that the Catholic style is monolithic. He asserts that the Catholic style of thinking cannot be based upon a "closed metaphysics."[5] The church as such, Balthasar states, possesses no such thing:

> [The church] tries in obedience to Christ to be what he called her to be: the custodian of his graces and the evangelist of his works and words. With the task of being an evangelist come healing, preaching, and pastoral responsibilities [*weiden*]. If she occasionally also has to take a position with respect to principles of thought, she will mainly do so where some way of thinking has circumscribed the broad compass of its proclamation and where she can knock an obstacle out of the way for the sake of achieving breadth.[6]

To be sure, Balthasar is not discounting metaphysics, but this particular endorsement of metaphysics is modest. The relationship between the obedience of the church to Christ and the task of metaphysics is by itself more fluid than a purely rationalist apologetics would permit. The church must concentrate on the breadth of what Christ accomplished in word and deed. Balthasar denies that the infinite mystery of God's revelation can be distilled into "an essence of Catholicism."[7] A Catholic form of thought remains open to a breadth that cannot be circumscribed. The Catholic form of thought is none other than the form of thinking that preserves this Catholic form of openness.

What form of Catholic thinking does Balthasar adopt as his own in the book on Barth? The thesis of this essay is that Balthasar does *not* adopt the

---

4. Balthasar, *Karl Barth. Darstellung und Deutung seiner Theologie*, pp. 266-67.
5. Ibid., p. 266.
6. Ibid. (my translation).
7. Ibid., p. 263.

194

style of thinking of Erich Przywara in formulating his Catholic response to Barth. His goal, rather, is to integrate elements of Barth's theology into a new Catholic synthesis. Let me be as precise as possible about what I mean. First, I am not saying that Balthasar is a crypto-Barthian, since the debt to Przywara and other Catholic thinkers who opposed Barth's rejection of the *analogia entis* is proudly acknowledged in part 3. Second, I am not saying that Balthasar's position in part 3 is something like a *via media* between Barthian theology and Przywara's *analogia entis.* Balthasar's style never broaches that of trying to mediate between two extreme positions, even though it is apparent that (like Barth himself) he inherited a penchant (sometimes Kierkegaardian and sometimes Hegelian) for overcoming problems in terms of sublating dual preconceptions expressed in a dialectical form.

Balthasar's method is that of Catholic integration. In the last section of the paper, I will explain what Balthasar meant by integration and how the integration of Barth into his thought must be situated in the context of the other works written by Balthasar in this period.

III. *Analogia Entis:* A Solution to the Problem of a Catholic *Denkform?*

Balthasar states very clearly that what Barth called "the great deception [*die große Truglehre*] of the *analogia entis*" *cannot* be taken to be "the fundamental schema behind Catholic thinking and teaching."[8] According to Balthasar, Barth misinterpreted the *analogia entis.* Balthasar calls Barth's version of the *analogia entis* an ogre (*Schreckgespenst*) compared to what Przywara himself taught.[9] But Balthasar is also making a larger point. Balthasar is also denying that Przywara's principle can be taken as the final solution to the Catholic way of thought.[10] In other words, Balthasar rises to the defense of Przywara in order to demonstrate the one-sidedness of Barth's interpretation of the Jesuit philosopher. But Balthasar ultimately does not defend the *analogia entis* in exactly the same way that Przywara did.

Balthasar notes that the book *Analogia Entis* (1932) concludes the one period of Przywara's thought. Przywara's later thought, including the 1940

8. Ibid., p. 266, citing Karl Barth, *Die Kirchliche Dogmatik,* II/1, 9th ed. (Zürich: TVZ, 1975-76), p. 658 (emphasis added).
9. Balthasar, *Karl Barth. Darstellung und Deutung seiner Theologie,* p. 269.
10. Ibid.

contribution "Reichweite der Analogie als katholischer Grundform," addresses more openly the specifically Christian dimension of analogy. But Balthasar thinks that Przywara's way of thinking can be defended against his Protestant critics in both periods. Barth was not the only Protestant who objected to what was taken to be problematic in Przywara's theology. Balthasar reminds us that Dietrich Bonhoeffer in *Akt und Sein* followed Barth's lead and made an even more direct attack on the Catholic principle of an *analogia entis*.[11] Bonhoeffer thinks that insufficient attention is paid to the "is," to the concept of existence itself in the metaphysical unfolding of an analogy of being. Balthasar says that this oversight is precisely what Przywara sought to avoid, starting with the publication of *Analogia Entis*, but concedes that Przywara's clearest response to that objection first appears in the works that followed *Analogia Entis*.

Balthasar begins his defense of Przywara by saying what the *analogia entis* is not. It is not the starting point of an absolute metaphysics. If one follows Przywara's interpretation, then analogy signifies "a creaturely principle and is therefore displayed in the illimitable openness of processual movement [*das unumgrenzbares Offensein der Werde-Bewegtheit*]."[12] Were this principle taken to be the sole formula for grasping creaturely being, then it would become the absolute starting point for an absolute metaphysics. But Balthasar strenuously objects to the idea that the principle of analogy is for Przywara the beginning of an absolute metaphysics. Instead, Balthasar says, analogy for Przywara is "only an expression for how the restless potentiality of the creaturely works itself out."[13] Moreover, Balthasar adds, the true principle of analogy is deconstructive vis-à-vis any preestablished metaphysical system.[14] The debates between Barth, Przywara, Söhngen, and others lie in the background of such a statement. The principle of analogy contributes a positive Catholic form to thinking about the world, but its function can also be purgative. In fact, for Balthasar once analogy is inserted into a system of thought or way of thinking that is purely objective, ready at hand, and *restlos* ("without rest"), then the principle ceases to reveal the dynamic rhythm of being itself. In his *Timaeus* Plato famously referred to time as a moving image of eternity. Przywara's analogy, according to Balthasar, is likewise a moving image of the inner dynamic structure of every and all being created by

11. Ibid., p. 403, n. 3.
12. Ibid., p. 267.
13. Ibid.
14. Ibid.: "Sie ist Destruktion jedes System zugunsten einer restlosen objektiven Verfügbarkeit des Geschöpfs zu Gott und zum göttlichen Maß hin."

God. The principle of analogy for Balthasar cannot be used as a means to evacuate created being of its inner mystery. Balthasar's 1947 *Wahrheit der Welt* had highlighted this mystery, and Balthasar does not retreat from that position in his book on Barth.

The case for Przywara and against Barth becomes even stronger when one turns to the works written after the publication of *Analogia Entis* (1932). Here the principle of analogy is not in any way abstracted from the specific contours and determinations of a distinctively Christian view of creation. Balthasar is not saying that Przywara imposed a Christian overlay on top of a preexisting metaphysical framework. Przywara's impulse toward Christo-centrism is present, if only in a somewhat muted form, in *Analogia Entis.* In his unfolding of the relationship between philosophy and theology in the works written after 1932, Balthasar invokes in his own expressionist language the Thomistic couplet whereby grace destroys nothing but presupposes and perfects nature. Grace, he says, lends to nature its final form, while bringing it to perfection.[15]

The process of seeing the final form of nature as an opening to a per-fection brought about by grace creates a new kind of philosophy. The exis-tential situation of the Christian philosopher for Przywara is accordingly cruciform.[16] Przywara had been Balthasar's highly acclaimed teacher in the Jesuit theologate in Pullach near Munich, and the mentor also would write later in his career a three-volume commentary on the *Spiritual Exercises.*[17] It is no wonder that Balthasar, who himself brought considerable erudition in arts and letters to the seminary, was still in awe of the one Jesuit who helped him during the bleak years of the war to escape the dry dust of scholastic manuals of philosophy: "Whoever . . . has gone through his school will re-main marked by this encounter," for "every return to the old master will leave one oddly shaken, perhaps because one comes to see how much youn-ger this old master has remained than all who have come after him."[18]

---

15. Ibid., p. 268: "Für diese Gestalt ist der Doppelsatz zuständig, der auf Thomas von Aquin zurückgeht. Die Gnade [Glaube] zerstört nicht, sondern setzt voraus und gibt, vollendend, die letzte Form der Natur."

16. See Peter Lüning, *Der Mensch im Angesicht der Gekreuzigten. Untersuchungen zum Kreuzesverständnis von Erich Przywara, Karl Rahner, Jon Sobrino und Hans Urs von Balthasar* (Münster: Aschendorff, 2007).

17. Erich Przywara, *Deus semper maior. Theologie der Exerzitien* (Vienna: Herold, 1964). On this see James V. Zeitz, *Spirituality and analogia entis according to Erich Przywara, S.J.* (Washington, D.C.: University Press of America, 1982).

18. Trans. by John Betz from *Erich Przywara, Sein Schriftum, 1912-1962,* ed. Leo

In what may be an evocation of the second week of the *Spiritual Exercises,* the philosopher according to Przywara stands before the concreteness of the cross and must choose between two and only two possibilities. From this vantage point, it is impossible to conceive of a purely natural or neutral philosophy of creation. Przywara, Balthasar reports, sees a necessary polarity between an originally sinful philosophy *(eine erbsündige Philosophie)* and a redeemed philosophy *(eine erlöste Philosophie).* Przywara's language to describe the alternatives is richly poetic. A philosophy of pure concepts is death. The "hell" of "pure criticism" stands and falls on the same grounds as the mortal punishment of abstraction. Each one endures a new condition of original sin on every occasion when it tries to resurrect itself wholly on its own terms.[19]

The Kierkegaardian phrase "either/or" appears in Przywara writings, and Balthasar connects the either/or in Przywara's mature philosophy to the debate between Karl Barth and Emil Brunner on the possibility of a natural knowledge of God. For Przywara, Balthasar states, there is no really existing purely natural religion. In a survey of religion or the religious impulse in humanity, there is an either/or between God and idols; one's approach is either truth-seeking *(catholicus)* or idol-worshipping *(paganus).* Przywara thus heralds the single true order and final form of being: God *in Christo* in the church. "There is really existing and without exception," Przywara says, "*only* the either/or of Yes or No to this one order."[20]

In the end Balthasar in his book on Barth still accepts Przywara's formulation of the *analogia entis* as an acceptable *katholische Grundform.*[21] Along the way to reaching this conclusion, Balthasar has highlighted the concrete, historical, and Christological aspects of the *analogia entis.* This point of view, he asserts, will meet the Barthian objection and display its one-sided interpretation. At the same time, the particular ecumenical spirit that inspired Balthasar to engage Barth is still present in the defense of Przywara. Balthasar's irenicism toward his neighbor and friend in Basel matches his loyalty to his teacher. He is *not* defending Przywara as a way to cast a shadow over the whole of the Barthian project. On the contrary, the most important conclusion of this section of the Barth book might very well

Zimmy, with an introduction by Hans Urs von Balthasar (Einsielden: Johannes Verlag, 1963), p. 18.

    19. See Balthasar, *Karl Barth. Darstellung und Deutung seiner Theologie,* p. 269.
    20. Ibid. (emphasis added).
    21. Ibid.

be the unequivocal assertion, pace Barth, that the principle of *analogia entis* no longer can be taken as a church-dividing difference.

In sum, Balthasar has transposed a difference that Barth took to be the critical difference between Catholicism and his own thought and turned it into a deep-rooted but essentially *stylistic* difference between two avowedly Christocentric thinkers. The important role of stylistic considerations in the book on Barth thus cannot be underestimated. The analysis of Balthasar's own literary form applies even more decisively to Balthasar's reformulation of Przywara's *Denkform* in the material just surveyed. In the process of defending his teacher, Balthasar redefines in very basic terms the meaning of a Catholic form of thought:

> But when Przywara still speaks about a *katholische Grundform,* then he obviously does not intend one form of thought alongside another. Instead he means the Catholic way in which the all-encompassing "yes" to revelation maintains room for every creaturely thought that can be saved and has been saved, given that the "yes" is a way of salvation from the ever-recurrent "no" of the sinner.[22]

The terms on which Balthasar accepts Przywara's way of thought as *the* Catholic way of thought depend upon a kind of Christian universalism. This theme occupies many of Balthasar's works completed just prior to the book on Barth, most notably *Das Herz der Welt* (1944) and *Theologie der Geschichte: Ein Grundriss* (1950).[23] It is also the overriding leitmotif of his first book on Reinhold Schneider, a work that was completed in 1953. In all of these works, as in the book on Barth (1st ed., 1951), Balthasar is concerned with integrating truths either that come from outside of the church or that have not been received by the church into a new, broader catholic unity.

IV. "Christ the Ground of Creation"

I would now like to consider two other critical texts, Balthasar's treatment in his book on Barth of Przywara's doctrine of creation and then his reconsideration twenty-seven years later of the paradigm of a Christological *analogia*

22. Ibid.

23. When Balthasar returns to Przywara's work in the *Theo-Drama,* he notes the importance of this work as the best expression of his achievement on Christian universalism in these early years. I return to this point below.

entis. These texts do not exhaust Balthasar's treatment of Przywara, but they indicate fairly clearly how his views changed. Przywara's doctrine of creation is just the first step in a much more comprehensive path that Balthasar followed in offering a response to the theology of Karl Barth. By showing that Przywara has something to say on Christ as the ground of creation, Balthasar is making the point that Przywara's philosophy is not only not inimical to the concrete, historical order of reality as revealed by Christ but that it contains the building blocks for a truly Christocentric view of creation. Przywara's is not the only or even the best Catholic Christocentrism available, for Balthasar also considers the Christocentric Catholicism of Romano Guardini, Michael Schmaus, Eucharius Berbuir, and Emile Mersch. Przywara is the first one treated by Balthasar in part because of the polemic with Barth. But Balthasar situates Przywara's Christocentrism in a broader context. That is to say, Przywara is introduced here as a badly needed new synthesis, a Catholic thinker who fully transcends the opposition between two extreme views that arose in the late Middle Ages — a Thomism that makes human sin the main reason for the incarnation of Christ, and a Scotism that raises the question of whether God would have become man if Adam had not sinned.[24] Balthasar is aware that the followers of Aquinas and of Scotus seldom do justice to the nuances in the theology of their respective masters. The constructive point that he seems to be making in taking his final cue from Przywara is to move beyond the school debates in order to underscore necessity in the one, historical order of creation and transcend what he calls "every theology of the possible."[25] The concrete *analogia entis* helps to perform this surpassing of entrenched positions.

In other words, Przywara grasps a new and much needed articulation of the dynamic interplay between Christ and creation. In the not-yet-promulgated language of Vatican II, Przywara implicitly understands the relative autonomy of the created order, even while positing Christ the new man as the one who truly illuminates the meaning of human existence and of the entire order of creation. Balthasar states:

> We already introduced textual evidence from Przywara that pointed to an interpretation of the *analogia entis* that was ultimately Christological.

24. Balthasar, *Karl Barth. Darstellung und Deutung seiner Theologie*, pp. 336-37. Balthasar writes: "In diese Perspektive jenseits von Thomismus-Skotismus, jenseits von jeder Possibilien-Theologie, um desto starker die Necessität in der einen faktischen Ordnung zu finden, stellt sich in seinem genzen Werk *Erich Przywara*" (p. 337).
25. Ibid.

> These texts can hardly be overlooked when dealing with the placing into opposition of Przywara and Barth. The major work *Deus semper maior* is a singular, inexorable reduction of all relations to one single relation: God in the crucified Christ in the cocrucified church, the intertwining of every direct statement about and relationship between God and man into the dialectic of the self-crossing beam of the cross (as the only concrete form of negative theology). . . . Przywara consequently takes the path of norming all logic (and thus ontology) by this Christological-historical-actualistic standard.[26]

Here the Przywara of *Deus semper maior* is applauded for having gone the same route as Barth in prioritizing the Christological and actualistic standard and for having seen (even if his achievement, according to Balthasar, seems to stop at that) an inner connection between the principle of analogy and the two natures of Christ.

Balthasar's defense of Przywara on these points needs to be seen in the context of two contemporaneous currents. First, Przywara remains a fundamentally Ignatian guide to the question of creation. For example, the paradoxical nature of the relationship between Christ and creation is illuminated by following the path of the *applicatio sensuum* and working out the tensions between flesh and spirit in the apperception of God's truth in the world. Second, and closely related to the first point, is the life and work of Henri de Lubac. Henri de Lubac's book on Origen, *Histoire et esprit,* was published just one year prior to the initial publication of the book on Barth. More important, one also sees here the effects of the controversy involving de Lubac that followed in the same year in the wake of the promulgation of *Humani generis.* In other words, it does not seem accidental that Balthasar highlights the aspects of Przywara's account of creation that accord best with the spirit of de Lubac, who in many ways is the true hero of the book on Barth, even when he is *not* mentioned. One more contemporary needs to be mentioned here. In the treatment of "Christ, the ground of creation," the section on Przywara is followed by one on Romano Guardini. Balthasar mentions in passing the difference between the two thinkers. In stark contrast to "the flamboyant, expressionistic style" of Przywara, Guardini, he says, is mellow *(abgeklärt).* It is always a mistake, I think, to read too much into student evaluations, especially one that is this candid. The reservations concerning the content of Przywara's thought that arise in later years are far more substantial.

26. Ibid., p. 338.

V. The Idea of a Christological *Analogia Entis* in *Theodramatik* II/2

In 1978 Balthasar returned to the question of the *analogia entis* while writing *Theodramatik* II/2 (which in English is the volume entitled *Theo-Drama* III).[27] By this time, the controversies surrounding Barth, Przywara, Brunner, and de Lubac had receded somewhat into the background, and the new problems of the postconciliar church were no doubt of far greater concern. The brief treatment of analogy is elucidating if one wants to consider the significance of the Barth book within Balthasar's overall work and the place of Przywara in that book. Written almost three decades later, the initial reservations about Przywara come into full view in *Theodramatik* II/2, even though Balthasar continues to defend and praise his teacher's lasting achievement.

The basic development concerns the explicitly Christological frame for the problem of the *analogia entis*. This theme needs to be seen in terms of the overall analysis of theological persons in the volume, as well as within the triptych as a whole, but I do not have the time to unpack those contexts except to say that the principle of analogy will now be connected to a new emphasis on the trinitarian foundations of and anthropological implications of the universal mission that Jesus Christ receives from the Father. I will concentrate rather on the new accents that appear with respect to Przywara.

Balthasar begins by stating that "between the divine and created natures there is an essential abyss."[28] The Barth book already included the proposal to think of the *duplex ordo cognitionis* of Vatican I as ultimately identical with the two natures of the Chalcedonian decree.[29] In that same context, Balthasar states that Maximus the Confessor preserved the soteriological essence of that decree with the dictum "Christ can save man only by preserving him,"[30] a maxim that points to the final pattern of human redemption within the unity of Christ's two natures.

Balthasar then connects the wholly otherness of the unmixed natures to the question of the principle of analogy in this way:

27. Hans Urs von Balthasar, *Theodramatik*, vol. 2, *Die Personen des Spiels*, pt. 2, *Die Personen in Christus* (Einsiedeln: Johannes Verlag, 1978; ET *Theo-Drama*, vol. 3, *Dramatis Personae: Persons in Christ*, trans. Graham Harrison [Ignatius: San Francisco, 1992]).

28. Balthasar, *Theo-Drama*, 3:220.

29. Balthasar, *Karl Barth. Darstellung und Deutung seiner Theologie*, p. 284.

30. Ibid., p. 282.

> However *analogia entis* may be defined in philosophical detail, it means
> that the terms employed cannot be traced back to a generic concept (for
> example, as if both God and the creature were to fall *under* the heading
> of "being as such": this is the danger of Scotism and late scholastic ratio-
> nalism). . . . Quite simply, this means that the person of the Logos in
> whom the hypostatic union takes place cannot function, in any way, as
> the ("higher") unity between God and man; this person, as such, is God.
> Since the person of the Logos is the ultimate union of divine and created
> being, it must constitute the final proportion *(Maß)* between the two
> and hence must be the "concrete *analogia entis*" itself. However, it must
> not in any way overstep this analogy in the direction of identity.[31]

The phrase "concrete *analogia entis*" signifies here that the one person of the
two natures tolerates no *Aufhebung* of humanity and divinity. To admit such
an overcoming of the difference within the union makes meaningless the
"the very presuppositions of the *pro nobis.*"[32] Different conceptualities arose
in the theological tradition to make this crucial point. Maximus the Confessor spoke of a chasm or abyss between the divine and created natures, and
scholastic theologians (a fortiori Nicholas of Cusa) denied any *proportio* (or
comparative relation) of the infinite to the finite.[33] Interestingly, the "synthesis" of natures in one person invented by Antiochene theologians and
carefully refined by Maximus, Peter Lombard, and Thomas Aquinas is not
the last word for the mature Balthasar, a point that may reflect his perduring
debt to Barth. Here Balthasar maintains that the view of a synthetic person
in the tradition is of less value for a Christology of mission than *a free act of
union by a divine person.* In other words, the dogmatic inadmissibility of a
notional ascent *from* two natures *to* one person opens up the domain of freedom. According to Balthasar, the "must" of Jesus' fulfillment of a mission
from the Father remains a wholly *free* act of obedience. In order to shed light
on the critical question of how freedom and obedience come into play with
one another, Balthasar provides an analogy drawn no doubt from his own
experience as a composer and as an author: "It is like the artist or scholar
who is so possessed by his vocation that he only feels free, only feels totally
himself, when he is able to pursue this task that is so much his own."[34]

31. Balthasar, *Theo-Drama,* 3:221-22, citing *Theologie der Geschichte* (Einsiedeln:
Johannes Verlag, 1959), pp. 53-54.

32. Ibid., p. 221.

33. Ibid., pp. 222-23.

34. Ibid., p. 225.

There is much more that could be said about the notion of a Christo-logical analogy of being in the *Theo-Drama*. As Pope Benedict XVI implied in his Regensburg address, the analogy of being (Benedict actually spoke only about the question of being) is the bulwark to defend against any nominalistic attempt to turn the singularity of Christ's sending as the determinative act in the history of salvation into a theory of an arbitrary, wholly irrational imposition of a divine will. What Balthasar's Christological *analogia entis* teaches us about his relationship to Przywara is equally interesting:

> The fact that the person of Jesus Christ bridges this abyss without harm to his unity should render us speechless in the presence of the mystery of his person. As E. Przywara tirelessly urged (even to the point of exaggeration), this all-embracing law of being both limits and acts as a stimulus to all philosophical and theological thought; in the face of this law, more than anywhere else, we discern the knife-edge between Nestorianism and Monophysitism that Christianity has to negotiate.[35]

Przywara recognizes the necessity and the limits of a philosophy of being within the concrete order of creation. Przywara preserves the Chalcedonian balance between similarity and difference in an overarching metaphysics of unity. So far Balthasar is only repeating what has already been developed in the book on Barth. Here he also notes that there is something slightly exaggerated in Przywara's thesis regarding the law of being. A footnote attempts to clarify the point.[36] The footnote states that Przywara relied upon the text of the Fourth Lateran Council and says that the phrase *tanta similitudo*, which Przywara took in an Ignatian fashion to signify that there is difference, no matter how great the similarity, has been altered in the new edition of Denzinger to simply *similitudo*. More to the point, Balthasar adds: "It is no accident that Przywara never produced a Christology."

So here we finally encounter the problem that Balthasar sees in the thought of Erich Przywara. He clearly does not intend to deliver a fatal blow either to Przywara's systematizing of analogy or to that of other Catholic thinkers. But a new accent has now been placed upon the work of Przywara. Przywara's metaphysics can be a great aid to a theologian to see the order of being in creation with Christ as its ground. His theory of analogy is grounded in the concreteness of revelation, but the living form of Christ and the Christological determinations of the analogy of being are still too vague.

35. Ibid., pp. 220-21.
36. Ibid., p. 220, n. 51.

In other words, Balthasar's final verdict seems to be that Przywara can take the theologian to this mountain, but he himself did not make the ascent.

VI. Truth as Integration

Let me bring this to a close by first reviewing the steps I have taken. The first point was that theological styles make a difference to Balthasar, and the stylistic considerations have a small but important role to play in the form and content of his analysis in the book on Barth. The second section demonstrated how effectively Balthasar defended his mentor against the caricature of the *analogia entis* that Barth had once drawn. In this section, I also made the claim that, even though Balthasar stands behind Przywara's assertion that the *analogia entis* can be taken as a *katholische Grundform,* I think that he is operating with notions of form and *Denkform* that are very different from those of his master. This is also true of Balthasar's defense of Przywara's understanding of Christ as the ground of creation. In the *Theo-Drama* Balthasar is extremely cautious in introducing any criticism of Przywara. At the same time, it is clear that Przywara's *analogia entis* is wholly inadequate to the task of articulating a Christology of mission that is robustly trinitarian and that simultaneously addresses fully the dilemma of human freedom as it needs to be understood today. Some sort of analogy of being needs to be incorporated into Christology, but Przywara's is only a first step toward reaching that goal.

The notion of integration is thus present in the entirety of Balthasar's consideration of both Barth and Przywara. This is a method quite central to Balthasar's project that only seldom gets mentioned by scholars working on his thought.[37] In sum, Balthasar conceives of the entire truth about God and humanity as a symphonic whole whose unity is greater than its parts. Przywara's principle of analogy is certainly one fragment of that whole and is a fragment in which one can even begin to view the whole as a whole. Balthasar argues, quite effectively in my estimation, that you cannot drive a wedge between Przywara's religious metaphysics and a Christocentric theology. Many of the resources needed for integrating the two are already present in Przywara.

---

37. See Holger Zaborowski, "Katholische Integration. Zum religionsphilosophischen Ansatz Hans Urs von Balthasars," in *Die Kunst Gottes verstehen. Hans Urs von Balthasars theologische Provokationen,* ed. Magnus Striet and Jan-Heiner Tück, pp. 28-48 (Freiburg: Herder, 2005).

Peter Casarella

One final point. What Balthasar takes from Przywara in the book on Barth is almost wholly determined by what he wants to take from Barth. One should not look to the book on Barth to understand the whole of Przywara. Balthasar badly needs to resurrect Przywara among the sympathizers with Barth's critique in order to develop a critical appropriation of Barth's own Christocentrism. I have not in this essay tried to develop this last point. It would require a separate study to lay this out. Balthasar's reading of Przywara is motivated by his ecumenical openness to certain aspects of Barth's thought. One of the main obstacles in achieving any rapprochement with Barth was removing the obstacle that Barth had placed in the way, namely, the notion that the *analogia entis* was the invention of the Antichrist and, as such, a defining moment in Catholic thought. Having removed that obstacle, Balthasar can now attend to his real agenda, namely, of engaging in dialogue with the Catholic substance and even the Catholic forms of thought in Barth's theology.

PART III

THE ANALOGY OF BEING AND
THOMISTIC *RESSOURCEMENT*

CHAPTER 6

Attending to the Wisdom of God — from Effect to Cause, from Creation to God: A *relecture* of the Analogy of Being according to Thomas Aquinas

Reinhard Hütter

In memoriam W. Norris Clarke, S.J.

Non enim possumus nominare Deum nisi ex creaturis.

— Thomas Aquinas, *Summa theologiae* I, q. 13, a. 5

I. Introduction: Two Protestant Objections to Analogical Predication of God in Thomas: Anthropomorphism (Pannenberg) and Apophaticism (Jüngel)

It is not altogether insignificant for the shape of the theological dispute over the *analogia entis* in the twentieth century that the arguably two most eminent German Protestant theologians of their period, Wolfhart Pannenberg and Eberhard Jüngel, in their early formative years as theologians both deeply immersed themselves in the doctrine of analogy. Maybe their early immersion in this (for Protestant theologians) arguably rather unlikely topic is not accidental, since after all, in Basel, Switzerland, each sat at the feet of the last century's greatest master of Protestant theology. And ever since, each — although arguably one more than the other — remained a close reader of that master's *opus magnum*, the *Church Dogmatics*. And so it happened that Wolfhart Pannenberg and Eberhard Jüngel wrote their respective *Habilitationsschriften* on the topic of analogy, Pannenberg's bearing the title *Anal-*

ogy and Revelation[1] and Jüngel's bearing the title *On the Origin of Analogy in Parmenides and Heraclitus*.[2]

And interestingly, neither Pannenberg nor Jüngel ever left the topic behind. Rather, each one in his respective *opus magnum* — Jüngel in his *God as the Mystery of the World*[3] and Pannenberg in his *Systematic Theology*[4] — develops his theology in marked contrast to what he holds to be profoundly problematic in the concept of analogy as it is used to predicate truths about God and, beyond that, to organize all theological knowledge itself.

There is something rather striking about the early Pannenberg's and Jüngel's respective accounts of the dangers of a theological use of analogy in what they identify as Thomas Aquinas's account of analogical predication. It is not that they differ somewhat in their respective post-Barthian assessments (which might be expected), but that their accounts of the use of analogy in Thomas Aquinas and of the detrimental theological problems arising from it are indeed diametrically opposed to each other. In a nutshell: The early Pannenberg of the unpublished *Habilitationsschrift* regards analogical predication in Thomas Aquinas as a subtly camouflaged version of univocal predication. Analogy allegedly always presumes a "common logos" between creature and Creator. Hence, for Pannenberg the very concept of analogy itself entails "the structure of 'spiritual assault'" upon the mystery of God.[5] If consistently employed in theology, analogical predication of God along Aquinas's

---

1. Wolfhart Pannenberg, "Analogie und Offenbarung" (Habilitationsschrift, Heidelberg, 1955), published in an altered and expanded version more than fifty years later, *Analogie und Offenbarung. Eine kritische Untersuchung zur Geschichte des Analogiebegriffes in der Lehre von der Gotteserkenntnis* (Göttingen: Vandenhoeck & Ruprecht, 2007).

2. Eberhard Jüngel, *Zum Ursprung der Analogie bei Parmenides und Heraklit* (Berlin: de Gruyter, 1964).

3. Eberhard Jüngel, *Gott als Geheimnis der Welt. Zur Begründung der Theologie des Gekreuzigten im Streit zwischen Theismus und Atheismus* (Tübingen: Mohr Siebeck, 1977; 5th ed., 1986; ET *God as the Mystery of the World: On the Foundation of the Theology of the Crucified One in the Dispute between Theism and Atheism*, trans. Darrell L. Guder [Grand Rapids: Eerdmans, 1983]).

4. Wolfhart Pannenberg, *Systematische Theologie*, vol. 1 (Göttingen: Vandenhoeck & Ruprecht, 1988), esp. pp. 372-73; ET *Systematic Theology*, trans. Geoffrey W. Bromiley (Grand Rapids: Eerdmans, 1991), pp. 342ff.

5. Elizabeth A. Johnson, "The Right Way to Speak about God? Pannenberg on Analogy," *Theological Studies* 43 (1982): 685. Johnson offers a lucid interpretation of Pannenberg's unpublished *Habilitationsschrift*. It is very instructive to see how deeply the early Pannenberg in his reading of Thomas on analogy was influenced by Barth's profound concern over the *analogia entis* allegedly enabling theology to take a conceptual hold of God, to submit God to our grasp ("Zugriff") by way of the concept ("Begriff").

lines must unavoidably end in anthropomorphism — the mystery of God in-eluctably drawn into the conceptual closure of the human mind and thus compromised in and eventually emptied of its infinite transcendence.

Jüngel, in contrast, regards Thomas as fatally implicated in the apophatic entailments of the analogy of attribution. Similar to Kant's ac-count of analogical predication of God at a later stage, he sees already Aqui-nas's account haunted by one central aporia culminating in the question "whether God is speakable only as the one who actually is unspeakable, and can be made known actually only as the one who is actually unknown."[6] Jüngel regards this aporia to be central to the analogy of attribution as — in his judgment — similarly employed by Aquinas and Kant: "The analogy of attribution defines so precisely the unknownness of God that it vastly in-creases that unknownness into God's total inaccessibility."[7] He concludes that analogy employed in divine predication by Aquinas as well as Kant "functions to keep God out of the world . . . and [thereby] to protect God from anthropomorphic talk — [from] dogmatic anthropomorphism."[8] For Jüngel, analogical predication in theology is a barely concealed version of equivocation — an instrument to prevent precisely what Pannenberg alleges it to lead into — anthropomorphism! If consistently employed in theology along Aquinas's lines, Jüngel claims, analogical predication ineluctably leads to a profound agnosticism irrevocably muting the God of the gospel.

A curious picture, to say the least, emerges: Thomas is charged by the one with exactly what, according to the other, Thomas is bent on avoiding at all costs. Of course, one reading might be right and the other wrong. But even if true — which it is not — such an answer would be less than satisfy-ing. For Pannenberg's and Jüngel's assessments of Thomas on analogical predication of God are not just variants but contradictories. And this cir-cumstance points to a deeper problem and hence invites the simple ques-tion, How come?

In the following I will advance an answer to this question from the posi-tion under critique by arguing that the best position from which to properly

6. Jüngel, *God as the Mystery of the World*, p. 277.

7. Ibid., p. 278.

8. Philip A. Rolnick, *Analogical Possibilities: How Words Refer to God* (Atlanta: Scholars Press, 1993), p. 208. I regard Rolnick's book as the most instructive analysis and dis-cussion available of analogy in David Burrell, W. Norris Clarke, and Eberhard Jüngel. I am gratefully indebted to his nuanced interpretation and acute critique of Jüngel's (mis-)read-ing of Thomas — a critique that still holds and that, in light of more recent research on the analogy of being in Aquinas, has become only more pertinent.

understand the reason for the contradictory assessment of Thomas is indeed Thomas's own, mature doctrine of the analogy of being and of analogical predication of God. I should like to propose that the very fact that Pannenberg and Jüngel misread Thomas in the precisely contrary way they do is profoundly indicative of the twin theological problems Thomas's doctrine of analogy is meant to address and avoid. Pannenberg and Jüngel, held captive by what both regard as the irreversible normative entailments of post-Cartesian philosophy, operate in their respective theologies from within the uniquely modern conceptualist metaphysical framework of what quite perceptively and famously has been diagnosed as the modern "forgetfulness of being." It strikes me as not an altogether unfair question to ask whether Pannenberg's and Jüngel's consistently modern rejection of the analogy of being might haunt their own respective theologies in problematic ways. In the following I will limit myself to the prolegomena of such an inquiry, that is, to reconsidering Thomas's mature doctrine of analogy. This account will unfold according to the usual three steps of exposition. First, I will offer a relecture of Thomas's mature doctrine of analogy; second, I will argue that Thomas's doctrine of analogy does not suffer from the flaws Pannenberg and Jüngel charge it to suffer from; and third, I will intimate the contours of a Thomist response to what amounts to the shared deficiencies in Pannenberg's as well as Jüngel's readings of Thomas's mature position on analogical predication of God.

My analysis will follow a line of recovery of Thomas's thought that (after certain recent detours around and flat denials of the central role of metaphysics in Thomas's synthesis) is returning to understanding his metaphysical insights as an integral part of his overall theological project. The following apt remark by Rudi te Velde captures well what I am going to argue: "Analogy, as applied to divine names, is firmly rooted in the metaphysical conception of being as the intelligible aspect under which the world of creatures is positively related to its divine origin."[9]

II. Analogy in Thomas Aquinas

Lest we cannot see the forest because of the trees, I shall first announce in broad sweeps the central themes that make up the core of this chapter. There

---

9. Rudi te Velde, *Aquinas on God: The "Divine Science" of the* Summa theologiae (Aldershot: Ashgate, 2006), p. 97. I am indebted to te Velde's excellent synthetic account of the metaphysics of participation and of transcendental analogy in Aquinas.

is, first, the theme of the *predicamental use of analogy;* here a "formal content" of existence is attributed horizontally across the various predicamental modes of being so as to attribute being as something intrinsic to all that exists across the diversity of genera, or categories. The predicamental use of analogy makes possible eventually an attribution of being to God in a sense that relates in some way analogically to what creatures are intrinsically. For this reason predicamental analogy avoids a "merely extrinsic" equivocation, pace Jüngel.

The second theme is the transcendental predication of being, from creatures to God, based upon causality and participation. Transcendental predication allows one to attribute perfections in creatures to God as "divine names." Because *transcendental analogy* is based on the creative causality of the transcendent first cause, it avoids any form of mere univocal assimilation of God to creatures, a "conceptual essentialism" of the kind the early Pannenberg greatly worried about in his first works on analogy.[10]

Those who have traveled this road know that the topic of analogy in Thomas is as notoriously complex as it is subtle. Thomas never wrote a treatise on analogy. But from his very first work on, he thought about analogy, and over time his thought did indeed develop in notable ways. I am not interested, however, in offering a genealogy of the overall development of the doctrine of analogy in Thomas's thought. For this I would like to direct the reader to the exhaustive scholarly accounts advanced by Hampus Lyttkens, George P. Klubertanz, Cornelio Fabro, Bernard Montagnes, Rolf Schönberger, Rudi te Velde, John F. Wippel, and Gregory P. Rocca.[11] Rather, I

---

10. See esp. Pannenberg's lengthy review essay "Zur Bedeutung des Analogiegedankens bei Karl Barth. Eine Auseinandersetzung mit Urs von Balthasar," *Theologische Literaturzeitung* 78 (1953): 17-24, as well as his essay "Analogy and Doxology," in *Basic Questions in Theology,* vol. 1, trans. George H. Kehm, pp. 212-38 (Philadelphia: Fortress, 1970), originally published in *Dogma und Denkstrukturen. Festschrift für Edmund Schlink,* ed. Wilfried Joest and Wolfhart Pannenberg, pp. 96-115 (Göttingen: Vandenhoeck & Ruprecht, 1963).

11. Hampus Lyttkens, *The Analogy between God and the World: An Investigation of Its Background and Interpretation of Its Use by Thomas of Aquino,* trans. Axel Poignant (Uppsala: Almqvist & Wiksells, 1952); George Klubertanz, *St. Thomas Aquinas on Analogy: A Textual Analysis and Systematic Synthesis* (Chicago: Loyola University Press, 1960); Cornelio Fabro, *Participation et causalité selon S. Thomas d'Aquin* (Paris: Béatrice-Nauwelaerts; Louvain: Publications Universitaires, 1961); Bernard Montagnes, *The Doctrine of the Analogy of Being according to Thomas Aquinas,* trans. E. M. Macierowski, reviewed and corrected by P. Vandervelde, with revisions by A. Tallon (Milwaukee, Wis.: Marquette University Press, 2004; French original: *La doctrine de l'analogie de l'être d'après Saint Thomas d'Aquin*

would like to content myself with offering the contours of what can reasonably be defended as Thomas's mature doctrine of analogy as it came to bear most significantly on his way of predicating divine names.

Thomas's mature doctrine of analogy arises from a distinct synthesis of two strands of metaphysical thought, a synthesis arguably prepared by the Neoplatonic commentators of the Aristotelian corpus. The one strand — that of the unity of order by reference to a primary instance — is of Aristotelian provenance and belongs primarily, albeit (as we shall see) not exclusively, to the order of predication. The other strand — that of participation — is of Neoplatonic origin and belongs exclusively to the order of being.[12] The first element of this synthesis — the unity of order by reference to a primary instance — permanently underlies all the later developments and is to be found in the early opuscula *De principiis naturae* and *De ente et essentia* (both probably written between 1252 and 1256), as well as in his late commentary on Aristotle's *Metaphysics* (1270-71). The second element of this synthesis, participation, which enriches and completes the Aristotelian strand, but also integrates it into a higher metaphysical synthesis, is already fully at work in the *Summa contra Gentiles* (1259-65) as well as the *Summa theologiae* (1265-73), but can as well be observed in the *De potentia* (1265-66) and in full maturity late in the *De substantiis separatis* (1271).

Any attempt to understand the analogy of being in Aquinas has to come to terms with the simple fact that the topic of analogy is present from the very first moment of Thomas's written work. At the danger of overstating the matter, there is simply no instance in Thomas's work where analogy is not tacitly presupposed or being treated without being named or simply being silently at work in the exercise of *sacra doctrina* itself.

Moreover, lest we immediately project definite preunderstandings of analogy onto Thomas — be they the mathematical analogy of the Pythago-

---

[Louvain: Publications Universitaires; Paris: Béatrice-Nauwelaerts, 1963]); Rolf Schönberger, *Die Transformation des klassischen Seinsverständnisses. Studien zur Vorgeschichte des neuzeitlichen Seinsbegriffs im Mittelalter* (Berlin: de Gruyter, 1986); Rudi te Velde, *Participation and Substantiality in Thomas Aquinas* (Leiden: Brill, 1995); John Wippel, *The Metaphysical Thought of Thomas Aquinas: From Finite Being to Uncreated Being* (Washington, D.C.: Catholic University of America Press, 2000); Gregory Rocca, *Speaking the Incomprehensible God: Thomas Aquinas on the Interplay of Positive and Negative Theology* (Washington, D.C.: Catholic University of America Press, 2004).

12. Montagnes, *The Doctrine of the Analogy of Being according to Thomas Aquinas*, p. 23. As will become clear in the following, on the relationship between the Aristotelian predicamental analogy and the transcendental analogy by way of participation I am substantively indebted to Montagnes's analysis.

rean school or analogy as the structural principle of the cosmos in Plato's *Timaeus* — let us first note that Aquinas's doctrine is part and parcel of a quite original interpretation of Aristotle advanced by the Christian school-men of the first half of the thirteenth century. Alexander of Hales, Albert the Great, and Bonaventure contribute to this emerging doctrine of analogy. In this Christian philosophical reception of Aristotle, analogy is first of all a distinct way of predication — in contrast with univocal predication — to be employed in transgeneric predication. The basis of such analogical predica-tion is the unity of many meanings of one common word by reference to a primary instance. Thomas was fully part of this emerging Christian tradi-tion of metaphysical inquiry and hence had no interest whatsoever in com-ing up with a new "theory" of analogy in the modern sense of philosophical patricide. Instead of aiming at intellectual replacement, Thomas aimed at a superior synthesis of what he regarded as the strongest strands of the re-ceived philosophical tradition, the Aristotelian account of the unity of order by reference to a primary instance, and the Neoplatonic account of ontologi-cal participation. I will first address the Aristotelian strand, then turn to the Neoplatonic one and the mutual integration of both, and finally to the pred-ication of divine names.

The fundamental axiom, ontological and epistemological in one, op-erative behind this analysis, and shared by the whole classical metaphysical tradition, is of an almost shocking naïvité for modern critical and skeptical sensibilities: the structure of the conceptual syntax that arises from the anal-ysis of the way we predicate reality is isomorphic to this very reality. Hence the very predication of being discloses and renders intelligible the structures of being itself. This axiom is understood to be operative not unlike a first principle of the intellect. Consequently, it cannot be proven. Rather, it as-serts itself in all modes of inquiry, including allegedly a priori inquiries into the conceptual structures of reason or the manifold complexities of lan-guage itself. The very cornerstone of metaphysical realism, this axiom, how-ever, can be reasonably accounted for and successfully defended against the criticisms raised against metaphysical realism from the perspectives of tran-scendental idealism, phenomenology, or poststructuralism. Such accounts and defenses have indeed been offered throughout the twentieth century.[13] The quite contingent but not altogether insignificant fact that only few con-temporary philosophers find such defenses convincing should not tempt us

---

13. Just to name one, by now classical, account: Jacques Maritain, *Distinguish to Unite; or, The Degrees of Knowledge,* trans. Gerald B. Phelan (New York: Scribner, 1959).

into assuming that therefore the axiom does not obtain. While I cannot get involved in any defense of metaphysical realism at this point, I should note that in the following I not only take this realist principle to be central to Thomas's metaphysical inquiry but also indeed to obtain per se. Hence the following presentation of Thomas on analogy, while primarily reconstructive, indeed holds the principle of Thomist realism to obtain and to enable a genuine inquiry into the structures of being.

A. Predicamental Analogy: The Likeness of Species and Genus

For Aristotle, being (ὄν) is predicated in irreducibly multiple ways. For being is primordially diverse. To put it in the terms of Aristotle's teacher, being does not have a single, pure, idea-like form and therefore cannot be determined by way of a definition. And consequently, neither can the unity of being be achieved by abstracting it like a genus from the multiplicity of beings — "being" (ὄν/*ens*) as something like the smallest common denominator of all beings. Rather, the very plurality of beings must be integrated into a differentiated unity of being by way of an analogy of proportion. Aristotle regarded this procedure as the only viable alternative to the procedure of definition — and the latter is obviously not possible. For in a definition, the specific difference is added *extrinsically* to the identity of the genus, while the multiplicity of being is *intrinsic* to the unity of being. Consequently, for Aristotle, the multiplicity of being presents itself irreducibly by way of the ten categories, or genera, of being (substance, quantity, quality, relation, place, time, position, action, passion/reception, possession/condition). Furthermore, the multiplicity of being presents itself as fundamentally differentiated between substance and accidents and in the modes of actuality and potentiality.[14]

Following Aristotle, Thomas understands the categories, or predicamentals, as the different ways of predicating. And because in each way of predicating ineluctably "being" is predicated, the various modes of being, the *modi essendi,* are always already included in these ways of predication. Hence, logically considered, the categories or predicamentals are the most comprehensive genera by way of which we conceptually understand all of contingent reality. Ontologically considered, the categories, or predicamentals, are the most universal modes of being and as such subsist indepen-

14. Aristotle, *Metaphysics* 5.7; 6.2.

dently of human conceptual formation. It is for this reason that Thomas never pursues a logical deduction of the categories (as Kant did famously, if erroneously, in his *Critique of Pure Reason*). Rather, according to Thomas, the deduction of the categories must follow the analysis of reality. For insofar as in each way of predicating a mode of being is entailed, the categories, or predicamentals, are grounded in the nature of being itself.[15]

We can find an immediate echo of these considerations in Thomas's early *De ente et essentia*:

> [T]he term "a being" [*ens per se*] in itself has two meanings. Taken one way it is divided by the ten categories; taken in another way it signifies the truth of propositions. The difference between the two is that in the second sense anything can be called a being if an affirmative proposition can be formed about it, even though it is nothing positive in reality. In this way privations and negations are called beings, for we say that affirmation *is* opposed to negation, and that blindness *is* in the eye. But in the first way nothing can be called being unless it is something positive in reality. In the first sense, then, blindness and the like are not beings.[16]

What matters for our consideration here is the first sense only, by way of which something positive in reality is predicated by way of the ten categories, or genera. For it is in the very context of this sense of "being" that Thomas conceives "analogy" in a largely unproblematic way as a property of common names and concepts — in short, as *predicamental analogy.* And it is for this reason that the division of predicates into three groups occurs — into univocal, equivocal, and analogous predicates. *Univocation:* a term is predicated of several subjects with exactly the same *ratio,* or meaning. *Equivocation:* there is no commonality of the *ratio* or meaning between the subjects predicated, only the same word is used accidentally. *Analogical* predica-

---

15. For a more detailed discussion of how the diverse modes of being are proportional to the ways of predicating, see Thomas's commentary on Aristotle's *Physics* 3.5.322.

16. Thomas Aquinas, *On Being and Essence,* trans. Armand Maurer (Toronto: PIMS, 1968), pp. 29-30; Thomas Aquinas, *De ente et essentia,* in *Opuscula philosophica* (Rome: Marietti, 1954), c. 1: "[E]ns per se dicitur *dupliciter: uno modo,* quod dividitur per decem genera; *alio modo,* quod significat propositionum veritatem. Horum autem differentia est, quia secundo modo potest dici ens omne illud de quo affirmativa propositio formari potest, etiamsi illud in re ponat; per quem modum privationes et negationes entia dicuntur: dicimus enim quod affirmatio est opposita negationi, et quod caecitas est in oculo. Sed primo modo non potest dici ens, nisi quod aliquid in re ponit. Unde primo modo caecitas et huiusmodi non sunt entia."

tion comes to stand in the middle between univocation and equivocation. It occurs when the analogous term comprises in its meaning some similarity-in-difference across the *predicamental range* (substance and accidents) or across the *transcendental range* (different levels/perfections of being).[17] Thomas never debates this division between univocal, equivocal, and analogical predication but always presupposes and uses it.[18]

B. De principiis naturae

In his very first work, *De principiis naturae*,[19] Thomas offers a brief but penetrating inquiry into the metaphysical principles that constitute reality as we

---

17. Thomas puts the matter succinctly in a late explanation of his mature doctrine of analogy in *Summa theologiae* I, q. 13, a. 10, c.: "Univocal terms mean absolutely the same thing, but equivocal terms are absolutely different; whereas in analogical terms a word taken in one signification must be placed in the definition of the same word taken in other senses; as, for instance, *being* which is applied to substance is placed in the definition of being as applied to accident; and *healthy* applied to animal is placed in the definition of healthy as applied to urine and medicine. For urine is the sign of health in the animal, and medicine is the cause of health." All citations from the *Summa theologiae (ST)* in English are taken from the translation of the Fathers of the English Dominican Province, *St. Thomas Aquinas Summa Theologica* (New York: Benziger Brothers, 1948). For a very clear rendition of this matter, one to which I am here indebted, see W. Norris Clarke, "Analogy and the Meaningfulness of Language about God," in *Explorations in Metaphysics: Being — God — Person* (Notre Dame, Ind.: University of Notre Dame Press, 1994), pp. 123-49.

18. As Montagnes has argued (*The Doctrine of the Analogy of Being according to Thomas Aquinas*, p. 24), this division was not introduced by Aristotle himself but by Arab Aristotelianism — to be precise, by Averroes. The other elements of predicamental analogy Thomas draws from Aristotle's *Metaphysics*. They pertain to the unity and diversity of the principles constituting reality, to the enumeration of the types of unity, and especially to the ordered diversity of the meaning of being. The doctrine of the unity and diversity of intrinsic principles appears in *Meta.* 12.4 and 5, 1070a31–1071b1; the enumeration of different types of unity appears in 5.6.1016b31–1017a2 and 5.9.1018a13, and the Aristotelian theory of the unity of the object of metaphysics (being is said in many ways but ways that are unified by reference to a fundamental meaning, which is that of substance) appears in 4.2.1003a33-b15; 7.4.1030a34-b3; 11.3.1060b31–1061a10.

19. Thomas Aquinas, *De principiis naturae*, in *Opuscula philosophica*, pp. 121-28; Saint Thomas d'Aquin, *Les principes de la réalité naturelle*, introd., trans., and notes by Jean Madiran (Paris: Nouvelles Éditions Latines, 1963); Thomas von Aquin, *De principiis naturae — Die Prinzipien der Wirklichkeit*, introd., trans., and commentary by Richard Heinzmann (Stuttgart: Kohlhammer, 1999). Heinzmann's commentary is as profound as it is lucid. I happily acknowledge my indebtedness to Heinzmann's insights.

perceive it by way of the senses. The last chapter of the opusculum, the one most pertinent to our topic, is devoted to the analogy of principles and causes. Thomas's metaphysical resolution toward the constitutive principles of sensibly perceptible reality leads him to form and matter.[20] Thomas then asks, What kind of unity obtains between the diverse things composed of form and matter we encounter?[21] In order to grasp the kind of unity we find between such diverse things as stones, trees, and human beings, Thomas appeals to the axiom of *proportional unity,* the unity of a standard-Aristotelian four-part proportion: The type of community and diversity of principles is identical to the type of community and diversity of the beings of which they are the principles. Thomas's late commentary on Aristotle's *Metaphysics* offers a helpful illustration for this axiom of predicamental analogy by way of proportion. Here he is defending the attribution of act and potency, not only to the accidents of a reality (its operations and powers), but also to substances. The ascription of act and potency is proportional and analogical, ascribed not only to accidents but also to substances:

> Then [Aristotle] shows that the term actuality is used in different senses; and he gives two different senses in which it is used. First, actuality means action, or operation. And with a view to introducing the different senses of actuality he says, first, that we do not say that all things are actual in the same way but in different ones; and this difference can be considered according to different proportions. For a proportion can be taken as meaning that, just as one thing is in another, so a third is in a fourth; for example, just as sight is in the eye, so hearing is in the ear. And the relation of substance (i.e., of form) to matter is taken according to this kind of proportion; for form is said to be in matter.[22]

There is a fundamental continuity between the early *De principiis naturae* and the late commentary on this crucial matter: *The principles of being for each of the categories identified by Aristotle are different, but they are*

20. *De principiis naturae,* chaps. 1-5.
21. Ibid., chap 6.
22. St. Thomas Aquinas, *Commentary on Aristotle's Metaphysics,* trans. John P. Rowan, preface by Ralph McInerny (Notre Dame, Ind.: Dumb Ox Books, 1995), 9.5.1828; S. Thomae Aquinatis, *In Duodecim Libros Metaphysicorum Aristotelis Expositio* (Rome: Marietti, 1950): "*Alius modus* proportionis est, ut dicamus quod sicut habet se hoc ad hoc, ita hoc ad hoc; puta sicut se habet visus ad videndum, ita auditus ad audiendum. Et per hunc modum proportionis accipitur comparatio motus ad potentiam motivam, vel cuiuscumque operationis ad potentiam operativam."

also proportionally similar.[23] Substances and their accidents are said "to be in act" in different ways. The very fact, however, that Aristotle already understands the principles of being to be *causal* principles allows Thomas to inquire more deeply into the precise nature of analogical unity. Following Aristotle, *he grounds the unity of proportion in the unity of order.*[24] For it is substance that gives causal order and unity to all the accidents of a specific being. Hence the principles of being relate not only proportionately to each other but also by way of the causality of the primary instance — substance.[25]

At this very point Thomas introduces Aristotle's famous example of health:

> While "healthy" can be predicated of an animate body as well as of its urine and its food, it does not mean in all three cases exactly the same. For "healthy" is predicated of the urine as a sign of health, of the animate body as its subject, and of its food as its cause. However, all these three meanings relate to one single end, that is, to health.[26]

It is of principal importance to grasp the profound metaphysical insight conveyed by this unassumingly simple example — and even more so by the deceptively simplistic explanation that Thomas adds. As Montagnes rightly stresses, Aquinas takes this reference to a primary instance of health as "a relation of ontological causality tying the analogates to the primary instance." For Thomas, most fundamentally, "analogical unity rests upon the causality that the primary instance exercises toward the analogates."[27] Notice, however, that

> the causality of the primary instance is not uniform. Sometimes it plays the role of final cause: in this way the different meanings of the term

23. Montagnes, *The Doctrine of the Analogy of Being according to Thomas Aquinas,* p. 25.

24. Ibid.

25. By extrapolating from the substance-accident relation of causal unity, Thomas arrives at the insight that the analogical way of predication "applies to different beings each of which has its own nature and a distinct definition, but which have in common the fact that they are all in a relation to the one among them to which the common meaning primarily belongs" (ibid., p. 26).

26. "Sicut sanum dicitur de corpore animalis et de urina et potione, sed non ex toto idem significat in omnibus tribus. Dicitur enim de urina ut de signo sanitatis, de corpore ut de subiecto, de potione ut de causa; sed tamen omnes istae rationes attribuuntur uni fini, scilicet sanitati" (*De principiis naturae*, no. 366, p. 127).

27. Montagnes, *The Doctrine of the Analogy of Being according to Thomas Aquinas,* p. 26.

"healthy" designate realities that are ordered to the health of a living being as their end; sometimes it is the efficient cause: in this way the meanings of the term "medical" are taken by derivation from the medical practitioner who is the agent; sometimes it is the receptive cause: this is the case with being, which is said primarily of substance, then secondarily of quantity, quality, and the other accidents by reference to the substance that is their subject, their material cause. This is why being is not a genus, because it is attributed unequally *(per prius et posterius)* to the various categories.[28]

We will discuss at a later point an important aspect that remains implicit in *De principiis naturae.* It is the precise way in which the analogy of being resembles the analogy of health and how it differs from it. Since health can properly belong only to a living thing and hence neither to urine nor to medicine, the analogy of health remains an *extrinsic* analogy. In the case of the analogy of being, however, there obtains a formal participation between the analogates; hence the analogy is *intrinsic.* While this important difference is developed only in later works, it is indeed the case that already in his very first work, "Thomas connects proportional unity to unity of order and defines analogical unity by reference to a primary instance."[29]

Notice that Thomas designates to these two kinds of unity, proportional unity and unity of order, the same name: *analogical unity.* There obtains, however, a subordination of the proportional unity to the unity of order, since, as Thomas argues, proportional unity depends upon the unity of order.[30] In short, *on the level of substance and accidents, the analogy of order by reference to a primary instance is ontologically primary. The analogy of proportion must be understood in light of the primordial, causal analogy of order or attribution.*

28. Ibid.
29. Ibid.
30. "[A]nalogical unity is first and foremost the unity that is established by the ontological relations of final, efficient and material causality with respect to a primary instance, whence proportional likenesses result among the analogates" (ibid., p. 27). "So, for Thomas, the name 'analogy' passes from proportion to relation: analogy is the theory laid out by Aristotle in book 4 of the *Metaphysics* to explain the diversity and unity of the meanings of being and secondarily mathematical proportion, i.e., the likeness of two or more relations. Each time that Thomas refers to the example of health and of the being of accidents and substance, he alludes implicitly but indisputably to Aristotle's *Metaphysics* and he understands analogy as unity of order by reference to a primary instance" (ibid., pp. 27-28).

C. De ente et essentia

While in *De ente et essentia*, the second of Thomas's early metaphysical works, the term *analogia* does not occur a single time, this opusculum amounts nevertheless to an extensive inquiry into analogy, namely, regarding the attributions of being in a unity of order by reference to a primary instance *(per prius et posterius)*. There are at least two aspects in *De ente et essentia* that pertain centrally to our topic: First, in continuity with *De principiis naturae* Thomas also argues in *De ente et essentia* that "the predicamental analogy of being is that which binds accidents to substance."[31] Substance is to be understood as principal being, being *in se*, and accident as relative being, ordered toward the substance. For its being the accident depends entirely upon substance; simultaneously, accident is the proper perfection of substance. Second, Thomas deepens his understanding of substance as principal being:

> In the order of being, there is a gradation by relation to a maximum that is cause: the perfection of being, realized without restriction in the substance, is participated derivatively by the accidents. The unity of order that relates accidental being to substantial being is no longer confined to an external relation of inherence; it is deeper: it is based upon a common nature, the *ratio entis*, unequally participated among the substance and the accidents.[32]

The key word in the last sentence is "participated": The *ratio entis* is unequally participated among the substance and the accidents. Already in *De ente et essentia* Thomas realizes that predicamental analogy must be conceived in terms of ontological participation. In the words of Bernard Montagnes, "If substance is the primordial being, it is no longer merely a subject of accidents, but a maximum degree of a perfection that the accidents possess by participation of a lesser degree. At the level of the categories, the unity of order rests on a relation of participation."[33]

---

31. Ibid., p. 29.

32. Ibid. Thomas puts the matter the following way in *De ente et essentia*, c. 6: "Sed quia illud quod dicitur maxime et verissime in quolibet genere, est causa eorum quae sunt post in illo genere . . . , ut etiam in II Metaphysicae dicitur, ideo substantia, quae est primum in genere entis, verissime et maxime essentia habens, oportet quod sit causa accidentium quae secundario et quasi secundum quid rationem entis participant" (ed. Roland-Gosselin, 44, lines 7-14).

33. Montagnes, *The Doctrine of the Analogy of Being according to Thomas Aquinas*, p. 29.

Let us step back for a moment and ask ourselves what the "analogy of being" signifies in Thomas's early philosophical work. Insofar as we can inquire into the causal principles of being, the unity and difference of being is reflected in the analogy of order that itself rests on the relation of participation. We are able to grasp the unity in difference because we understand the causal order that obtains between substance and accidents. Thomas always regards Aristotle's solution of predicamental analogy on the horizontal level as definitively established. From his early works on right up to his very last ones, he alludes to it in passing, clarifies it, but otherwise simply presupposes it.[34] However, what Thomas came increasingly to understand is that the relation of participation on which the analogy of order rests calls for further metaphysical resolution.

Now, let us prepare the transition from the predicamental to the transcendental order. Remember that in the predicamental order the predicates fall under a determinate category, or genus, with the exception of the most common predicate, being *(ens)*, which is analogously shared or participated by all things of whatever category. Hence the *predicamental analogy* is transgeneric, or transcategorical, insofar as it applies analogically to the substance and to all the accidents, across the various genera, or categories. Following his teacher Albert the Great, Thomas calls names that are common to all things in this transgeneric sense "transcendentals," *transcendentia* (next to "being," also "true," "good," and "one").[35] The transcendentals are *modes of being,* because they transcend everything that is, by being common to and contained in everything that is.[36] The turn to the transcendental order occurs in the realization that the same diversity of the transcendentals does not only obtain in relation to the diversity of created being but also obtains in their relation to the transcendent being of God as their ultimate cause.

At this point we have reached the threshold of the *transition from the predicamental to the transcendental order.* It is here, in light of the transcendentals, that for Christian thinkers in the medieval context the old meta-

---

34. In the most extensive treatments of this matter in his commentary on the *Metaphysics,* Thomas presents the predicamental analogy of being as a unity of order by relation to this primary form of being, which is substance: 1.14.223-24; 4.1.534-43 (commentary on 4.2); 7.1.1246-59 and 7.4.1334-38 (commentary on 7.1); and 11.3 (commentary on 11.3).

35. On the derivation of the transcendentals, see Wippel, *The Metaphysical Thought of Thomas Aquinas,* pp. 192-94.

36. See Thomas Aquinas, *De veritate,* q. 1, a. 1. For the overall topic of transcendentals in Aquinas, see the outstanding and, what strikes me as definitive, study by Jan Aertsen, *Medieval Philosophy and the Transcendentals: The Case of Thomas Aquinas* (Leiden: Brill, 1996).

physical problem of the one and the many takes on a new urgency. For by now creation *ex nihilo* is known definitively by virtue of divine revelation, as well as coherently defensible on the philosophical level. And consequently, the central metaphysical challenge is not anymore the reduction to unity of multiple meanings of being by way of substance but the reduction of diverse beings to unity in relation to God. Bernard Montagnes puts the matter succinctly and in such a way that we immediately realize its striking relevance for contemporary theology:

> How to conceive the relation of beings to Being? If they are homogeneous with it, the monism that results leads necessarily to pantheism. And if they are heterogeneous to it, the mind comes up against a pluralism such that makes God unknowable. A God too close or too far, pantheism or agnosticism: how can we find a passage between these two dangers?[37]

This is what is at stake in the question — Is being univocal or equivocal? — when understood to refer to transcendental analogy.

D. Is Analogy a Purely Logical Tool — or Does It Pertain to Reality As Well?

At this point — *the very transition from predicamental to transcendental analogy* — we have to pause briefly for a fundamental sort of clarification pertaining to predicamental as well as to transcendental analogy. Our reading of *De principiis naturae,* as well as of *De ente et essentia,* suggests that Thomas transitions in both works from logic to metaphysics, from the consideration of things according to the being that they have in the mind to a consideration of things according to their being in reality. And it is in the latter context, the metaphysical consideration, that Thomas develops the analogy of hierarchical participation of being. Some Thomists, however, deny such a transition from logic to metaphysics, from predicamental analogy that is concerned with logical *intentiones* to the analogy of being that is concerned with causal relations in reality. It is first and foremost Ralph McInerny who has extensively argued that the analogy of names belongs to logic alone, that it pertains exclusively to the mode of being things have in

37. Montagnes, *The Doctrine of the Analogy of Being according to Thomas Aquinas,* pp. 12-13.

human intellection.[38] While it would exceed the scope of this essay to enter into an extensive textual and speculative debate with McInerny, I shall rely in the following upon the extensive textual and speculative critique of his position advanced by Lawrence Dewan.[39] I find the latter persuasive as a reading of Thomas's texts, as well as a speculative position *secundum mentem S. Thomae* and in accord with major voices of the Thomist commentatorial tradition (John Capreolus and Sylvester of Ferrara). I shall briefly highlight three points as most salient for our concerns. They pertain to the fundamental relationship between metaphysics, or first philosophy, on the one hand, and logic, on the other hand. They make explicit the primordial nature of metaphysical inquiry of being as an inquiry that gives rise to notions that pertain properly to being and as defined by the metaphysician become the principles with which logic operates.

I also should stress that I do not regard these three points per se as advancing a probative argument against McInerny's position, though I think Dewan's developed position indeed does. All I regard these three points to do is, in light of McInerny's fundamental objection, to offer sufficient warrant to continue to maintain that there is terminologically as well as substantively speaking an analogy of being in Thomas Aquinas.

First, according to Thomas as well as Aristotle, logic as a science depends on metaphysics and not vice versa. Following Aristotle, Thomas regards metaphysics as the science that considers the principles common to all the other sciences.[40] Indeed, in some particular cases it is the metaphysician

38. Most recently Ralph McInerny, *Aquinas and Analogy* (Washington, D.C.: Catholic University of America Press, 1996). But see also Charles de Koninck, "Metaphysics and the Interpretation of Words," *Laval théologique et philosophique* 17 (1961): 22-34, and Hyacinthe-Marie Robillard, *De l'analogie et du concept d'être* (Montreal: Les presses de l'Université de Montréal, 1963).

39. Lawrence Dewan, "St. Thomas and Analogy: The Logician and the Metaphysician," in *Form and Being: Studies in Thomistic Metaphysics* (Washington, D.C.: Catholic University of America Press, 2006), pp. 81-95, and idem, "Does Being Have a Nature? (Or: Metaphysics as a Science of the Real)," in *Approaches to Metaphysics*, ed. William Sweet, pp. 23-59 (Dordrecht: Kluwer Academic Publishers, 2004).

40. "[T]hat science is pre-eminently intellectual which deals with the most universal principles. These principles are being and those things which naturally accompany being, such as unity and plurality, potency and act. Now such principles should not remain entirely undetermined, since without them a complete knowledge of the principles which are proper to any genus or species cannot be had. Nor again should they be dealt with in any one particular science; for, since a knowledge of each class of beings stands in need of these principles, they would with equal reason be investigated in every particular science. It follows, then,

Reinhard Hütter

who gives the principles of some sciences to these sciences, which is the case with logic. For, as Dewan emphasizes, the definition of the genus, the species, and the analogue falls under the responsibility of the metaphysician: "To investigate genus and species is proper to the metaphysician, since they pertain properly to being as being."[41]

Second, from logic's dependence upon metaphysics it follows that "more is included in the metaphysician's notions of univocity and analogy than the logician's notions of these *intentiones*."[42] This is a point as complex as it is crucial. Dewan draws upon Thomas's *Scriptum super libros Sententiarum* I, d. 19, q. 5, a. 2, ad 1 in order to substantiate it. Next to two classifications of analogy we are familiar with (according to notion only and not according to being; according to notion and according to being), Thomas introduces a third one:

> Or else, [something is said according to analogy] according to being and not according to notion [*secundum esse et non secundum intentionem*]; and this occurs when many things are taken as equal [*parificantur*] in the notion [*in intentione*] of something common, but that common item does not have being of one intelligible character [*esse unius rationis*] in all: for example, all bodies are taken as equal in the notion of corporeity [*in intentione corporeitatis*]; hence, the logician [*logicus*], who considers only notions [*intentiones tantum*], says that this name "body" is predicated of all bodies univocally; however, the being of this nature [*esse hujus naturae*] is not of the same intelligible character [*ejusdem rationis*] in corruptible and incorruptible bodies; hence for the metaphysician and the physicist, who consider things according to their being, neither this name "body," nor any other [name] is said univocally of corruptibles and incorruptibles, as is clear from *Metaph.* 10, text 5, from [both] the Philosopher and the Commentator.[43]

This classification is indeed crucial because here the difference between the metaphysician's consideration and that of the logician is starkest. There is

---

that such principles are treated by one common science, which, since it is intellectual in the highest degree, is the mistress of the others" (St. Thomas Aquinas, *Commentary on Aristotle's Metaphysics*, trans. Richard J. Blackwell, Richard J. Spath, and W. Edmund Thirlkel [Notre Dame, Ind: Dumb Ox Books, 1995], pp. xix-xx).

41. Dewan, "St. Thomas and Analogy," p. 84.

42. Ibid., p. 88.

43. Dewan's translation. He points to *Summa contra Gentiles* I, c. 32 and *De potentia* q. 7, a. 7, ad 6 for examples of this sort of analogy and Aquinas's explicit denial of its univocity.

one important instance, according to Thomas, where what is univocity for the logician is emphatically not univocity but analogy for the metaphysician. Hence, "there is a type of term that a logician sees as univocal and a metaphysician sees as analogical,"[44] and it is this latter instance that establishes the fact that more is included in the metaphysician's notions of analogy and univocity. In the case of corruptible and incorruptible bodies, Dewan rightly stresses, "It is not enough, according to the metaphysician, to have one *intentio* for *univocity*. One must have the same kind of matter."[45]

Third, because the metaphysician considers the constitutive causal principles of being and, by doing so, also investigates genus, species, and the analogue, Thomas properly uses the logical notions as "stand-ins" for metaphysical conceptions. As Thomas states in his commentary on Aristotle's *Metaphysics,* the metaphysician "considers the prior and the posterior, genus and species, whole and part, and other things of this sort, because these also are accidents of that which is inasmuch as it is that which is [*accidentia entis inquantum est ens*]."[46] As Thomas says elsewhere in his commentary, for the metaphysician's consideration "being *in* a subject" and "being *about* a subject"[47] do not differ. For genus and difference have a foundation in things, as it became clear in the connection of genus to matter in Thomas's treatment of "body" as an analogical name, metaphysically considered, when used in common for corruptible and incorruptible bodies.[48]

In conclusion, our transition from predicamental to transcendental analogy and from the logic of predication to the metaphysics of ontological

44. Dewan, "St. Thomas and Analogy," p. 89.

45. Ibid., p. 93. Dewan illustrates his point with *ST* I, q. 66, a. 2, ad 2, where Thomas argues that the word "genus" needs to be properly qualified according to its consideration by a logician compared to its consideration by a physicist, i.e., a natural philosopher: "If genus is taken in a physical sense, corruptible and incorruptible things are not in the same genus, on account of their different modes of potentiality, as is said in *Metaph.* x, text 26. Logically considered, however, there is but one genus of all bodies, since they are all included in the one notion of corporeity."

46. Thomas Aquinas, *Commentary on Aristotle's Metaphysics,* 4.4.587, concerning Aristotle's *Metaphysics* 1005a13-18. Dewan's translation, "St. Thomas and Analogy," p. 84, n. 14.

47. Thomas Aquinas, *Commentary on Aristotle's Metaphysics* 7.13.1576, concerning Aristotle's *Metaphysics* 1038b15-16.

48. Dewan is here in fundamental agreement with Montagnes. Cf. the latter's instructive n. 100 on p. 60, where, in reference to the passage of Thomas's Sentence commentary under discussion, he states: "The logical equality of the generic notion conceals a real hierarchy of species; whence the logician is more aware of the notional unity, whereas the metaphysician is more attentive to the real diversity."

participation merely reflects the *ordo doctrinae,* the pedagogical order from what is easier to what is more difficult. The order of being itself as it gives rise to the order of knowledge and of predication, in its distinction from the *ordo doctrinae,* is reflected in the hierarchical relationship between metaphysics as first philosophy to the science of logic, in that "it is the metaphysician who defines analogy, and does so in terms of *the foundations in reality* for the modes of discourse."[49] The analogy of being is the condition for the possibility of predicamental analogy and hence "the interest of the metaphysician in the *real* foundation for naming."[50] We understand *De principiis naturae* and *De ente et essentia* rightly only if we read them as exercises of a *metaphysical* inquiry into reality per se that provide the logician with the notions constitutive of his or her science but that simultaneously use these notions as "stand-ins" for metaphysical conceptions. It is for this very reason that in *Summa theologiae* I, q. 4, a. 3, when treating the metaphysical question of the likeness of some creature to God, Thomas identifies the similarity of the effect to the cause, the similarity of the creature to the Creator, as "according to a sort of analogy [*secundum aliqualem analogiam*]."[51] The question under consideration does not pertain exclusively to the analogy of names in the order of predication but indeed pertains first and foremost to the real relation of all beings insofar as they are beings to the first cause, the universal principle of being in its entirety. And it is the latter to which we shall now turn.

E. The Analogy of Participation:
The Likeness between Cause and Effect

It has been well established in recent scholarship on Thomas that, up to and including *De veritate,* he is intensely searching for the proper way to conceive of transcendental analogy and the ensuing analogical predication of God.[52] Eventually he integrates all major elements of the earlier solutions into a mature synthesis, fully articulated first in *Summa contra Gentiles* 1.34, a synthesis

49. Dewan, "St. Thomas and Analogy," p. 94.

50. Ibid., p. 95.

51. Also, as Dewan adds as additional text, Thomas characterizes the *natura entitatis* (i.e., the act of being) as one *secundum analogiam* in all creatures (*In II Sent.,* d. 1, q. 1, a. 1).

52. For the following, see Cornelio Fabro, "The Intensive Hermeneutics of Thomistic Philosophy: The Notion of Participation," trans. B. M. Bonansea, *Review of Metaphysics* 27 (1974): 449-91 (486ff.).

that presents "a general theory of the analogy of being that applies to transcendental unity as well as predicamental unity."[53] It is of paramount importance not to get sidetracked by the temporary solution entertained in the prior *De veritate*, where indeed for a brief period Thomas does consider the analogy of proportionality as the ultimate, overarching framework for transcendental analogy. In light of the late Scotus's critique of the analogy of attribution *ad alterum*, first Thomas Sutton and later Cajetan and the ensuing Cajetanian tradition of conceiving analogy anchor themselves in the particular proposal of *De veritate*.[54] Recent scholarship, however, has established that Thomas drops this proposal never to return to it again, except in those instances of transcendental analogy in which the analogy of proportionality is guided and controlled by the primordial analogy of causal participation.

It has been incontrovertibly demonstrated by L.-B. Geiger, Cornelio Fabro, W. Norris Clarke, John F. Wippel, Rudi te Velde, and others that the notion of ontological participation maintained by Neoplatonic philosophers — especially Proclus — and tacitly assumed by Aristotle's Neoplatonic commentators, became a central element in the development of Aquinas's mature position on the analogy of being.[55]

---

53. Montagnes, *The Doctrine of the Analogy of Being according to Thomas Aquinas,* p. 14.

54. See the important recent work of Joshua P. Hochschild on this complex and controversial issue: *The Semantics of Analogy: Rereading Cajetan's* De Nominum Analogia (Notre Dame, Ind.: University of Notre Dame Press, 2010).

55. L.-B. Geiger, *La participation dans la philosophie de S. Thomas d'Aquin* (Paris: J. Vrin, 1942); Cornelio Fabro, *Participation et causalité selon S. Thomas d'Aquin;* W. Norris Clarke, S.J., "The Limitation of Act by Potency in St. Thomas: Aristotelianism or Neoplatonism?" and "The Meaning of Participation in St. Thomas," in *Explorations in Metaphysics,* pp. 65-101; John F. Wippel, "Thomas Aquinas and Participation," in *Studies in Medieval Philosophy,* ed. John F. Wippel, pp. 117-58 (Washington, D.C.: Catholic University of America Press, 1987); Rudi te Velde, *Participation and Substantiality in Thomas Aquinas;* see also Fabro, "Intensive Hermeneutics," pp. 468-69. Notice, however, that deepening his inquiry into ontological participation by way of the Neoplatonic tradition did not mean for Thomas to replace the Aristotelianism of his youth with an allegedly more mature Neoplatonic view that eventually "Platonized" Thomas's whole metaphysical approach. On the contrary, the profoundly Aristotelian *De ente et essentia* already entailed the potential for the unique metaphysical synthesis Thomas achieves late in his work, especially in *De substantiis separatis.* In that work, see c. 3, "De convenientia positionum Aristotelis et Platonis." According to Fabro, the importance of this text for Thomas's synthesis cannot be overrated: "The Thomistic synthesis is absolutely original: it accepts the metaphysical nucleus of Platonic transcendence (notion of creation, composition of *esse* and essence, doctrine of analogy) and welds it with the act of Aristotelian immanence (the unity of the substantial form, the intellective soul as substantial

Thomas's decisive move was to deepen the analysis of *De ente et essentia* by way of the metaphysical method of resolution, that is, by tracing all things to the one first principle by which they are coordinated.[56] In the course of this inquiry toward increasing resolution — bearing fruit especially in *De potentia* — Thomas eventually realizes the following: *While God indeed is the source of all that exists with a formal or essential determination, God in his uniquely transcendent act of being as the efficient cause of their being is utterly distinct from the world of determinate created forms.* Such metaphysical resolution leads Aquinas eventually to the first substantial act, which is *esse.* And more important even, the final consequence of such metaphysical resolution is to reduce the act of being by participation, the *actus essendi,* to the first principle, the *esse per essentiam,* that which is the act of being by way of its very essence.[57]

Here we can see immediately why participation and transcendental analogy converge: To participate is to have partially what another is without restriction.[58] Since being is participated by degrees beginning with that

---

form of the body, the doctrine of abstraction). The originality of the dialectic of *esse* was fully developed by Aquinas especially in his later works because of a more direct knowledge of some Neoplatonic writings, such as those of Proclus and Porphyry. In *De substantiis separatis* (1272-73) he solves the classic Neoplatonic problem of the accord between Plato and Aristotle through his 'new' notion of participation. This he does in chapter 3, *De convenientia positionum Aristotelis et Platonis,* where he shows the agreement of the two philosophers on such important doctrines as the real composition of essence and *esse* in creatures, the absolute immortality of spiritual substances, and the notion of divine Providence, while in chapter 4, *De differentia dictarum positionum Aristotelis et Platonis,* he shows that their differences concern only very secondary points" ("Intensive Hermeneutics," pp. 468-69).

56. Saint Thomas Aquinas, *On the Power of God (Quaestiones Disputatae de Potentia Dei),* literally trans. by the English Dominican Fathers (Westminster: Newman Press, 1932), book I, q. 3, a. 6. In the body of the article he offers a highly condensed account of the discursive progress of metaphysical inquiry before Aristotle, at the end of which he states: "Consequently, all these various things must be traced to one first principle whereby they are co-ordinated: and for this reason the Philosopher concludes (*Meta.* 12.10) that there is one ruler over all" (p. 118; *De potentia,* q. 3, a. 6, c.).

57. "[T]he notion of *actus essendi* appears beginning with the *Contra Gentiles,* where we meet the decisive affirmation: *esse actus est*" (Montagnes, *The Doctrine of the Analogy of Being according to Thomas Aquinas,* p. 43). Hence, for Thomas participation by way of the *actus essendi,* the act of all acts, "concerns the transcendental analogy of being, or, more precisely, the communication of being according to degrees, from the divine being, in which being subsists without restriction right down to partial realizations in the different substances" (ibid., p. 34).

58. "Ens . . . de quolibet autem creatura praedicatur per participationem: nulla autem creatura est suum esse, sed *est habens esse*" (Quodl. II, q. 2, a. 1).

which is being by essence, there obtains simultaneously an essential diversity of participants and a unity of reference to the primary instance from which they obtain the common perfection.

Let us be very clear about one point here. For Thomas, being a creature means, not to be identical with one's *esse,* but to have *esse.* This *esse* is participated in by all creatures and hence is called *esse commune.* It is of central importance not to get the relationship wrong between the *esse commune* and God, *the esse ipsum subsistens.* Are the two identical, or is God even contained in the *esse commune?* In his commentary on Denys's *Divine Names,* Thomas explicitly rejects such an identification.[59] Rather, the *esse commune* is the first of created realities. As such, the *esse commune* is an effect of God's creative agency and hence has no part whatsoever in God's essence but participates in some of the perfections of the *ipsum esse subsistens.* Consequently, God and the *esse commune* are as fundamentally distinct from each other as cause and effect are. Moreover, the *esse commune* does not subsist on its own; rather, it is to be understood as a formal principle inherent in all beings.[60]

It is crucial to understand that in participation by way of the *actus essendi,* the act of being, there is no factor extrinsic to the *esse commune* itself that limits and pluralizes being. Rather, this limiting and pluralizing principle — in short, essence — must come by way of the *actus essendi* as the latter's proper perfection of differentiated subsistence. Remember what differentiates one thing from another. It is its essential determinations, that which makes it intelligibly different from something else.

But how exactly is this composite of the *actus essendi* and essence unified? It is in order to address this important metaphysical question that Thomas, in a rather bold speculative step of further metaphysical resolution, applies the Aristotelian principles of act and potency to the Neoplatonic dynamic of participation. We find this crucial move in *Summa contra Gentiles*

---

59. Thomas Aquinas, *In librum beati Dionysii de divinis nominibus expositio* (Rome: Marietti, 1950), 5.2.660: "Deinde, cum dicit [279]: *Et ipsum* . . . ostendit quomodo esse se habeat ad Deum; et dicit quod *ipsum esse* commune *est ex* primo Ente, quod est Deus, et ex hoc sequitur quod esse commune aliter se habeat ad Deum quam alia existentia, quantum ad tria: primo quidem, quantum ad hoc quod alia existentia dependent ab esse communi, non autem Deus, sed magis esse commune dependet a Deo; et hoc est quod dicit quod ipsum *esse* commune *est ipsius Dei,* tamquam ab Ipso dependens, *et non ipse* Deus *est esse,* idest ipsius esse communis, tamquam ab ipso dependens."

60. See the illuminating discussion of this difficult metaphysical point by Martin Bieler, "The Theological Importance of a Philosophy of Being," in *Reason and the Reasons of Faith,* ed. Paul J. Griffiths and Reinhard Hütter, pp. 295-326 (London: T. & T. Clark, 2005), pp. 314-15.

1.18: "Several things cannot become absolutely one unless among them
something is act and something potency."[61] Hence, this metaphysical resolution leads Thomas to the axiom of first composition: *the subject that participates is related to the participated perfection as potency to act.*[62]

It is indeed the case that, in this Aristotelian reconception of the Neoplatonic concept of participation, the primacy of act and the priority of efficient causality condition each other. In other words, in the process of
Thomas's metaphysical study of the composition of *esse* and essence in created things, participation remains governed by act and potency. *Participation signifies the communication of act to a subject in potency.*

Understanding participation rightly depends on not misunderstand-
ing *esse* as a quasi essence. Rather, *ens* is essence in act. It is the "in act" that
esse signifies. Let us unpack this fundamental point in three respects:

First, *esse* is always in act; hence a being *(id quod est)* can participate in
it, because a being is in potency to *esse*. God, who is *esse* without any potency
admixed whatsoever, has nothing by participation but is what he is by virtue
of his own essence: "As act free from potentiality, God grounds all participation and causes all beings."[63]

Second, *esse* as act is not to be conceived as some primordial, undifferentiated *esse* that would only subsequently actuate different essences "as it
were from the outside."[64] Rather, *esse* and essence are equally primordial and
hence each must be understood in light of the other. Essence itself comes on
the way of *esse* (Ferdinand Ulrich), the *esse commune*, for nothing falls out-

61. Saint Thomas Aquinas, *Summa contra Gentiles. Book One: God,* trans. Anton C.
Pegis (Notre Dame, Ind.: University of Notre Dame Press, 1975), p. 103 (SCG 1.18: "Non enim
plura possunt simpliciter unum fieri nisi aliquid sit ibi actus, et aliud potentia"). For this
point I am indebted to George Lindbeck's illuminating discussion in his essay "Participation
and Existence in the Interpretation of St. Thomas Aquinas," *Franciscan Studies* 17 (1957): 1-22
and 107-25.

62. "The participated perfection is the act of the subject in potency which receives it,
and it is limited to the measure of this subject" (Montagnes, *The Doctrine of the Analogy of
Being according to Thomas Aquinas,* p. 40).

63. Ibid., p. 41. "*Esse,* which is infinite when it is not received within a potency, can be
participated according to the indefinitely varied measures that the different essences are; beings are to the degree that they participate *esse,* and they are more or less perfect according as
they participate more or less the perfection of being that pertains to God by essence. Their
measure of being establishes their degree of likeness to the one who is *ipsum esse.* Thus, every subject that receives *esse* without being identical to it possesses being by participation.
This is why the essence of such a substance is to the *esse* that it participates as receptive potency to the act received" (ibid.).

64. Ibid.

side the act of being; hence neither does essence as the perfection of differentiated potency to subsistence. Now to invert the perspective, essence is the measure and degree in which *esse* is participated.[65] Consequently, the *perfectio essendi,* the act of being — terminating in a concrete being *(hoc ens)* — includes indissolubly *esse,* essence, and the subject.

Third, it is utterly crucial to understand that there is no "common logos" of an ever so subtly hidden univocity at play in Thomas's understanding of ontological participation. For beings, by way of the measuring perfection of essence, are *intrinsically* diversified. Hence, in analogical predication of existence there is no univocity of the nature of essence whatsoever involved. Nevertheless, there still obtains an analogical unity, since all intrinsically diversified beings receive their specific limited perfection from the primary instance in which the respective perfection subsists without limitation.[66] This is to say that all things resemble the primary cause of existence and, insofar as they participate in existence, resemble one another. In light of the correlation between act and form, *esse* and essence, Thomas conceives transcendental analogy as a causal, as well as formal, ontological dependence of every being *(id quod est)* with respect to the *ipse esse subsistens,* God. Being *(ens)* is never univocal because it is always participated. And because there obtain two dimensions of participation, predicamental and transcendental participation, there are two corresponding forms of the analogy of being, one between substance and accident, and the other between God and creature.

In his later works, that is, from the *Summa contra Gentiles* on, Thomas conceives of both dimensions of participation as an integral unity. In the order of knowledge, one ascends from predicamental to transcendental analogy. In the order of being, predicamental participation depends on the ontologically prior transcendental participation.[67]

Now, remember Aristotle's analogy of health as employed by Aquinas in *De principiis naturae.* Notice in what respect the analogy of being resem-

65. "The being that subsists in God without restriction communicates itself in virtue of the divine causality in a more or less limited way according to the measure of each being, and it is intrinsically and formally participated on each occasion" (ibid.).

66. Ibid.

67. Montagnes puts the matter well: "In order to elaborate a coherent and unified theory of the analogy of being, Thomas strove to apply the predicamental analogy discovered by Aristotle to the relation of beings to God, i.e., to transcendental analogy. By doing this the unified diversity that one encounters at the horizontal level of the categories and that one finds on the vertical plane of substances pertains to one and the same principle of explanation: analogy by reference to a primary instance" (ibid., p. 44).

bles the analogy of health and how it differs from it. Quite obviously, the analogy of health is an *extrinsic* analogy; there is no intrinsic formal participation involved, since health can belong only to a living thing. There would indeed be serious if not fatal consequences for transcendental analogy if all being were to belong only to the primary instance. For in this case it would be necessary to affirm that God is the only being, the only perfect thing, and that everything else has being and perfection only by extrinsic denomination. To emphasize divine transcendence in this way would deprive the universe of all reality. However, on this matter Thomas is as clear as can be desired. For he stresses that the analogy of health obtains "according to the intellectual conception only, but not according to being."[68] The analogy of being, in contrast, obtains "according to the intellectual conception as well as according to being,"[69] because it involves an intrinsic formal, as well as causal, participation. For this second kind of analogy by reference to a primary instance is constituted by causal dependence upon the first being and by an intrinsic possession of the perfection of being, albeit formally specified according to a hierarchy of essences.[70]

There is, however, one further step of differentiation necessary in the precise specification of the intrinsic analogy by reference to a primary instance. In an important discussion in *De potentia* Thomas identifies two ways to conceive such an analogy.[71] One is the analogy of two to a third

---

68. "*Secundum intentionem tantum et non secundum esse*" (*In I Sent.*, d. 19, q. 5, a. 2, ad 1).

69. "*Secundum intentionem et secundum esse*" (ibid.).

70. Montagnes, *The Doctrine of the Analogy of Being according to Thomas Aquinas*, pp. 44-45. In his instructive n. 100 on p. 60, Montagnes directs the reader to *De ver.*, q. 21, a. 4, ad 2, where Thomas distinguishes clearly between extrinsic and intrinsic analogy: "A thing is denominated with reference to something else in two ways. (1) This occurs when the very reference itself is the meaning of the denomination. Thus urine is called healthy with respect to the health of an animal. For the meaning of healthy as predicated of urine is 'serving as a sign of the health of an animal.' In such cases what is thus relatively denominated does not get its name from a form inherent in it but from something extrinsic to which it is referred. (2) A thing is denominated by reference to something else when the reference is not the meaning of the denomination but its cause. . . . It is in this way that the creature is called good with reference to God" (*Truth*, vol. 3, trans. Robert W. Schmidt, S.J. [Indianapolis: Hackett, 1994], pp. 20-21).

71. Saint Thomas Aquinas, *On the Power of God*, book 3, p. 43: "We must accordingly take a different view and hold that nothing is predicated univocally of God and the creature: but that those things which are attributed to them in common are predicated not equivocally but analogically. Now this kind of predication is twofold. The first is when one thing is predicated of two with respect to a third: thus being is predicated of quantity and quality

(duorum ad tertium). An example would be to call the accidents of quality and quantity as being in relationship to the substance. And it is this analogy of two to a third that Thomas decidedly rejects for use in the analogical naming of God. For according to this kind of analogy, the transcendental "being" *(ens)* would embrace God as well as beings and would be superior to them, since "being" *(ens)* would relate to God and creatures as substance would to quantity and quality.

What Thomas embraces in his later works is the second way of conceiving such an analogy, the analogy of *unius ad alterum,* which is established exclusively between a secondary analogate and the primary instance. The example for this kind of analogy is that between substance per se and accident per se. For substance exists of itself *(substantia est quod per se est),* and accident is in something else *(accidentis esse est inesse).* In this kind of predication one of the two precedes the other. Montagnes puts the matter succinctly:

> What it means is that on the categorical level accident and substance do not receive the attribution of being by reference to a form common to each term, namely, being; there is nothing prior to substance, and being is either substance in the first place *(per prius)* or else accident subsequently *(per posterius).* . . . In the same way, on the transcendental level, being does not encompass both beings and God, since being is not prior to God. It is God who grounds the analogy of being, since beings receive by participation what He is by essence; there is no primary instance of being other than He.[72]

Lest we misunderstand the analogy of being, however, as a ladder that, having made possible the necessary ascent, can now safely be discarded, let me reemphasize the following by way of a summary of what the analogy of being amounts to in Thomas's thought. It is fair to say that, ultimately, in light of the final metaphysical *resolutio,* for Thomas the unity of being rests

---

with respect to substance. The other is when a thing is predicated of two by reason of a relationship between these two: thus being is predicated of substance and quantity. In the first kind of predication the two things must be preceded by something to which each of them bears some relation: thus substance has respect to quantity and quality: whereas in the second kind of predication this is not necessary, but one of the two must precede the other. Wherefore since nothing precedes God, but he precedes the creature, the second kind of analogical predication is applicable to him but not the first" *(De potentia,* q. 7, a. 7, c.).

72. Montagnes, *The Doctrine of the Analogy of Being according to Thomas Aquinas,* p. 71.

on the unity of the first cause of being. For only when one has arrived at the real unity of being has the multiplicity of beings been reduced to one. Hence, there obtains a strict correspondence between the structure of analogy and the structure of participation, with analogy as the way of predicating the unity of being and participation as the real unity of being. In short, as a way of predication the analogy of being reflects the dynamic unity of causal order that obtains between beings and their first and universal principle.[73] Hence, for Thomas analogy is anything but a merely linguistic tool or logical operation in relation to divine predication. Rather, the analogy of being is the necessary predicamental entailment of an epistemological, as well as metaphysical, realism that finds its proximate metaphysical resolution in the *actus essendi* and its final resolution in the first and ultimate principle, *ipsum esse subsistens.*

F. The Analogical Predication of God: Transgeneric Likeness between Cause and Effect Based on the Analogy Unius ad Alterum

When we turn now to the analogical predication of God, we need to keep in mind that, according to Thomas's mature doctrine, such analogical predication occurs exclusively on the basis of this latter analogy of *unius ad alterum.* For being the first and universal principle of everything, God is "extra omne genus." Hence, in the analogy of divine predication, the whole of all categorically distinct things as such is transcended. As Rudi te Velde rightly observes:

> Seen in this light, it becomes clear why God cannot be addressed as some particular reality, the highest and first in the order of essences. God is not a being among others who is merely higher and more perfect than everything we know of. God cannot be approached in the line of "more of the same" — that is, the same as the perfections we encounter in the world of creatures, such as life, intelligence, goodness, and so on — but then enlarged to its maximum and purified from its imperfections.[74]

Rather than pursuing such a perfect-being ontology, as it won the day in later Leibnitzian and Wolffian metaphysics, Thomas conceives of created reality as *esse commune* in its differentiated unity and hence as a whole that *as such* is related to God as the first and universal principle of the *actus essendi.*

73. Ibid., p. 91.
74. Velde, *Aquinas on God,* p. 117.

Hence, there obtains a specific metaphysical order between the first principle or cause and its effect. Since this order is transgeneric, it escapes, on the one hand, the univocal identity of the genus. On the other hand, the likeness that it entails is "secundum analogiam tantum" (*ST* I, q. 4, a. 3, ad 3), only according to a certain analogy — that is, of course, the analogy "unius ad alterum."

At this point we need to come back to the first transcendental, "being" *(ens)*. Remember that for Thomas it was by way of considering the first transcendental as such, *ens inquantum ens,* that the final metaphysical resolution became possible, the resolution to the first and single universal principle of all being — God.

The entailment of this last resolution is that the relationship between God and the *esse commune* is a causal one. *Esse* designates the universal perfection, the perfection of all perfections that pertain to the essences of things. In the process of the metaphysical *resolutio* the many perfections of creatures are reduced to their one origin, the first causal principle. The very path of this *resolutio* consists in leaving behind, in bracketing, what pertains to the order of essence and its categorical differentiations.[75]

Now we have arrived at the key notion of analogical predication for Thomas — the names for divine perfections. These are names capable of signifying the very perfection of *esse* as the act of all acts and the perfection of all perfections. Hence they are not restricted to the categorically specified way in which we come to know these perfections. Because of their transcategorical nature the perfections they signify are not intrinsically finite, and therefore the names for divine perfections can properly be attributed to God.

Hence, Thomas emphasizes in *Summa theologiae* I, q. 13, a. 6 that

> these names are applied to God not as the cause only, but also essentially. For the words, God is good, or wise, signify not only that He is the cause of wisdom or goodness, but that these exist in Him in a more excellent way. Hence as regards what the name signifies, these names are applied primarily to God rather than to creatures, because these perfections flow from God to creatures; but as regards the imposition of the names, they are primarily applied by us to creatures, which we know first.[76]

---

75. See ibid., p. 116.

76. *ST* I, q. 13, a. 6, c.: "[H]uiusmodi nomina non solum dicuntur de Deo causaliter, sed etiam essentialiter. Cum enim dicitur *Deus est bonus* vel *sapiens,* non solum significatur quod ipse sit causa sapientiae vel bonitatis, sed quod haec in eo eminentius praeexistunt. Unde, secundum hoc, dicendum est quod, quantum ad rem significatam per nomen, per

Thomas draws here a clear distinction between the order of being and the order of knowledge in order to secure the absolute transcendence of God. In the order of being or participation, perfection belongs most eminently to God and is only participated in by the creature. Hence attributing perfection to God is not simply a virtual attribution. However, the perfection can be named only from the proximate context in which it is accessible to us as creatures. Rudi te Velde rightly stresses that all these multiple perfections are perfections of being, "which means that 'being' expresses their common unity in which they reflect their common origin in God. Perfection terms such as 'life,' 'wisdom,' 'good' signify more 'intense' aspects of the likeness creatures are said to have of God insofar as they are *beings*."[77]

Because of the simultaneity of the order of participation and the order of predication, the likeness of being has to find expression in a twofold analogous way. Regarding its *first* aspect, Thomas says: "Whatever is said of God and creatures is said according to the relation of a creature to God as its principle and cause, wherein all perfections of things preexist excellently."[78] Here we have the analogy of *unius ad alterum*. But remember now that all perfections are perfections of being, and because being is inherently and primordially predicated in an analogous way,[79] Thomas emphasizes that "a term [i.e., a perfection of being] that is thus used in a multiple sense signifies various proportions to some one thing; thus *healthy* applied to urine signifies the sign of animal health, and applied to medicine signifies the cause of that same health."[80] Because the perfections of being participate variously but similarly in their common first cause, they signify various but similar proportions to their common first cause. Hence there is a proportional likeness between God and creatures entailed in the analogy *unius ad alterum*. This kind of analogy by reference to a primary instance is constituted by

---

prius dicuntur de Deo quam de creaturis: quia a Deo huiusmodi perfectiones in creaturas manant. Sed quantum ad impositionem nominis, per prius a nobis imponuntur creaturis, quas prius cognoscimus."

77. Velde, *Aquinas on God*, p. 116.

78. *ST* I, q. 13, a. 5, c.: "[Q]uidquid dicitur de Deo et creaturis, dicitur secundum quod est aliquis ordo creaturae ad Deum, ut ad principium et causam, in qua praeexistunt excellenter omnes rerum perfectiones."

79. Ibid., a. 5, ad 1: "[A]ll univocal predications are reduced to one first non-univocal analogical predication, which is being." ("[I]n praedicationibus omnia univoca reducuntur ad unum primum, non univocum, sed analogicum, quod est ens.")

80. Ibid., a. 5, c.: "[N]omen quod sic multipliciter dicitur, significat diversas proportiones ad aliquid unum; sicut *sanum*, de urina dictum, significat signum sanitatis animalis, de medicina vero dictum, significat causam eiusdem sanitatis."

causal dependence upon the first being and by an intrinsic possession of the perfection of being, albeit formally specified according to a hierarchy of essences. Consequently, the analogy of attribution *unius ad alterum* by way of the *esse commune* always entails an analogy of proportion by way of reference to a primary instance. And this is the *second* aspect of the twofold way of the analogical predication of God. Because of the intrinsic possession of the perfection of being by way of participation, the proportion is *intrinsic* — quite unlike the analogy of health, where the proportion remains *extrinsic*. In short, the multiplicity of perfections (like life, goodness, being, etc.) all refer to God as "toward one" *(ad unum)* as proportional effects of God's being. The *proportio,* or relation, does not, however, depend on a "common logos," some shared identity, but only on a common first principle in the order of being. All that exists and all created ontological perfections refer to their one ultimate source, who as subsistent *esse* is perfect in an unsurpassable and ineffable way.

It is the order of being that requires the analogy of attribution *unius ad alterum* to be the logically primary one, and it is by way of this analogy that agnosticism as well as anthropomorphism is avoided. The logically subsequent analogy of intrinsic proportion secures that the perfections predicated of God are ascribed in a more than virtual sense such that a total apophaticism is also avoided.[81] God possesses the perfections we attribute to him in a preeminent way, from which creatures derive all that they are and all the perfections that pertain to them. Analogical names for divine perfection can be understood to refer to God not only eminently but indeed really and properly.[82] They truly signify God in himself as the *res significata* (the thing signified). But because God's essence indeed remains an utter mystery, the *modus significandi* of the perfection name (*how* the perfection exists in God) remains utterly unknown, hidden in the abyss of the *ipsum esse*

81. Eric L. Mascall, in his unjustly forgotten *Existence and Analogy: A Sequel to "He Who Is"* (London: Longmans, Green, 1949), rightly stressed this important point: "[I]n order to make the doctrine of analogy really satisfactory, we must see the analogical relation between God and the world as combining in a tightly interlocked union both analogy of attribution and analogy of proportionality. Without analogy of proportionality it is very doubtful whether the attributes which we predicate of God can be ascribed to him in more than a merely virtual sense; without analogy of attribution it hardly seems possible to avoid agnosticism. Which of the two forms of analogy is prior to the other has been, and still is a hotly debated question among scholastic philosophers. Sylvester of Ferrara, in his great commentary on the *Summa contra Gentiles,* asserted the primacy of attribution and alleged that in this he was expressing the true thought of St. Thomas" (pp. 113-14).

82. *ST* I, q. 13, a. 2, c.

subsistens — which is *not* the definition of God's essence but merely a circumscription of the first principle in its pure, subsisting actuality.[83] While we know that God truly is preeminently existent, good, wise, and so on, we do not know what this existence, goodness, and wisdom are in themselves. God in his perfection remains an unfathomable mystery.

III. Conclusion: A Response *secundum mentem S. Thomae* to the Two Protestant Objections to Analogical Predication of God in Thomas

We have reached the appropriate point in light of this *relecture* of Aquinas to reconsider the criticisms that Wolfhart Pannenberg and Eberhard Jüngel advanced against Aquinas's theological use of analogy.

The late Pannenberg in the significantly revised and recently published version of his 1955 *Habilitationsschrift* offers a much more nuanced and perceptive reading of Thomas's doctrine of the analogy of being than he did in his early work. Focusing in his critique of Thomas on the Neoplatonic causal scheme, he connects with it an axiom he sees entailed in Neoplatonic speculation, namely, that in us human beings capable of such rational speculation there must exist some identical core with the ultimate One. For without some point of identity of all things with the One, so Pannenberg maintains, an "Erfassung," that is, a proper speculative conceptual comprehension, of the One is impossible.[84]

In a nutshell, this is how Pannenberg's Hegelian argument goes: Any form of similarity presupposes a partial identity either of being or by way of a univocal conceptual comprehension. Since Thomas denies both, his analogical predication, says Pannenberg, is without any true conceptual traction and hence cannot deliver any genuine knowledge of God. In order to avoid this problem of a camouflaged equivocation, Pannenberg asserts that analogy has to be developed on the basis of a univocal concept of being (as Duns Scotus did). In this case, however, analogical predication of God becomes theologically problematic because of the serious danger of anthropomorphism entailed in this form of analogical predication. The one condition under which this double-pronged critique — either a univocal conceptual core or the meaninglessness of equivocation — gains true force is from the angle

83. Ibid., a. 3, c.
84. See Pannenberg, *Analogie und Offenbarung*, p. 122.

of a tacitly assumed, normative conceptualism: The question of analogous versus univocal predication is a question *exclusively* to be determined in relationship to the concept. Differently put, the concept by way of which essence is comprehended ("begriffen") becomes the *sole* normative metaphysical frame of reference — very much along the lines of Hegel's fatal identification of logic and ontology. However, Thomas's doctrine of analogy does not operate at all within this conceptualist metaphysical frame of reference for an analysis of analogical language. Rather, this frame of reference is decisively transcended in Thomas by the realization of the real distinction between *esse* and essence and the priority of order that obtains between the *actus essendi* and the essence. In the framework of these fundamental metaphysical principles, it becomes perfectly intelligible and defensible to understand analogy as a way of predicating in which an analogous term comprises in its meaning some similarity-in-difference across the transcendental range of perfections of being. As we have seen, for Aquinas the analogical naming of God from creatures is a transgeneric predication, not from one genus to another, but transcending all genera. The analogical naming occurs by way of the intrinsic attribution of a perfection name, where the similarity-in-difference expressed by the perfection comprises an intrinsic causal relation of participating in the *actus essendi*. In short, Thomas's analogy of being reaches to principles that decisively transcend the metaphysical conceptualism with its strong Hegelian undertones at work in Pannenberg's understanding of analogy.

Eberhard Jüngel, in his respective critique, reduces Aquinas's doctrine of analogy essentially to Kant's way of defending the possibility of an analogical predication of God.[85] What is quite obvious in Kant, he sees also at play in Aquinas, namely, that the analogy of attribution is of a purely *extrinsic* kind, functioning according to the logic of the analogy of proportionality: "God has a given perfection to God's being as the creature has the same perfection to that creature's being."[86] This reading and critique could perhaps

85. Jüngel, *Gott als Geheimnis der Welt*, pp. 358-63; *God as the Mystery of the World*, pp. 263-66.

86. Rolnick, *Analogical Possibilities*, p. 206; see Jüngel, *God as the Mystery of the World*, p. 276. While a theoretical proof of God's existence is impossible, according to Kant, he admits the possibility to think God coherently as a construct of pure reason by way of analogy. If such an analogy, however, is based upon concepts that (instead of receiving the intelligible by way of the sense data) impose intelligibility upon the sense data and hence when applied to that which lies outside the sensible world are entirely separate from it and receive no input of intelligibility from outside, the analogy of proportion based on these concepts of ex-

function against Cajetan's doctrine of analogy but misses Thomas's. Not unlike Pannenberg, Jüngel places Thomas into a tacitly assumed, overarching conceptualist framework — with the only difference that Pannenberg by putting Scotist pressure on Thomas forces on him the conceptualist alternative between either an analogous concept with a univocal core of identity or meaningless equivocation, while Jüngel, by mistaking Thomas for Cajetan — read in turn through Kant — reduces Thomas's way of analogical predication to conceptual proportionality.[87] Analogy is interpreted here merely as a mentally immanent system of comparison.

However, as we have seen, in Thomas the perfection names for God have a basis in the intrinsic being of creatures and their likeness to God through causal participation. This viewpoint (because of the intrinsicism due to causality) avoids the danger of an absolute apophaticism. For the analogy of intrinsic attribution reflects the dynamic of causal participation, and it is this causal connection that grounds the analogical naming of God from creatures.[88] Contrary to Jüngel's interpretation, Aquinas and Kant differ fundamentally in their respective doctrines of analogy. For, different from Kant, Aquinas regards metaphysical causality as reflected by the predicamentals to be indispensable for the analogy of intrinsic attribution. However, in his *Critique of Pure Reason*,[89] Kant famously *construes* — and, I would say, consequently *misunderstands* — the categories as categories of the understanding (quantity, quality, relation, and modality) as *constitutive* of experience. For Kant, the categories (including causality) are valid when applied to the phenomenal order, but not valid when applied beyond it to the noumenal order. Hence, for Kant the categories, by definition, cannot re-

---

perience must necessarily be an analogy of *extrinsic* proportionality. The result of such an analogical procedure can indeed be nothing but a "mere thought-entity" (cf. *Critique of Pure Reason* B 593-95).

87. The rejection of the real distinction between *esse* and essence and the denial of an analogous concept of being are at the core of this essentialist conceptualism: "Being is obviously not a real predicate, i.e., a concept of something that could add to the concept of a thing. It is merely the positing [*Position*] of a thing or of certain determinations in themselves. In the logical use it is merely the copula of a judgment" (*Critique of Pure Reason* B 626).

88. "God is the exceeding principle of all things contained under different genera. This causal connection grounds the analogical naming of God from creatures" (Velde, *Aquinas on God*, p. 112).

89. Immanuel Kant, *Kritik der reinen Vernunft* (Hamburg: Meiner, 1956), B 102-9; Immanuel Kant, *Critique of Pure Reason*, trans. Paul Guyer and Allen W. Wood (Cambridge: Cambridge University Press, 1997), pp. 210-14 (B 102-9).

flect causal principles in the order of being, and consequently the only form of analogy left for a predication of God is one of a purely formal, conceptual proportionality that indeed must — and here Jüngel is exactly right — end up in the apophaticism of an utterly mute God *supra nos*. A second reason is that "causality" for Kant is inapplicable to the trans-sensible realm, and therefore it is not only the case that predicamental analogy is inapplicable to the things themselves. In addition, causal and transcendental analogies from creatures to God are inapplicable, since we can never refer from sensible existents to the transcendent "cause" of existence.

Jüngel misses or chooses to ignore this fundamental difference between Kant on the one side and Aquinas on the other side when he argues that, in regard to analogical predication of truths about God, Kant, like Aquinas, seems to relate the analogy of proportion to the analogy of attribution or relation. He refers to a footnote in Kant's *Critique of Judgment* (B 448) where Kant considers the identity of the relationship between causes and effects.[90] While the categories of the understanding (including causality) can be applied validly only to the phenomenal order, they become invalid when applied to the noumenal order. Hence, because causes and effects cannot be extended beyond the sensible world, any supposed extension beyond it has to draw upon the pure (i.e., empty) conceptuality of reason. Correspondingly, any intrinsic proportion between finite effect and infinite first cause becomes impossible per se. Again, all we have here in Kant's discussion is the analogy of *extrinsic* proportionality that is explicitly excluded by Thomas in reference to God. (Moreover, the whole discussion in which this footnote occurs is part and parcel of Kant's consideration of the kinds of argument necessary for a valid *moral proof* of God's existence.) All of this is perfectly consistent within the specific conceptualism of Kant's critical transcendentalism. However, the whole approach rests on the unwarranted empiricist assumption that no intellectual nature can be abstracted from what the senses convey in combination with the rather unreasonable Cartesian mandate for clear and distinct ideas, as well as quasi-mathematical certitude in the deliveries of metaphysics. This unhappy union of two metaphysical reductions — empiricism and essentialist conceptualism — not only gave birth to the inherently patricidal monster of "modern philosophy" but remains under the fundamental critique of the uninterrupted tradition of Thomist metaphysics.[91]

---

90. Jüngel, *Gott als Geheimnis der Welt*, 363; *God as the Mystery of the World*, 266.
91. For a recent example of presupposing in a metaphysically unreflective way, that is,

And so the very difference between Aquinas's and Kant's ways of analogical predication of God offers quite a bit of evidence to what Bernard
Montagnes observes: "Each doctrine of analogy is a manifestation of a certain conception of being, of causality, of participation, of the unity of beings
in being."[92] Fundamentally different from Kant, for Aquinas analogical
predication reflects the causal structure of being in the existent world and
not merely a mentally immanent system of comparison.

Looked at from the Thomist perspective, Pannenberg's and Jüngel's
critical readings of Thomas on analogy are held captive by the implicit
Kantian and Hegelian presupposition that an essentialist notion of concept
holds the place of honor in philosophy, a notion they tacitly assume anteced-
ently also to be operative in Aquinas's way of analogical predication of God.
For Thomas, however, there is no concept of this kind operative in the analogical predication of God. Rather, the analogous term and concept comprises in its meaning some similarity-in-difference across the transcendental
range of perfections of being. Hence, the analogy of being is primordially
entailed in the concrete ways we ineluctably predicate being differently but
always in the differentiated unity of substance and accident, of cause and effect. W. Norris Clarke puts the matter that is at stake at this point between
univocity and analogy in the predication of God:

> The Scotus-Ockham analysis is geared primarily to the demands of de-
> ductive reasoning and the logical functioning of concepts. It also takes
> the word and concept as the fundamental unit of meaning, which re-
> mains intact in its own self-contained meaning no matter how it is
> moved around as a counter in combination with other concepts, includ-
> ing its use in a judgment, which is interpreted simply as a composition
> of two concepts, subject and predicate, without change in either. The

---

in a philosophically dogmatic way, the validity of the Kantian critique of the ascription of
causality to "supersensible" reality, see Archie J. Spencer, "Causality and the *analogia entis*:
Karl Barth's Rejection of the Analogy of Being Reconsidered," *Nova et Vetera*, Engl. ed., 6, no.
2 (2008): 329-76. However, the very presupposition of the validity of this Kantian critique
has been refuted consistently within the modern Thomist tradition, most recently by
Thomas Joseph White, O.P., *Wisdom in the Face of Modernity: A Study in Thomistic Natural
Theology* (Naples, Fla.: Sapientia Press, 2009). For a substantive interrogation of Spencer's
charges, see the astute response by Thomas Joseph White, O.P., "How Barth Got Aquinas
Wrong: A Reply to Archie J. Spencer on Causality and Christocentrism," in *Nova et Vetera*,
Engl. ed., 7, no. 1 (2009): 241-70.

92. Montagnes, *The Doctrine of the Analogy of Being according to Thomas Aquinas*,
p. 10.

Thomistic analysis is geared much more to the actual lived usage of the concept in a judgment, interpreted as an intentional act of referring its synthesis of subject-predicate to the real order, as it is in reality. Hence it tends to look right through the abstract meaning of the concept to what it signifies or intends to signify *(intendit significare)*, in the concrete, and so adjusts the content of the concept to what it knows about its realization in the concrete.[93]

According to Thomas, it is precisely by this way of understanding the analogy of being that rationalism and apophatic agnosticism are excluded in the analogous predication of God by way of perfection names. It is by way of the analogy of being that neither the mere metaphor nor the essentialist concept are granted predominance in the predication of God. This is the limited but indispensable role Aquinas assigns in *sacra doctrina* to the natural knowledge of God derived analogically from creatures by way of the transcendentals and the derived perfection names. But precisely because *sacra doctrina* is a subaltern *scientia* and as such essentially informed by the principles of the superior *scientia Dei et beatorum*, there is by definition no way that the analogy of being could ever determine or govern what infinitely surpasses it in dignity as well as depth. It is precisely because of the infinitely surpassing superintelligibility of the *scientia Dei et beatorum* and the simultaneous limitation of our understanding that the analogy of being remains a subaltern albeit integral *auxilium* in the science of theology. Short of the beatific vision, it is the case even in the state of grace that for a proper theological intelligibility of the revealed truths, the modest *auxilium* of the analogy of being proves indispensable. "For," as Thomas puts it very dryly in the famous question 13 of the Prima Pars of his *Summa theologiae*, "we can name God only from creatures."[94]

For Thomas, the analogy of being reflects in our very way of predicating our ineradicable creatureliness and hence the primordial relationship between creature and God as one of *causal participation*. And thus the analogy of being is indeed the always already operative metaphysical condition for the surpassingly gratuitous salvific relation of God *quoad nos* to become analogically intelligible while remaining essentially *mysterium*.

---

93. W. Norris Clarke, "Analogy and the Meaningfulness of Language about God," in *Explorations in Metaphysics*, pp. 126-27.

94. *ST* I, q. 13, a. 5: "Non enim possumus nominare Deum nisi ex creaturis."

CHAPTER 7

"Through him all things were made" (John 1:3): The Analogy of the Word Incarnate according to St. Thomas Aquinas and Its Ontological Presuppositions

Thomas Joseph White, O.P.

In the mid-twentieth century a string of Catholic authors such as Erich Przywara, Gottlieb Söhngen, Hans Urs von Balthasar, and Henri Bouillard emphasized the role that grace plays in the concrete historical formulation of all intellectual truths about God, even truths accessible to natural human reason.[1] For each of these thinkers — in differing ways — metaphysical aspirations to God seen in a theological light are understood as depending upon the stimuli of the grace of the incarnate Word, and as being exercised in view of that grace, such that any natural orientation toward God has as its unique condition of possibility and governing regulatory principle, the divine agency of the grace of Christ. Indeed, the First Vatican Council taught the capacity of the human person to arrive at certain natural knowledge of God by rational powers.[2] Nevertheless, this natural

---

1. Erich Przywara, *Analogia Entis. Metaphysik* (Munich: Kösel & Pustet, 1932) and "Reichweite der Analogie als katholischer Grundform," *Scholastik* 15 (1940): 339-62, 508-32; Gottlieb Söhngen, "Analogia fidei I. Gottähnlichkeit allein aus Glauben?" and "Analogia fidei II. Die Einheit in der Glaubenswissenschaft," *Catholica* 3 (1934): 113-36 and 176-208, and "Wunderzeichen und Glaube," *Catholica* 4 (1935): 145-64; Hans Urs von Balthasar, *Karl Barth. Darstellung und Deutung seiner Theologie* (Cologne: Verlag Jakob Hegner, 1951; ET *The Theology of Karl Barth,* trans. Edward Oakes [San Francisco: Ignatius, 1992]); Henri Bouillard, *Karl Barth. Genèse et évolution de la théologie dialectique,* 3 vols. (Paris: Aubier, 1957). See also the excellent Protestant study of Henry Chavannes, *L'analogie entre Dieu et le monde selon saint Thomas d'Aquin et selon Karl Barth* (Paris: Cerf, 1969).

2. "The same Holy Mother Church teaches that God, the source and end of all things, can be known with certainty from the consideration of created things, by the natural power

operation could never be properly exercised in man's fallen state, without the agency of grace.[3]

For the sake of argument, let us concede that basically there is a common theme present in these authors, and that it is theologically defensible. But let us then turn things around and ask the question from another point

---

of human reason (Rom. 1:20). . . . If anyone says that the one, true God, our Creator and Lord, cannot be known with certainty from the things that have been made, by the natural light of human reason, let him be anathema" (*Dei Filius,* chap. 2, and anathema 1, trans. N. Tanner, in *Decrees of the Ecumenical Councils* [London: Sheed & Ward; Washington, D.C.: Georgetown University Press, 1990]).

3. Such an idea certainly finds echoes in Aquinas's own thought, even if, within his historical context, the Angelic Doctor can be seen to emphasize the distinct powers of our philosophical knowledge of God over and against the Augustinian illuminism of his age. Aquinas clearly thinks that the human intellect is capable by its natural powers of attaining to some natural knowledge of God. See the helpful analysis of Aquinas's epistemology with respect to nature and grace by Santiago Ramírez, *De gratia Dei* (Salamanca: Editorial San Esteban, 1992), pp. 61-107, as well as the study by Paul Synave, "La révélation des vérités divines naturelles d'après saint Thomas," in *Mélanges Mandonnet,* vol. 1, pp. 327-71 (Paris: J. Vrin, 1930). Nevertheless, in *In Ioan.* 17.6.2265, Aquinas makes especially strong statements about the frailty of natural knowledge of God in the fallen state. Commenting upon John 17: 5: "Father, the world has not known you," he writes: "But this seems to conflict with Romans (1:19): 'For what can be known about God is plain to them. Ever since the creation of the world his invisible nature, namely, his eternal power, and deity, has been clearly perceived in the things that have been made.' We should say to this that knowledge is of two kinds: one is speculative, and the other affective. Through neither of these ways did the world know God completely. Although some Gentiles knew God as having some of those attributes which are knowable by reason, they did not know God as the Father of an only-begotten and consubstantial Son — and our Lord is talking about knowledge of these things. Again, if they did have some speculative knowledge of God, this was mixed with many errors: some denied his providence over all things; other said he was the soul of the world; still others worshipped other gods along with him. For this reason they are said not to know God. Composite things can be known in part, and in part unknown while simple things are unknown if they are not known in their entirety. Thus, even though some erred only slightly in their knowledge of God, they are said to be entirely ignorant of him. Consequently, since these people did not know the special excellence of God, they are said not to know him: 'For although they knew God they did not honor him as God or give thanks to him, but they became futile in their thinking and their senseless minds were darkened' (Rom. 1:21). . . . Furthermore, the world did not know God by an affective knowledge, because it did not love him. . . . So he says, 'the world has not known you,' that is, without error, and as a Father, through love" (trans. J. Weisheipl and F. Larcher, in Thomas Aquinas, *Commentary on the Gospel of St. John,* vol. 2 [Petersham, Mass.: St. Bede's Press, 2000], emphasis added). In *In Ioan.* 17.2.2195, Aquinas claims that Gentiles did know something of the Creator but did not worship him properly by the worship of exclusive *latria.* See also *ST* I-II, q. 109, a. 1, and *De divinis nominibus* 7.5.740.

of view. Let us take "nature" to designate the essential determinations of a created reality as it is constituted in existence, such that it can normally accomplish certain actions by its own intrinsic powers that tend toward such actions, and such that it behaves according to certain stable, integral ways of being. Let us take "grace" to be the life of God, transmitted to our created human nature in supernatural ways, through means and channels that we cannot obtain to naturally, but that can complement, heal, and elevate what we are naturally. If in the fallen state of our common human nature, grace is a great, perhaps even necessary, aid for the right exercise of any natural human knowledge of God, is there also the necessity of a human capacity for natural knowledge of God as a necessary condition for our intellectual understanding of divine revelation? If we have emphasized rightly the primacy of divine grace for a developed knowledge of God by nature, should we not also examine the question of the presuppositions of nature for a right knowledge of God by grace? In other words, in thinking out the *analogia fidei* (to use the term of Söhngen and Karl Barth), in what ways are we perhaps implicitly or explicitly committing ourselves to the *analogia entis?*

Let us again be clear from the beginning about the meaning of terms as I am using them here. By *analogia fidei*, I mean to denote ontological resemblances between creatures and God that are known to us uniquely by virtue of the supernatural revelation of God in Christ. By the term *analogia entis* I mean to denote ontological resemblances between creatures and God that can be discerned and understood by the powers of natural human reason — that is to say, by virtue of (1) the kind of thing we are and (2) the world we live in — and that resemblances are not given by supernatural revelation. In the case of analogies of faith and analogies of being, I am presuming that analogous propositional language (analogy as propositional naming) is distinct from, but also intrinsically related to, real analogies between things. Analogical propositional naming is capable of truly signifying analogical, ontological resemblances in realities themselves. Consequently, recourse to terms such as "the analogy of the incarnate Word" or "the analogy of being between creatures and God," as I am denoting them here, entails both an ontological foundation in the things themselves and a propositional mode of signifying this reality that is characterized by analogical terms.[4]

---

4. While "analogy" is sometimes meant to denote one of these two senses more precisely than another, neither sense of the word is meant to exclude the other, nor are they meant to be identical, but rather always interrelated, as the analogical mode of signifying realities as "being" is meant to signify in fact the real distinctions and likenesses between the

Here I will argue that the theological analogy of the incarnate Word (the *Logos ensarkos*) is not fully intelligible, even as a specifically Christian and dogmatic notion, without the capacity to ascribe to God analogical notions of being and unity, in comparison with creatures. Furthermore, we are capable of ascribing such analogical notions only if there is a real ontological resemblance between creatures and God that is naturally intelligible to the human intellect without formal recourse to divine revelation. Consequently, the knowledge of Christ's divinity that we are given by grace implies that we have a natural capacity for knowledge of God. Even more strikingly: if there were in our fallen condition no persisting capacity for natural knowledge of God (if we are not capable in principle of a so-called natural theology), then human beings would be radically and irremediably incapable of receiving knowledge of Christ by grace alone *under any form whatsoever*. The revelation of Christ would remain inextricably extrinsic to our human manner of knowing. Consequently, if in our concrete historical state as fallen creatures, the grace of Christ is necessary in one sense in order to cultivate a right understanding of the ontological similitudes between creatures and God, in

---

analogical modes of being in the things themselves. Interpreters of Aquinas such as Ralph McInerny (see esp. *Aquinas and Analogy* [Washington, D.C.: Catholic University of America Press, 1996]) have argued that analogy pertains especially to the logical structure of mental, intentional thinking, rather than to the nature of things in themselves. Bruce Marshall has presented a lucid version of this interpretation in his essay in this volume, "Christ the End of Analogy." While Aquinas clearly does use the term *analogia* to denote logical terms in many instances, he also quite clearly affirms that there exist ontological similitudes between realities themselves, or between accidents of substances, or between accidents and substances, as well as between creatures and God. In his *In meta.* 4.1.534-47 he makes quite clear that analogical naming ultimately derives from and refers back to ontological resemblances in realities, which result from causal dependencies. These realities and their similitudes are denoted by recourse to terms that are analogical, such that our discourse "by analogy" maps onto — and denotes insightfully — real resemblances and differences. See, for example, *ST* I, q. 4, a. 3, where Aquinas is speaking about a similitude in the order of being where there is no common *ratio* by which to denote this similitude because the agent is not of the same genus or species as the effect: "Si igitur sit aliquod agens, quod non in genere contineatur, effectus eius adhuc magis accedent remote ad similitudinem formae agentis: non tamen ita quod participent similitudinem formae agentis secundum eandem rationem speciei aut generis, sed secundum aliqualem analogiam, sicut ipsum esse est commune omnibus. Et hoc modo illa quae sunt a Deo, assimilantur ei inquantum sunt entia, ut primo et universali principio totius esse." See the helpful study of Lawrence Dewan, "St. Thomas and Analogy: The Logician and the Metaphysician," in *Form and Being: Studies in Thomistic Metaphysics* (Washington, D.C.: Catholic University of America Press, 2006), pp. 81-95, and the essay of Reinhard Hütter in this volume, "Attending to the Wisdom of God — from Effect to Cause, from Creation to God: A *relecture* of the Analogy of Being according to Thomas Aquinas."

another sense, our capacity of natural reason to attain to true analogical knowledge of God is a precondition in human beings for our capacity to receive grace.

I will make this argument in three stages, making appeal at each juncture to the perspectives of Thomas Aquinas, who on the theology of the incarnate Word is representative of the classical Christian tradition, and whose thought on the metaphysics of being is profoundly illuminating. The first stage will examine the properly theological analogy of the Word incarnate that originates, not from human philosophical ingenuity, but from divine revelation. What does it mean to say by analogy that the Son incarnate is truly God yet distinct from the Father *as his Word?* Here I will argue that a theological understanding of the incarnate Word *as God* necessarily implies an analogical analysis of the Word in his preexistence, and the ways that the eternal procession of the Word is both like and unlike a human intellectual "procession" of conceptual thought. The clarification of this later "analogy of faith" necessarily entails an understanding of the Word as the unoriginate (i.e., uncreated) ground or cause of existence in creatures.

The second stage will examine the metaphysical presuppositions necessary for the articulation of the transcendence and divinity of the incarnate Word in his likeness and difference with regard to creatures, illustrating how analogies of being and unity are implicit in any right understanding of the divinity of the Word as presented by Scripture itself. Use of the analogy of being is logically entailed by the articulation of the analogy of the Word. Without recourse to this form of thinking (which presupposes ontological analogies between creatures and God), the *theological* analogical knowledge of the Word as God *in faith* is literally unthinkable.

The third stage argues that the affirmation of divine revelation presupposes a minimal distinction between natural and supernatural modes of knowledge, as well as the understanding that our natural manner of knowing must be intrinsically capable of transformation by the knowledge of faith in grace. Yet if we are naturally capable of receiving grace so as to think truly of God by means of theological analogies of faith, then this presupposes a natural, epistemological capacity to conceive of God in terms of our experience of creatures. If these terms are either equivocal or univocal, rather than analogical, a capacity to cooperate intellectually with revelation is intrinsically neutralized. Correspondingly, while knowledge of Christ implies a natural capacity for knowledge of God by natural reason (natural theology), the absence of an intrinsic capacity for the latter would render belief in the divinity of Christ impossible. This suggests that, to the extent that there is a Christological *analogia entis* (an analogy between creation and God disclosed in Christ), this mystery presupposes a natural *analogia entis* intrinsic to creation. To believe in Christological knowledge of God, then, is to affirm the possibility, and necessity, of natural theology.

I

Aquinas holds to three principles for understanding the mystery of the Word incarnate, which places him in essential continuity with the patristic traditions of East and West, as well as with certain critical affirmations of Karl Barth. First, the knowledge of the Son and Word of God as distinct from the Father is a knowledge available to us only by means of the economy of the Word's visible mission. That is to say, it is only the Word incarnate, or *Logos ensarkos,* who makes known to us the immanent life of God as trinitarian. Commenting on the birth of Christ in the Gospel of Matthew, Aquinas appeals to Augustine's comparison of the manifestation of God in Christ with the manifestation of the mental concept in human speech through the spoken word:

> For in us there is a twofold word [*verbum*]: the word of the heart and the spoken word. The word of the heart is the intellect's concept, *which is hidden from human beings, unless it is expressed by the human voice or by the spoken word.* To the word of the heart is compared the eternal Word prior to the incarnation, *when he was with the Father and hidden from us;* but the spoken word is compared to the incarnate Word, which has already appeared to us and has been manifested.[5]

By way of complement to his statement, one can note that Aquinas argues (in distinction from Richard of St. Victor and Bonaventure) that the mystery of God as a Trinity of persons is a truth radically inaccessible to natural reason. That God is triune remains for us *naturally* unknown and indemonstrable even after revelation, even by way of *philosophical* arguments from reason given in light of the incarnation.[6]

---

5. Aquinas, *In Matt.*, c. 1, lec. 4. (emphasis added). Augustine employs the comparison, for example, in *De Trinitate* 9.12.

6. See *ST* I, q. 32, a. 1, in contrast with Richard of St. Victor, *De Trinitate* I, c. 4; III, c. 19; Bonaventure, *Itinerarium mentis in Deum* 6.2. See the helpful analysis of Bruce D. Marshall, "Putting Shadows to Flight: The Trinity, Faith, and Reason," in *Reason and the Reasons of Faith,* ed. Paul J. Griffiths and Reinhard Hütter, pp. 53-77 (London: T. & T. Clark, 2005).

Second, however, this revelation of the Word makes present to us the very life of God in the flesh, the life of God as he is in himself, as the eternal Son, in relation to the Father and the Holy Spirit. Aquinas states quite clearly that there is no ontological similitude between the Word incarnate and the Word of the immanent Trinity, but rather a pure identity: an economic presence in Christ of God as he truly is.[7] Consequently, the Word is manifest to us in his unity with the Father, but also in his distinctness, divine reciprocity, and mutual immanence. In short, the Son is revealed to us as truly God, equal to the Father, yet as personally distinct from the Father.

Nevertheless, our knowledge of the triune God transpires not through immediate vision but through an analogical, propositional form of knowing, derived from the divine economy. Based upon God's revelation in the flesh and the language of Scripture, the church has formulated propositions that prescribe true analogical names to the Son: he is identical in "nature" with the Father, yet "personally," or "hypostatically," distinct. Aquinas repeatedly makes this point by using Arianism and Sabellianism as a foil against this position to assert that the affirmations of doctrine really designate what God is in his immanent, trinitarian life.[8] There is a real unity of

---

7. Aquinas holds simultaneously that the Word incarnate is *known by us* through analogical comparisons but is himself the personal, eternal Word of the Father. Commenting on the above-mentioned similitude of the mental and spoken word, he writes in *De ver.,* q. 4, a. 1, ad 6: "Hoc quidem simile est in utroque, ratione cuius unum alteri comparatur: quod sicut vox manifestat verbum interius, ita per carnem manifestatum est verbum aeternum. Sed quantum ad hoc est dissimile: quod ipsa caro assumpta a verbo aeterno, non dicitur verbum, sed ipsa vox quae assumitur ad manifestationem verbi interioris, dicitur verbum; et ideo verbum vocis est aliud a verbo cordis; *sed verbum incarnatum est idem quod verbum aeternum,* sicut et verbum significatum per vocem, est idem quod verbum cordis." This seems to me to differ from Rahner's *grundaxiom,* not because it refuses an identification of the "economic Trinity" and the "immanent Trinity," but rather because it presupposes no "economic Trinity" at all that could be differentiated from God's immanent and transcendent life. Otherwise said, there is only the immanent, and incomprehensible, Trinity, who manifests himself to us imperfectly but truly in and through the economy, by means of the missions of the Son and Holy Spirit. I also think Aquinas would be unlikely to embrace the language of David Bentley Hart (*The Beauty of the Infinite* [Grand Rapids: Eerdmans, 2003], p. 165) when he refers to "the analogical interval between the immanent and economic Trinity, between timeless eternity and the time in which eternity shows itself," only because such language could give the impression of an ontological self-differentiation that takes place in God, between God in himself and God in his self-limiting decision to exist and reveal himself in time. The later idea is developed at painstaking length by Sergius Bulgakov, *The Lamb of God,* trans. Boris Jakim (Grand Rapids: Eerdmans, 2008), esp. chaps. 1, 3, and 4.

8. See, for example, *SCG* 4.11; *De rationibus fidei,* c. 9; *ST* I, q. 27, a. 1.

nature in God (against Arianism), but also a true distinction of persons (against Sabellianism). Such notions of nature and person are analogical (theological analogies), derived from a comparison of revelation and creation, and they are also true: They delineate in an imperfect and mediate fashion what God is in himself.

Third, then, the Word who is made known in the incarnation is truly the Word through whom God upholds all things in being. Being one with the Father, he is before all time (i.e., preexistent) and is the Creator himself, in whom all things were made.[9] In his reading of Philippians 2:6-7 ("though he was in the form of God . . . [he] emptied himself"), Aquinas is careful to exclude from theological understanding of the Son's kenosis any notion of the cessation or surrender of his divine prerogatives as God, instead attributing "humility" to God in the incarnation as an expression of the free condescension of divine love.[10] The Word who is incarnate is also the author of creation, who sustains all things in being as God, even as he experiences historical life, suffering, and death as a human being.[11] As God, he is one in es-

9. Aquinas explicitly employs the notion of preexistence; see *In Ioan.* 1.7.176: "If Christ was not God as to his person, he would have been most presumptuous to say 'I and the Father are one' (John 10:30) and 'Before Abraham came to be, I am,' as is said below (John 8:48). Now 'I' refers to the person of the speaker. And the one who was speaking was a man, who, as one with the Father, existed before Abraham. [homo autem erat, qui loquebatur; unum cum patre *praeexistebat* Abrahae]" (ET by J. Weisheipl and P. Larcher, *Commentary on John* [Albany, N.Y.: Magi Press, 1980]). This citation suggests that one must dispute Herbert McCabe's erroneous affirmation [*God Matters* (London: Continuum, 2005), pp. 48-51] that the notion of preexistence is a uniquely modern fabrication of nineteenth-century German Christology, alien to Aquinas's thought because of its usage of a temporal prefix to denote transcendent causality. Aquinas clearly is comfortable with using the term "preexistent" to denote the truth that God the Word in his eternal, transcendence precedes creation ontologically, not temporally.

10. On kenosis of the Son in Philippians 2:6-7, see, in particular, *In Phil.* 2.2; *SCG* 4.34.22, and the study of Emmanuel Durand, "La mission eschatologique du Christ implique sa préexistence ontologique. Un argument scripturaire de saint Thomas d'Aquin en prise avec le débat christologique actuel," *Revue Thomiste*, 108, 4 (2008): 467-96.

11. In his commentary on Hebrews 1:3 (*In Heb.* I, lec. 2, 30-36), Aquinas notes that if the Son "upholds all things by the word of his power," then he is God and "the cause of every substance," as well as its historical "operations." Yet this same verse claims that the Son "makes purgation for sins." Indeed, Aquinas will argue (37-39), these two things are understood to be simultaneously true, since the divinity of Christ is seen as the fitting precondition for the effectuation of our redemption through the Son's historical life in the flesh. See also I, lec. 3, 57: "He was first in the world invisibly by his power, [and subsequently] visibly by the presence of his humanity." For the English citations, see *Commentary on the Epistle to the Hebrews*, trans. C. Baer (South Bend, Ind.: St. Augustine's Press, 2006).

sence, power, and will with the Father and the Spirit, even as he empties himself by taking on the form of human nature out of divine compassion. Consequently, Aquinas could be said anachronistically to hold to what the Lutheran tradition has sometimes named the *extra Calvinisticum*.[12] This is the position not only of Calvin, but also of Athanasius, Augustine, Gregory of Nazianzus, the medievals, and, arguably, Karl Barth himself (although the reading of Barth on this topic is controverted).[13]

These three features are important because they suggest that, when Aquinas reflects upon the distinctly theological mystery of the Son incarnate as Word, he does so while being committed to two complementary truths. First, God the Son is known to us through his historical self-revelation. Second, however, because *in that revelation* he makes known to us who he is eternally, *therefore* we are permitted and invited to reflect upon the conditions of his existence as the true God and the ground of creation. We must pass from the visible mission of Christ in the flesh to the eternal procession of the Son that is truly revealed to us in that mission.[14] That is to say, we

12. See, for example, John Calvin, *Institutes* 2.13. 4. For Barth's analysis of the Calvinist notion that the Son while incarnate upholds all things in being as God, and the Lutheran reactions to this doctrine in the kenotic theories of the seventeenth-century schools of Giessen and Tübingen, see *Church Dogmatics* IV/1 (London: T. & T. Clark, 2004), pp. 180-83.

13. See, for example, the controversial interpretation of Barth on this question by Bruce McCormack in "Karl Barth's Christology as a Resource for a Reformed Version of Kenoticism," *International Journal of Systematic Theology* 8 (2006): 243-51.

14. For Aquinas, the missions of the trinitarian persons derive from the eternal processions of God, yet only insofar as these processions are made manifest to us in the human history of the Son incarnate and the visible mission of the Holy Spirit. *ST* I, q. 43, a. 1: "The mission of a divine person [denotes] (1) the procession of origin from the sender, and (2) a new way of existing in another. Thus the Son is said to be sent by the Father into the world, inasmuch as He began to exist visibly in the world by taking our nature." Consequently, the eternal processions of the persons are truly revealed to us within the economy *by the missions,* yet the immanent life of God is not identical with God's manner of existing in these visible missions, insofar as the latter imply the created order of grace and nature through which the triune God is revealed (*ST* I, q. 43, a. 8). (All translations of the *ST* are adapted from the 1920 English Province Dominican translation, *Summa Theologica* [New York: Benziger, 1947].) An interesting point of comparison can be found with Karl Barth, *CD* IV/1, 193: "It is His sovereign grace that He wills to be and is amongst us in humility, our God, God for us. But He shows us this grace, He is amongst us in humility, our God, God for us, as that which He is in Himself, in the most inward depth of His Godhead. He does not become another God. In the condescension in which He gives Himself to us in Jesus Christ He exists and speaks and acts as the One He was from all eternity and will be to all eternity. The truth and actuality of our atonement depends on this being the case. The One who reconciles the world with God is necessarily the one God Himself in His true Godhead. Otherwise the

must think analogically, by way of causality, negation, and preeminence (the threefold Dionysian *viae*), of what it must be for the Word to be eternally one in nature with the Father and distinct in person, and this in real distinction from (but not separation from!) and ontological priority to his human historical existence as Christ.[15] Even if we know the Son only in history, we must necessarily be able to think of him analogically through the medium of revelation from before history, as eternally God. Otherwise, we will not think rightly of the mystery of him who is truly *God* in history. We will not recognize him for who he is as one who is "among us," but who, in the words of John's gospel, existed "before" us as God's Word (John 1:14-15), the Word who was "in the beginning . . . with God" and who "was God" (1:1), through whom "all things were made" (1:3).

In his mature trinitarian theology, Aquinas understands the notion "Word" *(verbum)* to apply to Christ as a *proper* name.[16] Proper names here are to be distinguished from natural or essential names for God. Essential names pertain not to the trinitarian persons in their hypostatic distinctness but to the ineffable essence of God that is common to the Father, Son, and Holy Spirit, a mystery we designate when we speak about divine simplicity, goodness, unity, all-powerfulness, and so on. By contrast, the name "Word" is proper: it indicates the mystery of the person of the eternal Son alone. Furthermore, Aquinas makes a point to interpret systematically other scriptural proper titles for Christ — such as "Son" and "Image" — *in light of* the

---

world would not be reconciled with God. Otherwise it is still the world which is not reconciled with God." Evidently, the possibilities for identifying a close similitude between Aquinas and Barth depend in part on whether one reads such passages in light of Bruce McCormack's interpretations of Barth's doctrine of election, wherein election of humanity is *constitutive* of the life of the trinitarian God.

15. Aquinas takes as theologically normative the affirmation of a distinction between the humanity and divinity of Christ, according to the Council of Chalcedon. See *ST* III, q. 2, a. 1.

16. On Aquinas's evolution on this point, as well as for a more general exposition of his theology of Christ as the Word of God, see Gilles Emery, *The Trinitarian Theology of Saint Thomas Aquinas* (Oxford: Oxford University Press, 2007), pp. 176-218; *Trinity in Aquinas* (Naples, Fla.: Sapientia, 2005), pp. 71-120; See also Harm Goris, "Theology and Theory of the Word in Aquinas," in *Aquinas the Augustinian*, ed. Michael Dauphinais, Barry David, and Matthew Levering, pp. 62-78 (Washington, D.C.: Catholic University of America Press, 2007); L.-B. Geiger, "Les rédactions successives de *Contra Gentiles* I, 53 d'après l'autographe," in *Saint Thomas d'Aquin aujourd'hui*, ed. J. Y. Jolif et al., pp. 221-40 (Paris: Desclée de Brouwer, 1963); and Henri Paissac, *Théologie du verbe. St. Augustin et St. Thomas* (Paris: Cerf, 1951).

theological similitude of the Word. This theological decision has its precedent in the thought of Athanasius, transmitted to Aquinas by his reading of both Augustine and John Damascene.[17] In essence, against Sabellianism and Arianism, Aquinas wishes to maintain that there exist eternally in the mystery of God (1) a real relation of origin of the Son from the Father, who proceeds as a distinct hypostasis or person generated ineffably by the Father, and (2) a shared and identical, incomprehensible nature of the Father and Son. Following Athanasius and Augustine, Aquinas maintains that only the consideration of an analogy from human thought will allow us to understand something (albeit very imperfectly) of immaterial generation.[18] This in turn alone gives us the capacity to understand the mystery of the procession of the Son from the Father as one in which these persons of the trinitarian God share in one nature and being, without subordination or confusion.

To understand this revealed mystery theologically, then, Aquinas employs the similitude of the mental *verbum,* or "word," in the human person, where *verbum* denotes an intellectual concept proceeding from the mind, rather than a spoken word proceeding through speech.[19] The mental concepts in and through which we know things are expressions of our abstracted knowledge, drawn initially from the things themselves through the operation of the agent intellect. Just as our knowledge of a thing depends upon our abstracting its intelligible species or essence from multiple sensible experiences of the thing itself, so then the intellect, having abstracted the intelligible form, fashions a concept in and through which it proceeds back to the reality in order to think the experienced reality in overtly conceptual terms. This concept is generated from the mind, through an act of the mind. It is an accident of the being of the knower but also, in some fundamental sense, one in being with the knower. It contains the truth whereby the knower knows the essential properties of the reality in question. In addition, this interior word is the *terminus* of our act of understanding. It is not there-

---

17. Athanasius, *C. Arianos* I, para. 16: "If the Offspring of the Father's essence be the Son, we must be certain, that the same is the Wisdom and Word of the Father, in and through whom He creates and makes all things" (trans. by Atkinson, *Nicene and Post-Nicene Fathers,* vol. 4, ed. A. Richardson [New York: Charles Scribner, 1903]). See also I, n. 15; 24-29; II, n. 2; 5; 36ff. For an insightful discussion of these points, see Lewis Ayres, *Nicaea and Its Legacy* (Oxford: Oxford University Press, 2004), pp. 110-17. See also Augustine, *De Trin.* 15.10; John Damascene, *De fide orth.* I, cc. 6, 8, 13, 17.

18. *SCG* 4.11; *De pot.,* q. 9, a. 5; q. 10, a. 1; *ST* I, q. 27, a. 1; *Comp. theo.* 1.52; *In Ioan.* 1.1.23-66.

19. Cf. *ST* I, q. 34, a. 1.

fore something that precedes or leads to the act of understanding but is what the intellect produces when it understands.[20]

Once we have grasped this truth about the way our own intellect understands, we can then see why the interior word is a helpful analogy for us to grasp the procession of the Son in God: the Word in God proceeds, not as that by which the Father understands (the Father is the source of the Son; the Son cannot be a principle of anything in the Father himself), but rather as the perfect expression of what the Father understands about himself. Analogously, Aquinas argues, the Word, or *Verbum,* in God is the proper name for the Son, because it expresses the spiritual generation whereby the Son comes forth from the Father's knowledge of himself, as the expression of his own wisdom.[21] The Son possesses in himself the plentitude of the divine nature and wisdom — and therefore is equal to the Father, but as one who receives eternally all that he is from the Father, as his eternal Word, through whom the Father knows all things. The analogy of the Word thereby helps us interpret the analogy of sonship. "Sonship" entails begetting according to an identity of nature or essence (implying equality), while "Word" connotes the immateriality proper to spiritual intellect. Because the Word proceeds spiritually from the Father's wisdom, we can envisage a distinction of persons in God without quantity or spatiotemporal extension (without "history," if you will). Because the Son possesses in himself the plentitude of the Father's wisdom, the generation in question does not imply ontological inequality. The Father and Son are not merely one in kind but are one in being, *homoousios.*[22]

When we have said all this, however, we are not yet finished. For in order to convey the transcendent perfection of the Word of God, we must underscore not only the likeness but also the dissimilitude between God the Word and the created *verbum.* Only by means of the *via negationis* can we in

---

20. In his mature position on the subject, Aquinas distinguishes in human spiritual cognition the intelligible species abstracted from sensible phantasms *by which* the mind has understanding, and the expression of this same species in and through a concept *in which* the mind turns back to reality to think about it. It is the latter that is said to analogously "proceed" from the understanding by a relation of origin, not the former. *In Ioan.* 1.1.25: "The Philosopher says that the notion [*ratio*] which a name signifies is a definition. Hence what is thus expressed, i.e., formed in the soul, is called an interior word. Consequently it is compared to the intellect, not as that by which the intellect understands [i.e., the intelligible species], but as that in which it understands, because it is in what is thus expressed and formed that it sees the nature of the thing understood. Thus we have the meaning of the name 'word.'"

21. *ST* I, q. 34, a. 2.

22. See the beautiful and exacting analysis of this point in *SCG* 4.11.

turn arrive at the affirmation of the incomprehensibly unique perfection of the Son's generation, the *via eminentiae*.[23] These reflections are necessary in order to rightly contemplate the mystery of the filial generation of the Son in its uniqueness and transcendence, while safeguarding our understanding against improper anthropomorphisms.

Aquinas identifies three principal loci of theological dissimilitude between human thought and the eternal generation of the Word.[24] First, in ourselves the intellectual concept is merely a property or metaphysical "accident" of our being (a nonessential characteristic of our person) that qualifies our understanding in some way, through our acquired knowledge. In God, however, the Word is in no way accidental but is of the very substance of the Father (Heb. 1:3). In his incomprehensible perfection, the Father's generation of the Son communicates to him all that the Father has and is as God. And yet in differentiation from the procession of the word in ourselves, the Son who is God is truly eternally distinct from the Father hypostatically, or personally, even as he proceeds from him as his Word.[25]

Second, in ourselves, the generation of thought leads (eventually) to a greater maturity and perfection and thus actuates a latent intellectual potentiality. In our knowledge we pass from imperfection to greater perfection. In God, however, there is no potency of operation in the generation of the Word. Rather, in his transcendent perfection, the Word *is* the very act of being that the Father is.[26] He is light from light, or act from act, containing in himself the very existence, nature, and operation of the Father, all of which is hidden from our direct gaze. As such, he is without any perfection to acquire, being

23. Aquinas typically employs Dionysius's threefold *viae* in speaking about analogical names for the divine essence. (See, for example, *ST* I, q. 13, a. 2.) However, it seems to be clear that he employs a similar kind of thinking when speaking of the proper name of the Son as "Word" in *SCG* 4.11 and *In Ioan.* 1.1.

24. Aquinas's treatment of this subject is most extensive in the *Summa contra Gentiles*, 4.11, and the first *lectio* of his *Commentary on St. John's Gospel*. On these three dissimilitudes, see in particular *In Ioan.* 1.1.26-29. I am inverting the order of exposition of Aquinas's three arguments, and expressing them in a slightly different form, introducing complementary elements from *SCG* 4.11.

25. "Consequently, the word which our intellect forms is not of the essence of our soul, but is an accident of it. But in God to understand and to be are the same; and so the Word of the divine intellect is not an accident but belongs to its nature. Thus it must be subsistent, because whatever is in the nature of God is God. Thus Damascene says that God is a substantial Word and a hypostasis, but our words are concepts in our mind" (*In Ioan.* 1.1.28).

26. *In Ioan.* 1.1.27. See also *ST* I, q. 34, a. 3; q. 27, a. 1, ad 2; *SCG* 4.11.11.

in himself as God the source and summit of all lesser, created perfections, each of which participates in some way in his uncreated image.[27]

Third, our concepts are mere *intentiones* (mental intentionality, not reality), by and through which we aspire to know reality as it is, while the subjects of our thinking are (typically) realities distinct from ourselves and from our own thought. But in God, the Word himself contains the very truth of God. This truth in question is not abstract or intentional but is God's very essence, God's very being. Nor does God formulate his knowledge through a prior encounter with beings other than himself that he comes to know intentionally and from which he learns. Rather, God is the truth who created all things in the knowledge that he has of himself.[28] (All that exists depends upon God's self-knowledge, and not the inverse.) All that is in the Father, then, is present in the Son as the personal truth that proceeds forth from the Father, through whom he made all things.[29] In knowing himself (by means of the divine truth that he shares with the Father and the Spirit), the Son as God knows not only the Father and the Spirit but also all things that proceed forth from God as God's creatures.[30]

II

In the second section of this essay I examine some of the implicit logical consequences of the aforementioned analogy of the Word incarnate as I have briefly presented it above. Basically my argument will be that we cannot rightly conceive of the divinity of the Word without recourse to the analogy of being: the affirmation of an ontological likeness between creatures and God, specifically as applied to resemblances in the order of existence and unity. Following Aquinas, I am presuming here that unity, or oneness, is a

27. "Since we cannot express all our conceptions in one word, we must form many imperfect words through which we separately express all that is in our knowledge. But it is not that way with God. For since he understands both himself and everything else through his essence, by one act, the single divine Word is expressive of all that is in God, not only of the Persons but also of creatures; otherwise it would be imperfect" (*In Ioan.* 1.2.27).

28. *SCG* 4.11.9.

29. *In Ioan.* 1.2.76.

30. *ST* I, q. 34, a. 3: "Word implies relation to creatures. For God, by knowing himself, knows every creature. Now the word conceived in the mind is representative of everything that is actually understood. Hence there are in ourselves different words for the different things which we understand. But because God by one act understands himself and all things, his one only Word is expressive not only of the Father, but of all creatures."

transcendental notion coextensive with being. All that exists, *insofar as it exists,* has a certain unity. To say that "something exists" is to say also that it is in some sense "one."[31]

I am suggesting that discussion of the Trinity necessarily (logically) entails reference to the analogy of being. What does it mean to talk about an analogy of being, or unity, between the triune God and creatures? An ontological similitude — or analogy — between God and creatures exists because of God's causal creation of the world, because of which creatures participate in existence that they receive from the triune God. Accordingly, they in some way resemble God as effects resemble their cause. Yet such similitude between creatures and God simultaneously implies dissimilitude because of God's transcendence of this same creation. (Therefore it is best expressed in truly analogical names, rather than by means of an anthropomorphic univocity.) Because the Word and Son of God is himself very God, the articulation of his divine identity, unity with the Father, and causality with respect to creatures must be articulated in terms that imply a likeness between creatures' existence and oneness, and that of the Father and Son as God. The Son truly *is* God and, as God, is truly *one* with the Father. However, the Son and the Father do not exist and are not one as creatures are, as the effects of God fall infinitely short of their transcendent origin. Correspondingly, an analysis of the *analogia entis* is a dimension of the theological consideration of the *analogia Verbi/Filii.* It must occur as a means of understanding the Son as one with the Father and as God the Creator in such a way so as to safeguard a sense of the transcendence of the Son, who is not subject as God to the world of created dependency. I would like to illustrate

---

31. As Aquinas, following Aristotle, points out at some length, unity and being are coextensive concepts, which correspond to transcendental characteristics of being. The study of transcendentals — or notions "convertible" with being — has its prehistory in the philosophies of Plato and Aristotle. (See, for example, *Republic* 507b; *Sophist* 245c–255e, 260a; *Metaphysics* 4.2.1003b23–1005a18; 11.3.1061a15-17; *Nic. Ethics* 1.6.1196a23-34.) The basic text on the transcendentals in Aquinas is *De ver.,* q. 1, a. 1, where he justifies a fivefold distinction of terms coextensive with *ens* and *esse (res, unum, aliquid, bonum, verum)* through a series of "modes of differentiation." Being can be considered (1) either *per se* or with respect to another. If *per se,* then (2) either positively (as *res,* or "a determinate reality") or negatively (as *unum:* that which is indivisible), and if with respect to another, then either (3) in distinction from it (as *aliquid,* or "something other") or as fitted to it *(convenientia).* If the latter is the case, this can be with respect to appetite (*bonum:* all that is is somehow good) or with respect to intellect (*verum:* all that is is somehow true). On the coextensive character of unity and being in Aquinas, see the study of Jan Aertsen, *Medieval Philosophy and the Transcendentals* (Leiden: Brill, 1996), pp. 201-42.

this claim about the inevitability of a reference to the *analogia entis* within faith by a brief analysis of a central idea of New Testament teaching: the affirmation that the Son of God is the Lord (*Kyrios* → YHWH), and that the Lord is "He Who Is," he whom the Older Testament describes as the Creator of heaven and earth.

Recent biblical scholarship (N. T. Wright,[32] Larry Hurtado,[33] Richard Bauckham,[34] Simon Gathercole[35]) has underscored the fact that there exists an extensive divine-name theology in the New Testament, by which the sacred name of the God of Israel, "YHWH" (from Exod. 3:15), is in fact attributed directly to Christ in the euphemistic Septuagint form of the sacred name: *Kyrios,* or Lord.[36] In addition, the complementary gloss on the divine name from Exodus 3:14 ("I Am He Who Is") is also attributed directly to Christ in the New Testament.[37] Indeed, in John's gospel (as well as arguably

32. N. T. Wright, *The Climax of the Covenant* (Minneapolis: Fortress, 1993), pp. 56-98, 120-36.

33. Larry Hurtado, *Lord Jesus Christ* (Grand Rapids: Eerdmans, 2003), pp. 29-52, 108-17, 151-52, 364-72.

34. Richard Bauckham, *God Crucified: Monotheism and Christology in the New Testament* (Grand Rapids: Eerdmans, 1998).

35. Simon Gathercole, *The Preexistent Son: Recovering the Christologies of Matthew, Mark, and Luke* (Grand Rapids: Eerdmans, 2006).

36. Aquinas was in fact partially sensitized to this ascription as well. See esp. *SCG* 4.7.7, where Aquinas claims that Jeremiah 23:5-6 ascribes the Tetragrammaton to the incarnate Christ, mentioning that this is a term reserved for God alone.

37. Aquinas follows Maimonides (*Guide for the Perplexed* 1.60-62), as well as Origen and Jerome, in distinguishing between *YHWH* (from Exod. 3:15) and "I Am He Who Is" (Exod. 3:14) as distinct but interrelated divine names. See esp. Armand Maurer, "St Thomas on the Sacred Name 'Tetragrammaton,'" *Mediaeval Studies* 34 (1972): 275-86. Nevertheless, Aquinas also interprets the names as inseparable and mutually related. In his metaphysical exegesis in *ST* I, q. 13, a. 9 and a. 11, ad 1, he identifies the Tetragrammaton as the divine name that signifies the incommunicability of the divine nature in its individuality, just as a singular name signifies the incommunicability of the individual man. This contrasts with the name "God," which signifies the nature (a. 8), and the name "He Who Is," which signifies the uniqueness of the perfection of God as *Ipsum esse subsistens* (a. 11). Although these signifying terms are diverse, their multiplicity is derived from our human manner of knowing God based upon terms drawn from creatures that are themselves complex. For as *ST* I, q. 3 (esp. aa. 3-4) has already made clear, while in material creatures there is a real distinction between individuality and nature, as well as between essence and existence, there is no real distinction in God between either nature and individual, or essence and existence. Therefore, while we may rightly designate God in various senses (as existence, deity, or individual) under these terms, in their ultimate ontological ground, they signify He who is absolutely simple. By consequence, the multiplicity of terms can be seen only as complementary and interre-

in Mark's)[38] one finds Jesus attributing to himself this latter form of the name of God on several occasions: "For if you do not believe that I Am, then you will die in your sins" (8:24); "When you have lifted up the Son of man, then you will know that I Am" (8:28), and "Before Abraham was, I Am" (8:58). Commenting upon the first of these passages, Aquinas himself understands the "I Am He Who Is" of Exodus 3:14 and the "I Am" of the incarnate Christ as mutually self-interpreting.[39] The name of God in Exodus both reveals and conceals the unique identity of God as he who alone exists by nature, or by essence, who is not given existence. God in his existence is utterly distinct from all creatures visible and invisible, who receive their existence from him. His own essence remains hidden and incomprehensible as the unoriginate ground of all created, participated being.[40] John's gospel reveals to us that this same incomprehensible deity of God is in truth present in Christ. The person of the Son incarnate exists as a human being present in time. The human nature of Christ subsists hypostatically in the very person of the Son. Therefore, when Christ says, "Before Abraham was, I Am," or "I exist," he differentiates his own existence from that of others as the divine existence of the Son who was in the beginning with the Father, through whom all things were made (John 1:1-3). Aquinas comments: "For in all things that begin, there is a certain mutability, and a potency to nonexis-

---

lated, within a larger biblical and metaphysical framework of apophatic and kataphatic approaches to naming God. For a modern biblical treatment of the name "He Who Is" in the New Testament suggesting profound and necessary connections of this title with the Tetragrammaton (Lord), see Bauckham, *God Crucified*, pp. 63-77. I am grateful to Kendall Soulen for his discussions with me on this important point.

38. Cf. Mark 2:28; 5:19-20; 12:35-37; 14:62.

39. *In Ioan.* 8, lec. 3 and 8.

40. Ibid., 8.3.1179: "[Christ] says, I am, and not 'what I am,' to recall to them what was said to Moses: 'I am he who is' (Exod. 3:14), for existence itself [*ipsum esse*] *is* proper to God. For in any other nature but the divine nature, existence [*esse*] and what exists are not the same: because any created nature participates its existence [*esse*] from that which is being by its essence [*ens per essentiam*], that is, from God, who is his own existence [*ipsum suum esse*], so that his existence [*suum esse*] *is* his essence [*qua essentia*]. Thus, this designates only God. And so he says, 'For if you do not believe that I am,' that is, that I am truly God, who has existence by his essence, 'you will die in your sin.'" On Exod. 3:14 and the existence of Christ, see also *ST* I, q. 3, a. 4 and q. 13, a. 11, in reference to the metaphysics of *ST* III, q. 2, a. 3, and q. 17. For helpful studies of Aquinas's metaphysics of the incarnation as related to his metaphysics of *esse*, see the introduction to *Thomas d'Aquin, Question disputée: L'union du Verbe incarné*, ed. Marie-Hélèn Deloffre (Paris: Vrin, 2000), pp. 13-78; and Jean-Pierre, in *S. Thomas d'Aquin, Le Verbe incarné, Somme théologique IIIa q. 1-26, trad. et annotations* (Paris: Cerf, 2002), appendix 2, pp. 297-340.

tence; thus we can discern in them a past and a future, and so they do not have true existence in themselves. But in God there is no potency to non-existence, nor has he begun to be. And thus he is existence itself [*ipsum esse*], which is appropriately indicated by the present tense."[41] Christ, according to St. Thomas, reveals in a new way the unique God of Israel, who is able by virtue of his ordering wisdom and power to become human without undergoing any ontological self-alienation. God reveals his identity as Creator by being present at the deepest level of created existence, something only God the Creator (or YHWH) can do. Because he is the author of existence, God alone can truly exist as a human being without altering or forsaking his unique, transcendent existence as God.[42] Ultimately, of course, the "I Am" of the Son also reveals in a new way the very identity of the Lord, "He Who Is," of the Old Testament as trinitarian. God exists as Father, Son, and Holy Spirit eternally.[43] This truth of God's own eternal identity is most manifest to us in the physical elevation of the Son upon the cross, where we know that he is "He Who Is" (8:28), where the glory of YHWH as the Savior (foretold in Isa. 40:3) is unveiled as the glory of the Word of the Father (John 17:5; see 1:14), a glory that he had with the Father "before the world was made."[44]

It follows from this sound interpretation of the Johannine revelation that to think through the theological analogy of the Word as applied by Scripture to the crucified Lord is also to think of the Son with the Father as the preexistent causal origin of all that is, as He Who Is, and as the one upon whom all things depend for their existence (so-called Christological monotheism).[45] And so it is to claim theologically some real relation of dependence of all beings upon the transcendent, ineffable, and incomprehensible being of the Father, Son, and Holy Spirit, the God who alone is (or exists), in the superior sense of Exodus 3:14. This relation is designated by the Gospel of John itself, through the Christological gloss that is given on the name of God in Exodus, a text itself contextualized in turn by both Genesis 1:1-3 and

41. *In Ioan.* 8.3.1179.
42. Ibid., 8.8.1290: "For eternal existence knows neither past nor future time, but embraces all time in one indivisible [instant]. Thus it could be said: 'He who is, sent me to you,' and 'I am who am' [Exod. 3:14]. Jesus had being both before Abraham and after him, and he could approach him by showing himself in the present and be after him in the course of time."
43. Ibid., 8.3.1192.
44. See the exegesis congruent with this argument in Bauckham, *God Crucified*, pp. 63-68.
45. We can think here also of Hebrews 1:2: "In these last days, he has spoken to us by a Son, whom he appointed the heir of all things, through whom also he created the world."

John 1:1-3: in the beginning was the Word, the Word *through whom all things were made* (John 1:3; see Gen. 1:3), a phrase itself preserved in the Nicene Creed. We have here the affirmation of an ontological similitude (and corresponding conceptual analogy) between the existence of all things visible and invisible, on the one hand, and, on the other, the God who alone is, or who alone exists in the transcendent sense in which God alone exists as Creator. All that exists receives its existence from and through the Word and as such participates in being because of him as its transcendent efficient and exemplary cause. Reference to the analogy of being is logically entailed, then, by the affirmation of the divinity of the Word.

This point can be briefly restated negatively in a slightly more polemical way. If this relation between creatures and God on the level of existence is not conceivable in terms of an ontological analogy that is real between creatures and their transcendent cause, then the notion of the triune God as Creator is also not conceivable. Certainly God is ineffable and incomprehensible and as such cannot be captured or comprehended within any concept of being. Yet if between the notion of (1) God as one who eternally is and (2) creatures as beings that depend upon God there is such a dissimilitude that a pure equivocity is established between them, then we cannot speak in any intelligible way about what it means for God "to be" He Who "Is," nor even what it means for God "to be" the causal origin of the creation. Nor then could we speak intelligibly about the Word in the Father as the principle of creation, because it would mean nothing for us to signify that the Word is the source of all that exists, and that the Word is He Who Is. And so, finally, we would not be able to speak about the incarnation at all, since we would not be able to say that the one who is the Creator of the world (meaning what?) had become flesh.

Let me conclude this argument by putting things in a more concrete way. If we wish to affirm that Jesus Christ existed in history as a historical subject, then we must be willing to say at least minimally that he was truly crucified under Pontius Pilate. (Here I am appealing to Barth's minimal criteria for historical realism concerning the incarnation in his book on the Apostles' Creed.)[46] This means in turn that this same Jesus was truly cruci-

---

46. Karl Barth, *Credo*, trans. Robert McAfee Brown (New York: Scribner, 1962; German original, 1935), pp. 79-80: "How does Pontius Pilate get into the Credo? The simple answer can at once be given: it is a matter of date. The name of the Roman procurator in whose term of office Jesus Christ was crucified, proclaims: at such and such a point of *historical time* this happened. And the symbol intends to express just that: that what it has to say about Jesus Christ happened at a definite and definitively assignable time *within that time which is*

fied in our existent, physical world, in the common history that we share with Pontius Pilate, and the lineage of historical personages that have truly existed from his time down to our own. Correspondingly, the kind of singular existence each of us now has as a human being can be attributed analogically to Pontius Pilate, who really *existed* then, and to Jesus of Nazareth, who was crucified under the Roman procurator. To admit this is to accept already that there are analogical predications of existence that are presupposed by the historical realism of faith in the crucifixion of God. In fact, such thinking makes use of the analogy of being absolutely unavoidable at what modern Thomists (following Fabro and Montagnes) term the "predicamental level," because such a use is simply coextensive with rational thought.[47] Pontius Pilate exists, Jesus exists, Peter exists, and so do you and I, each in an analogically signified fashion. Unless we can think analogically about existence common to creatures, we cannot think about Jesus' existence in his shared history with us.[48]

---

ours also. With that a line is drawn, a polemic is directed against a Gnostic Christ-idealism. If the Word became flesh, then it became temporal, and the reality of the revelation in Jesus Christ was *what we call* the lifetime of a man" (emphasis added).

47. Here we are speaking about the so-called analogy of proper proportionality, employed by Aristotle and Aquinas to speak about the diverse predicamental categories of being (quality, quantity, relation, etc.) *or* the diverse individual realizations of a given substance. In this case, the latter is being employed. A is to B as C is to D; Pilate (A) exists and Peter (C) exists. The existence of these two is not identical, but each has something in common with the other. Therefore the existence of Pilate (B) is analogous to that of Peter (D). The attribution of existence to each transpires by a process of analogical thinking and is consistent with our sense of the real multiplicity of and likenesses between things. On the distinction between predicamental and transcendental analogies of being, see esp. Bernard Montagnes, *The Doctrine of the Analogy of Being according to Thomas Aquinas,* trans. Edward M. Macierowski (Milwaukee: Marquette University Press, 2004), pp. 43-112; and Cornelio Fabro, *Participation et causalité selon S. Thomas d'Aquin* (Paris: Béatrice-Nauwelaerts; Louvain: Publications Universitaires, 1961), pp. 319-412.

48. Bruce Marshall in his essay in this volume, "Christ the End of Analogy," has rightly emphasized that Aquinas attributes human nature to Christ univocally, as Christ partakes of the same human nature as all others. (See p. 304 below.) Yet when Aquinas writes that "Deus est homo" (*ST* I, q. 16, a. 1), I do not think (pace Marshall) this should be translated as "God is a human *being*," for being (*ens*), as we all know, is precisely that which is "said in many ways," according to Aristotle, or in Aquinas's terms, "analogically." (Aquinas is quite explicit about this in *In meta.* 4.1.534-35.) At any rate, nothing could be less controversial than to affirm that for Aquinas, *ens,* like *esse,* is predicated analogically of the diverse genera of being (which is precisely why *ens* and *esse* are not contained within a genus). It is true that some Thomists would dispute whether *ens* and *esse* are attributed to individuals of the same species in an analogical or in a merely univocal fashion. So, for example, one might argue that *esse* is attrib-

Now let us add to this the confession of faith: that in this historical Jesus, one of the Trinity was crucified. He who was crucified historically under Pontius Pilate was truly one with the Father and truly himself God, the Logos, through whom all things are made. In this case, this one here, Jesus of Nazareth, is distinct from Pontius Pilate and Peter and you and me, not only because he is a distinct human existent in history (the predicamental analogy mentioned above), but also because he is truly one in being with God, who is the origin of all that exists, and is himself God, through whom all things were made. And if this is the case, oneness and existence as they are applied to God alone must be applied to him. He is the one God. This occurs by what modern Thomists, following Aquinas, term an *ad alterum* analogy, or a "transcendental" analogy of being.[49] Since being and unity are coexten-

---

uted to Peter and to Paul univocally because of the commonality of their natural form, since both are human, even though, as concrete existents, they are of course truly distinct and do *resemble* one another ontologically. It seems to me, however, that this way of thinking would leave us with no way of allowing the full signification of *esse* to unfold, i.e., as signifying not only an existent natural kind but also as signifying the irreducible existence of *this* singular reality (Peter) in its ontological uniqueness, as both similar to and distinct from others (such as Paul). For a study of Aquinas's metaphysics that tends toward this sense, see Lawrence Dewan's "On Anthony Kenny's *Aquinas on Being*," *Nova et Vetera*, Engl. ed., 3, no. 2 (2005): 335-400. However, even if we concede the point about univocal attribution of *ens* and *esse* to individuals of the same species (uniquely for the sake of argument), the larger point I am making here would in no way be undermined. One could simply refer to the more common and irrefusable example of the analogical predication of *ens* to the diverse genera of being according to proportional analogy. Insofar as one would claim that (1) the qualities, (2) quantities, and (3) substantial beings of Pontius Pilate, Peter, and Jesus all "existed" in historical time, these diverse dimensions of their beings (as substances with certain diverse accidents that undergo change) were in fact ontologically complex, and the accidents of their beings participated in the existence of their substances, upon which they depended aitiologically, even while themselves truly existing as properties of those substances. If Pontius passed from a state of indetermined legal judgment to a state of determined legal judgment concerning Jesus, this was only possible because he first existed; but in making his decision, he did not cease to exist substantially or come to be. Consequently, the judgment has to be said to "exist" (as a quality of his soul) differently from his "existence" as a substantial being in time (a subsistent person). In short, *if* we accept the premise that *esse* is not in a genus but is attributed to the genera in ways that are analogical, *and* if we accept that the genera of being (qualities, quantities, relations, etc.) truly denote features of reality, then the analogical predication of being (and the implicit acknowledgment of the analogy of being) is unavoidable. Nor can it be absent from our discourse concerning the historical humanity of Christ, especially if he has taken on a human nature univocally identical with our own.

49. *ST* I, q. 13, a. 5; *De pot.*, q. 7, a. 7. See Montagnes, *The Doctrine of the Analogy of Being*, pp. 64-91.

sive notions common to every genus of being (transcendentals), an analogy of being also implies an analogy of unity. Jesus is truly one person like us, but in a wholly other way than us (analogical difference on the predicamental level) because he alone — as the Son eternally distinct from the Father — can say personally, "I and the Father are one." Yet we can understand that this man among us is truly one with the Father only if *their* oneness in being has something in common with unity-of-being as we otherwise experience it (analogical similitude on the transcendental level). In sum, if we are to claim both that he is one who exists in time whom we relate to historically and that *in him* the one God who is the cause of all that exists "exists" as man, then we must also posit an ontological similitude between all that exists and the existence of God present in Christ. Were this not the case, his presence in history would be for us utterly inconceivable (or indecipherable) and, therefore, ultimately meaningless.

III

To this point, I have argued that the ascription of an ontological analogy between creatures and God is logically implied by the realism of the incarnation and by the expression of a biblical understanding of God as the Word incarnate. In the third part of this essay, I turn to the epistemological presuppositions of this viewpoint. My claim is that the natural human capacity to think analogically about God in his unity and existence as the cause of the world — with the help of concepts drawn from creation — is a necessary epistemological presupposition for any scriptural or dogmatic account of the incarnate Word. The *analogia Verbi* presupposes the possibility of an analogical ascription of *esse* to God as a necessary (but not sufficient!) condition, just as grace presupposes created nature. It follows from such a claim that if we are able to come to a true theological — and even dogmatic — understanding of what it means for God to become man, we are also able in principle to achieve a distinctly philosophical understanding of God analogically (no matter how imperfect and indirect) from the consideration of creatures. That is to say, if Christianity is true, then human beings are necessarily capable of natural theology.

My argument for this claim is fairly simple. First, I will argue that the affirmation of a supernatural revelation (given in grace) presupposes the existence of knowledge in human persons that is not derived from revelation (so-called natural knowledge). Second, I will argue that there can be no correlation between the workings of the human mind and the grace of revelation unless the human mind is *naturally* capable *under grace* of recognizing such revelation *as grace,* that is to say, as something given from outside the ordinary spectrum of truths obtained by human reasoning and intraworldly experience. Third, however, this potentiality of the mind to receive a graced revelation is subject to such recognition of the gratuity of the gift of revelation only if it has in itself the natural or intrinsic capacity to recognize the existence of God as a reality that transcends the sphere of created existence. That is to say, only if we are intrinsically able to compare by analogy the existence of realities in our ordinary experience with the existence of God who is incomprehensible, and who utterly transcends the sphere of creaturely being, are we in turn able to recognize — in and by grace — the revelation of God's identity as a gift transcending the sphere of created being. Failing this natural openness to the mystery of God's transcendence, the recognition of God in Christ becomes epistemologically impossible.

First, let us begin with a presupposition from our earlier discussion. Aquinas rightly underscores the gratuity of the revelation of the triune God, which cannot be either predicted or derived from human rational reflection. God reveals his triune identity (the eternal generation of the Son and spiration of the Spirit) by the missions of the Son and Spirit within the divine economy. Consequently, because the missions alone truly reveal to us who God is in himself (albeit imperfectly and indirectly), they are also the basis for any such knowledge of this identity. To affirm this is to maintain with the First Vatican Council the supernatural character of revelation as something not derived from human ingenuity or deluded religious fancy.[50] At stake for Aquinas, as for Vatican I, is the claim that the revealed knowledge of God is a grace, and as such is unmerited and gratuitous (exceeding ordinary human powers).[51] Trinitarian truth is not to be considered some

---

50. *Dei Filius,* c. IV: "The perpetual agreement of the Catholic Church has maintained and maintains this too: that there is a twofold order of knowledge [*duplicem ordinem cognitionis*], distinct not only as regards its source, but also as regards its object. With regard to the source, we know at the one level by natural reason, at the other level by divine faith. With regard to the object, besides those things to which natural reason can attain, there are proposed for our belief mysteries hidden in God which, unless they are divinely revealed, are incapable of being known. . . . If anyone shall have said that no true mysteries properly so-called are contained in divine revelation, but that all the dogmas of faith can be understood and proved from natural principles, through reason properly cultivated, let him be anathema."

51. The latter claim, as regards Aquinas, is brought home in resolute fashion by the study of Joseph Wawrykow, *Grace and Human Action: Merit in the Theology of Thomas Aquinas* (Notre Dame, Ind.: Notre Dame University Press, 1996).

kind of unintelligible, purely equivocal discourse (dialectically opposed to our ordinary language). Nevertheless, it is situated beyond the horizon of our ordinary conceptual and linguistic capacities as a truth to which they can never attain by their own powers.

My first argument is that there is a necessary corollary to this last claim. If the revelation is given gratuitously, it is also something that is not possessed according to our ordinary form of human conceptuality. It is not identical with the banal or even the extraordinary knowledge that we have of the world or even (presupposing the possibility of such) of God the Creator, based upon his effects in the creation. If this is the case, then the affirmation of the gratuity and nonderived, transcendent origin of knowledge of the Son incarnate also entails the affirmation of an intraworldly, nonrevealed form of knowledge. Even if all things that we know belong to the world of Christ, the unique creation of the Logos, they are not all known directly and immediately through the encounter with Christ by grace and in faith. Thinking about unity in calculus or the philosophy of Plotinus is different from reflection upon the unity of the Father and the Son.[52] The ordinary knowledge we have of the world through our own powers, then, does not simply coexist along a gradient of degrees with the knowledge that comes through the light of faith in the incarnate Word. The two forms of knowledge are different in kind, or to use the phrase of Vatican I, there is a *duplex ordo cognitionis* in that each form of knowledge is distinguished by its originating principles as well as its objects.[53]

---

52. This position is illustrated by Aquinas's defense of the rationality of Christian belief in the Word as a person distinct from the Father. He follows the ancient Greek patristic tradition of showing in what ways it is not absurd to believe in a preexistent Logos in and through which God knows the world, but he qualifies this tradition so as to avoid any suggestion that the Logos of Christian revelation (the Logos as *personally* distinct from the Father) could be understood to exist necessarily by recourse to mere metaphysical analogy. *ST* I, q. 32, a. 1, ad 1: "The philosophers did not know the mystery of the triunity of the divine persons by its proper attributes, such as paternity, filiation, and procession. . . . Nevertheless, they knew some of the essential attributes appropriated [in Christian tradition] to the persons, as power to the Father, wisdom to the Son, goodness to the Holy Spirit. . . . In the Platonic books we find, 'In the beginning was the Word,' not as meaning the Person begotten in God, but as meaning the ideal type whereby God made all things." Contrast this with John Damascene, *De fide orth.* I, c. 6 (a text Aquinas was aware of), where the Greek doctor offers an argument (seemingly from reason) from the spiritual nature of God to the necessity of a subsistent *logos* in God, "differentiated in its subsistence from him from whom it derives." (Likewise, he argues for the procession of the Spirit in c. 7.) See the analysis of Bernard Lonergan on this point of Aquinas's teaching in *The Triune God: Systematics* (Toronto: University of Toronto Press, 2007), appendix 2B: "From the Image to the Eternal Exemplar," pp. 626-85.

53. For a Thomistic parallel, see *SCG* 4.1, esp. para. 5.

This brings us to the second stage of my argument. I have claimed above that to know the man Christ as God is to know him as one with the Father and the Holy Spirit and to know him as the Son and Word, through and in whom all things are given being. Consequently, to know the triune God revealed in the incarnate Son is to think analogically of God the Creator in terms of his unity and being, by comparison to the created order that depends upon him. How is this previous claim related to the argument that has just been made, the claim that there is knowledge of the world (in its existence and multiplicity) that does not derive epistemologically from the gift of faith in Christ? If we are able to recognize the triune God as being like the realities of our world, *even while recognizing* that the realities of this world *are known differently* (i.e., without explicit recourse to revelation), then we are also capable of recognizing a likeness and dissimilarity between the world as we know it naturally and God as he is revealed supernaturally (something akin to what Barth calls the "analogia fidei").[54] We come, then, to a second claim: If we receive knowledge of God through divine revelation, we must necessarily be capable of recognizing a comparison and contrast between God *as he is revealed to us in Christ,* and the world *as we know it by our ordinary powers of human reason.* We can judge, therefore, *from within the scope of our own natural reason* under grace that what we know by revelation is not the product of ordinary reflection but is a gift. And this means that in order to think rightly of the divinity of the man Christ by recourse to theological analogies of faith (the divinity of the Word, etc.), we must have *an intrinsic natural capacity of our minds* to recognize such revelation as something exceeding the scope of our ordinary natural powers of reflection and knowledge, *even while understanding it to be knowledge of a form that is not wholly alien to the human mind.*[55]

---

54. In his commentary on John 10:30 ("I and the Father are one"), Aquinas illustrates this truth very eloquently by way of a response to Arianism (*In Ioan.* 10.5.1451): "The Arians try to deny this [affirmation of divine unity], and say that a creature can in some sense be one with God, and in this sense the Son can be one with the Father. The falsity of this can be shown . . . from our very manner of speaking. For it is clear that 'one' is asserted as 'being'; thus, just as something is not said to be a being absolutely except according to its substance, so it is not said to be one except according to its substance or nature. Now something is asserted absolutely when it is asserted with no added qualification. Therefore, because 'I and the Father are one,' is asserted absolutely, without any qualifications added, it is plain that they are one according to substance and nature. But we never find that God and a creature are one without some added qualification, as in I Cor. 6:17: 'he who is united to the Lord becomes one spirit with him.' Therefore, it is clear that the Son of God is not one with the Father as a creature can be."

55. Aquinas typically addresses this question within the context of the medieval de-

This leads me to the third and final part of the argument. Knowledge of Christ is not wholly alien to us, because some dimension of the human mind is naturally open to knowledge of the Creator. Unless we have an intrinsic, natural capacity to think about God as the transcendent causal principle of existence in creatures, and therefore by recourse to analogical terms derived from creatures, revelation of God in Christ as the origin of the being of the world will remain something intrinsically unintelligible to the human intellect, something wholly extrinsic to our ordinary form of knowing. Such "epistemological extrinsicism" would in turn render knowledge of God as Creator impossible, even if it were given in Christ, and by consequence would impede our capacity to affirm the divinity of Christ, even if it were unveiled to us through the medium of divine revelation.

The reason for this is that Christian revelation stipulates that God, the triune God, has given being to all that exists. He is the cause of the world's coming into being. But if God is to be intelligible by comparison with all we know naturally of the existent world (as must be the case), and yet as not identical with, but utterly distinct from, the world (as must also be the case), then we must be naturally capable of thinking of God in comparison with creatures as something (or someone) that *is not created, but rather that is the source of all that exists in ontological dependence upon him.* Were this idea of causal dependency upon God for existence intrinsically unintelligible to us by means of natural, ordinary powers of reflection, the revelation of God *in Christ* as the Creator of the existent world *would remain inconceivable.* The "existence" of Christ *as God the Creator* (the source of created existence) would remain entirely alien to "existence" as we encounter it in creatures.

---

bate concerning whether the human person is naturally *capable* of receiving the grace of the beatific vision, or whether this gift (itself the final end of divine revelation) is something wholly extrinsic to the human mind, rendering Christianity philosophically untenable. At the same time, he wishes to underscore the traditional Augustinian understanding that the beatific vision is an absolute grace, one that our human powers are intrinsically incapable of procuring. He in fact resolves this seeming paradox by arguments that show that, from its knowledge of creatures that are God's effects, the human mind may naturally aspire to a perfect knowledge of God as their primary cause, since knowledge of God through his effects remains intrinsically unsatisfactory. Nevertheless, this aspiration may in no way be fulfilled by that same natural desire, and this has as a consequence to leave the mind naturally receptive both to divine revelation and to the grace of the immediate vision of God (in a way that nonrational creatures are not), even while underscoring the absolute gratuity of divine revelation and the vision as a gift that utterly transcend the powers and resources of created human nature. For examples of this argumentation, see *SCG* 3.50-54; *Comp. theo.* 1.104; *ST* I, q. 12, a. 1.

Consequently, one of two extremes would result. Either we would be forced to understand the existence of God in terms that are purely homogenous with those derived from the world (a form of univocal thinking effectively destroying the possibility of the knowledge of the transcendent otherness of God's existence as distinct from that of his creation), and in this case God's being would be intelligible only as a being among beings. Or else God would not be made known to us in any way that is in continuity with what we know naturally (an equivocal form of thinking making God's existence unintelligible to human thought). In this latter case, God's existence would remain so wholly other to the world as to be entirely inconceivable and alien.[56] To conceive of God, then, as the Creator of all that exists, doing so in terms drawn from the world as we ordinarily know it, requires that we can obtain true analogical knowledge of the existence of God, departing from existence in things that we experience and that are themselves derived from God.[57]

We can further clarify the form such analogical reflection must take by considering the following. Being, as both Aristotle and Aquinas rightly note, is not itself identical with any genus or species of thing.[58] Rather, every ge-

56. In this sense, I am arguing something that is logically contrary to Barth's claims in his criticisms of the *analogia entis* in *CD* II/1, pp. 82ff. There he suggests that the understanding of God attained from natural reason as "the first principle and final end of all things" (Vatican I) (1) introduces a mere abstraction into theology such that (2) we fail to understand God at all times uniquely as the God of salvation and reconciliation in Jesus Christ. This is to introduce an entirely "foreign god into the Church" (p. 84). No doubt false philosophical conceptions can render obscure Christian theological truths. However, it seems to me that there is also an inverse danger that Barth does not observe. (1) The negation of any capacity to conceive of God as the transcendent origin of the world brings with it (2) a radical "alienation" of the God of Jesus Christ from the world of human understanding, rendering him a "mere abstraction" or Gnostic deity, dialectically counterpoised to this world, and incapable of being understood by it in any way. Evidently, such perspectives remain entirely foreign to Barth's theological intentions. But if univocal conceptuality brings with it the danger of an abstract anthropomorphism, the dangers of agnosticism promoted by a thoroughgoing equivocity are not less great.

57. Restated in linguistic terms, we could say that (1) to speak of God we have to speak of creatures, but (2) to be able to speak of God in terms derived from knowledge of creatures, it has to be the case that creatures have to resemble God as their source. If there is a "divine grammar" given in revelation that is distinct from our ordinary human grammar, it is nevertheless not a substitute for the latter, and indeed in some real sense can be understood only in comparison with and by being grafted onto our preexistent, ordinary ways of speaking. This ordinary discourse must itself be capable of deriving terms for God that are true, if the divine grammar concerning God is to be able to take root adequately in our ordinary modes of discourse.

58. Aquinas, *In meta.* 5.9.889-90. A sign of this is that every genus of creature (whether

nus of being is rightly said to "exist" or to "be" in an analogical and non-generic fashion, without prejudice to any other mode of being or concrete existent. *Ens commune* (i.e., "being that is common to all creatures") transcends every genus but is also found within every genus of being.[59] However, if God is the Creator of all that exists, then not only is God not located within a genus or species of being (i.e., within *ens commune*) but God is the transcendent cause of *ens commune* as such, or all that exists.[60] Therefore, if the God who has been revealed in Christ is truly the Creator of all that exists, he is not conceivable for our human nature in his distinctness from creatures *as Creator* by recourse to univocal predication of any genus of created being, since he is not a being among beings in the created order.[61] Nor is he

---

substantial or accidental) may either actually exist or not exist. It is therefore composed of actuality and potentiality. *De pot.*, q. 3, a. 8, ad 12: "Actuality and potentiality are not different accidental modes of being, such as go to make an alteration: they are substantial modes of being. For even substance is divided by potentiality and act, like any other genus." Barth does not seem to have grasped this metaphysical point correctly. In *CD* III/3, p. 103, he suggests that within a Catholic theology "there is an *analogia entis* between God and the creature. To that extent there is a master-concept, a common denominator, a genus (being) which comprises both God and the creature. And it would be a really serious mistake if we were to adopt this argument." But no major Catholic metaphysician, including Aquinas, Scotus, or Suárez, has ever claimed even that being is in a genus (except by metaphorical comparison with other sciences), let alone that God and being are in a common genus. This portrayal of classical metaphysics is seriously problematic. See my study of this in Thomas Joseph White, O.P., "How Barth Got Aquinas Wrong: A Reply to Archie J. Spencer on Causality and Christocentrism," *Nova et Vetera*, Engl. ed., 7, no. 1 (2009): 241-70. (All citations from the *Church Dogmatics* are taken from the English translation of G. W. Bromiley and T. F. Torrance [London: T. & T. Clark; New York: Continuum, 2004].)

59. *ST* I, q. 4, a. 3.

60. *ST* I-II, q. 66, a. 5, ad 4; *ST* I, q. 3, a. 4, ad 1.

61. *ST* I, q. 3, a. 5: "All in one genus agree in the quiddity or essence of the genus which is predicated of them as an essential, but they differ in their existence. For the existence of man and of house is not the same; as also of this man and that man: thus in every member of a genus, existence and quiddity — i.e., essence — must differ. But in God [who does not receive his existence from another] they do not differ [because he exists necessarily, and his nature and existence are identical]; Therefore it is plain that God is not in a genus as if he were a species. *From this it is also plain that He has no genus nor difference, nor can there be any definition of him; nor, save through effects, a demonstration of him, for a definition is from genus and difference, and the mean of a demonstration is a definition.* That God is not in a genus, as reducible to it as its principle, is clear from this, that a principle reducible to any genus does not extend beyond that genus. . . . But God is the principle of all being. Therefore he is not contained in any genus as its principle" (emphasis added). Barth occasionally speaks about Aquinas's views in ways that suggest a serious miscomprehension in this re-

intelligible in his distinctness in comparison to the beings of this world merely by recourse to "proportional" analogical notions common to all that exists (transcendental notions such as being, oneness, goodness, and the like). God is not intelligible from within the *ratio* of these terms that are capable of signifying all created beings, for he is the transcendent source of all the realities that are designated by these common terms.[62] Rather, if God is conceivable in distinction to creatures *at all,* it is only as a heterogeneous cause is known analogically apart from his effects. That is to say, God is

---

spect. See, for example, *CD* II/1, p. 581: "For the Thomist conception of the relation of God and the creature also offers the picture of a system, of the relationship of two quantities which in the last resort are comparable and can be grouped together under one concept. God's infinite superiority and the infinite subordination of the creature are beautifully set out and secured in this system. Yet in this remarkable relationship the two quantities are embraced in the common concept of being. This is filled out by God in a divine manner and by the creature in a creaturely one, but at the same time it is described as the substance of both and therefore as a substance common to both." Of course, Aquinas refuses the reduction of divine unity to a concept of intraworldly material quantity precisely because quantity is generic (*ST* I, q. 11, a. 3, ad 2), but he also famously refuses to ascribe the term "substance" to God as such, precisely because God is outside of every known genus of being, including that of substance. *De pot.,* q. 7, a. 3, ad 4: "Substance is not rightly defined as a self-subsisting being: for being cannot be the genus of a thing according to the Philosopher, because nothing can be added to being that has not a share of being, and a difference should not be a part of the genus. If, however, substance can be defined notwithstanding that it is the most universal of genera, its definition will be 'a thing whose quiddity is competent to have being not in a subject.' Hence the definition of substance cannot be applied to God, whose quiddity is not distinct from his being. Wherefore God is not contained in the genus of substance, but is above all substance." Barth's portrayal of the Thomistic position on this point is caricatural. When in *CD* II/1, p. 237ff., Barth seeks to examine the doctrine of the analogy of being as employed in "natural theology," he studies the theory of the seventeenth-century Lutheran theologian A. Quenstedt (*Theol. did. pol.* [1685], I, c. 8, sect. 2, q. 1). In fact, as it turns out, Quenstedt's view on every point is simply that of Francisco Suárez. For an excellent study of Suárez, contrasting his views in many respects with those of Aquinas, see Jean-François Courtine, *Suarez et le système de la métaphysique* (Paris: Presses universitaires de France, 1990).

62. Aquinas, *In de causis,* prop. 6: "For what the intellect first grasps is being [*ens*]. The intellect cannot apprehend that in which the character of being is not found. . . . But, according to the truth of the matter, the first cause is above being [*supra ens*] inasmuch as it is itself infinite *esse.* 'Being,' however, is called that which finitely participates in *esse,* and it is this which is proportioned to our intellect, whose object is the quiddity or 'that which is' [*quod quid est*]. . . . Hence our intellect can grasp only that which has a quiddity participating in *esse.* But the quiddity of God is itself *esse.* Thus it is above intellect" (trans. V. Guagliardo, C. Hess, and R. Taylor, *Commentary on the Book of Causes* [Washington, D.C.: Catholic University of America Press, 1996], translation slightly modified).

known truly from creatures as containing in himself the perfections that are present within them, in a wholly other and preeminent way.[63] Yet he is not known as one possessing these perfections through a common participation in these attributes that is shared with creatures, but rather as their ineffable and incomprehensible source.[64]

In conclusion, we can say that if human beings can think by grace of Christ as the *Logos ensarkos* through whom all things were made, but we are not *naturally* able to think of things *as made* — as given existence — by God, who is one and who exists in a way analogous to creatures (transcending every genus of being, and even *ens commune* as such), then a contradiction results. Human beings cannot both think of things as given existence by and in the Word of the Father, who is the one God *(analogia fidei)*, and understand the existence of things in this world *without any possible reference to God* (prohibition on the *analogia entis*). In this conflict something is obliged to yield.[65] Even if God were to give to a human being in grace to know God in-

---

63. See *ST* I, q. 13, aa. 5-6, and Reinhard Hütter's analysis of Aquinas's *unius ad alterum* analogy in his essay in this volume. A. 6: "For the words, 'God is good,' or 'wise' signify not only that He is the cause of wisdom and goodness [though they also signify this!], but [also] that these exist in Him in a more excellent way."

64. See esp. *ST* I, q. 4, a. 3, ad 1, 2, and 3: "God is not related to creatures as though belonging to a different genus, but as transcending every genus, and as the principle of all genera. [Therefore,] likeness of creatures to God is not affirmed on account of agreement in form according to the formality of the same genus or species, but solely according to analogy, inasmuch as God is essential being, whereas other things are beings by participation. [Correspondingly,] although it may be admitted that creatures are in some sort like God, it must nowise be admitted that God is like creatures; because as Dionysius says (Div. nom. 9): 'A mutual likeness may be found between things of the same order, but not between a cause and that which is caused.' For, we say that a statue is like a man, but not conversely; so also a creature can be spoken of as in some sort like God; but not that God is like a creature."

65. It seems to me that this tension is manifest in Barth's *CD* I/1, in his simultaneous rejection of Emil Brunner's "point of contact [in created human nature] for the divine message" (p. 27) and his revelatory epistemology of the Holy Spirit as principal agent in the human subject's reception of revelation. P. 426: "The Spirit guarantees man what he cannot guarantee himself, his personal participation in revelation." P. 462: "Even in receiving the Holy Ghost man remains man, the sinner sinner. Similarly in the outpouring of the Holy Ghost God remains God. The statements about the operations of the Holy Spirit are statements whose subject is God and not man, and in no circumstances can they be transformed into statements about man. *They tell us about the relation of God to man, to his knowledge, will and emotion, to his experience active and passive, to his heart and conscience, to the whole of his psycho-physical existence, but they cannot be reversed and understood as statements about the existence of man.*" Barth seems to posit simultaneously a thoroughgoing ontological and epistemological extrinsicism of revelatory grace with respect to human natural pow-

tellectually as the Son and Word, and even if this gift were derived from an omnipotent freedom, this grace would necessarily be ineffective unless we were able by our natural powers to understand *something of* the oneness of God and of his transcendence as the Creator of existents. *Because* we can know something of God by our ordinary, natural powers, *therefore* we can receive knowledge of him by grace that is not wholly alien to our ordinary form of knowing. Correspondingly, if we do truly know God through the revelation of Christ given in grace, then we are also necessarily capable in principle of knowing God through the medium of our natural human powers by a knowledge derived from creatures. If we are able to affirm the divinity of Christ as "eternally begotten of the Father, begotten not made . . . true God from true God, through whom all things were made," then we are also necessarily capable of natural knowledge of God, or "natural theology."

*   *   *

Let me conclude the argument of this essay by adjoining a brief theological caveat. Nothing I have said above presupposes that human nature laboring under the effects of fallen existence and *acting without grace* might realize effectively in history a well-reasoned philosophical argument for the existence of God, or a lucid reflection on the analogical names for God as understood by comparison with creatures. Aquinas himself, who is not pessimistic about the human capacity to arrive at knowledge of God, notes the effects on the intellect in its concrete historical exercise by the draw of disordered passions,[66] the cupidity of the heart,[67] ignorance and laziness,[68] the difficulty of the subject matter,[69] and the weight of received opinions that are erroneous.[70] Nevertheless, Aquinas also recognizes that human beings remain es-

---

ers, even while maintaining a profound insistence on the thoroughly intrinsic character of the work of the Holy Spirit in the human person. What is the relation here between the extrinsicism of all God's action with regard to creaturely actions or dispositions, on the one hand, and God's work in and for the creature on the other? How might one coherently describe the work of God in the existence of man while simultaneously maintaining a prohibition on something existing in man that is potentially open to, or which stands in relation to, the work of God?

66. *Comp. theo.* 1.192.
67. *ST* I-II, q. 83, a. 3, c. and ad 3.
68. Ibid., q. 85, a. 3.
69. *SCG* 4.1.3.
70. *SCG* 1.4-5; *ST* I, q. 1, a. 1.

sentially the same *kind* of reality even after sin, and even in redemption.[71] Otherwise, neither prelapsarian humanity nor Christ would have been "human" as we are, in an unequivocal sense.[72] The metaphysical consequence of this is that the natural substrate of all divine agency, and of all human fallenness, is something: the human essence, a distinct human nature, which is not reducible either to the nothingness of sin that eats away at human being or to the graced life of Christ that re-creates the human substrate, healing and restoring a fallen human nature, turning it toward its final purpose. To claim that we have natural capacities for philosophical knowledge of God, then, implies that these capacities exist as properties intrinsic to the soul, even in its state of fallenness without grace. This does not mean, however, that we can employ them properly in our fallen state without the agency of the grace of Christ, or even flawlessly with such grace. Revelation, the illumination of faith, and the workings of hope and charity not only stimulate the human person's ascent to God in Christ but also facilitate his or her progressive recovery of the habitual exercise of natural capacities (virtues) that have been neglected because of sin. And yet again, when the pursuit of natural knowledge of God is inspired by revelation and stimulated by grace, it remains distinct from the knowledge of God given through revelation and accepted in faith. This distinctness in no way implies a rivalry, as if the *saving* knowledge or love of God occurs through recourse to the natural knowledge of God (whether within or apart from faith).[73] On the contrary,

71. *ST* I-II, q. 109, aa. 1-2.

72. *In II Sent.,* d. 28, q. 1, a. 1; *SCG* 4.30.3. In the latter text, Aquinas argues against Valentinus: "For in every single species there are determined essential principles . . . from which comes the essential constitution in things composed of matter and form. But just as human flesh and bone and the like are the proper matter of man . . . therefore, if the body of Christ was not earthly, it was not true flesh and true bone, but in appearance only. And thus, also, [Christ] was not a true, but an apparent man, whereas he himself nonetheless says: 'A spirit hath not flesh and bones, as you see me to have' (Luke 24:39)" (trans. C. J. O'Neill, *Summa contra Gentiles,* vol. 4 [Garden City, N.Y.: Doubleday, 1954]).

73. As was mentioned above, according to Aquinas, non-Christians have attained to some true knowledge of God — sometimes through philosophical reflection — yet, this knowledge was frequently admixed with errors and led to forms of religious practice that were inimical to the true Christian worship of God (*In Ioan.* 17.2.2195; 17.6.2265). In our fallen state, according to Aquinas's anti-Pelagian writing, a *natural* love of God above all things is impossible without grace (*ST* I-II, q. 109, aa. 1-4). This means that in the concrete historical order, in order to recognize God as one's true final end *even naturally,* some kind of *supernatural* grace of God (which itself presupposes the gift of supernatural faith) is necessary. Justification, meanwhile, occurs only through faith, informed by charity, and depends upon the revealed knowledge of God that accompanies this faith (*ST* I-II, q. 109, aa. 5-

the claim that there is a natural capacity for such knowledge is merely the mirror image of the claim that we are saved by grace and justified by faith, such that this grace and this faith *have* a true natural substrate that is sufficiently proportioned to them so as to be susceptible to redemption. It is not the claim that the latter substrate can in any way substitute itself for the redeemed state of being in Christ. The latter state is made possible uniquely because of God's incarnation and crucifixion, and through participation in the sacramental graces of Christ's church, the ecclesial body of the crucified and risen Lord.

Conclusion

I have argued above that some form of analogical, metaphysical thinking about God is in fact intrinsic to Christological dogmatic theology, and unavoidably so. We must be logically committed to a metaphysics of divine names if we wish to safeguard a true sense of the transcendent divinity of the Son as the incarnate Word, in and through whom all things were made. This means in turn that the analogical consideration of the Word incarnate by comparison with creatures requires of us the analogical consideration of the being of God by comparison with creatures.

Lest the conclusion of the argument seem insignificant, let me briefly note three fairly important consequences that follow from this line of thinking. First, statements concerning the natural capacity of the human intellect to attain to demonstrative knowledge of God have an irreducibly philosophical character and therefore cannot be justified uniquely by recourse to the intuitive, deductive, or moral force of theological arguments to which these philosophical claims are attached. We might wish, for example, to argue that, in light of *The Critique of Pure Reason,* theology must accept that it has been demonstrated that there is no possible speculative demonstration of the existence of God, nor any analogical naming of God from creatures that is other than conjectural, nor that we can appeal to "causality" in such a way as to speak of what transcends the realm of sensation. In doing so, however, we are at least implicitly accepting distinctly philosophical claims that are open to dispute or rebuttal from philosophical premises, and that cannot be maintained simply as an outcome of an

---

10). Therefore, if one were to know something true of God naturally, without authentic love for God above all things, this could potentially serve only to augment the soul's culpability before God by removing an excuse from ignorance (cf. Rom. 1:20-21).

aprioristic theological dogmatism. If Barthians frequently adopt Kantian epistemological premises, they do so not because of a theological understanding derived from divine revelation but because they have inherited a set of philosophical commitments and presuppositions from the German Enlightenment and modern liberal Protestantism.

Second, Christian theology cannot unfold in a congruent explanation of itself in relation to both God and ordinary knowledge and experience without the integration into itself of a lucid philosophical form of thought that is open to the knowledge of God that comes by way of grace. To the extent that profound philosophical errors or presuppositions emerge within a theology that do not relate to the theocentric tasks of theology, they will in fact anthropomorphize theology in erroneous and problematic ways.[74]

Finally, if what I have suggested in this essay is correct, then the progressive rejection of the classical analogical names of God in much of the modern philosophical tradition inexorably works to secularize Christian culture in a profound and unhealthy way. It does so because it habituates the mind to a form of thinking that continuously rejects in principle every point of contact for grace to work within the life of the human intellect, and consequently it renders basic facets of Christian dogma unintelligible. To the extent that postmetaphysical philosophy and its presuppositions are introduced into theology from within — even if such decisions are conducted in the name of Christocentrism — they have the capacity to obstruct and to undermine the very basis for a reception of the grace of Christ within the human mind and within ecclesial culture. Such features of an otherwise well-intentioned theology may in turn work to undermine the Christological confession that they are meant to serve. In thinking of this phenomenon, we may recall the pertinent saying of the Lord: "For those who have not, even what they have will be taken from them" (Mark 4:25). And perhaps correspondingly, and not wholly inappropriately, contemporary theology would do well to ponder anew words of Karl Barth: "Fear of scholasticism is the mark of a false prophet."[75] Christology and metaphysical reflection regarding creation are disciplines wed in an indissoluble fashion within the unique wisdom of God. The unity they share is a sign that God wishes to redeem rather than destroy our created nature. The distinction between them is an inalienable sign of the gratuity of the gift of Christ.

---

74. See in this respect the pertinent critical diagnostic of David Bentley Hart with respect to the theologies of Jürgen Moltmann, Eberhard Jüngel, and Robert Jenson in his "No Shadow of Turning: On Divine Impassibility," *Pro Ecclesia* 11 (2002): 184-206.

75. *CD* I/1, p. 279.

CHAPTER 8

Christ the End of Analogy

Bruce D. Marshall

I

For the last century or so, Catholic and Protestant theology has been marked by a recurring debate about "the analogy of being." Is this a high gift of divine wisdom, deep-laid in all the ways and works of God, or, on the contrary, the invention of Antichrist, a theological error than which none greater can be conceived? Many theologians have argued that the truth lies somewhere between these two extremes. Yet whatever they thought about the theological usefulness of the analogy of being, practically everyone engaged in this debate has agreed that all of our *talk* and thought about God is in some profound way analogical. Exactly how we can succeed in speaking and thinking about God without lapsing into univocity or equivocation remains contested. But that analogy furnishes the credible alternative to these dead ends, necessary for all successful discourse about God, has seemed obvious.

Thomas Aquinas has long been at the center of this argument. He provides the dominant paradigm for a theological and philosophical treatment of analogy, whether or not one thinks of the position he develops as "the analogy of being." His ideas are accordingly singled out for praise or blame, depending on the way his interpreters see the various theological and philosophical issues surrounding analogy. All the more remarkable, then, that Thomas himself emphatically rejects one of the few important assumptions on which both his partisans and his critics in the analogy debate have agreed: the notion that all our talk of God has to be analogical.

Aquinas insists, on the contrary, that for *Christian* theology all our speech about God cannot possibly be analogical. Quite a lot of Christian talk about God must, in fact, be univocal. To suppose otherwise is incompatible with faith in God's incarnation, and so with the most elemental Christian beliefs. Aquinas's dismissal of the omnipresence of analogy in Christian talk about God is not only explicit but utterly basic doctrinally, and of vital structural significance in his theology. We all have our blind spots. But how such an important matter could have gone unobserved in nearly a century's debate about Aquinas and analogy is nonetheless puzzling.

The failure of Aquinas's modern interpreters to connect his theological treatment of analogy in the Prima Pars with his Christological insistence on univocity in the Tertia Pars no doubt stems from the confluence of several different factors. At least in part, it seems to me, this problem typically follows from an inability — or unwillingness — to distinguish the linguistic and logical dimensions of analogy in St. Thomas from the metaphysical ones, and to appreciate the import of the former. In particular, that everything we say about God has to be analogical often looks to theologians like an unremarkable by-product of the fact that the relationship between God and the world is irreducibly analogical. Thomists like to think of this relationship as an analogy of being, while their opponents characterize it in some other way (e.g., as an analogy of faith), but both sides assume that the theologically significant issues about analogy belong in the domain of the real, not of the merely linguistic.

We can begin, then, by looking at how Aquinas treats the two sorts of things we most readily regard as analogous, or as having relationships of analogy to one another, namely, words and objects, or verbal and nonverbal sorts of things. I will first say something about verbal analogy and then talk about how this is, and is not, connected to analogy thought of as a real relation among things rather than words. We can then turn to Aquinas's Christological rejection of analogy in favor of univocity and conclude with some observations about the theological significance analogy does, and does not, have for Aquinas.

II

In the early 1960s, near the end of several decades of intense discussion about analogy among philosophers and theologians, Catholic and Protestant alike, Ralph McInerny published *The Logic of Analogy*, which offered a novel interpretation of St. Thomas's views on the subject.[1] Thirty-five years later, rather than reprint the earlier book, he rewrote it in light of what he had learned in the interim, under the title *Aquinas and Analogy*.[2] The two books make essentially the same argument, among the basic conclusions of which is that, for Aquinas, "the analogy of names" has to do with words and concepts, not objects and their properties, second intentional entities (to use Thomas's own idiom), not first intentional ones. Analogical naming — the issue treated so influentially by Aquinas in texts like *Summa theologiae* I, q. 13, aa. 5-6 — belongs in the domain of logic, not of metaphysics.

Especially in recent years attention to the logical and linguistic dimensions of Thomas's theology and philosophy has become widespread, often among interpreters interested in establishing connections between Aquinas and analytic philosophy. McInerny has no such interest; his two books on analogy in Aquinas are devoid of reference to Wittgenstein, Quine, or any other analytic philosopher, though there are extensive discussions of Aristotle and classical commentators on St. Thomas, especially Cajetan. Nor can McInerny be charged with a low regard for the metaphysics of Aquinas, either in these books or elsewhere. Taking "analogy" in Thomas to be at home in the discipline of logic rather than of metaphysics is not the same thing as claiming that metaphysics doesn't matter to Thomas, nor is it to deny that a metaphysics of participation plays a central role in his theology and philosophy. It is simply to claim that the distinction between the analogy of names and the metaphysics of being and participation does, in fact, matter to Thomas, and for good reason.

Still, as McInerny readily admits, his interpretation of Aquinas on analogy, especially his contention that the analogy of names is a logical rather than a metaphysical doctrine, has found few takers among those he most wants to convince, namely, committed Thomists.[3] This is due in part to questions about the interpretation of Thomas's texts. But many Thomists rule out such a reading of Aquinas on analogy long before specific exegetical questions come into play. For them the questions addressed by logical and

---

1. Ralph M. McInerny, *The Logic of Analogy: An Interpretation of St. Thomas* (The Hague: Martinus Nijhoff, 1961). The other papers in this volume all deal with important aspects of the twentieth-century debate about analogy.

2. Ralph McInerny, *Aquinas and Analogy* (Washington, D.C.: Catholic University of America Press, 1996).

3. See McInerny's "Analogy and Foundationalism in Thomas Aquinas," in *Rationality, Religious Belief, and Moral Commitment,* ed. Robert Audi and William J. Wainwright, pp. 271-88 (Ithaca, N.Y.: Cornell University Press, 1986), p. 271.

linguistic analysis are trivial at best, and so not the sort of matter in which a thinker of Thomas's significance could be seriously interested. Or worse, Thomists often seem to suppose, worrying about words competes with or even precludes a proper metaphysical attention to the real. Above all when applied to the divine names, the thought that analogy is a logical matter surely reeks of nominalism, and wherever that leads, it is away from Thomas Aquinas.

This disdain for logic and the philosophy of language quickly separates modern interpreters of Aquinas from the historical context in which he himself lived and thought. By the thirteenth century, logic was basic to all university education in Christian Europe, and recourse to logical and semantic analysis was basic to the work of philosophy and theology, regardless of whether one had a special interest in these topics and wrote treatises on them.[4] But evidently many modern Thomists either don't know this, or don't care.

The French Dominican Antonin-Dalmais Sertillanges (1863-1948) offers a delightfully candid example of this indifference to matters Thomas and his time thought worthy of painstaking reflection. In his commentary on the opening questions of the Prima Pars, Sertillanges observes that *ST* I, qq. 12-13 deals with the "grave and difficult question" of "what knowledge of God we can have in this life."[5] Among the topics treated by Aquinas in these two questions is "Whether the term 'God' is said univocally when it is predicated by participation, by nature, and by opinion" (I, q. 13, a. 10).[6] Thomas touches on this question a number of times in his writings. It deals with whether and how the unbeliever can succeed in denying the same things the

---

4. So, for example, deliberate analysis of language and the application of highly developed semantic theories became a standard feature of medieval sacramental theology, including that of St. Thomas. This is already clear from the debates over the interpretation of the consecration formula in the Berengarian controversy, well before specific utterances came to be thought of as the "form" of each sacrament, and thus as a constitutive element of all the sacraments, each requiring treatment in its own right. On this, see Irène Rosier-Catach, *La parole efficace. Signe, ritual, sacré* (Paris: Éditions du Seuil, 2004). On St. Thomas in particular see also Irène Rosier, "Signes et sacrements. Thomas d'Aquin et la grammaire spéculative," *Revue des sciences philosophiques et théologiques* 74 (1990): 392-436.

5. Saint Thomas Aquinas, *Somme théologique*, Éditions de la Revue des Jeunes, *Dieu II* (I, 12-17), trans. A.-D. Sertillanges, O.P., 3d ed. (Tournai: Desclée & Cie, 1926), p. 379.

6. Thomas's own title for the article is a bit different, though the difference is not substantive: "Utrum [hoc nomen 'Deus' — a. 9] accipiatur univoce vel aequivoce, secundum quod significat Deum per naturam et per participationem et secundum opinionem" (*ST* I, q. 13, prooem.).

Christian asserts (like "God exists"), and it bears on whether a natural theologian outside the Christian orbit (like Aristotle) can know enough about God to assert, by the statement "God exists," the same thing the Christian does. But here, at least, Sertillanges sees no grave matter at stake. In fact he disdains even to translate the article, in what is otherwise a bilingual *Summa,* dismissing it with the observation that this article "deals only with logic, and no longer holds any interest for us."[7] Sertillanges, I should stress, was an able theologian and philosopher, and an accomplished Thomist. That is what makes his comments telling. He thought being a Thomist had nothing important to do with being a logician. And he knows enough to recognize that in this he departs from St. Thomas, rather than supposing that indifference to matters of logic and language, or the reduction of these to metaphysics, is *secundum mentem Thomae.*

That Aquinas thinks it necessary to raise and answer questions about logic and language is not, of course, to say that he thinks of analogy in particular as a doctrine about words and their uses. Perhaps the easiest way to see that he does is to look at his standard example of an analogous term. This will help us grasp the important sense in which analogy is a linguistic, as distinguished from a metaphysical, issue.[8]

When Aquinas addresses a theological problem by recourse to analogy, he unfailingly introduces the same example to show what he means. "Healthy" *(sanus)* is said of an animal as the subject of health (thus "Ille homo est sanus"), of medicine as a cause of health ("Illa medicina est sana"), and of urine as a sign of health ("Eius urina est sana").[9] The conceptual content or meaning of "healthy" in each of these three statements (what Aquinas, following Aristotle, calls its *ratio,* or definition) is quite different.[10] Said of an animal, "healthy" denotes a flourishing bodily state (owing, as Aquinas understands it, to a right proportion among the humors). Neither medicine nor urine is a bodily state of an animal, so "healthy" said of each must de-

---

7. *Dieu II,* p. 142, n. 2: "Nous omettons de traduire l'article 10, de pure logique et qui n'a plus pour nous aucun intérêt."

8. The argument I offer in this section owes much to McInerny, though it is couched in my own terms.

9. Inter alia, see *In I Sent.,* d. 19, q. 5, a. 1, sol.; *SCG* 1.34 (297); *ST* I, q. 13, a. 5, c.; a. 6, c.; a. 10, c.

10. "[R]atio enim quam significat nomen, est definitio" (*ST* I, q. 13, a. 1, c.). Cf. *In IV meta.* 16 (733): "Nam ratio quam nomen significat est definitio rei." For the equivalence of "conceptual content" and *ratio,* see *ST* I, q. 13, a. 4, c.: "Ratio enim quam significat nomen, est conceptio intellectus de re significata per nomen."

note something different from "healthy" said of an animal. This rules out univocity and suggests equivocation. In fact Aquinas, again following Aristotle, grants that analogy is a kind of equivocation, taking the latter notion in a broad sense.[11] But an analogous term like "healthy," unlike a purely or strictly equivocal one (such as "dog," said of a fish and a quadruped), displays a definite order or connection among its various uses.[12] In this case, "healthy" said of medicine, urine, food, exercise, and so forth is always related in some specifiable way to "healthy" said of an animal: as a cause of health in an animal, a sign of health in an animal, or connected in some other specifiable way to health in an animal. When Aquinas equates analogy with "proportion," he's simply talking about this ordered relationship among uses of an analogous term.[13]

Despite the enormous complexity his interpreters sometimes introduce into the understanding of analogy, for Aquinas himself analogous language consistently follows this same straightforward pattern. A term is used (or as Aquinas characteristically puts it, "said" — *dicitur*) analogously when the *ratio*, or definition, it has in one application is included in the *rationes* it has in its other applications, whether there be many others or just one. Thus "healthy" as applied to an animal is included in the definition of "healthy" as applied to medicine (which is healthy in that it causes an animal's flourishing bodily state), urine (which is healthy in that it is a sign of an animal's flourishing bodily state), and so on. To recall Aquinas's familiar formulation of the point, "With *all* terms which are said analogically of more than one thing, the term must be applied to each of these things by reference to one of them. That one thing must therefore be included in the definition of them all" (my emphasis).[14]

An analogous term is said by Aquinas to be applied "in a prior way" *(per prius)* when the conceptual content *(ratio)* it has in that application is

---

11. *ST* I, q. 13, a. 10, ad 4: "Philosophus largo modo accipit aequivoca, secundum quod includunt in se analoga." The reference is to the opening lines of the *Categories* (1a 1-5).

12. The example of equivocation is Thomas's own, from *ST* I, q. 13, a. 5, obj. 1.

13. E.g., ibid., a. 5, c.: "huiusmodi nomina dicuntur . . . secundum analogiam, idest proportionem."

14. Ibid., a. 6, c.: "[I]n omnibus nominibus quae de pluribus analogice dicuntur, necesse est quod omnia dicantur per respectum ad unum, et ideo illud unum oportet quod ponatur in definitione omnium." Cf. ibid., a. 10, c.: "Quia univocorum est omnino eadem ratio, aequivocorum est omnino ratio diversa, in analogicis vero, oportet quod nomen secundum unam significationem acceptum, ponatur in definitione eiusdem nominis secundum alias significationes accepti."

included in the conceptual content of the others, and "in a posterior way" *(per posterius)* in those other cases. Thus "sanus" is said *per prius* of an animal, and *per posterius* of medicine, urine, food, exercise, and the like. The *ratio*, or definition, of an analogous term applied *per posterius* therefore depends on the definition it has when applied *per prius*. As Aquinas puts it: "Because the conceptual content signified by a term is its definition, as is said in *Metaphysics* IV, the term must be applied in a prior way to that which is placed in the definition of the others, and in a posterior way to those others, following the order in which the latter more or less approach that to which the term belongs in a prior way. Thus 'healthy' as said of an animal is included in the definition of 'healthy' as said of medicine, which is said to be 'healthy' in that it causes health in an animal, and it is also included in the definition of 'healthy' as said of urine, which is said to be 'healthy' in that it is a sign of health."[15]

For present purposes we need to notice two things about this stock example of an analogous name and Thomas's explanation of it. First, when we use a term analogically, it is not necessary that the various things of which we predicate the term all share a common quality in greater or lesser degree. More precisely, the quality or characteristic in virtue of which we apply the term primarily ("in a prior way") to one sort of thing need not be present at all in the rest of the things to which we apply the term ("in a posterior way"). This is obvious from Thomas's example, since having the quality of a flourishing animal body is not present at all in medicine, urine, and other things called "healthy" by analogy. Therefore — and this point needs to be underlined — ontological similarity is not necessary for analogy. Neither, therefore, is ontological participation necessary among things spoken of analogously, since participation requires similarity.

Analogy's indifference to real resemblance is evident from the standard example Aquinas uses, but in any case he is explicit about the point. In an early text on analogy, Thomas characterizes the standard example ("sanitas") as precisely a situation in which there is a relationship of ordered dependence, of the prior and the posterior, "only with respect to conceptual

---

15. Ibid., a. 6, c.: "Et quia ratio quam significat nomen, est definitio, ut dicitur in IV Metaphys. [c. 7], necesse est quod illud nomen per prius dicatur de eo quod ponitur in definitione aliorum, et per posterius de aliis, secundum ordinem quo appropinquant ad illud primum vel magis vel minus, sicut sanum quod dicitur de animali, cadit in definitione sani quod dicitur de medicina, quae dicitur sana inquantum causat sanitatem in animali; et in definitione sani quod dicitur de urina, quae dicitur sana inquantum est signum sanitatis animalis."

content [*intentionem*], and not with respect to reality [*esse*]," since what is grasped in the concept actually exists in only one of the many things to which the concept is applied: "health only exists in the animal."[16]

Conversely, there can be real order and similarity among the objects to which a concept or intention is applied, and yet the concept can quite correctly be attributed univocally to all the objects. Thomas's example is "body" *(corpus)*, which is applied univocally to all three-dimensional objects in virtue of their possession of a common property *(corporeitas* — "bodiliness"), even though, in Aquinas's metaphysics and cosmology, some objects possess this common property with greater degrees of perfection than others. Corruptible bodies like ours, for example, have bodiliness in a less perfect way than the incorruptible bodies existing in the heavens, and so are ontologically inferior to the heavenly bodies. But this ordered ontological diversity is no barrier to predicating "body" univocally of both. While ontologically diverse, and rightly spoken of as such by the metaphysician and the natural scientist, they are generically equal *(parificantur)* and so are rightly spoken of univocally by the logician, and anyone else who has reason to consider them generically.[17] Whether language is being used analogically or univocally thus

---

16. There can be analogy "secundum intentionem tantum, et non secundum esse; et hoc est quando una intentio refertur ad plura per prius et posterius, quae tamen non habet esse nisi in uno; sicut intentio sanitatis refertur ad animal, urinam et dietam diversimode, secundum prius et posterius; non tamen secundum diversum esse, quia esse sanitatis non est nisi in animali." *In I Sent.,* d. 19, q. 5, a. 2, ad 1 (*Scriptum super libros Sententiarum,* vol. 1, ed. P. Mandonnet, O.P. [Paris: Lethielleux, 1929], p. 492). On the equivalence of "intentio" and "ratio" in this context, and thereby of "intentio" and "conceptual content" (cf. n. 10), see *SCG* 1.53 (443): "[I]ntellectus, per speciem rei formatus, intelligendo format in seipso quandam intentionem rei intellectae, quae est ratio ipsius, quam significat definitio."

17. There can be analogy "secundum esse et non secundum intentionem; et hoc contingit quando plura parificantur in intentione alicuius communis, sed illud commune non habet esse unius rationis in omnibus, sicut omnia corpora parificantur in intentione corporeitatis. Unde Logicus, qui considerat intentiones tantum, dicit hoc nomen corpus de omnibus corporibus univoce praedicari: sed esse huius naturae non est eiusdem rationis in corporibus corruptibilibus et incorruptibilibus. Unde quantum ad metaphysicum et naturalem, qui considerant res secundum suum esse, nec hoc nomen corpus, nec aliquid aliud dicitur univoce de corruptibilibus et incorruptibilibus, ut patet X *Met.* [c. 10], ex Philosopho et Commentatore" (*In I Sent.,* d. 19, q. 5, a. 2, ad 1).

St. Thomas here says that the metaphysician and the natural scientist, "who consider things according to their being [*esse*]," speak nonunivocally even where the logician speaks univocally. This has given rise to a conflict of interpretations. Since Thomas begins this passage by saying "aliquid dicitur secundum analogiam tripliciter," it may seem fair to suppose that this present case (the second of the three) involves metaphysical analogy *secundum esse,*

floats free of whether the term in question denotes a property shared, in greater or lesser degree, by the objects to which it is applied. There can be analogy without any such common property, and univocity even where a term denotes a property shared with varying degrees of perfection.

Of course there are analogous terms that denote properties really common, though in different degrees, to all the things of which the term is said. Aquinas's standard example is "being," said analogously of Aristotle's ten categories, with substance as the *per prius* of the term. *Ens* is really common to all the categories, but the nine genera of accidents have it only insofar as they belong to substance in some way. Correlatively, "substance" is placed in the definition of "being" as predicated of the different sorts of accident.[18] The difference in reality between cases where a common characteristic is present and those where it is not makes, however, no difference to the analogous character of the term and its use. The logic of analogy is the same in both cases and is not affected by the ontological disparity. Thus, having characterized analogy in the way we have identified, where the primary *ratio*

---

even though there is logical univocity *secundum intentionem*. This evidently led Cajetan to hold, influentially, that analogy in its fullest and most proper sense (what he calls the "analogy of proportionality") always involves a similarity *secundum esse* among the things spoken of analogously. Recently Lawrence Dewan argues for a similar reading of this text, holding (against McInerny) that Aquinas is here grading types of analogy according to their metaphysical depth, rather than forcing them into a single logical mold (see "St. Thomas and Analogy: The Logician and the Metaphysician," in *Form and Being: Studies in Thomistic Metaphysics* [Washington, D.C., Catholic University of American Press, 2006], pp. 81-95).

St. Thomas, however, gives no indication that he thinks the logician is wrong to use the term "body" univocally, any more than he thinks the metaphysician is wrong not to. His reply assumes, on the contrary, that there are cases where it is perfectly in order to speak univocally, even though the things spoken of have differences in *esse* that are important enough to block univocity when these differences are taken into account. It seems to me that McInerny is basically right, therefore, to read this text as describing three different ways the order of language and concepts (what we say *secundum intentionem*) can be related to the order of things (what we say *secundum esse*), rather than as introducing a threefold metaphysical classification of analogy (see *The Logic of Analogy*, pp. 1-23, 90-95, and *Aquinas and Analogy*, pp. 3-29). In any case, Aquinas later makes it quite clear that the use of terms *per prius et posterius* is not only necessary, but suffient, for analogy, regardless of whether the order of being matches the order of naming. See the texts cited below, nn. 22-23.

18. Thus the last of the three ways in which "something is said analogically" according to *In I Sent.*, d. 19, q. 5, a. 2, ad 1: "Vel secundum intentionem et secundum esse; et hoc est quando neque parificatur in intentione communi, neque in esse; sicut ens dicitur de substantia et accidente; et de talibus oportet quod natura communis habeat aliquod esse in unoquoque eorum de quibus dicitur, sed differens secundum rationem maioris vel minoris perfectionis."

of the analogous term is included in the way the term is defined in its other applications, Aquinas can straightaway introduce *ens* and *sanus* as equivalent exemplifications of the logical point: "*Just as* 'being' said of substance is placed in the definition of 'being' said of an accident, *so also* 'healthy' said of an animal is placed in the definition of 'healthy' said of urine and medicine" (my emphasis).[19] In at least this sense "analogy," as Thomas conceives it, is indifferent to ontology. As a logical and linguistic procedure it works the same way regardless of the situation in reality that it characterizes. This is part of what it means to say that the analogy of names is a logical rather than a metaphysical doctrine for Aquinas.

A second feature of the standard example further specifies the way in which Aquinas thinks of analogy as a matter of words rather than objects. Analogical predication does not require that there be any particular relationship in reality among things spoken of analogously. We have just observed that analogical speech does not require the quality or property designated by the analogical term to be shared by all the analogates. As a result, the analogous term need not designate a qualitative similarity or resemblance among the things to which it is applied. Equally important for theological purposes, analogy need not involve a causal relationship among the various analogates, though of course it can. Still less does it require that those things to which the term is applied "in a posterior way" be causally dependent on, participate in, or otherwise be ontologically beholden to that of which it is said primarily.

This is again obvious from the example. "Sanus" is *said* primarily of an animal and derivatively *(per posterius)* of medicine, but in reality medicine is a cause of health in an animal, and not the other way around. "Sanus" is also said derivatively of urine, which, while a by-product of health in an animal, is called "healthy" because it signals the animal's state, not because of the causal relationship between the animal's state and its urine.[20] Or, to recall a

19. "*Sicut* ens de substantia dictum, ponitur in definitione entis secundum quod de accidente dicitur; *et* sanum dictum de animali, ponitur in definitione sani secundum quod dicitur de urina et de medicina; huius enim sani quod est in animali, urina est significativa, et medicina factiva" (*ST* I, q. 13, a. 10, c.).

20. Thus the *per posterius* of an analogous term can be a sign of the *per prius* of the term without being caused by it at all. Observing the stars and stripes up and down my street on Memorial Day, I might say to my daughter, "The flag is patriotic." In that case the *per prius* of "patriotic" is a human attitude (love of country), and the *per posterius* is an object (the flag) called patriotic because it signals love of country. But no one on my street made their own flag, nor is there a causal connection between love of America and the stars and

theologically and philosophically freighted way Aquinas applies the example "sanus," an utterance is "true" as a sign of the intellect's true apprehension of things. Utterances are thus called "true" analogically, by reference to the *per prius* of "true," namely, the intellect's apprehension. But the apprehension isn't the *cause* of the utterance; otherwise we would never be able to stop talking. The cause of the apprehension itself is the reality apprehended, but this reality, like the medicine that causes health, is not the *per prius* (or, as it is sometimes put, the "prime analogate") of "true." The reality apprehended by the intellect, like the utterances that signal the intellect's apprehension, is called "true" only derivatively *(per posterius)*, even though the apprehension itself derives from the reality.[21]

The dependence of the "posterior" applications of an analogous term on its primary application is thus logical and semantic, not ontological. That is, whether an ontological dependence (causal or otherwise) runs parallel to the logical dependence among applications of the term is accidental and so does not enter into the definition of analogy. In analogical predication, as Thomas says, sometimes the order of naming and the order of being are the same, and sometimes they are not.[22] The logic and semantics of analogy are the same, regardless of this difference.

Aquinas illustrates this point by invoking, once again, the standard examples of *ens* and *sanus*. Both are cases of analogical predication in just the same sense: the same term used to characterize many things by reference to one, *per prius et posterius*. In the first case the order of predication follows the ontological order. As the cause of its accidents, substance is prior to accident in the order of being (prior *secundum rei naturam*, as Aquinas puts it), and since "substance" enters into the definition of "accident," it is also prior in the order of naming. Thus "*ens* is said to be prior to accident both in real-

---

stripes, as there is between natural signs (like urine) and what they signal (health). The U.S. flag might, of course, have been very different, and still have signaled the same attitude.

21. "Unde dico, quod verum per prius dicitur de veritate intellectus, et de enuntiatione dicitur inquantum est signum illius veritatis; de re autem dicitur, inquantum est causa" (*In I Sent.*, d. 19, q. 5, a. 1, sol.). Cf. *ST* I, q. 16, a. 1, ad 3: "[L]icet veritas intellectus nostri a re causetur, non tamen oportet quod in re per prius inveniatur ratio veritatis, sicut neque in medicina per prius invenitur ratio sanitatis quam in animali; virtus enim medicinae, non sanitas eius, causat sanitatem, cum non sit agens univocum. Et similiter esse rei, non veritas eius, causat veritatem intellectus. Unde philosophus dicit [*Cat.* 3] quod opinio et oratio vera est 'ex eo quod res est, non ex eo quod res vera est.'"

22. Cf. *SCG* 1.34 (298): "In huiusmodi autem analogica praedicatione ordo attenditur idem secundum nomen et secundum rem quandoque, quandoque vero non idem."

ity and in the meaning *(rationem)* of the term." In the second case, by contrast, the order of predication reverses the ontological order. As a cause of health, medicine is ontologically prior to its effect, namely, health in an animal. But we put "animal health" in the definition of "medicine," in this case naming the cause from the effect. "Thus, while the cause of health is prior ontologically *(in ordine rei)*" to the animal health it brings about, "when it comes to the meaning of the term, 'animal' is prior, since 'health' is said primarily of it."[23]

That the order of naming need not correspond to the order of being is only to be expected, since for Aquinas, as for Aristotle, we talk about things after the fashion in which we know them. "To the extent that our intellect can know something, we can name it."[24] And, to recall one of Aquinas's most basic epistemic assumptions, "The known is in the knower according to the mode of the knower," and thus "in accordance with the knower's nature."[25] Therefore we know, and name, both material things below us and divine things above us in a manner different from that in which they actually exist.[26] The linguistic order follows, indeed coincides with, our order of knowing, rather than the order of being.

Thomas, then, gives us good reasons to distinguish clearly the analogy of names from ontological similarity and participation. In so doing, he shows that this distinction is basic to his own understanding of language, reality, and the connections between the two. There's nothing wrong with calling on-

23. Ibid.: "Quando igitur id quod est prius secundum rem, invenitur etiam cognitione prius, idem invenitur prius et secundum nominis rationem et secundum rei naturam: sicut substantia est prior accidente et natura, inquantum substantia est causa accidentis; et cognitione, inquantum substantia in definitione accidentis ponitur. Et ideo ens dicitur prius de substantia quam de accidente et secundum rei naturam et secundum nominis rationem. Quando vero id quod est prius secundum naturam, est posterius secundum cognitionem, tunc in analogicis non est idem ordo secundum rem et secundum nominis rationem: sicut virtus sanandi quae est in sanativis, prior est naturaliter sanitate quae est in animali, sicut causa effectu; sed quia hanc virtutem per effectum cognoscimus, ideo etiam ex effectu nominamus. Et inde est quod sanativum est prius ordine rei, sed animal dicitur per prius sanum secundum nominis rationem."

24. "Secundum igitur quod aliquid a nobis intellectu cognosci potest, sic a nobis potest nominari" (*ST* I, q. 13, a. 1, c.). Cf. *SCG* 1.34 (298): "Nam ordo nominis sequitur ordinem cognitionis"; *In I Sent.*, d. 22, q. 1, a. 1, sc 2: "omne quod cognoscitur, potest etiam voce significari."

25. "Cognitum autem est in cognoscente secundum modum cognoscentis. Unde cuiuslibet cognoscentis cognitio est secundum modum suae naturae" (*ST* I, q. 12, a. 4, c.).

26. "Alius est enim modus intellectus in intelligendo, quam rei in essendo" (ibid., q. 13, a. 12, ad 3).

tological similarity "analogy." Aquinas himself occasionally talks this way, though his more usual term for these ontological relationships, especially when the similarity involves causal dependence, is "participation."[27] The point, in any case, is to see that linguistic analogy, the analogy of names, is simply a different matter from relationships of similarity among things. The analogy of names neither requires, nor is it required by, ontological similarity.

III

What difference does any of this make? Even if Thomas regards analogy as a doctrine about the way thought and language work rather than a doctrine about the way the world is, he clearly thinks that there are relations of similarity among creatures, and of creatures with God. These similarities among nonverbal sorts of things are, moreover, tied up in various ways with causal relations, relations both among creatures and between creatures and God.[28] Ontological similarity, in other words, often involves participation, and when the similarity of creatures to God is at issue, it always does. Our labors so far might therefore seem to have done nothing more than establish a terminological point. Even supposing the account I have given of Aquinas on analogy is right, why not simply agree to call the structured use of words *per prius et posterius* "analogy," and relationships of likeness and causality among real entities "similarity" and "participation"? Or, if we are wedded to the idea that being, and not simply "being," is analogous, we could call naming *per prius et posterius* "logical analogy," and relationships of similarity and participation "ontological analogy." We could then get on with the theological work analogy needs to do.

The importance of keeping straight the difference between linguistic analogy and ontological participation comes to light in the most famous ap-

---

27. "[A]liquid dicitur secundum analogiam tripliciter: vel . . . non secundum esse . . . vel . . . secundum esse" (*In I Sent.*, d. 19, q. 5, a. 2, ad 1; cf. above, nn. 16-17).

28. The likeness creatures have to God, rooted in their causal dependence on God, Aquinas does not regard as reversible. Creatures as such are similar to God in various ways, but God just is not similar to creatures: "[L]icet aliquo modo concedatur quod creatura sit similis Deo, nullo tamen modo concedendum est quod Deus sit similis creaturae" (*ST* I, q. 4, a. 3, ad 4). This is tied up with Aquinas's semantic contention that terms said "temporally" of God (like "Creator" and "Lord") connote relations that are real in creatures, but not in God; these relations are attributed to God conceptually or notionally, not "really" (cf. I, q. 13, a. 7). What to make of these much-disputed claims I will not go into here.

peal to analogy Thomas makes. In his treatment of the divine names, Thomas defends the claim that we human beings can make affirmative substantial predications about God that yield true statements. That is, we can actually speak of God, and not simply of creatures, as the substance or subject to whom our predicates refer (or, to use the very broad medieval term, whom they signify). Thus when we say "God is good" or "God is wise," the terms "good" and "wise" refer to *God's* goodness and wisdom, and so to the substance or reality God is. These statements cannot be interpreted simply as a negative way of referring to creatures, so that "God is good" means "Creatures are evil, and God is not." Nor can such statements be taken simply as a causal way of referring to creatures, so that "God is good" means "Creatures are good, and God causes their goodness." Instead we have to insist that "terms of this kind signify the divine substance, and are predicated of him substantially [and not just negatively or causally], even though they fail to represent him."[29]

As examples like "Deus est sapiens" suggest, the statements we can make about God are not only substantial but affirmative. "God is wise" cannot be interpreted simply to mean "God is not foolish"; it means there is a wisdom that really belongs to God. This is basic to Christianity: "To faith belong affirmative propositions, for example that God is one and triune, and that he is omnipotent."[30] And by God's free grace, whether in the Church or in nature, we are able to form statements that are not only substantial (really about God) and affirmative (they really attribute perfections) but true.[31] The

29. The quoted sentence concludes the following passage from *ST* I, q. 13, a. 2, c.: "Quidam enim dixerunt quod haec omnia nomina, licet affirmative de Deo dicantur, tamen magis inventa sunt ad aliquid removendum a Deo, quam ad aliquid ponendum in ipso. Unde dicunt quod, cum dicimus Deum esse viventem, significamus quod Deus non hoc modo est, sicut res inanimatae, et similiter accipiendum est in aliis. Et hoc posuit Rabbi Moyses. Alii vero dicunt quod haec nomina imposita sunt ad significandum habitudinem eius ad creata, ut, cum dicimus Deus est bonus, sit sensus, Deus est causa bonitatis in rebus. Et eadem ratio est in aliis, . . . [H]oc est contra intentionem loquentium de Deo. Aliud enim intendunt dicere, cum dicunt Deum viventem, quam quod sit causa vitae nostrae, vel quod differat a corporibus inanimatis. Et ideo aliter dicendum est, quod huiusmodi quidem nomina significant substantiam divinam, et praedicantur de Deo substantialiter, sed deficiunt a repraesentatione ipsius."

30. "[P]ropositiones quaedam affirmativae subduntur fidei, utpote quod Deus est trinus et unus, et quod est omnipotens" (*ST* I, q. 13, a. 12, sc).

31. "Ergo propositiones affirmativae possunt vere formari de Deo" (ibid.). The true statements we can make in virtue of God's ecclesial gift of truths about himself (that is, in virtue of the revelation made to the authors of Holy Scripture; cf. *ST* I, q. 1, a. 8, ad 2; II-II, q. 171, a. 5, c.) are the needed means to a share in his own knowing; they help give us

whole of *ST* I, q. 13 can be seen as a defense of the claim that we can speak truly of God in a substantial and affirmative way, complementing the claim of *ST* I, q. 12 that in this life we can know God, even if imperfectly, and not only creatures.

Thomas employs a number of strategies in defense of the deep-laid Christian conviction that we can make true statements about God. Analogy is only one of them, but it's the role of analogy, the theological work it can be expected to do, that we're trying to figure out. We can focus the issue by asking whether analogy can serve as a procedure for generating concepts of God's perfections (analogous concepts, naturally). Or, a bit more in Thomas's own idiom, is it the business of analogy to provide us with *rationes* for the perfections we attribute to God, so that we can say, albeit analogically, what the conceptual content of (for example) "good" and "wise" is when applied to God?[32]

To many Thomists, it has seemed quite obvious that the answer to this question must be yes. We must have some grasp of what our concepts contain and our words mean when applied to God, lest we lapse into equivocation, and thus into fallacy. At just this point, so the typical argument goes, recourse to metaphysical analogy (or ontological participation) is indispensable. Creatures really resemble God, and they do so because every perfection they possess, and their possession of it, comes to them from God, as a limited creaturely participation in his own unlimited perfection. The task of analogy is to mount upward from creatures to God by an array of metaphysical attributions and proportions, ascending in thought and language the road God has already established downward by allowing perfections to flow from himself to creatures. No merely linguistic or logical procedure can accomplish this ascent to the *ratio* of what we say about God; it can only stipulate a way of talking. Aquinas apparently says as much, when he holds that "whatever is said of both God and creatures is said insofar as there is some order of the creature to God, as its source and cause, in whom all the perfections of created things preexist in a more excellent way."[33]

"quaedam impressio divinae scientiae" (I, q. 1, a. 3, ad 2). As such they are far more extensive, certain, and precise than the statements we can make in virtue of God's gift of truths about himself in creation. But this does not mean that there are no truths of the latter kind, or that they have no theological significance. I will return to this point.

32. On the *ratio* of a term as its conceptual content for Aquinas, see above, n. 10.

33. "[Q]uidquid dicitur de Deo et creaturis, dicitur secundum quod est aliquis ordo creaturae ad Deum, ut ad principium et causam, in qua praeexistunt excellenter omnes rerum perfectiones" (*ST* I, q. 13, a. 5, c.).

All of this may seem too plain to need comment, but Thomas's insistence that we distinguish the order of knowing and naming from the order of being should perhaps give us pause. The correct application of predicates to God is one of those cases, like the application of the predicate "health" to men and medicine, where the order of naming and knowing reverses the order of being. The perfections we attribute to God, like "good" and "wise," belong to him by nature, and to creatures by his generous bestowal of them. In the order of being, that is, these perfections belong first to God, and only derivatively to creatures.[34] But we can name God only from creatures.[35] When we seek to know God analogically, the terms we use inevitably apply, in the order of naming, primarily to creatures and derivatively to God. In Thomas's vocabulary for analogy, we apply perfection *terms* to creatures *per prius* and to God *per posterius*, even though the *perfections* we are referring to exist first of all in God, and only derivatively in creatures. The logic of the situation is just the same as with the application of the analogous term "health." It is said primarily of the bodily flourishing of an animal, and only derivatively of medicine, spoken of as healthy by reference to the animal's flourishing, even though in the order of being animal health is derived from medicine, and not medicine from health.[36]

Thomas's standard way of spelling this point out is to say that, in analogical language about God, the "mode of signification" is that which belongs to creatures, even though the perfection of which we're speaking belongs primarily, and in an immeasurably higher way, to God.[37] The medieval

---

34. "[Q]uantum ad rem significatam per nomen, per prius dicuntur de Deo quam de creaturis, quia a Deo huiusmodi perfectiones in creaturas manant" (ibid., a. 6, c.).

35. As a revealed self-designation for God, the Tetragrammaton might be an exception to this principle. But even if that is the case, it does not help with the present question, since taken in this way, the Tetragrammaton has no *ratio* (or at least none we can apprehend). That is, it designates God not in his nature in any respect (even as possessed by a person), but in his sheer individuality, as "this something *(hoc aliquid)*" (*ST* I, q. 13, a. 9, c.). As such, it is the name most uniquely suited to God *(magis proprium)*, just because it designates God's very substance, singular and incommunicable: "Et adhuc magis proprium nomen est tetragrammaton, quod est impositum ad significandam ipsam Dei substantiam incommunicabilem, et, ut sic liceat loqui, singularem" (I, q. 13, a. 11, ad 1). Since the individual as such can be designated but not defined ("hoc singulare vel illud definiri non possit," I, q. 29, a. 1, ad 1), and a *ratio* is precisely a definition, the Tetragrammaton has no *ratio*.

36. "[Q]uantum ad impositionem nominis, per prius a nobis imponuntur creaturis, quas prius cognoscimus" (*ST* I, q. 13, a. 6, c.). In this passage Thomas has already used "health" as the example illustrative of his point about the divine names.

37. "Unde et modum significandi habent qui competit creaturis, ut supra dictum est"

term "modus significandi" basically captures the thought that we can talk about the same object or state of affairs (the *res significata*) in many different ways (the *modi significandi*). The idea is not simply that we can have multiple descriptions of the same thing, but that the descriptions themselves will refer to one and the same thing differently. Thus a native Latin speaker, noticing a bird fall from the sky, might say "Cadit!" ("It's falling!"), "Cadens!" ("Look, falling!"), or "Casus!" ("Lo, a fall!"). One and the same reality, or state of affairs *(res)*, is referred to in three irreducibly different ways *(modi significandi)*, embodied in the grammatical distinction between finite verb, participle, and noun: as a passion undergone by a substance, as an event in progress, and as a particular kind of thing. As this example suggests, talk about the "modi significandi" was originally at home in grammatical theory, when medieval grammarians started attending systematically to the differences of meaning that go with using the same root word in different declensions, parts of speech, and sentential locations. But it soon began to be used much more widely, not least by theologians.[38]

Any *ratio* includes a mode of signification. Or more precisely, whatever we think of, we conceive as existing in a certain way, and this conceived manner of being is captured by the *modus significandi* of the term we use to express our thought. Since the difference between univocal, equivocal, and analogous terms is the difference between terms with one *ratio*, diverse *rationes*, and diverse *rationes* ordered to one, the difference between the three types of terms will be that between having the same mode of signification across multiple applications, diverse and unrelated modes of signification, and diverse but ordered and related modes. Thus the analogous term "healthy," said primarily of an animal, has a qualitative mode of signification

---

(ibid.), referring to I, q. 13, a. 3, c.: "In nominibus igitur quae Deo attribuimus, est duo considerare, scilicet, perfectiones ipsas significatas, ut bonitatem, vitam, et huiusmodi; et modum significandi. Quantum igitur ad id quod significant huiusmodi nomina, proprie competunt Deo, et magis proprie quam ipsis creaturis, et per prius dicuntur de eo. Quantum vero ad modum significandi, non proprie dicuntur de Deo, habent enim modum significandi qui creaturis competit."

38. The *modi significandi* have been the subject of extensive research since the appearance of Jan Pinborg's *Die Entwicklung der Sprachtheorie im Mittelalter* (Münster: Aschendorff, 1967). On some of the theological uses of the distinction, see, for example, Irène Rosier, "*Res significata* et *modus significandi*. Les implications d'une distinction médiévale," in *Sprachtheorien in Spätantike und Mittelalter*, ed. Sten Ebbesen, pp. 135-68 (Tübingen: Gunter Narr, 1995). On one of St. Thomas's applications of the distinction, see my essay "In Search of an Analytic Aquinas: Grammar and the Trinity," in *Grammar and Grace* (FS Victor Preller), ed. Robert MacSwain and Jeffrey Stout, pp. 55-74 (London: SCM Press, 2004).

(i.e., its way of signifying health is as the quality of an animal). Said derivatively of medicine, it has a causal mode of signification, in that it signifies health as caused in an animal by medicine. The distinctions and relations among the different *rationes* of an analogous term depend, therefore, on the distinctions and relations among its various modes of signifying.

Well and good, the metaphysical analogician may say. This is just a second-order reiteration of what is already going on metaphysically. We start with goodness or wisdom as it exists in creatures, and accordingly it is known and named by us in a creaturely mode of signification. Since God is ultimately the cause of these and all perfections existing in creatures, we can mount up metaphysically to an analogical apprehension of these perfections as they exist in their first cause — to a grasp, in other words, of the *rationes* of "bonus" and "sapiens" as applied to God.

Tempting as this is, it clearly will not work, at least as far as Thomas is concerned. As he always insists when he talks about analogous names for God, "cause of the goodness in creatures" is precisely *not* what we mean or intend when we say "God is good."[39] We aim to speak of the goodness God has by nature, and substantially — of the goodness God would have even if there were no creatures. But since we can attribute goodness to God only *per posterius,* based on a grasp of "good" as applied to creatures, the goodness of creatures will in one way or another always be included in the *ratio* of "good" when we apply it to God. That's what it *means* to say that a term is applied *per posterius,* and thus analogously: the *ratio* of the primary, or *per prius,* application has to be contained in all other applications of the term.

As we have observed, the mode of signifying of any *per posterius* use of an analogous term consists in some specific relation to the primary *ratio,* or meaning. So when we say "God is good" *per posterius* — the only way we can — we have to include in what we mean by "good" a reference to some sort of created goodness, as caused, exemplified, or perfected by God. Even when we intend to leave creatures and their derivative goodness behind and speak only of God's goodness, we cannot. Whatever meaning "good" has for us when applied to God depends on its reference to a specific *per prius:* created goodness. The same goes for all other perfection terms, that is, for any term we can apply to God *proprie,* rather than in a simply metaphorical way.

This is what Thomas means when he observes that, in everything we say of God, the mode of signifying is fit for creatures, and not for God. "No

39. Cf. *ST* I, q. 13, a. 2, c.; 6, c.

term has a mode of signifying that belongs to God."[40] And since we cannot have a mode of signifying, we cannot have what metaphysical analogy is looking for: the *ratio* of our terms as applied analogically to God, an analogical concept of God's own wisdom or goodness.

At this point have we not openly embraced equivocation, and thus departed from the manifest teaching of St. Thomas? Thomas does, no doubt, turn to the analogy of names in order to ease the worry that there is no ordered relationship between the meaning or *ratio* of our predicates when we apply them to creatures and when we apply them to God. Appealing to analogy does not, however, actually supply a *ratio* for perfection terms when predicated of God. That is not how the analogy of names answers the objection that our language about God is wholly equivocal. Its point, rather, is to supply a reason for thinking that there must be a *ratio* for the application of these terms *in divinis*, even though we do not know what it is.

The analogy of names does the simple but needed work of identifying a semantic pattern, other than pure equivocation, into which language about God may reasonably be said to fit. To say that God is, for example, analogically wise is simply to say that "wise," as applied to Socrates and to God, conforms to the semantic pattern exemplified by "healthy," as applied to Socrates and his diet, and not to the one exemplified by "dog" when we speak of "the dog star" and "the dog Fido." Observing that there are genuinely analogous names supplies warrant for our conviction that what we mean when we say "God is wise" bears an ordered and intelligible relationship to what we mean when we say "Socrates is wise," just as, in general, the *per posterius* application of an analogous term is related to the *per prius* application. What "wise" must mean when applied to God so far exceeds what it means when applied to Socrates that it leaves God's wisdom "ungrasped" by us *(incomprehensam)*.[41] "Analogy" gives us a way of saying that "wise" nonetheless does have a *ratio* when attributed to God, one genuinely related to the wisdom we know and name in creatures, however much that relationship eludes us in this life.

The metaphysics of participation and similarity also plays a role here, though not that customarily attributed to it by Thomists. It supplies no *ratio* for perfection terms used *in divinis*. Here the notion that matters of logic and language are trivial and no longer hold any interest for us, regularly gets

---

40. Ibid., a. 12, ad 1: "[N]ullum nomen Deo competit secundum modum significandi." Cf. I, q. 13, a. 3, c.; a. 6, c.
41. *ST* I, q. 13, a. 5, c.; cf. below, n. 48.

its revenge on interpreters of St. Thomas. Failing to distinguish questions about language from questions about the real, they fail to notice that ontological participation, no matter how robustly affirmed, is no warrant for the claim that analogy supplies us with a mode of signification, and thus a meaning, or *ratio,* for what we say of God. As we have already seen (in section II), participation and analogy are simply two different matters, neither of which requires the other. Still less does one (the causal dependence of creatures on God) tell us what to say about the other (the *ratio* of a term as applied *per posterius* to God). Nor, conversely, does denying that we can know the *rationes* of perfection terms applied to God require denying that creatures are in any way similar to God, or that God himself possesses, in an immeasurably higher way, the perfections we find in creatures. Distinguishing between the order of being and the order of logic and language, as Thomas does, helps one see how he can insist without contradiction both on the similarity of creatures to their Creator and on our inability to come up with concepts for the creative perfections on that which similarity depends.

The import of ontological participation for "the divine names" is more modest, but still indispensable. Basic Christian teaching requires that whatever perfections are found in the world among the material objects connatural to our intellect must be thought of as created by God. As an element in the theology of creation, the notion of participation supplies the conviction that every perfection found in creatures must preexist in God and "flow" from God to creatures.[42] Some of these perfections, moreover, preexist in God, not simply in that God understands them and accordingly makes things that possess the perfection he understands (like the hardness of the stone), but that he himself possesses them (like being, goodness, and wisdom).[43]

The metaphysics of creation deals with beings and their perfections, while the analogy of names deals with *rationes* and their logical relationships. When it comes to understanding the import of our speech and thought about God, metaphysics and analogy, while quite distinct, comple-

---

42. Thus ibid., a. 6, c.; see above, n. 34.

43. Cf. ibid., a. 3, ad 1: "[Q]uaedam nomina significant huiusmodi perfectiones a Deo procedentes in res creatas, hoc modo quod ipse modus imperfectus quo a creatura participatur divina perfectio, in ipso nominis significato includitur, sicut lapis significat aliquid materialiter ens, et huiusmodi nomina non possunt attribui Deo nisi metaphorice. Quaedam vero nomina significant ipsas perfectiones absolute, absque hoc quod aliquis modus participandi claudatur in eorum significatione, ut ens, bonum vivens, et huiusmodi, et talia proprie dicuntur de Deo."

ment one another. The metaphysics of creation having assured us that God himself possesses some of the same perfections we see in creatures, the analogy of names backs up the complementary thought that there must be a *ratio* for these perfections as possessed by God, one uniquely adequate to these perfections in their divine manner of being, more excellent than any *ratio* by which we apprehend created qualities. Analogy does not offer us a way of figuring out, under the epistemic conditions by which we are presently bound, what the divine *ratio* of our perfection terms actually is. Analogy does help assure us, though, that there is a divine *ratio* for us to know when our present epistemic limitations pass away.

Here too the distinction between the *modus significandi* of our terms and their *res significata* does useful work. It gives us a way of saying that our perfection terms succeed in referring to God — he, and not any creature, is the *res* of whom "wise" is true when we say "God is wise" — even though we cannot specify the manner in which they do so, since our predication unavoidably imports a mode of signifying that "belongs to creatures."[44]

As Thomas sees it, we cannot seek refuge from this cognitive limitation in the thought that our minds can attain an intuitive grasp of, or insight into, God's perfections that goes beyond what we can express in language. Whatever we can know, indeed whatever we can think *(cognoscere)*, we can also name. God's essence and perfections are simply "beyond what we understand of God, as well as what we signify by our speech."[45] We will have to content ourselves, as Aquinas often does, with the thought that when we speak truly of God, the *ratio* of our terms is "higher" or "more eminent" than the best *ratio* we ourselves can conceive, starting as we must from material creatures and speaking of their transcendent source only *per posterius.*[46] Such epistemic and linguistic modesty does not place in question the real similarity of creatures to God or their causal dependence on God. We can grant, indeed, the "analogy of being," as Scripture invites us to do.[47] But it will not tell us, or give us a basis for finding out, what the divine mode of being is of these creaturely perfections, which speak so eloquently of him.

It seems, then, that even our best thought and speech about the only wise God, while substantial, affirmative, and true, leaves God's wisdom, and

44. Ibid., a. 3, c.: "creaturis competit" (cf. above, n. 37).
45. Ibid., a. 1, ad 1: "[E]ssentia eius est supra id quod de Deo intelligimus et voce significamus." On knowing and naming, cf. above, n. 23.
46. "[S]ecundum modum altiorem" (ibid., a. 2, c.); "eminentius" (a. 6, c.).
47. "For from the greatness and the beauty of created things their original author, by analogy, is seen" (Wis. 13:5).

so God himself, "ungrasped, exceeding the signification of our term."[48] Thus Aquinas bids to guard both God's epistemic availability to creatures (indeed fallen creatures) and God's radical transcendence to creatures (even those immediately united to him in glory).[49] He accordingly sees no special difficulty in saying both that we are cognitively united to God already in this life and that, even by faith (let alone natural knowledge), we cannot know what God is, and so "are joined to him as to one unknown."[50]

In fact we can no more have a *ratio* or concept in this present life for what we rightly say of God than we can know God's essence, what he is *(quod quid est)*. This only stands to reason, since a definition gives the essence of the thing defined, and our predicates stand for *rationes*, that is, definitions.[51] If we could have a concept for wisdom, goodness, or any other divine perfection, it would be a definition of that perfection as it exists in God, no matter how stringently analogical the concept might be. As such it would be a definition of what God is in that respect, an account, in other words, of what it is for *God* to be wise, to be good, and so forth. But we are presently united to God "as to one unknown" just because we can have no such concept, and so cannot know what God is.[52]

Our cognitive limitation does not lie only in the fact that our knowledge, proportioned to the essence (the *quid est*) of material creatures, inevitably imports a defective mode of signification when we form concepts of created perfections and attribute them to God. Nor does it lie in any lack of ingenuity in the construction of analogical concepts. However analogically refined, any concept we can form in our minds and signify by our words is itself a created reality, the product of our own thought and speech. But in the

---

48. "[R]elinquit rem significatam ut incomprehensam, et excedentem nominis significationem" (*ST* I, q. 13, a. 5, c.).

49. Even though the *beati* know God in the highest possible way, the divine essence itself having become the intelligible form of their intellects ("Cum autem aliquis intellectus creatus videt Deum per essentiam, ipsa essentia Dei fit forma intelligibilis intellectus"; *ST* I, q. 12, a. 5, c.), it remains impossible for any created intellect to comprehend God ("[C]omprehendere Deum impossibile est cuicumque intellectui creato"; I, q. 12, a. 7, c.).

50. *ST* I, q. 12, a. 13 ad 1: "Licet per revelationem gratiae in hac vita non cognoscamus de Deo quid est, et sic ei quasi ignoto coniungamur; tamen plenius ipsum cognoscimus . . . inquantum ei aliqua attribuimus ex revelatione divina, ad quae ratio naturalis non pertingit, ut Deum esse trinum et unum."

51. So, for example, the term "human being" *(homo)* "exprimit sua significatione essentiam hominis secundum quod est, significat enim eius definitionem, declarantem eius essentiam; ratio enim quam significat nomen, est definitio" (ibid., q. 13, a. 1, c.; cf. above, n. 10).

52. Ibid., q. 12, a. 13, ad 1; cf. n. 50.

nature of the case no created reality can serve as a means for knowing what God is, and so for knowing what his perfections are, as they exist in him. Thus Aquinas, reflecting near the end of the *Scriptum* on the vision of God, observes that

> God subverts every form in our intellect, just as Augustine says. Whatever form our intellect conceives, that form does not belong to the *ratio* of the divine essence. Therefore our intellect has no way into God. Rather, we think of him most perfectly in this life by knowing that he is beyond all that our intellect can conceive. For this reason we are joined to him as to one unknown. But in heaven we will see him through that form which is his own essence, and then we will be joined to him as to one known.[53]

Much of the motivation for taking analogy as a metaphysical doctrine lies in the hope of finding *rationes,* always analogically tied to creatures, for God's perfections. As it turns out, though, the only *ratio* for God's wisdom, goodness, or any other divine perfection is the divine essence itself. God's essence alone can be the means by which we know in what God's own wisdom or goodness consists. The divine nature, and nothing less, is the *ratio* of God's perfections. For just this reason, it is the sole *ratio* left for us to know when faith gives way to sight.

In fact any analogical *ratio,* or definition, we can have of a perfection does not yield knowledge of God but guarantees that what we know is precisely not that perfection as it exists in God. Our *rationes,* or definitions, as Thomas sees it, are potent tools. When rightly deployed, they enable us not only to know the essence of (created) beings but to comprehend or circumscribe what we know. If we can rightly define a particular reality or substance, we may not know everything about it, but we know its limits, the boundaries imposed on it by what it is — by the essence our definition enables us to grasp. God's essence cannot be bounded in this way, that is, it cannot be comprehended by creatures. So it is not simply the case that we

---

53. *In IV Sent.,* d. 49, q. 2, a. 1, ad 3: "[S]icut dicit Augustinus, Deus omnem formam intellectus nostri subterfugit: quia quamcumque formam intellectus noster concipiat, illa forma non pertingit ad rationem divinae essentiae; et ideo ipse non potest esse pervius intellectui nostro; sed in hoc eum perfectissime cognoscimus in statu viae quod scimus eum esse super omne id quod intellectus noster concipere potest; et sic ei quasi ignoto coniungimur. Sed in patria id ipsum per formam quae est essentia sua videbimus, et coniungemur ei quasi noto." On the impossibility of knowing what God is through any created medium, see, for example, *ST* I, q. 12, a. 2; *In I Cor.* 13, lec. 4 (803).

currently lack a definition, and in that sense a *ratio,* for God's perfections. For these there can be no definition, and in that sense no *ratio.* When the blessed see God's essence, they know what he is indeed, but they cannot comprehend him (which is part of knowing what he is). To see God by way of his own essence, and so to grasp the *rationes* of his perfections, is thus to enjoy a way of knowing quite different from grasping or giving a definition.

In Thomas's own terms: "Just as the saints see the divine essence but do not comprehend it, so also they see what God is but do not comprehend this. Therefore God is not seen by them in the manner in which a thing whose essence is comprehended is seen by way of its definition."[54] Just as we can have a *ratio* for God's perfections only by knowing what God is, the *quid est* of God, so also any essence or quality we can define is, conversely, not God's own. In order to have *rationes* for God's perfections, we do not need a theory of analogy — semantic, metaphysical, or otherwise. We need to see God. The root of our inability to have a *modus significandi* or an analogical *ratio* for what we say of God in this life is nothing less than our inability to see God and live.

IV

Aquinas thus offers a quite austere understanding of analogy and, with that, of the content we can ascribe to our thought and talk about God by analogical means. His logical and semantic account of analogy aims, it appears, only to block the suggestion that, having rejected univocity, we are stuck with pure equivocation. There must be a *ratio* of perfection terms rightly ascribed to God, even if we don't presently know what it is and must await the light of glory to reach such knowledge. It may come as a surprise, therefore, to observe that Aquinas in fact has no difficulty at all speaking univocally of God and creatures.

In the *Summa theologiae*'s Tertia Pars, after discussing a number of issues

---

54. *In IV Sent.,* d. 49, q. 2, a. 3, ad 5: "[E]odem modo aliquis cognoscit quid est res quo cognoscit essentiam rei, cum ipsa essentia sit quidditas rei; et ideo ille solus comprehendit quid est res, qui comprehendit essentiam; unde sicut sancti videbunt essentiam divinam, sed non comprehendent ipsam; ita videbunt quid est Deus, sed non comprehendent; et ita non videbitur Deus ab eis sicut videtur res per suam definitionem, cuius essentia comprehenditur." The objector here (obj. 5) had argued, drawing on Augustine's *Ep.* 147 (known to Aquinas as the book *De videndo Deo*) that to "comprehend" the essence of a thing is to be able to specify the thing's limits.

concerning the incarnation — the hypostatic union, the grace of Christ as an individual human being and as head of the church, Christ's knowledge and other aspects of his humanity — Aquinas turns to a series of Christological questions that are explicitly semantic in character. The first of these is whether the statement "God is a human being" *(Deus est homo)* is true. All Christians hold that it is, Thomas observes, but not all understand it properly — *secundum eandem rationem*.[55] Some, for example, suppose that "human being" said of Jesus Christ means something different than it does when said of the rest of us. The Manichaeans furnish Thomas's example. They held, as he understands it, that the Son of God assumed a fictive humanity. But any suggestion that "homo" when applied to Jesus Christ has a different *ratio* than it does when applied to any other person of flesh and blood must be firmly set aside by all who share the Catholic faith in the incarnation. "Human being" has just the same meaning when applied to God the Son as it has when applied to the rest of us. It is, in other words, said univocally of God and creatures. Otherwise it would simply be false to believe that the Word has become our flesh and is *inventus ut homo*.[56] "Homo," Thomas insists, is predicated *vere et proprie* — in its full signification, and so as to form a true proposition — of God the Son, "just as it is said of Socrates and Plato."[57]

Aquinas does not simply hold that "homo" can be predicated univocally of God and creatures. Jesus Christ is like us in all things save sin. Everything done and suffered by the incarnate Son of God in the humanity he assumed, everything that belongs to his humanity, is said *vere et proprie* — univocally — of God and any human creature of whom it is also true.[58]

---

55. *ST* III, q. 16, a. 1, c.

56. Ibid., a. 1, sc (Phil. 2:7).

57. Thus ibid., a. 1, c.: "De quolibet autem supposito alicuius naturae potest vere et proprie praedicari nomen significans illam naturam in concreto, sicut de Socrate et Platone proprie et vere praedicatur homo. Quia ergo persona filii Dei, pro qua supponit hoc nomen Deus, est suppositum naturae humanae, vere et proprie hoc nomen homo potest praedicari de hoc nomine Deus, secundum quod supponit pro persona filii Dei." Of the three Christological opinions considered by the Lombard (*Sententiae* III, d. 6), only the second can be true, because it alone verifies "Deus est homo" without equivocation: "[S]ola opinio secunda vera est, quae verificat eam: potest enim ponere, quod cum dicitur, 'Deus est homo,' est praedicatio per informationem essentialem, quia ly Deus supponit suppositum personae filii; et hoc idem est suppositum humanae naturae per illam naturam informatum, secundum modum intelligendi, inquantum subsistit in ea. Unde sicut haec est vera et propria, 'Petrus est homo,' ita et ista, 'Deus est homo'" (*In III Sent.*, d. 7, q. 1, a. 1, sol. [no. 33]; cf. ad 7 [no. 41]). See also *SCG* 4.39 (3772); *ST* III, q. 2, a. 6, c.

58. Cf. *ST* III, q. 27, pro.: "[R]estat considerandum de his quae filius Dei incarnatus in

Thus Aquinas asks whether whatever belongs to human nature can be said of God. He takes the answer to be an obvious yes, calling on John of Damascus for support. "God accepted all that is characteristic of the flesh . . . 'for God is termed passible, and the God of glory was crucified.'"[59]

To think otherwise is the error of the Nestorians. It is basic to Catholic faith, Aquinas observes, that all the particular human properties, actions, and passions of Jesus be ascribed to God the Son. All that the human being Jesus does and suffers is true of God in just the same sense as — and just because — it is true of the human being Jesus. All that God the Son does, conversely, is true of the human being Jesus. This is the elemental *modus loquendi* of Scripture, the repeated pattern in which Scripture speaks to us of Jesus Christ. In Thomas's formulation of the rule: "Those things that belong to the divine nature can be said of the human being, and those things that belong to the human nature can be said of God."[60] In Thomas's lexicon, a "Nestorian" is anyone who refuses to follow this rule, and so denies that

---

natura humana sibi unita fecit vel passus est" — a consideration which takes up over thirty questions in the *Summa theologiae,* and embraces everything from the sanctification of Christ's virgin mother to his ascension, session, and return in judgment.

59. Ibid., q. 16, a. 4, sc: "Deus suscepit ea quae sunt carnis idiomata, id est proprietates, 'dum Deus passibilis nominatur, et Deus gloriae crucifixus est.'" The citation of John of Damascus is from *De fide orthodoxa* 3.4, alluding to 1 Cor. 2:8. As Aquinas's language here suggests, we are in the vicinity of the so-called *communicatio idomatum.* Aquinas occasionally picks up this phrase from John of Damascus, but for him it involves no mysterious metaphysical intermingling of divine and human attributes, as it sometimes does in more recent theology. The term refers to a logical rule for identifying true statements about Jesus Christ, of just the sort we are looking at: "[I]n Christo est communicatio idiomatum. Non quod sit aliqua proprietatum naturalium confusio, sed quia proprietates utriusque naturae *dicuntur* de eodem supposito" (*De unione Verbi incarnati* a. 5, ad 9, my emphasis).

60. "Et ideo de homine dici possunt ea quae sunt divinae naturae: et de Deo possunt dici ea quae sunt humanae naturae" (*ST* III, q. 16, a. 4, c.). For a different formulation of the same rule, cf. *SCG* 4.39 (3771): "Cum enim Scriptura sacra indistincte quae sunt Dei homini illi attribuat, et quae sunt illius hominis Deo, ut ex praemissis patet; oportet unum et eundem esse de quo utraque dicantur." This way of stating the rule classes the predicates concretely ("Deus" instead of "divina natura" and "homo" instead of "humana natura"), and so points to an important feature the rule has for Aquinas: it works only when terms referring to the human and the divine in Christ are concrete. Thus "Deus est homo" is true, but "Deus est humanitas" is not, nor is "Divinitas est humanitas." On this see, for example, *ST* III, q. 16, a. 5. For a more detailed discussion of Aquinas's semantics of concrete and abstract terms, and of the importance it has in his theology, see my essay "Utrum Essentia Generet: Semantics and Metaphysics in Later Medieval Trinitarian Theology," in *Trinitarian Theology in the Medieval West,* ed. Pekka Kärkkäinen, pp. 88-123 (Helsinki: Luther-Agricola Society, 2008).

Bruce D. Marshall

statements like "God was born of a virgin" and "This human being existed from all eternity" are true.[61]

Univocal human speech about God becomes possible, then, from the moment the Word becomes flesh — at the moment, in other words, of Mary's *fiat* to the announcing angel (Luke 1:38). For us to actualize this possibility, however, requires that we know God has become a human being, and that we know the human being God has become. Coming to know these truths about God and our own humanity depends not only on the incarnation but on the human action of the incarnate Word.[62]

Jesus Christ, Aquinas emphasizes, is a single existing subject or person (one *suppositum*, in his terminology). As such, Jesus is, like any individual subject, a single agent, and therefore his actions are always single, or one in number. At the same time, his mode or manner of action is unique among human beings: here one subject acts in an irreducibly twofold way. Following John of Damascus in particular, but also the Sixth Ecumenical Council (681), Aquinas cleaves to the Chalcedonian tradition for which Jesus Christ, as he is one person existing in two complete natures, divine and human, is also one agent who acts in two complete ways, divine and human. With his two natures he possesses, to recall the traditional terms, two wills and two "operations," or ways of acting.[63] While he is a single agent, each of his actions is always "theandric," as Aquinas puts it (picking up a term from Pseudo-Dionysius much used by defenders of Chalcedon), at once human and divine, or "divino-human." Concretely, this means that he does human things (like walk) in a divine way (on

---

61. *ST* III, q. 16, a. 4, c.: "[N]on tamen concedebant vel Deum natum de Virgine, vel hominem ab aeterno fuisse." This article contains one of Thomas's many critical discussions of Nestorianism; cf. III, q. 2, a. 6; *SCG* 4.34 & 38; *In Ioan.* 1.7 (170-71); *In Rom.* 1.2 (35-36); *In I Cor.* 2.2 (92).

62. I am grateful to Emmanuel Perrier, O.P., for underlining this point. Note Thomas's remarks in his *Lectura* on John. "Nullum enim tam evidens indicium de natura alicuius rei esse potest quam illud quod accipitur ex operibus eius." This general principle applies to any agent at all. But its application to the human being Jesus is momentous: "Evidenter ergo cognosci potest de Christo et credi quod sit Deus, per hoc quod facit opera Dei" (*In Ioan.* 10.6 [1466]).

63. On the unity of Christ's person and action in its dual mode or species, cf. *ST* III, q. 19, a. 1, ad 3: "[O]perari est hypostasis subsistentis, sed secundum formam et naturam, a qua operatio speciem recipit. Et ideo a diversitate formarum seu naturarum est diversa species operationum, sed ab unitate hypostasis est unitas secundum numerum quantum ad operationem speciei. . . . [I]n Christo oportet quod sint duae operationes specie differentes, secundum eius duas naturas, quaelibet tamen operationum est una numero in Christo, semel facta, sicut una ambulatio et una sanatio."

water), and that he does divine things (like heal a leper in an instant) in a human way (at a touch).[64] These actions teach us that specific ways of willing and acting belong univocally to us and to God the Son, and thus they teach us that "Homo est Deus" and "Deus est homo" are true.

Take, for example, Jesus' act of forgiving the sins of a paralyzed man (Matt. 9:2-8; Mark 2:4-12; Luke 5:18-25). As the New Testament narratives of this event clearly attest, only the God of Israel can forgive sins on his own authority and by his own power. The forgiveness granted by the one true God does not ignore or overlook sin but actually removes it, healing the interior wound of sin.[65] This no merely human agent can do, as the scribes of the Gospel accounts rightly realize when they accuse Jesus of blasphemy. A merely human agent can act as an instrument or mediator of God's forgiveness, but only an agent who possesses God's own nature can actually forgive effectively, repairing the ontological damage wrought by sin. Jesus says to the paralytic, "Your sins are forgiven." If this statement is true (as the Gospel accounts clearly aim to show, against the doubts of the scribes), then Jesus must be God by nature.

Yet Jesus acts in an entirely human way, making a simple declarative statement in a natural human language. This one must possess a human nature to do, and any other human being could do the same (i.e., make the statement). Thus an utterly ordinary human act (speech) is at one and the same time an act of which God alone is capable (the forgiveness of sins). Jesus does this divine thing in a human way; here God forgives sin by speaking Aramaic to a paralyzed man. "Speaks Aramaic" is here true of God (the Son) and the scribes univocally. Otherwise Jesus would not undertake the divine act of forgiveness in a genuinely human way, and his act would not teach us that he is God incarnate — that "Deus est homo" and "Homo est Deus" are true.[66]

---

64. Cf. ibid., a. 1, ad 1: "Dionysius ponit in Christo operationem 'theandricam,' id est 'divinam-virilem' vel 'divinam-humanam,' non per aliquam confusionem operationum seu virtutum utriusque naturae, sed per hoc quod divina operatio eius utitur humana eius operatione, et humana operatio participat virtutem divinae operationis. Unde, sicut ipse dicit in quadam epistola [Ep. 4], 'super hominem operabatur ea quae sunt hominis, quod monstrat virgo supernaturaliter concipiens, et aqua terrenorum pedum sustinens gravitatem.' Manifestum est enim quod concipi est humanae naturae, similiter et ambulare, sed utrumque fuit in Christo supernaturaliter. Et similiter divina operabatur humanitus, sicut cum sanavit leprosum tangendo. Unde in eadem epistola subdit, 'sed, Deo homine facto, nova quadam Dei et hominis operatione.'"

65. As Aquinas puts it, "[F]ecit Deus sicut bonus medicus qui causam curat" (*In Matt.* 9.1 [746]).

66. "Per hoc manifestat se Deum," says Thomas, here speaking of the healing of the

Bruce D. Marshall

Commentators on Aquinas's account of analogy have tended not to notice the exuberant embrace of univocity in his Christology. There are no doubt several reasons for this. The simple fact that the Tertia Pars seems, especially in recent times, to be *terra incognita* to students of Aquinas on analogy may explain much. But the modern tendency generally to ignore Aquinas's deliberate analysis of language (it "deals only with logic, and no longer holds any interest for us") surely plays an important role as well. Thomas's Christological endorsement of univocal speech about God emerges, naturally enough, only from an explicit analysis of specific statements concerning Christ (e.g., "Deus est homo"). No amount of reflection on the metaphysics of the incarnation is likely to bring it directly to light. Thomas himself evidently regards the analysis of Christological language (e.g., in *Summa theologiae* III, q. 16) as a needed complement to a properly developed Christological metaphysics (e.g., in *Summa theologiae* III, q. 2). Declining to follow him in this, or taking linguistic analysis to be a needless repetition of truths about the metaphysics of the incarnation, many of Thomas's interpreters seem unable to see his Christological univocity.

Perhaps the tendency to conflate linguistic analogy with metaphysical participation also plays a role here. Thinking only or chiefly in metaphysical terms, Thomists often seem to assume that (linguistic) "univocity" must be some inherent or necessary sameness of ontological determination between God and creatures, a sameness that belongs to God and creatures by nature. This they emphatically, and rightly, reject. As Thomas sees it, though, the doctrine of the incarnation requires that there be extensive sameness of ontological determination or attribute between God and creatures: God "est homo," just as Peter, James, and John are; and God "speaks Aramaic," just as Peter, James, and John do. There need be no conflict between the metaphysical denial of sameness in ontological determination between God and creatures and the Christological affirmation of it. That the eternal Son is a human being and speaks Aramaic is true of neither God nor creatures by nature, and so it is not an inherent ontological determination of either. Rather, the identity of ontological determination between God and us, which the incarnation brings about, is freely willed by God, without any

paralytic, which attests Jesus' authority to forgive sins (ibid. [750]). This Aquinas connects to the name of Jesus in Matt. 1:21, on which he comments, "Ecce quod ille idem homo, qui natus est de virgine, qui vocatur Iesus, ipse salvum faciet populum suum a peccatis eorum. Unde cum peccata dimittere non possit nisi solus Deus, oportet dicere quod iste homo sit Deus, et quod ea, quae Dei sunt, ei verissime convenient" (*In Matt.* 1.4 [138]).

change in his divinity — in what makes him God.[67] God brings about this sameness of attribute or determination between himself and us by willing to be, in the person of the Son, the subject of a human nature, and so to make "est homo" and "speaks Aramaic" true of himself in just the same sense in which they are true of us.[68] Analogical metaphysicians have nothing to fear — at least when they believe in the incarnation — from univocity. Recognizing that univocity is not a metaphysical matter may help in seeing this.

Thomas's Christological embrace of univocity also, of course, poses a problem. One might get the impression that he forgot in the Tertia Pars what he so clearly insisted on in the Prima Pars, namely, that we cannot speak univocally of God. How shall we square Aquinas's vigorous Christological affirmation of univocity with his equally vigorous denial of it in the question on the divine names?

In an earlier treatment of how to take "Deus est homo," Thomas addresses this question explicitly. In book 3 of the *Scriptum,* an objector proposes that the locution must simply be false, because nothing is rightly said univocally of God and creature, and "homo" is presumably a term applied univocally to God the Son and us.[69] Thomas replies: "'Homo' is predicated univocally of God and other human beings. The objection that nothing is said univocally of God and creatures pertains to those things that are said of him insofar as he is God."[70]

This reply is no doubt puzzling, to say the least — one of those quintessentially terse Thomistic answers that says either nothing or everything needed. We can perhaps clear up the mystery by recalling that "insofar

67. On this last point, see my essay "The Dereliction of Christ and the Impassibility of God," in *Divine Impassibility and the Mystery of Human Suffering,* ed. James F. Keating and Thomas Joseph White, O.P., pp. 246-98 (Grand Rapids: Eerdmans, 2009).

68. This is one of many places where the doctrine of the two natures in Christ — one of which he possesses necessarily or inherently (the divine), the other freely (the human) — plays a needed systemic role in theology. Without a real distinction of natures, both fully possessed by the person of the Son, it would evidently be impossible to hold both that God is transcendent (by [divine] nature he has no ontological determination in common with creatures) and that God is incarnate (he has freely but irrevocably accepted a whole range of ontological determinations that goes with having a human nature).

69. *In III Sent.,* d. 7, q. 1, a. 1, ob 3: "Praeterea, nihil praedicatur univoce de creatore et creatura. Sed homo univoce praedicatur in Christo et in nobis. Ergo non praedicatur de Deo" (no. 24).

70. Ibid., a. 1, ad 3: "Ad tertium dicendum, quod homo univoce praedicatur de Deo et aliis hominibus. Quod autem dicitur, quod nihil dicitur univoce de Deo et creaturis, intelligendum est de illis quae praedicantur de ipso inquantum est Deus" (no. 36).

as he is God" *(inquantum est Deus* here, or more commonly *secundum quod Deus)* is a technical locution for Aquinas, with a stipulated sense. We might be inclined to suppose that when we say (for example) "The God of glory was crucified" but deny (with Aquinas) that he was crucified "as God," we are actually denying that "God" is the subject of "crucified." This would be to say that "The God of glory was crucified" is in fact false, and so to deny that God was really crucified. If we read Thomas in this way, we would not be interpreting his claim that "homo," and thereby all the *acta* and *passa* that go with being this particular man, are predicated univocally of God and us. We would be repudiating it.

For Aquinas, however, to say that the God of glory was crucified "as man" but not "as God" has a different sense. The locutions "as man" *(secundum quod homo)* and "as God" *(secundum quod Deus)* do not specify the *subject* of "was crucified" or of any other predicate we might apply to God incarnate. Rather, they always specify the respect in which the *predicate* applies to the subject. So when we say, "The God of glory was crucified" but not "as God," our statement means that God was crucified all right, but that he was crucified (more exactly, able to be crucified) on account of having a human nature, and not on account of his having the divine nature.[71] More generally: nothing is said univocally of creatures and God in virtue of his divine nature, but rather in virtue of the human nature he has in the person of the Son. Thus everything that is said univocally of the human being Jesus and of us is said univocally of God.

The question on the divine names in the Prima Pars, then, is not the sum of Thomas's treatment of our language about God. It is what we could say of God if the Word had not become flesh. Apart from the incarnation of the Word and the sacramental economy that anticipates it (in Israel) and expresses it (in the Church), any human attempt to speak univocally of God, rather than by an analogy that leaves the *rationes* for what we say of God "ungrasped," would be idolatry. This applies not only to what we can say of

---

71. More technically put, the rule for interpreting reduplicative expressions like "Christus secundum quod homo . . ." is: "nomen sic resumptum in reduplicatione magis proprie tenetur pro natura quam pro supposito, resumitur enim in vi praedicati, quod tenetur formaliter; idem enim est dictu, Christus secundum quod homo, ac si diceretur, Christus secundum quod est homo" (*ST* III, q. 16, a. 10, c.). For Thomas's application of this rule to statements like "The Lord of glory was crucified," see *In I Cor.* 2.2 (92); *ST* III, q. 46, a. 12. On the interpretation of these standard medieval Christological formulae in Aquinas, see Bruce D. Marshall, *Christology in Conflict: The Identity of a Saviour in Rahner and Barth* (Oxford: Blackwell, 1987), chap. 6.

God by way of natural reason but to what we may be able to say by way of any religion that does not know of the incarnation of the Word.[72] Conversely, to deny that we can in fact speak univocally of God is by implication (and perhaps unwittingly) to deny that the Word has become incarnate. That Christians can and do speak univocally of God, not lapsing into idolatry but from the heart of their faith in God's incarnation, is one way of saying what's *different* about Christianity — what marks Christianity off from any other religion, real or possible, natural or revealed.[73]

To be sure, all of this leaves intact Thomas's claim that, even by revelation, we are joined to God in this life "as to one unknown." Nothing it is true for us to say univocally of God in virtue of the humanity of the Logos tells us of God *quid est,* what he is in his divine nature.[74] The human nature of the incarnate Word gives us numerous univocal *rationes* for God (in the person of the Son), but we remain without a *ratio* for the divine essence and its perfections. Thus the human wisdom we ascribe to Jesus (e.g., in the Sermon on the Mount) is univocally the wisdom of God the Son, but this human wisdom is not the same as the wisdom the Son possesses eternally, in virtue of his divine nature. Of this even the incarnation allows us to speak only analogically, that is to say, without knowing what it is.

We are not, however, simply back with the analogical austerity with which we began. Even though faith, as well as natural knowledge, leaves the divine nature unknown to us in this life, "nevertheless we know God more fully" by faith than by natural reason, since "in the revelation of grace . . . more, and more excellent, effects of God are shown to us."[75] The most excellent effect of God in creation — not simply the highest we know of, but the highest conceivable — is the hypostatic union of the human nature of Jesus

72. Here, as elsewhere, Judaism fails to fit straightforwardly into the distinctions Christian theology rightly makes. The Jewish people and the Jewish religion cannot, from a Christian point of view, be fully abstracted from the becoming flesh of the Word, but rather belong to the sacramental economy ordered to the incarnation. Christian theology therefore cannot rule out true univocal speech about God within Judaism.

73. Here too I am grateful for a suggestion by Emmanuel Perrier.

74. "[P]er revelationem gratiae in hac vita non cognoscamus de Deo quid est, et sic ei quasi ignoto coniungamur" (*ST* I, q. 12, a. 13, ad 1; cf. n. 50).

75. "[P]er revelationem gratiae . . . tamen plenius ipsum cognoscimus, inquantum plures et excellentiores effectus eius nobis demonstrantur; et inquantum ei aliqua attribuimus ex revelatione divina, ad quae ratio naturalis non pertingit, ut Deum esse trinum et unum" (ibid.). As the latter half of this sentence suggests, revelation also enables us to know things about God that are not, in themselves, effects at all, such as that God is the Trinity.

to the person of the Word. By God's assumption of a human nature into personal unity with the Word is brought about, in other words, the most intimate relationship possible between God and a creature.[76] Just this relationship enables us to speak univocally of God.

Among the excellent "effects" of this supreme unity with our nature is that the wisdom and goodness of Jesus are the wisdom and goodness of God himself. God fully possesses this human goodness and wisdom in time, as much as he eternally possesses infinite divine goodness and wisdom. They are God's human goodness and wisdom, and so not to be equated with the goodness and wisdom God has by (divine) nature, and would have even if he had created no world. But they are truly his own, no less than what belongs to him on account of his divine nature. They too are God's hypostatic wisdom and goodness and as such are as close to the eternal divine exemplars of those perfections as any created wisdom and goodness could be. Jesus' goodness and wisdom, his righteousness, holiness, and redemption — all the human perfections we see in him — express as nearly as possible the perfections that are eternally God's by nature, which we must yet wait to see.

Because Jesus Christ is God incarnate, we do know God "more fully" than we can by natural knowledge. This does not simply mean that we acquire more items of which we can speak only analogically, but that we come to know God in a more excellent way, befitting the supreme excellence of what he is, and does, in Christ. We acquire univocal predicates by which to know him. The faith that lays hold of God incarnate thus forms a genuine middle step between natural knowledge and the vision of God *in patria*. Faith gives us a univocal grasp of God's human perfections, exceeding the merely analogical apprehension we can have of any divine perfection by natural reason alone, or apart from faith in the incarnation. And faith itself will be exceeded by the final vision, where we will grasp God's divine as well as his human wisdom and goodness as they are.

As it turns out, Aquinas's account of language about God is not nearly so spare as his treatment of the divine names, all by itself, might lead us to suppose. We can have a *ratio* for talk about God in this life after all. But we do not acquire it by mounting up analogically to make the *rationes* of God's natural perfections our own. Rather, God has condescended in love to make his own that of which we can have a *ratio*: our birth, infancy, speech, prayer, suffering, and more.

76. "Non potest autem esse, nec intelligi, maior unio creaturae rationalis ad Deum quam quae est in persona" (*ST* III, q. 7, a. 12, c.; cf. III, q. 2, a. 9).

It is perhaps unusual to conclude a paper on Aquinas by quoting Bernard of Clairvaux. But Thomas clearly regards Bernard as an authority, not least on the incarnation.[77] St. Bernard vividly captures, it seems to me, the logic of St. Thomas's position on the divine names — both the limitations on our speech about God apart from the incarnation and the depth of what we can say because of it. We can leave the last word with him.

> Once God was incomprehensible and inaccessible, invisible and entirely unthinkable. But now he wanted to be seen, he wanted to be understood, he wanted to be known. How was this done, you ask? God lay in a manger and rested on the Virgin's breast. He preached on a mountain, prayed through the night, and hung on a cross. He lay pale in death, was free among the dead, and was master of hell. He rose on the third day, showed the apostles the signs of victory where nails once were, and ascended before their eyes to the inner recesses of heaven. . . . When I think on any of these things, I am thinking of God, and in all these things he is now my God.[78]

77. In fact Aquinas invokes St. Bernard (*De consideratione* 5.9) as authoritative support for taking the basic Christological sentence "Deus est homo" *vere et proprie:* "Bernardus dicit, in lib. *De consid.,* 'Tantam et tam expressam vim unionis in se praefert illa persona quae Deus et homo unus est Christus, ut si alterum de altero praedices, non erres.' Ergo Deus est homo, et e converso" (*In III Sent.,* d. 7, q. 1, a. 1, sc 2 [no. 26]).

78. *Sermo in nativitate B. Mariae,* 11: "Incomprehensibilis erat et inaccessibilis, invisibilis et inexcogitabilis omnino. Nunc vero comprehendi voluit, videri voluit, voluit cogitari. Quonam modo, inquis? Nimirum iacens in praesepio, in virginali gremio cubans, in monte praedicans, in oratione pernoctans, aut in cruce pendens, in morte pallens, liber inter mortuos et in inferno imperans, seu etiam tertia die resurgens et Apostolis loca clavorum victoriae signa demonstrans, novissime coram eis caeli secreta conscendens. Quid horum non vere, non pie, non sancte cogitator? Quidquid horum cogito, Deum cogito, et per omnia ipse est Deus meus." *Sancti Bernardi Opera* V, ed. J. Leclercq, O.S.B., and H. Rochais (Rome: Editiones Cistercienses, 1968) p. 282.19-26.

CHAPTER 9

Analogia Entis as an Expression of Love according to Ferdinand Ulrich

Martin Bieler

Et ex amore facit omnia dans eis esse.

— Thomas Aquinas, *In De divinis nominibus* 4.9.409

I. An Unknown Important Thinker

The German philosopher Ferdinand Ulrich (born 1931) is a rather unknown figure in the American discussion of Thomistic metaphysics.[1] Actually, he is not very well known in Europe either.[2] Until 1996 he taught philosophy at the University of Regensburg, but his writings have only recently become more accessible. The Johannes Verlag in Einsiedeln engaged in the project of editing his writings, an edition that so far contains five

1. But see Thomas Prufer, *Recapitulation: Essays in Philosophy* (Washington, D.C.: Catholic University of America Press, 1993), p. xii; David C. Schindler, *Hans Urs von Balthasar and the Dramatic Structure of Truth: A Philosophical Investigation* (New York: Fordham University Press, 2004), p. 455; Adrian J. Walker, "Love Alone: Hans Urs von Balthasar as a Master of Theological Renewal," *Communio* 32 (Fall 2005): 521; Reinhard Hütter, "St. Thomas on Grace and Free Will in the *Initium Fidei*: The Surpassing Augustinian Synthesis," *Nova et Vetera*, Engl. ed., 5, no. 3 (2007): 543.

2. But see Stefan Oster, *Mit-Mensch-Sein. Phänomenologie und Ontologie der Gabe bei Ferdinand Ulrich* (Freiburg: Karl Alber, 2004); André Léonard, *Métaphysique de l'être* (Paris: Cerf, 2006), p. 359.

314

substantial volumes.[3] It is not by chance that Ulrich's books were edited in the publishing house founded by Hans Urs von Balthasar. It is undisputed that the German philosopher Gustav Siewerth had an important influence upon Balthasar, especially in the development of the latter's philosophical stance in volume III/1 of his *Theological Aesthetics*. It is less well known that Ulrich was an even more crucial interlocutor for Balthasar when he wrote his *Theodramatics*.[4] Ulrich is not cited too often throughout the *Theodramatics*, but his influence is apparent in important passages of this centerpiece of Balthasarian theology.

Ulrich's working relationship with Balthasar is an example of his influence as an interlocutor. Ulrich was probably more influential as a teacher in direct encounters than as a writer. But that does not mean that his writings are unimportant. They deserve close attention, for Ulrich presents a most interesting and, in its consequences, far-reaching philosophy that centers upon Aquinas's insight into *esse* as "similitudo divinae bonitatis," a similitude of divine goodness.[5] It is also a philosophy containing a developed critique of modern thinkers like Hegel, Nietzsche, and Freud. In many ways Ulrich makes Balthasar's concern with concrete contexts of human existence accessible. (See, for example, Balthasar's discussion of sociological and psychological issues in the first volume of his *Theodramatik* [Einsiedeln: Johannes Verlag, 1973], pp. 463-511.) This is also true for the discussion of the *analogia entis*, which is so controversial between Catholics and Protestants.

On the Protestant side, it is first of all Karl Barth who never lost his reservations against the *analogia entis*. He first got acquainted with it in his conversations with Erich Przywara, whom he described to his friend Eduard Thurneysen with a mixture of admiration and dismay.[6] The result of Barth's dispute with Przywara is his famous statement that the *analogia entis* is the invention of the Antichrist.[7] Even though Barth could endorse at a later date much of what Gottlieb Söhngen said about the *analogia entis* — up to the point of taking back what he, Barth, said about the *analogia entis* earlier on

3. *Homo abyssus* (1998); *Leben in der Einheit von Leben und Tod* (1999); *Erzählter Sinn* (2002); *Logo-Tokos* (2003); *Gabe und Vergebung* (2007).

4. On Siewerth, see Manfred Lochbrunner, *Hans Urs von Balthasar und seine Philosophenfreunde. Fünf Doppelporträts* (Würzburg: Echter, 2005), pp. 143-88.

5. *De ver.*, q. 22, a. 2, ad 2.

6. Karl Barth, *Karl Barth–Eduard Thurneysen Briefwechsel*, vol. 2, *1921-1930* (Zürich: TVZ, 1974), pp. 651-54.

7. *Kirchliche Dogmatik* I/1, 9th ed. (Zürich: TVZ, 1975), p. viii.

— he never gave up his critique of the *philosophical* undertaking of an *analogia entis.*[8]

In one of his last statements on the issue, Barth names the one whom he sees behind Przywara and others: Thomas Aquinas.[9] Barth feared that an *analogia entis* as Aquinas understood it would establish a neutral ground between Creator and creature, which would allow the creature to get hold of God. But this was not Barth's only concern. The second major concern was the view of God that an *analogia entis* might foster. What does it mean for our view of God if we call him the "ipsum esse subsistens"? With such an abstract notion of God, are we not very far from the Father of Jesus Christ? What Barth feared in both cases was a distortion of God by a philosophizing creature unable to escape the fate of sin (Rom. 1:18-23).[10] According to Barth, it does not make sense to approach God in a different way than the one chosen by God himself in his revelation in Jesus Christ. For Barth, a philosophical *analogia entis* is not only harmful but simply superfluous, because the light of Christ can enlighten everything in creation.[11]

It was particularly Hans Urs von Balthasar who challenged Barth's rejection of a Thomistic account of created being, an *analogia entis ad mentem Sancti Thomae.* For Balthasar the metaphysics of being is an integral part of God's revelation in our world. It is not only possible but necessary to deal with the philosophical *analogia entis.* For Balthasar, Christ himself is the concrete *analogia entis,* because he measures all dimensions between God and human beings through his own person in the unity of his divine and his human nature. The philosophical *analogia entis* has the same relation to Christ as world history has to the history of Christ: It is like promise to fulfillment, and like provisional to final.[12] Yet it is precisely the philosophical

---

8. *Kirchliche Dogmatik* II/1, 4th ed. (Zürich: TVZ, 1958), p. 90.

9. "Meine Kritik gegenüber der analogia entis war, dass darin — so wie Thomas sie verstanden hat, von einem gemeinsamen Grund zwischen Gott und Mensch gesprochen wurde; und dieser Grund wurde im Begriff des Seins gefunden. Gott ist, der Mensch ist auch. Insofern gibt es eine Analogie von Gott und Mensch usw. Und gegen diesen Begriff musste ich kämpfen" (*Gespräche, 1959-1962* [Zürich: TVZ Verlag, 1995], p. 294).

10. This concern is not foreign to Aquinas. See Eugene F. Rogers Jr., *Thomas Aquinas and Karl Barth: Sacred Doctrine and the Natural Knowledge of God* (Notre Dame, Ind.: University of Notre Dame Press, 1995).

11. See Martin Bieler, "Karl Barths Auseinandersetzung mit der analogia entis und der Anfang der Theologie," *Catholica* 40 (1986): 241-45.

12. Hans Urs von Balthasar, *Theologie der Geschichte* (Einsiedeln: Johannes Verlag, 1959), pp. 53-54. The term "provisional" might be misleading, for philosophy is not replaced by Christ, as Balthasar knows very well. In the first volume of his *Theologik*, Balthasar un-

analogia entis that is disputed by Barth. As Stephen D. Wigley recently stated, Balthasar's way of structuring his trilogy according to the transcendentals *pulchrum, bonum,* and *verum* is a large-scale attempt to resolve Barth's reservations about the philosophical knowledge of God.[13] But Barth's reaction to the first volumes of Balthasar's trilogy was rather chilly. He did not feel at home in this kind of thinking.[14]

I think the way Ferdinand Ulrich unfolds the philosophical *analogia entis* of Aquinas is of great help for spelling out the concrete relevance of the *analogia entis* Balthasar had in mind. Ulrich is a Christian philosopher, which means that for him the philosophical act as an existential act is rooted in grace.[15] It also means that he develops his philosophy in close contact with theology. But this does not mean that he confounds in any way the formal object of theology with the formal object of philosophy. Rather, he offers a genuine *praeambula fidei,* not unlike the sort that Ralph McInerny has recently advocated. As a result, Ulrich's philosophy is by no means a neutral philosophy but an appraisal of the gift of being, a philosophy of love based on the insight that being *(esse)* is a gift. In the following I will present Ulrich's interpretation of Aquinas mainly according to his magisterial work, *Homo abyssus.* The accompanying presentation of Aquinas's views serves to establish the starting points for Ulrich's reflections.

II. *Ens, Esse,* and the Philosophical Beginning

As it was for Barth, the quest for the right beginning is also crucial for the philosopher. In an important article on the nature of the philosophical beginning *(Anfang),* Ulrich shows that *esse,* as Aquinas understands it, is the

folds the relationship between truth, measure, and being: "Truth is the revealed or just about to be revealed being, or shorter: It is the measure of being" (*Theologik,* vol. 1 [Einsiedeln: Johannes Verlag, 1985], p. 35; translations in this essay from German are my own unless otherwise noted). For the term "measure," see also James McEvoy, "The Divine as the Measure of Being in Platonic and Scholastic Thought," in *Studies in Medieval Philosophy,* ed. John F. Wippel, pp. 85-116 (Washington, D.C.: Catholic University of America Press, 1980).

13. Stephen D. Wigley, *Karl Barth and Hans Urs von Balthasar: A Critical Engagement* (London: T. & T. Clark, 2007), p. 48.

14. Karl Barth, *Briefe, 1961-1968,* ed. Jürgen Fangmeier and Hinrich Stoevesandt (Zürich: TVZ, 1975), pp. 145-46.

15. This is also conceded by Ralph McInerny, who is critical toward the idea of a Christian philosophy. See *Praeambula fidei: Thomism and the God of the Philosophers* (Washington, D.C.: Catholic University of America Press, 2006), p. 107.

beginning of finite being insofar as *esse* is the free beginning of the absolute in the finite, the free gift of being.[16] Human beings are challenged to receive this beginning and to "perform" it in freedom as the realization of their own nature.[17] As the beginning, *esse* connects and divides the beginner and the being with which he began. *Esse (commune)* cannot be substantiated as something between God and finite being, and yet it also cannot be substantiated into God or finite being.[18] But the latter does not mean that *esse* remains inaccessible to us or that it is a mere concept. *Esse* cannot be grasped as a fixed point, but it is fully present in finite beings that — drawn by the love of their Creator[19] — tend back to the source of their being and in this way represent in themselves the difference between being *(ens)* and *esse*.[20] As a result of his reflections, Ulrich denotes the human being as an "in-between" who represents the ontological difference between *esse* and being.[21] "In this way philosophy reaches its beginning in the always already-in-advance [!] realized act of transcendence of the embodied spirit into the ungraspable mystery of being [*Sein*] as love."[22]

It is first of all the other human being we encounter who represents to us the mystery of *esse* as the beginning. As modern research in childhood development has shown, "infants with harmonious relationships with their mothers develop 'person permanence' prior to 'object permanence.'"[23] So it is in a very literal sense that other human beings are the first objects for us.

16. Ferdinand Ulrich, "Über die spekulative Natur des philosophischen Anfangs," in *Innerlichkeit und Erziehung. In Memoriam Gustav Siewerth*, ed. Franz Pöggeler, pp. 27-72 (Freiburg: Herder, 1964), p. 40. For the term "beginning" as a theological and philosophical category, see Klaus Hemmerle's reflections on Bonaventure, which are close to Ulrich's view (*Theologie als Nachfolge. Bonaventura — ein Weg für heute* [Freiburg: Herder, 1975], 63-99).

17. Ulrich, "Über die spekulative Natur des philosophischen Anfangs," p. 46.

18. Ibid., p. 55. In *Homo abyssus. Das Wagnis der Seinsfrage*, 2d ed. (Einsiedeln: Johannes Verlag, 1998), p. 15, Ulrich cites *De ver.*, q. 8, a. 17, c.: "Non potest aliquid esse medium inter creatum et increatum."

19. Albert Ilien, *Wesen und Funktion der Liebe im Denken des Thomas von Aquin* (Freiburg: Herder, 1975). As John Calvin puts it: "Deinde ab his bonis quae guttatim e caelo ad nos stillant, tanquam a rivulis ad fontem deducimur" (*Institutio Christianae religionis* 1.1.1, in *Joannis Calvini Opera selecta*, vol. 3, ed. Peter Barth and Wilhelm Niesel [Munich: Chr. Kaiser Verlag, 1928], p. 31).

20. Ulrich speaks in this context of "circulating thinking" (*Homo abyssus*, pp. 10-14).

21. Ulrich, "Über die spekulative Natur des philosophischen Anfangs," p. 56. Ulrich refers to Przywara for this thought (*Homo abyssus*, p. 9).

22. Ulrich, "Über die spekulative Natur des philosophischen Anfangs," p. 57.

23. Margaret S. Mahler, Fred Pine, and Anni Bergman, *The Psychological Birth of the Human Infant: Symbiosis and Individuation* (New York: Basic Books, 2000), p. 111.

According to Thomas Aquinas, "Id autem quod primo intellectus concipit quasi notissimum, et in quo omnes conceptions resolvit, est ens."[24] What "ens" means appears first of all in another human being. As soon as we consciously reflect on the wonder of the presence of a human being and of beings in general, we are philosophizing.

In the encounter with the *ens,* we have the intuitive knowledge of what Aquinas calls the first principles ("primorum principiorum notitia"), without which there would be no human thinking.[25] But by this *notitia* we do not yet recognize the problem of being as such *(ens inquantum ens)* explicitly. It is only in the process of abstraction and separation, as Aquinas called it, that we discover *ens* as such. The *esse* that we discover in being *(ens)* transcends the difference between material and immaterial.[26] We touch here something inexhaustible, yes, even absolute.[27] We do not have to first recognize the possibility of immaterial beings in order to enter metaphysics, for the *ens* itself as the font and origin of *esse* itself ("fons et origo ipsius esse") opens up the way to metaphysics.[28] The *esse* we touch upon in every *ens* transcends all creaturely differences. It makes it possible for Aquinas to say

---

24. *De ver.,* q. 1, a. 1, c.

25. *SCG* 2.83 (Torino: Marietti, 1961): "Naturaliter igitur intellectus noster cognoscit ens, et ea quae sunt per se entis inquantum huiusmodi; in qua cognitione fundatur primorum principiorum notitia, ut non esse simul affirmare et negare, et alia huiusmodi."

26. L.-B. Geiger, "Abstraction et séparation d'après s. Thomas *In de Trinitate,* q. 5, a. 3," *Revue des sciences philosophiques et théologiques* 31 (1947): 22.

27. *De ver.,* q. 1, a. 1, c.: "Aliquid affirmative dictum absolute."

28. *In Peri hermeneias* 1.5.70. Ulrich would agree with John Wippel and Lawrence Dewan, who have shown against the River Forest School that we do not have to prove immateriality by natural philosophy in order to enter metaphysics. See John F. Wippel, *The Metaphysical Thought of Thomas Aquinas: From Finite Being to Uncreated Being* (Washington, D.C.: Catholic University of America Press, 2000), pp. 44-62; and Lawrence Dewan, *Form and Being: Studies in Thomistic Metaphysics* (Washington, D.C.: Catholic University of America Press, 2006), pp. 47-60. For the River Forest School, see Benedict Ashley, *The Way toward Wisdom: An Interdisciplinary and Intercultural Introduction to Metaphysics* (Notre Dame, Ind.: University of Notre Dame Press, 2006). The research of the River Forest School is important for metaphysics with respect to the notion of substance, as the metaphysical notions of *substantia* and *essentia* are questioned by many modern natural scientists. This is not irrelevant for metaphysics. Lawrence Dewan, *St. Thomas and Form as Something Divine in Things* (Milwaukee: Marquette University Press, 2007), p. 21: "It is only inasmuch as one appreciates the *unity* of the things we call 'dogs' and 'cats' and 'human beings' that one will be obliged to treat them as 'beings' in the unqualified sense of that word, and that one will be obliged to do the intellectual work involved in understanding how unqualified coming to be and ceasing to be are possible."

that to be caused is *not* intrinsic to the notion of being as such ("de ratione entis simpliciter").[29] This insight carries us in a certain sense into a realm before creation.[30]

We encounter the perfection of *esse* in the subsisting *ens* because the gift of existence common to all beings *(ipsum esse commune)* connecting us with every other being is present in every single being.[31] Jacques Maritain is right when he emphasizes the difficulty of coming to this understanding of being, which he characterizes as "a gift bestowed upon the intellect."[32] It is difficult to grasp being as such because it implies an understanding of the character of "being given" in every *ens*. Therefore the experience of grasping *ens* as such, the *conceptio entis,* very often happens as an insight into the wonder of one's own existence that is accompanied not only by amazement but also by awe.[33]

Ulrich particularly emphasizes the importance of receiving one's being as a gift and the dangers connected to this challenge. He pointedly speaks of temptation in this context (see below).[34] The intellectual grasp of being with its existential connotations is the center of the philosophical act. This understanding, or *conception,* gives us access to the *analogia entis* in its whole range.

Analogy is the adequate form of thinking for this *conceptio* because it expresses the presence of *esse* in *ens* and the difference between *ens* and *esse* at the same time — in a way that makes it necessary even to go beyond *esse commune* to the *esse subsistens.*[35] Analogy can be treated as a logical concept, as Ralph McInerny treats it in his book *Aquinas and Analogy.*[36] But analogy must also be treated as a metaphysical doctrine, as John Wippel rightly points out.[37] Aquinas clearly distinguishes the two points of view: The logician considers the ways in which we predicate being to reality (the *modus praedicandi*); the

29. *ST* I, q. 44, a. 1, ad 1.

30. Ulrich, *Homo abyssus,* p. 129.

31. Johannes B. Lotz, *Transzendentale Erfahrung* (Freiburg: Herder, 1978), pp. 108-15.

32. Jacques Maritain, *A Preface to Metaphysics: Seven Lectures on Being* (New York: Mentor Omega Book, 1962), p. 52.

33. Ibid. See also Victor Emil von Gebsattel, *Imago Hominis. Beiträge zu einer personalen Anthropologie* (Salzburg: Otto Müller, 1968), pp. 308-23.

34. Ulrich, *Homo abyssus,* p. 2.

35. Ibid., p. 250.

36. Ralph McInerny, *Aquinas and Analogy* (Washington, D.C.: Catholic University of America Press, 1996).

37. Wippel, *The Metaphysical Thought of Thomas Aquinas,* p. 87. See also Gregory Rocca, *Speaking the Incomprehensible God* (Washington, D.C.: Catholic University of America Press, 2004), pp. 127-34.

philosopher, the very existence of things (the *existentia rei*).[38] In both cases we have to deal with analogy, hence also when we consider the *existentia rei*.[39] For Aquinas it is quite clear that the metaphysical point of view is normative for all other realms of natural knowledge, including logic.[40] Therefore the way in which Bernard Montagnes and others deal with the issue of analogy as a metaphysical doctrine is legitimate and necessary.[41]

According to Aquinas, we grasp not only being as such but also being as having a given determination, or as *res*. "Res" signifies the *quidditas*, the *essentia*, by which *esse* is conceived in being. The *essentia* shows that we have *esse* only inside the limitations of our nature. The first judgment is therefore a negative judgment, which not only grasps *esse* in being but also shows that every being is "something other," an *aliquid* to other beings and hence not the totality of being *(esse)*.[42] A given being *(ens)* does not exhaust the act of being *(esse)*, and yet *esse* is exactly also due to the *limits* of *ens* fully present in *ens*, because *esse* can be conceived only inside the limitations of a being.[43] This is the reason why we are urged by *ens* itself to transcend *ens*. As a reality that contains something absolute but in a limited mode, *ens* appears as a reality having being, as an "esse habens," but not as being *(esse)* itself.[44] But what is this *esse* that *ens* participates in? In clarifying this question, Ulrich makes his most original contribution to philosophy.

38. Aquinas, *In meta.* 7.17.1658. For the relationship between these two points of view, see Gyula Klima, "Ens multipliciter dicitur: The Semantics and Metaphysics of Being in St. Thomas Aquinas," www.fordham.edu/gsas/phil/klima/FILES/Ens-multiplicter-dicitur.doc. The nature and danger of a "pure logic" that is dissociated from the *conceptio entis* are forcefully analyzed by Ulrich in *Homo abyssus*, pp. 452-64.

39. McInerny's statement that "the question of analogy does not arise in discussing things as they exist but as they are known and named" (*Aquinas and Analogy*, p. 101) stands in opposition to the view of Aquinas: "Est autem veritas, quod unum et ens non sunt genera, sed sunt omnibus communia analogice" (*In meta.* 11.11.2170; see also 7.7.1576); *ST* I, q. 4, a. 3, c. and *De pot.*, q. 3, a. 4, ad 9).

40. See, for example, *In meta.* 4.1 and the *prooemium* of this book; *In Boethii De Trin.* II, q. 5, a. 1.

41. See Bernard Montagnes, *The Doctrine of the Analogy of Being according to Thomas Aquinas*, trans. Edward M. Macierowski (Milwaukee: Marquette University Press, 2004), and the essay in this volume by Reinhard Hütter, "Attending to the Wisdom of God — from Effect to Cause, from Creation to God: A *relecture* of the Analogy of Being according to Thomas Aquinas."

42. Léon Elders, *Autour de saint Thomas d'Aquin*, vol. 1, *Les commentaires sur les oeuvres d'Aristote; La métaphysique de l'être* (Brugge: Tabor; Paris: FAC, 1987), pp. 187-206.

43. Martin Bieler, *Freiheit als Gabe* (Freiburg: Herder, 1991), p. 247.

44. "Nam ens dicitur quasi esse habens, hoc autem solum est substantia, quae subsistit" (*In meta.* 12.1.2419).

Martin Bieler

III. *Completum et simplex sed non subsistens*

When we attempt to identify the act of being, or *actus essendi,* that every being participates in, we notice that it does not subsist as a thing in itself. How
could it, if it is not just yet another being with its own limiting *essentia?* But
at the same time it is more than an empty concept. It is truly present as actu-
ating power in every being, as "actualitas omnium actuum."[45] It is not
subsistens but *inhaerens,* as Aquinas formulates it: it inheres in all things.[46] It
is not the absolute because it "is" only in the *entia.* Ulrich postulates that *esse*
"is always in the plurality of beings . . . itself."[47] It relies, so to speak, on the
substance of each thing with its *respective form* for its subsistence. In *De
Potentia,* q. 1, a. 1, c., Aquinas gives the decisive clue how to understand *esse.*
It is a "completum et simplex sed non subsistens."[48] It is complete and simple, but not a subsistent thing. For Ulrich, the importance of this sentence
cannot be overestimated. It designates the very core of his philosophy, on
which he dwells particularly in his main work, *Homo abyssus.*

    Esse is a *completum* because it contains all things. Nothing is outside
of *esse* apart from nonbeing.[49] And *esse* is a *simplex* because it is the one
unified outpouring by which God creates all things, itself a pure mediation
of being.[50] *Esse* is a *non subsistens* because it is poured out into all beings
without withholding anything. For Ulrich it is very important that *esse* is
not a thing. It is not *esse* that "puts" things into being, but *esse* is that
through which all things are given by God. So it is not *esse* that strives for
being *(ens),* for *esse* is not a subject.[51] "Being [*esse*] as being [*esse*] is superessential and cannot be substantiated."[52] *Esse* is not a hypostasis. The two
aspects of *esse* — the *completum et simplex,* on the one hand, and the *non*

45. *De pot.,* q. 7, a. 2, ad 9.
46. Ibid., a. 2, ad 7.
47. *Homo abyssus,* pp. 67-68.
48. The importance of this thought has also been noticed by Louis-Bertrand Geiger,
La participation dans la philosophie de S. Thomas d'Aquin (Paris: J. Vrin, 1942), pp. 351-52.
49. *De pot.,* q. 7, a. 2, ad 9.
50. *Homo abyssus,* p. 24. The single outpouring of the *communicatio totius esse* is described by Aquinas with the metaphor of light. See Martin Bieler, "The Theological Importance of a Philosophy of Being," in *Reason and the Reasons of Faith,* ed. Paul Griffith and
Reinhard Hütter, pp. 295-326 (London: T. & T. Clark, 2005), pp. 316-17; Antoine Levy, "An Introduction to Divine Relativity: Beyond David Bradshaw's *Aristotle East and West," Thomist*
72 (2008): 173-231.
51. *Homo abyssus,* p. 65.
52. Ibid., p. 70.

subsistens, on the other — do not contradict each other. They are, rather, the two necessary aspects of a single phenomenon. The nonsubsistence of *esse* shows that it is always, already poured out into substantial beings, and that it is poured out as a *completum et simplex,* as what is common to all that exists. That is why beings really are and why they contain this perfection in themselves. It is in the unity of *completum et simplex* (or ontological "wealth," as Ulrich often calls it) and nonsubsistence (or poverty) that *esse* is the similitude of the divine goodness, the gift in its radical givenness. In this unity *esse* reflects in the end the life of the Trinity, in which each person possesses the fullness of the divine nature (wealth) only in ecstatic and "kenotic" openness (poverty) toward the other two persons. Particularly important is the fact that the nonsubsistence of *esse* is not first of all a deficiency but rather a perfection. It shows that the gift is really given and is not held back in any way. Hence we encounter in our fellow beings the Creator himself, who is present in his creature through being:[53] "Because being [*Sein*] 'outside' of God is always already finite being [*Seiendes*], the research of the inherence of being [*Sein*] 'in' finite being [*Seiendes*] is already the touching of God by the intellect, the transcendental deduction of being [*Sein*]." This "already" of the presence of God through the *completum et simplex* of *esse* in everything that exists in creation explains why *esse* as created *actuality* can be a "fixum et quietum in ente," an unchanging testimonial of the quiet of God himself.[54]

As soon as we substantiate *esse* as a hypostasis between God and finite beings, the two aspects mentioned contradict each other. *Esse* loses its character of *pure* outpouring, and the *completum et simplex* is no longer totally present in beings through the nonsubsistence of *esse.* Then we get the structure that the snake in paradise insinuates, namely, the gift of *esse* is given in beings and held back at the same time in the hypostasis of *esse:* We can eat from the trees (beings), but the most important (this one tree, the hypostasis of *esse,* which makes us godlike) we don't get. So right from the beginning the snake can draw the conclusion that God must have said, "Ye shall not eat of *every* tree of the garden" (Gen. 3:1), for if we don't have access to *esse,* all the beings are not of any accessible value for us either. Therefore we have to grasp on our own what we are entitled to (instead of receiving it). *Esse* is no longer a gift but a prey we can dispose of on our own. And now *esse* becomes a means to mediate between God and beings on our terms — which is ex-

53. *Comp. theo.* 1.130.
54. *SCG* 1.20; *Homo abyssus*, p. 146.

actly what Barth had in mind as a danger.[55] That's also what Ulrich means when he speaks about the "temptation" associated with the consideration of the *analogia entis.*[56] It is the temptation to no longer receive one's freedom as a gift from the gracious God whom we love in return, but to consider our freedom as something that we owe to no one and that we even have to defend against an envious God. The consequence of philosophical stances of this sort is that the structures of creation break apart and force the human being to re-create them anew in an act of desperation. What is not a gift is no longer an expression of love but actually a threat we have to deal with, something we have to re-create *for ourselves* on our own terms. Ulrich analyzed this in a long chapter in his work *Logo-Tokos.*[57]

The nonsubsistence of *esse* shows that *esse commune* is not God himself, who is *ipsum esse subsistens.* Aquinas is very clear on the difference between *esse commune* and *esse subsistens.*[58] Since *esse commune* relies on the *essentia* (which itself presupposes intelligence) in order to subsist in finite things, *esse commune* carries us back to *ipsum esse subsistens* — God, who alone is the final origin of the creature's *essentia.* For Aquinas, *forma* is a *divinum quoddam,* an imprint of the Creator in the creature.[59] Because *esse commune* and *essentia* have to be differentiated in this way, the question arises whether there is something like a double participation in creatures — one of *esse,* and one of *essentia.* Ulrich shares the concern of Rudi te Velde not to ascribe this kind of duplicity to Aquinas.[60]

Here again the nonsubsistence of *esse* helps us to understand how the *essentia* can be different from *esse* and belong at the same time totally to *esse.* The essence *(essentia)* of each thing proceeds from *esse,* as the plurality of beings proceeds from the totality of *esse* as *completum et simplex.* This giving of being implies the nonsubsistence of *esse,* which is poured out into all things.[61] "In the real difference of the instituted essence toward being [*esse*], the not-

---

55. For the critique of this kind of mediation, Ulrich's dispute with Hegel is essential.

56. *Homo abyssus,* p. 103.

57. Ulrich, *Logo-Tokos. Der Mensch und das Wort* (Einsiedeln: Johannes Verlag, 2003), pp. 507-693.

58. See Fran O'Rourke, *Pseudo-Dionysius and the Metaphysics of Aquinas* (Leiden: Brill, 1992), pp. 143-55; Jan Aertsen, *Medieval Philosophy and the Transcendentals: The Case of Thomas Aquinas* (Leiden: Brill, 1996), pp. 387-95.

59. *SCG* 1.50.

60. Rudi te Velde, *Participation and Substantiality in Thomas Aquinas* (Leiden: Brill, 1995), p. 90.

61. *Homo abyssus,* pp. 72-74.

being-able-to-dispose-of-itself-in-suspension of being, the speculative seriousness of self-surrender is expressed."[62] The term "suspension" or "balance" is crucial for Ulrich. It expresses the indecision, the holding back of a substantiated *esse* between creature and Creator. (In reality there is no indecision, because there is no such thing as a substantiated *esse* between creature and Creator. But we can interpret *esse* in this way and create the *illusion* of indecision and suspension.) The nonsubsistence of *esse* shows that it is in fact already intended and given by God. This being intended and given by God contributes a precise meaning to *esse*: the sense of being the *similitudo divinae bonitatis,* the sense of being an expression of love. This decision, not made by *esse* but by God, explains how the *essentia* that is given through *esse* and belongs to *esse* can be one by itself and is hence also different from *esse*: "Essentia rei est una per seipsam, non propter esse suum."[63] The essence is one by itself because the form is the "seal [*sigillatio*] of Divine knowledge in things,"[64] which stands (in unity with God's will) at the beginning of the communication of *esse.*

Ulrich goes yet a step further and points out that, according to Aquinas, the true receiver of *esse* is not a free-floating *essentia* but the full-fledged *substantia,* the *ens:* "Substantia completa est proprium susceptivum ipsius esse."[65] This means that the difference between *esse* and *essentia* in creatures is, so to speak, "embedded" in the wider difference between *esse subsistens* and *ens,* for the *ens,* the *tota substantia rei,* is the actual aim of creation.[66] It is not as if a preexisting *essentia* is created and then put together with *esse,* but rather the *substance* is created together with its principles. Therefore *esse* and *essentia* are "con-created," as Aquinas puts it, rather than created.[67] But this does not diminish the role of the *essentia,* for it is the *essentia* by which *ens* receives its *esse* and by which *esse* is contracted *(coarctatio)* and limited *(limitatio).*[68] By its *essentia* the individual *ens* can be a mode of being.[69] By this pluralization of *esse* into the different beings, the *esse* as *completum et*

---

62. Ibid., p. 73.

63. Ibid., p. 74. Citation from *De ver.,* q. 21, a. 5, ad 8.

64. *De ver.,* q. 2, a. 1, ad 6.

65. *SCG* 2.55. "Esse non est formae, sed subiecti per formam" (*De virtutibus in communi;* q. 1, a. 11, c.).

66. *ST* I, q. 45, a. 1, c.

67. Ibid., a. 4, c. "Creatio non dicit constitutionem rei compositae ex principiis praeexistentibus: sed compositum sic dicitur creari, quod simul cum omnibus suis principiis in esse producitur" (ibid., a. 4, ad 2).

68. *De spiritualibus creaturis,* q. 1, a. 1, ad 15.

69. See Dewan, *Form and Being,* pp. 229-47.

simplex fully reaches each individual substance. Therefore Ulrich emphasizes with Aquinas that *esse* is not participated by being split into parts — which would be the impossible fragmentation of *esse,* the loss of the *completum et simplex* in the *entia* — but rather through its proceeding from God.[70]

The plurality of beings is instituted through *esse* by the Creator.[71] In this procession of beings *esse* "results from below" through the principles of *essentia,* as Ulrich says in accordance with Aquinas.[72] In this derivation of being, *forma* and *materia* are poured out through nonsubsisting *esse* in order to fuse with *esse* in the receiving *ens.* This happens in such a way that created causes (Aquinas's *causae secundae*) can be involved in the coming about of other beings, as is apparent, for example, in the relationship between parents and child.[73] Hence from a Thomist point of view, it is quite natural to think of a natural evolution of species.[74] The superessentiality of *esse* and the *uninformed potency* of the *materia prima,* which both result from the nonsubsisting character of *esse,* guarantee the possibility of such a process. But at the same time the evolutionary process is not aimless, for it aims at the development of human beings.[75]

70. *ST* I, q. 75, a. 5, ad 1.

71. *SCG* 2.45; *De pot.,* q. 3, a. 1, ad 8; *ST* I, q. 47, a. 1, c.

72. *Homo abyssus,* pp. 81, 91, 153-54. See *In III Sent.,* d. 6, q. 2, a. 2, c.: "Et est actus entis resultans ex principiis rei." And *In meta.* 4.2.558: "Esse . . . quasi constituitur per principia essentiae." But at the same time: "Impossibile est autem quod esse sit causatum tantum ex principiis essentialibus rei" (*ST* I, q. 3, a. 4, c.).

73. *Homo abyssus,* pp. 322-23. For the ontological presuppositions of the involvement of the *causae secundae* in the emergence of new life, see Joseph Bobik, *Aquinas on Matter and Form and the Elements: A Translation and Interpretation of the Principiis Naturae and the De Mixtione Elementorum of St. Thomas Aquinas* (Notre Dame, Ind.: University of Notre Dame Press, 1998).

74. *Homo abyssus,* pp. 333-34, 400-412. "The work of secondary causes is not envisaged by Thomas as in a context of evolution, that is, with the appearance of new species; however, he does not rule out such events, as is clear in *ST* 1.73.1 *ad* 3 (ed. Ottawa, p. 431b10-22), and the sort of active power considered in *ST* 1.110.2 *ad* 3 would allow the angels, working through the celestial bodies, such a role" (Dewan, *St. Thomas and Form,* p. 91). See also *De pot.,* q. 3, a. 8, ad 17: "Sicut virtus divina, scilicet primum agens, non excludit actionem virtutis naturalis, ita nec prima exemplaris forma, quae est Deus, excludit derivationem formarum ab aliis inferioribus formis, quae ad sibi similes formas agunt." For Aristotle and evolution, see Fran O'Rourke, "Aristotle and the Metaphysics of Evolution," in *Review of Metaphysics* 58 (2004): 3-59. Quite close to an Aristotelian view is J. Scott Turner's understanding of evolution, *The Tinkerer's Accomplice: How Design Emerges from Life Itself* (Cambridge, Mass.: Harvard University Press 2007).

75. *Homo abyssus,* p. 404. "In quo apparet quod tota operatio inferioris naturae

The connection between exemplarity *(completum et simplex)* and out-pouring *(non subsistens)* of *esse* not only sheds light on the relationship between form *(forma)* and *esse* but enables also a speculative interpretation of the *materia* as real pure potency *(potentia pura realis)*. Taken in isolation, *completum et simplex* or *non subsistens* alone must lead to an entitative interpretation of matter (matter as a "thing") because the superessentiality of *esse* is destroyed, the *informitas* of the *similitudo divinae bonitatis,* which is neither a *nihil negativum* nor a hypostasis.[76] As an "almost nothing" *(prope nihil),*[77] which doesn't exist by itself, the *materia prima* is the dimension of the transformability of bodily things, that which cannot be completely realized by any form.[78] Therefore it safeguards the possibility of change, the openness for future things to come, the openness for the ever richer being *(esse).* Like the *bonum* and its causality, which aim at that which is not yet, the *materia prima* is in a certain sense wider than being.[79] In consequence Aquinas can link the *informitas* of *materia prima* to the divine goodness.[80]

> The "emanatio totius esse," so to speak, keeps open the room for the emanation of a dimension of possibility, which is not essentially [*essentiell*] determined, even if it is not only the emanation of this nonessential dimension of possibility of being [*Sein*] to its concrete subsistence that reveals the superessentiality of being [*Sein*]! Also the subsistence of being [*Sein*] in pure essence, which means in pure spirit, stems from the superessentiality of participated being [*Sein*]. Nevertheless, being would not have been revealed in its final superessentiality if it only came to subsistence in pure spirit, because love has the diversity and multiplicity of being [*Seienden*] in mind, which result from the total givenness of being, the *emanatio totius esse.* Hence in the emanation of matter from being [*Sein*], the love of God revealed in the emanation of being itself is revealed in an unspeakable way. Therefore Thomas says: "Even if the spiritual nature has a higher rank than the corporal, the world in which there would be only spiritual natures would still not be better but less perfect."[81]

---

terminatur ad homines sicut ad perfectissimum" (*Quaestio disputata De anima*, a. 8 c.). From a modern perspective, see Simon Conway Morris, *Life's Solution: Inevitable Humans in a Lonely Universe* (New York: Cambridge University Press, 2003).

76. *Homo abyssus,* pp. 323-24.
77. *ST* I, q. 54, a. 3, *argumentum* 3.
78. Ibid., q. 66, a. 2, c.
79. *SCG* 2.20.
80. *In De div. nom.* 4.2.297.
81. *Homo abyssus,* p. 325. The quote at the end of the citation refers to *SCG* 3.136.

Martin Bieler

Matter, however, is not only the realm of possibility and diversity but also the realm of necessity, through which decisions of life and death are enacted, suffered, and enjoyed, the fulfillment of which we find in the Eucharist of Christ.[82] Thanks to *materia,* a special depth of outpouring into creation is possible.

Since the aim of creation is the giving of concrete substance through the *emanatio totius esse,* and since the highest form of being we know in our realm ("apud nos non subsistunt nisi composita")[83] is the human being, we have to understand creation, according to Ulrich, from within the framework of the relationship between absolute and human freedom. Ulrich is aware of the fact that *esse simpliciter est superior ad esse hominem,* but this does not mean that human freedom could not be the measure and the guideline for our understanding of the communication of *esse.*[84] His philosophy, like Balthasar's, is a meta-anthropology. But this is already the case for Aquinas, as can be seen in Aquinas's treatment of the transcendentals in *De ver.,* q. 1, a. 1.[85] From within the mentioned framework all dimensions of metaphysics take on a dialogical-personal meaning, and metaphysics proves to be the unfolding of the gift-character of being, which is imprinted in every aspect of creation.

Considered from the perspective of the relationship between God and human beings, the givenness of *esse* as *completum et simplex sed non subsistens* is something decided and willed by God.[86] Therefore *esse* is actually a likeness of the divine goodness *(similitudo divinae bonitatis),* an expression of God's love. But how do we gain access to this truth? For Ulrich it is decisive that the "movement" of the communication of being (not to be confused with *"motus,"* or "change," in Aquinas)[87] tends toward the giving of concrete *subsistence* to humans, and subsistence in turn implies *action.* This freedom in creatures is more than the mere *substantia rei,* which Ulrich calls their "reality," for it emphasizes their goodness and therefore testifies explicitly to the *similitudo divinae bonitatis.*[88]

82. *Homo abyssus,* pp. 328-34.
83. *ST* I, q. 3, a. 3, ad 1.
84. *Homo abyssus,* p. 359; *ST* III, q. 16, a. 9, ad 2.
85. *Homo abyssus,* pp. 235-88.
86. Ibid., pp. 41-44.
87. *In IV Sent.,* d. 1, q. 1, a. 4, 2 c.: "Motus autem non est ens completum, sed est via in ens."

88. *Homo abyssus,* pp. 96-168. Ulrich sees three aspects in the movement by *esse* into finite being: ideality, reality, and the aspect of the *bonum.*

IV. Subsistence and *Bonitas*

The whole range of the communication of *esse* — from God to finite composite beings — is expressed in the things of our world, in the *entia*. But in human beings the divinely willed character of *esse* is supposed to be explicitly accepted and affirmed by them.[89] The subsistence of beings is not without activity, or *operatio:* "Cum omnis res sit propter suam operationem."[90] This is true a fortiori for human beings, who have to use their freedom in order to become who they are. A fundamental *operatio* proper to the nature of human beings is their own affirmation of the communication of *esse*. Human beings have to receive their being in freedom, and by doing so, they confirm or consent to the divinely willed character of *esse* as truly given, and yet, as relative to God, as *completum et simplex sed non subsistens*. This consent and affirmation mark the difference between *bonum secundum quid* and *bonum simpliciter*.[91] Every being in this world is good insofar *(secundum quid)* as it is a creature of God. But only the free positive response to the communication of being *(esse)* is the *bonum simpliciter* at which this communication aims. The difference between *bonum secundum quid* and *bonum simpliciter* leaves open the room for evil in this world without revoking the goodness of creation, and it gives us the room we must have in order to really be free.[92]

The free reception of being as the loving response to the love of God makes the meaning of the *esse* as *completum et simplex sed non subsistens* accessible to us. Therefore the human being is what Ulrich calls the measure and guideline of creation.[93] The creation aims at this free reception, at this *bonum simpliciter,* in which the *similitude divinae bonitatis* is expressed explicitly in finite freedom. Ulrich emphasizes time and again that not the reality, the mere *substantia*, is the final aim of creation, but the *substantia* bring-

89. Ibid., pp. 36-37.
90. *ST* I, q. 105, a. 5, c.
91. *Homo abyssus*, p. 160; *ST* I, q. 5, a. 1, ad 1.
92. Martin Bieler, "Seinsmitteilung und Bonität," in *Das Sein als Gleichnis Gottes*, ed. Michael Schulz, pp. 164-69 (Freiburg: Verlag der Katholischen Akademie der Erzdiözese Freiburg, 2005).
93. Ulrich uses the word "Richte" to describe the status of human nature in creation (*Homo abyssus*, p. 295). "Richte" is the straight line one uses to straighten out things. "The human being contains in himself the whole dimension of the participation of being. It is his mandate to cosmically guard the movement of being [*Sein*] to become finite: in passing the test of the emptying of being [*im Bestehen der Entäusserung des Seins*], which means the ontological difference" (ibid.).

ing forth accidents: the *substantia* acting in freedom.[94] Far from being static, the analogy of being shows how being and action are inseparable.[95] Every aspect of metaphysics, every aspect of creation is an expression of the loving communication of being by the Creator aiming at the loving response of his creature. How could the drama of history not unfold from here? This kind of philosophy is particularly apt to relate to the grand narrative of the biblical tradition, and it has far-reaching consequences for understanding our world and for the discussion between different sciences.[96]

According to Ulrich, the confirmation of the communication of being has to be lived in the self-communication toward our fellow beings, in relating to another "thou." The substance develops through its accidents, in which it flows out and receives itself. This horizontal structure of the *substantia-accidentia* relation is the continuation of the communication of being.[97] By relating to the other in affirming him or her in love, we follow in the wake of the movement of the communication of being by which he or she is affirmed by God. Our affirmation is only a posteriori. "Though the being comes to its word 'through' the human being, [it does not come] from the human being."[98] By the affirmation of the other we follow the attraction of being toward mutual accord, or *convenientia,* and unite with the other as a "we."[99] By following this attraction, we agree to assume and realize what we are meant for by the Creator. He is therefore the *tertium inter nos* who enables the saving *quality* of our relationship with others and with ourselves.[100] It is truly by this kind of relationship that we return to our origin.[101]

In accordance with this insight, Ulrich develops in his work *Homo abyssus* an extensive analysis of the transcendentals and of human potencies as being structured according to the logic of the gift-character of being. He

---

94. Ibid., pp. 93, 153.

95. *SCG* 3.65: "Quia inquantum sunt, divinae bonitatis similitudinem gerunt." *ST* II-II, q. 34, a. 1, ad 3: "Omnia, inquantum sunt, tendunt in Dei similitudinem, qui est ipsum esse." *ST* I-II, q. 55, a. 2, ad 3: "Cum Dei substantia sit eius actio, summa assimilatio hominis ad Deum est secundum aliquam operationem." *ST* I-II, q. 18, a. 1, c.: "De ratione boni est ipsa plenitudo essendi."

96. I have tried to show this for the discussion between metaphysics and psychology in a forthcoming article: "Attachment Theory and Aquinas's Metaphysics of Creation."

97. *Homo abyssus,* pp. 158-63.

98. Ibid., p. 308.

99. *De ver.,* q. 1, a. 1; *ST* I-II, q. 29, a. 1, ad 1.

100. Ferdinand Ulrich, "Sein und Mitmensch," *Salzburger Jahrbuch für Philosophie* 19 (1974): 93-128; *Logo-Tokos* (Einsiedeln: Johannes Verlag, 2003), pp. 523-26.

101. *In De div. nom.* 4.11.450.

shows how in humans the relation between *esse* and *essentia* finds its representation in the relationship between man and woman, who — being equal in dignity as persons and in their nature — represent different aspects of the communication of being.[102] This difference testifies to the truth that we cannot find fulfillment in ourselves but only in the other, who is really different from us. Especially here it is true what Ulrich writes: "In the face of the human being, the mutual accord [*convenientia*] of beings has reached its last order and unity. Not in a general image of a human being, but in a concrete face of a concrete human being in her historicity."[103]

V. Metaphysics of Gift and Analogy

Ulrich's treatment of the *analogia entis* corresponds to the view expressed by Bernard Montagnes: "The structure of analogy and that of participation are rigorously parallel: they correspond to each other as the conceptual aspect and the real aspect of the unity of being."[104] The main focus for Ulrich lies, of course, on the correct understanding of *esse commune* as God's gift: "The analogy of being stands and falls with the movement of being [*Sein*] into the finite."[105]

The intricate question of analogy in Ulrich's book does not become clear unless one knows the starting point from which he is reasoning. Otherwise one gets lost in a maze of technicalities. Already in *Homo abyssus* Ulrich puts the central reality of the relation between giver and gift in the foreground.[106] In his book *Leben in der Einheit von Leben und Tod,* he develops explicitly the structure of this relationship, the logic of giving, which also stands behind the reality of the participation of being. In a small but decisive

102. *Homo abyssus*, pp. 406-12; *Der Mensch als Anfang. Zur philosophischen Anthropologie der Kindheit* (Einsiedeln: Johannes Verlag, 1970), pp. 47ff.

103. *Homo abyssus*, p. 293.

104. Montagnes, *The Doctrine of the Analogy of Being according to Thomas Aquinas*, p. 91. Montagnes offers a very comprehensive and concise presentation of Aquinas's view and is systematically more satisfying than the lengthy study by Hampus Lyttkens, *The Analogy between God and the World: An Investigation of Its Background and Interpretation of Its Use by Thomas of Aquino*, trans. Axel Poignant (Uppsala: Almqvist & Wiksells, 1952). See also Geiger, *La participation dans la philosophie de S. Thomas d'Aquin*, p. 318: "Le fondement ontologique de l'analogie est la participation. L'analogie est la logique, plus précisément, une partie de la logique de la participation."

105. *Homo abyssus*, p. 224.

106. Ibid., pp. 52, 128.

section of this book, Ulrich describes "the giver and the gift of being [*Sein*] in the unity of life and death."[107] First he treats the exemplary unity of giver and gift: The deeper a gift comes from within the heart of the giver, the deeper is the exemplary unity of the two. The giver is then really *present* in his gift.[108] The *life* of the giver is present in his gift.[109] But this life is accessible for the receiver of the gift only if the giver *separates* the gift from himself, if the giver is ready to die the *death* of pouring himself out, or expending himself on behalf of the other.[110] Ulrich can use different terms in order to describe this phenomenon: presence and separation, richness and poverty, life and death. All these terms are meant to render transparent the wholeness of being as *completum et simplex* ("life") and the nonsubsistence of being ("death"), but they are also transparent to the one who gave his life on the cross as the one who has life in himself (John 5:26). Presence and separation include each other, for only by separation is the presence for the other realized. Only if the giver himself is present in the gift does the separation of the gift carry something valuable across to the other. True giving is always both: presence and separation, presence *through* separation.[111]

When the communication of *esse* is seen in the context of the logic of giving, it becomes apparent how Aquinas can state that analogy is the adequate expression of the relationship between Creator and creature. Geiger has shown that there are two different kinds of participation in Aquinas, a "participation by similitude" and a "participation by composition."[112] The participation by composition implies the duality of a receiver and something received. If the receiver limits what he or she receives by his or her nature, the limitation of the received element is due to the composition of receiver and received. In the participation by similitude, in contrast, the limitation of the participated reality is grounded in a formal inequality between similar natures, in a difference in nature that precedes the composi-

---

107. *Leben in der Einheit von Leben und Tod,* p. 70.

108. Ibid., pp. 70-71.

109. Ulrich often refers to *SCG* 4.11 for this presence.

110. This "separation" is not self-annihilation but self-affirmation: I reach out to the other *by* saying "yes" to myself.

111. When Balthasar, who was talking with Ulrich on these issues, speaks in volume 3 of his *Theodramatik* (Einsiedeln: Johannes Verlag, 1980), pp. 297-305, about the separation between Father and Son — even to the point of a kenosis — as a presupposition for the possibility of the cross, we should not think first of all of a separation *from* the other, but of a separation *toward* the other. Only then the separation from the other can be understood not as an estrangement but as a positive letting be of the other, which connects with the other.

112. Geiger, *La participation dans la philosophie de S. Thomas d'Aquin,* pp. 26-38.

tion.[113] The composition has to follow the inequality of nature if *esse* is supposed to be received by a finite subject. However, if the similarity of natures is lost, there can be no genuine reception of *esse* through composition. Both forms are interconnected, and they both are indispensable aspects of the communication of *esse*. If one of the aspects is given up, the analogy is destroyed. If there was only a *participatio per similitudinem*, the result would be univocation. If there was only a *participatio per compositionem*, the result would be equivocation — that is to say, God would be rendered unintelligible. Ulrich connects this with his understanding of *esse:* The aspect of univocation in metaphysical thinking corresponds to the overemphasis of the *completum et simplex,* whereas the overemphasis of the *non subsistens* of *esse* leads to equivocation. The *modus medius* of analogy is reached only if one maintains the unity of the *completum et simplex* with the *non subsistens,* of presence and separation.[114]

Ulrich cites the following text of Aquinas in order to characterize thinking based upon univocation, equivocation, and analogy: "Aliter dividitur aequivocum, analogum et univocum. *Aequivocum* enim dividitur *secundum res significatas, univocum* vero dividitur *secundum diversas differentias,* sed *analogum* dividitur *secundum diversos modos*" (emphasis added by Ulrich).[115] In univocation things are divided "according to diverse *differences*" because there is in the univocal thinking a commonality according to a shared nature, a "communitas secundum rationem naturae."[116] This would mean that Creator and creature would share the same nature, because the creature would be a mere extension of the Creator, who would not be ready to *separate* the gift from the receiver. Equivocal thinking, in contrast, divides "according to the things signified," because here the beings are only divided, cut-away pieces from the Creator, into which the Creator has not invested himself. The *completum et simplex,* the fullness of being, is lost and the giver is not present in being.[117] Only analogy is the true expression of the givenness of *esse,* because in analogy the *completum et simplex* and the *non*

113. Ibid., pp. 26-29.
114. *Homo abyssus,* pp. 216-17.
115. Ibid., 217. See *In I Sent.,* d. 22, q. 1, a. 3, ad 2.
116. *Homo abyssus,* pp. 219-20. "In processione creaturarum, ipsa divina Essentia non communicatur creaturis procedentibus, sed remanet incommunicata seu imparticipata; sed similitudo eius, per ea quae dat creaturis, in creaturis propagatur et multiplicatur et sic Divinitas per sui similitudinem non per essentiam, in creaturis procedit" (*In De div. nom.* 2.3.158).
117. *Homo abyssus,* p. 219. Ulrich cites *In I Sent.,* d. 3, q. 5, a. 1, ad 4.

subsistens of *esse* are saved at the same time: Analogy shows that *esse* is fully present inside the limits of *ens,* because *esse* is poured out *(non subsistens)* without loosing its unity *(completum et simplex).* So in analogy the individual appears as a mode of being ("secundum diversos modos") to whom the gift of being *(esse)* is really given.

The true givenness of *esse* excludes a (pre-)determined outpouring of the Creator toward the creature *(excessus determinatus)* through which the creature could determine God's nature by drawing — in a Hegelian manner — a straight line from the infinite to the finite and in reverse. The metaphysics of *esse* should not be mistaken for Hegel's attempt to tie together the absolute and the finite in a way that destroys the difference between God and the world: "The 'pure mediation' [sc. "esse," MB] can never be determined as the speculative turning point of a mediation of the finite into the infinite. It is not the 'metaphysical joint,' in which the absolute and the finite are bound together."[118] Only univocal thinking could offer such a direct road to the absolute. But this would also imply that nothing is given by God. In the context of the gift of being it might appear that univocation expresses the idea that *everything* is given, whereas equivocation would express the thought that *nothing* is given. As the middle way, analogy would express the idea that at least *something* is given. But in reality the univocal as well as the equivocal construal of being would mean that nothing is given. The univocal would mean that finite being is only a mere extension of absolute being and no reality "on its own" (lack of the separation of the gift with respect to the receiver), whereas the equivocal would mean that absolute being in no way reaches finite being (lack of the presence of the giver in the gift). In contrast to this, the analogy of being shows how *truly everything* is given (presence of the giver in the gift through loving separation of the gift with respect to the receiver).

The impossibility of a (pre-)determined outpouring of the Creator to the creature also excludes a simple *analogia proportionis* in which each pole can be determined by the other, for no creature can determine the divine perfection.[119]

---

118. *Homo abyssus,* pp. 224-25. See also Montagnes, *The Doctrine of the Analogy of Being,* p. 71, who puts it very well: "In the same way, on the transcendental level, being does not encompass both beings and God, since being is not prior to God. It is God who grounds the analogy of being, since beings receive by participation what He is by essence; there is no primary instance of being other than He."

119. But see the comment by Montagnes, who shows that Aquinas knows a narrow and a wide use of "proportio," so as to allow a legitimate use of "proportio" for the characterization of the relation between Creator and creature *(causa ad causatum) (The Doctrine of the Analogy of Being,* p. 76).

Only an *analogia proportionalitatis* that refers all beings back to God by corresponding to the real distinction between *esse* and *essentia* in creatures allows for a genuine analogy between creation and God. The *analogia proportionalitatis* particularly respects the nonsubsistence of *esse*. But this also means that an isolated *analogia proportionalitatis* is in danger of neglecting the *completum et simplex* of *esse*, the real subsistence of creatures by virtue of their *esse*. Therefore the *analogia proportionalitatis* has to be combined with an *analogia attributionis* that gives due expression to the *completum et simplex*. As Ulrich says, the *analogia attributionis* is fulfilled in the *analogia proportionalitatis* because *esse* as *completum et simplex* is only in beings by its nonsubsistence.[120]

VI. *Analogia Entis* and *Analogia Fidei*

Ferdinand Ulrich is a devout Christian who wrote not only a book on prayer but also a long interpretation of the parable of the lost son (Luke 15:11-32).[121] He is familiar with trinitarian speculations, the theology of the cross, and Mariology as well. So it is no surprise that Ulrich offers some reflections as a philosopher on the relationship between the metaphysics of *esse (analogia entis)* and the likeness between the world and God unveiled in faith (the *analogia fidei*). Already the weight of the theme of temptation in his thinking shows how aware Ulrich is of our status as fallen creatures. He knows that this status does have a profound impact on our philosophy *and* theology. And he knows that we can endure the temptations in this state only by the help of God's grace. Therefore he consciously relates as a philosopher to the gospel of Christ and to theology. He does not shy away from utterances that most of his colleagues in today's universities would consider totally embarrassing. He mentions, for example, the mother of Jesus in an interpretation of Hegel in order to elucidate a philosophical issue with a Mariological thought.[122]

120. *Homo abyssus,* p. 231. In reverse, Ulrich can formulate from the side of participation that the *participatio per compositionem* is contained [*aufgehoben*] in the *participatio per similitudinem* (ibid., p. 130). Cornelio Fabro also sees the necessity of a connection between *analogy attributionis* and *analogia proportionalitatis* (*Participation et causalité selon S. Thomas d'Aquin* [Paris: Béatrice-Nauwelaerts; Louvain: Publications Universitaires, 1961], pp. 510-35).

121. *Gebet als geschöpflicher Grundakt* (Einsiedeln: Johannes Verlag, 1973); *Gabe und Vergebung* (Einsiedeln: Johannes Verlag, 2007).

122. See, for example, Ferdinand Ulrich, "Hegel und die Frage nach der reinen Endlichkeit," *Theorein,* 1972, pp. 65-97.

One might therefore suspect that he is trying to instrumentalize philosophy for religious purposes — by which the difference between the *analogia entis* and the *analogia fidei* would be dangerously blurred. One may also suspect, however, that he is trying unduly to turn theology into philosophy. But Ulrich keeps the *analogia entis* and the *analogia fidei* distinct and connects them with each other in a helpful way. He even dares to challenge theology from a philosophical point of view (an action that should not be alien to theology) when he states that theology must be subject to speculative measurement based upon the ontological difference between *ens* and *esse*.[123] This is not erroneous because we do not have two different Gods in creation and redemption, although God shows himself differently in both realms, and redemption as re-creation is a greater work than creation.

Ulrich also knows the other side of the coin: Philosophy must open itself up toward theology and receive its own fulfillment from God's revelation in Christ.[124] Philosophy can see that the difference between God and the world must be somehow contained in God *as a difference,* if the unity of God should not be destroyed by the difference between Creator and creature.[125] Philosophy can in no way anticipate God as Trinity, as he revealed himself in Christ. But once God is revealed in this way, it helps philosophy to maintain the unity of its vision of created being as *completum et simplex sed non subsistens* instead of yielding to the temptation — out of angst — to close the gap between the finite and the absolute in a move toward univocation, which then must be counterbalanced by equivocation.[126] The latter possibility leads to a dialectics between God and the world that seems to safeguard the freedom of both. However, it is actually only the oscillating suspension of the right awareness concerning the divinely willed character of *esse* as gift, and it reflects a conscious or unconscious attempt to keep God away from the world and to deliver him to the world at the same time. In this move philosophy becomes pseudotheology instead of sticking to its own

---

123. *Homo abyssus,* p. 81. He mentions this in the discussion of the incarnation of the Son of God, who cannot fall from heaven like a meteorite but has to come from above by coming from us according to the resulting of *the act of being,* from the principles of the thing *(res),* as Aquinas puts it. See n. 72 above.

124. *Homo abyssus,* pp. 110-11.

125. Ibid., pp. 42, 56, 317, 412.

126. Ibid., p. 168: "The passing of the test [*Bestehen*] of the phases of the move of being to the finite, in which neither the setting of essence over against superessential being is played out nor being as being is hypostasized against the essence, has its last condition of possibility in the abyssal unity and difference of person and nature in God experienced in faith."

formal object.[127] German Idealism is such a turn of philosophy into pseudotheology — starting with Immanuel Kant — which in the end leads to a powerless eternal Father unable to express himself.[128] (The implicit or explicit understanding of the Son and the Spirit are affected by this deformation of philosophy as well.)[129]

Ulrich strongly emphasizes that grace comes to us "along the pathway of being [*auf dem Weg des Seins*]," as is radically shown by the eternal Son becoming a human being.[130] Therefore it is impossible to ignore the philosophical *analogia entis* when we talk of grace and the *analogia fidei*. The movement into the finite by *esse* has as its most perfect theme the gift of existence to the human being. This gift in turn is recapitulated in Christ. And philosophy has to surpass itself by moving into this dimension, into this "medium and root of all analogy."[131] But this does not mean that the ontological difference between *ens* and *esse* is closed and replaced by grace. The ontological difference is, on the contrary, confirmed by grace and gains by it a depth never known before.[132]

127. Ibid., pp. 112, 207, 233. The suspension oscillates between the isolated elements of the broken unity: "completum et simplex" in the sense of univocity and "non subsistens" in the sense of equivocity.

128. Ibid., pp. 57-60, 179, 206-8, 273, 336, 358.

129. Ibid., pp. 60, 206, 336, 410-12.

130. Ibid., p. 93: "We must always keep in mind, that the grace of God received in faith is not experienced beyond being [*jenseits des Seins*] but 'along the pathway of being.'" See also ibid., pp. 111, 172, 180.

131. Ibid., pp. 232-33.

132. Ibid., pp. 112-22.

PART IV

THE ANALOGY OF BEING AND THE RENEWAL OF CONTEMPORARY THEOLOGY

CHAPTER 10

Creation as Aesthetic Analogy

Michael Hanby

I. *Analogia et Creatio Convertuntur:*
Analogy, Science, and the Recovery of Creation

I begin this essay in a sort of *via negativa,* specifying what I do not intend to do in order to circumscribe my actual, positive concerns. It is not my intention here to engage, at least directly, in the usual polemics and controversies surrounding the *analogia entis,* be they the controverted points at issue between Barth and Balthasar or the contested question of whether, in fact, an ontological doctrine of analogy can even be found in St. Thomas, though I would concur with Reinhard Hütter and others in this volume who claim that it can. Nor is it my intention to offer a detailed explication of this doctrine, whether in a strictly Thomist, Przywarean, or Balthasarian vein. Others in this volume are undoubtedly doing this much better than I can.

Instead I wish in the first place simply to take for granted what Balthasar claims in *The Theology of Karl Barth,* namely, that the entire point of the doctrine of *analogia entis* is to insist upon and protect the infinite difference between God and the world;[1] to note, in the second place, that this is also the first logical function of the doctrine of creation *ex nihilo* demanded by a coherent and orthodox doctrine of God;[2] and to acknowledge in the

---

1. Hans Urs von Balthasar, *The Theology of Karl Barth,* trans. Edward Oakes (San Francisco: Ignatius Press, 1992), p. 50.
2. I note the "logical" function of creation, or the function of creation in the order of

third place that it is by virtue of this infinite difference from the world that God is able be intimate and immanently present within the world — superlatively and paradigmatically in Christ. I also wish to assert, with both St. Thomas and Balthasar, that this negative or apophatic function itself, and indeed God's infinite surpassing of the world, can be secured only by affirming kataphatically the supereminence of the divine perfections after the fashion of the Areopagite and insisting on the world's goodness "in its own right" as something other to and different from God and thus somehow "like God" in and through this very difference. It is the hypostatic union in Christ, whose incarnation, passion, and resurrection discloses God's judgment of the world as the fruit and object of love, that fully discloses this difference, generating a revolution in thought. This is my final point of assertion. Étienne Gilson argues that "the ancient philosophers, in fact, never succeed in conceiving of a production of things complete and integral not only as to their order and their form, but also as to their being; so they taxed their ingenuity to assign to them a form of production from some principle both different from themselves and other than the void."[3] David Bentley Hart perhaps goes even further, contending in this volume and elsewhere that the claim animating the trinitarian and Christological debates of the third and fourth century — a claim that was scarcely intelligible in the terms of Greek metaphysics — allowed this difference and thus allowed genuine divine transcendence to appear to thought for the first time.[4] For entailed in the claim that Christ is at once very God and very man without admixture, blending, or diminution was not only an acknowledgment of the full divinity of the second hypostasis of the Trinity but a transcendence so radical as to include reflexivity and reciprocity within itself and the capacity for intimate relation to what is not itself, without losing its own otherness or dialectically negating the world.[5] David L. Schindler puts the Christological point very well, "Thus the mutuality of God-centeredness and world-centeredness means that the world's (destined) ever-greater union with God coincides

---

reason, in order to distinguish my meaning both from its strictly theological function (in the order of revelation) and from its historical development, from which the logical function is at least somewhat independent.

3. Étienne Gilson, *The Philosophy of St. Bonaventure,* trans. Dom Illtyd Trethowan and Frank J. Sheed (Paterson, N.J.: St. Anthony Guild Press, 1969), p. 168.

4. David Hart, *The Beauty of the Infinite: The Aesthetics of Christian Truth* (Grand Rapids: Eerdmans, 2003), pp. 179-249.

5. See, for example, Ps.-Dionysius, *The Divine Names* 712A-713A, in *Pseudo-Dionysius: The Complete Works,* trans. Colm Luibheid (New York: Paulist Press, 1987), pp. 82-83.

with, even as it provides the anterior condition for, the world's ever-deeper integrity as world."[6]

So far as I can gather, all that Przywara himself says about the need for a "creaturely metaphysics" that is neither a priori nor a posteriori, and yet somehow also both at once — a metaphysics of the "suspended middle" operating within the license St. Thomas grants to "philosophical theology" and undertaken "groundlessly," as it were, from within this surpassing difference — simultaneously stems from and points toward this basic understanding of the demands of creation, even though it is not simply deduced from this understanding.[7]

Assuming, then, that analogy names "the ontological relation that obtains between God and creation" manifest without parallel in Christ and drawing rather impressionistically upon St. Thomas, Przywara, and Balthasar (and Aristotle too, for that matter), I would like to indicate how I think a recovery of analogy as the form of Christian metaphysics and the form of the God-world relation might assist in recovering a conception of creation that is neither fideistic nor rationalistic, but one that mediates "aesthetically" between these untenable extremes.[8] That is, I wish to suggest first that analogy is indispensable to recovering a notion of creation as a claim about the surpassing difference of God as ever greater and wholly other. Second, I wish to suggest that analogy is therefore indispensable to recovering creation as a claim about the true meaning of the world. And finally, I maintain that this notion of creation so understood can claim at least theoretical credibility in a world still firmly in the grips of scientific positivism and a corresponding "technologism" — the "sick blindness," as Balthasar puts it, that is the very death of philosophical wonder and that "arises from regarding reality as raising no questions, being 'just there.'"[9] Of course the qualifier "theoretical" is crucial here. The odds of theology's reinstatement as queen

---

6. David L. Schindler, "Trinity, Creation, and the Order of Intelligence in the Modern Academy," *Communio* 28 (Fall 2001): 408.

7. All references to Przywara are from the forthcoming translation by David Bentley Hart and John Betz, who graciously allowed me to see the unfinished manuscript prior to the conference that occasioned this volume. I regret that for this reason the references cannot be more exact.

8. On Balthasar's conception of the *analogia entis,* see Nicholas J. Healy, *The Eschatology of Hans Urs von Balthasar: Being as Communion* (Oxford: Oxford University Press, 2005), pp. 19-90.

9. Hans Urs von Balthasar, *Theo-Drama,* vol. 2, *Dramatis Personae: Man in God,* trans. Graham Harrison (San Francisco: Ignatius Press, 1990), p. 286.

of the sciences are, shall we say, rather slim. There is a great deal at stake in our remaining barbarous.

That this credibility is all but lost, that it is no longer clear just what if anything "creation" adds to our knowledge of the world as such, I take to be self-evident. This is true, however, not only for scientific positivism but for much of modern theology, which, in full retreat from the "success" of science, has largely forsaken the metaphysical and cosmological ambitions characteristic of the Fathers. Henri de Lubac claimed that the "pure nature" posited by some neoscholastics, instituted in order to protect the gratuity of grace, had the opposite effect of rendering grace "accidental" to the meaning of the world in both the scholastic and the ordinary sense.[10] And more recently, (then Cardinal) Ratzinger has lamented "the practical abandonment of creation in influential modern theology," claiming that with the frequent "existential reduction of the creation theme, there occurs a huge (if not a total) loss of the reality of the faith, whose God no longer has anything to do with matter" — a loss, he makes clear, that takes the world in train.[11]

Though de Lubac was obviously preoccupied with preconciliar Catholic theology, his concern that heroic attempts to secure the gratuity of the supernatural result ironically in its exile seems to apply perforce on the Protestant side to the commanding Christocentrism of Barth's theology and its suggestion that creation exists simply, even instrumentally, for the sake of redemption.[12] This is of course not to deny the Christological center of cre-

---

10. "People took hasty flight to what seemed the 'safest' position, and felt that they thereby possessed dogmatic truth in peace. But by this over-simple method of preserving the gratuitousness of the supernatural order, they were, to put it mildly, lessening its meaning. They were making it not merely an 'accident' in the scholastic sense — which is understandable — but in the ordinary sense, and therefore, one must admit, something superficial. It followed inevitably that man could not only have managed quite well without it, but that even now he could with impunity disregard it. It was deprived of any hold on human thinking or human existence. Christian thought was thus bounded by a narrow circle, in a quiet backwater of the intellectual universe, where it could only waste away. By the good offices of some of its exponents, who were aiming to preserve its transcendence, it became merely an 'exile.'" Thus, de Lubac concludes, "here lies one of the deepest roots of all that is negative in modern secularization" (Henri de Lubac, *The Mystery of the Supernatural,* trans. Rosemary Sheed [New York: Crossroad Herder, 1999], pp. 177-78).

11. Joseph Cardinal Ratzinger, *"In the Beginning . . .": A Catholic Understanding of the Story of Creation and the Fall,* trans. Boniface Ramsey (Grand Rapids: Eerdmans, 1995), pp. x, xii, 100.

12. See, for example, Barth, *Church Dogmatics* III/1, trans. G. W. Bromiley and T. F. Torrance (London: T. & T. Clark; New York: Continuum, 2004), p. 18. "He it is for whose

ation; that creation and covenant, as Barth says, do indeed belong to each other.[13] Nor do I pretend to offer a summary interpretation, much less a dismissal, of Barth's theology. Yet it can hardly be denied that the way in which Barth viewed creation, apart from an avowal of faith and explicit reference to redemption in Christ, was inherently vulnerable to conceptions of nature that condition and delimit revelation, and ultimately divine sovereignty, a priori. Nor can it be denied that Protestant thought in Barth's wake has tended to subordinate creation to redemption and to regard the assertion of the "in-itselfness" of creation, in distinction from redemption, as tantamount to a "separation" that grants creation independence and relegates redemption to a marginal realm. It is worth asking whether such assumptions, in their logic and not their intent, effectively deny the real difference between God and the world and undercut the grounds for a truly adequate — and adequately revolutionary — Christocentrism. For inasmuch as creation is subordinated without remainder to redemption, inasmuch as creation is denied the integrity of having being-in-itself, anything theology says to the world will appear to it as fideistic and moralistic and thus accidental and irrelevant to the world's own meaning.

Again, I will leave it to others in this volume to take up the finer points of these dogmatic controversies. It is rather my intent in this essay to address these concerns more to science or at least to the metaphysics of science than to philosophy or theology per se. My justification in doing so should be self-evident. In the first place, I have already noted the seemingly unshakable grip that scientific positivism and technologism maintain upon Western culture and imagination. In the second place, one might well argue that these and other theological controversies of recent vintage are themselves subtly occasioned in part by the advance of this outlook, though this would require a detailed consideration of how theology itself has been conditioned by the "Copernican turn," the separation of faith, philosophy, and the sciences, and the institutionalization of this schism in the guild divisions of the modern academy, where theology finds an uneasy home.[14] Could the notion of pure nature in a dialectical relation to grace have ever taken hold, had Cartesian man not been invented to complement Galileo's cosmos, which

---

sake God loved man from eternity and for whose sake He willed and as the Creator gave reality to the existence and being of man as this creature on earth and under heaven."

13. Ibid., p. 48.

14. For an important meditation on this subject, see Hans Urs von Balthasar, "Theology and Sanctity," in *The Word Made Flesh*, vol. 1, *Explorations in Theology*, trans. A. V. Littledale and A. Dru (San Francisco: Ignatius Press, 1989), pp. 181-209.

had already rendered theology extraneous and redundant?[15] Does the very conception of theology enunciated at the outset of the *Church Dogmatics* — not as "a link in an ordered cosmos, but only as a stop-gap in a disordered cosmos"[16] — where theology exists as an "emergency measure" alongside other sciences, seemingly indifferent to their axioms and methods, not preserve some trace of this Copernican turn?[17]

In any event, conventional ways of separating philosophy, theology,

---

15. See de Lubac, *The Mystery of the Supernatural*, pp. 179, 222-38.

16. Barth, *CD* I/1, p. 10.

17. Ibid., p. 7. The central problem, so John Milbank contends, consists not in Barth's assigning theology "emergency status" but, first, in the way theology's relation to the sciences is conditioned by Barth's very conception of the theological task as "measur[ing] . . . its talk about God against its being as the church" and, secondly, in the way Barth's differentiation of the sciences by object precludes a genuine theological critique of the science's axioms and methods. This is effectively denied in the citation from the main text, and one can speculate that Barth would have to preclude this possibility because allowing it would require the mediation of something like the *analogia entis*. To the extent that "all sciences might be theology" (p. 7), this is presumably because the other sciences in principle might be capable of performing this task within their own domains. Thus Milbank contends, "What is lacking here is an older understanding of Christ as restoring us to participation in the mind of God: thus Christ *himself as theologic (logos),* not the 'object' of theology. Theology is *not* positive knowledge of an object, but finite intimation of infinite understanding. (Barth grasps, indeed, that God is not an object, yet only in a post-Kantian manner which confines God in himself to a formally known and uncharacterisable source; inversely, when God is shown, it is in the realm of objects which are in no sense transparent to Being as Being, the ground of the objective.) Hence, indeed, as Barth says, theology is no special science, but the perspective to which all disciplines are orientated. However, since this is an all-inclusive (but not fully graspable) perspective, not just one perspective among many, other disciplines, especially philosophy, would become theological when they were *utterly transfigured,* when the infinite transformed their sense of their finite objects and methods, and in ever unpredictable ways. They would not become theological through applying their perspectives to Christ-as-object: here Barth reveals himself as thoroughly late-scholastic, thoroughly positivist, thoroughly muscle-bound by the constricting 'professional' norms of theology faculties." I would wish to draw certain qualifications omitted by Milbank about the nature of both theology and the sciences. With regard to the former there is more to say, consonant with a proper construal of the grace-nature distinction, about how theology both is and is not "a link within an ordered cosmos." With regard to the latter, it would be necessary to show how the sciences become more properly scientific (and to that extent, *autonomos*) to the extent they become more theological in Milbank's sense, but otherwise Milbank's criticism seems more or less on target. See Milbank, "Knowledge: The Theological Critique of Philosophy in Hamann and Jacobi," in *Radical Orthodoxy: A New Theology,* ed. John Milbank, Catherine Pickstock, and Graham Ward (London: Routledge, 1999), p. 33, n. 1.

and the sciences are finally somewhat dubious anyway, as modern science from its very inception usurped the prerogatives of philosophy (as well as theology) and continues to remake philosophy (as well as theology) even now. This is not to minimize the complexity of their interrelation, and it would be silly and unmeaning to deny the stunning success of modern science in opening to view aspects of the world's truth that would otherwise remain hidden. I would certainly wish to uphold distinctions, moreover, between science and metaphysics, further distinctions between modern and premodern science, as well as distinctions between the various modern sciences and, within the practice of modern science, between relatively more theoretical and more practical applications.[18] From the claim that metaphysical and theological judgments are inherent in all scientific theorizing, whether in the act of cognition formally considered or in the various sciences' conceptions of their objects and methods, it does not follow that these judgments are univocally operative *in the same way* in all the sciences, irrespective of whether the scientific enterprise is in what Mikael Stenmark calls the problem-stating, development, justification, or application phases.[19]

These qualifications notwithstanding, however, I would nevertheless insist with Aristotle that science by whatever definition — beginning in principle from preexistent, nonscientific knowledge, whose truths remain operative within the science from beginning to end — is inexorably and constitutively related to metaphysics and theology.[20] That is, I wish to reassert the increasingly commonplace observation that science cannot do without and indeed never does without a metaphysics, and therefore ultimately a theology, whose axioms with respect to being, time, space, matter, motion,

---

18. The work of Mikael Stenmark, which can be seen as an attempt to improve upon the groundbreaking work of Ian Barbour in this field, is helpful in focusing our attention on the complex ways in which science as practiced "interacts" in its various phases with "religion," noting that this "interaction" differs depending upon whether we are referring to science in its "problem-stating phase," its "development phase," its "justification phase," or its "application phase." This is fair enough and to be born in mind in any material engagement with science, but in my estimation this project is nevertheless destined to fall short from the outset, even when it recognizes the implicit metaphysical commitments of modern naturalism, because it regards the question of the relation between science and religion as a (neutral) methodological question rather than a metaphysical one, thus betraying a metaphysics of its own, which negatively prejudices the project in advance. See Stenmark, *How to Relate Science and Religion: A Multidimensional Model* (Grand Rapids: Eerdmans, 2001), pp. 209-50.

19. Ibid., p. 215.

20. Aristotle, *Post. anal.* 1.77a25ff., 99b15ff.; *Meta.* 4.1005b–1006a29.

truth, knowledge, and ultimately God are more than simply "presupposed" at the boundaries of the science, where they can be bracketed in the name of methodological purity but, like Aristotle's principle of noncontradiction, are operative throughout. This last qualification is important, because there remains a pervasive temptation to treat the question of the relation between science and theology as a matter of each keeping its proper limits. It is then assumed that reductionism and other problems associated with scientific positivism could be avoided "were it recognized that science does not claim to exhaust the intelligibility of an object in the integrity of its existing being: were physics or biology, for example, to remain just physics or biology and not venture onto the terrain of philosophy or theology."[21] Whereas David L. Schindler has shown in an important article that while there is a real and legitimate distinction between theology and science and therefore an important sense in which this is true, it is not sufficient, inasmuch as it fails to attend to the nature of abstraction and therefore of limit, which always carries within it a tacit relation to what lies just beyond it and thus, ultimately, to God.[22] In other words, a philosophical — and ultimately theological — ontology is implicit and operative within the most mundane act of scientific abstraction.

> Abstractions and distinctions, which involve separating x or pulling it out or excluding from the web of relations to non-x that characterize x's concrete existence at any moment, necessarily evoke the notion of limit: of a boundary that sets x off from non-x. This idea of limit, even if intended to be only disciplinary in nature, will inevitably carry some tacit conception of what (non-x) lies beyond the limit of x: some tacit conception of the relation of x to non-x, and so far some conception also of both x and non-x. The idea of limit presupposed in any abstraction of x from non-x will imply x in a way that makes a difference already from within the limit that constitutes x relative to the (possible) existence and nature of God and a universe of beings under God (non-x): in a word some ontology of creation.[23]

21. David L. Schindler, "The Given as Gift: Creation and Disciplinary Abstraction in Science," in "Ordering Love" (forthcoming), p. 1

22. Wittgenstein had once made a similar remark in a quite different context: "Insofar as people think they can see 'the limits of understanding,' they believe of course that they can see beyond these" (*Culture and Value*, trans. Peter Winch [Chicago: University of Chicago Press, 1975], p. 15).

23. Schindler, "The Given as Gift."

Relation to God (as Augustine realized) is inherent in the most primitive act of cognition, a claim that is at once philosophical, theological, and historical. The claim for this necessary and inexorable relation is philosophical inasmuch as the very act of making distinctions or abstractions formally entails this relation to being as such and therefore to God (though it remains to be seen how being as such — *esse* — entails relation to God). Moreover, this relation can be seen to hold both "subjectively" with respect to the act and "objectively" of the cognized as it appears to thought distinct from the order in which it is always concretely located, and though I intend to confine my comments mostly to this latter aspect,[24] this way of putting the matter should not be taken as an endorsement of any "strong" subject-object dualism, itself the consequence of abstraction badly conceived.

The claim also follows theologically from an adequate understanding of creation. Viewed theologically, thought's inherent relation to God is but an aspect of the world's real relation to God (though again one need not be thinking theologically to see this relation). Inasmuch as the world is inexorably and constitutively related to God, such that this relation is implicated in all its dimensions as world, science is inexorably and constitutively related to theology.

What is true of thought and being we should expect to see in time, and so science's inexorable relationship to theology is a historical claim evidenced by the actual history of modern science, which was intimately bound up from the outset with changed metaphysical and theological understandings. It is not only that theology has been profoundly conditioned by the original Copernican turn; it is that this turn is intimately bound up with deviations from sound theology.[25]

24. With respect to the "subjective" pole of this distinction, see Schindler, "The Given as Gift," and Michael Hanby, "These Three Abide: Augustine and the Eschatological Non-obsolescence of Faith," *Pro Ecclesia* 14 (2005): 340-60, though the latter would require some revision to deal directly and fully with the point at issue.

25. Much good work has been done in recent years exploring the (sometimes) latent theology of seventeenth-century natural philosophy. Among the numerous examples, see Amos Funkenstein, *Theology and the Scientific Imagination: From the Middle Ages to the Seventeenth Century* (Princeton: Princeton University Press, 1986); Simon Oliver, *Philosophy, God, and Motion* (London: Routledge, 2005). What is true of modern science in general, that it is constitutively and inexorably related to theology, is especially true of Darwinian biology in particular, as it appropriates the Newtonian paradigm of explanation and systems dynamics and constitutes itself in opposition to the natural theology paradigmatically represented by William Paley. In appropriating Paley's mechanical conception of organisms and "adaptation" as the defining problem of biological explanation, Darwinian evolutionary bi-

Michael Hanby

The question, then, is not *whether metaphysics* but rather *what metaphysics* is adequate to the actual ontological situation in which science actually commences and what metaphysics can actually protect science's true nature and genuine achievements. I wish to suggest that the *analogia entis,* as the metaphysics adequate to a coherent doctrine of creation, not only can restore the credibility of this doctrine but in "saving the appearances" can perform this latter service as well, though it should be obvious from our brief excursus on abstraction in science that this will also mean recuperating more expansive notions of reason and truth, as indeed Pope Benedict XVI has been arguing, which take into account the implicit reference to God in every act of cognition, the "subjective" entailment of desire (and faith) in knowledge, and their "objective" correlate in the convertibility of beauty, goodness, truth, and unity in the transcendental attributes of being.[26]

Finally, I take it as no less evident that recovery of a meaningful doctrine of creation is *at least* as urgent, for example, as pinning down the precise position of St. Thomas relative to modern doctrines of "analogy," worthy and crucial though this is. It is surely no accident that the loss of a credible understanding of the world as creation and the doctrine of God entailed in it has been accompanied by a crisis of intelligibility that now besets every facet of contemporary life. Just as it is no longer clear what if anything "creation" could add to our knowledge of the world as such, so it is no longer clear what if anything it means to be a human being *as such* — a notion in-

---

ology appropriates important metaphysical and theological predecisions discussed below, and even offers in natural selection what is arguably a secularized providence in conformity with those predecisions. This is especially and ironically true of professional atheists and neo-Darwinian apologists, such as Richard Dawkins, who imagine themselves to be free of theological contamination. See, for example, Dawkins, *The Blind Watchmaker: Why the Evidence of Evolution Reveals a World without Design* (New York: W. W. Norton, 1996), pp. 1-21, in which he both assumes that Paley represents the apex of Christian thought on creation and appropriates Paley's problem of "apparent design" as his own defining problematic. Though he does not grasp the significance of the point, there is a good account of Darwin's debts to Paley in Stephen Jay Gould, *The Structure of Evolutionary Theory* (Cambridge, Mass.: Harvard University Press, Belknap Press, 2002), pp. 116-24, 251-61. On Darwin's debts to Newton, see David Depew and Bruce Weber, *Darwinism Evolving: Systems Dynamics and the Genealogy of Natural Selection* (Cambridge: MIT Press, 1997), pp. 56-139.

26. This has been a persistent theme of the first two encyclicals of Pope Benedict XVI (*Deus caritas est* and *Spe salvi*), as well as the famous Regensburg address. To see these issues treated more extensively, see Joseph Ratzinger, *Introduction to Christianity,* trans. J. R. Foster (San Francisco: Ignatius, 2004), pp. 57-81. I have also treated this at more length in Hanby, "The Logic of Love and the Unity of Catholic Truth: Reflections on *Deus caritas est,*" *Communio* 33 (Fall 2006): 400-422.

deed that is increasingly regarded as merely an antiquated piece of "folk biology." We cannot cultivate hope in humanity's salvation, nor can we be delivered from our pathological attempts to erase the memory of God by eradicating all traces within ourselves unless we can make this doctrine integral once again to our understanding of the world. To paraphrase then-cardinal Ratzinger, we cannot win the future if we do not recover creation.[27]

II. "Theological" Science, the Evacuation of the World, and the Incredibility of Creation

I want to open up how I think analogy might help recover the intelligibility of creation first by briefly sketching the metaphysical foundations of modern life and science that I take to be most responsible for the incredibility of creation in modernity. The features most immediately relevant to our problem are fairly well summed up in what Pope Benedict, following Francis Bacon, has recently called "the triumph of art over nature," whereby the seventeenth-century natural philosophers first inverted the traditional relation of nature and art before collapsing them entirely, with profound repercussions both for the order of being and for the order of knowledge.

With respect to the order of knowledge, the transposition of nature into artifice effected a transformation of what Amos Funkenstein called both the *ideas* and *ideals* of science,[28] the former referring to the actual content of scientific theory, and the latter both to what scientists think it is worthy and possible to know and what methods are appropriate to attaining it. In the process, this double revaluation transformed the very meaning of truth, whose substance is no longer being *(ens)* — and no longer convertible with the other transcendentals — but the made *(factum)*. It would likewise transform what it would mean to know truth, replacing a contemplative conception of knowledge with an *ergetic* one and insinuating technological manipulation, and its attendant mechanistic ontology, into the heart of scientific knowing.[29] "To know a thing is to know how it is or can be made and

27. Ratzinger, *"In the Beginning . . . ,"* p. 100.

28. See Funkenstein, *Theology and the Scientific Imagination,* pp. 18-22.

29. Benedict XVI, *Spe salvi,* sect. 26; Bacon, *Novum Organum* 1.117. On the relation between the contemplative and the *ergetic,* see Funkenstein, *Theology and the Scientific Imagination,* pp. 290-99. The relationship between these two modes of truth and knowledge, while too complex to receive full attention here, nevertheless should not be passed over lightly. Robert Miner has argued that the connection between knowing and making is not

therefore means being able to repeat or vary or anticipate the process of making. . . . To put it in the form of a slogan, the modern knowledge of nature, very unlike the classical one, is a 'know-how' and not a 'know what,' and on this basis it makes good Bacon's contention that knowledge is power."[30]

There are a couple of crucial points to note here. First, apropos of our earlier point concerning science's inexorable relationship to theology, the triumph of art over nature — in both knowledge and being — was as much the effect of theological deviance as its cause; for Ockham and other late-medieval voluntarists had already done much to make straight the path for Descartes and Newton. Amos Funkenstein notes "the radical change in the

---

per se problematic, that "making" (or doing: John 3:21) truth need not be equated with "making up" truth. One reason for this is that the connection between knowing and making had already been effected by orthodox theologies of creation as God's knowledge of creation "extends as far as his causality extends" (Aquinas, *ST* I, q. 14, a. 11, c.), which is not merely to the form or the universal, but to the entire being *(esse)* of each singular, whereby God, for Aquinas, has knowledge of singulars otherwise inaccessible to us. Inasmuch as God's gratuitous generation of *esse* from nothing is the precondition for all created agency (see Aquinas, *In II Sent.*, d. 1, q. 1, a. 4) — and I would contend that creation in this sense is necessary for the difference intrinsic to all causality — then the way is open to see in the apprehension of truth space for a genuinely creative human contribution, irreducible to *technē* ancient or modern, which nevertheless does not violate the priority that should be accorded to the receptive, contemplative "moment" within the creature's being and knowledge, does not fail to presuppose (and thus imitate) nature, and thus does not deny the "being-in-itselfness" of the object. Indeed D. C. Schindler contends for something along these lines, in very different terms, in his development of Balthasar's conception of truth as *Gestalt*. For Miner, then, the problem is not that secular modernity, paradigmatically represented by Bacon, Descartes, and Hobbes, connects knowing and making, but rather that "its particular mode of connecting the two ultimately serves to deny the dignity of making itself" because they "engage in the willful detachment of human ratio from divine ratio . . . through preserving the constructive character of reason while severing construction with connection to recollection and illumination." See Miner, *Truth in the Making: Creative Knowledge in Theology and Philosophy* (London: Routledge, 2004), pp. xv, 3, 127. See also Schindler, *Hans Urs von Balthasar and the Dramatic Structure of Truth: A Philosophical Investigation* (New York: Fordham University Press, 2004), pp. 163-254, esp. 245-50. All English references to the *Summa* are from the translation by the Fathers of the English Dominican Province (Westminster, Md.: Christian Classics, 1981).

30. Hans Jonas, "The Practical Uses of Theory," in *The Phenomenon of Life: Toward a Philosophical Biology* (Evanston, Ill.: Northwestern University Press, 2001), pp. 203-4. However, one may ask — as Leon Kass does — whether mechanistic accounts, abstracting phenomena such as metabolism from the whole that is the lived life of an organism, are adequate to explain "how things work." See Kass, *Life, Liberty, and the Defense of Dignity: The Challenge for Bioethics* (San Francisco: Encounter Books, 2002), pp. 277-97.

perception of the world that occurred between the generation of Thomas and that of Ockham . . . embodied by the latter's 'principle of annihilation.'"[31] Employed by Ockham in a counterfactual thought experiment to secure the liberty of God's *potentia absoluta,* the principle asserted that "every absolute thing, distinct in subject and place from another absolute thing, can exist by divine power even while [any] other absolute thing is destroyed."[32] As Funkenstein notes, "The difference between them is not that Ockham's world is more contingent than that of his predecessors. It is rather a difference in the meaning of 'contingent orders' and 'things.'" For Aquinas, the world is one because "things in it are structured in a mutually supporting order *(ordo ad invicem),* they are 'ordained toward each other' *(ad alia ordinantur)."*[33] While Aquinas placed no extrinsic limits on God's ability to create other possible worlds, he would regard "absolute things" as imagined by Ockham as nonsense, for a subject that actually contradicts itself is not a thing. Since actual things are such that they are intrinsically and constitutively related to their world as their presupposition, to annihilate those relations and presuppositions is to annihilate the very notion of "thing."[34] By contrast, Ockham's nominalism and (untrinitarian) voluntarism presupposes and, combined with the principle of annihilation, makes possible the notion of a "thoroughly individualized thing." In so doing, he ascribes to matter a fully actualized status apart from and prior to form, natures, or relations, which have been deprived of ontological status, anticipating both the Newtonian conception of body and Hume's skeptical demolition of causality.[35] Ockham's world is "one" because it is an aggregate, "held together," as it were, by the power of God.

31. Funkenstein, *Theology and the Scientific Imagination,* p. 135.

32. Ibid.

33. Ibid., p. 136.

34. See ibid., pp. 137-44. Nor would such singular things be immediately recognizable for Aquinas, since material objects are sensed through the mediation of sensible species and known through the mediation of intelligible species. With the advent of Ockham's thoroughly individualized thing, and with form and nature denied any ontological basis, the question of the knowledge of singulars loses its context of intelligibility.

35. This also had ramifications for the order of knowledge. See ibid., p. 144: "Ockham, however, believed it to be the case: namely, that the criterion of isolation through imaginary destruction of contexts was necessary to save the utter contingency of the world. But his very insistence, in the name of saving the contingency, on the primacy of concrete singular things led him to postulate another kind of necessity. What guarantees our intuitive notions? Not their logical independence — it may serve only as a clue. Nor indeed any *adaequatio rei ad intellectum* through the mediation of species: there is no similarity or

Modern science in its origins is premised upon such nominalism.[36] Counterfactual worlds, principles of annihilation, and thoroughly individualized things, aided and abetted in each case by voluntaristic and essentially untrinitarian conceptions of God,[37] would be put to dramatic new uses in the endeavor of seventeenth-century natural philosophy to convert Aristotelian nature into a mechanical artifact. It is important to note, secondly, that artifice was so able to triumph in the order of knowledge precisely because the very conceptions of knowledge operative in Descartes, Bacon, and others had already transformed nature into artifice in the order of being.[38] "I do not," wrote Descartes in the *Principles of Philosophy,* "recognize any difference between artifacts and natural bodies except that the operations of artifacts are for the most part performed by mechanisms which are large enough to be easily perceivable by the senses."[39] What does this mean? In re-

---

identity between concepts and things. Left only is a strictly causal dependence." This is instrumental in paving the way for Descartes. See Roger Ariew, *Descartes and the Last Scholastics* (Ithaca, N.Y.: Cornell University Press, 1999), pp. 39-76.

36. Nominalism, a common assumption of Galileo, Bacon, Descartes, Newton, Hobbes, and later Darwin, is a warrant for both the mathematical and the experimental methods.

37. On the untrinitarian nature of voluntarism, see my *Augustine and Modernity* (London: Routledge, 2003), pp. 134-77.

38. This is to say that the very conception of abstraction at the heart of modern science is itself an expression of a mechanistic ontology, characterized above all, perhaps, by theological extrinsicism and the externality of matter. In the aforementioned essay by David L. Schindler, "The Given as Gift" (p. 11), he writes that the notion of limit inherent in the position criticized above is one in which "the limit of *x* is thus conceived in terms of an original indifference hence closure of *x* toward what (non-*x*) (possibly) lies beyond and hence transcends x. This notion of limit presupposes a Cartesian understanding of distinction. Distinction for Descartes is conceived in terms of the straight lines proper to geometry (in the form in which he studied it). Straight lines enable clarity. How so? By virtue of what is (as conceived by Descartes) a line's externality — its purely abstract externality. A line so conceived establishes a limit that externalizes the relation between *x* and non-*x,* thus enabling *x* to be and to be known without any admixture of non-*x,* and vice versa. Hence we have the mechanistic idea of limit as simple closure of *x* to non-*x,* and vice versa."

39. Descartes, *Principles of Philosophy,* in *The Philosophical Writings of Descartes,* vol. 1, trans. J. Cottingham, R. Stoothoff, and D. Murdoch (Cambridge: Cambridge University Press, 1985), p. 288. He continues, "Moreover, mechanics is a division or special case of physics, and all the explanations belonging to the former also belong to the latter; so it is no less natural for a clock constructed with this or that set of wheels to tell time than it is for a tree which grew from this or that seed to produce the appropriate fruit." See also the work of Claude Bernard, who wrote: "I propose, therefore, that the science of vital phenomena must have the same foundations as the science of inorganic bodies, and that there is no difference

jecting Aristotle's conception of substantial form, seventeenth-century science emptied beings of the self-transcending unity and interiority heretofore distinguishing "things existing by nature" from artifacts, thereby effacing any essential difference between motion and rest or the animate and the inanimate[40] and rendering accidental the relation of each thing to its own form.[41] Each natural thing would thus eventually stand to its own quiddity in more or less the same external and artificial relation as obtained between Antiphon's bed and its wooden substrate.[42] Yet in contrast to the

---

in this respect between the principles of biological science and those of physic-chemical science" (Bernard, *An Introduction to the Study of Experimental Medicine*, trans. H. C. Greene [New York: Dover Publications, 1957], p. 60).

40. I do not wish to be misinterpreted here. While it is essential to insist upon (indeed to recover) a distinction between the animate and the inanimate (and thus a distinction between I-thou and I-it knowledge), it is equally essential that this difference not be exaggerated and that it not be thought that this distinction is necessarily mechanistic in character, which would simply push the prevailing dualism deeper into the order of nature. Rather, I would wish to suggest that insofar as anything is an *unum per se*, it is possessed of its own being and therefore interiority (and is thus analogously the subject of I-thou knowledge), though clearly an animate thing, and particularly persons, possess their being more interiorly — and move and transcend themselves more profoundly — than inanimate ones.

41. On the demise of interiority and a meaningful distinction between the animate and inanimate, see the work of Hans Jonas in general but particularly Jonas, "Is God a Mathematician? The Meaning of Metabolism," in *The Phenomenon of Life*, pp. 64-98. For more on the conflation of nature and artifice in the orders of being and knowledge, see also Jonas, "The Practical Uses of Theory," in *The Phenomenon of Life*, pp. 188-210. On the loss of the distinction between motion and rest, see Simon Oliver, *Philosophy, God, and Motion*, pp. 156-90. For hints at the correlation between these and the demise of the act-potency distinction, though it is a bit dated, see E. A. Burtt, *The Metaphysical Foundations of Modern Science* (Mineola, N.Y.: Dover, 2003), pp. 72-104. For the lineaments of a contemporary retrieval of interiority, properly understood, see Kenneth L. Schmitz, "Immateriality Past and Present," in *The Texture of Being: Essays in First Philosophy* (Washington, D.C.: Catholic University of America Press, 2007), pp. 168-99.

42. As an illustration of this point, consider the following passage from Darwin's 1868 work *The Variation of Animals and Plants under Domestication*, vol. 2 (London: Murray, 1868), pp. 248-49, cited by Stephen Jay Gould, in which Darwin prioritizes the agency of natural selection as an external artificer in bringing about evolutionary development over the contributions of internal "laws of form": "Throughout this chapter and elsewhere I have spoken of selection as the paramount power, yet its action absolutely depends on what we in our ignorance call spontaneous or accidental variability. Let an architect be compelled to build an edifice with uncut stones, fallen from a precipice. The shape of each fragment may be called accidental; yet the shape of each has been determined by the force of gravity, the nature of the rock, and the slope of the precipice — events and circumstances, all of which depend on natural laws; but there is no relation between these laws and the purpose for

tree from which it was made, Antiphon's bed is not an *unum* per se. It does not move or transcend itself; it does not grow and develop according to its own identity — in short, it does not possess its own being. For as Aquinas says in commenting on the distinction in a passage that inadvertently sheds light on the technological *pathos* at the heart of Baconian nature, "We are in a sense the end of all artificial things."[43] Hence, Robert Spaemann notes, we may ask, in the words of Thomas Nagel's famous essay, "What is it like to be a bat?" "But nobody would ask what it is like to be a car. Being a car is not like anything, because a car does not exist in other than a purely logical sense."[44]

Spaemann is here calling our attention to the fact that natural beings, and particularly those peculiar beings — persons — discovered by Christian theology, "exist in other than a purely logical sense," the implication being that a loss of the distinction between the artificial and the natural entails within it a loss of the being-in-itselfness — the interiority and unity — of nature.[45] Thus Bacon makes the truly remarkable claim, "Nature reveals herself more through the harassment of art than in her own proper freedom."[46]

---

which each fragment is used by the builder. In the same manner the variations of each creature are determined by fixed and immutable laws; but these bear no relation to the living structure which is slowly built up through the power of selection, whether this be natural or artificial selection" (Gould, *The Structure of Evolutionary Theory*, p. 341).

43. Aquinas, *In meta.* 2.4.173.

44. Robert Spaemann, *Persons: The Difference between "Someone" and "Something,"* trans. Oliver O'Donovan (Oxford: Oxford University Press, 2007), p. 30. Tellingly, Richard Dawkins, who ironically stresses to a much greater degree than Darwin the "artificial" character of organisms that originated in British natural theology and who obliterates any meaningful distinction between the living and the nonliving in the process, entirely misses the significance of Nagel's point, which is not simply that we cannot "imagine" what it is like to be a bat or that we might be able to reconstruct the "type of computer model . . . suitable for the internal representation of the changing positions of objects in three-dimensional space" accomplished for us in vision. It is rather, as Conor Cunningham, suggests, to demonstrate "that perspective is an ontologically rich notion," as irreducible as the act of being peculiar to each irreducible subject. See Dawkins, *The Blind Watchmaker*, pp. 21-41; Cunningham, "Trying My Very Best to Believe Darwin; or, The Supernaturalistic Fallacy: From Is to Nought," in *Belief and Metaphysics*, ed. Peter M. Candler Jr. and Conor Cunningham (London: SCM, 2007), p. 120.

45. It is crucial here that for Spaemann, following Ratzinger and ultimately Richard of St. Victor, "person" is an existential, rather than essential, category. See Joseph Cardinal Ratzinger, "Retrieving the Tradition: Concerning the Notion of Person in Theology," *Communio* 17 (Fall 1990): 439-54.

46. Francis Bacon, *The New Organon*, ed. Lisa Jardine and Michael Silverthorne (Cambridge: Cambridge University Press, 2000), p. 21.

What we see here consequent upon a rejection of Aristotelian substance (or its replacement by Cartesian substance) is a trajectory toward an "accidental world" in the scholastic sense of a world of unnecessary parts belonging to no real wholes; wholes, that is, that are but the end result and aggregation of these parts and the various, largely extrinsic agencies that produce them — an ontology, we have seen, that is already noetically inscribed in the notion of abstraction-as-separation.[47] This would later make possible an "accidental world" in the ordinary sense as it would be articulated by Jacques Monod — a world existing by mistake. Events were pushed further along this trajectory by the elimination of the act-potency distinction and the substitution of homogeneous and indifferent Newtonian space for heterogeneous Aristotelian *topos*, which had provided the contextual (and thus relational) presupposition for the distinction between natural and violent motion.

All this effectively dispensed with the uni-verse, both in (1) the metaphysical sense implied by the etymology of a "turning" of all things toward a "one," by virtue of which they are established as a unity, and in (2) the complementary natural sense of a single order in which anything could ever properly belong. Aristotle's notion of heterogeneous "places" had captured this notion of "belonging," as had his very notion of act. Aristotle illustrates this by considering a builder as the (efficient) cause of a house. Strictly speaking, it is not the builder but the builder *building* who causes the house, and his activity in causing the house is contemporaneous with the house *being* built. In brief, when viewed in act rather than in potency, causes and effects belong to a single actuality.[48] So too the soul and its "external" objects, when in the second actuality of knowing, touching, seeing, hearing, eating, and living — dare we say, when in the act of be-ing — comprise a single actuality while nevertheless remaining distinct.[49] In a move that tellingly mirrors de Lubac's persistent complaints against proponents of *natura pura*,

47. On distinction and separation and its relation to both the transformation of causality and the demise of the act-potency distinction, see, in addition to the Schindler article, Kenneth Schmitz, "Analysis by Principles and Analysis by Elements," in *The Texture of Being*, pp. 21-36.

48. Aristotle, *Physics* 2.195b5ff.

49. Aristotle, *On the Soul* 2.417a, 425b26–426b3. A fully mature conception of the universe arguably fully emerges only in consequence of the acknowledgment that all things similarly receive their existence entirely from God. "The unmistakable sign of this," in the twelfth century, "was the spread of the word *universitas* employed independently and as a concrete noun (not *universitas rerum*) to designate the universe in descriptions or systematic treatises" (M.-D. Chenu, *Man, Nature, and Society in the Twelfth Century*, ed. J. Taylor and L. K. Little [Toronto: University of Toronto Press, 1997], p. 5).

namely, that they attempt to premise the actual concrete order of graced nature on a counterfactual pure nature that never existed,[50] seventeenth-century philosophers, employing their own variations of the "principle of annihilation," demolished the *actual* world,[51] the intelligible whole of lived experience, replacing it with a counterfactual world of inertial singulars, whose second-order unity must then be accounted for on the basis of extrinsic and accidentally related forces or mechanisms.[52]

50. See de Lubac, *Mystery of the Supernatural,* pp. 53-74, 222-38. Balthasar would echo this point in articulating a Catholic conception of nature in *The Theology of Karl Barth,* p. 267.

51. There are, of course, key differences. "Bendetti and Galileo, Huygens and Descartes, Pascal and Newton used their imaginary experiments in a definite way which differs *toto caelo* from their medieval predecessors not in discipline and vigor, but in physical interpretation. Counterfactual states were imagined in the Middle Ages — sometimes, even, we saw, as limiting cases. But they were never conceived as commensurable to any of the factual states from which they were extrapolated. No number or magnitude could be assigned to them, even if schoolmen were to give up their reluctance to measure due to their conviction that no measurement is absolutely precise. For Galileo, the limiting case, even where it did not describe reality, was the constitutive principle in its explanation. The inertial motion of a rolling body, the free fall of a body in a vacuum, and the path of a body projected had to be assigned a definite, normative value. . . . In the Middle Ages, the function of imaginary experiments was critical — except for some of the work of the fourteenth century. In the seventeenth century's science and philosophy, they became a tool for the rational *construction* of the world, of the *machina mundi.* This is true of the principle of annihilation in Descartes's or Hobbes's philosophy. This is true of imaginary motions of simple bodies in Galileo's physics. This is also true in the actual construction of experiments in chemical laboratories, under the useful fiction that one can isolate a system of chemical substances and construct them in such conditions as to study pure processes. The study of nature in the seventeenth century was neither predominantly idealistic nor empirical. It was first and foremost *constructive,* pragmatic in the radical sense. It would lead to the conviction that only the doable — at least in principle — is also understandable: *verum et factum convertuntur*" (Funkenstein, *Theology and the Scientific Imagination,* pp. 177-78). This premising of the actual world upon the counterfactual would find paradigmatic expression in Newton's formulation of the principle of inertia, which would be extended analogously to the relations governing political economy and evolutionary development.

52. For an insightful and succinct summation of the basic principles governing mechanism, see David Bohm, "The Implicate Order: A New Approach to the Nature of Reality," in *Beyond Mechanism: The Universe in Recent Physics and Catholic Thought,* ed. David L. Schindler (Lanham, Md.: University Press of America, 1986), pp. 14-15. The essentials are these: "[1.] The world is reduced as far as possible to a set of basic elements. Typically these have been taken as particles, such as atoms, electrons, protons, quarks, etc., but to these may be added various kinds of fields that extend continuously through space, e.g., electromagnetic, gravitational, etc. [2.] These elements are basically *external* to each other,

Aquinas is clear that neither *esse* nor *essentia* subsists on its own, but rather that the composite subject subsists *through* them. Thus while *esse* and *essentia* depend upon each other for the constitution of the composite subject, they cannot simply be derived from each other. Even so, I wish to suggest that, in eliminating the interiority of *esse* and its concomitant notions of act and potency, early modern science turned a blind eye to the even deeper interiority and actuality of *esse*, through the giving of which God grants it to the creature freely "to be" — and to be uniquely this — in an act more intimate and more interior, as Aquinas says, "than those things by which being is specified."⁵³ Of

---

not only in the sense of being separate in space, but more important, in the sense that the fundamental nature of each is independent of that of the other. [3.] The elements interact mechanically, and are thus related only by influencing each other externally, e.g., by forces of interaction that do not deeply affect their inner natures. [4.] It is admitted that such a goal is yet to be fully achieved . . . but it is essential for the *mechanistic reductionistic* program to assume that there is nothing that cannot eventually be treated in this way." As we have seen, these features are inherent in the normal scientific conception of limit and abstraction, which is basically Cartesian.

53. See Aquinas, *In II Sent.*, d. 1, q. 1, a. 4; *ST* I, q. 8, a. 1, in *Aquinas on Creation: Writings on the Sentences of Peter Lombard, Book 2, Distinction 1, Question 1*, trans. Steven E. Baldner and William E. Carroll (Toronto: Pontifical Institute of Mediaeval Studies, 1997), p. 85. Balthasar calls attention to the marvel of the real distinction from the inside, as it were, and in so doing attempts to retrieve genuine wonder from mere positivist admiration in his "phenomenological" consideration of this distinction, and the ever-greater difference between God and the world, in the fourfold distinction: "The fact that I find myself within the realm of a world and in the boundless community of other existent beings is astonishing beyond measure and cannot be exhaustively explained by any cause that derives from within the world. In surveying Western metaphysics in its entirety, we must be amazed at how little the enigma of reproduction — not only of organic natural creatures but above all of man, who is Spirit — has concerned philosophers. From the infinite prodigality of an act of generation — prodigality in the male as well as the female organism resulting in a 'chance hit' — a 'new' being is created which, reflecting upon its personal ego, cannot interpret itself in any way as a product of chance; for it possesses the capacity to view the world as a whole, indeed Being as a whole, from its unrepeatable perspective and thus to effect a unification of what it sees (Leibniz). Nothing within (world-)Being indicates that this had the 'personal' intention of producing precisely this unique and as such irreplaceable person through that game of chance; there is nothing to prove that this unique person receives a kind of necessary place through his incorporation into a (wholly hypothetical) series of monads, as a number receives its necessity within a totality of a series of numbers. I could imagine (and there is nothing to conflict with this idea) that an infinite number of 'others' could have occupied this 'same' place in the universe instead of me. Why it should have been me, I do not know" (Hans Urs von Balthasar, *The Glory of the Lord*, vol. 5, *The Realm of Metaphysics in the Modern Age*, trans. O. Davies, A. Louth, B. McNeil, C.R.V., J. Saward, and R. Williams [San Francisco: Ignatius Press, 1991], p. 615).

course, this claim could just as easily be reversed, as the history of modern philosophy and certainly modern science has shown us that whenever being is lost sight of, essence too is soon obscured.[54]

It was thus through this real distinction that Thomas had made more precise Augustine's confession that God's presence is more interior to the creature than the creature is to itself, a gift and presence made possible in both instances by God's transcending and surpassing difference. It was on the basis of this most interior gift of *esse* that Thomas had been able to sustain the remarkable twofold claim demanded by creation: first, that the world is really distinct from God, with its own being, integrity, and causal order that are knowable by the various sciences; and second, that this worldly order has its own freedom and integrity, not despite, but just *because,* God is immediately present to the world, indeed closer to it than it is to itself, granting it the *esse* through which it is able to be all that it is. As he states in his commentary on the *Sentences:*

> The fact, therefore, that a creature is the cause of some other creature does not preclude that God operate immediately in all things, insofar as His power is like an intermediary that joins the power of any secondary cause with its effect. In fact, the power of a creature cannot achieve its effect except by the power of the Creator, from whom is all power, preservation of power, and order to effect. For this reason, the causality of the secondary cause is rooted in the causality of the primary cause.[55]

I will eventually have more to say about the implications of St. Thomas's claims in these last two sentences. Suffice it for now to say that the eventual elimination of *both poles* of the real distinction would likewise open up a twofold possibility, though I'm speaking theoretically and not strictly historically. First, dispensing with the question of *being,* or at least relegating it to a philosophical ghetto outside the commanding precincts of modern science, would usher in just that form of positivism decried by Balthasar, helping further to pave the way for the ascendancy of physics, now understood as

54. One thinks here of the "war on essentialism" waged in both contemporary philosophy and throughout the sciences, exemplified in Ernst Mayr's famous prohibition against "typological thinking" in biology. Of course, in this prohibition Aristotelian forms are often mistakenly treated as universals and species as classes of individuals bound together by common features. See Mayr, *One Long Argument: Charles Darwin and the Genesis of Modern Evolutionary Thought* (Cambridge, Mass.: Harvard University Press, 1991), pp. 26-34; Depew and Weber, *Darwinism Evolving,* pp. 35-40, 299-328.

55. See Aquinas, *In II Sent.,* d. 1, q. 1, a. 4, in Baldner and Carroll trans., pp. 85-86.

mechanics, to the position of first philosophy.[56] Or in what amounts to the same thing, the concomitant reduction of truth to function would allow for the pragmatic jettisoning of the notion of first philosophy altogether — and arguably truth as well, if subsequent philosophical and scientific history is any indication.[57] Second, this evacuation of interiority would transpose the creature's relation to God from an intrinsic and constitutive relation into an extrinsic and accidental one that would no longer deeply inform the meaning of the created and natural world *as* created and natural. The eighteenth- and nineteenth-century project prominent particularly among Broad Church Anglicans but with analogies among some Continental romantics of seeking to re-found "creation" either in an extrinsic designer or in an immanent providence whose invisible hand in either case mechanically procures unintended benefits from heterogeneous pursuits would die under the weight of its own irrelevance, often enough by being translated into a purely secular idiom without loss of substance.[58] Not that such "design" or "cun-

---

56. On natural philosophy as first philosophy, see Bacon, *Novum Organum*, 1.80; Newton, *Principia Mathematica*, trans. I. Bernard Cohen and Anne Whitman (Berkeley: University of California Press, 1999), pp. 939-43.

57. See Ratzinger, *Introduction to Christianity*, pp. 57-69.

58. For the relation between (1) the advent of mechanism and the consequent relocation of nature from an immanent and interior principle of things to an external law; (2) the concomitant transformations to the meaning of nature, time, space, and causality; and (3) the rise of new conceptions of providence in the form of "invisible hand" or "cunning of history" explanations, see Funkenstein, *Theology and the Scientific Imagination*, pp. 202-89. John Milbank notes the theological character of such arguments and the role they played in giving rise to "political economy" as a "scientific" discourse. We could extend this to include the advent of evolutionary biology, which is "the doctrine of Malthus, applied to the whole animal and vegetable kingdoms" (Darwin, *The Origin of Species*, 6th ed. [Amherst, N.Y.: Prometheus, 1991], p. 3). Milbank observes, "A whole important chapter of 'natural theology,' constantly rewritten all the way from Derham in the seventeenth century to Sumner in the nineteenth, concerned the demonstration of design not just in the natural world but also in the social order. This reinsertion of 'providence' into scientific discourse means that one cannot tell the story of the development of 'social science' simply under the rubric of the substitution of human for divine agency. Indeed, divine agency is invoked much more *directly* as an explanatory cause in the eighteenth century (both in natural and social science) than in the middle ages." Milbank then goes on to describe how such "providence" supplied a kind of "social theodicy," immanently and mechanically procuring goodness and social equilibrium (notice the latent Newtonianism here) from self-interested, heterogeneous pursuits. "This fact has been very well delineated by Milton L. Myers, among others. However, Myers attempts to distinguish a tendency, culminating with Adam Smith, to conceive the heterogenesis of ends in gradually more 'natural' and 'realist' terms and so finally to dispense with the theological fiction which had nonetheless heuristically assisted the final sci-

Michael Hanby

ning" ever really was creation, or that its basic extrinsicism was a purely Protestant phenomenon. Once again, Henri de Lubac thought he could detect more than a whiff of it in the neoscholastic notion of *natura pura,* though the revived debate over de Lubac's reading of St. Thomas tends to minimize this larger — and arguably more important — point.[59]

It is difficult to overstate, I think, the extent to which this extrinsicism still governs, occasionally even subtly, what is left of modern thought about creation, certainly enough outside theology but often enough within it. Even in those rare instances where contemporary discussion of the matter attains to the properly metaphysical question "Why something rather than nothing?" its pertinence is relegated to the margins of time and thought, with no expectation that its answer might be immanently visible *in* the world. From a modern point of view, the world's inner nature and meaning are no longer deeply informed by its relation to God for the simple reason that, from within the scientific outlook governing modern thought and life, the world now *has no* inner meaning and nature, no inherent unity, no being in itself that might make visible the invisible or provide (in principle) a limit to our ability to command it. The incredibility of creation stems not from science having rendered God's existence doubtful. Rather it is that science in its positivism has so defined the world, and so emptied it of its unity and interiority in defining it, that we can no longer imagine what difference God's existence or nonexistence might make to it. In a world so construed, talk of creation as a mere

---

entific 'discovery.' Whereas in truth there was *no* point at which a theological or metaphysical thesis got translated into a scientific and empirical one, no Bachelardian 'epistemological break.' The only change was a relatively trivial one, from ascribing design to a transcendent God, to ascribing it to an immanent 'nature'" (Milbank, *Theology and Social Theory: Beyond Secular Reason* [London: Blackwell, 1990], pp. 38-39).

59. See Ralph McInerny, *Praeambula fidei: Thomism and the God of the Philosophers* (Washington, D.C.: Catholic University of America Press, 2006). The treatment of de Lubac is questionable on several counts. For instance, McInerny says, "In de Lubac's account, man no longer has a natural end. His actual call to the vision of God is the basis for a natural potency to achieve that end. It is almost as if the supernatural replaces the natural." The first claim is true, though de Lubac would likely add such qualifiers as "purely" and "ultimate"; the second and third result from imposing on de Lubac the assumption — not de Lubac's own (and arguably not that of St. Thomas if the first question of the *Summa* is to be taken at face value) — that a nature must have an ultimate end proportionate to it in order to be natural. And nowhere that I am aware of — certainly not in the crucial fifth chapter of *The Mystery of the Supernatural* — does de Lubac actually say that man has a "natural potency to achieve" a supernatural end. More pertinent to our point, however, is the fact that McInerny merely notes the concern highlighted here in order to dismiss it. See, for example, p. 87.

"theater" for redemption cannot help coming off as fideistic, pietistic, or moralistic, and so as inherently unrelated to the so-called real world.

III. Saving the Appearances and the Gift of Science

Crude as this little sketch may be, I hope it goes some distance in indicating just how the *analogia entis* might come to our aid and just what demands it must meet in order to be theologically coherent in doing so. These demands, it turns out, are entailed in the *analogia entis* itself.

First of all, I hope it is clear that I am urging the *analogia entis* as crucial for recovering a credible account of creation both because it expresses the infinite and surpassing difference of God as ever greater and wholly other and because, in so doing, it supplies what is finally the only adequately non-reductive account of the world as *world* and so the only account of a world in which science is finally justified. And I hope it is equally clear that I take the real distinction between *esse* and essence to be integral both to an adequate sense of analogy and to this nonreductive account of the world. Of course, it is currently quite fashionable to oppose reductionism from within science; few would admit to being what Richard Dawkins calls a "baby-eating" reductionist, who "tries to explain complicated things *directly* in terms of their smallest parts."[60] Yet from within the mechanistic ontology that continues to govern science it is impossible to account for the "more" characteristic of a real *unum per se* without regarding it as merely "supervenient" upon lower-level phenomena, such that it remains either epiphenomenal with respect to those phenomena or simply the product of external addition and thus ultimately and in principle reducible to them through the discovery of the necessary "bridge laws" governing the relationship between levels. Claude Bernard, nineteenth-century pioneer of experimental medicine, sums this up perfectly: "If a phenomenon, in an experiment, had such a contradictory appearance that it did not connect itself with determinate causes, then reason should reject the fact as non-scientific."[61] And despite Dawkins's own protests, he does not depart far from this basic position. If reality does not submit to science's self-understanding, deny reality.

Obviously, a great deal of technical specification, more than I can sup-

---

60. Dawkins, *The Blind Watchmaker*, p. 13.
61. Bernard, *An Introduction to the Study of Experimental Medicine*, p. 54. See also p. 83.

ply here, is required both to fill out the implications of the real distinction in its relation to analogy and to say how it might help bridge the abyss of incommensurability now separating theology and the natural sciences. Much of that metaphysical work has already been done in the contributions that John Betz, Martin Bieler, and Reinhard Hütter have offered in this volume — though I do not mean by referring to their contributions to command their assent to mine — and the bridge work remains an enormously tall order, as it entails a fundamental renegotiation of the very meaning of truth and knowledge so as to bring science to see what it cannot but presuppose, even as it is blinded by its own constitutive first principles.

Two points apropos of our remarks at the outset of this essay nevertheless bear mentioning. First, to follow Aquinas in recognizing a real distinction between *esse* and *essentia* in the nonidentical and nonnecessary relation of "thisness" and "whatness," and to follow him further in regarding *esse creatum* as nonsubsistent,[62] to see *esse,* that act of acts formal in respect of every form,[63] as nevertheless, in Balthasar's words, paradoxically "dependent upon its explication in the existent"[64] is at once to see *esse* as "the foundation of the most interior unity of every singular and particular essence" and to deny *esse* its own ground in itself.[65] Inherent in *esse,* in other words, is a twofold, constitutive relation to its subject and source. We can say in St. Thomas's terms that *esse,* like form, only is "in" something else, namely, the "composite" creature.[66] Hence, according to Balthasar, "*esse,* as Thomas understands it, is at once both total fullness and total nothingness: fullness, because it is the most noble, the first and proper effect of God, because 'through being God causes all things and being is prior to and more interior than all other effects.' But being is also nothingness, since it does not exist as such, 'for just as one cannot say that running runs, but rather that the runner runs,' so, 'one cannot say that existence exists.'"[67] The nonsubsistence of

62. See Aquinas, *De pot.,* q. 1, a. 1; q. 7, a. 2, ad 7. "Esse non est subsistens sed inhaerens."

63. Aquinas, *ST* I, q. 8, a. 1.

64. Balthasar, *The Glory of the Lord,* 5:619.

65. Balthasar, *The Glory of the Lord,* vol. 4, *The Realm of Metaphysics in Antiquity,* trans. O. Davies et al. (San Francisco: Ignatius Press, 1989), p. 402.

66. See Aquinas's *In meta.* 7.2.1293, and esp. 7.7.1423. Here, though, Aquinas corrects Aristotle. "Yet it must be noted that even though it is said in the text that form comes to be in matter, this is not a proper way of speaking; for it is not a form that comes to be, but a composite. Thus the proper way of speaking is to say that a composite is generated from matter according to such and such a form."

67. Balthasar, *Glory of the Lord,* 4:404. The relevant citations from St. Thomas are *De*

esse thus opens it up from the inside, as it were, to a double convertibility with gift. On the one hand, *esse* "is" as giving, as radical self-emptying, which means that it is only in the creature and in the form of being received. And yet, on the other hand, for precisely this reason neither the *esse* nor the creatures who participate in it are sufficient to ground themselves. Of its own inner necessity, then, *esse* is internally open and constitutively related to a gift from beyond itself. In its wealth and poverty it "is" as received as a participation in and imitation of the *ipsum esse subsistens,* who is God himself.

Second, at the point of this interior reception of being as gift, we converge once again upon the "Christian difference" we encountered in our brief consideration of the metaphysical revolution instigated by the incarnation, a difference we saw to be at work more generally in Aquinas's understanding of creation as a certain giving and receiving of *esse.* This time it is Balthasar who sums up that difference:

> It is precisely here [as the giving of *esse* grounds both act and potency] that a new kind of intimacy of God to the creature becomes clear, an intimacy that is only made possible by the distinction between God and *esse.* Allowing natures to participate in reality — God's most proper prerogative — is not to be understood as the disintegration or diminution (on the part of the creature) of God's being and unicity (which is how it is invariably seen outside the Christian tradition) and the essences of things must not appear as the fragmentation of reality, in a negative sense, but must be seen positively as posited and determined by God's omnipotent freedom and therefore are grounded in the unique love of God. In what we might call the "real distinction" (circumspectly, because here we are dealing with an inexplicable mystery) God contemplated his creation with free, so to speak, stereoscopic sight, which means at the same time that God preserves for the creature this wholly new plasticity: it is precisely when the creature feels itself to be separate in being from God that it knows itself to be the most immediate object of God's love and concern; and it is precisely when its essential finitude shows it to be something quite different from God that it knows that, as a real being, it has had bestowed upon it that most extravagant gift — participation in the real being of God.[68]

---

pot., q. 7, a. 2, ad 9; *Comp. theo.* 1.68; *In De div. nom.* 5.1; *De pot.,* q. 3, a. 7; *In Boeth. De Heb.,* lec. 2.

68. Balthasar, *Glory of the Lord,* 4:404.

Michael Hanby

"Analogy" names the unity-in-difference characteristic of the gift of being, and I would suggest that it is in this twofold character as gift, though not necessarily by that name, that *esse* can be the subject matter of a limited science of *being qua being* that nevertheless remains, in itself, groundless. I will say more about this momentarily, but we are now in a position to state the implications of all this a bit more fully.

It is precisely through the receiving of *esse* that creation is intrinsically and thus constitutively related to God as gift. This constitutive relation, as Henri de Lubac points out, is almost impossible to capture in language because the ordinary disjunction of giver, gift, and recipient makes it appear as if there is a recipient outside of and prior to the gift. In the case of the gift that is creation *ex nihilo,* this difficulty compromises both the depths of the gift's gratuity and the transcendence and freedom of God as giver. Thus, as de Lubac says, while the model of a parent giving a present to a child is perhaps the best we have for expressing this profound gratuity:

> [it nevertheless] would not adequately express, in all its force, the radical gift of being which God has given me (inevitably we fall back into this language) by creating me. For it is a gift totally interior to me; nothing is left out of it, and nothing of myself is without it. It is incomparably more a gift than any outward, additional gifts which may later be given me by men. There is no proportion between them; as an analogy they are infinitely inadequate.[69]

Now we may state the demands and implications of creation, understood as entailing analogy, for the relationship between theology and the sciences. Inasmuch as this gift that is my being — and my being related to God — really constitutes me, it must really be "in" me, and so it must be both (subjectively) implied in the most basic act of cognition by which the world is apprehended and (objectively) "visible" in principle to the world known by the sciences and thus visible to the sciences themselves, according to the formal principles that distinguish them one from another.[70] And yet, precisely

69. De Lubac, *The Mystery of the Supernatural,* p. 77.
70. Kenneth Schmitz helpfully distinguishes between the modern sense of "object," as that which stands over against a possible knower, and the medieval sense, in which "something other than the knower made itself present to the knower," a possibility only because the object is first a *subject (suppositum)* of its own being and therefore possessed of "an interiority and depth that wove the web of a certain natural mystery." This notion is in the background when Aquinas (*ST* I, q. 1, a. 7), arguing that God is the object of *sacra doctrina,*

because it is *gift* expressing and preserving God's infinitely surpassing difference *from* me, it cannot be visible in such a way so as to collapse this difference, any more than the incarnation can simply be derived from creation, or *sacra doctrina* from the "theology" belonging to metaphysics. However we understand this constitutive relation, this gift is visible to the sciences; it can neither collapse the world into God in a pure a priori metaphysics that would pretend to deduce the world from its divine idea, nor collapse God into the world in a metaphysics purporting to infer the divine essence from worldly particulars. Its visibility must take the form of invisibility — or rather, hypervisibility; putting the matter somewhat differently, the invisible must be made visible precisely as invisible, without ceasing to be such.

How, then, might the real distinction help us register this visibility in thought so as to acknowledge the creature's constitutive relation to God without compromising, on the ontological side, God's free and infinite surpassing of the world or, what amounts to the same thing, erecting a barrier between them that makes their relation extrinsic? And how, on the noetic side, might we retain science's inexorable and constitutive relationship to metaphysics and theology while maintaining the distinction between them and their nonderivability from each other? To fail to meet either set of demands is to fail to meet both and ultimately to compromise the difference between God and the world, doing so, ironically, in the name of protecting it.

The key, in the first instance, is the way in which this formulation of the

---

says, "The relation between a science and its object is the same as that between a habit and its faculty and its object. Now properly speaking the object of a faculty or habit is the thing under the aspect of which all things are referred to that faculty or habit, as man and stone are referred to the faculty of sign in that they are colored." The upshot of this point for our purposes is twofold. First, to distinguish this science by their objects, *on this understanding of objects is also to distinguish them formally,* that is, *according to the aspect under which they disclose themselves as subjects.* While it is therefore true to say that "different sciences look at the same object differently," this is not *simply* a matter of "subjective" point of view such that each is simply left to its own. Secondly, this is because *distinguishing* the sciences through abstraction is not the same thing as *separating* them in the Cartesian manner noted above, wherein *x* is *simply* divided from non-*x* (making the relation between them a secondary and extrinsic qualification of simple identity). Why so? While there is a certain truth to the notion that the various sciences refer to the "parts" of being while metaphysics attends to "being as such," it is *never* the case that all the sciences, in dealing with the "parts," do not also in a sense have the whole as their object. In consequence, sciences differentiated by virtue of the "parts" of being with which they deal are differentiated by the way the whole makes itself visible in one of its aspects, or, conversely, sciences are differentiated by how they deal with the whole, to which both the part and the science remain intrinsically related, *through* the part. See Schmitz, *The Texture of Being,* pp. 187-88.

real distinction as a kind of groundless, asymmetrical reciprocity between *esse* and *essentia* opens up what Przywara calls the "back-and-forth *within the immanence of creatureliness itself*: an 'immanent dynamic middle of actuality *(energia)* between dynamic possibility *(dynamis)* and inner end-directedness *(entelechia).*'"[71] Precisely because this dynamic as dynamic is "middle" and thus does not ground itself, each pole being dependent upon the other — and thus on the Wholly other — in the "composite" that they comprise, this analogy internal to the creature opens up of its own inner necessity to a still higher analogy, "as a dynamic back and forth between the above-and-beyond (a transcending immanence) and the from-above-into," the transcendence of a divine other internal to the creature itself.[72] At the heart of each creature lies an enigma, as Augustine realized, for at the heart of each creature is a relation to God that makes the creature more than itself.[73]

This "suspended" ontological position, for Przywara, is reflected in the creature's paradoxical noetic suspension between — and need for — an equally impossible a priori and a posteriori metaphysics, or, perhaps what is not exactly the same thing, between the two legitimate kinds of theology or divine science differentiated by Aquinas.[74] And here, precisely as "sus-

---

71. Przywara, *Analogia Entis,* p. 113.

72. Ibid.

73. Augustine, *Confessions* 10.8.15; 10.17.26; 10.3.49.

74. Aquinas, *In Boethii De Trin.,* q. 5, a. 4, in *The Division and Methods of the Sciences,* trans. Armand Mauer (Toronto: Pontifical Institute of Mediaeval Studies, 1986), p. 52: "Accordingly, there are two kinds of theology or divine science. There is one that treats of divine things, not as the subject of the sciences but as the principles of the subject. This is the kind of theology pursued by the philosophers and that is also called metaphysics. There is another theology, however, that investigates divine things for their own sakes as the subject of the science. This is the theology taught in Sacred Scripture. Both treat of beings that exist separate from matter and motion, but with a difference, for something can exist separate from matter and motion in two distinct ways: first because by its nature the thing that is called separate in no way can exist in matter and motion, as God and the angels are said to be separate from matter and motion. Second, because by its nature it does not exist in matter and motion; but it can exist without them, though we sometimes find it with them. In this way being, substance, potency, and act are separate from matter and motion, because they do not depend on them for their existence, unlike the objects of mathematics, which can only exist in matter, though they can be understood without sensible matter. Thus philosophical theology investigates beings separate in the second sense as its subjects, and beings separate in the first sense as the principles of its subjects. But the theology of Sacred Scripture treats of things separate in the first sense as its subjects, though it concerns some items in matter and motion insofar as this is needed to throw light on divine things." There is much to sort through in relating these two sorts of "theology," especially in light of the

pended," I want to claim that this ontological position can become visible and creation made once again credible, in different ways, not just in the "divine science" proper to revelation, but also in the "divine science" invariably presupposed and operative within the other sciences,[75] and this in such a way so as to preserve and authorize a *legitimate* form of scientific abstraction, and thus a relative "legitimate autonomy" for the sciences.[76] Let me try to state what I mean more clearly and simply.

As I argued earlier, the theological precondition for all forms of so-called naturalism is an extrinsicist conception of the God-world relationship that finitizes God often enough in the name of protecting his transcendence, a gesture we find recapitulated, or so I have suggested, in so-called dialectical theology. The metaphysical correlate of this theology is a positivism devoid of all real wonder at the mystery of being. This positivism evacuates beings of the unity and interiority of *essence* and the irreducible novelty of every concrete act of existence, reconceiving the unity of the *per se unum* as the unity of an aggregate and reducing beings to the sum of their antecedent causes and the interactions of component parts only indifferently and externally related to each other.[77]

To recuperate the "back-and-forth within the immanence of creatureliness itself," this asymmetrical reciprocity between *esse* and *essentia*, is, in more mundane terms, to recuperate precisely the coincidence of interiority, essential intelligibility, and existential novelty, the common "whatness" and incomprehensible, irreducible "thisness" characterizing the actual world of elementary experience that science, even in its blindness, cannot help but presuppose. Plainer still, it is to "save the appearances" by recovering the world as subject of its own being, possessed of its own freedom distinct, though not separate or independent, from God (and distinct from human

---

Barthian objection to the *analogia entis*. Let it suffice for now to briefly reiterate three points. First, precisely inasmuch as the world is distinct from God with *esse* of its own, a philosophical metaphysics, like a worldly science, is both necessary and legitimate. Second, inasmuch as *esse* does not suffice as its own ground but opens of its own necessity to a gift from beyond itself that remains beyond comprehension even in its apprehension, so this philosophy finds its completion as philosophy only in its intrinsic openness to theology at once apophatic and kataphatic. Third, with Aristotle, relation to being and thus metaphysics in the first sense is intrinsic to reason and the other sciences as such, through which they are also related intrinsically to theology. Thus metaphysics and theology are inexorably implicated in all sciences.

75. See Aristotle, *Meta.* 4.2.1004b4–1005a18; Aquinas, *In Boeth. De Trin.*, q. 5, a. 4.

76. Second Vatican Council, *Gaudium et spes*, 36, 59.

77. On the difference between genuine wonder and the circumscribed "admiration" consequent upon scientific positivism, see Balthasar, *The Glory of the Lord*, 4:613.

subjectivity), with its own irreducible mystery always pressing toward expression as form, a mystery that is neither the opposite of truth and knowledge nor the unknown awaiting discovery just beyond their boundaries but an immanent feature of them.[78] Indeed, as Balthasar realizes, it is precisely this coincidence of mystery and truth in the being-in-itselfness of the world exhibited in the "interplay" between essence and existence that makes real knowledge possible, inasmuch as it protects the actuality of the world from the homogenizing violence of technological abstraction.[79] And it is this same interiority, this same being-in-itselfness, that likewise authorizes the sciences and metaphysics and prevents their reduction to theology, even as it is itself the interior gift of God and recognized fully as such only by theology proper consequent upon revelation.[80]

In the beginning I claimed that the function of analogy is the same as the doctrine of creation, expressing what is revealed to us fully in the incarnation: that God can be intimately present to creation — can indeed become man and enter into his suffering and death — in virtue of being wholly other to it. Later on I supplemented this claim with the insight variously stated by St. Thomas, Przywara, and Balthasar that this first analogy of the dynamic interplay between being and essence opens of its own inner necessity to the higher analogy, the likeness within surpassing difference of the creature's relation to God — that is, creation.

At the risk of oversimplification, I wish nevertheless to amplify this by saying that to recover the actuality of the world in its fullness simply *is* to recover creation. It is to recover and make visible the world's interior, constitutive relation to God, not least by making the world visible to itself. This is because the "act of creation" is not an extrinsic qualification of the world but its most interior, constitutive gift, and the doctrine of creation does not sup-

---

78. On the immanence of mystery within truth, see Balthasar, *Theologic,* vol. 1, *The Truth of the World,* trans. Adrian J. Walker (San Franscisco: Ignatius Press, 2000), pp. 206-25.

79. See Balthasar, *Theologic,* 1:79-226; Michael Hanby, "A Few Words on Balthasar's First Word," in *How Balthasar Changed My Mind: Fifteen Scholars Reflect on the Meaning of Balthasar for Their Own Work,* ed. Rodney Howsare and Larry Chapp, pp. 74-90 (New York: Crossroad, 2008).

80. Thus, the crucial teaching of *Gaudium et spes* 22 — that "Christ the Lord, Christ the new Adam, in the very revelation of the mystery of the Father and his love, fully reveals man to himself and brings to light his most high calling" — can be extended analogously to the world as such. The full revelation of God is simultaneously the revelation of the meaning of the world as world. Hence, to paraphrase Aquinas (*ST* I, q. 1, aa. 4-7), all things are potentially *revelabilia.* See *Vatican Council II: The Conciliar and Post Conciliar Documents,* vol. 1, ed. Austin Flannery (Grand Rapids: Eerdmans, 1992), p. 922.

ply a mechanism for the being of the world, as if the interior act of God in making the world to be were an alternative to some natural process. This is what I take David Burrell to mean when he says that the relationship expressed by creation "makes its appearance within the world as we know it and yet does not express a difference within that world."[81] There are at least two reasons why this is the case, one from God's side, and another from ours. Because God as *ipsum esse subsistens* is *actus purus,* he need "do" nothing further than be in order to cause the world. Moreover, creation, according to St. Thomas, is not action or passion or motion or change but simply a relation of effect to cause; change is always *from* some potency *to* some actuality, while the gift of *esse* is the cause not the consequence of potency.[82] Hence creation is not a discrete event qualifying the world from within the world but the event *of* the world, and it can be said to have occurred whenever anything genuinely new appears, which happens to be every concrete act of existence. And yet to see creation is also to see analogy, for the "new" would not even be intelligible as such were it not for the "memory," the anterior relations that both the knowing subject and the *novum* carry within themselves. To see creation, then — indeed, simply to see the world — is to see the unity of anterior relation and the irreducible novelty of difference in every concrete act of existence and in every concrete causal transaction inasmuch as effects are genuinely different from and thus irreducible to their causes and to every concrete act of existence insofar as these are genuinely different from and irreducible to their antecedent causes, component parts, or even their own "natures." And inasmuch as real, positive difference is intrinsic to causality as such — otherwise every effect would be but a manifestation of its cause — this irreducibility characteristic of creation, this genuine difference between and indeed this surplus of effect to cause, is necessary for there to be causality at all. "The causality of the secondary cause is rooted in the causality of the primary cause."[83]

81. David Burrell, *Knowing the Unknowable God: Ibn-Sina, Maimonides, Aquinas* (Notre Dame, Ind.: University of Notre Dame Press, 1986), p. 20.

82. Aquinas, *ST* I, q. 44, a. 3.

83. See Aquinas, *In II Sent.,* d. 1, q. 1, a. 4. This is how I interpret St. Thomas in his *Sentences* commentary (II, d. 1, q. 1, a. 4, ad 4), when he says that Anaxagoras failed to hold a true account of generation that occurs when "a *new* substantial form is acquired in matter" (emphasis mine). It is also what I take it to mean when he says (II, d. 1, q. 1, a. 4) "that the causality of the secondary cause is rooted in the causality of the primary cause." In other words, creation is the presupposition of causality as such.

However, this raises numerous questions that I can barely acknowledge here. Chief

Creation does not therefore tell us "how the world came to be" or, strictly speaking, "why there is something rather than nothing," since God in

---

among these is the ontological status of the novelty — which I am claiming is characteristic of creation — of every causal transaction and concrete act of being. In what sense is each concrete act of existence new, not simply with respect to us, but in the order of being and therefore to God? Nothing less than both poles of the difference between God and the world seem to hinge on this. We have already indicated the paradoxical demand entailed in this difference. On the one hand, God, as *ipsum esse subsistens,* the ineffable I-Am in whom all the perfections of being reside, must be so wholly other to the world that it cannot add or subtract from these perfections, a conviction encapsulated in St. Thomas's denial of God's real relation to the world. On the other hand, the world must really have its own positivity — and thus goodness, beauty, and truth — precisely in its difference from God. It is my claim that it is the revelation of the world as creation and the articulation of this claim through the real distinction that uniquely uphold both demands.

And yet, with this doctrine of the precontainment of the perfections of the effect in the cause, one sometimes detects an ambiguity with respect to difference, such that defects can appear "defective" insofar as they differ from their cause, an echo, perhaps, of the pre-Christian tendency to regard multiplicity as a "fall" from unity. When, for instance, Aristotle says that "the most natural act is the production of another like itself . . . in order that, as far as its nature allows, it may partake in the eternal and divine" (*On the Soul* 2.415a29), it becomes tempting to regard the novel element in natural generation — namely, the signate matter that individuates — as preventing the formative element (sperm, in human generation) from inducing a perfect likeness of itself. (See, for example, Aquinas, *In meta.* 7.7.1433.) This "negative" impression is sometimes compounded in Aristotle by the incomprehensibility of the particular *qua* particular (e.g., Socrates *qua* Socrates), inasmuch as this forestalls the unity of thought and being. Kenneth Schmitz, who would never commit the "act of philosophical injustice and impiety to suggest that Aristotle ever lost sense of the concrete individual," nevertheless notes the ambiguity that, when Aristotle "came to formulate the essential meaning of the individual, he turned very quickly to the universal in the form of the specific nature — in a word, the *ti*" ("Neither with nor without Foundations," in *The Texture of Being,* p. 57). One can even detect a measure of it in Pseudo-Dionysius (see, for example, Ps.-Dionysius, *Divine Names* 645c), who is unparalleled in commending the unity-in-difference and who attributes the goodness of the world to the difference inherent in divine love, which is at once *eros* and *agape,* calling God "beyond himself" where there is no "beyond" (see *Divine Names* 712a–713a).

I also would not wish to commit this impiety, and in addition to the Areopagite's virtues, I recognize (with Schmitz) a certain equi-primordiality of the singular *(tode)* and the communal *(ti)* in Aristotle's individual, a recognition brought to full fruition, so I am claiming, by St. Thomas's discovery of *esse.* Moreover, on St. Thomas's terms the question of difference as defect can be finessed somewhat by recourse to a distinction between perfection with reference to the particular subject as in the question of "whether one man can be happier than another?" (*ST* I-II, q. 5, a. 2). Finally, any orthodox and coherent theology obviously would want to insist upon the precontainment of all perfections in the cause and the communication of form to the effect. God in his fullness *does* infinitely surpass all his effects

creating the world cannot act for an end otherwise lacking. Rather, precisely in not telling us these things, creation tells us, as Pope Benedict reminds us in the homilies noted above, what the world is.[84] And what is the world? A novel and gratuitous "surplus" of being, a "pointless" abundance of good-

---

and cannot be added to or diminished by them. Nevertheless, it seems that this ambiguity can finally be dispensed with only when the world is acknowledged as good not simply in spite of but also because of its very difference from God, or, rather, when the *difference (and therefore relationality and love) intrinsic to goodness as such* in its self-communication is brought to bear without remainder on the world. On these terms it seems we can, and perhaps even must, hold that the world, precisely in its positivity as something "other" than God, is somehow "new to" or "more than" God, without this in any way diminishing the fullness of divine perfection or God's surpassing otherness. In other words, we must think creation through the Trinity, in which infinite otherness and receptivity are perfections internal to the fullness of the love that God is in himself. The Son is from the Father. He is all things that the Father is, and yet he is *not* the Father, remaining infinitely irreducible to him, and this "not" is not a "negation" but the inverse side of a mutual embrace and affirmation, the fruit of which is the Holy Spirit. Precisely because God *is* infinite love, ever greater difference coincides with ever greater unity. Thus, in that Word through whom all things were made, the world can be "more than God" — having being in itself and capable of giving to God, who can really "receive" from it — because God as "ever greater" is infinitely more than himself, without this implying that he is ever less than himself, ever less than the surpassing fullness of *ipsum esse subsistens*. This should be seen as a promissory note to allay the earlier "Barthian" concerns about an "abstract" or "independent" creation. The only doctrine of creation that can uphold its own internal demands must be thoroughly trinitarian and hence Christological. I have reflected a bit more on this in "A Few Words on Balthasar's First Word."

I would argue that the capacity for the doctrine of creation to "save the appearances" hinges upon its ability to insist upon the reality of created novelty that is everywhere present and everywhere denied. I have argued in the body of this essay that modern science has succeeded in conquering the world by suppressing its actuality and turning a blind eye to the novelty necessary for the causal transactions upon which it depends. All that exists is merely rearranged stuff, whose novelty and existential significance can be reduced to those configurations. Indeed, in Jacques Monod, Richard Dawkins, and others we see a perverse reincarnation of the ancient tendency, as apparent novelty is merely the result of mistakes in reproduction, "defects" in matter, as it were, which prevent "form" (DNA in Dawkins's case) from reproducing itself perfectly. See Richard Dawkins, *The Selfish Gene* (Oxford: Oxford University Press, 1989), pp. 17-18, 21-45. "What I am doing is emphasizing the potential near-immortality of a gene, in the *form* of copies, as its defining property" (p. 35, emphasis mine). There are a great many problems with Dawkins's genetic reductionism, not least in that it is not an accurate picture of how genes "work." (See Lenny Moss, *What Genes Can't Do* [Cambridge, Mass.: MIT Press, 2004], pp. 75-116, 183-98.) What is interesting in this case is his use of "form" and the metaphysics of an account — wholly unexplained, of course — of how a thing can survive, not materially, but in the *form* of another.

84. Ratzinger, *"In the Beginning . . . ,"* p. 50.

ness, truth, and beauty, which is not God and which is good and indeed "like God" in its very difference from God. Hence St. Thomas tells us that there is a multitude of creatures because no one creature could adequately represent the divine goodness and beauty.[85]

Simply put, to see each irreducible, concrete act of existence is to *see* creation, for to see the being-in-itselfness, the gratuitous novelty — in short, the beauty — of every concrete act of existence, to see the infinite existential difference between every cause and effect and the irreducibility of the latter to the former, is to *see* this surplus. "Ever since the creation of the world, his eternal power and divine nature, invisible though they are, have been understood and seen through the things he has made."[86] This is why creation is an *aesthetic* analogy, in both the objective sense that the world simultaneously hides and manifests itself as creation in an infinite depth of interplay between being and ground, and in the subjective sense by which we apprehend and exhibit the truth of this mystery in the primitive cognitive act of wonder, which require us to let the world be before forcing it to be, in Heidegger's words, a "standing reserve."[87] This further is why to recover creation we must also recover the coincidence of beauty and truth and rescue the contemplative dimension of knowledge from the grips of a debased *technē*.[88]

To say that this surplus is visible, however, is not to say that this surplus is seen in the same way by that theology, implicit in all the other sciences, which is proper to metaphysics and which treats of divine things as an inexorable aspect of their treatment of the world[89] and that theology disclosed in the person Christ himself, which treats and reveals the world as a gratuitous aspect of its revelation of God. Nor is it to suggest that either can simply be derived from the other, that the first theology is enough, or that the fullness of the second can be attained without subjective preparation through the gift, virtue, and objective content of faith.

85. Aquinas, *ST* I, q. 47, a. 1.

86. Rom. 1.20.

87. Martin Heidegger, "The Question concerning Technology," in *Basic Writings*, trans. David Farrell Krell (San Francisco: Harper, 1993), p. 322.

88. This is by no means to suggest that *technē* is debased *in principle*; to the contrary, it belongs to the original order of nature and stands in a relation to it, so I would argue, analogous to grace. A central problem consists in the fact that human artifice now imitates a nature that is regarded as nothing but artifice — as "parts outside of parts." The question in this context is what a properly human making would look like, but that is too vast a subject to take up here. See David L. Schindler, "The Meaning of the Human in a Technological Age," *Anthropotes* 15 (1999): 31-51.

89. Aquinas, *In Boeth. De Trin.*, q. 5, a. 4.

I want to suggest a final analogy between the knowledge of the God-world relationship in the two theologies that will hopefully help illuminate these different forms of visibility. I have suggested, loosely following Balthasar, that the restoration of the world's interiority entails within it the immanence of mystery, the distance between ground and manifestation, *within* the world's truth, that this mystery of interiority is indeed the precondition for the world's truth. Put plainly, the world must always and in principle be infinitely more than our knowledge of it, and this "more," which provides the basis for the distinction between truth *and* appearance, which is itself the condition of possibility for the truth *of* appearance and the further possibility that our knowledge may indeed be knowledge. Whereas the first theology, implicit in science as such, will tend to see this "more" negatively as limit — for example, as the incomprehensibility of Socrates *qua* Socrates — or perhaps even positively as the beauty of Socrates *qua* Socrates, theology proper sees in the very incomprehensibility of Socrates the reverse side of an affirmation of the gratuitous goodness and beauty and the infinite depth proper to every concrete act of being as such: in short, as the unity of a gift, the fruit and object of love that is the ground of his comprehensibility as Socrates.[90]

90. I am rather skeptical that contemporary "emergence theory," which seems to be finding a place both in physics and in the attempt in some quarters of biology to "recover the organism," is adequate to the task of giving a scientific account or description of this "more." Inasmuch as "higher levels of organization," irreducible to their material bases, are merely "supervenient" (i.e., additive) on those bases, it is difficult to see how supervenient "form" finally remains anything but consequent upon — and therefore incidental to — a more basic mechanism, in other words, how it could ever recover a conception of form adequate to an *unum per se*. The sorts of causal descriptions that attach to emergence theory may be harmless enough in the order of efficient causes, but this would need to be integrated into a more robust causal order, and the notion of cause itself would need to be reexamined. Even so, I find the recognition of the phenomenon encouraging, particularly among physicists, and it serves to illustrate the point as to how creation might be seen from within different sciences. While I would not want to overstate the congruence, the following remarks by Robert Laughlin, Stanford professor and 1998 Nobel laureate in physics (*A Different Universe: Reinventing Physics from the Bottom Down* [New York: Basic Books, 2005], pp. xiv-xv), are at least grounds for hope:

> I think primitive organizational phenomena such as weather have something of lasting importance to tell us about more complex ones, including ourselves: Their primitiveness enables us to demonstrate with certainty that they are ruled by microscopic laws but also, paradoxically, that some of their more sophisticated aspects are insensitive to the details of those laws. In other words, we are able to prove in these simple cases that the organization can acquire meaning and life of its own and begin to transcend the parts from which it is made.
>
> What physical science thus has to tell us is that the whole being more than the

Simply put, if the basic form of analogy, and of the analogy between God and creatures, is captured in the negative theology of the Areopagite, wherein the *apophatic* negation of not-knowing is always the reverse side of a *kataphatic* affirmation of the surpassing and ineffable perfection of divine being, I am suggesting that this form holds not simply for the relation between created and uncreated being but also analogously — by virtue of that relation — *within* the truth of created being itself, such that in the dynamic interplay between essence and existence there is a certain bottomless depth, a certain infinity *within* the being of the creature itself, that is phenomenologically and analogically visible, as it were, and that opens of its own inner necessity into the gift of *esse* and the dependence of the creature upon the gratuity of the Creator.

The theological recognition of *esse* as gift, I want to suggest, is not simply a "supernatural" addition, tacked on to the more austere philosophical or scientific recognition of this surplus. Rather, it is integral to the nature of the metaphysical or the scientific *qua* metaphysical and scientific. For the same gift that, in giving *esse,* gives metaphysics and the science their objects, in this very same act gives it to metaphysics and the sciences to be and to be other than theology.[91] But their being "other than theology" is not *external* to theology, any more than their objects are external to the gift of *esse.* Consequently, "scientific autonomy" is not found in some illusory freedom from and indifference to metaphysical and theological assumptions. To the contrary, the freedom of metaphysics and the sciences not to be theology is itself theologically granted — not, of course, in a juridical sense by theologians and ecclesiastics but by the metaphysical and theological truth of the created order itself, which gives the sciences their being and subject. Hence meta-

---

sum of its parts is not merely a concept but a physical phenomenon. Nature is regulated not only by a microscopic rule base but by powerful and general principles of organization. Some of these principles are known, but the vast majority are not. New ones are being discovered all the time. At higher levels of sophistication the cause-and-effect relationships are harder to document, but there is no evidence that the hierarchical descent of law found in the primitive world is superseded by anything else. Thus if a simple physical phenomenon can become effectively independent of the more fundamental laws from which it descends, so can we. I am carbon, but I need not have been. I have a meaning transcending the atoms from which I am made.

91. It is also given to theology to be other than science, but this too is within the context of a fundamentally theological relation. So the theological still retains what David L. Schindler has referred to as its "absolute priority" over the scientific, even when science maintains a "relative priority" over theology.

physics and science alike can only do justice to this gift, to their own nature and to their objects, and thus resist the temptation of simultaneously becoming theology and making the world less than the gift and mystery that it is, by accepting the gift and seeing in the beauty of their objects the visibility of the invisible. So there is nothing here to prevent physics from being physics or biology from being biology, though we should expect of each of these to be transfigured internally *qua* physics and *qua* biology by this relation in ways that it is not up to theology to specify. Nor is there anything here to deny the legitimacy of scientific abstraction of parts from the whole of reality. St. Thomas himself allowed for this when he correlated Aristotle's distinction between understanding and judgment to the two poles of the real distinction.[92] It is surely possible to study form in abstraction from its matter and parts in isolation from their wholes — or for that matter to experimentally isolate natural phenomena — without losing one's grip on the priority of the "single actuality," the one single concrete, existing order, composed from them. In other words, scientific abstraction need not entail the Cartesian illusion that abstraction itself is indifferent or the Cartesian conceit that one can destroy the one actual existing universe and rebuild it as merely the aggregation of so many indifferent parts.

The legitimate autonomy of science, in other words, is not to be found in opposition to metaphysics and theology — an opposition that can finally be only a *theological stance.*

> The positive definition of grace can only be given through grace itself. God must himself reveal what he is within himself. The creature cannot delimit itself in relation to this Unknown reality. Nor can the creature, as a theologically understood "pure" nature, ever know wherein it specifically is different from God.[93]

Relation to God is constitutive of the creature as such and thus implicated in his most basic acts and in all other relations. Attempts *by science* to separate the natural and the supernatural therefore always have something of the character of Jonah about them, running to elude a relationship they can never escape, but can only distort. So the more vehemently a Richard Dawkins protests his atheism, the more definitive and grotesque his theology becomes. Such distortions of theology are always accompanied by a corresponding distortion of the world, the willful suppression and blindness to

92. Aquinas, *In Boeth. De Trin.,* q. 5, a. 3.
93. Balthasar, *The Theology of Karl Barth,* p. 279.

a world that — even now — screams "God!" even if we are no longer able to ascend the ladder it provides to us. Bonaventure's chastisement falls hard on us all now. "Whoever is not enlightened by such great splendor in created things is blind; whoever remains unheedful of such great outcries is deaf; whoever does not praise God in all these effects is dumb; whoever does not return to the First Principle after so many signs is a fool."[94] If in this scientific and technological age we are to entertain any hope of salvation from such foolishness, science must abandon the false freedom promised by the metaphysics and theology in which it is constituted and must embrace a metaphysics and theology at once adequate to the surpassing transcendence of God and the gratuitous beauty of the world, a metaphysics and theology adequate to the gift and beauty of creation.

This is the analogy of being.

94. Bonaventure, *The Journey of the Mind to God*, trans. Philotheus Boehner, O.F.M. (Indianapolis: Hackett, 1990), p. 10.

CHAPTER 11

Perfection and Participation

John Webster

I

Working in recent years on topics in dogmatics and moral theology, as well as on the exegesis of a number of New Testament texts, I have found myself placing some reliance on a theology of God's perfection, understood as God's wholly realized triune life in himself, which is infinitely full and infinitely loving, gracious, and creative. God's perfection is an immensely compelling concept, both intellectually and spiritually; used well, it can do what all good theological concepts should do, namely, assist in an intelligent grasp of the instruction concerning the ways and works of God that we find in the prophets and apostles. Furthermore, it can also have the subordinate function of assisting discrimination about contemporary theological proposals. I have found that, coordinated with a cluster of related concepts such as divine aseity, election, and covenant, the theology of divine perfection can both illuminate and enable critical engagement with conceptions of the relation of God and creatures that I do not find myself able fully to share.

The shape, flow, and proportions of a systematic theology are determined both by judgments of material content (that which the Christian faith teaches) and by judgments of circumstance (that which ought to receive especial emphasis here and now). Material judgments should carry greater weight, partly because theology properly understands its circumstances only from the illumination of the gospel, of which it is a conceptual celebration, and partly because apologetic gestures of concord or polemical gestures of defiance ought not to distort theology's relation to its proper object. That being said, the material judgment about the consequence of the concept of divine perfection for theology proper and for its dogmatic derivatives does lead to a distance from some prominent theological trends. From this point of view, for example, the stress in some recent (chiefly Protestant) trinitarian theology and Christology that the real is the historical offers little protection against seeing the temporal career of the Incarnate One as a kind of theogony. Or again, I remain uneasy with at least some uses of the idiom of participation in the theology of creation and salvation, chiefly because of its slender exegetical foundation, but also because of its sometimes hectoring and often drastically schematic history of Christian thought, and its apparent lack of concern with the hypertrophy or atrophy of some tracts of Christian teaching. By way of contrast, I have come to think that the rather strictly drawn demarcations between Creator and creature in some classical Calvinist divinity — in its doctrine of God, its account of the hypostatic union, its doctrine of election and covenantal fellowship, and the modesty of its theology of *unio* and *inhabitatio* — bring a good deal more to the table than is generally allowed. This tradition has few takers in contemporary constructive dogmatics, despite the continuing influence of its most sublime modern exposition in the work of Barth. It is commonly thought that it commits some serious errors (spectacularly so in the case of Barth) — that, far from offering a way out of the disarray of theology in modernity, it is a transcription of modernity's defects. My reflections on divine perfection suggest that these judgments cannot easily be sustained, and that there are more options available to us than extrinsicism or emanationism. Some of those options can be mined from the various seams of the Reformed tradition. In its most measured and intelligent expositions, when it has been determined to keep its eye on Scripture and eager to learn from catholic Christianity, that tradition has been able to shake itself free from a dialectical metaphysics without recourse to the opposite, and to commend a theology of God's perfection, which is the eternal depth of his creative triune goodness as the one who loves, elects, accompanies, reconciles, and glorifies creatures, so making resplendent his own inherent glory.

II

God's perfection is the limitless abundance of his life, the sheer plenitude that he is in himself as Father, Son, and Spirit. It is the infinite ocean from which flows the tide of God's loving acts toward creatures. God's perfection is the wholly realized fellowship of the eternal three, extended by virtue of his goodness into fellowship with creatures, a goodness that, in the wake of Adam's defection, takes redemptive form. God's perfection is the eternal rest and movement of his blessedness, life, and therefore movement, which are not simply self-revolving because they include the uncaused generosity with which, in correspondence to his own blessedness, God blesses creatures with life and new life. To speak of God's perfection is, therefore, simply to attempt a conceptual expansion of the statement in the Johannine prologue: "from his fullness we have all received, grace upon grace." God is full in himself; his fullness is, Calvin comments with one of his favorite images, "the fountain of life . . . a truly inexhaustible fountain."[1]

To expand on this: because God's perfection is the fullness with which he is and acts as the one he is, it is a positive, material concept. It does not first and foremost indicate negative characteristics such as absence of restriction or potentiality in God; rather, it indicates God's wholly realized identity as *himself.* "Things are called perfect when they have achieved actuality," says Thomas, "the perfect being that in which nothing required by the thing's particular mode of perfection fails to exist."[2] The concern of a dogmatics of God's perfection is to specify the particular *modus perfectionis* proper to God; in this matter, its first task is not *disputatio* (though that may come at some later point) but *explicatio,* repetition and expansion of the divine self-naming and self-indication: "I am he" (Isa. 41:4).

A Christian theology of God's perfection asks, Who is this God? In Christian theological usage, the conception of perfection can be filled out only very clumsily by magnifying what are taken to be attributes of greatness. The triune God is not a "perfect being," that is, one who instantiates great-making properties. Accounts by philosophers of religion along these lines are flawed in a double way. They are rarely able to extricate themselves from an abstract concept of *deitas,* a preconception of divinity that is not generated from or corrected by God's evangelical self-enactment and self-communication but emerges out of the need for a perfect being as a causal explanation of features of the contingent world: God's perfection is a necessary property of the world's origin. A second weakness is that — in contrast to the premodern Christian thinkers to whom "perfect being" theorists often

---

1. John Calvin, *The Gospel according to St John 1–10* (Edinburgh: St. Andrew Press, 1959), p. 23.

2. Thomas Aquinas, *Summa theologiae* I, q. 4, a. 2.

appeal (Anselm especially) — the doctrine of the Trinity plays little role, the weight of the edifice being borne by *deity*, its logical structure and cosmological function. God's special character, the particular mode of perfection confessed of him as Father, Son, and Spirit, the one who has life in himself and gives life to creatures, is subsumed beneath the project of determining the necessary attributes of a supreme causal power from which all things can be explained. The resultant notion of God is synthetic rather than analytic, built out of observations upon creaturely realities and their lack, and so an insufficiently determinate concept of *divine* perfection. Over against this: God's perfection is his singular, noncomparative, nonderivative identity. Tautology — God is God — rather than comparison or contrast is basic to the dogmatic logic of Christian teaching about God, concerned as it is with the sheer originality and singularity of the one who displays and magnifies his inherent perfection in the history of the covenant and supremely in the missions of the Word and the Spirit.

In ordering its thinking in this way, dogmatics is simply acknowledging that it stands within the domain of revelation. Revelation is God's communicative and intelligible presence, and this presence disciplines theological reason, commanding its attention and directing it to the place where God's majestic condescension is to be found: in the external works of God. But theological reason attends to those works in their depth, investigating them not only in their temporal occurrence but also in terms of their reference back to the groundless, infinite life of God disclosed in them. The economy of God's works is a making known of "the mystery of [God's] will" (Eph. 1:9); it is a "setting forth" (Eph. 1:9), a projection into the temporal realm of the fathomless reality of God's eternal, antecedent determination, which is "mystery," exceeding any comprehension, even as it presents itself for our knowledge and delight. Dogmatics attends to God's self-expressive form — his being with us in his works — in which the one who is in utter sufficiency makes his approach as the creature's Lord and reconciler.

But more may be said by way of positive transcription. God is one God as Father, Son, and Spirit. The relations between the triune persons are God's undivided perfection. They do not flow from it, as secondary realities underpinned by a simple divine substrate, for they *are* the one God. God's perfection is his abundant life in himself as the Father, the unoriginate one who is eternally the Father of the Son and the one from whom the Spirit proceeds; God's perfection is his life as the Son, who is eternally generate of the Father and who, with the Father, breathes the Spirit; God's perfection is his life as the Spirit, who proceeds from them both. The perfection of God is this life of his; it is this plenitude of processions, wholly realized communion, spontaneous, replete, glorious.

There is a necessary indirectness to what dogmatics is able to say about this immanent perfection of God. The processions of the eternal Son and the eternal Spirit from the eternal Father become matters of theological intelligence only as the mind follows the beckoning of God's economic form. Yet — this point is crucial — the priority of the economy in the order of the intellect should not be mistaken for the drastically different (and calamitous) dogmatic claim that the only significant distinctions are those enacted in the theater of God's external works. God's triunity is not simply his threefold external actuality. What takes place in the economy is not a history in which God, as it were, evacuates himself, but a history precipitated by divine capacities and movements "outside" creation, on the basis of which God reaches down or out toward or into creaturely time. There really is a history of God among creatures, though it is a strange history, strangest of all in its supreme moment, which is the history of God among creatures *as* a creature; but this takes place only because of God's anterior perfection, from which the history comes (this is why it is so strange). The Son is "in" the world, but he is so only because "I *proceeded* and *came forth* from God" (John 8:42); the Spirit is "with" the disciples, dwelling with them, being in them; but only because he is *given* (John. 14:16ff.). Proceeding, coming forth, being given — they all point *back*. Following this line of retrojection, we can come to see that the differentiated presence of the Son and the Spirit in the world is the external realization of eternal movements and distinctions within the being of God.

This being so, we may fittingly (i.e., nonspeculatively) move to indicate something of the particular inner life of the one-in-three. As the Father, Son, and Spirit, who in his self-utterance names himself as such in our hearing, God's life is constituted by his personal works, the *opera Dei personalia*, that is, the *ad intra* operations, enactments, or mutual address and response of the triune persons in which their personal characteristics can be discerned. Reticence is imperative: whatever is said of the properties of each person and of their relations must not suggest a society of essentially distinct centers of will and action bound by relations into a federal unity. God's unity is not the *product* of his immanent relations. Yet the indivisibility of the substance of the one God does not disallow fitting differentiation of God's personal works. Each of the persons may be identified in terms of its hypostatic character *(character hypostaticus sive personalis)*, that is, by properties that distinguish that person and so are incommunicable. Thomas spoke of these personal properties as "notions,"[3] and his usage, which echoes the Greek patristic concept of the *idioma* of each triune person, found its way into later Protestant scholastic theology. "Notions" do not compromise simplicity; they simply indicate what each divine person is in relation to the other persons, showing not only the differentiation within the being of the one God but also the kind of unity that God has, namely, unity-in-distinction.

God's perfect life is the life of God the Father. The Father is the principle of the Trinity "in reference to the persons proceeding from him by fatherhood and common spiration"; because the Father is "principle without a principle," he is identified "by his not being from another."[4] The Father is characterized by innascibility *(innascibilitas)*, the property of not being begotten *(agennēsia)*.[5] This, in turn, does not mean that, as principle, the Father is superior to the Son and the Spirit, for all the persons are *a se* according to their common divine essence, but the Father alone is ingenerate, no other substance having been given to him. Yet fatherhood is predicated of the first person because of his eternal relation to the second and third persons; he is not Father in isolation but as the one who begets the Son and with the Son breathes the Spirit. Begotten of the Father, the Son is the perfect counterpart of the Father, his "passive generation" or "filiation" corresponding to the Father's "active generation." Similarly, the Spirit's "passive spiration," his proceeding from the Father and the Son, corresponds to their "active spiration." Paternity, filiation, and spiration are the fullness of God; being begotten and being breathed are eternal relations in the simple essence of God, not acts of self-creation; in his inner relations God is not *causa sui*, for the relations do not effect a coming-to-be or suggest precedence in time or superiority of nature on the part of the one who begets and breathes, nor do they denote lack on the part of Son and Spirit, for they are modes of God's eternal perfection, the limitless mobility of God's life in himself.

One could extend this in a number of directions, for example, by looking at the concepts of aseity or divine *apatheia;* but enough may already have been said to draw forth an objection: do we really need to insist on this dogmatic move? Does not the desire to make it threaten to lead Christian doctrine into captivity to Eleatic metaphysical assumptions about the gulf between the permanence of being and the transience of appearance? Does not this separation insinuate itself into the Christian doctrine of God whenever

3. *ST* I, q. 32, aa. 2-4.
4. *ST* I, q. 33, a. 4, ad 1.
5. *ST* I, q. 33. a. 4.

God's immanent life is conceived as the immutable substrate of his historical manifestation? May not the sharp distinction between uncreated and created mount resistance to the gospel's instruction to look for the gospel's God in temporal appearance? Perhaps temporal appearance is of itself sufficient; perhaps the economy of God's presence exhausts God's perfection. God's "hypostatic being, his self-identity, is constituted in *dramatic coherence*": so Jenson. He continues: "Aristotle . . . regarded liability to historical contingency as an ontological deficit. . . . But since God is himself identified by contingencies, Aristotle's prejudice need not hinder us. Why should commitment in a history not be instead an ontological *perfection?*"[6]

The answer to Jenson's question is straightforward: it is precisely because God is not *liable* to historical contingency — because he has life in and of himself apart from creatures and time — that his commitment in a history can be an ontological perfection (this is the point of the so-called *extra Calvinisticum*). God's eternal triune aseity is the capacity and authority of the Son and the Spirit to bring a divine blessing to creatures in their missions of love. A more extended response would identify three matters for reflection. First, to speak of God's perfect life in himself as the infinite ground of God's works is not to demote these works to the status of mere epiphenomena. Only a seriously reduced dogmatics would do that — one in which the only relations within God would be relations of origin, one that accorded no significance to the divine missions in determining the properties of the persons and their common divine essence, one that had purged the eternal divine counsel of all reference to the appointment of creatures to fellowship with God. Second, the "drama" of the economy has not only events but *agents, dramatis personae* who come into this history without coming to themselves for the first time in its execution. A doctrine of the perfect life of the immanent Trinity furnishes a description of these persons and of what we may expect of them. It does not reduce the drama to mere appearance, nor its agents to masks; it tries, rather, to indicate that the evangelical saving force of the drama draws momentum from the eternal repleteness of these agents and their acts of "sending" and "coming" — from the divine missions and their temporal execution — in which the eternal God reaches out to bless creatures. Accordingly, third, there are no realities beyond God that provide the occasion for the perfecting of God's love. The love of God is wholly original and wholly originating. In terms of trinitarian

6. Robert Jenson, *Systematic Theology,* vol. 1 (Oxford: Oxford University Press, 1997), p. 64.

dogma, the divine processions are "extended" (not "supplemented" but "set forth") in the divine missions or temporal processions into the creaturely domain. Yet this does not entail that creatures somehow co-constitute God, but simply that the relations of origin between the persons of the Trinity are the unfathomable, free source of the economy. To speak of creatures and created history, we need only speak of the perfect God.

But how is the movement from the uncreated to the created to be conceived? Through some variant of the metaphysics of participation? Theologians in the Reformed tradition — notably, of course, Calvin himself — have not been unremittingly hostile to such ideas in soteriology and sacramental theology, though they have not commonly sought to extend them into a theology of created being as such, typically preferring to tie participation very tightly to soteriology, that is, to "union with," "partaking of," or "being in" Christ. The larger setting of a Reformed theology of participation has characteristically been a "dramatic" conception of the economy of divine grace, organized around two basic principles: (1) the history of God's dealings with creatures is "covenantal," that is, an ordered moral history between personal agents (the uncreated God and his creatures) and not a process of diffusion of being; (2) the course of this history is shaped by God's good pleasure, the eternal divine counsel executed in the *opera Dei externae.* If within such an overall conception of the economy, divine election acquires some prominence, this is not because it is thought of as an implacable force that crushes the creature, but because election helps characterize the kind of fellowship that takes place between the triune God and the creature, namely, one that is a history of gracious divine making and active creaturely gratitude, and one in which the creature's attempt at self-destruction cannot thwart the divine purpose to bestow life.

Such a conception of the overall shape of the relations of God and creatures is not widely shared and has received rather rough treatment at the hands of its objectors. The objection, at heart, is that when the movement from God to creatures is conceived of as a matter of God's free self-determination, divine perfection is understood contrastively, as discontinuous with or antithetical to created reality. To speak in such terms seems unilateralist; there appears — at least from a casual glance — to be no proper creaturely counterpart to the divine will, and so no reciprocity in the fellowship of God and creature, no active reception of the divine gift but mere passivity before a force that smashes everything in its path — in the end, therefore, no *grace* in the sense of creative, life-bestowing goodness but just a divine will in a void (the privileging of the forensic element in justification is taken to be an egregious instance). The point can be made in historical form: Reformed theology seems to be the triumph of nominalist metaphysics, which replaced an earlier theology of participation with a voluntarist scheme, according to which Creator and creature are understood as infinite and finite causes operating in the same terrain, collaborating or contrasting or conflicting, negatively or dialectically related as two objects — wills — set in opposition. And if this is the case, then may it not be that the *analogia entis* — properly understood not as subsuming God and creatures under a general category of being but as a teaching about God's abundance, according to which "creatures . . . belong to the infinity of God"[7] — offers relief from the separated philosophy and theology by which the Reformed tradition is ensnared?

What might Reformed dogmatics make of this? There are some preliminaries to be noted — that the critiques are often stronger on the *grandes lignes* than on the textual details, that the genetic fallacy is not always kept at bay, that many of the criticisms are anticipated (and prosecuted rather more accurately) by Barth, in his doctrines of election and providence, for example, as well as by earlier Reformed theologians. These matters need not detain us; better to indicate in more general terms something of the temper of a dogmatic response.

We may begin by observing that a prudent and modest Reformed dogmatics will feel no compelling need to rush to its own defense in these matters but will be open to learn from its interlocutors, however hostile or underinformed they sometimes prove to be. It is undoubtedly the case that some of what the Reformed tradition has had to say about the perfection of God and the supremacy of God's good pleasure has been unguarded and subject to distortion. Furthermore, Reformed dogmatics would do well to look for what is of value in the very different conceptions of its critics. There is nothing self-evidently panentheistic about theologies of participation, no obvious compromise of the distinction between the agenetic and the genetic orders of reality. God does not need to be protected from degradation by establishing a caesura between the divine and the creaturely; "uncreated" is not necessarily a counterpoint to "contingent": it may mean plenitude as *source.* To protect God may simply be to imprison him in a separate domain, incapable of free generous self-communication. All this is simply a necessary corrective to a tradition that has not always found it easy to do justice to the self-correcting impulse that is claimed as one of its hallmarks.

---

7. David Bentley Hart, *The Beauty of the Infinite: The Aesthetics of Christian Truth* (Grand Rapids: Eerdmans, 2003), p. 242.

At the same time, a fittingly confident Reformed dogmatics will not make hurried, impetuous adjustments to its construal of the gospel. To listen carefully to interlocutors does not entail prima facie acceptance of the terms of the questions posed to dogmatics, or of the descriptions of its own tradition offered by those interlocutors, be they historical or conceptual. Simply to concede that one's tradition is trapped by philosophical defect is inadequate for reasons that are as much spiritual as intellectual: precipitate concession to criticism can inhibit the stability of intelligence; eagerness to admit objections and make corresponding corrections can mean inattention to the genuine instruction offered by one's tradition, and so a *diminishment* of catholicity; above all, swift surrender to critique can presume an impossible ideal of the perfectibility of Christian dogmatics or a less than providentialist reading of one's theological situation and history, which ought properly to fall under the rule of all human endeavor, namely, *Dei providentia et hominum confusione.*

With this in mind, here are some rules of thumb for how a discussion might proceed from the side of an unpretentious and critically alert Reformed dogmatics. The first and primary directive is that any account of the relation of God's perfect life in himself to created reality will be adequate to the degree to which it is shaped and normed by the biblical canon. Any such account will have to commend itself by a capacity to illuminate that by which it is itself illuminated, namely, Holy Scripture. This means, on the one hand, that, both in its scope and its details, any such account must be *warranted* by Scripture as the law of theological intelligence and judgment. It means, on the other hand, that any such account must demonstrate that it is *required* by Scripture and must respect the reticence or silence of Scripture: this is the extension into dogmatic and speculative divinity of the principle of the sufficiency of Scripture, that is, that Scripture prescribes the topics for and limits to theological reasoning. The application of this directive is, of course, more a matter of art than of calculus; establishing biblical warrants for doctrinal proposals is not a straightforward matter (though more straightforward than some like to think); nor is it always self-evident what constitutes straying beyond the scriptural territory (and maybe, some say, "territory" is too bounded a way of thinking about the operations of Scripture in theology). What is clear is that, as servants in the domain of Word and Spirit, the prophets and apostles are the masters of divinity, and that, by reading their several witnesses, we may legitimately expect to solve theological problems. The question then becomes: to what extent does a particular theology of divine perfection emerge from disciplined, Spirit-governed reading of (say) Exodus, Isaiah, John, Ephesians, Hebrews, and 1 Peter? To what extent are systematic and speculative theology paraphrases of the scriptural testimonies?

A second directive is that we may expect to make progress by material dogmatic description, that is, by the kind of theology whose concepts are secondary to the scriptural rendering of God and God's relations to creatures. Alongside exegesis, we require a descriptive anatomy of the economy to which Scripture testifies: this is who God is, these are his creatures, this is the unfolding history between them. By way of illustration, this means that the twin topics of election and reconciliation will assume prominence, since the canon is in large part a narrative of how the eternal loving purpose of God for fellowship with creatures triumphs in the face of the creature's treachery. The relation of agenetic and genetic is not simply a matter of co-ordinated or coinherent or competing orders of being; it is a moral history that flows from the first to the second Adam and on into the communion of saints.

A third directive follows: it is imprudent for dogmatics to expect too much from inquiry into the metaphysics of the matter. Of course, dogmatics needs an operative metaphysics in order to do its job — and not just in cosmology: how could it make any headway in the doctrines of the Trinity or of the person and work of Christ without extensive deployment of metaphysical intelligence? But because the office of metaphysics is ministerial, not magisterial, it is important not to think of dogmatics as a set of problems for whose resolution we must await an improved *philosophical* apparatus. A corollary here is that genealogies of modern theology that trace its putative disarray to earlier philosophical compromise (with nominalism or whatever) have limits; this, because dogmatic failure is not only the outworking of philosophical error but also — more often — the consequence of thin, tired, or unexpectant exegesis in which interpretative convention replaced reading, and which kept dogmatics away from the tense readiness for correction that is the proper stance of theological intelligence before the embassy of the prophets and apostles.

III

How, then to proceed? By listening to Holy Scripture. Here is Ephesians 1:3-14:

³Blessed be the God and Father of our Lord Jesus Christ, who has blessed us in Christ with every spiritual blessing in the heavenly places, ⁴even as he chose us in him before the foundation of the world, that we should be holy and blameless before him. ⁵He destined us in love to be his sons through Jesus Christ, according to the purpose of his will, ⁶to the praise of his glorious grace which he freely bestowed on us in the Beloved. ⁷In him we have redemption through his blood, the forgiveness of our trespasses, according to the riches of his grace ⁸which he lavished upon us. ⁹For he has made known to us in all wisdom and insight the mystery of his will, according to his purpose which he set forth in Christ ¹⁰as a plan for the fullness of time, to unite all things in him, things in heaven and things on earth. ¹¹In him, according to the purpose of him who accomplishes all things according to the counsel of his will, ¹²we who first hoped in Christ have been destined and appointed to live for the praise of his glory. ¹³In him you also, who have heard the word of truth, the gospel of your salvation, and have believed in him, were sealed with the promised Holy Spirit, ¹⁴which is the guarantee of our inheritance until we acquire possession of it, to the praise of his glory.

Drawing, perhaps, on the form of the *berakah*, this single loose, unwieldy sentence is a magnification of the redemptive grace accomplished in Jesus Christ in fulfillment of the will of the Father, that all things should be drawn into unity in the eternal Son. God's fullness is assumed throughout. The obliqueness of what is said about this fullness in its interior and exterior aspects — as the fullness of God in himself before creation — ought not to lead us to minimize its pervasive importance. As often in Scripture, what is most important in the order of being does not necessarily manifest itself on the surface (this is why speculative exegesis is necessary). The passage is scattered with gestures toward God's wholly realized life. The blessings with which God has blessed us in Christ are "in the heavenly places" (3) — in the "highest heavens," that is, the place where God and his Christ are ineffably exalted, "far above" (4:10), from where Christ exercises his universal and supreme lordship over "things in heaven and things on earth" (10). These divine blessings flow, moreover, from the eternal relations of Father and Son: God the Father chose us in Christ "before the foundation of the world" (4); created circumstance follows and does not cause or shape divine election. And so God the Father is "the Father of glory" (1:17), the inextinguishable source of light and radiant presence; God the Son is one who is again "far above" (1:21) — not a mere competing power or name, not circumscribed by spatial or temporal locale, but the universal and self-authored presence that can emerge only from the infinite recesses of God's own life. What is manifest, therefore, in the mission of Christ is God's *mysterious* will (9): Christ's work flows from and makes apprehensible the antecedent divine purpose, which is not reactive but which comprehends and forms created history. All this, then, indicates that the condition for there being an economy, and the shape of that economy, are both to be found in the plenitude of God. He "who fills all in all" (1:23) is in himself replete, filling all things but filled by none; and so there is a creation and a redemptive history and a church. There is a twofold order here: in the order of knowing, economy precedes theology, for God who is himself blessed conducts us to himself by blessing us; in the order of being, theology precedes economy, for only because God is in himself infinitely rich is he the one who enriches creatures.

What ties together the realities of God in himself and God's economic presence is God's *will*, directed to creatures as sovereign decision and determination in their favor. God "chose" us (4); God "destined us" and did so "according to his good pleasure," setting creatures under a divine "purpose" (5); this choice and foreordination — that is, God's "will" and "purpose" (9) — are made known in Christ, in whom there is brought to enactment God's "plan," that is, his economy, in which he governs and administers creation in accordance with his eternal will (10). And so to hope in Christ is not to be a self-originating and self-directing subject and agent but to find oneself, as it were, anticipated by universal and irresistible love, to become aware that creaturely history runs "according to the purpose of him who accomplishes all things according to the counsel of his will" (11); more specifically, it means to have one's life on the basis of having been "destined and appointed" (12).

But how is this divine will to be understood? We must allow ourselves to be led to the identity of the divine agent; this willing, destining, purposing are acts of the God and Father of our Lord Jesus Christ, acts of the Father "in him." Little can be determined about the nature and operation of God's will if we seize upon some formal characteristic (causal force, perhaps, or influence). Instead, we must be directed by the divine subject, the one of whom we are required to say that he is "self-moved and moving" being.[8] The movement of divine grace, and what it manifests about the source of grace in

8. Karl Barth, *Church Dogmatics* II/1, trans. G. W. Bromiley and T. F. Torrance (Edinburgh: T. & T. Clark, 1957), p. 268.

God's life in himself, must govern theological reason, ensuring that only after contemplating the actual accomplishment of God's will may we speak intelligently of its nature. Much follows from this.

1. God's will is his determination to *bless* and *love* creatures (3, 5). It ought not to be conceived as sheer force obliterating everything that stands in its way, as an assertive movement with no term other than its own unhindered enactment. It is fathomless generosity. This generosity is "willed," not in the sense that it might *not* have been, had God directed his will to different objects, but in the sense that it is personal determination, undeflectable goodness: this will be!

2. God's will is *gracious,* known in the act of praise as free bestowal of glorious grace (6). It is unbidden and undeserved, not a reaction to desert or need, and only so a matter for praise rather than expectation. Grace is sheer creativity requiring nothing beyond itself; but it is not thereby an act of impoverishment but an enrichment. Grace is *lavish* (8); to be its recipient is to know "the riches of his glorious inheritance in the saints, the immeasurable greatness of his power in us who believe" (1:18, 19), and to be given status as those seated with Christ (1:20, 2:6). Grace, in short, means that creatures are destined to become the sons of God (5). Adoptive grace dignifies; God's gracious will does not devour everything; it gives being and activity.

3. If we inquire into the specific direction taken by the gracious divine determination to bless and dignify creatures, we receive a strangely specific answer: redemption through the shedding of blood, the forgiveness of trespasses (7). In "the Beloved" — that is, in the personal acts of the one who is the unique object of the Father's regard, and who is one with the Father's being — God fulfills his eternal counsel by interposing himself into the midst of the creature's jeopardy. The creature has so acted as to need deliverance from bondage and remission of offenses. God does not defeat the creature's self-defeat by diffusion of being but by a moral act undertaken by one other than the fallen creature: by "blood" — by the personal, historical, and external act of obedient self-sacrifice on the part of the beloved Son.

4. This opens out into the most comprehensive characteristic of the divine will: both in its inner divine depth and its historical form, it is inseparable from the name of Jesus Christ. God chose us *in him* (4); God destined us for adoption *through Jesus Christ* (5); God set forth his plan *in Christ* (9); God unites all things *in him* (10); it is *in him* that we

are appointed to live for the praise of the Father's glory (11-12). "In him" is a fluid term here, and its range should not be restricted to straightforward incorporation; indeed, the term presupposes the *difference* between Christ and believers, as much as their union. We are chosen in him, but he is not chosen; we are adopted through him, but he is himself the eternal Son. "In him," therefore, indicates not substantial union so much as intimate, asymmetrically ordered fellowship between uncreated and created.

5. Of course, there is much more that needs to be said: substantial union is not a stable concept, and it may admit of senses that are not simply *methexis*. In reaching a judgment about that, it is important to bear in mind that, for the apostle's *berakah*, the *telos* of God's will for creatures is *moral fellowship;* at the very least, any theology of *inhabitatio* would have to prove itself capable of embracing this. Thus the counterpart of election is not creaturely passivity but ethics. God chose us "before the foundation of the world that we should be holy and blameless before him" (4) — holiness and blamelessness are not simply infused virtues or a situation into which believers are dropped; they are aspects of a mode of life stemming from the divine alteration of the condition of creatures. This is why they are the legitimate basis for the moral exhortation of the second half of the letter. Destiny is appointment to life, namely, life "for the praise of his glory" (12). This is not the Ritschlian moralism so deplored by revisionist Lutherans and others — that is, God as an external causal impulse upon a creaturely will, generating a *Tatgemeinschaft* rather than ontological communion. It is, rather, simply to observe that alongside "in him" we also have to say "before him" (4) — in his presence, before his face: the note of moral answerability ought not to be missed.

So far, Ephesians 1: what does it indicate about divine perfection? A dogmatic paraphrase of the flow of the material might go something like this: There is the perfect life of God, the Father of glory, the Beloved, the Spirit given in him. There is the eternal divine determination in which God loves creatures by electing them for life before him in holiness. That determination receives temporal fulfillment in the history of redemption in Christ, a history that generates a moral fellowship, whose social form is the body over which Christ is head, the communion of saints. This is not bare extrinsicism but the history of creatures with God. That history is not an interplay of causal forces, still less a contest of wills; whatever other distortions may be attributable to Reformed federal dogmatics, that, surely, may not. God is not one element in a synthesis of uncreated and created powers. Nor is God's will to be considered simply in terms of its inward quality of freedom from determination — in terms, that is, of abstractly conceived unconditionedness, absoluteness, independence, and infinity, for God is without counterpart. God's will is effortless, self-moved, outward movement, flowing from abundance of life and therefore a determination of himself for generosity that does not violate the creature because God is not a rival occupant of some territory in which the creature can also be found struggling to preserve itself. The creature's increase neither decreases nor increases God, because God's perfect bliss blesses; it is his nature to be ever more fruitful, and so he is Creator of heaven and earth and redeemer of the children of Adam.

If this, or something like it, is what is meant by the *analogia entis,* then the polemical situation looks rather different; if this is what Barth failed or refused to see, then he deserves to be taken to task. But Ephesians ought at least to register the question whether God's goodness is such that he is beyond ontological difference. It is without doubt easy to slide into a mythological account of the divine economy, in which God is simply a magnified voluntary agent, contracted to certain relations and acts; however infinite the magnification, it always misses God's true infinity. Yet the history set out in Ephesians 1 is neither myth nor projection but apostolic embassy to which we are to direct our contemplation.

Is the analogy of being the invention of the Antichrist? Hardly: it is a theologoumenon, no less and no more; surely the Antichrist would unleash something a bit more destructive than a somewhat recherché bit of Christian teaching? Is it the wisdom of God? Surely that title is reserved for one alone, Jesus Christ, and him crucified. This is why the rule for theological intelligence — and, we might add, for theological metaphysics — is: "Let him who boasts, boast of the Lord" (1 Cor. 1:31).

CHAPTER 12

The Destiny of Christian Metaphysics: Reflections on the *Analogia Entis*

David Bentley Hart

I. The Analogy as a Principle of Christian Thought

In that small, poorly lit, palely complected world where the cold abstractions of theological ontology constitute objects of passionate debate, Erich Przywara's proposal regarding the *analogia entis* is unique in its nearly magical power to generate inane antagonisms. The never quite receding thunder of Karl Barth's cry of "Antichrist!" hovers perpetually over the field of battle; tiny but tireless battalions of resolute Catholics and Protestants clash as though the very pith and pulp of Christian conviction were at stake; and even inside the separate encampments, local skirmishes constantly erupt among the tents. And yet it seems to be the case that, as a rule, the topic excites conspicuous zeal — especially among its detractors — in directly inverse proportion to the clarity with which it is understood; for in itself, there could scarcely be a more perfectly biblical, thoroughly unthreatening, and rather drably obvious Christian principle than Przywara's *analogia entis*.

What, after all, are the traditional objections to the analogy? What dark anxieties does it stir in fretful breasts? That somehow an ontological analogy between God and creatures grants creaturely criteria of truth priority over the sovereign event of God's self-disclosure in time, or grants the conditions of our existence priority over the transcendent being of God, or grants some human structure of thought priority over the sheer *novum* of revelation, or (simply enough) grants nature priority over grace. Seen thus, the *analogia entis* is nothing more than a metaphysical system (which we may vaguely denominate "Neoplatonist") that impudently imagines there to be some ground of identity between God and the creature susceptible of human comprehension, and that therefore presumes to lay hold of God in his unutterable transcendence. But such objections are — to be perfectly frank — total nonsense. One need not even bother to complain about the somewhat contestable dualities upon which they rest; it is enough to note that such concerns betray, not simply a misunderstanding, but a perfect ignorance, of Przywara's reasoning. For it is precisely the "disjunctive" meaning of the analogy that animates Przywara's argument from beginning to end; for him, it is the irreducible and, in fact, *infinite* interval of difference within the analogy that constitutes its surprising, revolutionary, and metaphysically shattering power. Far from constituting some purely natural conceptual scheme to which revelation must prove itself obedient, the *analogia entis*, as Przywara conceives of it, is nothing more than the largely apophatic, almost antimetaphysical ontology — or even meta-ontology — with which we have been left, now that revelation has obliged us to take leave of any naive metaphysics that would attempt to grasp God through a conceptual knowledge of essences or genera. A more plausible objection to the analogy might be the one that Eberhard Jüngel attributed (unpersuasively) to Barth, and that even Hans Urs von Balthasar found somewhat convincing: that so austere and so vast is the distinction between the divine and human in Przywara's thought that it seems to leave little room for God's nearness to humanity in Christ. This is no less mistaken than other, more conventional views of the matter, but at least it demonstrates some awareness of the absolute abyss of divine transcendence that the analogy marks.

At its most elementary, what Przywara calls the *analogia entis* is simply the scrupulous and necessary rejection of two opposed errors, each the mirror inversion of the other: the equally reductive and equally "metaphysical" alternatives of pure identity and pure dialectic. For neither approach to the mystery of God — neither the discourse of God as the absolute One nor the discourse of God as the absolute "Wholly Other" — can by itself truly express the logic of divine transcendence; both resolve the interval of difference between God and creation into a kind of pure and neutral equivalence, somehow more original and comprehensive than that difference, and so more original and comprehensive than God in himself *as God* (though this is perhaps easier to see in the case of the metaphysics of identity).

As Przywara understands the analogy, it is first and foremost an affirmation that creation comes about *ex nihilo*, and that God therefore is not merely some "supreme being," but is at once utterly transcendent of all beings and also the only source of all beings. Thus the analogy presumes what no self-sufficient and perfectly systematic metaphysics could ever properly admit into its speculations: the radical contingency and nonnecessity of the created order. One cannot begin to understand the principle of the *analogia entis* unless one first grasps that, before all else, it is the delightful and terrible principle of the creature's utter groundlessness; it is the realization that we possess no essence, no being, no foundation that is not always, in every moment, imparted to us from beyond ourselves, and that does not therefore always exceed everything that we are in any moment of our existence. Or, said differently, essence and existence never coincide in us as they do in God but subsist, from our perspective, only in an altogether fortuitous synthesis, and are given to us at once, separately and together, in a movement of purest gratuity, from a transcendent source upon which we have no "natural" claim. Thus the sheer dynamism of creaturely existence (which is the constant and guiding theme of Przywara's thought) can never be resolved into the stability of any ground of identity belonging to us; only in him do we live, and move, and have our being. Of course, to understand even this much, one must avoid falling into any of the common misunderstandings that have attached themselves to the concept of the *analogia entis* since at least the days of Barth. Before all else, one must grasp that, for Przywara, the ontological analogy does not treat "being" as some genus under which God and the creature — or the infinite and the finite — are placed as distinct instances. Quite the reverse, in fact: it is precisely *being* that is to be understood as analogous; and it is precisely any univocal concept of being — any notion that God and creatures alike are "beings" comprehended by "being as such" — that the *analogia entis,* as a principle, denies. The proper proportion of the analogy, after all, is that of the *maior dissimilitudo* (or, as Przywara would prefer, the *semper maior dissimilitudo*) that separates God from any creature. So transcendent is God, one might say, that *even being* — that barest, most basic, most primordial of attributions — is *only analogous* between him and his creation. And this is an absolute impoverishment for any traditional metaphysics that would hope to lay hold of God within human concepts, for there is no discrete being called God, within the fold of "being as such," whose nature we can conceive *per analogiam essentiarum.*

Nevertheless — and this touches upon the other "false path" to transcendence — the being of the creature must indeed be *analogous to* God's pure act of being; otherwise all talk of God would be confined within an arid dialectical theology of the "Wholly Other" so extreme as to posit — even if only tacitly — a logically absurd equivocity of being. Absolute otherness is not transcendence but merely a kind of "negative immanence," for true transcendence must be beyond all negation. If creation were somehow something simply "outside of" or "other than" God, like one object outside another, then logically one would have to say that there is something more than — something in addition to — God; God, thus conceived, would be a kind of thing, less than the whole of things, a being embraced within whatever wider abstract category is capacious enough to contain both him and his creatures under its canopy, without confusing their several essences (and inevitably that category will be called "being," in the barren univocal sense). It is one of the great oddities of most debates concerning the *analogia entis* that those who reject the principle in order to defend God's sovereign transcendence against the encroachments of human reason are in fact effectively denying God's fully ontological transcendence and replacing it with a concept of mere ontic supremacy. If being is not susceptible of the interval of the analogy (even though it is an interval of ever greater unlikeness), then God and creation exist in a reciprocal real relation to one another, which means an extrinsic relation between two mutually delimiting objects; not only is this a degrading concept of God, but inevitably it must presuppose the mediations of some *tertium quid,* some broader context of "reality" that somehow exceeds the difference between God and creatures. Nor is it enough to answer such concerns with the essentially magical claim that the "divine will" alone mediates between God and world; for unless God is understood as the ontological source and ground of creation, creation itself must be understood as a thing separate from God, founded upon its own potentiality, and the creative will of God must then be understood simply as the spontaneous and arbitrary power of conjuration possessed by a very impressive — but still finite — divine sorcerer.

The actual terms of the analogy, moreover, are of a sort that could not possibly give offense to any Christian, however piously certain he or she is of personal nothingness before God. The proportion of likeness within the analogy subsists simply in the recognition that God alone is the source of all things, while we are contingent manifestations of his glory, destined for a union with him that will perfect rather than destroy our natures; entirely dependent as it is upon his being — receiving even its most proper potentiality from him as a gift — our being declares the glory of He Who Is. The proportion of unlikeness, however, which is the proportion of infinite transcendence, subsists in the far more vertiginous recognition that God is his own being, that he depends upon no other for his existence, that he does not become what he is not, that he possesses no unrealized potential, that he is not a thing set off against a prior nothingness, that he is not an essence joined to existence, and that he is not a being among other beings; and that we, in our absolute dependence upon him, are not timeless essences who "demand" existence or who possess any actuality of our own; neither essence nor existence belongs to us, and their coincidence within each of us is an entirely gratuitous gift coming to us from beyond ourselves; we have no power to be, no *right* to be, no independent ground that gives us some sort of natural claim on being.

Of all the accusations laid against the *analogia entis* by its most redoubtable foes, none is more peculiar (nor, in my experience, more common) than the claim that the analogy is simply a pagan — specifically Neoplatonist — metaphysics of participation, to which Christian motifs have been at best cosmetically applied. I am not entirely certain, however, what reply to make to such an indictment. It is so thoroughly irrelevant to Przywara's argument that it is not even clear that it could be characterized as wrong; one must simply assume at this point that the very concept of an "analogy of being" has become equivocal, since those who reject it on these grounds are clearly talking about something altogether different from what Przywara means when he uses the same words. It is true that Przywara presumes some sort of "metaphysics of participation," as any clear theological concept of the contingency of finite existents must involve some idea that all finite things "partake of" being rather than intrinsically possess it, and that God alone — and in himself — is the source of all being as such. And it may be perfectly fair to describe many of the philosophical premises of Przywara's thought as — in a very general and excruciatingly imprecise sense — "Platonist" or "Neoplatonist," since some such metaphysical scheme has been part of Christian discourse since the days of the New Testament itself. But this most definitely has nothing to do with the distinct and distinctive principle of the *analogia entis*, which no one (at least, no one who actually understands the concept as Przywara does) could possible mistake for some metaphysical system of natural likenesses established upon and sustained by the supposition of a prior identity between the absolute and the contingent. In fact, it is precisely this that the analogy is not and can never be.

I say this with some care, I should add, since — anxious though I am to do full justice to Przywara's insight — I am equally anxious to avoid conceding any legitimacy to the terms in which this particular rejection of the analogy is couched. Speaking entirely for myself, I am quite happy to embrace a metaphysics that might loosely be called the metaphysics of traditional Platonism, or even the metaphysics of certain kinds of Vedanta philosophy; indeed, I would argue that, as far as a philosophy of essences goes, any attempt to speak intelligibly of God and creation, one that does not ultimately dissolve into childish mythology, requires some such metaphysics. And in fact, if we confine ourselves entirely to questions of the causality of created things, we must ultimately conclude that, speaking purely logically — purely metaphysically — there is no significant difference between the idea of creation and that of emanation (unless by the latter one means some ridiculously crude, intrinsically materialist concept of a divine substance that merely "expands" into universal space and time). The basic structure of *exitus* and *reditus, diastole* and *systole* — as, among many others, the Areopagite and Thomas both understood — is as inevitable for a doctrine of *creatio ex nihilo* as it is for a Plotinian metaphysics of the One. Moreover, I would go on to say that it is impossible to speak meaningfully of a God who is all Goodness and Truth, the source of all being and knowing, without acknowledging that our being and our knowing are sustained from within by a God who is for each of us *interior intimo meo,* and that at the level of *nous* or spirit (or whatever one would call the highest intellective principle within us) there is that place where the *Fünklein* or *scintilla* resides, where our ground is the divine ground, where (as Augustine says) *nihil intersit,* where Brahman and Atman are one, and in regard to which one may say of all things "Tat tvam asi." Indeed, if we were simply to confine ourselves to purely *metaphysical* questions regarding the relation between the Absolute and the dependent, and never asked the still more fundamental *ontological* questions regarding the difference between divine and human being or the difference between God as God and each of us as *this* particular being, we would never have to venture speculatively beyond the conceptual law of *methexis,* within which both absolute dialectic and absolute identity have their parts to play, as the two mutually sustaining poles of a single philosophical grammar. For both are equally true, in their distinct ways, of the unmoving ground of being: we are wholly other than God ("He is in heaven and thou art on earth," he is all and we are nothing, he is absolute and we are contingent), and at the same time, the highest level of our being abides in God (in the eternal act of God being and knowing God). And, indeed, if we were never to concern ourselves with anything other than the unmoving ground — if we were to regard the givenness, fortuity, transience, and irreducible particularities of our being as utterly subordinate and even subphilosophical matter for thought — we would never be obliged to consider many subtler, more disturbing questions of difference or identity, or of what real divine transcendence ultimately entails. We could remain ever thus, at the level of a purely natural metaphysics. But the *analogia entis* is not a principle native to any purely natural metaphysics.

Again, this is the wonderful — and, in a sense, liberating — novelty of the ontology Przywara finds within the Christian philosophical tradition. Any metaphysics can discern some order of participation uniting the here below to the there beyond, but not every metaphysics can grasp the analogical interval that disrupts the continuity of being within that order of participation. And this is a distinction of the greatest spiritual import. To the degree that any metaphysics remains confined to the oscillation between total otherness and total identity, it can conceive of no "resolution" of the difference between the absolute and the contingent that is not in some sense tragic; for — as both Western and Eastern philosophies attest — such a metaphysics must affirm either the "necessary" violences of historical dialectic or the final nothingness of perfect identity or the perfect void. Without the interval of ontological analogy, the only alternative to the interminable and pointless disruptions of multiplicity is the final repose of simple unity. The ascent from unlikeness and finitude is necessarily a retreat, not only from all transient attachments, but also from the disposable chrysalis of one's empirical self; within the terms of such a metaphysics, to find identity there is to negate it here. The *nous* must leave soul and body behind to enter into a bliss beyond self, in the journey of the alone to the alone. Atman must pass beyond the veil of *maya* and the boundless play of Isvara in order to return to its deep and dreamless sleep in Brahman, and so pass from self to Self. Or if not this, the force of becoming — the ceaseless phenomenal succession of mental and physical states — must finally be extinguished in the *nibbana* of the Hinayana. Whatever the case, the nearer the creature approaches that ultimate terminus, the less creaturely it becomes.

The *analogia entis,* however, introduces an unclosable ontological caesura into what mere metaphysics treats (quite unconsciously) as a seamless ontological continuum. And this is the interval of being that lets us *be* as the creatures we are, that sets us free from our "own" ground; for without it, all we are — insofar as any one of us is "this" rather than "that" — deficient, remote, but ultimately recuperable moments within the eternal odyssey of the One's alienation from and return to itself, and our "redemption" in God is our annihilation as beings. This disruption — this infinite qualitative distinction between God and creatures — is one that, within the *ordo cognoscendi,* we must call "analogy," but only in order that we may see it properly as, within the *ordo essendi,* the mystery of the perfect gift: the gift of real difference whose "proportion" is that of infinite charity. For if there is no simple, uninterrupted ontological continuum as such between God and creation, and no sense in which the divine is diminished in the created, then creation is a needless act of freely imparted love, and so can be understood as an act not of alienation from God but of divine expression. In this utter ontological difference from God — this merely analogous relation of our being to the God who is his own being — our identity is given to us as the creatures we are, who precisely as such give glory to and manifest God. The other language of identity — of simple unity or simple negation — belongs (again) to the unmoving ground of being. But in truth — so says the analogy — the ceaseless dynamism of our existence is not something accidental to what we "more truly" are, dissembling a more essential changelessness within; we *are* that dynamism, liberated in every instant from nothingness. Our "return" to God is nothing other than our emergence into our own end, and our difference from God is the very revelation of the God who infinitely transcends us and who freely gives us to ourselves.

All of which, in the abstract, seems as if it ought to be quite inoffensive to those who persist in their distrust of the "invention of Antichrist"; but I suspect that, as yet, this would still not be enough to calm their fears. So it would probably not go amiss to note that, for Przywara, the *analogia entis* is not a principle simply consistent with Christian thought but is in fact a principle uniquely Christian, one that follows from the entire Christian story of creation, incarnation, and salvation; as such, it describes a vision of being that is not merely an option for Christian thought but an ineluctable destiny.

II. The Analogy as the Destiny of Christian Thought

I think it fairly uncontroversial to say that, in the intellectual world of the first three centuries before Nicaea, especially in the Eastern half of the empire, something like a "Logos metaphysics" was a crucial part of the philosophical lingua franca of almost the entire educated class — pagan, Jewish, Christian, and even Gnostic (even though the term generally preferred was rarely "logos"). Certainly, this was case in Alexandria: the idea of a "derivative" or "secondary" divine principle was an indispensable premise in the city's native schools of trinitarian reflection, and in the thought of either "Hellenized" Jews like Philo or of the Platonists, middle or late. And one could describe all of these systems, without any significant exception, pagan and Jewish no less than Christian, as "subordinationist" in structure. All of them attempted, with greater or lesser complexity, and with more or less vivid mythical adornments, to connect the world here below to its highest principle by populating the interval between them with various intermediate degrees of spiritual reality. All of them, that is, were shaped by the same basic metaphysical impulse, one sometimes described as the "pleonastic fallacy": the notion that, in order to overcome the infinite disproportion between the immanent and the transcendent, it is enough to conceive of some sort of *tertium quid* — or of a number of successively more accommodating quiddities — between, on the one hand, the One or the Father or ὁ Θεός and, on the other, the world of finite and mutable things. In all such systems, the second "moment" of the real — that which proceeds directly from the supreme principle of all things: *logos,* or *nous,* or what have you — was understood as a kind of economic limitation of its source, so reduced in "scale" and nature as to be capable of entering into contact with the realm of discrete beings, of translating the power of the supreme principle into various finite effects, and of uniting this world to the wellspring of all things. This derivative principle, therefore, may not as a rule properly be called ὁ Θεός, but it definitely is θεός: God with respect to all lower reality. And this inevitably meant that this secondary moment of the real was understood as mediating this supreme principle in only a partial and distorted way; for such a Logos (let us settle upon this as our term) can appear within the totality of things that are only as a restriction and diffusion of — even perhaps a deviation or alienation from — that which is "most real," the Father, who, in the purity of his transcendence, can never directly touch this world. For Christians who thought in such terms, this almost inevitably implied that the Logos had been, in some sense, generated *with respect to* the created order, as its most exalted expression, certainly, but as inseparably involved in its existence nonetheless. Thus it was natural for Christian apologists of the second century to speak of the Logos as having issued from the Father in eternity shortly before the creation of the world. And thus the essentially Alexandrian theology of Arius inevitably assumed the metaphysical — or religious — contours that it did: the divine Father is absolutely hidden from and inaccessible to all beings, unknowable even to the heavenly powers; and only through the mediation of an inferior Logos is anything of him revealed. What was fairly distinctive in Arianism was the absence of anything like a metaphysics of participation that might have allowed for some sort of real ontological continuity (however indeterminate) between the Father and his Logos; consequently the only revelation of the Father that Arius's Logos would seem to be able to provide is a kind of adoring, hieratic gesture toward an abyss of infinitely incomprehensible power, the sheer majesty of omnipotent and mysterious otherness.[1] The God (ὁ θεός) of Arius is a God revealed *only* as the hidden, of whom the Logos (θεὸς ὁ λόγος) bears tidings, and to whom he offers up the liturgy of rational creation; but as the revealer of the Father, his is the role only of a celestial high priest, the Angel of Mighty Counsel, the coryphaeus of the heavenly powers; he may be a kind of surrogate God to the rest of creation, but he too, logically speaking, cannot attain to an immediate knowledge of the divine essence.

Even, however, in late antique metaphysical systems less ontologically austere than Arius's, in which the economy of divine manifestation was understood as being embraced within a somewhat more generous order of μετοχή or μετουσία, the disproportion between the supreme principle of reality and this secondary principle of manifestation remains absolute. Hence all revelation, all disclosure of the divine, follows upon a more original veiling. The manifestation of that which is Most High — wrapped as it is in unapproachable darkness, up upon the summit of being — is only the paradoxical manifestation of a transcendence that can never become truly manifest: perhaps not even to itself, as it possesses no Logos immanent to itself. It does not "think"; it cannot be thought. This, at least, often seems to be the case with the most severely logical, and most luminously uncluttered, metaphysical system of the third century, that of Plotinus. For the One of Plotinus is not merely *a* unity, not merely solitary, but is oneness as such, that perfectly undifferentiated unity in which all unity and diversity here below subsist and by which they are sustained, as at once identity and difference. Plotinus recognized that the unity by which any particular thing is what it is, and is at once part of and distinct from the greater whole, is always logically prior to that thing; thus, within every composite reality, there must always also be a more eminent "act" of simplicity (so to speak) that makes its being possible. For this reason, the supreme principle of all things must be the One that requires no higher unity to account for its integrity, and that therefore admits of no duality whatsoever, no pollution of plurality, no distinction of any kind, even that between the knower and the known. This is not, for Plotinus, to deny that the One is in some special and transcendent sense possessed of an intellectual act of self-consciousness, a kind of "superintellection" entirely transcendent of subjective or objective knowledge.[2] But the first metaphysical moment of *theoria* — reflection and

---

1. I am largely persuaded by the portrait of Arius that Rowan Williams paints in his *Arius: Heresy and Tradition,* rev. ed. (Grand Rapids: Eerdmans, 2002).

2. See Plotinus, *Enneads* 6.7.37.15–38.26; 6.9.6.50-55.

knowledge — is of its nature a second moment, a departure from unity, Nous's "prismatic" conversion of the simple light of the One into boundless multiplicity; the One itself, possessing no "specular" other within itself, infinitely exceeds all reflection. Nor did philosophy have to await the arrival of Hegel to grasp that there is something fundamentally incoherent in speaking of the existence of that which is intrinsically unthinkable, or in talking of "being" that possesses no proportionate intelligibility: for in what way is that which absolutely — even within itself — transcends intuition, conceptualization, and knowledge anything at all? Being *is* manifestation, and to the degree that anything is *wholly* beyond thought — to the degree, that is, that anything is not "rational" — to that very degree it does not exist. So it was perhaps with rigorous consistency that the Platonist tradition after Plotinus generally chose to place "being" second in the scale of emanation: for as that purely unmanifest, unthinkable, and yet transfinite unity that grants all things their unity, the One can admit of no distinctions within itself, no manifestation *to* itself, and so — in every meaningful sense — *is* not (though, obviously, neither is it not *not*).

In truth, of course, even to speak of an "ontology" in relation to these systems is somewhat misleading. Late Platonic metaphysics, in particular, is not so much ontological in its logic as "henological," and so naturally whatever concept of being it comprises tends toward the nebulous. "Being" in itself is not really distinct from entities, except in the manner of another entity; as part of the hierarchy of emanations, occupying a particular place within the structure of the whole, it remains one item within the inventory of things that are. Admittedly, it is an especially vital and "supereminent" causal liaison within the totality of beings, but a discrete principle among other discrete principles it remains. What a truly ontological metaphysics would view as being's proper act is, for this metaphysics, scattered among the various moments of the economy of beings. One glimpses its workings now here and now there: in the infinite fecundity of the One, in the One's power to grant everything its unity as the thing it is, in the principle of manifestation that emanates from the One, in the simple existence of things, even in that unnamed, in some sense *unnoticed*, medium in which the whole continuum of emanations univocally subsists. But ultimately, the structure of reality within this vision of things is (to use the fashionable phrase) a "hierarchy within totality," held together at its apex by a principle so exalted that it is also the negation of the whole, in all of the latter's finite particularities.[3]

---

3. Ibid., 6.7.17.39-43; 6.9.3.37-40; cf. 5.5.4.12-16; 5.5.11.1-6.; etc.

What has never come fully into consciousness in this tradition is (to risk a grave anachronism) the "ontological difference" — or, at any rate, the analogy of being. So long as being is discriminated from the transcendent principle of unity, and so long as both figure in some sense (however eminently) within a sort of continuum of metaphysical moments, what inevitably must result is a dialectic of identity and negation. Again, this is the special pathos of such a metaphysics: for if the truth of all things is a principle in which they are grounded and by which they are simultaneously negated, then one can draw near to the fullness of truth only through a certain annihilation of particularity, through a forgetfulness of the manifest, through a sort of benign desolation of the soul, progressively eliminating — as the surd of mere particularity — all that lies between the One and the noetic self. This is not for a moment to deny the reality, the ardor, or the grandeur of the mystical elations that Plotinus describes, or the fervency with which — in his thought and in the thought of the later Platonists — the liberated mind loves divine beauty.[4] The pathos to which I refer is a sadness residing not within Plotinus the man but within any logically dialectical metaphysics of transcendence. For transcendence, so understood, must also be understood as a negation of the finite, and a kind of absence or positive exclusion from the scale of nature; the One is, in some sense, *there* rather than *here*. To fly thither one must fly hence, to undertake a journey of the alone to the alone, a sweetly melancholy departure from the anxiety of finitude, and even from being itself, in its concrete actuality: self, world, and neighbor. For so long as one dwells in the realm of finite vision, one dwells in untruth.

It is precisely here, however, that the advent of Nicene theology began to alter — altogether fundamentally — the conceptual structure of the ancient world. The doctrinal determinations of the fourth century, along with all of their immediate theological ramifications, rendered many of the established metaphysical premises upon which Christians had long relied in order to understand the relation between God and the world increasingly irreconcilable with their faith, and at the same time suggested the need to conceive of that relation — perhaps for the first time in Western intellectual history — in a properly "ontological" way. With the gradual defeat of subordinationist theology, and with the definition of the Son and then the Spirit as coequal and coeternal with the Father, an entire metaphysical economy had implicitly been abandoned. These new theological usages — this new Chris-

---

4. There are rather too many passages on this mystical *erōs* in the *Enneads* to permit exhaustive citation, but see esp. 6.7.21.9–22.32; 6.7.31.17-31; 6.7.34.1-39; 6.9.9.26-56.

tian philosophical grammar — did not entail a rejection of the old Logos metaphysics, perhaps, but certainly did demand its revision, and at the most radical of levels. For not only is the Logos of Nicaea *not* generated with a view to creation, and *not* a lesser manifestation of a God who is simply beyond all manifestation; it is in fact the eternal reality whereby God is the God he is. There is a perfectly proportionate convertibility of God with his own manifestation of himself to himself; and in fact, this convertibility is nothing less than God's own act of self-knowledge and self-love in the mystery of his transcendent life. His being, therefore, is an infinite intelligibility; his hiddenness — his transcendence — is always already manifestation; and it is this movement of infinite disclosure that is his "essence" as God. Thus it is that the divine persons can be characterized (as they are by Augustine) as "subsistent relations": for the relations of Father to Son or Spirit, and so on, are not extrinsic relations "in addition to" other, more original "personal" identities, or "in addition to" the divine essence; rather, they are the very reality by which the persons subsist. Thus the Father is eternally and essentially Father *because* he eternally has his Son, and so on.[5] God *is* Father, Son, and Spirit; and nothing in the Father "exceeds" the Son and Spirit. In God, to know and to love, to be known and to be loved are all one act, whereby he is God and wherein nothing remains unexpressed. And if it is correct to understand "being" as in some sense necessarily synonymous with manifestation or intelligibility — and it is — then the God who is also always Logos is also eternal Being: not *a* being, that is, but transcendent Being, beyond all finite being.

Another way of saying this is that the dogmatic definitions of the fourth century ultimately forced Christian thought, even if only implicitly, toward a recognition of the full mystery — the full transcendence — of Being within beings. All at once the hierarchy of hypostases mediating between the world and its ultimate or absolute principle had disappeared. Herein lies the great "discovery" of the Christian metaphysical tradition: the true nature of transcendence, understood not as mere dialectical supremacy, and not as ontic absence, but as the truly transcendent and therefore utterly immediate act of God, in his own infinity, giving being to beings. In affirming the consubstantiality and equality of the persons of the Trinity, Christian thought had also affirmed that it is the transcendent God alone who makes creation to be, not through a necessary diminishment of his own presence,

---

5. See Augustine, *De Trinitate* 7.1.2. Or, as John of Damascus puts it, the divine subsistences dwell and are established within one another (*De Fide Orthodoxa* 1.14).

and not by way of an economic reduction of his power in lesser principles, but as the infinite God. He is at once *superior summo meo* and *interior intimo meo:* not merely the supreme being set atop the summit of beings, but the one who is transcendently present in all beings, the ever more inward act within each finite act. This does not, of course, mean that there can be no metaphysical structure of reality, through whose agencies God acts; but it does mean that, whatever that structure might be, God is not located within it but creates it, and he does not require its mechanisms to act upon lower things. As the immediate source of the being of the whole, he is nearer to every moment within the whole than it is to itself, and is at the same time infinitely beyond the reach of the whole, even in its most exalted principles. And it is precisely in learning that God is not situated within any kind of ontic continuum with creation, as some "other thing" mediated to the creature by his simultaneous absolute absence from and dialectical involvement in the totality of beings, that we discover him to be the *ontological* cause of creation. True divine transcendence, it turns out, transcends even the traditional metaphysical divisions between the transcendent and the immanent.

As I have said, this recognition of God's "transcendent immediacy" in all things was in many ways a liberation from the sad pathos native to metaphysics described above; for with this recognition came the realization that the particularity of the creature is not in its nature a form of tragic alienation from God, which must be overcome if the soul is again to ascend to its inmost truth. If God is himself the immediate actuality of the creature's emergence from nothingness, then it is precisely through becoming what it is — rather than through shedding the finite *idiomata* that distinguish it from God — that the creature truly reflects the goodness and transcendent power of God. The supreme principle does not stand over against us (if secretly within each of us) across the distance of a hierarchy of lesser metaphysical principles but is present within the very act of each moment of the particular. God is truly Logos, and creatures — created in and through the Logos — are, insofar as they participate in the Logos's power to manifest God. God is not merely the "really real," of which beings are distant shadows; he is, as Maximus the Confessor says, the utterly simple, the very simplicity of the simple,[6] who is all in all things, wholly present in the totality of beings and in each particular being, indwelling all things as the very source of their being, without ever abandoning that simplicity.[7] This he does, not as a sub-

---

6. Maximus, *Ambigua*, PG 91:1232BC.
7. Ibid., 1256B.

lime unity absolved of all knowledge of the things he causes, but precisely *as* that one infinite intellectual action proper to his nature, wherein he knows the eternal "logoi" of all things in a single, simple act of knowledge.[8] God in himself is an infinite movement of disclosure, and in creation — rather than departing from his inmost nature — he discloses himself again by disclosing what is contained in his Logos, while still remaining hidden in the infinity and transcendence of his manifestation. When we become what we are, it is through entering ever more into the infinitely accomplished plenitude of his triune act of love and knowledge. And to understand the intimacy of God's immediate presence *as God* to his creatures in the abundant givenness of this disclosure is also — if only implicitly — to understand the true difference of Being from beings.

For Przywara, however, even this trinitarian warrant for the *analogia entis* would be invisible to us were it not for the full revelation of God's transcendent immediacy to his creatures provided by the incarnation of the Son of God — understood in a truly Chalcedonian way. Balthasar's claim that Christ is in fact the "concrete *analogia entis*" is far more than a vague but pious nod in the direction of Scripture. Fully developed Christology is, when all is said and done, impossible to conceive apart from a proper understanding of the true difference between transcendent and immanent being. Of course, it is not entirely clear that Balthasar himself always grasped this, inasmuch as he did occasionally wonder whether a coherent Christology could be enucleated from Przywara's principle of the "*ever* greater difference" between God and creatures. In truth, it is precisely this word "ever" that lifts the doctrine of the incarnation out of the realm of myth, for it marks the difference between the divine and the human as an infinite qualitative distance, and as such makes intelligible the claim that there is no conflict or rivalry between Christ's divinity and his humanity, and that the latter participates in the former so naturally that the one person of the Son can be both fully divine and fully human at once. If the difference between God and man were a merely quantifiable difference between extrinsically related beings, the incarnation would be a real change in one or both natures, an amalgamation or synthesis; but then Christ would be not the God-man but a monstrosity, a hybrid of natures that, in themselves, would remain opposed and unreconciled. But because the difference between the divine and human really is an infinite qualitative difference, the hypostatic union involves no contradiction, alienation, or change in the divine Son. Because the difference between

---

8. See Maximus, *Centuries of Knowledge* 2.4, PG 90:1125D-1128A.

God and creation is the difference between Being and created beings, Christ is not an irresoluble paradox fixed within the heart of faith, or an accommodation between two kinds of being; in his one person — both God and man — there is neither any diminishment of his divinity nor any violation of the integrity of his humanity. In a sense, in Christ one sees the analogy with utterly perspicuous brilliance: that is, one glimpses at once both the perfect ontological interval of divine transcendence and also the perfect fittingness of the divine image to its archetype. For the perfect man is also God of God: not a fabulous demigod but human in the fullest sense because divine in the fullest sense. And it is here, ultimately, in the mystery of Christ the incarnate God, the irreducible *concretum* of infinite, self-outpouring charity, that the analogy of being finds its true and everlasting proportion.

Analogy of Being — Invention of the Antichrist or the Wisdom of God? Looking Back, Looking Forward

Richard Schenk, O.P.

What have we gained? Where have we come with the essays collected here? Hans Urs von Balthasar once suggested a metaphor that can help us answer that question. In 1961, beginning the preface to the second edition of his epoch-making book *Karl Barth*, Balthasar defended his use of the term *theological constriction* ("Engführung") to describe the structure of Barth's developing thought at that time. Balthasar tells us here that he meant the term in the sense it can be used in music theory to describe one dynamic in the structure of the fugue.[1] Given Balthasar's own dedication to music and music theory,[2] and given what Bruce McCormack and Peter Casarella elucidate in this volume about the election-driven direction of Barth's Christology and the degree to which Balthasar was willing to follow him on this Christological "arcta via," there is no reason to doubt his explication.

---

1. Hans Urs von Balthasar, *Karl Barth. Darstellung und Deutung seiner Theologie,* 2d ed. (Einsiedeln: Johannes Verlag, 1961), p. ii, n. 1: "Das von mir verübelte Kennwort Engführung stammt natürlich aus der Theorie der musikalischen Fuge." The remark is not contained, or at least is not obvious, in the English translation.

2. For Balthasar's use of musical metaphors (not, however, including "Engführung"), cf. Camille Dumont, "Ein musikalisches Genie," in *Hans Urs von Balthasar. Gestalt und Werk,* ed. Karl Lehmann and Walter Kasper, pp. 223-36 (an essay not contained in the parallel English text) (Cologne: Communio, 1989). Dumont also refers to Balthasar's first work, *Die Entwicklung der musikalischen Idee. Versuch einer Synthese der Musik* (1925), reprinted now together with the 1955 essay "Bekenntnis zu Mozart" in *Studienausgabe der frühen Schriften* (Einsiedeln: Johannes, 1998).

Richard Schenk, O.P.

Balthasar's remark that Roman-Reformed conversation can be described in terms of a fugal theme suggests, too, the path that the conversations presented in this book have taken. A fugal theme of this kind needs to be developed by several "voices," since the contrast will never stay just between two discussion partners. If ecumenism is a back-and-forth of convergent and relational methods, stressing first a growing closeness, then the need for difference, it is always concerned with seeking one's own identity by seeking to identify the other as well; if the latter project fails, the former will evaporate as well. The search for proper identity soon reveals different understandings of one's own confessional identity, and these understandings correspond in turn to different views of the identities of other confessions as well. The voices multiply, varying the basic theme in point and counterpoint.[3]

This collection begins by recalling the fugal theme developed by Przywara and Barth in their important books of 1932: *Analogia Entis* I and *Church Dogmatics* I/1, with the point and counterpoint expressed in the programmatic terms of *analogia entis* and *analogia fidei*. We owe to these two forceful books and their authors the importance still sensed in this question. This volume looks then at some of the older sources that the framers of the question initially drew upon to give their compositions depth: especially Thomas Aquinas and John Calvin. Then, as if in pairs of voices, the following chapters expand and vary the basic theme identified in 1932. In its development, the fugal tension does not for long remain one just between Protestant and Catholic voices.

John Betz treats of Erich Przywara's life and work, centered on the early development of his views on analogy;[4] Kenneth Oakes follows the later Przywara, whose sense of the *Deus semper maior* in the midst of Europe's darkening history leads him to an increasing skepticism about the reliability

---

3. In other early, poetic remarks "The Art of the Fugue," which situated J. S. Bach in a wider overview of intellectual and musical history, Balthasar had drawn a parallel to Leibniz's monadology and commented that in the fugue "the voice does not get submerged beneath the all-important position of harmony, but rather is incalculably significant both as a part of the whole and at the same time as its mirror, both wedged into the order of the development and yet at the same time effecting, commanding, that development." The loss of the popularity of the fugue would follow upon alienation from a sense of dialogue or conversation ("Zwiesprache") in favor of romantic individualism (Balthasar, "Die Kunst der Fuge," *Schweizer Rundschau* 28 [1928]: 85). It would not be too difficult to identify parallels in contemporary ecumenical discourse.

4. John R. Betz, "After Barth: A New Introduction to Erich Przywara's *Analogia Entis*."

of the *analogia entis*.[5] Providing an alternative reading to the one made famous by Balthasar's book on Karl Barth, Bruce McCormack first argues that the reasons for Barth's rejection of Przywara's claims on analogy are to be found in the alternative Christology that Barth was still working out in light of his developing views on election;[6] John Webster then returns to Calvin as a prior measure of Reformed teaching on Trinity, Christ, creation, and fellowship.[7] In a close reading of Thomas Aquinas, Reinhard Hütter shows that analogy was strong enough to help us come to know God;[8] looking at other texts by Thomas, Bruce Marshall makes clear how the *analogia nominum* was "weak" enough to be a gift to and from human language.[9] Reflecting again upon Thomas Aquinas, Thomas Joseph White elucidates how *esse* can manifest the Word of God.[10] Presenting the thought of Ferdinand Ulrich, Martin Bieler discusses how *esse* can manifest the love of the Crucified Lord.[11] David Bentley Hart reflects upon how the memory of the struggle for an adequate Christology can manifest otherwise unsuspected dimensions of Being, underlining the ongoing need for something like analogy to mediate the transcendent without precluding a genuine sharing in it.[12] Michael Hanby speaks of analogy as a means of furthering the reenchantment of the search for nature in philosophies inspired by natural science.[13] Richard Schenk treats of analogy as a means of furthering the reenchantment of the search for a Roman Catholic theology of grace as distinct from nature; and of faith, as distinct from experience.[14] Peter Casarella speaks of the close affinity of Hans Urs von Balthasar to Karl Barth, inscribing *analogia entis*

5. Kenneth Oakes, "The Cross and the *analogia entis* in Erich Przywara."

6. Bruce L. McCormack: "Karl Barth's Version of an 'Analogy of Being': A Dialectical No and Yes to Roman Catholicism."

7. John Webster, "Perfection and Participation."

8. Reinhard Hütter, "Attending to the Wisdom of God — from Effect to Cause, from Creation to God: A *relecture* of the Analogy of Being according to Thomas Aquinas."

9. Bruce D. Marshall, "Christ the End of Analogy."

10. Thomas Joseph White, O.P., "'Through him all things were made' (John 1:3): The Analogy of the Word Incarnate according to St. Thomas Aquinas and Its Ontological Presuppositions."

11. Martin Bieler, "The *analogia entis* as an Expression of Love according to Ferdinand Ulrich."

12. David Bentley Hart, "The Destiny of Christian Metaphysics: Reflections on the *analogia entis*."

13. Michael Hanby, "Creation as Aesthetic Analogy."

14. Richard Schenk, O.P., "Analogy as the *discrimen naturae et gratiae*: Thomism and Ecumenical Learning."

Richard Schenk, O.P.

into the *analogia fidei* of a prior Christology.[15] At another juncture,[16] the volume reviews the close affinity of Gottlieb Söhngen to Karl Barth, both of whom sought to subordinate the *discrimen legis et evangelii* to the *tertius usus legis,* the gospel sense that reveals a new law of its own, as had been urged by Karl Barth in the characteristically Reformed tradition.[17] While at first unsure how much to appropriate from Barth's critique of Emil Brunner's sense of the natural or cultural presuppositions of Christian faith, Gottlieb Söhngen, distancing himself from the Thomism of his day, suggested a deep affinity between Calvin and Bonaventure's alternative of a programmatic analogy of faith.[18]

The name of Gottlieb Söhngen brought an additional note to the symposium that has led to this volume. The Pope John Paul II Cultural Center in Washington, D.C., where the discussions took place, was just about to host that student of Gottlieb Söhngen who three years to the month before the symposium had been elected as John Paul II's successor. Although Pope Benedict XVI was scheduled to speak at the center some two weeks after the symposium not on ecumenical but on interreligious concerns, he would do so as the pope who, arguably more than any other since the sixteenth century, had developed his own theological understanding in the context of Roman-Reformed discussions; and in particular, through Söhngen, who directed Joseph Ratzinger's dissertation on Augustine and his habilitation on Bonaventure, in the context of the debate on the two analogies that had been taken up by the Barth-friendly thought of Söhngen. A comprehensive assess-

15. Peter Casarella, "Hans Urs von Balthasar, Erich Przywara's *analogia entis,* and the Problem of a Catholic *Denkform.*"

16. Schenk, "Analogy as the *discrimen naturae et gratiae.*"

17. Famously in his 1935 essay "Evangelium und Gesetz," in *Gesetz und Evangelium. Beiträge zur gegenwärtigen theologischen Diskussion,* ed. Ernst Kinder and Klaus Haendler, pp. 1-29 (Darmstadt: Wissenschaftlichen Buchgesellschaft, 1986).

18. Cf. Gottlieb Söhngen, "Bonaventura als Klassiker der Analogia fidei," *Wissenschaft und Weisheit* 2 (1935): 97-111, e.g., 105, n. 17: "Im übrigen stellt die Kritik der Reformatoren an der *theologia naturalis* keinen so eindeutigen Bruch mit der Tradition Augustins und der augustinischen Scholastiker dar, wie es protestantische Theologen selbst wahrhaben wollen. Wer einigermaßen vertraut mit dem Schrifttum Augustins und Bonaventuras die Calvin-Texte liest, die Peter Barth in dem Heft *Das Problem der natürlichen Theologie bei Calvin* (1935) beibringt, wird nicht wenige und nicht unwichtige Stellen mit Texten Augustins und Bonaventuras zusammenhalten können und so urteilen müssen, daß Peter Barth Emil Brunners katholisierende Calvin-Interpretation in *Natur und Gnade* (2/1935) zum mindesten nicht ganz aus dem Sattel gehoben hat." Cf. from the same year Gottlieb Söhngen, "Natürliche Theologie und Heilsgeschichte. Antwort an Emil Brunner," *Catholica* 4 (1935): 97-114.

ment of Ratzinger's early involvement in the analogy controversies can now benefit from the recent publication of the initial 1955 draft of the habilitation on revelation and history in Bonaventure,[19] as it is considered alongside the earlier, published portion of the habilitation,[20] Ratzinger's following publications on Bonaventure,[21] and the essay he contributed as coeditor of Söhngen's 1962 Festschrift.[22] All of these writings point to a reading of Bonaventure that place the Seraphic Doctor in a position designed to mediate between an understanding of God based on an autonomous, "natural" understanding of the world and a revealed grasp of God and the world that would be largely unencumbered by historical and worldly constraints. Developing Söhngen's programmatic sense of Bonaventure as a defender of the profound contribution of faith to reason,[23] yet showing already a certain distance from the terms of the debates in the 1930s, the work of the young Ratzinger views analogy first as God's own expression of himself in creation and history and only then as the language God gives us by which to answer his self-communication. The insights that the young professor developed in his work on Bonaventure would flow into the controversial discussions of revelation at the Second Vatican Council, beginning just three years after the publication of the final sections of Ratzinger's habilitation. Today's task of working out a Roman Catholic theology of revelation revolves in no small part around the legacy of that council and our need today to negotiate in

19. Joseph Ratzinger (Benedict XVI), *Offenbarungsverständnis und Geschichtstheologie Bonaventuras*, vol. 2 of *Gesammelte Schriften* (Freiburg: Herder, 2009).

20. Joseph Ratzinger, *Die Geschichtstheologie des heiligen Bonaventura* (Munich: Schnell & Steiner, 1959; St. Ottilien: EOS, 1992; ET *The Theology of History in St. Bonaventure*, trans. Zachary Hayes [Chicago: Franciscan Herald Press, 1971]).

21. Cf. especially Joseph Ratzinger, "Offenbarung — Schrift — Überlieferung. Ein Text des hl. Bonaventura und seine Bedeutung für die gegenwärtige Theologie," *Trierer theologische Zeitschrift* 67 (1958): 13-27; idem, "Der Mensch und die Zeit im Denken des hl. Bonaventura," in *L'homme et son destin d'après les penseurs du moyen âge* (Louvain: Nauwelaerts, 1960), pp. 473-83; idem, "Wesen und Weisen der auctoritas im Werk des hl. Bonaventura," in *Die Kirche und ihre Ämter und Stände. Festgabe für Joseph Kardinal Frings zum goldenen Priesterjubiläum*, ed. W. Corsten, A. Frotz, and P. Linden, pp. 58-72 (Cologne: Bachem, 1960); idem, "Der Wortgebrauch von *natura* und die beginnende Verselbständigung der Metaphysik bei Bonaventura," in *Die Metaphysik im Mittelalter*, ed. Paul Wilpert, pp. 483-98 (Berlin: de Gruyter, 1963).

22. Joseph Ratzinger, "Gratia praesupponit naturam. Erwägungen über Sinn und Grenze eines scholastischen Axioms," in *Einsicht und Glaube. Festschrift G. Söhngen zum 70. Geburtstag*, ed. Joseph Ratzinger and Heinrich Fries, pp. 75-97 (Freiburg: Herder 1962).

23. Ratzinger drew above all on the essay cited above by Gottlieb Söhngen, "Bonaventura als Klassiker der Analogia fidei."

light of postconciliar developments between the claims of what were majority and minority positions, both of which found expression and legitimation in the final, much debated text of *Dei Verbum,* the Dogmatic Constitution on Revelation. The ecumenical dimension of the conciliar debates, which includes their background in the controversies on analogy, has become an elemental moment of Roman Catholic reflection on the meaning of revelation.

The title of the present volume might seem to suggest a clear alternative between two understandings of analogy — "invention of the Antichrist" or "the wisdom of God" (cf. Wis. 13:5). But if, as is well known by the authors represented here, there is after the fall from innocence no possible return to neutral innocence but only the possibilities of virtue and vice,[24] then there is a sense in which we always already are usurpers of the divine glory. The question is how we might find our way to the *timor Dei filialis* that can enable us to resist such usurpation. "The fear of the LORD is the beginning of Wisdom" (Ps. 111:10), and the Lord who is so revered ("feared") is the Lord who is in-and-above his creatures (Przywara). How can our thoughts be modified so that the world might become ever more an icon (as his creatures) and ever less an idol (as if his equivalent)? Does the "analogy of being" necessarily favor the temptation to idolatry, or can it not help theology and theologians to resist the illusion of excessive epistemological claims? Is it not precisely the memory of the *analogia entis* that keeps alive our theological sense of that *extra nos* of grace and revelation that was so dear to the Reformation, not just among its Lutheran proponents: by identifying and pointing beyond the limits of what is ours to recall the Word of God? In characteristic formulas, Barth taught Protestants and Catholics alike to "let God be God," to "give God the glory," just as already the early Przywara's hopes were *sub signo crucis.* The essays gathered in this volume seek to remember these two theologians, who — by the debate they initiated, the debate recalled here, and the inter- and intraconfessional discussions they help us to hope for in our shared future — have both helped show us the path to wisdom.

---

24. Cf. Robert Kilwardby, *Quaestiones in lib. IV Sententiarum,* 22: ". . . postquam semel homo convertit se ad bonum vel ad malum, non fuit status innocentiae, sed immediate se habuit semper humana natura in omni persona ad gratiam vel culpam. Unde quamvis fuerit ille status forte in primordio naturae institutae, deinceps tamen non fuit" (Robert Kilwardby, *Quaestiones in librum quartum Sententiarum,* ed. Richard Schenk, Bayerische Akademie der Wissenschaften, Veröffentlichungen der Kommission für die Herausgabe ungedruckter Texte aus der mittelalterlichen Geisteswelt, vol. 17 [Munich: Bavarian Academy of Sciences, 1993], p. 89, lines 143-47).

Select Bibliography

Aertsen, Jan. *Medieval Philosophy and the Transcendentals: The Case of Thomas Aquinas.* Leiden: Brill, 1996.

Althaus, Paul. "Theologie und Geschichte. Zur Auseinandersetzung mit der dialektischen Theologie." *Zeitschrift für systematische Theologie* 1 (1923): 741-86.

Antweiler, Anton. *Die Anfangslosigkeit der Welt nach Thomas von Aquin und Kant.* Trier: Paulinus, 1961.

Ashley, Benedict. *The Way toward Wisdom: An Interdisciplinary and Intercultural Introduction to Metaphysics.* Notre Dame, Ind.: University of Notre Dame Press, 2006.

Auer, Johann. *Das Evangelium der Gnade.* 2d ed. Regensburg: Pustet, 1980.

Ayres, Lewis. *Nicaea and Its Legacy: An Approach to Fourth-Century Trinitarian Theology.* Oxford: Oxford University Press, 2004.

Balthasar, Hans Urs von. "Analogie und Dialektik. Zur Klärung der theologischen Prinzipienlehre Karl Barths." *Divus Thomas* (Fribourg) 22 (1944): 171-216.

———. "Analogie und Natur. Zur Klärung der theologischen Prinzipienlehre Karl Barths." *Divus Thomas* (Fribourg) 23 (1945): 3-56.

———. *The Glory of the Lord: A Theological Aesthetics.* 7 vols. Translated by Erasmo Leiva-Merikakis, Oliver Davies, and others. San Francisco: Ignatius Press, 1983-91.

———. *Karl Barth. Darstellung und Deutung seiner Theologie.* Cologne: Verlag Jakob Hegner, 1951.

———. "Die Kunst der Fuge." *Schweizer Rundschau* 28 (1928): 84-87.

———. *Theo-Drama: Theological Dramatic Theory.* 5 vols. Translated by Graham Harrison. San Francisco: Ignatius Press, 1988-98.

———. *Theodramatik.* 3 vols. Einsiedeln: Johannes Verlag, 1973-80.

————. *Theologic.* Vol. 1, *The Truth of the World.* Translated by Adrian J. Walker. San Francisco: Ignatius Press, 2000.

————. *Theologie der Geschichte.* Einsiedeln: Johannes Verlag, 1959.

————. *Theologik.* Vol. 1. Einsiedeln: Johannes Verlag, 1985.

————. *The Theology of Karl Barth.* Translated by Edward Oakes. San Francisco: Ignatius Press, 1992.

————. *The Word Made Flesh.* Vol. 1 of *Explorations in Theology.* Translated by A. V. Littledale and A. Dru. San Francisco: Ignatius Press, 1989.

Barth, Karl. *Briefe, 1961-1968.* Edited by Jürgen Fangmeier and Hinrich Stoevesandt. Zürich: TVZ, 1975.

————. *Church Dogmatics.* Translated by G. W. Bromiley and T. F. Torrance. London: T. &T. Clark; New York: Continuum, 2004.

————. *Credo.* Translated by Robert McAfee Brown. New York: Scribner, 1962.

————. *The Epistle to the Romans.* 6th ed. Translated by Edwyn C. Hoskins. Oxford: Oxford University Press, 1968.

————. "Evangelium und Gesetz." In *Gesetz und Evangelium. Beiträge zur gegenwärtigen theologischen Diskussion,* edited by Ernst Kinder and Klaus Haendler, pp. 1-29. Darmstadt: Wissenschaftlichen Buchgesellschaft, 1986.

————. *The Göttingen Dogmatics.* Vol. 1, *Instruction in the Christian Religion.* Translated by Geoffrey W. Bromiley. Grand Rapids: Eerdmans, 1990.

————. *The Holy Spirit and the Christian Life: The Theological Basis of Ethics.* Translated by R. Birch Hoyle. Louisville, Ky.: Westminster/John Knox Press, 1993.

————. *Kirchliche Dogmatik.* 9th ed. Zürich: TVZ, 1975-76.

————. *Nein! Antwort an Emil Brunner.* Munich: C. Kaiser, 1934.

————. "No! Answer to Emil Brunner." In *Natural Theology: Comprising "Nature and Grace" by Professor Dr. Emil Brunner and the Reply "No!" by Dr. Karl Barth,* translated by Peter Fraenkel. Eugene, Ore.: Wipf & Stock, 2002.

————. "Offener Brief an Professor D. Dr. G. Wobbermin." *Theologische Blätter* 11 (1932): 186-87.

————. *Prolegomena, 1924.* Edited by Hannelotte Reiffen. Zürich: TVZ, 1985.

————. *Die protestantische Theologie im 19. Jahrhundert. Ihre Vorgeschichte und ihre Geschichte.* Zürich: Evangelischer Verlag, 1947.

————. *Protestant Theology in the Nineteenth Century: Its Background and History.* Translated by Brian Cozens and John Bowden. London: SCM Press, 1973.

————. *Der Römerbrief, 1922.* Zürich: TVZ, 1940.

————. *Theologische Fragen und Antworten.* 2d ed. Zürich: TVZ, 1986.

Barth, Karl, and Rudolf Bultmann. *Karl Barth–Rudolf Bultmann: Letters, 1922-1968.* Translated by Geoffrey Bromiley. Grand Rapids: Eerdmans, 1981.

Barth, Karl, and Eduard Thurneysen. *Karl Barth–Eduard Thurneysen Briefwechsel.* Vol. 2, *1921-1930.* Edited by Eduard Thurneysen. Zürich: TVZ, 1974.

Bauckham, Richard A. *God Crucified: Monotheism and Christology in the New Testament.* Grand Rapids: Eerdmans, 1998.

Bauhofer, Oskar. *Das Metareligiöse. Eine kritische Religionsphilosophie.* Leipzig: J. C. Hinrichs, 1930.

Beintker, Michael. *Die Dialektik in der "dialektischen Theologie" Karl Barths.* Munich: C. Kaiser, 1987.

Berlinger, Rudolf. "Absconditum sub contrario. Philosophische Bemerkungen zur Methode Erich Przywaras." *Philosophisches Jahrbuch* 62 (1953): 86-95.

Betz, John R. *After Enlightenment: The Post-Secular Vision of J. G. Hamann.* Oxford: Blackwell, 2008.

———. "Beyond the Sublime: The Aesthetics of the Analogy of Being." *Modern Theology* 21 (July 2005): 367-411 and 22 (January 2006): 1-50.

Beumer, B. "Gratia supponit naturam. Zur Geschichte eines theologischen Prinzips." *Gregorianum* 20 (1930): 381-406 and 535-52.

Bieler, Martin. "Karl Barths Auseinandersetzung mit der analogia entis und der Anfang der Theologie." *Catholica* 40 (1986): 241-45.

———. *Freiheit als Gabe.* Freiburg: Herder, 1991.

———. "Seinsmitteilung und Bonität." In *Das Sein als Gleichnis Gottes,* edited by Michael Schulz, pp. 164-69. Freiburg: Verlag der Katholischen Akademie der Erzdiözese Freiburg, 2005.

———. "The Theological Importance of a Philosophy of Being." In *Reason and the Reasons of Faith,* edited by Paul J. Griffiths and Reinhard Hütter, pp. 295-326. London: T. & T. Clark, 2005.

Blondel, Maurice. *L'action* (1893 ed.). Paris: Presses universitaires de France, 1995.

Bonhoeffer, Dietrich. *Act and Being.* Edited by Hans-Richard Reuter and Wayne Whitson Floyd Jr. Translated by H. Martin Rumscheidt. Minneapolis: Fortress Press, 1996.

Bouillard, Henri. *Karl Barth. Genèse et évolution de la théologie dialectique.* 3 vols. Paris: Aubier, 1957.

———. *The Knowledge of God.* Translated by Samuel D. Femiano. New York: Herder & Herder, 1968.

Brito, Emilio. *La christologie de Hegel. Verbum Crucis.* Paris: Beauchesne, 1983.

———. "Dieu en mouvement? Thomas d'Aquin et Hegel." *Revue des sciences religieuses* 62 (1988): 111-36.

———. *Dieu et l'être d'après Thomas d'Aquin et Hegel.* Paris: PUF, 1991.

Brunner, Emil. *Natur und gnade. Zum gespräch mit Karl Barth.* Zürich: Zwingli-Verlag, 1935.

———. *Religionsphilosophie evangelischer Theologie.* Munich: R. Oldenbourg, 1928.

Bulgakov, Sergius. *The Lamb of God.* Translated by Boris Jakim. Grand Rapids: Eerdmans, 2008.

Burrell, David B. *Freedom and Creation in Three Traditions.* Notre Dame, Ind.: University of Notre Dame Press, 1993.

———. *Knowing the Unknowable God: Ibn-Sina, Maimonides, Aquinas.* Notre Dame, Ind.: University of Notre Dame Press, 1986.

Chavannes, Henry. *L'analogie entre Dieu et le monde selon saint Thomas d'Aquin et selon Karl Barth.* Paris: Cerf, 1969.

Clarke, W. Norris. *Explorations in Metaphysics: Being — God — Person.* Notre Dame, Ind.: University of Notre Dame Press, 1994.

Courtenay, William J. "Dominicans and Suspect Opinion in the Thirteenth Century: The Cases of Stephen of Venizy, Peter of Tarentaise, and the Articles of 1270 and 1271." *Vivarium* 32, no. 2 (1994): 186-95.

Courtine, Jean François. *Inventio analogiae. Métaphysique et ontothéologie.* Paris: J. Vrin, 2005.

De Koninck, Charles. "Metaphysics and the Interpretation of Words." *Laval théologique et philosophique* 17 (1961): 22-34.

Dewan, Lawrence. "Does Being Have a Nature? (Or: Metaphysics as a Science of the Real)." In *Approaches to Metaphysics,* edited by William Sweet, pp. 23-59. Dordrecht: Kluwer Academic Publishers, 2004.

———. *Form and Being: Studies in Thomistic Metaphysics.* Washington, D.C.: Catholic University of America Press, 2006.

———. "On Anthony Kenny's *Aquinas on Being.*" *Nova et Vetera,* English edition, 3, no. 2 (2005): 335-400.

Diem, Hermann. "Analogia fidei gegen analogia entis. Ein Beitrag zur Kontroverstheologie." *Evangelische Theologie* 3 (1936): 157-80.

Driel, Edwin C. Van. "Karl Barth on the Eternal Existence of Jesus Christ." *Scottish Journal of Theology* 60 (2007): 45-61.

Dumont, Camille, "Ein musikalisches Genie." In *Hans Urs von Balthasar. Gestalt und Werk,* edited by Karl Lehmann and Walter Kasper, pp. 223-36. Cologne: Communio, 1989.

Ebeling, Gerhard. "Der hermeneutische Ort der Gotteslehre bei Petrus Lombardus und Thomas Aquinas." *Zeitschrift für Theologie und Kirche* 61 (1964): 283-326.

Elders, Léon. *Autour de saint Thomas d'Aquin.* Vol. 1, *Les commentaires sur les oeuvres d'Aristote; La métaphysique de l'être.* Brugge: Tabor; Paris: FAC, 1987.

Emery, Gilles. *The Trinitarian Theology of Saint Thomas Aquinas.* Translated by Francesca Murphy. Oxford: Oxford University Press, 2007.

———. *Trinity in Aquinas.* Naples, Fla.: Sapientia, 2005.

Faber, Eva-Maria. "Skandal und Torheit. Katholische Kreuzestheologie bei Erich Przywara." *Geist und Leben* 69 (1996): 338-53.

Fabro, Cornelio. "The Intensive Hermeneutics of Thomistic Philosophy: The Notion of Participation." Translated by B. M. Bonansea. *Review of Metaphysics* 27 (1974): 449-91.

———. *Participation et causalité selon S. Thomas d'Aquin.* Paris: Béatrice-Nauwelaerts; Louvain: Publications Universitaires, 1961.

Fackre, Gabriel J., and Michael Root, *Affirmations and Admonitions: Lutheran Decisions and Dialogue with Reformed, Episcopal, and Roman Catholic Churches.* Grand Rapids: Eerdmans, 1998.

Gathercole, Simon. "Pre-existence and the Freedom of the Son in Creation and Redemption: An Exposition in Dialogue with Robert Jenson." *International Journal of Systematic Theology* 7, no. 1 (2005): 38-51.

———. *The Preexistent Son: Recovering the Christologies of Matthew, Mark, and Luke.* Grand Rapids: Eerdmans, 2006.

Gebsattel, Victor Emil von. *Imago Hominis. Beiträge zu einer personalen Anthropologie.* Salzburg: Otto Müller, 1968.

Geiger, L.-B. "Abstraction et séparation d'après s. Thomas *In de Trinitate*, q. 5, a. 3." *Revue des sciences philosophiques et théologiques* 31 (1947): 3-40.

———. *La participation dans la philosophie de S. Thomas d'Aquin.* Paris: J. Vrin, 1942.

———. "Les rédactions successives de *Contra Gentiles* I, 53 d'après l'autographe." In *Saint Thomas d'Aquin aujourd'hui,* edited by J. Y. Jolif et al., pp. 221-40. Paris: Desclée de Brouwer, 1963.

Gertz, Bernhard. "Erich Przywara (1889-1972)." In *Filosofía cristiana en el pensamiento católico de los siglos XIX y XX. Vuelta a la herencia escolástica,* edited by Emerich Coreth and translated by Eloy Rodríguez Navarro, pp. 523-39. Madrid: Ediciones Encuentro, 1993.

———. *Glaubenswelt als Analogie. Die theologische Analogie-Lehre Erich Przywaras und ihr Ort in der Auseinandersetzung um die analogia fidei.* Düsseldorf: Patmos Verlag, 1969.

Goebel, Hans Theodore. "Trinitätslehre und Erwählungslehre bei Karl Barth." In *Wahrheit und Versöhnung. Theologische und philosophische Beiträge zur Gotteslehre,* edited by D. Korsch and H. Ruddies, pp. 147-66. Gütersloh: Gütersloher Verlagshaus Gerd Mohn, 1989.

———. *Vom freien Wählen Gottes und des Menschen. Interpretationsübungen zur "Analogie" nach Karl Barths Lehre von der Erwählung und Bedenken ihrer Folgen für die Kirchliche Dogmatik.* Frankfurt: Peter Lang, 1990.

Goris, Harm. "Theology and Theory of the Word in Aquinas." In *Aquinas the Augustinian,* edited by Matthew Dauphinais, Barry David, and Matthew Levering, pp. 62-78. Washington, D.C.: Catholic University of America Press, 2007.

Graf, Josef. *Gottlieb Söhngens (1892-1971) Suche nach der "Einheit in der Theologie." Ein Beitrag zum Durchbruch des heilsgeschichtlichen Denkens.* Frankfurt: Peter Lang, 1991.

Gundlach, Thies. *Selbstbegrenzung Gottes und die Autonomie des Menschen.* Frankfurt: Peter Lang, 1992.

Hammer, Karl. "Analogia relationis gegen analogia entis." In *Parrhesia. Karl Barth zum achtzigsten Geburtstag,* edited by E. Busch, pp. 288-304. Zürich: EVZ, 1966.

Hanby, Michael. *Augustine and Modernity.* London: Routledge, 2003.

———. "A Few Words on Balthasar's First Word." In *How Balthasar Changed My Mind: Fifteen Scholars Reflect on the Meaning of Balthsar for Their Own Work,* edited by Rodney Howsare and Larry Chapp, pp. 74-90. New York: Crossroad, 2008.

————. "The Logic of Love and the Unity of Catholic Truth: Reflections on *Deus caritas est.*" *Communio* 33 (Fall 2006): 400-422.

————. "These Three Abide: Augustine and the Eschatological Non-obsolescence of Faith." *Pro Ecclesia* 14, no. 3 (2005): 340-60.

Härle, Wilfried. *Sein und Gnade. Die Ontologie in Karl Barths "Kirchliche Dogmatik."* Berlin: de Gruyter, 1975.

Hart, David Bentley. *The Beauty of the Infinite: The Aesthetics of Christian Truth.* Grand Rapids: Eerdmans, 2003.

————. *The Doors of the Sea: Where Was God in the Tsunami?* Grand Rapids: Eerdmans, 2005.

————. "No Shadow of Turning: On Divine Impassibility." *Pro Ecclesia* 11 (2002): 184-206.

Healy, Nicholas J. *The Eschatology of Hans Urs von Balthasar: Being as Communion.* Oxford: Oxford University Press, 2005.

Hector, Kevin W. "God's Triunity and Self-Determination: A Conversation with Karl Barth, Bruce McCormack, and Paul Molnar." *International Journal of Systematic Theology* 7, no. 3 (2005): 246-61.

Hemmerle, Klaus. *Theologie als Nachfolge. Bonaventura — ein Weg für heute.* Freiburg: Herder, 1975.

Hemming, Laurence Paul. *Worship as a Revelation: The Past, Present, and Future of Catholic Liturgy.* London: Burns & Oates, 2008.

Hittinger, Russell. "*Pascendi Dominici Gregis* at 100: Two Modernisms, Two Thomisms; Reflections on the Centenary of Pius X's Letter against the Modernists." *Nova et Vetera,* English edition, 5, no. 4 (2007): 843-80.

Hochschild, Joshua Peter. *The Semantics of Analogy: Rereading Cajetan's De Nominum Analogia.* Notre Dame, Ind.: University of Notre Dame Press, 2010.

Humbrecht, Thierry-Dominique. *Théologie négative et noms divins chez saint Thomas d'Aquin.* Paris: J. Vrin, 2006.

Hunsinger, George. "Election and the Trinity: Twenty-five Theses on the Theology of Karl Barth." *Modern Theology* 24 (2008): 179-98.

Hütter, Reinhard. "St. Thomas on Grace and Free Will in the *Initium Fidei:* The Surpassing Augustinian Synthesis." *Nova et Vetera,* English edition, 5, no. 3 (2007): 521-54.

Ilien, Albert. *Wesen und Funktion der Liebe im Denken des Thomas von Aquin.* Freiburg: Herder, 1975.

Israel, Jonathan I. *Radical Enlightenment: Philosophy and the Making of Modernity, 1650-1750.* Oxford: Oxford University Press, 2001.

Jenson, Robert. *Systematic Theology.* Vol. 1. Oxford: Oxford University Press, 1997.

Johnson, Elizabeth A. "The Right Way to Speak about God? Pannenberg on Analogy." *Theological Studies* 43 (1982): 673-92.

Johnson, Keith. "Analogia Entis: A Reconsideration of the Debate between Karl Barth and Roman Catholicism, 1914-1964." PhD diss., Princeton Theological Seminary, 2008.

Jüngel, Eberhard. *Barth-Studien*. Gütersloh: Benziger, 1982.

―――. *God as the Mystery of the World: On the Foundation of the Theology of the Crucified One in the Dispute between Theism and Atheism*. Translated by Darrell L. Guder. Grand Rapids: Eerdmans, 1983.

―――. *God's Being Is in Becoming*. Translated by John Webster. Grand Rapids: Eerdmans, 2001.

―――. *Gott als Geheimnis der Welt. Zur Begründung der Theologie des Gekreuzigten im Streit zwischen Theismus und Atheismus*. 7th ed. Tübingen: Mohr Siebeck, 2001.

―――. *Unterwegs zur Sache. Theologische Bemerkungen*. Munich: C. Kaiser, 1972.

―――. *Zum Ursprung der Analogie bei Parmenides und Heraklit*. Berlin: de Gruyter, 1964.

Kasper, Walter. *The God of Jesus Christ*. Translated by Matthew O'Connell. New York: Crossroad, 1989.

Klubertanz, George. *St. Thomas Aquinas on Analogy: A Textual Analysis and Systematic Synthesis*. Chicago: Loyola University Press, 1960.

Koch, Hugo. "Proklus als Quelle des Pseudo-Dionysius Areopagita in der Lehre vom Bösen." *Philologus* 54 (1895): 438-54.

Kühn, Ulrich. *Natur und Gnade. Untersuchungen zur deutschen katholischen Theologie der Gegenwart*. Berlin: Lutherisches Verlagshaus, 1961.

―――. *Via caritatis. Theologie des Gesetzes bei Thomas von Aquin*. Göttingen: Vandenhoeck & Ruprecht, 1965.

Léonard, André. *Métaphysique de l'être*. Paris: Cerf, 2006.

Levy, Antoine. "An Introduction to Divine Relativity: Beyond David Bradshaw's *Aristotle East and West*." *Thomist* 72 (2008): 173-231.

Lindbeck, George. "Participation and Existence in the Interpretation of St. Thomas Aquinas." *Franciscan Studies* 17 (1957): 1-22 and 107-25.

Lochbrunner, Manfred. *Hans Urs von Balthasar und seine Philosophenfreunde. Fünf Doppelporträts*. Würzburg: Echter, 2005.

Loewenich, Walther von. *Luther's Theology of the Cross*. Translated by Herbert Bouman. Belfast: Christian Journals, 1976.

Lonergan, Bernard. *The Triune God: Systematics*. Toronto: University of Toronto Press, 2007.

Lösel, Steffen. "Love Divine, All Loves Excelling: Balthasar's Negative Theology of Revelation." *Journal of Religion* 82, no. 4 (2002): 586-616.

Löser, Werner. *Kleine Hinführung zu Hans Urs von Balthasar*. Freiburg: Herder, 2005.

―――. "Von Balthasars Karl-Barth-Buch — eine theologische Würdigung." In *Karl Barth — Hans Urs von Balthasar. Eine theologische Zwiesprache*, edited by Wolfgang W. Müller, pp. 71-96. Zürich: TVZ, 2006.

Lotz, Johannes B. *Transzendentale Erfahrung*. Freiburg: Herder, 1978.

Luciani Rivero, Rafael Francisco. *El misterio de la diferencia. Un estudio tipológico de la analogía como estructura originaria de la realidad en Tomás de Aquino, Erich*

Przywara y Hans Urs Von Balthasar y su uso en teología trinitaria. Rome: Editrice Pontificia Universitá Gregoriana, 2002.

Lüning, Peter. *Der Mensch im Angesicht des Gekreuzigten. Untersuchung zum Kreuzesverständnis von Erich Przywara, Karl Rahner, Jon Sobrino und Hans Urs von Balthasar.* Münster: Aschendorff, 2007.

Lyttkens, Hampus. *The Analogy between God and the World: An Investigation of Its Background and Interpretation of Its Use by Thomas of Aquino.* Translated by Axel Poignant. Uppsala: Almqvist & Wiksells, 1952.

McCormack, Bruce L. "Barths grundsätzliche Chalcedonismus?" *Zeitschrift für dialektische Theologie* 18 (2002): 138-73.

———. "Divine Impassibility or Simply Divine Constancy? Implications of Karl Barth's Later Christology for Debates over Impassibility." In *Divine Impassibility and the Mystery of Human Suffering,* edited by James F. Keating and Thomas Joseph White, O.P., pp. 150-86. Grand Rapids: Eerdmans, 2009.

———. "Grace and Being: The Role of God's Gracious Election in Karl Barth's Theological Ontology." In *The Cambridge Companion to Karl Barth,* edited by John Webster, pp. 92-110. Cambridge: Cambridge University Press, 2000.

———. "Karl Barth's Christology as a Resource for a Reformed Version of Kenoticism." *International Journal of Systematic Theology* 8 (2006): 243-51.

———. *Karl Barth's Critically Realistic Dialectical Theology: Its Genesis and Development, 1909-1936.* New York: Oxford University Press, 1995.

———. "The Ontological Presuppositions of Barth's Doctrine of the Atonement." In *The Glory of the Atonement: Biblical, Historical, and Practical Perspectives,* edited by Charles E. Hill and Frank A. James III, pp. 346-66. Downers Grove, Ill.: InterVarsity Press, 2004.

———. "Participation in God, Yes, Deification, No: Two Modern Answers to an Ancient Question." In *Denkwürdiges Geheimnis. Beiträge zur Gotteslehre; Festschrift für Eberhard Jüngel zum 70. Geburtstag,* edited by Ingolf U. Dalferth, Johannes Fischer, and Hans-Peter Großhans, pp. 347-74. Tübingen: Mohr Siebeck, 2004.

———. "Seek God Where He May Be Found." *Scottish Journal of Theology* 60 (2007): 62-79.

———. *Theologische Dialektik und kritischer Realismus. Entstehung und Entwicklung von Karl Barths Theologie, 1909-1936.* Zürich: TVZ, 2006.

———. " 'With Loud Cries and Tears': The Humanity of the Son in the Epistle to the Hebrews." In *The Epistle to the Hebrews and Christian Theology,* edited by Richard Bauckham, Daniel R. Driver, Trevor A. Hart, and Nathan MacDonald, pp. 37-68. Grand Rapids: Eerdmans, 2009.

McEvoy, James. "The Divine as the Measure of Being in Platonic and Scholastic Thought." In *Studies in Medieval Philosophy,* edited by John F. Wippel, pp. 85-116. Washington, D.C.: Catholic University of America Press, 1980.

McGinn, Bernard. *The Calabrian Abbot: Joachim of Fiore in the History of Western Thought.* New York: Macmillan, 1985.

McInerny, Ralph. "Analogy and Foundationalism in Thomas Aquinas." In *Rational-*

ity, Religious Belief, and Moral Commitment, edited by Robert Audi and William J. Wainwright, pp. 271-88. Ithaca, N.Y.: Cornell University Press, 1986.

———. *Aquinas and Analogy.* Washington, D.C.: Catholic University of America Press, 1996.

———. *The Logic of Analogy: An Interpretation of St. Thomas.* The Hague: Martinus Nijhoff, 1961.

———. *Praeambula fidei: Thomism and the God of the Philosophers.* Washington, D.C.: Catholic University of America Press, 2006.

MacIntyre, Alasdair. *Three Rival Versions of Moral Enquiry.* Notre Dame, Ind.: University of Notre Dame Press, 1990.

Maréchal, Joseph. *Le point de départ de la métaphysique.* Vol. 5. Paris: Librairie Félix Alcan, 1926.

Marga, Amy. "Partners in the Gospel: Karl Barth and Roman Catholicism, 1922-1932." PhD diss., Princeton Theological Seminary, 2006.

Maritain, Jacques. *Distinguish to Unite; or, The Degrees of Knowledge.* Translated by Gerald B. Phelan. New York: Scribner, 1959.

———. *A Preface to Metaphysics: Seven Lectures on Being.* New York: Mentor Omega Book, 1962.

Marmann, Michael J. "Praeambula ad gratiam. Ideengeschichtliche Untersuchung über die Entstehung des Axioms *gratia praesupponit naturam.*" PhD diss., University of Regensburg, 1974.

Marshall, Bruce, *Christology in Conflict: The Identity of a Saviour in Rahner and Barth.* Oxford: Blackwell, 1987.

———. "In Search of an Analytic Aquinas: Grammar and the Trinity." In *Grammar and Grace: Reformulations of Aquinas and Wittgenstein,* edited by Jeffrey Stout and Robert MacSwain, pp. 55-74. London: SCM Press, 2004.

———. "Putting Shadows to Flight: The Trinity, Faith, and Reason." In *Reason and the Reasons of Faith,* edited by Paul J. Griffiths and Reinhard Hütter, pp. 53-77. London: T. & T. Clark, 2005.

———. "The Trinity." In *The Blackwell Companion to Modern Theology,* edited by Gareth Jones, pp. 183-203. Oxford: Blackwell, 2004.

———. *Trinity and Truth.* Cambridge: Cambridge University Press, 2000.

———. "*Utrum essentia generet:* Semantics and Metaphysics in Later Medieval Trinitarian Theology." In *Trinitarian Theology in the Medieval West,* edited by Pekka Kärkkäinen, pp. 88-123. Helsinki: Luther-Agricola Society, 2008.

Mascall, E. L. *Existence and Analogy: A Sequel to "He Who Is."* London: Longmans, Green, 1949.

———. *He Who Is: A Study in Traditional Theism.* London: Longmans, Green, 1945.

Maurer, Armand. "St Thomas on the Sacred Name 'Tetragrammaton.'" *Mediaeval Studies* 34 (1972): 275-86.

Mechels, Eberhard. *Analogie bei Erich Przywara und Karl Barth. Das Verhältnis von Offenbarungstheologie und Metaphysik.* Neukirchen: Neukirchener Verlag, 1974.

Mietke, Juergen. "Papst, Ortsbischof und Universität in den Pariser Theologenprozessen des 13. Jahrhunderts." In *Die Auseinandersetzungen an der Pariser Universität im XIII. Jahrhundert,* edited by Albert Zimmermann, pp. 52-94. Berlin: de Gruyter, 1976.

Milbank, John. *The Word Made Strange: Theology, Language, Culture.* Oxford: Blackwell, 1997.

Molnar, Paul. *Divine Freedom and the Doctrine of the Immanent Trinity: In Dialogue with Karl Barth and Contemporary Theology.* London: T. & T. Clark, 2002.

————. "The Trinity, Election, and God's Ontological Freedom: A Response to Kevin W. Hector." *International Journal of Systematic Theology* 8 (2006): 294-306.

Mondin, Battista. *Storia della teologia.* Bologna: Edizioni Studio Dominicano, 1997.

Montagnes, Bernard. *La doctrine de l'analogie de l'être d'après Saint Thomas d'Aquin.* Louvain: Publications Universitaires, 1963.

————. *The Doctrine of the Analogy of Being according to Thomas Aquinas.* Translated by E. M. Macierowski, reviewed and corrected by P. Vandervelde, with revisions by A. Tallon. Milwaukee, Wis.: Marquette University Press, 2004.

Naab, Erich. *Zur Begründung der analogia entis bei Erich Przywara. Eine Erörterung.* Regensburg: Pustet, 1987.

Negel, Joachim. *Ambivalentes Opfer. Studien zur Symbolik, Dialektik und Aporetik eines theologischen Fundamentalbegriffs.* Paderborn: Ferdinand Schöningh, 2005.

Neuser, W. H. "Karl Barth in Münster, 1924-1930." *Theologische Studien* 130 (1985): 37-40.

Nichols, Aidan. *No Bloodless Myth: A Guide through Balthasar's Dramatics.* Washington, D.C.: Catholic University of America Press, 2000.

————. *Scattering the Seed: A Guide through Balthasar's Early Writings on Philosophy and the Arts.* Washington, D.C.: Catholic University of America Press, 2006.

————. *The Word Has Been Abroad: A Guide through Balthasar's Aesthetics.* Washington, D.C.: Catholic University of America Press, 1998.

Nieborak, Stephan. *"Homo analogia." Zur philosophisch-theologischen Bedeutung der "analogia entis" im Rahmen der existentiellen Frage bei Erich Przywara, S.J. (1889-1972).* Frankfurt: Peter Lang, 1994.

Oakes, Kenneth. "The Question of Nature and Grace in Karl Barth: Humanity as Creature and as Covenant-Partner." *Modern Theology* 23 (2007): 595-616.

Oh, Peter S. *Karl Barth's Trinitarian Theology: A Study in Karl Barth's Analogical Use of the Trinitarian Relations.* London: T. & T. Clark, 2006.

O'Meara, Thomas. *Erich Przywara, S.J.: His Theology and His World.* Notre Dame, Ind.: University of Notre Dame Press, 2002.

O'Rourke, Fran. "Aristotle and the Metaphysics of Evolution." *Review of Metaphysics* 58 (2004): 3-59.

————. *Pseudo-Dionysius and the Metaphysics of Aquinas.* Leiden: Brill, 1992.

Oster, Stefan. *Mit-Mensch-Sein. Phänomenologie und Ontologie der Gabe bei Ferdinand Ulrich.* Freiburg: Karl Alber, 2004.

Paissac, Henri. *Théologie du verbe. St. Augustin et St. Thomas.* Paris: Cerf, 1951.

Palakeel, Joseph. *The Use of Analogy in Theological Discourse: An Investigation in Ecumenical Perspective.* Rome: Editrice Pontificia Università Gregoriana, 1995.

Pannenberg, Wolfhart. *Analogie und Offenbarung. Eine kritische Untersuchung der Geschichte des Analogiebegriffs in der Lehre von der Gotteserkenntnis.* Göttingen: Vandenhoeck & Ruprecht, 2007.

———. *Basic Questions in Theology.* Vol. 1. Translated by George H. Kehm. London: SCM Press, 1970.

———. "Eternity, Time, and the Trinitarian God." In *Trinity, Time, and Church: A Response to the Theology of Robert W. Jenson,* edited by Colin E. Gunton, pp. 62-70. Grand Rapids: Eerdmans, 2000.

———. Review of Hans Wagner, *Existenz, Analogie and Dialektik,* vol. 1. *Theologische Literaturzeitung* 79 (1954): 318ff.

———. *Systematic Theology.* 3 vols. Translated by Geoffrey W. Bromiley. Grand Rapids: Eerdmans, 1991-98.

———. *Systematische Theologie.* 3 vols. Göttingen: Vandenhoeck & Ruprecht, 1988-93.

———. "Zur Bedeutung des Analogiegedankens bei Karl Barth. Eine Auseinandersetzung mit Urs von Balthasar." *Theologische Literaturzeitung* 78 (1953): 17-24.

Peterson, Erik. *Theologische Traktate.* Munich: Kösel, 1951.

Pinborg, Jan. *Die Entwicklung der Sprachtheorie im Mittelalter.* Münster: Aschendorff, 1967.

Prufer, Thomas. *Recapitulation: Essays in Philosophy.* Washington, D.C.: Catholic University of America Press, 1993.

Przywara, Erich. *Alter und Neuer Bund. Theologie der Stunde.* Vienna: Herold Verlag, 1956.

———. *Analogia Entis. Metaphysik.* Vol. 1. Munich: Kösel & Pustet, 1932.

———. *Analogia Entis. Metaphysik; Ur-struktur und All-Rhythmus.* Rev. ed. Einsiedeln: Johannes Verlag, 1962.

———. *Christentum gemäss Johannes.* Nürnberg: Glock & Lutz, 1955.

———. *Crucis mysterium. Das Christliche Heute.* Paderborn: Schöningh, 1939.

———. *Deus semper maior. Theologie der Exerzitien.* Freiburg: Herder, 1938.

———. "Drei Richtungen der Phänomenologie." *Stimmen der Zeit* 115 (1928): 252-64.

———. *Gott. Fünf Vorträge über das religionsphilosophische Problem.* Munich: Oratoriums-Verlag, 1926.

———. *Gottgeheimnis der Welt. Drei Vorträge über die geistige Krisis der Gegenwart.* Munich: Theatiner-Verlag, 1923.

———. "Gott in uns oder Gott über uns? (Immanenz und Transzendenz im heutigen Geistesleben)." *Stimmen der Zeit* 105 (1923): 343-62.

———. "Der Grundsatz. Eine ideengeschichtliche Interpretation." *Scholastik* 17 (1942): 178-86.

———. *In und Gegen. Stellungnahmen zur Zeit.* Nürnberg: Glock & Lutz, 1955.

————. "Das katholische Kirchenprinzip." *Zwischen den Zeiten* 7 (1929): 277-302.

————. *Katholische Krise.* Düsseldorf: Patmos-Verlag, 1967.

————. *Logos, Abendland, Reich, Commercium.* Düsseldorf: Patmos-Verlag, 1964.

————. *Nuptiae agni. Liturgie des Kirchenjahres.* Nürnberg: Glock & Lutz, 1948.

————. *Polarity: A German Catholic's Interpretation of Religion.* Translated by A. C. Bouquet. London: Oxford University Press, 1935.

————. "Reichweite der Analogie als katholischer Grundform." *Scholastik* 15 (1940): 339-62, 508-32.

————. *Religionsphilosophie katholischer Theologie.* Munich: R. Oldenbourg, 1927.

————. *Ringen der Gegenwart. Gesammelte Aufsätze, 1922-1927.* 2 vols. Augsburg: Benno Filser, 1929.

————. *Schriften.* 3 vols. Einsiedeln: Johannes Verlag, 1962.

————. *Was ist Gott? Eine Summula.* Nürnberg: Glock und Lutz, 1947, 2d ed., 1953.

————. "Wende zum Menschen." *Stimmen der Zeit* 119 (1930): 1-10.

Rahner, Karl. *Foundations of Christian Faith: An Introduction to the Idea of Christianity.* Translated by W. V. Dych. New York: Crossroad, 1978.

————. *Gnade als Freiheit. Kleine theologische Beiträge.* Freiburg: Herder, 1968.

————. *Hearers of the Word.* Translated by Michael Richards. New York: Herder & Herder, 1969.

————. *Hörer des Wortes.* Edited by J. B. Metz. Munich: Kösel, 1963.

————. *Theological Investigations.* Vol. 5. Translated by K. H. Kruger. London: Darton, Longman & Todd, 1966.

Ramírez, Santiago. *De gratia Dei.* Salamanca: Editorial San Esteban, 1992.

Ratzinger, Joseph (Benedict XVI). *Daughter Zion: Meditations on the Church's Marian Belief.* Translated by John M. McDermott. San Francisco: Ignatius Press, 1983.

————. *Die Geschichtstheologie des heiligen Bonaventura.* Munich: Schnell & Steiner 1959; St. Ottilien: EOS, 1992.

————. *God's Word: Scripture, Tradition, Office.* Translated by Henry Taylor. San Francisco: Ignatius Press, 2008.

————. "Gratia praesupponit naturam. Erwägungen über Sinn und Grenze eines scholastischen Axioms." In *Einsicht und Glaube. Festschrift G. Söhngen zum 70. Geburtstag.* Edited by Joseph Ratzinger and Heinrich Fries, pp. 75-97. Freiburg: Herder, 1962.

————. *"In the Beginning . . . ": A Catholic Understanding of the Story of Creation and the Fall.* Translated by Boniface Ramsey. Grand Rapids: Eerdmans, 1998.

————. *Introduction to Christianity.* Translated by J. R. Foster. San Francisco: Ignatius, 2000.

————. "Offenbarung — Schrift — Überlieferung. Ein Text des hl. Bonaventura und seine Bedeutung für die gegenwärtige Theologie." *Trierer theologische Zeitschrift* 67 (1958): 13-27.

————. *Offenbarungsverständnis und Geschichtstheologie Bonaventuras.* Vol. 2 of *Gesammelte Schriften.* Freiburg: Herder, 2009.

―――. "Retrieving the Tradition: Concerning the Notion of Person in Theology." *Communio* 17 (Fall 1990): 439-54.

―――. *Theologische Prinzipienlehre. Bausteine zur Fundamentaltheologie.* Munich: Wewel, 1982.

―――. *The Theology of History in St. Bonaventure.* Translated by Zachary Hayes. Chicago: Franciscan Herald Press, 1971.

―――. "Wesen und Weisen der auctoritas im Werk des hl. Bonaventura." In *Die Kirche und ihre Ämter und Stände. Festgabe für Joseph Kardinal Frings zum goldenen Priesterjubiläum.* Edited by W. Corsten, A. Frotz, and P. Linden, pp. 58-72. Cologne: Bachem, 1960.

―――. "Der Wortgebrauch von *natura* und die beginnende Verselbständigung der Metaphysik bei Bonaventura." In *Die Metaphysik im Mittelalter.* Edited by Paul Wilpert, pp. 483-98. Berlin: de Gruyter, 1963.

Ratzinger, Joseph, and Heinrich Fries, eds. *Einsicht und Glaube. Festschrift G. Söhngen zum 70. Geburtstag.* Freiburg: Herder, 1962.

Rendtorff, Trutz. *Theorie des Christentums. Historisch-theologische Studien zu seiner neuzeitlichen Verfassung.* Gütersloh: Gütersloher Verlagshaus Gerd Mohn, 1972.

Robillard, Hyacinthe-Marie. *De l'analogie et du concept d'être.* Montreal: Les presses de l'Université de Montréal, 1963.

Rocca, Gregory. *Speaking the Incomprehensible God: Thomas Aquinas on the Interplay of Positive and Negative Theology.* Washington, D.C.: Catholic University of America Press, 2004.

Rogers, Eugene F., Jr. *Thomas Aquinas and Karl Barth: Sacred Doctrine and the Natural Knowledge of God.* Notre Dame, Ind.: University of Notre Dame Press, 1995.

Rolnick, Philip A. *Analogical Possibilities: How Words Refer to God.* Atlanta: Scholars Press, 1993.

Rosier, Irène. "Signes et sacrements. Thomas d'Aquin et la grammaire spéculative." *Revue des sciences philosophiques et théologiques* 74 (1990): 392-436.

Rosier-Catach, Irène. *La parole efficace. Signe, ritual, sacré.* Paris: Éditions du Seuil, 2004.

Schaeffler, Richard. *Die Wechselbeziehungen zwischen Philosophie und katholischer Theologie.* Darmstadt: Wissenschaftliche Buchgesellschaft, 1980.

Scheffczyk, Leo. "Die Frage nach der 'Erfahrung' als theologischem Verifikationsprinzip." In *Dienst der Vermittlung.* Edited by Wilhelm Ernst, pp. 353-73. Leipzig: Benno, 1977.

Schenk, Richard. "Eine Ökumene des Einspruchs. Systematische Überlegungen zum heutigen ökumenischen Prozess aus einer römisch-katholischen Sicht." In *Die Reunionsgespräche im Niedersachsen des 17. Jahrhunderts. Rojas y Spinola, Molan, Leibniz,* edited by Hans Otte and Richard Schenk, pp. 225-50. Göttingen: Vandenhoeck & Ruprecht, 1999.

―――. *Die Gnade vollendeter Endlichkeit. Zur transzendentaltheologischen Auslegung der thomanischen Anthropologie.* Freiburg: Herder, 1989.

―――. "Option für den Thomismus in der Enzyklika?" In *Die Vernunft des*

Glaubens und der Glaube der Vernunft. Die Enzyklika Fides et Ratio in der Debatte zwischen Philosophie und Theologie, edited by P. Koslowski and A. M. Hauk, pp. 59-81. Munich: W. Fink, 2007.

Schindler, David C. *Hans Urs von Balthasar and the Dramatic Structure of Truth: A Philosophical Investigation.* New York: Fordham University Press, 2004.

Schindler, David L. "The Meaning of the Human in a Technological Age." *Anthropotes* 15 (1999): 31-51.

———. "Trinity, Creation, and the Order of Intelligence in the Modern Academy." *Communio* 28 (Fall 2001): 406-29.

Schmitz, Kenneth L. *The Texture of Being: Essays in First Philosophy.* Washington, D.C.: Catholic University of America Press, 2007.

Schönberger, Rolf. *Die Transformation des klassischen Seinsverständnisses. Studien zur Vorgeschichte des neuzeitlichen Seinsbegriffs im Mittelalter.* Berlin: de Gruyter, 1986.

Schreiter, Michael. "Zur geschichtstheologischen Ausdeutung der ignatianischen Exerzitien bei Erich Przywara und Karl Rahner." In *Zur grösseren Ehre Gottes. Ignatius von Loyola neu entdeckt für die Theologie der Gegenwart,* edited by Thomas Gertler et al., pp. 368-88. Freiburg: Herder, 2006.

Schumacher, Thomas. *In-Über. Analogie als Grundbestimmung von Theo-Logie. Reflexionen im Ausgang von Erich Przywara.* Munich: Institut zur Förderung der Glaubenslehre, 2003.

Siewerth, Gustav. *Der Thomismus als Identitätssystem.* Frankfurt: Verlag Schulte-Bulmke, 1939.

Söhngen, Gottlieb. "Analogia entis in analogia fidei." In *Antwort. Karl Barth zum siebzigsten Geburtstag am 10. Mai 1956,* edited by E. Wolf, pp. 266-71. Zurich: Evangelischer Verlag, 1956.

———. "Analogia entis oder analogia fidei?" *Wissenschaft und Weisheit* 9 (1942): 91-100.

———. "Analogia fidei I. Gottähnlichkeit allein aus Glauben?" *Catholica* 3 (1934): 113-36.

———. "Analogia fidei II. Die Einheit in der Glaubenswissenschaft." *Catholica* 3 (1934): 176-208.

———. "Analogie." In *Handbuch theologischer Grundbegriffe,* vol. 1, edited by Heinrich Fries, pp. 49-61. Munich: Kösel, 1962.

———. "Bonaventura als Klassiker der Analogia fidei." *Wissenschaft und Weisheit* 2 (1935): 97-111.

———. *Gesetz und Evangelium. Ihre analoge Einheit. Theologisch, philosophisch, staatsbürgerlich.* Freiburg: Alber, 1957.

———. "Natürliche Theologie und Heilsgeschichte. Antwort an Emil Brunner." *Catholica* 4 (1935): 97-114.

———. "Wunderzeichen und Glaube." *Catholica* 4 (1935): 145-64.

Spencer, Archie J. "Causality and the *analogia entis:* Karl Barth's Rejection of Analogy of Being Reconsidered." *Nova et Vetera,* English edition, 6, no. 2 (2008): 329-76.

Spieckermann, Ingrid. *Gotteserkenntnis. Ein Beitrag zur Grundfrage der neuen Theologie Karl Barths.* Munich: C. Kaiser, 1985.

Stein, Edith. *Finite and Eternal Being.* Translated by Kurt F. Reichardt. Vol. 9 of *The Collected Works of Edith Stein.* Washington, D.C.: ICS Publications, 2002.

Stertenbrink, Rudolf. *Ein Weg zum Denken. Die "analogia entis" bei Erich Przywara.* Salzburg: Pustet, 1971.

Stiglmayr, Josef. "Der Neuplatoniker Proclus als Vorlage des sogenannten Dionysius Areopagita in der Lehre vom Übel." *Historisches Jahrbuch* 16 (1895): 253-73 and 721-80.

Stoeckle, Bernhard. *Gratia supponit naturam. Geschichte und Analyse eines theologischen Axioms.* Rome: Orbis Catholicus, 1962.

Stolina, Ralf. *Niemand hat Gott je gesehen.* Berlin: de Gruyter, 2000.

Synave, Paul. "La révélation des vérités divines naturelles d'après saint Thomas." In *Mélanges Mandonnet. Études d'histoire littéraire et doctrinale du Moyen Age,* vol. 1, pp. 327-71. Paris: J. Vrin, 1930.

Taylor, Charles. *Sources of the Self: The Making of the Modern Identity.* Cambridge, Mass.: Harvard University Press, 1989.

Terán-Dutari, Julio. *Christentum und Metaphysik. Das Verhältnis beider nach der Analogielehre Erich Przywaras.* Munich: Berchmanskolleg, 1973.

———. "Die Geschichte des Terminus 'Analogia entis' und das Werk Erich Przywaras." *Philosophisches Jahrbuch der Görres-Gesellschaft* 77 (1970): 163-79.

———. *Participation and Substantiality in Thomas Aquinas.* Leiden: Brill, 1995.

Ulrich, Ferdinard. *Erzählter Sinn.* Einsiedeln: Johannes Verlag, 2002.

———. *Gabe und Vergebung.* Einsiedeln: Johannes Verlag, 2007.

———. *Gebet als geschöpflicher Grundakt.* Einsiedeln: Johannes Verlag, 1973.

———. "Hegel und die Frage nach der reinen Endlichkeit." *Theorein,* 1972, pp. 65-97.

———. *Homo abyssus. Das Wagnis der Seinsfrage.* Einsiedeln: Johannes Verlag, 1998.

———. *Leben in der Einheit von Leben und Tod.* Einsiedeln: Johannes Verlag, 1999.

———. *Logo-Tokos. Der Mensch und das Wort.* Einsiedeln: Johannes Verlag, 2003.

———. *Der Mensch als Anfang. Zur philosophischen Anthropologie der Kindheit.* Einsiedeln: Johannes Verlag, 1970.

———. "Über die spekulative Natur des philosophischen Anfangs." In *Innerlichkeit und Erziehung. In Memoriam Gustav Siewerth,* edited by Franz Pöggeler, pp. 27-72. Freiburg: Herder, 1964.

Velde, Rudi te. *Aquinas on God: The "Divine Science" of the "Summa theologiae."* Aldershot: Ashgate, 2006.

Wagner, Hans. *Existenz, Analogie, Dialektik. Religio pura seu transcendentalis.* Munich: Ernst Reinhard, 1953.

Webster, John. *Barth's Ethics of Reconciliation.* Cambridge: Cambridge University Press, 1995.

————. *Barth's Moral Theology: Human Action in Barth's Thought.* Edinburgh: T. & T. Clark, 1998.

White, Thomas Joseph, O.P. "How Barth Got Aquinas Wrong: A Reply to Archie J. Spencer on Causality and Christocentrism." *Nova et Vetera,* English edition, 7, no. 1 (2009): 241-70.

————. "Intra-Trinitarian Obedience and Nicene-Chalcedonian Christology," *Nova et Vetera,* English edition, 6, no. 2 (2008): 397-402.

————. *Wisdom in the Face of Modernity: A Study in Thomistic Natural Theology.* Naples, Fla.: Sapientia Press, 2009.

Wigley, Stephen D. *Karl Barth and Hans Urs von Balthasar: A Critical Engagement.* London: T. & T. Clark, 2007.

Wippel, John F. *The Metaphysical Thought of Thomas Aquinas: From Finite Being to Uncreated Being.* Washington, D.C.: Catholic University of America Press, 2000.

————. "Thomas Aquinas and Participation." In *Studies in Medieval Philosophy,* edited by John F. Wippel, pp. 117-58. Washington, D.C.: Catholic University of America Press, 1987.

Witherington, Ben, III. *The Christology of Jesus.* Minneapolis: Fortress Press, 1990.

————. *Jesus the Sage: Pilgrimage of Wisdom.* Minneapolis: Fortress Press, 1994.

————. *The Many Faces of the Christ.* New York: Crossroad, 1998.

Zaborowski, Holger. "Katholische Integration. Zum religionsphilosophischen Ansatz Hans Urs von Balthasars." In *Die Kunst Gottes verstehen. Hans Urs von Balthasars theologische Provokationen,* edited by Magnus Striet and Jan-Heiner Tück, pp. 28-48. Freiburg: Herder, 2005.

Zechmeister, Martha. *Gottes-Nacht. Erich Przywaras Weg negativer Theologie.* Berlin: LIT Verlag, 1997.

————. "Karsamstag. Zu einer Theologie des Gott-vermisses." In *Vom Wagnis der Nichtidentität,* edited by Johann Reikerstofer, pp. 50-78. Berlin: LIT Verlag, 1998.

Zeitz, James V. *Spirituality and analogia entis according to Erich Przywara, S.J.: Metaphysics and Religious Experience, the Ignatian Exercises, the Balance in Rhythm in "Similarity" and "Greater Dissimilarity" according to Lateran IV.* Washington, D.C.: University Press of America, 1982.

Zimny, Leo. *Erich Przywara. Sein Schriftum, 1912-1962.* Einsiedeln: Johannes Verlag, 1963.

Contributors

John R. Betz is Professor of Theology at the University of Notre Dame, Notre Dame, Indiana. He is the English translator (with David Bentley Hart) of the forthcoming *Analogia Entis* of Erich Przywara (Grand Rapids: Eerdmans). He has also written numerous theological articles on modern German theology in journals such as *Modern Theology* and *Pro Ecclesia*. He is the author of *After Enlightenment: The Post-Secular Vision of J. G. Hamann* (Oxford: Wiley-Blackwell, 2009).

Martin Bieler, Privatdozent in systematic theology at the University of Bern, Switzerland, is an ordained pastor of the Swiss Reformed Church. A friend and former interlocutor of Hans Urs von Balthasar, he is the author of *Freiheit als Gabe. Ein schöpfungstheologischer Entwurf* (Freiberg: Herder, 1991) and *Befreiung der Freiheit. Zur Theologie der stellvertretenden Sühne* (Freiburg: Herder, 1996).

Peter Casarella, Professor of Catholic Studies at DePaul University, Chicago, Illinois, is the editor and coeditor of several books, including *Cusanus: The Legacy of Learned Ignorance* (Washington, D.C.: Catholic University of America Press, 2006) and *Christian Spirituality and the Culture of Modernity: The Thought of Louis Dupré* (Grand Rapids: Eerdmans, 1998). He has published articles in *Communio, Thomist,* and other journals.

J. Augustine Di Noia, O.P., is the Secretary Archbishop of the Congregation for Divine Worship and the Discipline of the Sacraments of the Roman Catholic Church. He served as the undersecretary of the Congregation for the Doctrine of the Faith from 2001 to 2009, and as executive director of the Secretariat for Doctrine for the National Conference of Catholic Bishops (NCCB) from 1993 to 2001. He was the editor-in-chief for many years of the *Thomist* and is the author of many books and articles, including *The Diversity of Religions: A Christian Perspective* (Washington, D.C.: Catholic University of America Press, 1992).

Michael Hanby is Assistant Professor of Biotechnology and Culture at the John Paul II Institute for Studies on Marriage and the Family, Catholic University of America, Washington, D.C. He is the author of *Augustine and Modernity* (London: Routledge, 2003), and his articles have appeared in journals such as *Pro Ecclesia, Theology Today, Communio,* and *Modern Theology.* A forthcoming volume on the doctrine of creation, modern science, and evolutionary biology will be published by Blackwell.

David Bentley Hart, 2006-7 Robert J. Randall Chair in Christian Culture at Providence College, Providence, Rhode Island, has previously taught at the University of Virginia; the University of St. Thomas, St. Paul; Duke University Divinity School; and Loyola College, Baltimore. He is Eastern Orthodox and, among his books, are *The Beauty of the Infinite: The Aesthetics of Christian Truth* (Grand Rapids: Eerdmans, 2003) and *Atheist Delusions: The Christian Revolution and Its Fashionable Enemies* (New Haven: Yale University Press, 2009).

Reinhard Hütter, Professor of Christian Theology at Duke University Divinity School, Durham, North Carolina, is the coeditor of several books, including *Reason and the Reasons of Faith* (ed. with Paul J. Griffith; London: T. & T. Clark, 2005) and *Ressourcement Thomism: Sacred Doctrine, the Sacraments, and the Moral Life* (ed. with Matthew Levering; Washington, D.C.: Catholic University Press, 2010). He is also coeditor of the theological journal *Nova et Vetera: The English Edition of the International Theological Journal* and the author of numerous books, most recently *Dust Bound for Heaven: Explorations in the Theology of Thomas Aquinas* (Grand Rapids: Eerdmans, forthcoming). He is a member of the Roman Catholic Church, an ordinary academician of the Pontifical Academy of Saint Thomas Aquinas, and was the 2010-11 president of the Academy of Catholic Theology.

434

Bruce D. Marshall, Professor of Historical Theology in the Perkins School of Theology, Southern Methodist University, Dallas, Texas, is the author of *Trinity and Truth* (Cambridge: Cambridge University Press, 2000) and *Christology in Conflict: The Identity of a Saviour in Rahner and Barth* (Oxford: Blackwell, 1987), and is currently at work on a book on Aquinas and the renewal of Catholic Theology. He was the 2008-9 president of the Academy of Catholic Theology.

Bruce L. McCormack is the Frederick and Margaret L. Weyerhaeuser Professor of Systematic Theology at Princeton Theological Seminary, Princeton, New Jersey, and a member of the Presbyterian Church (USA). He is the author of *Karl Barth's Critically Realistic Dialectical Theology: Its Genesis and Development, 1909-1936* (New York: Oxford University Press, 1995).

Kenneth Oakes is a Protestant theologian who has studied and taught at the University of Aberdeen, Scotland. His doctoral dissertation, entitled "The Positive Protest: Karl Barth on Theology and Philosophy," considered among other topics the ecumenical ramifications of Barth's fundamental theology. He has published essays in *Modern Theology, Thomist,* and the *International Journal of Systematic Theology.*

Richard Schenk, O.P., is Professor of Philosophy and Theology at the Dominican School of Philosophy and Theology, and the Graduate Theological Union, Berkeley, California. He is author and editor of numerous books in English and German, including *Der Gnade vollendeter Endlichkeit. Zur transzendental-theologischen Auslegung der thomanischen Anthropologie* (Freiburg: Herder, 1989). He has also written numerous articles, many pertaining to contemporary Lutheran-Catholic debates on justification. He was the 2007-8 president of the Academy of Catholic Theology.

John Webster is Professor of Systematic Theology at King's College, University of Aberdeen, Scotland, and is an ordained minister in the Church of England. He has published numerous articles and books on Christian doctrine, many pertaining to the theology of Karl Barth and Eberhard Jüngel. These include *Barth's Moral Theology: Human Action in Barth's Thought* (Grand Rapids: Eerdmans, 1998) and *Word and Church: Essays in Church Dogmatics* (Edinburgh: T. & T. Clark International, 2006). He is the cofounder, with Colin Gunton, of the *International Journal of Systematic Theology.* In 2005 he was elected a fellow of the Royal Society of Edinburgh.

Thomas Joseph White, O.P., is Director of the Thomistic Institute at the Pontifical Faculty of the Immaculate Conception, Dominican House of Studies, Washington, D.C. He is the author of *Wisdom in the Face of Modernity: A Study in Thomistic Natural Theology* (Naples, Fla.: Sapientia Press, 2009) and coeditor, with James F. Keating, of *Divine Impassibility and the Mystery of Human Suffering* (Grand Rapids: Eerdmans, 2009).

Index of Names

Anselm, 183
Aquinas. *See* Thomas Aquinas
Aristotle, 4, 46-47, 63, 66, 214-23, 227, 233, 260n.31, 272, 284-85, 291, 355, 357
Arius, 403-4
Augustine, 5-6, 11-13, 15-16, 51-52, 96, 102

Balthasar, Hans Urs von, 18-19, 40-41, 82, 88-89, 108-17, 180-83, 192-206, 315-17, 343-44, 365, 411
Barth, Karl, 1-23, 36-38, 53, 70-87, 88-144, 172-74, 180-81, 254, 315-16
Bauhofer, Oskar, 105
Benedict XVI (Joseph Ratzinger), 25-26, 149, 204, 344, 350-51, 373, 414-16
Bernard of Clairvaux, 313
Blondel, Maurice, 177
Bonaventure, 184-87, 190
Bonhoeffer, Dietrich, 196
Brunner, Emil, 36, 105-6

Cajetan, 47-48, 229, 282
Calvin, John, 254, 380, 386
Clarke, W. Norris, 244-45

Dawkins, Richard, 349n.25, 363
De Lubac, Henri, 366

Descartes, 354
Dewan, Lawrence, 225-28, 319n.28
Diem, Hermann, 183, 191
Dionysius the Areopagite, 54, 184-90, 306, 376

Funkenstein, Amos, 351-53

Gertz, Bernard, 179
Gilson, Etienne, 342
Goebel, Hans Theodore, 132-34
Gogarten, Friedrich, 105
Gregory the Great, 184
Groche, Robert, 99
Gundlach, Thies, 134

Härle, Wilfried, 127-32
Hegel, Georg Wilhelm Friedrich, 5-6, 54, 65, 95, 241, 315, 334, 405
Heraclitus, 44-45
Hunsinger, George, 120n.92

Ignatius of Loyola, 54, 154, 178, 204

Jenson, Robert, 385
Joachim of Fiore, 151

437

Index of Names

Jüngel, Eberhard, 23, 35, 44-45, 123-27, 131, 209-12, 241-44, 396

Kant, Immanuel, 5, 10-11, 61, 95, 211, 242-44

Luther, Martin, 96, 148, 164-65, 174, 182

Marga, Amy, 100n.35
Maréchal, Joseph, 177
Maximus the Confessor, 408-9
McInerny, Ralph, 224, 281-82, 317, 320
Montanges, Bernard, 29, 213, 220-24, 235, 244, 365, 321, 331

Ockham, 352-53

Pannenberg, Wolfhart, 209-12, 240-41
Parmenides, 44-45
Paul, 86, 165-66
Peterson, Erik, 105-6
Plato, 46, 196
Plotinus, 404-6
Proclus, 187-88
Przywara, Erich, 1-23, 35-87, 88-108, 147-71, 172-79, 195-99, 205-6, 343, 368, 395-97, 399

Rahner, Karl, 14-15, 43
Ratzinger, Joseph. *See* Benedict XVI
Root, Michael, 173

Schindler, David L., 342-43, 348
Schleiermacher, Friedrich, 9, 53, 72, 109
Sertillanges, Antonin-Dalmais, 283-84
Söhngen, Gottlieb, 17-18, 87, 89, 180-83, 190, 246, 315, 414-15
Spaemann, Robert, 356-57
Spieckermann, Ingrid, 92-93
Stein, Edith, 41-42

Thomas Aquinas, 19-20, 61-62, 82, 156, 175-76, 188-91, 209-45, 246-79, 280-313, 315-35, 343, 359-60, 365, 368, 377, 384
Thurneysen, Eduard, 93, 101, 174, 315

Ulrich, Ferdinand, 29, 232, 314-37

Velde, Rudi te, 212, 238

Wippel, John, 320
Wobbermin, Georg, 105-7

Index of Subjects

analogia attributionis, 47, 69, 76, 106,
221, 236-40, 284-88, 335
analogia fidei, 9, 18, 71, 87, 89, 91, 92-117,
159-69, 173, 181-82, 248, 335-37, 414
analogia proportionalitatis, 47-48, 69,
76, 221, 235-36, 334-35
analogia relationis, 71, 91, 135-39, 164,
181-82
analogia verbi, 260, 267
Analogy: as pertaining to logic vs.
metaphysics, 224-28, 248n.4, 281-92,
320-21; between creation and God, 6,
9-10, 52, 73, 102-3, 228, 236-40, 294,
322-28, 325, 341-78, 396-97; concept
of, 4, 44-50, 63, 122-23, 176, 272-75,
284-92, 320, 366, 397-98; extrinsic vs.
intrinsic, 216, 221; in Aquinas's
thought, 209-45, 280-303; predicamental vs. transcendental, 213, 217,
266-67; use within dogmatic theology, 48-49, 67-70, 74, 150, 245, 246-79,
389
Anknüpfungspunkt ("point of contact"),
16, 79, 275n.65, 279
Arianism, 403-4
Aristotelianism, 165, 186, 214

Chalcedon (Council of): 115-16, 202,
204, 306, 409
Christ: as the concrete *analogia entis,*
83-86, 169, 198-205, 316, 410; as resolution of philosophy's quest, 15, 59,
84, 197, 336-37; bodily resurrection of,
97; *esse* of, 261-65; historicity of, 264-
65; incarnation of, 7, 14, 80-81, 112,
168, 251-53, 281, 304; and knowledge
of God, 9, 11-13, 93, 281, 310-12, 316;
obedience of, 139-43, 203; ontology
of, 90-91, 203; and theandric acts,
304-7; two natures of, 115-16, 164, 203,
310, 409
Christocentrism, 18, 77n.140, 197, 200-
206, 279, 344-45
Church, 7-8, 40, 42, 151, 153, 194, 201,
252, 391
Creation, 6-7, 11, 16-18, 36, 48, 51-53, 72,
102, 117, 150-58, 200, 299-300, 325,
322-37, 341-78

Dialectical theology, 16, 44n.29, 57n.74,
71, 92, 94-97, 112
Divine name, 260-64
Divinization, 153, 158

439